Lecture Notes in Computer Science 2163

Edited by G. Goos, J. Hartmanis, and J. van Leeuwen

Springer

Berlin
Heidelberg
New York
Barcelona
Hong Kong
London
Milan
Paris
Tokyo

Panos Constantopoulos
Ingeborg T. Sølvberg (Eds.)

Research and Advanced Technology for Digital Libraries

5th European Conference, ECDL 2001
Darmstadt, Germany, September 4-9, 2001
Proceedings

 Springer

Series Editors

Gerhard Goos, Karlsruhe University, Germany
Juris Hartmanis, Cornell University, NY, USA
Jan van Leeuwen, Utrecht University, The Netherlands

Volume Editors

Panos Constantopoulos
University of Crete, Department of Computer Science
Leof. Knossou, P.O. Box 1470, 71409 Heraklion, Greece, and
Foundation for Research and Technology - Hellas
Institute of Computer Science
Vassilika Vouton, P.O. Box 1385, 71110 Heraklion, Greece
E-mail: panos@ics.forth.gr

Ingeborg T. Sølvberg
The Norwegian University of Science and Technology
Department of Computer and Information Science
7491 Trondheim, Norway
E-mail: ingeborg.solvberg@idi.ntnu.no

Cataloging-in-Publication Data applied for

Die Deutsche Bibliothek - CIP-Einheitsaufnahme

Research and advanced technology for digital libraries : 5th European
conference ; proceedings / ECDL 2001, Darmstadt, Germany, September 4 - 9,
2001. Panos Constantopoulos ; Ingeborg T. Sølvberg (ed.). - Berlin ; Heidelberg ;
New York ; Barcelona ; Hong Kong ; London ; Milan ; Paris ; Tokyo : Springer, 2001
    (Lecture notes in computer science ; Vol. 2163)
    ISBN 3-540-42537-3

CR Subject Classification (1998): H.3, H.2, H.4.3, H.5, J.7, J.1, I.7

ISSN 0302-9743
ISBN 3-540-42537-3 Springer-Verlag Berlin Heidelberg New York

Springer-Verlag Berlin Heidelberg New York
a member of BertelsmannSpringer Science+Business Media GmbH

http://www.springer.de

© Springer-Verlag Berlin Heidelberg 2001
Printed in Germany

Typesetting: Camera-ready by author, data conversion by Boller Mediendesign
Printed on acid-free paper   SPIN 10840321   06/3142   5 4 3 2 1 0

Statement of the Chairpersons

ECDL 2001 was the 5th conference in the series of European Conferences on Research and Advanced Technology for Digital Libraries. Following previous events in Pisa (1997), Heraklion (1998), Paris (1999), and Lisbon (2000), this year ECDL was held in Darmstadt, Germany, and was co-organized by the Technical University of Darmstadt, GMD-IPSI, and Die Deutsche Bibliothek (the German National Library), Frankfurt. The overall objective of the ECDL series is to foster the formation of a multi-disciplinary scientific community in Europe specific to digital library research, development, and deployment. The ECDL series is supported by the DELOS Network of Excellence in Digital Libraries.

ECDL 2001 was seen as a good opportunity to review the impact that DLs have had on science, technology, and society in general. The call for papers therefore placed emphasis on applications of DL systems and on their integration into practical work. Looking to the future from the same perspective, we feel it is timely for the DL community to discuss such issues as the possible convergence of libraries, museums, and archives in their capacity as carriers of collective memories, which will yield large digital information spaces, and will encourage future co-operation in information spaces. This process seems, important as it is, to be only at its beginning.

The Programme Committee, comprised of 36 members from 14 countries, selected 39 papers, 22 for regular and 17 for short presentations, out of a total of 79 submissions coming from 21 countries and 4 continents, in the following areas:

- User modelling
- Digitisation
- Interpretation and annotation of documents
- Knowledge management
- Data and metadata models
- Integration in user communities
- Information retrieval and filtering
- Multimedia digital libraries
- Multilinguality.

Besides the technical papers, the programme also featured three invited talks by Mike Keller, Stanford University, Eric Miller, W3C, and Dr. Michael Türkay, Senckenberg Museum, Frankfurt, three panel discussions, and a poster and demonstration session. Moreover, tutorials and workshops conveniently arranged immediately before and after the conference extended the range of subjects and opportunities for exchange of knowledge and opinions offered by the conference.

July 2001

P. Constantopoulos
E.J. Neuhold
E. Niggemann
I. Sølvberg

Organisation

General Chairs

Erich J. Neuhold, GMD-IPSI, Darmstadt
Elisabeth Niggemann, Die Deutsche Bibliothek Frankfurt a. M.

Programme Chairs

Ingeborg Torvik Sølvberg, Norwegian University of Science and Technology,
Trondheim
Panos Constantopoulos, FORTH, Crete

Demo & Poster Chairs

Dan Atkins, University of Michigan
Karsten Wendland, Darmstadt University of Technology, Darmstadt

Tutorial Chairs

Norbert Fuhr, University of Dortmund
Richard Furuta, Texas A&M University, USA

Workshop Chair

Carol Peters, IEI-CNR, Pisa

Organisation Chairs

Rudi Schmiede, Darmstadt University of Technology, Darmstadt
Matthias Hemmje, GMD-IPSI, Darmstadt

Publicity Chairs

Thomas Baker, GMD, Sankt Augustin
Nick Belkin, Rutgers University, USA

Programme Committee

T. Aalberg, NTNU, Norway
D. E. Atkins, University of Michigan, USA
Th. Baker, GMD, Germany
N. Belkin, Rutgers University, USA
J. Borbinha, INESC, Portugal
A. Brüggemann-Klein, Technical University of Munich, Germany
P. Constantopoulos, FORTH, Greece, (co-chair)
L. Dempsey, King's College London, UK
M. Doerr, FORTH, Greece
M. Dovey, Oxford Univ., UK
E. Fox, Virginia Tech, USA
N. Fuhr, University of Dortmund, Germany
R. Furuta, Texas A&M University, USA
H. Haddouti, Bavarian Research Center, Germany
P. Hansen, SICS, Sweden
L. Hardman, CWI, The Netherlands
M. Hedstrom, University of Michigan, USA
M. Hemmje, GMD, Germany
L. Hill, University of California at Santa Barbara, USA
O. Husby, BIBSYS, Norway
L. Kalinichenko, Russian Academy of Sciences, Russia
T. Koch, Lund University, Sweden
L. Kovacs, SZTAKI, Hungary
S. Krause, Germanisches Nationalmuseum, Germany
C. Lagoze, Cornell Univ., USA
P. Miller, UKOLN, UK
A. Paepcke, Stanford University, USA
C. Peters, IEI-CNR, Italy
C.J. van Rijsbergen, University of Glasgow, UK
L. Rold, National Museum, Denmark
Ch. Rusbridge, University of Warwick, UK
D. Soergel, University of Maryland, USA
I. Sølvberg, NTNU, Norway, (co-chair)
S. Sugimoto, ULIS, Japan
C. Thanos, IEI-CNR, Italy
U. Thiel, GMD, Germany
A.-M. Vercoustre, CSIRO, Australia
S. Weibel, OCLC, USA

Steering Committee

Costantino Thanos, Chair, DELOS director, CNR-IEI, Italy
Yannis Yoannidis, DELOS Research Forum leader, University of Athens, Greece
Alan Smeaton, University of Dublin, Ireland
Hans-Jörg Scheck, ETHZ, Switzerland
Serge Abiteboul, ECDL 1999 Programme Chair, INRIA, France
Jose Borbinha, ECDL 2000 Programme Chair, BN-IST-INESC, Portugal
Erich Neuhold, ECDL 2001 General Chair, GMD-IPSI, Germany
Ingeborg Sølvberg, ECDL 2001 Programme Chair, NTNU, Norway
Panos Constantopoulos, ECDL 2001 Programme Chair, FORTH, Crete
Nick Belkin, JCDL representative, Rutgers University, USA

Additional Reviewers

Andre Everts
Anna Tonazzini
Claudio Gennaro
Donna Bergmark
Fernando Adrian Das Neves
Ingo Frommholz
Giuseppe Amato
Marcos André Gonçalves
Jörg Cassens
Marcello L'Abbate
Mingfang Wu
Naomi Dushay

Table of Contents

Knowledge Management I

Data and Metadata Models

Integration in User Communities

Information Retrieval and Filtering

Knowledge Management II

Multimedia Digital Libraries

Multilinguality

Evaluating Electronic Textbooks: A Methodology

Ruth Wilson[1] and Monica Landoni[2]

[1] CDLR: Centre for Digital Library Research, University of Strathclyde
[2] Department of Information Science, University of Strathclyde

ruth.m.wilson@strath.ac.uk
monica@dis.strath.ac.uk

Abstract. EBONI (Electronic Books ON-screen Interface) [1] builds on the premise to emerge from the Visual Book [2] and WEB Book projects [3], that appearance is important in the design of electronic textbooks, and offers an evaluation model, or general methodology, from which ebook usability experiments in a range of areas can be extracted and remain comparable at a basic level. The methodology sets out options for selecting material, participants, tasks and techniques, which vary in cost and level of sophistication. Results from each study will feed into a set of best practice guidelines for producing electronic textbooks on the Web, reflecting the requirements of students and academics throughout the UK.

1 Introduction

The Visual Book and the WEB Book experiments have demonstrated that appearance is a critical factor in the design of effective electronic textbooks [4]. The Visual Book experiment studied the application of the paper book metaphor to the design and production of electronic books, particularly focusing on the role of visual components such as size, quality and design, as well as the way in which people interact with them. It was found that users felt familiar with the representation of the book on screen and were able to rely on their experience with paper books to interact with the electronic book. The WEB Book experiment, on the other hand, focused on the impact of appearance on the usability of textbooks on the Web. Two electronic versions of the same text, one in a very plain scrolling format, the other made more "scannable" according to Morkes and Nielsen's Web design guidelines [5], were selected as the material for evaluation, and the scannable text proved to be 92% more usable.

At a time when the place of the book in the digital world is changing [6], it is important that the role of appearance in the design of ebooks is explored thoroughly in order that commercial publishing developments are fully informed from a design, as well as a content and technology perspective, and are delivered to the end-user in a form which maximises their usability.

EBONI (Electronic Books ON-screen Interface), funded under the JISC DNER Programme for Learning and Teaching [7], builds on the experience of the Visual Book, the WEB Book and related projects [8], and will conduct a large-scale

P. Constantopoulos and I.T. Sølvberg (Eds.): ECDL 2001, LNCS 2163, pp. 1-12, 2001.

evaluation of electronic textbooks, assessing the usability requirements of students and academics throughout the UK. This will be achieved through one core experiment in one academic discipline, and a number of "satellite" studies in other disciplines. In order to provide cohesiveness to the project, a general ebook evaluation model has been developed, from which each experiment will be extracted. This comprises a wide variety of techniques including "low cognitive skill" tasks measuring participants' ability to retrieve and recall information, "high cognitive skill" tasks set by lecturers to measure students' understanding of concepts in the texts, and questionnaires designed to measure user satisfaction. In addition, some users will be filmed during the experiment and others will be asked to participate in "think-aloud" procedures. As such, it will aim to measure "usability" comprehensively and at a variety of levels, incorporating traditional IR concepts as well as users' satisfaction and lecturers' pedagogical objectives.

This evaluation model is outlined below. The quantity and combination of elements employed will depend on:

- Appropriateness to the specific objectives of the study. For example, an investigation into pure HCI issues when reading texts on the Web may wish to measure the speed and accuracy of retrieval of information, and users' subjective satisfaction, but be less concerned with the completion of high cognitive skill tasks set by lecturers. Studies into the application of material for educational purposes, however, will adopt measures which reflect the requirements of learners and teachers in Higher Education; and
- Availability of resources. Every study varies in the resources (space, time, people and tools) it has at its disposal. Therefore, for some experiments adopting evaluation techniques such as interviews and think aloud sessions, which are costly in terms of space and time, may not be possible.

2   Selection of Material

Electronic books offer a diverse array of material for evaluation. The term "electronic book" is used throughout professional literature and popular culture to refer variously to hardware, software and content. As Tony Cawkell notes [9], the traditional concept of the book includes novels, dictionaries, telephone books, textbooks, anthologies, instruction manuals, proceedings of meetings, and directories. The phrase "electronic books", however, has been applied to some types of CD-ROM systems, palm-top CD players, on-demand text, electronic documents systems of various kinds, and nearly any kind of computer-based text system that needs "hyping up" for marketing purposes.

Broadly, the term can be applied to the following categories:

- **Hardware devices.** Electronic books can be read on electronic handheld devices, which replicate the size and portability of paper books. Some, such as Gemstar's REBs [10], the eBookman [11] and the goReader [12], are dedicated primarily to reading books. Increasingly, reader software is also available on Pocket PCs or PDAs, which typically perform a host of other functions;
- **Ebook reader software**. A variety of proprietary formats, such as Microsoft Reader [13], Adobe Acrobat Ebook Reader [14] and the TK3 Reader [15], have

been developed, designed to make electronic texts easier to read by preserving the logical structure of the paper book and some of its visual features such as typefaces, colour images and page layout. This software can run on any laptop or desktop PC and is often intended for use on handheld devices, such as the PDAs and Pocket PCs described above;

- **Web books**. Electronic books are accessible via the Web in a number of forms, for free, to borrow, or at a price. Some are simply scrolling pages of text; some incorporate paper book features such as tables of contents, indexes, and page numbers; others exploit Web technology and features of HTML through hyperlinks and frames, and by incorporating search facilities.

EBONI is interested in each of these categories, and the methodological model outlined here can be adapted to them all. However, the core experiment to be extracted from the model is concerned with Web books and, in particular, educational texts produced on the Internet. This is free material published by lecturers and academics to aid the learning and teaching of students at all stages and in all disciplines. Because it is produced by individuals, groups or departments, this material is characterised by its diversity: rather than adhering to a proprietary format, resources employ a variety of styles and techniques, such as frames, hypertext, tables of contents, indexes, internal search mechanisms, navigation icons, interactive elements, and so on. Inevitably, material which displays so much diversity in its presentation will also vary in the success with which it provides help to students. EBONI's aim is to identify those styles and techniques which maximise information intake by users, in order to provide the creators of online learning and teaching content with guidance on how to produce usable, effective material.

The process of selecting particular textbooks for evaluation will be directed by the objectives of the investigation and it is important that the chosen material will enable those objectives to be met in full. In an e-book evaluation, texts may be selected for comparison according to three parameters:

- Format/appearance;
- Content;
- Medium.

For example, the Visual Book experiment compared the same text in electronic and paper media, while the WEB Book experiment compared two electronic versions of the same text, each of which exhibited different styles of presentation (or formats). EBONI's core study, on the other hand, has selected texts which vary according to two parameters: appearance and content. Several texts (different in content) representing different styles have been selected for evaluation, all of them aimed at the same level of students in the same discipline.

In all, the possible combinations of objects selected for comparative evaluation in an e-book usability study include:

- The same text in electronic and paper formats;
- Different electronic versions of the same text;
- Different electronic texts exhibiting different styles/techniques, in the same discipline;
- Different electronic texts exhibiting similar (or the same) styles/techniques, in different disciplines;

- The same electronic texts on different monitors or hardware devices (such as portable e-books).

3 Selection of Actors

Ebook evaluations will vary in terms of the effort and skills required to set up an experiment. In general, though, four main roles, or possible actors, can be distinguished:

3.1 The Participant

Participants interact with the selected texts during a structured evaluation session and their feedback, derived through a variety of techniques, forms the results of the experiment.

Different experiments will have different requirements in terms of the characteristics of the groups of individuals they wish to select. For example, in the WEB Book study participants were asked to read and perform tasks using a textbook on Information Retrieval; therefore, it was important that participants had some knowledge of the subject matter in order that they could engage effectively with the content of the textbook. Other ebook evaluations might require participants of a certain age, or with a certain level of experience with the Internet, or to be undergraduates or postgraduates in a particular discipline.

Preliminary questionnaires can be used to glean more specific information about participants. They can help to distinguish between different "groups" of participants, identify significant differences in population samples, and record any other user needs, characteristics or abilities which may affect the results of the experiment. The information gathered as a result of a pre-questionnaire will usually be factual and, in the case of electronic book evaluations, is likely to fall into two broad categories, both of which may be relevant when interpreting results: background information about the user, and details of the equipment he or she is using to conduct the experiment.

3.2 The Evaluator

The evaluator coordinates all aspects of the experiment, from the selection of material and participants, to the design of the methodology and the selection of evaluation techniques and tasks. More than one evaluator may be needed to supervise studies involving a large number of participants, or if it is felt appropriate for more than one to be present at an interview or think-aloud session.

In a less sophisticated experiment, the evaluator may also take on the role of task developer and assessor. For example, in the WEB Book experiment, the same person devised tasks, arranged the experiment and assessed the feedback. This is possible in cases where:

- The tasks are simple Scavenger Hunt or memory tasks which don't require a subject expert to set them;

- The evaluator has sufficient understanding of the experimental material and with the requirements of lecturers and students to set high cognitive skill tasks himself.

3.3 The Task Developer

The task developer devises and sets tasks for the participant to carry out, using the selected texts. The role of task developer is particularly important in developing high cognitive skill tasks, intended to reflect the more complex uses of material by HE students (see below).   The task developer should be a lecturer or tutor in the appropriate discipline who:

- Is aware of the goals of the experiment;
- Understands the level of knowledge and ability of the participants;
- Is willing to devise tasks which will require participants to use the test material critically, in a way which meets the learning requirements for the level of participants selected.

For developing Scavenger Hunt and memory tasks, it may be possible for this role to be performed by the evaluator.

3.4 The Task Assessor

The assessor accumulates and interprets the evaluative data provided by the participant. Like the task developer, the assessor of high cognitive skill tasks will be a teacher in the appropriate discipline who understands the objectives of the study and the expected level of ability of the participants. He will adopt a marking scheme which is consistent both within the realms of the experiment and which enables results to be compared across other ebook studies derived from this methodology.

4 Selection of Tasks

A number of methods for measuring the usability of user interfaces have been inherited from the field of Human Computer Interaction [16]. Certain of these tasks and techniques are particularly appropriate to extracting evaluative information from electronic books, and these are described below.

Tasks are a way of bringing together participants and the test material in a structured manner, enabling quantitative data about particular aspects of interacting with the electronic book to be gathered. Three types of task are outlined here, intended to measure usability at different levels:

4.1 "Scavenger Hunt"

Scavenger Hunts involve participants in hunting through the material selected for evaluation in search of specific facts without using the browser's "Find" command.

This method is suggested by Spool et al [17] as a means of learning how easy it is for participants to find information in a Web site, and is of particular relevance to electronic textbooks, which are often used for the retrieval of facts and pieces of information. Scavenger Hunts are appropriate in all cases where it is important to the goals of the experiment to determine the accuracy and/or speed with which information can be retrieved from the test material, and the level of difficulty of tasks set will change according to the level of knowledge and expertise of the participants. Coupled with participant observation or the think-aloud technique, they can provide valuable information about how people search an electronic text and what factors help or hinder them.

The results of the Scavenger Hunt will feed directly into two measures of usability:

- **Task time:** the number of seconds it takes users to find answers to the search tasks and one judgment task;
- **Task success:** a percentage score based on the number of correct answers users give in the search tasks.

Although the cost of implementing Scavenger Hunts varies according to the type and quantity of material selected for evaluation, overall they are the least expensive of the types of tasks outlined in this methodology. They can easily be implemented in a group laboratory evaluation session, and require little time and expertise to assess. The questions participants are asked can be derived by the task developer directly from the test material, and so should be quick and easy to devise. Further, responses can be quickly checked against a list of correct answers by the task assessor.

4.2 Memory Tasks

Memory tasks involve the participant reading a chapter or a chunk of text for a short period of time, learning as much as possible in preparation for a short exam. The exam will comprise a set of multiple-choice questions (measuring recognition) and a question asking them to recall a list of items. These tasks are suggested by Morkes and Nielsen as a method of measuring a participant's ability to recognise and recall information from an electronic text, after spending a specified amount of time reading it [18]. Data gathered from such tasks can be used to infer how the appearance of information on screen affects users' ability to remember that information.

As with Scavenger Hunts, memory tasks are quick to devise and assess, and require little expertise on the part of the task developers and assessors. They are derived directly from the test material, and answers can be checked quickly and effortlessly. Memory tasks are more demanding in terms of the environment required to implement them, however, because exam conditions must be enforced. It is still possible for many participants to complete the tasks at once, but quiet surroundings will be required with sufficient personal space for each participant, and more input will be required from the evaluator, who will be required to supervise the exam and enforce exam conditions.

These tasks will comprise two more measures: recognition and recall.

- **Recognition memory**: a percentage score based on the number of correct answers minus the number of incorrect answers to the multiple-choice questions;

- **Recall memory**: a percentage score based on the number of items correctly recalled minus the number incorrectly recalled.

4.3 High Cognitive Skill Tasks

Scavenger Hunts and memory tasks involve participants in interacting with the text in a relatively straightforward manner, searching for facts, or reading and trying to remember information.   Textbooks, however, are often put to more complex uses by students and lecturers, and high cognitive skill tasks are intended to measure participants' ability to engage with the selected material in a manner which requires a higher degree of cognitive skill. In devising such tasks, the roles of task developer and task assessor become key.

Lecturers in the appropriate discipline are asked to read the test material and to assign tasks, the results of which will indicate students' understanding of the concepts in that material. These "high cognitive skill" tasks should reflect the more complex uses to which HE material is often put and measure the effectiveness of the electronic textbook in enabling participants successfully to engage in processes involving skills appropriate to their Higher Education course. A lecturer will also be asked to assess the results of these tasks. Adoption of the same marking scheme across all evaluations which implement high cognitive skill tasks will enable results from different experiments to be compared easily and effectively.

High cognitive skill tasks are the most costly of the types of task outlined here, primarily due to the time and expertise required to develop and assess them. Because they are intended to reflect the learning requirements of students and teachers, at least one lecturer in the relevant discipline will be heavily involved in the development of tasks which will elicit responses from participants that indicate their ability to use the text material critically.   A lecturer will also be required to assess participants' responses.   This is a time-consuming process that requires heavy communication between the evaluator and the lecturer(s) developing tasks in order to:

- Discuss the goals of the experiment;
- Discuss the learning requirements of the lecturer; and
- Incorporate the lecturer's requirements into the high cognitive skill tasks.

5   Selection of Evaluation Techniques

The following procedures are suggested by EBONI for obtaining qualitative feedback about the selected material:

5.1 Subjective Satisfaction Questionnaire

Questionnaires are a relatively inexpensive evaluation technique.   They can be completed by many participants at once and, as demonstrated by the WEB Book experiment, it is possible to distribute them over the Internet, effectively reducing space costs to zero.

Satisfaction is measured after participants have used the test material and carried out any tasks which form part of the experiment, so that their responses are informed and based on experience. Morkes and Nielsen suggest using indices such as quality, ease of use, likability and user affect to measure satisfaction [19]. Studies especially concerned with learning and teaching aspects of the test material (such as those employing high cognitive skill tasks) may find it appropriate to engage the help of a lecturer in the relevant discipline in devising the questionnaire; he or she may be able to advise, for example, on items to include in an index measuring participants' satisfaction with the educational elements of the test material.

5.2 Behaviour Observation

Observation is appropriate to investigations which are particularly concerned with HCI issues, and can be used in e-book evaluations to examine closely the interaction between users and the test material. While interviewing and think-aloud procedures discover information about participants' thoughts, views and opinions, covert observation enables participants' physical behaviour to be studied and draws attention to specific problems. Using video as an observation tool will enable the evaluator to investigate interaction issues that are not easily studied by any other method, and will therefore provide additional data to that derived from other evaluation techniques. Observation is costly in terms of the equipment (a video camera) required to record participants' behaviour, and the time involved in scrutinising the footage after the evaluation session.

5.3 Think-Aloud

The "think-aloud" technique involves at least one participant in thinking aloud to explain what he or she is doing at each stage of performing the tasks, and why, to at least one evaluator. This provides qualitative information about the participant's cognitive processes, explanations of how he or she is navigating the test material, and reasons for difficulties. The evaluator can observe the participant's behaviour at the time of the task, which adds another source of data.

Implementing this technique is more expensive than questionnaires and covert observation in terms of space. Sessions require quiet surroundings, separate from other participants in the evaluation, in order that:

• The "thinking-aloud" procedure does not distract the other participants;
• The think-aloud participant can be heard clearly by the evaluator; and
• The think-aloud participant is not influenced or distracted by the other participants.

Think-aloud sessions will be conducted while the participant completes the tasks although, as explained above, they cannot easily be integrated into a laboratory session with other participants present; therefore, they must occupy a separate "time-slot" and are relatively costly. Moreover, this technique requires the presence of at least one evaluator for every think-aloud participant, in order to record everything that occurs during the session. However, this method can be used effectively with little training on the part of the evaluator [20, 21]. The more participants selected to take part in this procedure, the more expensive it will be in terms of people, time and space.

5.4 Interviews

Interviews will be conducted on a one-to-one basis after any tasks have been performed and the subjective satisfaction questionnaire has been completed. They use a "script" or set of clear instructions and cover a list of questions in a predetermined order, but the interviewer and respondent are free to follow leads [22]. Patrick Dilley suggests structuring the flow of questions to lead the conversation pointedly yet comprehensively toward the larger research questions of the study [23]. Even if the interviewer deviates from the script later, a printed list of questions serves as a guide to return to should he lose his way in the course of listening to answers. They can, therefore, be used to elicit full feedback on selected aspects of the experiment, and to follow leads on additional themes raised by the participant.

Of all the evaluation techniques discussed in this methodology, interviews are the most expensive. As with think-aloud sessions, interviews are costly in terms of space, requiring quiet surroundings, separate from the other participants. They will be conducted after the completion of tasks and questionnaires, and in-depth discussions will be time-consuming for the evaluator. Transcribing the interview later will be an additional cost. Interviews require the presence of at least one evaluator for every participant, skilled in interview techniques. Like think-aloud sessions, the more participants interviewed, the more expensive this technique will be in terms of people, time and space.

6 Conclusions

The tasks and evaluation techniques described above differ in terms of cost, level of sophistication, and the criteria they intend to measure or evaluate. Therefore, depending on the objectives of each ebook evaluation and the resources at its disposal, the implementation of different combinations of tasks and/or evaluation techniques will be appropriate, and the total expense of each experiment will vary across two dimensions:

- Task complexity, ranging from simple retrieval (Scavenger Hunt) tasks to more complex high cognitive skill tasks; and
- Technique complexity, from inexpensive questionnaires to interviews requiring time and expertise.

Although the cost of each element is not quantifiable, Figure 1 provides a rough indication of the relationship between these two dimensions, and is a crude indication of the relative total costs of implementing different combinations of tasks and techniques in an experiment derived from this methodology.

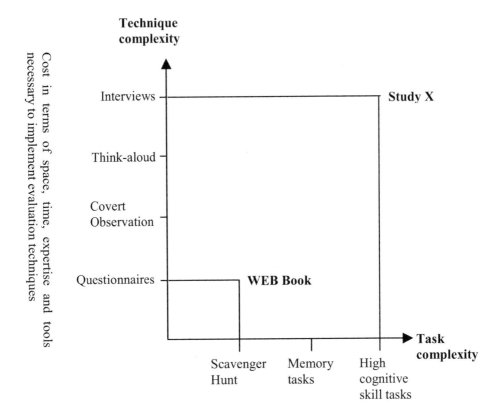

Cost in terms of space, time, expertise and tools
needed to develop and assess tasks

Fig. 1. Relative total costs of the WEB Book experiment and Study X

An experiment implementing a Scavenger Hunt and a questionnaire (such as the WEB Book) will have low scores on both dimensions, indicating a relatively inexpensive experiment. On the other hand, a study which employs high cognitive skill tasks and conducts interviews with participants (Study X) will score highly in terms of task complexity and technique complexity, indicating a relatively costly experiment.

Note that the incremental costs of implementing more than one element from a dimension (for example, questionnaires and think-aloud sessions) are not indicated in this Figure. EBONI's core experiment, therefore, which employs all the tasks and all the evaluation techniques, scores very highly on both axes, yielding a very large total area.

EBONI's hypothesis is that reductionist principles can be applied to the evaluation model so that very sophisticated experiments with unlimited resources which comprise many of the tasks and techniques described above, can be broken down to their constituent elements and "mapped" to simple, unsophisticated experiments employing only one task or technique. Following this logic, the results of EBONI's core study, The WEB Book, and the various ebook satellite studies which will employ other combinations of elements from the two dimensions, will all be comparable at some level.

This will enable the results of all user evaluations to feed directly into a set of best practice guidelines for producing educational material on the Web. Available in January 2002, these will be sent to relevant organisations, targeting publishers of electronic material, similar or related programmes, libraries and museums involved in digitizing collections and interested parties in the HE community in general. In addition, they will be available from the project Web site, together with an example of a text on which they have been implemented.

EBONI is based at the Centre for Digital Library Research [24], University of Strathclyde. The project welcomes feedback at all stages, and interested parties are invited to join the project mailing list [25].

References

1. EBONI (Electronic Books ON-screen Interface), http://eboni.cdlr.strath.ac.uk/
2. Landoni, M.: The Visual Book system: A study of the use of visual rhetoric in the design of electronic books. Glasgow: Department of Information Science, University of Strathclyde (PhD Thesis) (1997).
3. Wilson, R.: The importance of appearance in the design of WEB books. Glasgow: Department of Information Science, University of Strathclyde (MSc Diss.) (1999).
4. Landoni, M., Wilson, R. and Gibb, F.: From the Visual Book to the WEB Book: the importance of good design. Proceedings of the Fourth European Conference on Research and Advanced technology for Digital Libraries, Lisbon, Portugal, 18-20 September 2000.
5. Morkes, J. and Nielsen, J.: Concise, SCANNABLE, and objective: how to write for the Web, http://www.useit.com/papers/webwriting/writing.html (1997)
6. Lynch, C.: The battle to define the future of the book in the digital world. First Monday. 6 (6) (2001)
7. JISC (Joint Information Systems Committee) DNER (Distributed National Electronic Resource) Programme for Learning and Teaching. Available at: http://www.jisc.ac.uk/dner/ (Last visited 14/06/01)
8. Landauer, T., Egan, D., Remde, J., Lesk, M., Lochbaum, C. and Ketchum, D.: Enhancing the usability of text through computer delivery and formative evaluation: the SuperBook project. In: McKnight, C., Dillon, A. and Richardson, J. (eds.): Hypertext: A Psychological Perspective. Available: http://telecaster.lboro.ac.uk/HaPP/happ.html (Last visited 14//06/01)
9. Cawkell, T.: Electronic books. Aslib Proceedings. 51 (2), 54058. (1999)
10. Gemstar REBs. Available: http://www.ebook-gemstar.com/ (Last visited 14/06/01)
11. Franklin's eBookMan. Available: http://www.franklin.com/ebookman/ (Last visited 14/06/01)
12. goReader. Available: http://www.goreader.com/ (Last visited 14/06/01)
13. Microsoft Reader. Available: http://www.microsoft.com/READER/ (Last visited 14/06/01)
14. Adobe Acrobat eBook Reader. Available: http://www.adobe.com/products/ebookreader/main.html (Last visited 14/06/01)
15. Night Kitchen's TK3 Reader. Available: http://www.nightkitchen.com/ (Last visited 14/06/01)

16. Hilbert, D and Redmiles, D.: Extracting usability information from user interface events. ACM Computer Surveys. 32 (4). Baltimore (2000)
17. Spool, Scanlon, Schroeder, Snyder and DeAngelo.: Web site usability: a designer's guide. California: Morgan Kaufmann (1999)
18. Morkes, J. and Nielsen, J. (1997). *op.cit.*
19. *ibid.*
20. Jorgensen, A.K.: Thinking-aloud in user interface design. Human-Computer Interaction – INTERACT '90. D. Diaper et al. (eds.), Elsevier Science Publishers B.V. (North-Holland) (1990) 351-356
21. Wright, P.C., and Monk, A.F.: The use of think-aloud evaluation methods in design. SIGCHI Bulletin. 23 (1) (1991) 55-57
22. Russell, Bernard, H.: Social research methods: qualitative and quantitative approaches. London: Sage Publications (2000) 189-225
23. Dilley, P.: Conducting successful interviews: tips for intrepid research. Theory into Practice. 39 (3) (2000) 131-7
24. Centre for Digital Library Research (CDLR). Available: http://cdlr.strath.ac.uk/ (Last checked 14/06/01)
25. For details of how to join the EBONI mailing list, see the JISCmail Web site: http://www.jiscmail.ac.uk/lists/open-eboni.html (Last checked 14/06/01)

Search Behavior in a Research-Oriented Digital Library

Malika Mahoui[1], Sally Jo Cunningham[2]

[1]Department of Computer Science, Purdue University,
West Lafayette, Indiana, USA 47907
mmahoui@cs.purdue.edu
[2]Department of Computer Science, University of Waikato,
Private Bag 3105, Hamilton, New Zealand
sallyjo@cs.waikato.ac.nz

Abstract. This paper presents a transaction log analysis of ResearchIndex, a digital library for computer science researchers. ResearchIndex is an important information resource for members of this target group, and the collection sees significant use worldwide. Queries from over six months of usage were analyzed, to determine patterns in query construction and search session behavior. Where appropriate, these results are compared to earlier studies of search behavior in two other computing digital libraries.

1. Introduction

Understanding the information behavior of digital library users is central to creating useful, and usable, digital libraries. One particularly fruitful area of research involves studying how users interact with the current library interface, with a view to using the insights gained from the study to improve the library's interface or the collection's contents.

Many different techniques exist to study the behavior of library users: focus groups, talk-aloud protocols, and post-search interviews. These techniques are rich sources of data for gaining insight into users' search intentions and high level strategies, but they are also highly intrusive—and so the data gathering itself may skew the search/browsing tasks, or it may be subject to faulty memories or retroactive re-interpretation of search behavior.

Transaction log analysis—examining information behavior through the search artifacts automatically recorded when a user interacts with a library search system—offers an unobtrusive means for finding out *what* users are doing in a digital library. Although log analysis cannot provide insight into the *why* of search behavior, this method supports examination of very large numbers of search sessions and queries, on a scale that more qualitative studies cannot match.

Although transaction log analysis (TLA) has been applied extensively to the study of search behavior on conventional library OPACs, few studies of digital libraries (for example, ([2], [5]) or other large-scale WWW-based document collections (for example, [8]) exist. Presumably few log analyses exist because digital libraries have only recently seen usage levels warranting analysis. Other search interfaces, such as

P. Constantopoulos and I.T. Sølvberg (Eds.): ECDL 2001, LNCS 2163, pp. 13-24, 2001.

WWW search engines, tend to be commercial enterprises, and are generally reluctant to allow research access to their usage logs.

In this paper, we use TLA techniques to study usage patterns in the ResearchIndex (formerly known as CiteSeer) digital library (http://www.researchindex.org/cs). ResearchIndex (RI) has been developed and maintained by the NEC Research Institute, Inc. It is a large digital library; at the time of the data collection, it provided access to over 290,000 full text documents. This analysis is compared with results from previous studies of two other digital libraries: the Computer Science Technical Reports (CSTR) collection developed by the New Zealand Digital Library project[1]; and the Computer Science Bibliographies[2] (CSBIB) maintained by Alf-Christian Achilles at Karlsruhe University. The CSTR log analysis statistics described in this paper are presented in more detail in [2]; the CSBIB results were previously published in [5].

All three digital libraries are intended to support the same type of user: computer science researchers and tertiary computing students. The comparison of log analysis results is of significance, then, as it highlights the common search behavior shown by this group. Differences in behavior across the three systems can, in some cases, be trace to differences in the search interfaces.

In the following section, we describe the ResearchIndex digital library, and briefly outline the interface and collection characteristics of the CSTR and CSBIB digital libraries. Section 3 describes the collection of the usage data from these three digital libraries. Sections 4 – 6 present the results of the analysis of the ResearchIndex logs, describing user demographics, user session lengths, query complexity, and query refinement patterns. Where applicable, these results are compared to previous results from analysis of CSTR and CSBIB usage logs.

2. Three Computer Science Digital Libraries: RI, CSTR, CSBIB

ResearchIndex (RI), previously known as CiteSeer ([3], [4]), is a digital library focusing on computer science research documents. During the period in which the transaction logs were collected, the collection included more than 290,000 documents. These documents are not assumed to have any bibliographic record available; instead, the document's text is extracted and then parsed to extract the document's bibliographic details and its list of references to other documents. This information is then used to build a citation index and a full text index. Given a search query, ResearchIndex retrieves either the documents (document option) for which the content match best the query terms, or the citations (citation option) that best matches the query terms.

Using the document option, the user can browse through each document; information displayed includes the first lines of the documents, the list of references cited in the paper, the list of papers citing the document and the list of other related documents. The user may select any of these entries for further browsing. He/she also may download the paper or choose to display further extracted text.

---

[1] http://www.nzdl.org
[2] http://liinwww.ira.uka.de/bibliography/index.html

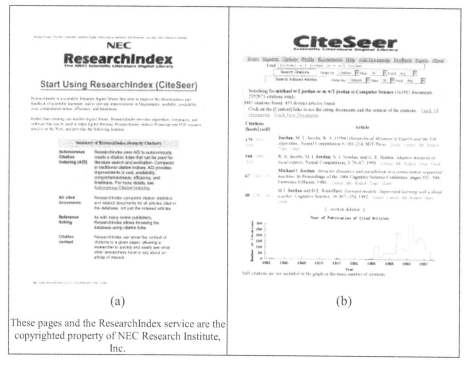

(a)   (b)

Fig. 1. (a) the RI 'welcome page, and (b) the RI main search page, during the data gathering period (figures taken from Lawrence et al, [3]).

Using the citation options, the user may retrieve for any citation the context in which the citation appears, or the document that corresponds to the citation. Additional information about each citation (i.e. number of cited papers, number of citing papers) is also displayed.

Figure 1 show the interface as it appeared during the logging period. The welcome page is a brief description of the ResearchIndex system and its features. A link takes the user to the main page where he/she can either choose to search the indexed citations (citation option) or the indexed articles (document option). Other options include ordering of the query results, maximal hits to return and the search scope within a document (i.e., title, header, any).

The CSTR digital library also provides a full text index to computer science research material. At the time of the usage logging, the CSTR indexed nearly 46,000 technical reports, harvested from over 300 research institutions. The CSTR search interface is based solely on keyword searching; no bibliographic records are provided by the sites from which the documents are harvested, and, unlike the RI system, CSTR does not parse documents to automatically extract bibliographic details. The CSTR has two search options: the simple search (a ranked search), and the advanced search (offering a choice between ranked or Boolean, stemming on/off, specifying proximity of search terms within the documents, etc.).

By contrast with the RI and CSTR digital libraries, CSBIB documents are primarily bibliographic records, rather than full text documents. The CSBIB collection, at the time of the data logging, included approximately 1,000,000 references. Approximately 9% of the references included a link to an online version of the corresponding paper. However, the full text of the online papers was not searchable. CSBIB also offers a simple and an advanced search interface. The simple search screen for the CSBIB is similar to the advanced search option of the CSTR; users can select a number of options, including stemming, number of documents in the result set, etc. The CSBIB advanced search supports the simple search options, and also allows a user to limit searches by bibliographic field (author, title, date, etc.).

3. Data Collection

User activity was automatically logged on all three digital libraries. At the times that the log files were collected, the CSTR and the RI systems were undergoing testing by the digital library developers. For that reason, local queries for these two collections were excluded from this analysis, as during the period studied many local queries were submitted as system tests.

The total number of queries and the time period of study are summarized in Table 1. For all three digital libraries, user activities are timestamped and include the machine identifier (IP address) from which the query was issued, the query text, and all query options selected (for example, ranked or boolean). The users themselves remain anonymous. Since users do not log in or out of the system, it is problematic to identify the beginning/end of a session. A simple heuristic was used to approximate session limits: a session is assumed to be a series of queries containing the same machine identifier, and with no more than a 30 minutes lapse between consecutive queries.

The logs from all three systems were taken over significant periods of time, allowing us to view user activities across more than one session. This longer time period also reduces the possibility that the logs represent an atypical or unrepresentative set of queries and usage patterns.

Table 1. Summary of data collection

Digital Library	Period of study	No. of weeks	No. of queries/ accesses	No. of user sessions	Average no. of queries per week
RI	Aug 99 – Feb 2000	29	1,541,148	46,486	53,143
CSTR	Apr 96 – Jul 97	61	32,802	26,128	428
CSBIB	Sept – Dec 99	17	251,878	54,671	14,816

4. ResearchIndex User Demographics

Since the RI collection is freely accessible—users do not register for the collection—the only information held on a user is the IP address through which that user accessed the RI digital library. This is one significant drawback to studying search behavior that is shared by many digital collections: it is not possible to incorporate detailed user demographics into the transaction log analysis.

However, this user anonymity has its advantages: anonymous access appears likely to prove attractive to computing digital library users, and to increase the appeal of a particular library. In all three collections studied in this paper, users appear to prefer brief interactions with the search systems—and so would likely prefer a system that allows them to immediately begin searching, without spending time registering or verifying their account. Other research suggests that digital library users may be concerned about privacy [7]—and so users may prefer a system that prevents user interest profiles from being linked to a particular individual.

Examination of user domain codes indicates that educational (.edu) institutions form the largest identifiable group of users—suggesting that the RI digital library is indeed reaching its intended users in tertiary institutions. A similar proportion of commercial (.com) users presumably indicates that the RI collection is seeing use in corporate research and development units.

The remaining domain codes primarily indicate national origin, with the highest proportion of use by country coming from users located in Europe (particularly Germany, France, and the UK). RI is truly receiving worldwide attention: the top 24 domains are drawn from such linguistically diverse and geographically dispersed countrues as Japan, Brazil, Israel, and Greece.

Table 2. RI usage by domain.

Domain	Sessions (%)	Domain	Sessions (%)
edu	17.04	pt (Portugal)	1.31
com	16.76	gr (Greece)	1.27
net	10.29	br (Brazil)	1.17
de (Germany)	4.27	se (Sweden)	1.13
fr (France)	4.18	ch (China)	0.94
uk (United Kingdom)	3.18	gov (Government)	0.79
ca (Canada)	2.84	es (Spain)	0.78
it (Italy)	2.52	at (Austria)	0.58
nl (Netherlands)	1.97	fi (Finland)	0.57
au (Australia)	1.94	il (Israel)	0.56
jp (Japan)	1.69	All others	22.54

5. User Sessions

The 1,541,148 queries or browsing accesses logged for the RI digital library are divided into 46,486 sessions. The first, startling, result from the analysis of these sessions is only about 6% of the total number of sessions started with a citation/document search query—that is, from the main search page for the digital library! 4.17% of the total number of user sessions began with a citation search query, and 1.85% started with a document search query; the vast majority of sessions began with a search that bypassed the main query screen. If the users don't enter the digital library through the initial search page, then how do they get in?

We suggest two possible explanations for this situation: either technique that we use for identifying the start of a session is not appropriate for ResearchIndex data, or that the majority of the sessions have been initiated by linking through the results of a previously executed query from a search engine such as Altavista or Google. Setting the timeout between two user sessions to 30 minutes is a heuristic that is plausible from a commonsense point of view, and this heuristic has been adopted by most of the community working on TLA and Web mining (see, for example, [9]). Further, an earlier study of computing researchers indicated that many of these researchers used general purpose search engines to locate research papers more frequently than they used 'formal' computing subject indexes [1]. We therefore tend to the second conjecture, particularly as an examination of the results from popular search engines for queries containing computing-related term reveals the frequent presence of links to RI search result pages.

This observation is emphasized by the total number of sessions including either citation or document search queries as shown in Table 3 (53.31%). When combined with the number of sessions that started with citation/document search queries, we conclude that about 47.31% of the sessions originated by loading results of a 'ready made' search query, and then included at least one citation or document search query later in the session. This suggests that links from general purpose search engines are an effective way to draw users into a digital library, as nearly half of the sessions are initiated in this way and then include further exploration of the RI collection.

Table 3. Summary of session activity

Total number of sessions	% sessions *not including* search queries	% sessions *including* search queries
46,486	46.69	53.31

Table 4 shows the percentage of search sessions not including citation search queries (9.4%) compared to the percentage of search sessions not including document search queries. Recall that 4.17% of the total number of user sessions began with a citation search query, and 1.85% started with a document search query. Taken together, these results indicate that users tend to explicitly change the default search type (citations search) and prefer to run a document type search.

Table 4. frequency of the query types in sessions including search queries

% sessions starting with a search query	% sessions including both citation and document queries	% sessions not including document queries	% sessions not including citation queries
6.02	19.87	24.12	9.4

This is an interesting observation, since the CSTR and CSBIB users, in the overwhelming majority of cases, do *not* change default settings ([1], [5]). The movement of the RI users from the default citation search to the (full text) document search therefore gains significance: the changing of the default is unlikely to occur unless a clear, strong preference exists for full text search. Perhaps the common usage of full text search through general purpose search engines such as Google or AltaVista when conducting a literature survey plays a part in this preference for document search [1]. Or perhaps researchers do not normally begin a search with citation links: the computing researchers studied in the Cunningham and Connaway [1] investigation used citation links, but only by following links within documents that they had read and found relevant. Again, a limitation of transaction log analysis is that it can tell us *what* occurs in a search session, but not *why* those actions occurred; we must therefore be cautious in ascribing motivations to the patterns of action that we observe. On the other hand, the volume of data that is analyzed in these transaction logs, and the length of time over which the logs were gathered, gives confidence that the observed pattern is not a product of coincidence or chance.

Table 5. Frequency distribution of the number of queries issued in user session for RI

Number of search queries issued in user sessions	Adjusted number of Search queries issued in user sessions	Sessions (%)
0	1	46.69
1	2	11.51
2	3	7.48
3	4	5.42
4	5	3.86
5	6	3.10
6	7	2.63
7	8	2.07
8	9	1.63
9	10	1.50
10	11	1.21
10<x<31	11<x<32	9.59
>30	>31	3.24

The analysis of the frequency distribution of queries issued in user sessions for ResearchIndex (Table 5) presented challenges, mainly because of the large portion of sessions that did not include a search query (46.69%). One way to compute the percentages is to discard the sessions that strongly suggest the presence of outliers. This category refers not only to sessions not including any search query (46.69%), but also those that present an extraordinarily large number of queries (3.24%).

A second approach to creating a frequency distribution would be to consider a session that didn't initiate any search query as being a result of a query made by a third party (i.e., a search engines) on behalf of the user. So, from the user's point of view, the session includes a search query, even though this query hasn't been explicitly created by the user through a RI query page. Furthermore, as the number of sessions that include search queries but didn't start with an explicit search is high (47.31%), compared to the number of sessions (6.02%) that started with an explicit search query, it is reasonable to include a 'third party' query as one of the series of queries issued in user sessions. We choose to work with the second approach; it is shown in the 'adjusted' column in Table 5. A final advantage of this approach is that it allows us to easily compare ResearchIndex results with those from the CSBIB and CSTR collections.

Table 6. Frequency distribution of the number of queries issued in user sessions

No queries issued in a user session	Percentage of sessions			
	RI	CSTR	CSBIB (advanced search)	CSBIB (simple search)
1	46.69	43.89	35.97	29.95
2	11.51	21.95	20.02	20.43
3	7.48	12.1	12.19	12.88
4	5.42	7.76	8.51	8.46
5	3.86	4.88	5.84	5.82
6	3.10	2.90	3.83	4.22
7	2.63	1.92	2.68	3.14
8	2.07	1.53	2.13	2.35
>8	17.17	2.41	8.81	12.71

The majority of ResearchIndex sessions (74.96%) include fewer than six queries. This behavior is similar to that of CSBIB and CSTR users (Table 7). However, the RI query frequency distribution contains a far longer 'tail' of than the CSTR and CSBIB distributions (Table 6). In particular, RI sessions including between 9 and 30 queries account for 12.3% of the total number of sessions. The largest number of queries issued in a single session is 18,359—surely beyond the limits of even the most dedicated human researcher!

Table 7. Percentage of sessions including fewer than six search queries

RI	CSTR	CSBIB (advanced search)	CSBIB (basic search)
74.96	90.58	82.53	77.54

An examination of the user session lengths in minutes tells a similar story: the majority of RI sessions are relatively brief, and the distribution for sessions lasting less than 10 minutes is strikingly similar to the distributions for the CSTR and CSBIB collections. Users for all three digital libraries tend to run short sessions containing relatively few queries; presumably these users either quickly find relevant documents to satisfy their information need, or quickly decide that the digital library will not provide useful documents for this need. The exceptionally long 'tail' for the RI sessions includes a maximum session length of nearly 25 days.

Table 8. Session lengths in minutes

	Percentage of sessions			
Number of minutes	RI	CSTR	CSBIB (advanced search)	CSBIB (simple search)
<1	46.90	29.16	47.10	44.18
1	10.57	7.59	7.39	9.07
2	6.48	5.88	4.97	5.38
3	4.87	4.81	3.41	3.68
4	3.70	4.03	2.71	2.58
5	2.89	2.87	2.04	2.05
6	2.61	3.05	1.67	1.68
7	2.08	2.60	1.54	1.29
8	1.93	2.38	1.26	1.15
9	1.50	1.99	1.23	0.91
10	1.46	2.07	1.02	0.90
10<x<30	15.00	24.19	12.37	7.79
>= 30	28.54	9.38	13.30	19.28

A manual examination of the transaction logs supports the conjecture that the majority of lengthy sessions including a large number of queries are the results of robot actions, submitting non related queries to satisfy a broad range of topics. We intend to pursue our tests to assess the validity of this conjecture or find evidence of more convincing explanations for this behavior.

6. Query Complexity

The analysis of the distribution of the number of query terms for ResearchIndex confirms previous results gathered from CSBIB and CSTR collections: user queries are short. For each collection, at least 80% of users queries contain three or fewer terms (Table 9). The average number of query terms is 2.32% in ResearchIndex queries, compared to 2.5% in the CSTR collection and 1.8% in the CSBIB collection. The distribution of the number of query terms in ResearchIndex is closer to that of CSTR collection than to that of CSBIB collection. The number of query terms in CSBIB may have been affected by a quirk in the CSBIB syntax, which enters author names as initials appended to the family name (for example, as the one term SmithJ rather than the two terms J Smith)—which will have the effect of reducing the number of query terms in many author queries. An alternative explanation is that users tend to enter more query terms when searching full text systems (such as RI and

CSTR) than when searching a bibliographic database (such as CSBIB). This hypothesis is supported by many OPAC transaction log studies, which report extremely brief queries as the norm (see, for example, [6]).

The total percentage of queries including three or four queries is more evenly distributed in ResaerchIndex collection than in CSTR collection; more precisely, there are more queries with four terms in ResearchIndex. The analysis of a sample of these queries revealed that many of these queries are in the form "Lee w/2 Giles OR L w/2 Giles". In this example the query includes four terms used in combination with the union and search proximity (i.e., w/n or within n words) logical operators.

Table 9. Distribution of the number of query terms (RI, CSBIB simple search, CSTR)

No of terms in query	0	1	2	3	4	5	6	>6
RI % of queries	0.07	37.02	30.98	12.44	13.34	2.16	1.37	2.67
CSTR % of queries	1.59	27.06	34.04	19.76	8.98	4.26	2.06	2.25
CSBIB (simple search) % queries	0	52.72	28.10	10.8	4.18	1.75	1.02	1.41

In all three systems the default Boolean operator is the union operator; that is, if no operator is explicitly specified in a Boolean search, then the union operator is assumed. Overall, RI users tend to use more operators than CSTR and CSBIB users (Table 10). The search proximity operator is available in the ResearchIndex system, but not in the CSTR and CSBIB interfaces. Over 9% of RI Boolean queries include at least one search proximity operator. The relative popularity of this operator is likely due to the prominent message explaining the operator, which is positioned prominently on search result pages for searches that yield no or few matches. It appears that the users are taking into account this search refinement strategy proposed by the RI interface.

Surprisingly, the union operator is explicitly included in 12.78% of ResearchIndex Boolean queries, despite being the default operator. A further analysis revealed that more than 8% of the total queries included both the union operator and search proximity operator. Note that this percentage also accounts for most of the queries including the search proximity operator—so the bulk of the union operators are included in support of the proximity operator.

Table 10. Frequency of operators in Boolean queries

Percentage of queries containing	RI	CSTR	CSBIB
at least one intersection operator	14.73%	25.8%	14.18%
at least one union operator	12.78%	2.5%	1.69%
parentheses for compound expressions	0.75%	4.6%	0.01%
at least one proximity (NEAR) operator	9.32%	Nil	Nil

7. Conclusions

This paper examines user search behavior in the ResearchIndex digital library. This library is a significant resource for researchers and tertiary students working in computing, and it indeed sees significant usage worldwide. Usage of ResearchIndex is compared to usage in two other digital libraries intended to support this same user group: the Computer Science Technical Reports collection, and the Computer Science Bibliographies. For all three systems, user activities were logged over an extended period, to allow us to examine user behavior over time, and also to minimize the possibility that the period of study is in some way uncharacteristic.

Results from the log analysis of the RI collection indicates that RI users prefer relatively brief queries (fewer than 3 words), and relatively short search sessions (measured both in clock time and in number of queries per session). This pattern of behavior is also noted in the CSTR and CSBIB collections.

Most RI user sessions appear to have been initiated through links from general search engine result pages—indeed, only about 6% of users enter ResearchIndex through the 'front door' of the digital library, so to speak. The links from search engine result pages are extremely effective in bringing searchers into RI; nearly half of the sessions begin with a link from a search engine and then continue with one or more additional queries.

The RI search refinement hint about use of the proximity operator appears to be highly effective: this operator is not common in general search engines and digital libraries, but is used in one-eighth of the RI squeries.

Acknowledgements

We are greatly indebted to the NEC Research Institute, Inc., who have created and maintained the ResearchIndex digital library, for providing access to ResearchIndex transaction logs and for their immense help in interpreting those raw logs. Alf-Christian Achilles has developed and maintained the CSBIB collection since 1995; he generously provided the CSBIB transaction logs described in this paper. We gratefully acknowledge Steve Jones, Roger McNab, and Stefan Boddie, who have worked with us in earlier analysis of CSTR logs. The New Zealand Digital Library project members have inspired us with their enthusiasm and ideas. Zayed University (Abu Dhabi, UAE) provided support and resources for the second author during the final stages of this work.

References

1. Cunningham, S.J., and Connaway, L.S.: Information searching preferences and practices of computer science researchers. Proceedings of OZCHI '96 (Hamilton, New Zealand) (1996) 294-299.
2. Jones, S., Cunningham, S.J., McNab, R.J., and Boddie, S.: A transaction log analysis of a digital library. International Journal on Digital Libraries 3(2) (2000) 152-169.

3. Lawrence, S., Bollacker, K., and Giles, L.C.: Indexing and retrieval of scientific literature. Proceedings of the Eighth ACM International Conference on Information and Knowledge Management (Kansas City MO, November) (1999) 139-146.
4. Lawrence, S., Giles, L.C., and Bollacker, K.: Digital libraries and autonomous citation indexing. IEEE Computer, 32: 6 (1999) 67-71.
5. Mahoui, M., and Cunningham, S.J.: A Comparative Transaction Log Analysis of Two Computing Collections. Research and Advanced Technology for Digital Libraries: Proceedings of the 4th European Conference, ECDL (Lisbon, Portugal, Sept.) (2000) 418-423.
6. Peters, T.A.: The history and development of transaction log analysis. Library Hi Tech 42(11:2) (1993) 41-66.
7. Samuelson, P.: Legally speaking: encoding the law into digital libraries. Communications of the ACM 41:8 (1998) 13-18.
8. Spink, A., Bateman, J., and Jansen, B.J.: Searching heterogeneous collections on the web: behavior of EXCITE users. Information Research: an electronic journal, 4:2 (1998). http://www.shef.ac.uk/~is/publications/infres/paper53.html
9. Tan, Pang-Ning, and Kumar, Vipin.: Discovery of Web Robot Sessions based on their navigational patterns. Technical Report, University of Minnesota (2001). Available at http://www.cs.umn.edu/~ptan/dmkd.ps.

A Combined Phrase and Thesaurus Browser
for Large Document Collections

Gordon W. Paynter and Ian H. Witten

Department of Computer Science, University of Waikato, New Zealand.
{paynter, ihw}@cs.waikato.ac.nz

Abstract. A browsing interface to a document collection can be constructed automatically by identifying the phrases that recur in the full text of the documents and structuring them into a hierarchy based on lexical inclusion. This provides a good way of allowing readers to browse comfortably through the phrases (all phrases) in a large document collection.

A subject-oriented thesaurus provides a different kind of hierarchical structure, based on deep knowledge of the subject area. If all documents, or parts of documents, are tagged with thesaurus terms, this provides a very convenient way of browsing through a collection. Unfortunately, manual classification is expensive and infeasible for many practical document collections.

This paper describes a browsing scheme that gives the best of both worlds by providing a phrase-oriented browser and a thesaurus browser within the same interface. Users can switch smoothly between the phrases in the collection, which give access to the actual documents, and the thesaurus entries, which suggest new relationships and new terms to seek.

1.   Introduction

Browsing is an important activity in any large document collection (Chang and Rice, 1993). Previous work has shown how a browsing interface to a document collection can be constructed by extracting the phrases that occur more than once in the full text of the documents and structuring them into a hierarchy based on lexical inclusion—a phrase points to longer, and hence generally more specific, phrases that include it (Nevill-Manning *et al*, 1999; Paynter *et al.*, 2000a). The scheme is fully automatic and the phrase structure can be created without any manual intervention. Although it works on a purely lexical basis, it creates and presents a plausible, easily-understood, hierarchical structure for documents in the collection—a structure that conventional keyword queries could never reveal. This technique helps bridge the gap between standard term-based query methods and the more complex topics or concepts that readers employ.

Manually constructed subject thesauri also provide a very useful browsing structure. They provide a topic-oriented arrangement of documents, akin to a standard library subject heading scheme, that will generally be completely different from that described above—and far more soundly based. The thesaurus terms themselves constitute a carefully-constructed controlled vocabulary. Most thesauri identify, for each term, broader and narrower terms, and these permit users to navigate from broad groups of items down to more manageable subsets in a well-defined topic-oriented

P. Constantopoulos and I.T. Sølvberg (Eds.): ECDL 2001, LNCS 2163, pp. 25-36, 2001.

Figure 1 The FAO on the Internet (1998) collection

hierarchy. Subject-oriented thesauri have been refined over decades to provide extremely useful browsing structures, and are universally used in all physical libraries—and many digital libraries—as the fundamental basis for the logical and physical organization of library holdings.

Clearly, high-quality subject headings that describe document content should be used wherever they are available, to assist users in their browsing activities. But manually classifying documents according to a thesaurus is expensive. In many digital library or Web-based document collections, subject heading information is unavailable, and infeasible to produce. Machine-readable subject thesauri provide invaluable searching and browsing tools for exploring document collections topically, but documents in digital libraries are rarely tagged with thesaurus metadata, and doing so manually is extremely time-consuming. Automated classification, an active research topic with great promise for the future (Giles, 1998), gives a handle on the problem, but it unlikely to solve it fully.

This paper describes an interface that combines a browsing hierarchy constructed from the full text of a document collection with a completely different hierarchy supplied by a standard subject thesaurus. Users can examine the phrases in the document collection, which give access to the actual documents that contain them. They can also examine the thesaurus terms, which are tagged with information about how often and in which documents they occur. Thesaurus entries suggest new relationships and new terms to seek. The user can switch smoothly between document phrases and thesaurus phrases. The result is a combined hierarchical browser based on both thesaurus phrases and all phrases that occur in the document collection.

Figure 2 Browsing a list of *Title* metadata

The structure of the paper is as follows. The next section describes the document collection that we use as an example throughout the paper, and briefly discusses conventional non-hierarchical metadata-based browsing. Following that we describe the phrase interface, which is called Phind for "phrase index," and convey how it feels to browse a collection using it. We then discuss the process of identifying the phrase hierarchy in a document collection. Next we discuss a particular thesaurus that is used as an example, and show how thesaurus entries are presented, along with phrases, in the same interface.

2.   Example Document Collection

Figure 1 shows the introductory page of a collection called *FAO on the Internet (1998)*, which forms the principal example used throughout this paper. It contains of the Web site of the Food and Agriculture Organization (FAO) of the United Nations, in a version that was distributed on CD-ROM in 1998. This is not an ordinary, informally-organized Web site. Because the mandate of the FAO is to distribute agricultural information internationally, the information included is carefully controlled, giving it more of the characteristics of a typical digital library collection. With 21,700 Web pages, as well as around 13,700 associated files (image files, PDFs, etc.), it corresponds to a medium-sized collection of approximately 140 million words of text. The Web site (*www.fao.org*) has since grown to many times this size, but we

Figure 3 Browsing for information about *forest*

use the 1998 version because it was selected by editors at the FAO, and contains no dynamic content.

Figure 2 shows a typical non-hierarchical browsing display, an ordered list of titles broken down by initial letter (*A* has been selected in the Figure) (Witten *et al*, 1999). This ordered list is selected by clicking the *titles a–z* button in Figure 1. However, it does not scale well (Paynter *et al.*, 2000a). A user browsing the titles will find far too many to view at once—Figure 2, for example, goes only a very small distance through the *A*s. It is necessary to focus the browsing task, while retaining the simplicity and transparency of the interface presented to the user. Further refinement based on more initial letters is not a satisfactory solution.

3.   Browsing the Phrase Interface

Clicking on the *phrases* button in Figure 2 takes users to an automatically-constructed phrase browser that lets them explore the collection according to a hierarchical structure built from all the phrases that occur in the full text of the documents. Unlike the title browsing discussed above, this does scale very well in practice and we have used it on some fairly large (around 0.5 Gb) document collections.

Figure 3 shows the interface in use. It is designed to resemble a paper-based back-of-the-book subject index. The user enters an initial term in the search box at the top. On pressing the *Search* button, the upper panel appears. This shows the phrases at the top level in the hierarchy that contain the search term—in this case the word *forest*.

Figure 4 Expanding on *sustainable forest*

The list is sorted by phrase frequency; on the right is the number of times a phrase appears, and preceding that is the number of documents in which it appears.

Only the first ten phrases are shown, because it is impractical with a Web interface to download a large volume of text, and many of the phrase lists are very large. The total number of phrases appears above the list: in this case 10 phrases are displayed of an available 1632 top-level phrases that contain the word *forest*. At the end of the list is an item that reads *Get more phrases* (displayed in a distinctive color). Clicking it downloads a further ten phrases, which will be accumulated in the browser window so that the user can scroll through all phrases that have been downloaded so far.

The lower panel in Figure 3 appears when the user clicks one of the phrases in the upper list. In this case the user has clicked *sustainable forest* (which is why that line is highlighted in the upper panel), causing the lower panel to display phrases that contain the text *sustainable forest*. The text above the lower panel shows that the phrase *sustainable forest* appears in 36 larger phrases, and in 258 documents.

If one continues to descend through the phrase hierarchy, ever longer and more specific phrases will be found. The page holds only two panels, and if a phrase in the lower panel is clicked the contents of that panel move up to the top panel to make way for the phrase's expansion in the lower panel. In Figure 4, for example, the user has expanded *sustainable forest management*, and begun scrolling through its expansions.

The interface not only presents the expansions of the phrase, it also lists the documents in which the phrase occurs. Each panel shows a phrase list followed by a document list. The first ten document titles are loaded immediately, and become visible when the list is scrolled. In the lower panel of Figure 4, the user has scrolled

Figure 5 Example Web page

down so that the first six document titles are visible. Document titles are easily distinguished on the screen because they appear in a different color from phrases. On the black-and-white rendition in Figure 4 they are distinguished by the absence of a "document" count, because this, by definition, is equal to 1 for the phrase in question (otherwise the document would appear not under the phrase itself but under an expansion of it.) Only the first ten document titles are downloaded, and (as with phrases) users can *Get more documents* by clicking on a special entry at the end of the list (which would become visible if the panel were scrolled down a little more).

Clicking on a document title opens that document in a new window. In fact, in Figure 4 the user has clicked on *Unasylva 182 * Sustainable forest management*, which highlights the phrase and brings up the page shown in Figure 5. As Figure 4 indicates, that document contains 20 occurrences of the phrase *sustainable forest management*. In Figure 5, each occurrence in the document text has been underlined (this can be turned off by clicking the *no highlighting* button).

4.   Identifying Phrases

Underlying the Phind user interface is a hierarchy of phrases that appear in the document collection. For the purposes of this work, a "phrase" is a sequence of words that occurs more than once in the text—that is, we are talking about any phrases that repeat. To include *every* such phrase would clutter the interface with trivial phrases,

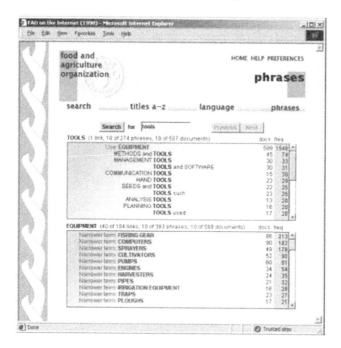

Figure 6 The Phind user interface again

so we add three further conditions to the definition. Phrases must be *maximal-length*, must not contain *phrase delimiters*, and must begin and end with a *content word*.

Phrases are *maximal-length* sequences if they occur in more than one context, where by "context" we mean the words that flank the phrase where it appears in the text. Phrases that are not maximal-length—ones that occur in a single unique context, in other words ones that are flanked by the same two words wherever they appear—are expanded to encompass that context. In the FAO collection, for example, the phrase *forest industries strategy* occurs only in the longer phrase *forestry industries strategy study*, so the latter term is displayed at the top level of the hierarchy in place of the former. On the other hand, the phrase *sustainable forest* occurs in many different contents—ten examples can be seen in the bottom pane of Figure 3.

If the text were treated as an undifferentiated stream of words, many of the phrases extracted from it would cross syntactic boundaries. To take an extreme example, the last word of one document and the first word of the next are unlikely to form a meaningful two-word phrase. For this reason, we impose the constraint that phrases may not include delimiters. Delimiters are defined as the end of documents, the end of sentences, and any punctuation characters. In practice, we tune the punctuation rule to account for common (and language-dependent) usage: in English, for example, neither the apostrophe in *don't* nor the hyphen in *language-dependent* are interpreted as phrase boundaries.

To suppress trivial phrases, we impose the condition that phrases must begin and end with "content words." Function words like *the*, *of*, and *and* occur very frequently (in English) but have no intrinsic semantic value. Without special treatment, the phrases that are extracted would include a myriad of trivial expansions like *the forest*

Figure 7 The Phind interface with thesaurus data

and *of forest*—which would displace more useful terms by taking up space in the phrase list. For each language we further expand phrases whose first or last word appears in a predefined list of stopwords.

At the core of the phrase extraction process is a program that extracts the phrase hierarchy from a sequence of input symbols. It must identify the set of phrases that occur more than once, are maximal length, do not contain delimiters, and begin and end with content words. We will not describe the details of this lengthy and rather intricate process here, but refer the reader to other papers on the subject (Nevill-Manning *et al*, 1999; Paynter *et al.*, 2000a).

The result is a data structure that supports the online browsing interface. As well as the text of the phrases, the interface needs to know the structure defined by the subphrase relation, and what documents each phrase appears in. For every word and phrase there is a list of phrases in which that word or phrase occurs, and with each word or phrase is stored a list of the documents in which it occurs.

5. Thesauri

AGROVOC is a multilingual thesaurus for agricultural information systems, developed by the FAO to provide subject control for the AGRIS agricultural bibliographic database and the CARIS database of agricultural research projects (FAO, 1995). The thesaurus supports the three working languages of the FAO—English, French, and Spanish—and versions in Arabic, German, Italian, and Portuguese are under construction. AGROVOC is actively supported by the FAO and

Figure 8 The Phind interface with thesaurus data.

its international community of users, and is periodically updated to reflect changing terminology or shifts in the boundaries of the research field.

Thesaurus terms are nouns or noun phrases, and are divided into "descriptors," which are the preferred terms that the thesaurus compilers think should be used to describe documents, and "non-descriptors," which are synonyms that are linked to a preferred descriptor that should be used in their place. Despite their name, non-descriptors are extremely useful when searching: they are meaningful domain terms that searchers might use in a query or that document authors might include in their writing. We have in fact studied the relationship between thesaurus phrases and the phrases extracted from a document collection as described above, and conclude that there is a significant degree of overlap (Paynter et al., 2000b). However, many descriptors are rarely used in an actual document collection. For example, descriptors are often scientific names that do not form part of normal discourse, and equivalent non-descriptors may be far more prevalent in actual documents.

Each language version of AGROVOC includes approximately 15,700 descriptors and 10,000 non-descriptors. The terms were designed to be brief (three or fewer words if possible) and compact (at most 35 characters) due to limitations imposed by the original thesaurus software (FAO, 1995). The strict upper limit on characters requires that lengthy terms (such as the names of organizations, enzymes, chemical compounds, etc.) have had to be abbreviated, sometimes in arbitrary or non-standard ways. This impacts the overlap between extracted and AGROVOC phrases, though only slightly.

Manually constructed thesauri include a wealth of potentially useful terms and detailed information about their interrelations. Carefully compiled and edited by hand, they are an authoritative source of subject information and structure. Given a specialist thesaurus that relates to the area covered by a particular document collection, such as the AGROVOC thesaurus for the FAO collection, it seems likely that a phrase browsing scheme would be greatly improved by enriching the phrases with information from the thesaurus—such as descriptors, synonyms, and their relationships.

6. Thesaurus Integration

We have enhanced the Phind interface by including relevant information from the AGROVOC thesaurus alongside phrases extracted from the document collection itself. Given a search term, entries from the thesaurus that include the term are displayed first, followed by the phrases from the document that contain the term, extracted as described above, followed, finally, by documents that contain the term, also described above. The first ten items on each of these three lists are displayed immediately; more can be obtained by clicking the *Get more* links.

In the example of Figure 6, the user has performed a search for *tools*. The first result is a *Use* entry from the thesaurus; the results below are phrases from the document collection. The *Use* entry recommends that the term *equipment* be substituted for *tools* in the query (and states that it occurs 1548 times, in 599 documents). The user clicks on *equipment* and a list of narrower terms are displayed in the bottom pane.

The lower pane in Figure 6 is entirely taken up by thesaurus links. The user has expanded the thesaurus list to 40 terms by clicking the *Get more thesaurus links* bar; in fact, there are a total of 184 thesaurus links for *equipment*. These terms describe a diverse range of equipment, the vast majority of which would not be found by the phrase browser on its own because they do not include either of the words *tools* or *equipment*. Under the thesaurus links appear phrases containing the term; however none of these are currently visible in the Figure because too many thesaurus terms appear.

In Figure 7 the user is searching for information on locusts, using the Latin name *robinia*, which is the preferred descriptor in the AGROVOC thesaurus. On its own, the phrase browser would not lead the user to much useful information, because the term hardly appears at all in the documents in the collection. As the text above the first panel indicates, it occurs in only three documents, and one phrase. However, it also appears in seven thesaurus links, which are shown as the first seven lines in the upper panel. The eighth entry gives the only longer phrase extracted, *robinia pseudoacacia*, which occurs twice, and in two documents (as noted in the columns on the right).

The thesaurus links given in the first seven entries in the top panel, however, provide several alternatives. The first entry indicates that *robinia* is used for the term *locust*, which occurs far more frequently in the text (1417 occurrences, 312 documents). Merely clicking on this term would bring up the display in Figure 8. Subsequent entries state that *acacia* is a synonym (and appears 406 times in 93 documents), that *robinia pseudoacacia* is a narrower term (which appears in two documents), and that several other terms in the thesaurus may be of interest but do not appear in the text of the collection. Clicking on the narrower term *robinia pseudoacacia*, the user discovers from its thesaurus entry that it is used for *black locust*, a subspecies (Figure 7, bottom pane).

The user is not interested in subspecies, so instead clicks on *locust*, the most frequently used term. The result, shown in the lower panel of Figure 8, gives only one thesaurus entry, which directs the user back to the preferred term *robinia*. However, there are 158 expansions, including *desert locust*, *locust numbers*, and *locust control*. The user can explore any of these topics, which may or may not have further expansions and thesaurus entries. Alternatively, they can explore another link from *robinia*, including those that occur in the thesaurus but not in the document text. For example, they may click on the broader term *papilionoideae*, which does not occur in the collection, but has 76 thesaurus entries for broader terms, narrower terms, and synonyms, many of which do occur.

These examples show how manually constructed thesauri can be used to significantly enrich the phrase browsing experience.

7. Conclusion

Both phrase browsing, based on phrases automatically extracted from the documents, and thesaurus browsing, based on manually tagging documents with thesaurus terms, are useful ways of examining the content of a document collection in a way that is more informal, but in many cases far more useful, than full-text searching. Manual tagging is the more powerful technique if the appropriate information is available and accurate, partly because it uses a controlled vocabulary and partly because it is based more directly on the content of the documents. Automatically extracted phrases are lexically based, which could prove limiting—even occasionally misleading—in the normal free-vocabulary situation. But manual tagging needs to be accurate, and is expensive.

We have demonstrated a novel interface that combines automatic phrase extraction, which is very cheap because it requires no manual processing, with the semantic benefits of a manually-constructed thesaurus, which normally presupposes expensive manual tagging of documents. Rather than tagging documents with thesaurus terms manually, the documents in which these terms occur are identified. The thesaurus hierarchy is presented in tandem with the automatically-extracted phrase hierarchy, and smooth transitions from one to the other are provided. For example, the number of occurrences of thesaurus terms and number of documents in which they occur are noted in the display, just as they are for phrases. Thesaurus links are presented explicitly in the display. Clicking on a link to a non-descriptor, or a narrower term, or a broader term, or a related term, brings up all phrases that contain that term—just as clicking on an automatically-extracted phrase brings up all phrases that contain it.

A combined thesaurus/phrase browser gives the best of both worlds: an accurate, cheap, automatically-constructed phrase hierarchy, alongside a carefully-constructed and well-thought-out thesaurus.

References

1. Chang, S.J. and Rice, R.E. (1993) "Browsing: a multidimensional framework." *Annual Review of Information Science and Technology*, Vol. 28, pp. 231–276.
2. FAO (1995) *AGROVOC: multilingual agricultural thesaurus*. Food and Agriculture Organization of the United Nations, Rome, Italy.
3. Giles, C.L., Bollacker, K. and Lawrence, S. (1998) "CiteSeer: An automatic citation indexing system." *Proc ACM Digital Libraries*, Pittsburgh, PA, pp, 89–98.
4. Nevill-Manning, C.G., Witten, I.H. and Paynter, G.W. (1999) "Lexically-generated subject hierarchies for browsing large collections." *Int J Digital Libraries*, Vol. 2, No. 2/3, pp. 111–123; September.
5. Paynter, G.W., Witten, I.H., Cunningham, S.J. and Buchanan, G. (2000a) "Scalable browsing for large collections." *Proc ACM Digital Libraries*, San Antonio, TX, pp. 215–223.
6. Paynter, G.W., Cunningham, S.J. and Witten, I.H. (2000b) "Evaluating extracted phrases and extending thesauri." Proc Asian Digital Libraries Conference, Seoul, Korea, pp. 131–138.
7. Witten, I.H., McNab, R.J., Boddie, S., Bainbridge, D. (1999) "Greenstone: a comprehensive open-source digital library software system." *Proc ACM Digital Libraries*, San Antonio, TX, pp. 113–121.

Customizable Retrieval Functions Based on User Tasks in the Cultural Heritage Domain

Holger Brocks, Ulrich Thiel, Adelheit Stein and Andrea Dirsch-Weigand

GMD-IPSI, German National Research Center for Information Technology, Integrated
Publication and Information Systems Institute, Darmstadt
{brocks, thiel, stein, dirsch}@darmstadt.gmd.de

Abstract. The cultural heritage domain dealing with digital surrogates of rare
and fragile historic artifacts is one of the most promising areas for establishing
collaboratories, i.e. shared virtual working environments for groups of users.
However, in order to be considered a useful tool, such a system must reflect and
support the specific tasks which are typical for the domain. The system design
presented here takes into account a variety of activities, e.g., source analysis,
which are supported by a task-specific selection of appropriate retrieval
functions, e.g., access to OCR results and annotations. The tasks are explicitly
modeled, thus the corresponding user interfaces can be automatically generated.

Keywords. Cultural Heritage, Collaboratory, Task-based Retrieval

1 Digital Libraries in Cultural Heritage

The cultural heritage domain differs considerably from "classical" application
scenarios for digital libraries. Access to existing collections of historical archive
material is severely impeded due to the unavailability of electronic versions of the
rare and fragile source artifacts. The digitization of such material and the storage into
a digital library only represent the most basic prerequisites for solving this access
problem. Appropriate search and retrieval functionality is a fundamental requirement
for enabling the users of such a repository to beneficially employ their personal
expertise and professional knowledge. They need relevant content-based information
and are willing to employ their domain knowledge in order to find what they are
really looking for. If the material to be retrieved consists of digitized documents,
additional information in the form of metadata is necessary for reasonable access
capabilities. To allow for advanced content-based and context-based search the
documents in the digital collection must be indexed by content and subject matter,
whether manually/intellectually or by automatic reasoning procedures.

An adequate working environment for scholarly research in cultural heritage also
has to offer support for typical archival tasks like title cataloguing, formal and
content-based indexing, and several others. In traditional archives, domain experts
perform these tasks referring to the physical objects. This expert knowledge about
procedures and methodology is extremely valuable and should feasibly be elicited and
mapped onto a virtual knowledge environment. However, common workflows in the

P. Constantopoulos and I.T. Sølvberg (Eds.): ECDL 2001, LNCS 2163, pp. 37–48, 2001.

cultural heritage domain, especially in the Arts and Humanities, are difficult to capture in a generic model. To ensure the acceptability of a digital working environment at least the following two factors have to be taken into account:

- Cultural archiving institutions maintain very effective – but mostly informal and very personal – collaborations and connections. Tacit expert knowledge often is made explicit only by face-to-face communication on the occasion of conferences, workshops and professional meetings.
- Arts and Humanities are interpreting sciences, mainly based on the intense and acute interpretation of historical-cultural materials, including primary sources as well as secondary materials, e.g., documentation of cultural objects.

The need for collaboration support has resulted in the introduction of the concept "collaboratory" (a merger of collaboration and laboratory) to the digital library world. Collaboratories can be defined as "virtual centers in the Web, where professionals and lay persons are provided with means for interacting with colleagues, accessing instrumentation, sharing data and computational resources, and accessing information stored in digital libraries and archives" (cf. [1], [2]).

For an adequate "cultural" collaboratory in Arts and Humanities a wide variety of different types of scholarly users – ranging from archivists to historians – together with their specific tasks and conventions must be taken into account. Thus, to ensure the acceptability within the cultural domain, a collaborative environment should maintain a model of its target domain. This model should include the roles of its users as well as relevant aspects of their real-life working environments.

Collaboration can be regarded as a social process where individuals or groups contribute unpublished parts of their work on material in the digital collection or just comment on certain issues, hence complementing the original digitized documents with value-added information, which can then in turn be accessed by other users. In this way discussion amongst scholarly professionals can be incorporated as metadata into the virtual environment of a collaborative digital library.

2   The COLLATE Project

Using the World Wide Web as gateway for document-centered digital library applications and as standard communication, the COLLATE[1] project set out to design and implement a collaboratory for archives, researchers and end-users working with digitized historic-cultural material.

As example domain COLLATE uses historic film documentation, employing digitized multi-format documents on several thousand European films of the early 20th century. Three major European film archives from Germany, Austria and Czechia provide the source material and contribute their professional expertises as initial users of the prototype system.

COLLATE supports the transfer of hitherto tacit expert knowledge of film professionals into explicit knowledge through semantic in-depth indexing. Annotations represent the core concept in COLLATE for implementing collaborative

---

[1] *COLLATE: Collaboratory for Annotation, Indexing and Retrieval of Digitized Historical Archive Material* (IST-1999-20882)

semantic indexing functionality. They can be notes and comments added to a document or its associated metadata (e.g., source of origin) in order to explain and interpret it. COLLATE thus implements – through its inherent annotation support – a collaborative environment for heterogeneous types of users (e.g., archivists, film scholars or just interested laymen). User knowledge is continuously integrated into its repository, forming a continually growing shared information space. COLLATE thus enables its users to create and share valuable knowledge about the cultural, political and social contexts of its application domain.

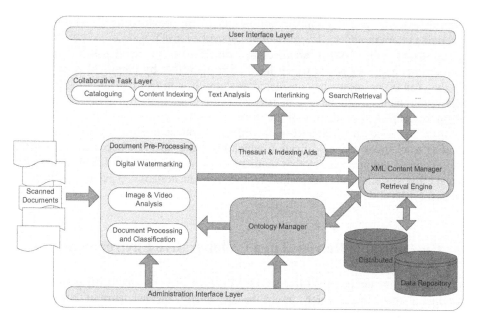

Figure 1:   Overall architecture of the COLLATE system

The COLLATE system is under development. *Figure 1* illustrates its overall architecture that was designed to meet user requirements elicited during the first phase of the project. We will briefly summarize the workflow within the system and describe the function of the contained modules and their interrelations.

Information Capturing. After the historical documents are scanned in they have to pass through a pre-processing module, which automatically extracts relevant information about the documents. Domain knowledge contained in the *Ontology Manager* is used by the *Automatic Document Processing and Classification module* as well as by the *Image & Video Analysis module*. Optionally, the documents can be supplied with *digital watermarks*. The meta-information discovered during pre-processing is then stored (digitally signed) together with the corresponding documents in the repository. The storage will be carried out by the *XML Content Manager* which serves as mediating management layer between the COLLATE system and its underlying databases.

User Interaction. As regards user interaction COLLATE provides appropriate task-based interfaces (*Interface Layer*). These interfaces are dynamically generated according to the specific task the user is trying to perform. Support for several domain-specific tasks – based on a generic task model – is incorporated in the system. Input which is to be stored (e.g., keywords, annotations) is supplied with digital signatures to enable collaborative work on documents and their metadata (*Collaborative Task Layer*). Certain tasks like indexing are supported by *thesauri and indexing aids*. Document retrieval is managed by the *XML Content Manager*. Depending on the issued retrieval request domain information (*Ontology Manager*) as well as *controlled vocabularies* (*Thesauri and Indexing Aids*) may also be consulted. A standard *Retrieval Engine* (e.g., INQUERY) can be used for free text search within the COLLATE repository.

Administration. Special administration interfaces are provided for the configuration of certain system modules (*Administration Interface Layer*).

The COLLATE system architecture was developed on basis of the user requirements and user needs which have been identified by empirical field studies. But they can by no means be considered as static. It is in fact realistic to assume that these requirements might have to be revised as more and more information is gathered during the empirical evaluation of the system. For this reason the COLLATE system has been specified as a framework flexible and scaleable enough to be capable of adapting to changes and modification which may turn up to be necessary during the progression of the project. Another motivation for structuring COLLATE this way is to make the system easily adaptable to other content domains, types of applications and user types.

3   Customizable Retrieval in a Collaborative Environment

In a collaborative environment like COLLATE each actor maintains her own view on the digital repository, which might be dependent on her current role in the collaboration process as well as on the actual task she is trying to perform with the system. Users might even switch roles during the interaction with the system. Contemporary groupware products take neither the heterogeneous user roles nor the social aspects of collaborative work into account. In order to cope with spontaneously emerging profiles of interest and information needs an adequate collaborative environment has to maintain a model of the roles its users can take up. An interested layperson, for example, can be treated as a consumer of the information contained in the repository. Film experts (e.g., archivists, film scientists), on the other hand, also provide additional knowledge through annotating the digitized documents or their associated metadata, thus producing even more information.

These domain experts cannot be treated as a coherent group. Depending on their professional background these people have different motivations and requirements towards utilizing COLLATE as a virtual environment for their daily work. Typical tasks would comprise, e.g., the analysis of source material, the cataloguing of the original documents, or the – formal or semantic – indexing of the documents. All these domain-specific work processes have to be implemented and managed by the system in order to provide reasonable support for the various roles and tasks of its users. In this sense COLLATE provides its users with documents, knowledge about these documents and appropriate interfaces which enable the user to apply their methodological domain knowledge by working with the system.

Despite the inherent differences between the user roles and the corresponding tasks one can identify a single basic requirement which they all share: *The need for advanced embedded retrieval functionality.* This means that in order to maintain the flow of information between the system and its users, COLLATE has to provide advanced retrieval capabilities to allow for a direct and indirect access to the digitized documents and the corresponding secondary material, i.e. their associated metadata. Experts as well as laypersons – assuming proper usage – are thus enabled to satisfy their information needs, which in turn forms the basis for the extending the repository with new knowledge derived from the material accessed before.

3.1   Example Working Scenario: Source Analysis and Interpretation

Scientific *source analysis and interpretation* is one of the most challenging scenarios in film documentation to be supported by the COLLATE system. Scientific source analysis and interpretation can be considered as being composed of at least the following two complex tasks:

Subjective object assessment describes the identification, rating, evaluation and selection of documents according to personal, vague, not predefined and possibly subjective ad-hoc criteria (e.g., the "most typical" censorship case for a short publication about film censorship, the "most impressing" photo of Greta Garbo for a retrospective exhibition, the most optically "attractive" censorship document for a Website or a poster, etc.).

Selecting by criteria paraphrases the retrieval and further selection of relevant documents. The difference between fetching a document in an archive and retrieving a document in a collection is that in the former case the document is already formally identified by its signature, i.e., it is known in advance. In the latter case the need for information can only be vaguely specified. In depends on the tacit knowledge and intuition of the individual film scientist whether any documents matching the request can be found.

In common digital library systems source analysis and interpretation is supported by maintaining a content representation of the document in the form of metadata, which is searchable by keywords. Thus the retrieval of documents in a digital library application is typically performed by simply matching query terms with the document representations and their associated metadata.

The document types in COLLATE differ from the ones normally found in digital libraries. The collection comprises digitized versions of historic film censorship cards, judgments about the prohibition of certain films, newspaper articles, pictorial material and much more. As these documents are quite antique they hardly share any common layout structure or standardized typeface. OCR – if at all – can only be partially employed with a high probability of failure. Thus full-text representations of the digitized documents will be the exception rather than the rule. For this reason retrieval in COLLATE has to rely mainly on the information extracted during document preprocessing and the metadata provided through manual indexing or in the form of annotations.

Metadata standards like Dublin Core (see http://purl.org/DC/) or TEI (see http://www.uic.edu/orgs/tei/) define how to represent textual documents in digital form. They provide – for pre-specified purposes – sets of appropriate metadata elements to capture additional information which is not contained in the original documents. The information represented this way is largely extensional, i.e. it is related to the document as an "object" which has parts and attributes like title, author, affiliation, intellectual property (e.g., creator, publisher) or the concrete instantiation (e.g., date, type) of the document itself. But COLLATE focuses on content-based analysis and indexing, not on cataloguing. Because Dublin Core and TEI are inadequate for the representation of semantic information, they have been extended by a separate document classification schema for the censorship documents.

In order to be also able to embody non-structural information within the metadata associated to a digital document it is necessary to provide a conceptual representation of the domain. One way to structure this domain knowledge is to model it into an ontology, a taxonomy of concepts and their relations (cf. [3]). Keyword lists and thesauri can be – in this sense – considered as low level-concepts within a restricted context.

3.2   The Retrieval Approach in COLLATE

Retrieval in COLLATE can be roughly structured into two levels:
On the *content level* the user can enter terms which are expected to be found in relevant documents. Navigational thesauri structures can be used to enhance recall by adding related keywords to the query terms (*query expansion*). COLLATE can also take advantage of conceptual information stored in the domain ontology and use it to enhance the retrieval capabilities. If the user has, for example, only a vague idea of what she is looking for the system will offer possible interpretations of the otherwise too unspecified query. One of these interpretations can then be selected and used to narrow the search. Thus COLLATE will interactively guide its (inexperienced) users in their retrieval tasks. However, content-based retrieval might also consider structural information of the documents as well as of their associated metadata. Therefore, it will also be possible to restrict the search according to structural criteria, e.g., just searching within annotations or looking for a specific title. As annotations can be employed to express subjective assessments these personalized evaluations can be specifically searched for.

Another alternative to perform search within COLLATE is based on the *active working context*. Already retrieved documents and their metadata can be used to express a new query. Desired features of the active document set can be selected and utilized to retrieve similar documents. As documents can also be interlinked by annotations it might be possible to retrieve all documents which are potentially relevant to the actual working context.

3.3   Document Access

In COLLATE we provide the end user with appropriate search and retrieval functionalities, i.e., conceptual, content-based and context-based, which can be customized by the role of the current user as well as by the task she tries to perform. This means that we also have to take the users' tasks into account when defining the retrieval capabilities of the system. The current task the user is trying to accomplish plays in fact a dominant role as it specifies the view on the domain objects in the repository and the relevant retrieval operations on them. Pre-constructed retrieval forms would offer only insufficient support under these multifaceted conditions. For this reason dynamically constructed retrieval interfaces (see next section), which are highly adaptive to the specific retrieval situation, are provided for. The offered search options will comprise situation-dependent access modes, such as:

- **Full-text** – If OCR techniques were successfully applied to certain document groups, full-text retrieval might yield expedient results. But of course these results have to be treated with care, as full-text search is only capable of identifying whether certain keywords are contained within a document or not, but any information about the semantic context, in which these words occur, is neglected.

- **Structural** – Automatic document processing and classification techniques (see [4]) is used to partition the document collection into classes of documents with similar structure. It is possible to associate certain parts and attributes of the document "object" like concern, type of request or legal motivation with layout elements, which can be identified and marked correspondingly. These layout elements have thereby been transformed into addressable entities. The attributes of these components can then be individually queried according to the document class.

- **Metadata** – Searching on metadata can be treated quite similarly to structural retrieval. By metadata we mean here metadata as defined by the library community, i.e. bibliographic information, index terms or keyword lists. This kind of information is generally entered manually by certain user types, e.g., film scientists. Metadata – as defined in this way – is not necessarily disjunct from the structural information described above. In fact, structural entities have to be indexed manually if automatic classification fails or is unreliable with respect to a certain document type.

- **Annotation** – Annotations are the core elements within the COLLATE environment. They can be notes and commentaries added to a document to explain and interpret it, e.g., transcriptions, translations, summaries, and – in the broader sense – any kind of free text comments or keywords added to describe and index a given document or part of it. To ensure the authenticity of the individual author's contribution and the integrity of the data (annotations can also be nested) each annotation is marked with a digital signature. This impedes any interpretation ambiguities from treating annotations out-of-context.

- **Conceptual** – Retrieval on the conceptual level represents one of the most challenging features within the COLLATE system. Yet it is also is the most promising approach in a domain, where semantics play an important role. The introduction of the intensional level to the retrieval task greatly enhances the querying facilities for the user. Exploiting the ontology to identify ambiguous word meanings, the system can use the information provided in annotations, meta data entries referring to document type (indicating preferred meanings), and factual databases, to select the most probable interpretation. A method to implement this kind of semantic interpretation was prototypically implemented in an earlier project based on a specific logical model, called "abductive inference" (cf. [5], [6], [7]). Thus, search is no longer restricted to the selection of certain attributes which have to be matched by the objects in the database in order to be retrieved. It is now possible to search for documents that represent a certain concept the user might be interested in. Conceptual retrieval – in this sense – can be employed in order to assist inexperienced users.

Future versions of the system will also offer multimedia support. Multimedia material like stills, posters, photos or video fragments can – to some extent– be treated like their textual counterparts. It can be indexed and annotated as well as conceptually indexed and classified by means of automatic image and video analysis (see [8]). Thus, retrieval on these objects can also be performed according to semantic criteria.

These above mentioned set of basic retrieval activities can be considered as the functional core of retrieval primitives in the COLLATE system. These activities are compositional, thus more complex retrieval tasks could be derived out of them. It is in fact difficult to distinguish between them in a non-ambiguous way because they are interrelated on a certain level. Therefore, we consider retrieval in COLLATE as a complex feature which is determined by the task the user is currently pursuing. In this sense the retrieval functionality the system offers is parameterized by the context (task, active documents, user type) of the active environment. By adopting this user-centered perspective we can ensure to be compliant with the requirements and expectations the end user has towards the system.

3.4   Task-Based Generation of User Interfaces

Ensuring usability of a software system is the core objective in user interface design. This can be achieved through the application of design guidelines and heuristics during the development phase of a user interface. The resulting interface has then to be evaluated in practice and, if necessary, refined. As the refinement process usually has to undergo several iterations, recoding the interface by hand can be very time-consuming. The intended functionality of a software system is strongly connected to the tasks users are supposed to perform. Therefore, it is feasible to capture this information within a task model which describes the users, their work, the objects they use, and maybe even the organization they are part of. Task modeling has a strong background in cognitive psychology and focuses on how users perform their work and think about it (cf. [9]).

The formalization of such a task model then serves as the foundation for the generation of appropriate task-based user interfaces. UML has been established as the principal object modeling language. UML offers effective techniques for the modeling of complex workflows at different levels of abstraction. These techniques can also be exploited for the representation of task-models. So-called activity diagrams are applied to model the flow of control of whole tasks, but complex tasks might also be described in decomposed form. *Figure 2* illustrates the representation of the "annotation task" as an UML activity diagram. In our notation activities (the rounded rectangles) are denoting (sub-)tasks which are related by the arrowed lines. Rectangles represent instantiated objects which can be associated to task by the dotted lines. Swim lanes indicate alternatives in the task-flow whereas the diamond depicts a decision to be made. Bullets indicate the start/end states of the task-flow.

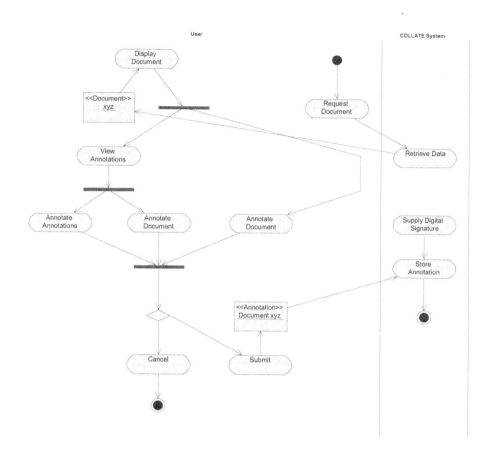

Figure 2:   Sample Task: Annotation

By choosing UML as a standard notation for the task model we can use existing graphical editors and CASE tools, e.g., Rational Rose, as modeling environments, thus saving efforts for designing a custom model editor for COLLATE. The representation of user tasks as UML diagrams yields other benefits as well: instead of explaining proprietary task representation schemas we can share our designs in a declarative, systematic and standardized way. As collaboration is a central feature of COLLATE, our approach is also capable of dealing with multiple actors within the task model.

However, the task model alone is not sufficient for defining the concrete interaction between the user and the system. To effectively support users and their specific role in accomplishing their tasks a comprehensive dialogue model is also required. The dialogue model we intend to employ comprises two tiers that mutually constrain each other. 1) The Conversational Roles model (COR, cf. [5], [6]) specifies the general local interaction options (dialogue acts, embedded clarification dialogues) for all possible dialogue states. 2) Scripts are used as global task-oriented plans to guide the user through the (sub-)tasks to be accomplished. This form of user guidance, recommending appropriate problem-solving steps, is helpful to users unfamiliar with the system. However, it is impossible to anticipate all of the problematic situations that can occur during interaction. To also cover unexpected situations, COR is capable of modeling additional dialogue options not included in any script specification (cf. [10], [11]). This dialogue model therefore allows for a very general specification of kinds of resources and interactions among those resources that are necessary for a flexible account of dialogue. This is achieved by constraining the selection of appropriate interaction patterns with respect to the dialogue context (active task, user role).

In order to allow for uniform processing both – task model and dialogue model – are transformed into equivalent XML representations. These representations, together with the domain model (document/object structures), serve as knowledge bases for the interface generation process. By means of abductive inference the available conceptual information structures can then be mapped to an abstract specification of the user interface design (cf. [6]). Abduction is generally used to infer explanations for a given observation or reasons why a proposition holds. This proposition might be a formal specification of a certain system behavior, and the abduction process yields possible ways to implement this behavior using given elementary functions. In our case the model for a given task, the corresponding dialogue model and the domain model can be considered as the specification. What we are basically trying to find are reasonable designs (i.e. possible interface constructs) for our given "observation". The mapping from task model, dialogue model and domain model to the interface model can therefore be reformulated as an abductive inference process. Since an abductive system generates all feasible hypotheses, several interface designs can be proposed. These interface designs can then be previewed and interactively selected.

The resulting interface model is an abstract representation, which consists of a hierarchical decomposition of different interaction objects (i.e. widgets, dialogue boxes, etc.) and their relations to each other. We adopted XML as the representation language for the interface design to ensure maximum flexibility with regard to presentation styles and operating systems.

By being capable of dynamically constructing user interfaces, customization according to the active task, its context and the role of the current user can be accomplished by simply selecting the appropriate parameters the underlying task/dialogue model representation.

4   Related Work

In order to support situation-dependant task-related retrieval functions, the documents need to be represented in a format which is far more complex that the standard inverted file approach in IR. In some systems, the idea of transforming a collection of documents into "text knowledge bases" has been explored (e.g., CODER [12], CONCERTO [3]). While sophisticated document modeling extends the potential for semantic retrieval, other AI techniques can be employed to achieve even more inferential power (for an overview see, e.g. [5]). Exploiting the knowledge about a specific problem domain and typical user tasks, some systems were able to efficiently assist inexperienced users in query formulation and searching (e.g., CANSEARCH [13]).

It is generally accepted that tasks the user has to fulfill with a system should play an important role in its design. Knowing the user's tasks therefore enables the designer to construct user interfaces reflecting the tasks' properties, including efficient usage patterns, easy-to-use interaction sequences, and powerful assistance features. To accomplish this a systematic transition has to be made from task identification to user interface construction. Hence, a task model of how users perform their tasks with the future system has to be defined. This model contains the task structure, the division of labor between user and system, as well as information about the objects used within tasks (cf. [14]).

Currently, different approaches to model-based user interface development exist, which utilize a great variety of techniques and notations. For a detailed survey on the more recent projects see Da Silva ([15]).

5   Conclusions

The COLLATE system provides appropriate task-based interfaces which offer a situation-adequate choice of retrieval options to a user. Our flexible knowledge-based approach guarantees conformance with the end user's requirements and to be able to adapt to changes in these requirements in a dynamic way.

The identified user requirements for the COLLATE system will be detailed according to experiences gathered in further field evaluation studies. This – of course – also influences the COLLATE task model. The tasks initially modeled in the system may have to be revised, modified or completely redeveloped. In COLLATE we are able to restrict these revisions to the model of the corresponding user task. The matching interfaces are then derived (semi-) automatically. Thus the COLLATE task model can also be seen as a rapid prototyping environment for user interface design.

The individual retrieval operations are implemented as separate components within a generic framework. They can be composed and grouped in order to adequately support the more complex search tasks required by the COLLATE end users (cf. [16]).

References

1. Kouzes, R.T.; Myers, J.D. & Wulf, W.A. (1996). Collaboratories: Doing science on the Internet. In: *IEEE Computer*, Vol. 29, No. 8, August 1996.
2. Wulf, W. A. (1989). The National Collaboratory – A White Paper. In: *Towards a National Collaboratory*. Unpublished report of a workshop held at Rockefeller University, March 17-18, 1989 (co-chaired by J. Lederberg and K. Uncapher).
3. Zarri, G.P.; Bertino, E.; Black, B.; Brasher, A.; Catania, B.; Deavin, D.; Di Pace, L.; Esposito, F.; Leo, P.; McNaught, J.; Persidis, A.; Rinaldi, F. & Semeraro, G. (1999). CONCERTO, An Environment for the "Intelligent" Indexing, Querying and Retrieval of Digital Documents. In *LNAI 1609: Foundations of Intelligent Systems, Proceedings of the 11th Int. Symp. ISMIS'99*, pp. 226-234, Warsaw, Poland, June 1999.

4. Semeraro, G., Ferilli, S., Fanizzi, N. & Esposito, F. (2001). Document Classification and Interpretation through the Inference of Logic-based Models. *This volume.*

5. Stein, A., Gulla, J.A., Müller, A. & Thiel, U. (1998). Abductive dialogue planning for concept-based multimedia information retrieval. In: Fankhauser, P. & Ockenfeld, M. (Eds.), *Integrated Publication and Information Systems. 10 Years of Research and Development* (pp. 129-148). Sankt Augustin: GMD – Forschungszentrum Informationstechnik.

6. Thiel, U., Everts, A., Lutes, B. & Tzeras, K. (1998). A logic-based approach to search in digital libraries. In: Fankhauser, P. & Ockenfeld, M. (Eds.), *Integrated Publication and Information Systems. 10 Years of Research and Development* (pp. 169-186). Sankt Augustin: GMD – Forschungszentrum Informationstechnik.

7. Gulla, J.A, Vos, A.J. & Thiel, U. (1997): An Abductive, Linguistic Approach to Model Retrieval. *Data and Knowledge Engineering*, 23(1): 17-31.

8. Hollfelder, S.; Everts, A. & Thiel, U. (2000). Designing for Semantic Access: A Video Browsing System. *Multimedia Tools and Applications*, 11(3): 281-293.

9. Van Welie, M.; van der Veer, G.C. & Eliens, A. (1999). Breaking down Usability. In *Proceedings of Interact 99*, pp. 613-620, Aug 30 – Sep 3 1999, Edinburgh, Scotland.

10. Stein, Adelheit; Gulla, Jon Atle & Thiel, Ulrich (1999). User-Tailored Planning of Mixed Initiative Information-Seeking Dialogues. *User Modeling and User-Adapted Interaction*, 1999, 9(1-2): 133-166.

11. Belkin, Nicholas J.; Cool, Colleen; Stein, Adelheit & Thiel, Ulrich (1995). Cases, Scripts and Information Seeking Strategies: On the Design of Interactive Information Retrieval Systems. *Expert Systems and Applications, 9*(3): 379-395.

12. Fox, E. A. (1987): Development of the CODER System: A Testbed for Artificial Intelligence Methods in Information Retrieval. *Information Processing & Management* 23 (4). 341-366.

13. Pollitt, S: (1987): CANSEARCH: An expert system approach to document retrieval. *Information Processing & Management* 23 (2): 119-138.

14. Bomsdorf, B. & Szwillus, G (1999). From Task to Dialogue Modelling Based on a Tool-Supported Framework. In *CHI '99 Workshop "Tool Support for Task-Based User Interface Design"*, May 15-20 1999, Pittsburgh/PA, USA.

15. Da Silva, P.P. (2000). User Interface Declarative Models and Development Environments: A Survey. In *7th International Workshop on Design, Specification and Verification of Interactive Systems (DSV-IS2000)*, June 2000, Limerick, Ireland.

16. Sonnenberger, G. & Frei, H.P. (1995). Design of reusable IR framework. Proceedings of the 18th annual international ACM SIGIR conference on Research and development in information retrieval, 1995, Pages 49 – 57.

Digital Watermark

Hamid Reza Mehrabi

The Royal Library
P.O.Box 2149, Denmark-1016 Copenhagen
TEL +45 33474842
hrm@kb.dk

Abstract. Cultural institutions have an increasing need for protection of copyright on the internet. Digital images are easily downloaded and thus need to be protected from misuse. This project will develop a method for provision of protection.

An invisible signal, known as a digital watermark, is a mark placed on a still image. In a project Culture Net Denmark at The Royal library in Copenhagen a method for copyright protection of digital colour images is analysed and implemented.

The signature bits are embedded by modifying the blue channel in the image. A generator that produces random locations in the image, where the signatures bits are embedded, is chosen to prevent any removal of the signature. Specifically, a secret key determines where the signatures bits are embedded in the image.

To extract the signature a user needs to know the secret key.

Furthermore, a method is implemented to retrieve the signature without reference to the original image.

The robustness of the method against possible attacks via geometrical transformation or filtering is analysed.

1 Introduction

The usage of digital media has increased tremendously in the last ten years. Great investments have been made in the production of digital images, sound and video. Big companies and libraries are in the process of converting their image and video archives to an electronic form. Already in the early 90s, World Wide Web started its wide- spread popularity. Digital media has numerous advantages over analogue media. The quality of digital sound, image and video is higher than the corresponding analogue. It is easier to manipulate digital media or make copies without loosing data. A copy of a digital media is identical to its original and can be easily transmitted over a network.

These advantages create new possibilities. It is possible to hide data (information) in a digital sound, image or video. This hidden information cannot be detected by human senses. Embedding of digital data can be used for numerous purposes, one of which is copyright protection.

The electronic representation and transformation of digital media has created possibilities for misuse. Therefore the owners of digital media need to provide a form

P. Constantopoulos and I.T. Sølvberg (Eds.): ECDL 2001, LNCS 2163, pp. 49-58, 2001.
© Springer-Verlag Berlin Heidelberg 2001

of proof for their ownership in order to protect their ownership rights. Digital watermarks can very well serve this purpose.

M. Kutter, F. Jordan, F. Bossen [1] have introduced a watermark technique based on *amplitude modulation*. The method of embedding a watermark is based on adding or subtracting a fraction of the luminance for a given pixel in its blue channel. The retrieving algorithm retrieves the watermark without reference to the original image. Most methods use the original image to retrieve the watermark, and it is therefore we have chosen this method, in the case of any corruption of the original.

At The Royal Library in Denmark we have implemented the method with slight modifications in a prototype available for all culture Net Denmark's governmental institutions.

The prototype works on a JPEG image which is supplied by the true colour space (RGB). The prototype is in use at the library website **www.kb.dk** .

This paper describes the method used and the results obtained.

2 Watermark in General

A digital watermark is a digital signal or pattern placed on a digital media. As the watermark is located on every copy of the watermarked media, this signal can be used as a digital signature. This digital signature can be used as an identification for owners, users or both.

The signature should be similar and unique on every copy for the owner's identification. But in any case, the embedding of a digital watermark can be described as a transformation from the original media to the new media which is completely recognizable compared to the original. Figure 1 demonstrates this transformation, and figure 2 shows the retrieving of the watermark. As figure 1 shows, certain elements (i.e. pixels from a digital colour image) are chosen from the original media. These elements are arbitrary and can be chosen by the use of a *random generator* that gets a secret key (an integer number) as an input.

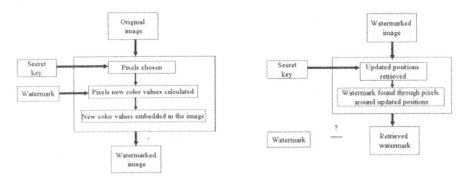

Fig. 1. Watermark process   **Fig. 2.** Retrieving process

These elements will be used to embed the watermark. The length of the watermark and the number of positions are not necessarily the same. The embedding of the watermark in the selected positions (pixels) creates new updated positions which will be replaced with the corresponding original positions.

This transformation is absolutely different from the transformation that takes place in cryptography, which also transforms the original document to the new document that is completely unrecognisable in comparison to the original document.

There are two types of watermarks (visible and invisible). Visible watermarks are basically similar to stamps used on documents. Due to the high contrast between background and foreground in the watermarked image, a visible watermark can be easily observed. The advantage of a visible watermark is that it destroys the commercial value of the digital image. An example is TV stations that use logos.

An invisible watermark can be potentially used to identify the owner or user of a digital image or both. The digital signature is hidden in the image in such a way that human eye cannot detect it. Whenever an image is misused, the owner can retrieve the digital signature by the retrieving algorithm in order to prove his ownership.

3 Human Visual System

One of the important characteristics of the human visual system is the capacity called *masking*. Masking occurs when a component in a given visual signal becomes invisible in the presence of another signal. An example is the reduction of the visibility of the pixels around edges with high contrast. There are different models for the description of masking effects. Giord [2] has presented the model *spatial masking* which is based on threshold vision model. The model is claimed to be able to predict masking effects around edges. B. Zhu, A. Tewfik, O. Gerek [3] have linearized Giord's model in order to determine the tolerable error level for the coefficients. Further calculations result in the determination of tolerable error level for each pixel.

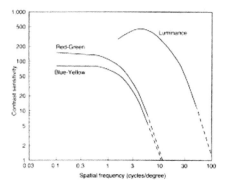

Fig. 3. Spatial frequency

There is another model based on discrete cosine transformation (DCT). In this model the contrast threshold in frequency f is expressed as a function of f, masking frequency f_m, and masking contrast c_m [4]. The graph in figure 3 [5] shows the human eye's sensitivity to luminance intensity. As the graph shows, contrast sensitivity appears around 5 cycle/degree, and sensitivity is 0 around 100 cycle/degree. This shortcoming in the human eye can make it possible to embed data (which is hidden to the eye) in the image.

4 Demands on Digital Watermark

As digital watermarks serve different purposes, we cannot set up a number of unique demands. Digital watermarks can be used to identify the owner or user of digital media. They can also be used for secret communication, as well as pay per use. Our purpose here, however, is to use the watermark to identify the owner or user of the digital image. Therefore, we can have particular demands as shown in the following:

1. A digital watermark is in fact invisible if the human eye is unable to differentiate between the original image and the watermarked image. However, the quality of the image should not be affected after the watermark is embedded.
2. We do not always have access to the original image to enable us compare it to the watermarked image while retrieving the watermark. Therefore, we need certain methods to retrieve the watermark without any reference to the original image.
3. The length of the watermark cannot be arbitrarily long. The longer the watermark, the more difficult it will be to retrieve it. If the purpose is to identify the user of a particular digital media, a 32-bit-watermark can be long enough to identify 2^{32} users.
4. The robustness of a watermark is another issue to be considered. An opponent tries to destroy the watermark through image processing. The watermark should be robust over following:

    1. Linear filter
    2. Non-linear filter
    3. Compression
    4. Quantization
    5. Additive Gaussian or Non-Gaussion noise
    6. Translation, rotation, and cropping

5 Watermark Technique

Three processes are involved in every watermark system:
1. Generating of watermark
2. Embedding of watermark
3. Retrieving of watermark

The generating of a watermark is dependant on its purpose. The obvious method is to use a bit pattern of a particular length, if the purpose is to identify the owner or user of digital media.

The digital watermark can be embedded either in a suitable transform domain like DCT, Wavelet, Fourier, or a spatial domain. In this paper, we have concentrated on the watermark technique used in the spatial domain.

The most important part of a watermark system is the retrieving part. This retrieving part may or may not have reference to the original image to retrieve the watermark. The algorithm that has been implemented retrieves the watermark without any reference to the original image.

6 Implementing of the Watermark Technique Suggested by Martin Kutter, F. Jordan, and F. Bossen

6.1 Single Embedding of a m-bit Watermark

Consider a m-bit watermark $S = \{s_1,...,s_m\}$ that will be embedded in the image $I = \{R,G,B\}$, where R, G, and B stand for the red, green and blue channels. A random generator starts with a *secret key* (an integer number) as input and as output obtains a number of arbitrary positions (as shown in figure 4). In this case the number of positions is equal to the length of watermark. Call these positions **P(i,j).** The first bit s_1 from S is embedded in position **P(i,j)** with modification of the blue channel in position **P(i,j)** through equation 1 :

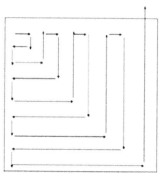

Fig. 4. Searching in the image to choose positions

$$B_{ij} = B_{ij} + (2s-1)L_{ij}q \qquad (1)$$

Where

$$L_{ij} = 0.299R + 0.587G + 0.114B \qquad (2)$$

and **q** determines the fraction of luminance that has to be added or subtracted .

According to equation (1), if **s=0**, a fraction of luminance is subtracted from and if **s=1**, a fraction of luminance is added to the blue channel. The more one adds to or subtracts from the original pixel under modification (according to equation 1), the more robust the watermark becomes, and the greater the difference will be between the original image and the watermarked image (the watermark becomes more visible).

It is the value of **q** that determines the amount of the luminance that should be added or subtracted.

We have to find an optimal value for **q** in equation (1) that gives less difference between the watermarked image and the original image, and gives more robustness to the watermark.

6.1.1 Single Retrieving of a m-bit Watermark

As mentioned earlier, the retrieving algorithm retrieves the watermark from the watermarked image without any reference to the original image. It uses a kind of prediction based on the watermarked image to retrieve the watermark.

Consider the followings equations:

$$\widehat{B}_{ij} = \frac{1}{4c} (\sum_{k=-c}^{c} B_{i+k,j} + \sum_{k=-c}^{c} B_{i,j+k} - 2B_{ij}) \qquad (3)$$

$$\widehat{B}_{ij} = \frac{1}{4c} (\sum_{k=-c}^{c} B_{i-k,j-k} + \sum_{k=-c}^{c} B_{i+k,j-k} - 2B_{ij}) \qquad (4)$$

where B_{ij} is the value of the blue channel of pixel **P(i,j)** which has been used to embed one bit (1 or 0) under the embedding process. Equation (3) makes an average of blue values (which have not been modified under the embedding process) located on the vertical and horizontal lines in figure 6. For example, for c=3 equation (3) makes an average of 12 blue values, 6 on each line. $\widehat{B}_{ij}$ is the prediction of the original blue value for **P(i.j)** before the modification. In order to find out whether a 0 or a 1 has been embedded in **P(i.j)**, we consider the following:

$$\text{If } B_{ij} - \widehat{B}_{ij} < 0 \text{ then 0 has been embedded} \qquad (5)$$

$$\text{If } B_{ij} - \widehat{B}_{ij} > 0 \text{ then 1 has been embedded} \qquad (6)$$

Equation (4) is another model which makes the average of blue values in a different way (Figure 5). We have implemented both models, and come to the conclusion that the model corresponding to equation 3 gives better results as Martin Kutter, F. Jordan, and F. Bossen postulate.

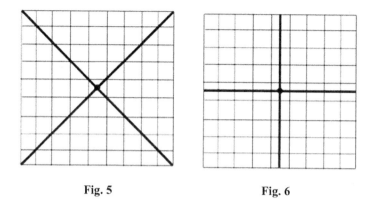

Fig. 5   Fig. 6

As we can see, the retrieving algorithm is not exactly the inverse of the embedding algorithm. Therefore while retrieving the watermark from the watermarked image we expect possible errors. These errors can be reduced by embedding each single bit in more pixels.

6.2 Multiple Embedding

Consider again a m-bit watermark $S = \{s_1, ..., s_m\}$. The principle of multiple embedding is the same as single embedding with the only difference that in multiple embedding, one bit is embedded in more pixels to make the watermark more robust. We use two more bits, one of which is always 0, and the other is 1. These are embedded in the same way as the bit from the watermark **S** is embedded in the image. These will be used for a different purpose that will be discussed later on in the paper.

The number of pixels we want to use for embedding one bit is a critical parameter because it interacts with the value of q from equation (1) and the way in which we search to choose the positions (Figure 6). While retrieving the watermark, the more pixels chosen for embedding, the greater the risk of using pixels that have already been updated. Fewer pixels result in less robustness of the watermark, and this results in more error in the retrieving process. A good combination of the number of pixels and the value of q in equation (1) gives suitable robustness and less invisibility to the watermark.

There is another parameter to consider. We have implemented a dynamic multiple embedding algorithm which means the watermark is embedded in the image when a user, through a WEB browser on the internet, requests for an image from our image base (Figure 7). Therefore running time of the embedding algorithm is an important parameter to consider. The more pixels chosen, the longer the running time will be.

6.2.1 Dynamic Embedding of Watermark

As a consequent of the current development, it is important for the library to have a model in which images and watermark technology are kept separate, so that the library's policy with regard to watermarking can be changed or adjusted, should either technological or legal development require it. Therefore we have developed a dynamic watermark system at The Royal Library. An illustration of the system is showed in figure 7.

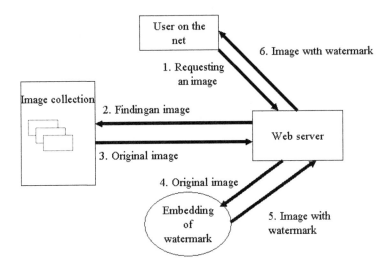

Fig. 7. Dynamic embedding of watermark

6.2.2 Retrieving of a m-bit Watermark in the Case of Multiple Embedding

Here again, the principle is the same as a single retrieving. Each bit is embedded in n pixels under the embedding process. If the length of the watermark is m, then n*m pixels have been updated under the embedding process. All the n*m pixels are accessible through the secret key. Consider the first n pixels where the first bit is embedded. We take an average of blue channels around every pixel which has been updated (exactly the same as the single case, Figure 3) from the n pixels.

We take an average ($\widehat{B}_{ij}$) of all the averages mentioned. We also take an average (B) of the blue channels for the updated pixels where the first bit is embedded. The sign of $(B - \widehat{B}_{ij})$ determines whether 0 or 1 has been embedded in the first n positions. We do the same for the next m-1 bit. It has already been mentioned that in addition to the m-bit watermark, two other bits are also embedded, one of which is always 0 and the other is 1. These two bits are used to retrieve the watermark when the watermarked image is rotated, translated, or cropped. This results in a repositioning of pixels in the watermarked image. We use these two bits for the detection of translation, cropping, or the degree of rotation. 0 and 1 are each embedded in n positions. We call the average of the blue channels of the n updated positions B_0 where 0 is embedded, and B_1 where 1 is embedded.

In the case of rotation, we rotate the watermarked image to a certain degree and measure the difference between B_0 and B_1. We repeat this a number of times. Where the difference between B_0 and B_1 is the greatest, the degree of rotation can be detected. We can implement the same technique for translation. The next problem occurs when we apply the *blur* filter on the watermarked image. To retrieve the watermark from this image, we use again the two additional bits as in the following:

$$\text{If } (B - \widehat{B}_{ij}) > \frac{B_0 + B_1}{2} \text{ then 1 is embedded} \tag{7}$$

$$\text{If} (B - \widehat{B}_{ij}) < \frac{B_0 + B_1}{2} \text{ then 0 is embedded} \tag{8}$$

7 Conclusion

We have implemented a watermark technique that is working on a JPEG image, which is supplied with RGB color space. The watermark system is tested on JPEG images with size up to 600x800 DPI. As mentioned, we had to find an optimal value of q in equation (1) and a suitable number of pixels for the embedding process.

The system is tested in two different ways:

1. With a fixed number of pixels for embedding, fixed value of q (equation 1), c=3 equation (3) and a watermark of length 32 which gives the following results:

Number of pixels for embedding	256	512	1024	2048	16384	16384
Invisibility of watermark	Invisible	Invisible	Invisible	Invisible	Invisible	Invisible
Value of q	0.4	0.4	0.4	0.5	0.1	0.15
Robust over rotation	No	No	No	No	Yes	Yes
Robust over translation	No	Yes	Yes	Yes	Yes	Yes
Robust over blur filter 5x5	No	No	No	No	No	Yes
Robust over blur filter 3x3	No	No	No	No	Yes	Yes
Robust over JPEG compression 60%	No	No	No	No	Yes	Yes
Robust over quantization	No	No	Yes	Yes	Yes	Yes

2. With dynamic size of number of pixels for embedding which is 35 % of the total pixels of the image of size up to 600x800, c= 3 and q=0.2.

The latter model gave the best result, which means that:

- The watermark is completely invisible in the watermarked image
- The watermark is robust over blur filter (3x3)
- The watermark is robust over rotation
- The watermark is robust over translation
- The watermark is robust over compression at 60%
- The watermark is robust over quantization

Limitation in this method.

- The algorithm cannot be applied on B/W and greyscale images. The reason is that these types have not RGB colour space.
- Applying the dynamic model on a coloured image over 600x800 pixels results in higher running time. In this case the static model should be applied.
- Applying the model on an image with white background results in yellow stripes in the watermarked image. If you have many images with white background the parameter q in equation (1) has to be reduced.

The system is implemented in Linux operative system and running time in our dynamic model for embedding the watermark is under 2 seconds.

8 Literature

[1]   Digital Signature of Color Images using Amplitude Modulation, Martin Kutter, Frederic Jordan, Frank Bossen, Signal Processing Laboratory, EPFL 1015 Lausanne Switzerland.

[2]   The information theoretical significance of spatial and temporal masking in video signals.k in Proc. SPIE Human Vision, Visual Processing, and Digital Display, 1989, vol. 1077, pp 178-187. B. Giord.

[3]   Low bit rate near-transparent image coding, in Proc. SPIE Int. Conf. Wavelet Appls. For dual Use, 1995, vol, 2491, pp. 173-184.

[4]   Low bit rate near-transparent image coding, in Proc. SPIE Int. Conf. Wavelet Appls. For dual Use, 1995, vol, 2491, pp. 173-184.

[5]   JPEG STILL IMAGE DATA COMPRESSION STANDARD. William B. Pennebaker, Joan L. Mitchell.

Document Classification and Interpretation through the Inference of Logic-Based Models

Giovanni Semeraro, Stefano Ferilli, Nicola Fanizzi, and Floriana Esposito

Dipartimento di Informatica, Università di Bari, Via Orabona 4, 70125 Bari, Italy
{semeraro,ferilli,fanizzi,esposito}@di.uniba.it

Abstract. We present a methodology for document processing that exploits logic-based machine learning techniques. Our claim is that information capture and indexing can profit by the identification of the document class and of specific function of its single layout components. Indeed, the application of incremental and multistrategy machine learning techniques, rather than the classic ones, allows for an efficient solution to the problem of information capture.

1 Introduction and Motivation

Digitization of real world artifacts has witnessed an increasing interest in recent times, due to the worldwide availability of large corpora of paper documents to be converted in digital form. Indeed, this task is prior to any advanced technologies for intelligent digital libraries [6], as it affects the representation, organization and indexing of the information.

In a nutshell *Classification* and *Interpretation* of documents can be regarded as the problem of labelling the documents according to one of some predefined classes and then eliciting the function of the various layout components [11, 8] and relating the content (*semantics*) to spatial information coming from layout analysis. State-of-the-art machine learning methods have recently been applied to the task, leading to systems of increased sophistication and effectiveness (see, e.g., [4, 7]). Yet most of the current work has been carried out following pattern analysis or single-strategy learning approaches.

Our claim here is that a solid methodology should profit by the application of various machine learning schemes based on a common symbolic language representation. First order logic, as a well-founded knowledge representation offers a unique and natural infrastructure both for describing the document structure and for detecting its content in order to categorize it. We intend to show how this can be achieved through incremental algorithms, which comply with domains where there is a continuous flow of new incoming evidences, while maintaining comparable performance in time and predictive accuracy of the model with respect to theories learned by systems that follow a *batch* approach.

After the various components of a document have been singled out, OCR can be applied only to the ones recognized as textual so to perform categorization also on the ground of this information [9]. Two more phases can be devised, that

P. Constantopoulos and I.T. Sølvberg (Eds.): ECDL 2001, LNCS 2163, pp. 59–70, 2001.

can be regarded as the counterparts, at a higher semantic level, of the two tasks described above. The former aims at identifying the subject of the document, among a given set of possibilities (e.g., a commercial letter could be a job request or a meeting announcement, etc.). Then, knowing what the document is about, one might want to single out information that is significant for that particular concern (e.g., in the job request case, the specialization and past experiences could be searched for).

Also from the perspective of a semi-automatic solution to the problem, a logic-based approach can be very advantageous. Indeed, a logic representation allows for an easy understanding of the model inferred by the learning system employed. Thus, when the human intervention is required to refine such a model, as well as for any other kind of fine-tuning and adjustment, manipulating logic representations of the model at hand can be far more manageable than acting on the parameters of a numeric approach.

The remainder of the paper is organized as follows. In Section 2 our methodology for document processing is summarized. Section 3 presents a multi-purpose tool for inferring the logic models incrementally. In Section 4 we show an experiment where our incremental model inference approach is compared to a proprietary batch system in terms of both efficiency and accuracy of the model inferred. Finally, Section 5 draws the conclusions and outlines possible developments.

2   Document Processing

Document processing as a research area has a tradition of many decades, during which it has been carried out exploiting a variety of tools and techniques [11, 8]. It seems a real world problem that is suitable for an extensive application of logic-based techniques.

After a proper pre-processing phase has been carried out for obtaining the digital representation from the physical form, it is possible to infer models (in the form of rules) for recognizing the class they belong to, among a given set of significant ones. For instance, in an office it would be useful to separate the incoming mail into bills, commercial letters and advertisements; in an academic library, it would make sense to divide the incoming papers and journals according to their series for cataloguing and indexing purposes. Once the document class has been identified, a further step is to understand the logical function of its components. This phase must necessarily follow the previous one, since for each document type it makes sense to search for different kinds of semantic components. For instance, in a commercial letter we may expect to find sender address, receiver address, possibly the logo of the sender company, body, date and signature; conversely, standard logical components in a scientific paper are title, authors, their affiliation and address, an abstract and the various (sub-)sections.

The tasks described above are referred to as *document image understanding*, intended as the formal representation of the abstract relationships indicated by the two-dimensional arrangement of the symbols [8], and can be carried out based only on the layout structure of the document. Some authors single out from the larger task of document image understanding the specific sub-phase of *document classification*, that corresponds to assigning a document to its class [9]. In the following, such a distinction will be made.

2.1 Pre-processing

Information capture, as a task of setting information items free of the physical medium on which they are stored, involves the conversion of data from a paper format into a digital one. Such a transformation requires a solution to several problems, such as the separation of text from graphics. In the literature, the process of breaking down a document image into several layout components is known as *document analysis*. This process is summarized here since it is prior to model inference; more details can be found in [4].

WISDOM [3, 1] is the system used to transform printed information into a symbolic representation. In fact, it is also able to carry out Document Image Understanding by means of a batch symbolic learning system. It can manage multi-page documents (the definition of the right sequence of the single scanned pages is a responsibility of the user).

Initially, each document page is scanned and thresholded into a binary image. Then, the bitmap representation is converted into a structured set of symbolic entities, that is appropriate for computerized information processing, by a *segmentation* phase. Since the result of the segmentation algorithm used in WISDOM depends on both the *skew angle* (i.e., the orientation angle of text lines in the page), and the choice of some critical parameters, the system was made less vulnerable to non-zero skew angles and/or arbitrary parameter definitions. The page is segmented by means a fast top-down technique, the Run Length Smoothing Algorithm (RLSA).

It is important to label the blocks according to the type of content (text or graphic information), so that subsequent processing stages may operate exclusively on the appropriate type of information (e.g., an OCR will be applied only to textual components). This separation problem can be reformulated as a classification (or discrimination) one, where the classes are *text block*, *horizontal line*, *vertical line*, *picture* (i.e., halftone images) and *graphics* (e.g., line drawings).

2.2 Layout Analysis

A segmented page is still too detailed. Generally, there is no need of so much information for the subsequent phases of document processing. *Layout analysis* is the perceptual organization process for detecting structures among blocks.

The result is a hierarchy of abstract representations of the document image, called the *layout* (or *geometric*) *structure* of the document. The leaves of the layout tree (lowest level of the abstraction hierarchy) are the (*basic*) blocks, while the root represents the whole document. A page may group several layout components, called *frames*, which are still rectangular areas of interest in the image of a document page. An ideal layout analysis process should produce a set of frames, each of which can be associated with a distinct semantic label,

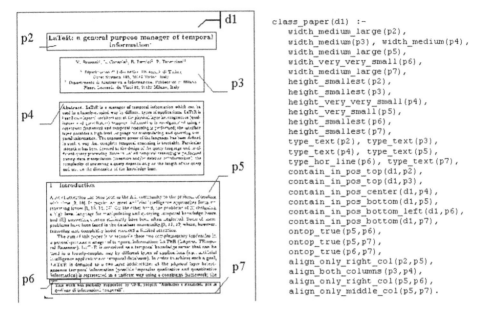

```
class_paper(d1)  :-
      width_medium_large(p2),
      width_medium(p3),  width_medium(p4),
      width_medium_large(p5),
      width_very_very_small(p6),
      width_medium_large(p7),
      height_smallest(p2),
      height_smallest(p3),
      height_very_very_small(p4),
      height_very_small(p5),
      height_smallest(p6),
      height_smallest(p7),
      type_text(p2),  type_text(p3),
      type_text(p4),  type_text(p5),
      type_hor_line(p6),  type_text(p7),
      contain_in_pos_top(d1,p2),
      contain_in_pos_top(d1,p3),
      contain_in_pos_center(d1,p4),
      contain_in_pos_bottom(d1,p5),
      contain_in_pos_bottom_left(d1,p6),
      contain_in_pos_bottom(d1,p7),
      ontop_true(p5,p6),
      ontop_true(p5,p7),
      ontop_true(p6,p7),
      align_only_right_col(p2,p5),
      align_both_columns(p3,p4),
      align_only_right_col(p5,p6),
      align_only_middle_col(p5,p7).
```

Fig. 1. A document and its description

such as title and author of a scientific paper. In practice, however, a suboptimal layout structure in which it is still possible to distinguish the logical meaning of distinct frames should be considered a good output of the layout analyzer.

To extract the layout structure from the digital image a knowledge-based approach was adopted, that exploits generic knowledge and rules on typesetting conventions in order to group basic blocks together into frames.

The result of the layout analysis process is a file describing the hierarchy of layout components, made up of blocks (at the bottom), lines, sets of lines, first frames and second frames (at the top). The 'second frame' level of the layout hierarchy is described by means of

attributes: *height* and *width* of a frame (numeric), *type* of a frame (text, horizontal line, and so on), *coordinates* of the centroid of a frame (numeric);

binary relations: *part-of*, *on-top*, *to-right* and relative *alignment* (only by left column, only by right column, by both columns, by middle column, only by upper row, only by lower row, by both rows, and by middle row).

Each document can be represented as a logical conjunction of literals, by means of predicates that express the above properties (numeric features are discretized in a finite number of values). Figure 1 shows the first page of a scientific paper along with the frames identified and the corresponding description.

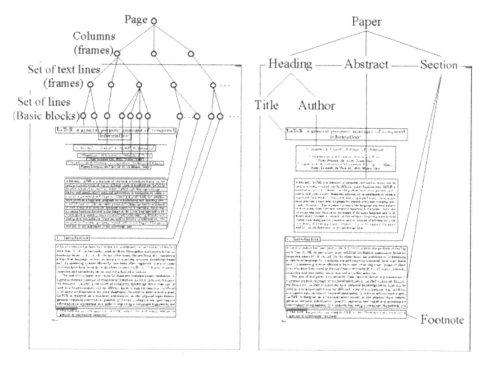

Fig. 2. Layout and Logic structure of a document

2.3   Document Classification and Interpretation

After detecting the layout structure, the logical components of the document can be identified (such as title, authors, sections of an article). Also these components can be arranged hierarchically in the so-called *logical structure*, by repeatedly dividing the content of a document into increasingly smaller parts, based on its human-perceptible meaning. The leaves of this structure are the basic logical components, such as authors and title. Internal nodes represent structured logical components (e.g. the heading of an article, that encompasses the title and the author). The root is the document class, such as *scientific-paper*. Figure 2 shows the two structures as detected in a scientific paper.

The problem of finding the logical structure of a document can be cast as the problem of associating layout components with a corresponding logical component. In the case at hand, this mapping is limited to the association of a page with a document class (*classification*) and the association of second frames with basic logical components (*interpretation*). Both the rules used for the classification and interpretation process are automatically learned from a set of training documents for which the correct class and frame labels are already provided. By looking at each class or frame label as a distinct concept to be learned, it is possible to apply conceptual learning algorithms (see the next section) whose final product are rules expressed in high-level, human-oriented terms and forms.

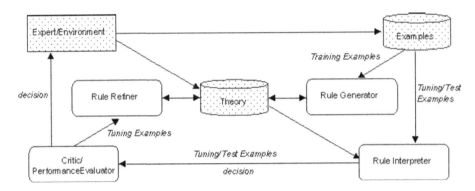

Fig. 3. INTHELEX closed-loop architecture

Once the logical components have been detected, the OCR can be selectively applied to variable areas of the raster image corresponding to the significant logical components.

3   The Incremental Learning System INTHELEX

In this section we present INTHELEX (*INcremental THEory Learner from EXamples*), a multi-purpose system that is able to infer rules from (positive and negative) examples in the form of first-order logic theories (more technical details about INTHELEX can be found in [5]). Since it can be exploited for document processing, it was embedded in the Learning Server module of our prototypical digital library CDL [10, 4] and is going to be integrated in the Document Processing and Classification module of the COLLATE system [2].

The system can learn simultaneously rules for describing *multiple concepts*, that are possibly related to each other; furthermore, it is a *fully incremental closed loop* system, meaning that it is able to revise a previous model, as well as to start from an empty one, and that the model inferred is checked for validity on any new example; in case of failure, a revision process is activated in order to restore the consistency of the model. Incremental learning is necessary when either incomplete information is available at the time of model generation, or the nature of the concepts evolves dynamically. In particular, INTHELEX adopts a *full memory storage* strategy (i.e. it retains all the available examples), and incorporates two inductive refinement operators, one for generalizing hypotheses that reject positive examples, and the other for specializing hypotheses that explain negative examples. Another feature is the integration of abstraction and abduction operators that allow for the solution of the theory revision problem in a multistrategy perspective [5]. They aim at reducing the computational effort required to learn a correct theory with respect to the incoming examples.

The system architecture is depicted in Figure 3. A set of examples of the concepts to be learned, possibly selected by a domain EXPERT, is provided by the ENVIRONMENT. This set can be subdivided into three subsets, namely *training*, *tuning*, and *test* examples, according to the way in which examples are exploited during the learning process. Specifically, training examples, previously classified by the EXPERT, are exploited by the RULE GENERATOR to produce a theory that is able to account for them. The initial theory can also be provided by the EXPERT. Subsequently, the current theory is used by the RULE INTERPRETER to check its validity even against new available examples. This module makes a decision according to the current theory for any incoming tuning/test example. The CRITIC/PERFORMANCE EVALUATOR compares this decision to the correct one. In case of incorrectness, it can locate the cause of the wrong decision and choose the proper kind of correction, initiating the theory refinement process. In such a case, tuning examples are exploited incrementally by the RULE REFINER to modify incorrect theory rules according to a data-driven strategy. The RULE REFINER consists of two distinct modules, a SPECIALIZER and a GENERALIZER, which attempt to correct too weak and too strong rules, respectively. Test examples are exploited to check the predictive capabilities of the theory, i.e. the behavior of the theory on previously unseen examples.

To perform its task, INTHELEX exploits a previous candidate theory, a graph concerning the relations among the concepts to be learned, and a historical memory of all the past examples that led to the current theory.

Example 3.1. Suppose that the available theory for the concept *bicycle* is
`bicycle(X) :- two_wheels(X),red(X).`
(i.e., an object is a bicycle if it has two wheels and is red) when the new positive example $\{bicycle(b), two\_wheels(b), blue(b)\}$ becomes available. Since the current theory wouldn't account for it, the Critic locates the problem in the color requirement, so that the Generalizer can drop this condition, leading to a new revised theory
`bicycle(X) :- two_wheels(X).`
Now, suppose that the description of a motorcycle becomes available as a negative example: $\{not\ bicycle(m), two\_wheels(m), yellow(m), has\_engine(m)\}$. It satisfies all the conditions required by the current theory to be recognized as a bicycle, and hence the Specializer must add to the theory the condition that a bicycle has no engine, thus obtaining
`bicycle(X) :- two_wheels(X), not has_engine(X).`

4   Experiments

Experiments were performed to evaluate the effectiveness of the incremental approach on the problem of document classification and interpretation. In particular, the experiments concerned the induction and performance evaluation of rules for the identification of the class of a document, according to its logical components organized in a logical structure.

Indeed, the computational strategy adopted consists of a hierarchical model fitting, which limits the range of labeling possibilities. More precisely, the document is first matched against models of classes of documents and then against models of the logical components of interest for that class. Since models are rules expressed in a first-order logic language, the operation of model fitting becomes a matching test of a logic formula describing a model against another logic formula that represents the document layout.

4.1   Identification of the Document Class

Like in [10], a database of 92 scientific paper front pages was considered, whose description was automatically derived based on the geometrical properties and relationships of their layout components as described above. The documents in the database belong to three different classes: 30 instances of class *SVLN* (*Springer-Verlag Lecture Notes* series), 34 of class *IEEE* (*IEEE Transactions*) and 28 of class *ICML* (*Proceedings of the International Conference on Machine Learning*). Each paper is a positive example for the class it belongs to and, at the same time, is a negative example for the other classes.

We performed 33 runs of the experiment, by randomly splitting the dataset of 92 papers into a learning set and a test set, composed respectively of 70% and 30% of the whole dataset. In turn, the learning set has been subdivided into training and tuning sets, made up respectively of 30% and 70% of the whole learning set. In each of the 33 runs the composition of document samples was changed, while keeping fixed set sizes.

The learning set has been exploited in three ways, according to the mode - batch or incremental - adopted for the learning process. In the first case, this set has been entirely processed by INDUBI [3], an empirical learning system in order to generate a theory for classification operating in a batch way (i.e., starting from scratch and knowing the whole set of examples since the beginning). In the second case, the same set has been entirely processed by INTHELEX to perform the same task according to its incremental algorithm. Finally, in a hybrid mode, only the training set has been used by INDUBI in order to produce rapidly the first version of the classification theory, and then the resulting rules were refined incrementally by INTHELEX, exploiting the tuning set made up of both positive and negative examples. At the end, the test set has been exploited to evaluate the predictive accuracy of the theories thus learned on document instances that had not been employed during the previous phase. The average results of the experiments, as regards the predictive accuracy of the generated theories on the test set (i.e., the ratio of correctly classified test examples over the whole test set), are shown in Table 1.

As expected, the batch theories generated by INDUBI were more accurate than those generated incrementally by INTHELEX, even though, as regards the class IEEE, the difference was not considerable. This is probably due to the fact that, being IEEE a journal, it has a strict layout standard imposed by the publisher, while both the other classes are printed from camera ready copies provided by the authors, and thus suffer from more variability in following the guidelines. For this reason, few examples are sufficient to characterize the class IEEE, while, for the other classes, having all the examples available allows to

Table 1. Average results on document classification (predictive accuracy %) and t-test

	INDUBI	INTHELEX	Both	INDUBI vs. INTHELEX	INDUBI vs. Both	INTHELEX vs. Both
SVLN	89.63	82.17	91.33	*2.42E-06*	0.28802	*0.000159*
IEEE	88.93	86.70	88.87	0.203127	0.970127	0.399112
ICML	96.23	83	90.13	*4.43E-06*	*0.002864*	*0.02268*

focus on the most characterizing features. The worse predictive accuracy (if compared to that of the theories produced in batch mode) reached by the incremental system starting from the empty theory probably suffers from the order in which examples are presented to the system. On the other hand, predictive accuracy when INTHELEX refines a theory initially generated by INDUBI is very close to that obtained by running the batch system on the whole learning set.

Table 1 also shows the results of the t test, exploited to evaluate the significance of the average differences in predictive accuracy observed along the runs, according to the learning schemas adopted. This test has been performed as a two-sided paired test at a 0.05 level of significance, by considering the predictive accuracy achieved by the theories produced in each run along the modes already mentioned and comparing them pairwise. It is possible to note that in all statistically significant cases (emphasized entries in Table 1) the difference is in favor of INDUBI, which showed a higher average predictive accuracy in all of the runs. On the contrary, for the IEEE class, where INTHELEX showed a better performance on the average with respect to the other classes, the results are not statistically significant, both starting from an empty theory and refining a theory previously generated by INDUBI.

4.2   Identification of the Logical Components

INTHELEX has been evaluated and compared to INDUBI also on the task of document interpretation. Differently from the case of document classification, logical components of a document may be related to each other (e.g., in standard scientific papers the author's affiliation is above the abstract and under the title). Thus, it would be more appropriate to learn models that reflect these dependencies among components of the logical structure, in which case the learning system has to be provided with a graph reporting all possible dependencies between logical components. Future experimental results inducing both independent and dependent models will check whether taking into account the dependencies between logical components improves the accuracy and the comprehensibility of the models as well as the efficiency of the learning process. The presented experimentation was run under the assumption that the various logical components that make up a given document are independent of each other, thus it is not possible that one component is defined by referring to another one.

Table 2. Document interpretation results for class SVLN

		Time (min - max)	P.A. (min - max)	avg. difference Time	P.A.
title	Batch	823.576 (228 - 1483)	91.273 (84 - 97)	488.79	4.879
	Incr.	334.788 (65 - 1578)	86.394 (76 - 95)	t-test significance 0.0001	0.0001
authors	Batch	606.758 (183 - 1238)	92.909 (84 - 98)	218.73	6.121
	Incr.	388.03 (88 - 1768)	86.788 (74 - 95)	t-test significance 0.0011	0.0001
abstract	Batch	434.576 (90 - 876)	95.212 (85 - 100)	271.79	3.727
	Incr.	172.788 (23 - 838)	91.485 (84 - 98)	t-test significance 0.0001	0.0004
paper	Batch	753.515 (168 - 1802)	93.394 (82 - 100)	426.49	3.333
	Incr.	327.03 (48 - 1786)	90.061 (80 - 98)	t-test significance 0.0001	0.0036

The experiment has been carried out on the subset of 30 SVLN documents used for classification. In such a class, four logical components make sense, and hence can be recognized and learned by the system: *title*, *authors*, *abstract* and *paper*. Each document description was associated to as many logical components as those that were recognizable in it. Hence, for each of such associations an example was created, having the same description of the document as for the previous task, but the head representing the involved logical component, properly instantiated with the frame associated to that component in the document.

Also in this case, 33 runs were executed, by randomly splitting the database of 30 SVLN documents into learning set and test set, made up by 21 and 9 documents, respectively. While the learning set was, as usual, entirely given to INDUBI to generate a theory in a batch way, for the incremental modality it was further split into a training set of dimension 6 (to be provided to INDUBI in order to generate an initial set of rules to work on) and a tuning set of 15 documents to be exploited by INTHELEX in order to refine the rules by correcting omission and commission errors, if any. The test set was exploited, in both modalities, to check the predictive accuracy of the rules thus generated. Note that both the learning and the test set for the batch experimentation on document interpretation are the same as those used in the experimentation on document classification. The evaluation was performed as regards both computation timings and predictive accuracy for the two learning systems, as summarized in Table 2.

In this case, the t-test reveals that all differences are statistically significant, both at a 0.01 and at a 0.05 significance level. Before commenting the experimental outcomes, it is useful to recall that the SVLN class is based on author-prepared camera ready layout of the papers, and hence has not a rigid schema as in the IEEE journals. This should account for a more difficult learning task, and hence result in a slightly worse performance in document interpretation just like for document classification. This choice was purposely made, to test the effectiveness of the system on a more difficult environment.

Predictive accuracy is always statistically significant in favor of the batch approach, which is not surprising. In particular, the greatest difference among the two approaches happens for the *title* and *author* labels. A possible explanation lies in the fact that these two kinds of components show the greatest variability in size: a two-line title is just twice in height than a one-line title, as well as many authors may cause a high growth in the corresponding frame dimension.

The time elapsed for the computation is always statistically significantly different too, but in favor of the incremental system. It is noteworthy that in this case the difference is far higher, and in all cases but the *author* label the incremental system requires less than half a time than the batch one. A possible explanation for this is that, for the incremental modality, the batch system works only on 30% of the learning set, which greatly reduces the complexity of consistency checks of the generated rules and, hence, computational times (specific experiments are planned to assess how computational time varies according to a reduction of the training set). Moreover, if the theory learned on the training set only is sufficiently accurate, the incremental system will mostly perform single-example cover checks, and very few refinements will be needed, which again significantly reduces running time. Anyway, the fact that the computation timings are far in favor of the incremental system is very encouraging, since there are tasks whose nature, for instance because of the variability of the observations, is such that they are infeasible in batch mode and calls for continuous refinement of the generated theories.

5   Conclusions and Further Work

We have presented an approach to document processing problems exploiting incremental learning. Our logic-based approach has a double advantage, namely, it can exploit entirely the organization present in a document at many levels of grain size and it produces first order logic models, that are easily understandable and directly manageable by humans (in the perspective of a semi-automatic approach to the problem). An experiment proved the effectiveness of our incremental approach with respect to a traditional model inference system.

The presented techniques have, thus, good chances of being useful to make automatic the tasks of information capture and indexing of documents that are to be included into a digital library. However, further potential application areas must be recognized, in order to compare our approach to the problems treated in this paper with completely different ones and to ascertain its absolute effectiveness. Moreover an experimentation is needed following up the entire process from the paper up to the textual categorization of the digitized documents [9].

We are also working on the integration of external knowledge that can speed up and improve the performance of the incremental algorithms. In particular, in a multistrategy perspective, we are investigating how to plug in ontologies as abstraction theories.

Acknowledgments

The work illustrated in this paper was partially funded by the EC project IST-1999-20882 *COLLATE a Collaboratory for Automation, Indexing and Retrieval of Digitized Historical Archive Materials.*

References

[1] O. Altamura, F. Esposito, and D. Malerba. Transforming paper documents into XML format with WISDOM++. *International Journal on Document Analysis and Recognition*, 2001. To appear.

[2] H. Brocks, U. Thiel, A. Stein, and A. Dirsch-Weigand. Customizable retrieval functions based on user tasks in the cultural heritage domain. In *this book*.

[3] F. Esposito, D. Malerba, and F.A. Lisi. Machine learning for intelligent processing of printed documents. *Journal of Intelligent Information Systems*, 14(2/3):175–198, 2000.

[4] F. Esposito, D. Malerba, G. Semeraro, N. Fanizzi, and S. Ferilli. Adding machine learning and knowledge intensive techniques to a digital library service. *International Journal of Digital Libraries*, 2(1):3–19, 1998.

[5] F. Esposito, G. Semeraro, N. Fanizzi, and S. Ferilli. Multistrategy Theory Revision: Induction and abduction in INTHELEX. *Machine Learning*, 38(1/2):133–156, 2000.

[6] E.A. Fox. How to make intelligent digital libraries. In Z.W. Raś and M. Zemankova, editors, *Proceedings of the 8th International Symposium on Methodologies for Intelligent Systems*, volume 869 of *LNAI*, pages 27–38. Springer, 1994.

[7] X. Li and P. Ng. A document classification and extraction system with learning ability. In *Proceedings of the 5th International Conference on Document Analysis and Recognition*, pages 197–200, 1999.

[8] G. Nagy. Twenty years of document image analysis in PAMI. *IEEE Transactions on Pattern Analysis and Machine Intelligence*, 22(1):38–62, 2000.

[9] F. Sebastiani. Machine learning in automated text categorization. Technical Report Technical Report IEI:B4-31-12-99, CNR - IEI, Pisa, Italy, 1999. Rev. 2001.

[10] G. Semeraro, F. Esposito, D. Malerba, N. Fanizzi, and S. Ferilli. Machine learning + on-line libraries = IDL. In C. Peters and C. Thanos, editors, *Research and Advanced Technology for Digital Libraries. First European Conference - ECDL97*, volume 1324 of *LNCS*, pages 195–214. Springer, 1997.

[11] Y. Tang, S. Lee, and C. Suen. Automatic document processing: A survey. *Pattern Recognition*, 29(2):1931–1952, 1996.

The Cervantes Project: Steps to a Customizable and Interlinked On-Line Electronic Variorum Edition Supporting Scholarship

Richard Furuta, Siddarth S. Kalasapur, Rajiv Kochumman, Eduardo Urbina,
Ricardo Vivancos-Pérez[*]

Center for the Study of Digital Libraries
Texas A&M University
College Station, TX 77843-3112, USA
{furuta, ssk9770, rajiv, e-urbina, rv} @csdl.tamu.edu

Abstract. The Cervantes Project, housed under the auspices of the Center for
the Study of Digital Libraries at Texas A&M University, aims to provide a
comprehensive on-line research and reference site on the life and works of the
author Miguel de Cervantes Saavedra (1547-1616). This activity is a joint
collaboration among researchers in the Department of Computer Science and
the Department of Modern and Classical Languages, Texas A&M University.
This paper outlines the work being conducted by the project, focusing on the
creation of an Electronic Variorum Edition of Cervantes' *Don Quixote*.

1   Introduction

Miguel de Cervantes Saavedra (1547-1616), one of the world's greatest and most
influential authors, is generally-recognized as a central figure in Hispanic literature
and culture. His best-known work, *Don Quixote*, first published in two parts in 1605
and 1615, has been called the first modern novel and has been translated into more
languages than any other literary text except the *Bible*.

The Cervantes Project, initiated in 1995, has as goal the creation of a
comprehensive Web-accessible reference and research site dedicated to the study of
Cervantes' works and life. To this end, the Cervantes Project is supporting a number
of different components: the Cervantes Digital Library (CDL), an electronic
collection of Cervantes' plays, novels, and other writings;[1] the Cervantes Digital
Archive of Images (CDAI), an online archive of photographic images related to the

---

[*] Authors are listed in alphabetical order. Richard Furuta, Siddarth S. Kalasapur, and Rajiv
Kochumman also are affiliated with the Department of Computer Science. Eduardo Urbina
and Ricardo Vivancos-Pérez also are affiliated with the Department of Modern and Classical
Languages. The project's Web pages are at http://www.csdl.tamu.edu/cervantes/
[1] The Cervantes Project and the CDL are unrelated to the University of Alicante's similarly-
named "Biblioteca Virtual Miguel de Cervantes," which is building a general electronic
library of Hispanic literature.

P. Constantopoulos and I.T. Sølvberg (Eds.): ECDL 2001, LNCS 2163, pp. 71-82, 2001.
© Springer-Verlag Berlin Heidelberg 2001

life and works of Cervantes; and the Cervantes International Bibliography Online (CIBO), a comprehensive annotated bibliography on the studies, works and life of Cervantes. All of these components are constantly growing, with new records being added to the bibliography on an annual basis, in parallel with the publication of the "*Anuario Bibliográfico Cervantino*"[2], the annual Cervantes bibliography.

A current focus of the project is the creation of an Electronic Variorum Edition (EVE) of *Don Quixote*. To this end we are developing computer-based tools that support the tasks of creating and accessing the EVE. These are a Multi-Variant Document Editor (MVED), which aids scholars in detecting and evaluating the differences among the various versions of *Don Quixote*, and the Virtual Edition Reader's Interface (VERI), which enables users to view texts along with the comments and emendations made by the scholars. Both these tools will be described in more detail subsequently.

2   Electronic Variorum Editions

The digital environment allows the conception of new document forms in support of scholarship. Once such form is the Electronic Variorum Edition (EVE)—an electronic edition containing all existing editions of a text, annotation of the variances present among the editions to allow for their comparison, derivative editions, generated as the result of scholarly analysis of the variances and bearing supporting reasoning, and scholarly commentary by expert editors that illuminates elements of the texts and of the comparisons among editions. The reader of the EVE should be able to customize the text presentation, perhaps selecting different interpretations for different applications, as well as annotate the results. Furthermore, all components in the EVE should be interlinked, allowing easy traversal among the representations.

The EVE is a general representation, allowing the specification of collections that parallel the traditional notions of Documentary Edition, Critical Edition, and Variorum Edition.[3] The application of these distinctions within the EVE is discussed in this section.

---

[2] The "*Anuario Bibliográfico Cervantino*" is published by the Universidad de las Islas Baleares (Spain). Three volumes (1996, 1998, and 1999) are available at present.

[3] Definitions, adopted and adapted from [11], for some of the terms we used are contained in this footnote. *Critical edition*: A scholarly edition that presents a text constructed by adopting readings from one or more documents and by correcting readings determined to be errors, and accompanied by apparatus explaining editorial principles and procedures, lists of emendations, and a historical collation of the text. *Documentary edition:* Also known as diplomatic edition; a scholarly edition that presents the text of a particular document without emendation. It includes an apparatus describing the document, the basis for its selection, the principles of transcription used, and a list of variants found in other documents. *Variorum edition*: A scholarly edition in which a base text (not necessarily critically edited) is annotated with a record of critical and textual commentary on particular passages, of editors' emendations, or of variant readings present in other texts. A critical variorum edition includes primarily critical commentary; a textual variorum edition primarily reports textual variation.

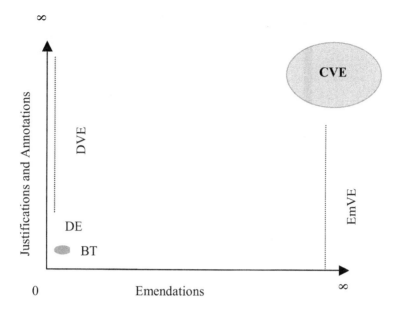

Figure 1. The relationship between Base Text (BT), Critical Variorum Edition (CVE), Documentary Variorum Edition (DVE), and Emended Variorum Edition (EmVE).

Any commentary made by an editor or a scholar that either describes the text or a variant, but does not make any changes to the text is called an annotation. On the other hand, the editorial alteration of the text to adopt readings from other documentary texts or to adopt readings not present in any document but arrived at through editorial conjecture is called an emendation. Thus while an annotation serves to describe or elaborate the underlying text, an emendation changes the same.

A direct transcription of an edition, without any modifications, is a Documentary Edition (DE). In terms of annotations and emendations, none exist as far as documentary editions are concerned. We identify one of the DEs to serve as a *base text* (BT). The base text is used as the source or reference to compare with other texts during the collation process, as will be elaborated later. During the process of editing the base text, or while comparing with other texts, scholars may annotate the base text, or make changes to the same, along with a justification for the corrections. An electronic edition that comprises of the base text, with changes made to the same is called an Emended Variorum Edition (EmVE). Cross-linking of a base text with other documentary editions and association of annotation constitutes a Documentary Variorum Edition (DVE). Finally, a collection of a base text, emendations of the base text, along with justifications, and annotations to either the text or the emendations, constitutes a Critical Variorum Edition (CVE). The Critical Variorum Edition, which includes all emendations and annotations, represents a scholar's complete interpretation of the underlying text. Figure 1 illustrates the relationships among these terms.

Figure 2. A representative page.

3   An EVE of *Don Quixote*

We are preparing an Electronic Variorum Edition of key editions of *Don Quixote*, specifically of the significant editions that were published during Cervantes' lifetime. Since no manuscripts are known to survive, the available textual resources for *Don Quixote* begin with the first published editions of its two volumes (these are called the *princeps*), which appeared in Madrid in 1605 and 1615. The significant editions for Volume 1, then, are Madrid 1605 (*princeps*), Madrid 1605 (2nd edition), Valencia 1605, Brussels 1607, and Madrid 1608 (3rd edition). For Volume 2, the significant editions are Madrid 1615 (*princeps*) and Brussels 1616. Additionally, a combined edition (Madrid 1637), containing both volumes, is included in our collection. Although this edition appeared after Cervantes' death, scholarly consensus (e.g., see [9]) indicates that its contents provide additional insight into the early development of the work. Each edition is about 700 pages long.

We have obtained multiple microfilmed copies of these editions. Because changes may be made during a print run, established scholarly practice is to consult multiple copies of an edition. We currently possess, and have digitized, six copies of each of the two *princeps* and at least two copies of each of the other editions. We hold microfilmed copies of two other editions (Lisbon 1605 and Madrid 1647), which we are not including in our initial efforts since scholarly analysis indicates that they are of limited significance. The Lisbon 1605 edition is a pirated reproduction of the Madrid 1605 and the Madrid 1647 combined edition adds little additional insight beyond that provided by Madrid 1637.

Figure 2 shows a typical page from our collection. Note that numerous artifacts exist on the image. Some artifacts are easy to handle, for example the dark region around the manuscript and the skewing of the image. Others are more difficult, for example the dark spots in the image's text area. Removing artifacts in the latter category will take great care in processing as improper adjustment may result in changes to the text's semantics (see, for example, Donaldson's description of semantic differences introduced by interpretation of an ambiguously printed character as "f" or "s" in a Shakespeare text [1]). Processing of digitized microfilms raises questions that still remain unanswered. One clear implication, however, is that we will need to make images available in both their original and also their processed form.

Our use of microfilmed sources represents a compromise position. On the one hand, the image quality of the microfilms is not as good as would be obtainable from customized digitizing. On the other hand, microfilm copies often are already available and do not subject the original volumes to the potential of damage—a risk that many of the editions' owners are unwilling to take. The 1605 *princeps*, for example, is quite rare, with only 18 copies known to exist. Even with image compromises, our combined archive already is of great significance to the Cervantes scholar and far more extensive than that formerly available.

Given a collection of digitized editions, we must support several tasks in creating an EVE. The first is to interlink the editions and their different representations (textual, original image, and modified image). A second is support for the creation of a unified text. This requires first that the scholar selects the base text. Given the base text, it is then necessary to detect differences between it and the other texts in the collection, to enable the scholar's emendation of the base text (along with justification), and to allow the association of general commentary. This set of functions is supported by the MVED, which will be described in the next section.

Given the participation of one or more scholars serving as editors, we also must provide a means for readers to examine the texts and commentary. This is provided by the Reader's Interface, which will be discussed later in the paper

The initial implementations of the MVED and the VERI were completed by Shueh-Cheng Hu, and were reported earlier [5]. In the following sections, we review the interfaces and the modifications that we have made to them as we gained experience with their use.

3.1   MVED

The MVED (the Multi Variant Document Editor) is a software tool intended for use by scholars to aid them in collating different editions of the same text. It helps scholars in identifying, analyzing, and editing variances between a base text and different editions of the same.

3.1.1   Motivation behind the MVED

Access to old documents is rare and restricted. To prevent damage to these rare documents, and also to make them widely accessible, facsimile copies are taken and textual transcriptions are made. Scholars then need an interface they can use to relate the actual image and its textual transcription, and the MVED provides this facility.

Also, there might be multiple versions of a single document, with no sure mechanism to detect the original. In some cases like *Don Quixote*, the original itself

Figure 3. A collation session in progress, with the images and the corresponding texts displayed by the dual-form *document viewer* of the MVED. The base text, on the right of the figure, is shown in with a uniquely colored background.

might be lost. In such cases, scholars require a mechanism to compare the many versions of the same document, and make emendations to the underlying text, with an aim to develop their understanding of the document. The MVED provides the facility to compare and edit multiple documents simultaneously, with provisions to associate annotations and emendations.

The MVED was thus developed with the intention of providing an environment for creating and presenting electronic variorum editions originating from document facsimiles stored in microfilms. Starting from a base text, the scholar can make emendations to the text, and create an Emended Variorum Edition. The scholar can also annotate the text, adding valuable commentary, without actually emending it, thereby creating a Documentary Variorum Edition. A combination of emendations, annotations and justifications yields what is called a Critical Variorum Edition. Readers can then read the newly created editions, using the VERI.

3.1.2   MVED Data Entities
MVED uses data entities like the textual image and its plain-text transcription, and creates additional data entities like editing records during the process of collation. It is necessary to maintain a relationship between these data entities, for example between the text portion and its annotation. The centralized data entity management framework within the MVED achieves just this, maintaining a tight coupling between the steps in the collation process. All data entities created within a collation session can be viewed within the *data entity browsing interface*, a component of the MVED that enables editors to view the existing entities and the relationships among them.

3.1.3   Components of the MVED
The MVED has a set of tools to aid the scholar in the collation process. It has a dual-form *document viewer* that displays both an image and its textual transcription (see Figure 3). The document viewer synchronizes the text and the corresponding image portion.

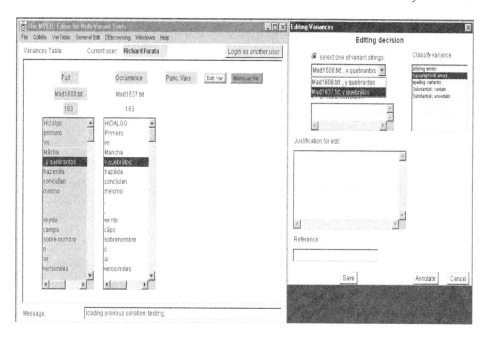

Figure 4. The left portion of the figure shows the list of variants resulting from Figure 3's collation. The scholar then uses the interface on the right to classify the variances and to specify emendations.

Synchronization between two texts under collation is achieved by means of the *text synchronizer*. This enables scholars to compare two or more texts simultaneously, so that variances can be detected and corrected.

Another tool called the *collator* helps in identifying the variances among the collated texts. This tool automatically identifies variances between the base text, and the other texts (called comparison texts) under collation, and presents the list of variances to the scholars, who can then make decisions on the validity of variants. This is illustrated in Figure 4, which shows automatically generated variances from all texts involved in the collation. The editing scholar can see the variances from different versions simultaneously in "full" form, or can view them in compact form, using an expandable tree structure. The MVED provides additional modifications to the display, for example detection (or not) of punctuation variances and case-sensitivity, so that the scholars can view variances in a flexible format.

At any time during the collation process, a comprehensive summary of the collation session in progress is available for the scholar, who can view the same using the earlier-described data entity browsing interface.

3.1.4   Annotations

Annotations are an important part of the new editions; annotations made by scholars are especially valuable because they give the reader an insight into the text. The MVED provides a facility for the user to attach annotations to a variance, or to a selected text portion, or to an emendation to the text. An annotation can be classified as historical, geographical, cultural, biographical, linguistic, or literary, based on its significance, or may be attached to a base text or a variant without any classification (generally unclassified annotations can be avoided, since the classification categories can be extended by the scholar if necessary). Thus the MVED allows the editing scholar to not only annotate the base text itself, but also to annotate his own emendations of the text.

3.2   VERI

The Virtual Edition Reader's Interface (VERI) is a WWW front end for the data sets produced by the MVED, so that any user who wishes to view the results of collations can do so. It is instructive to compare the view of the information space as shown in Figure 1, as perceived within the MVED and as presented in the VERI. The goal of the editors using the MVED is to produce a Critical Variorum Edition. In accomplishing this task, an editor begins in the lower left hand corner of Figure 1, and associates annotations, emendations, categorizations and justifications while approaching the CVE in the upper right hand corner of the Figure. The reader, on the other hand, has goals that may favor examination of the CVE, of an EmVE, or of an intermediate state. Consequently, the VERI should support flexible traversal of the space represented in the Figure.

Our initial model of the VERI was intended to do just this, by providing a "category-centric" selection mechanism. In that version of the VERI, each of the categories of editing decisions made by an editor (or editors) could be manipulated separately. However, our evaluation of the interface demonstrated that exercising some degrees of flexibility result in semantically-inconsistent representations, as an editor's actions were generally unified rather than discrete. Consequently by default, we now support an "editor-centric" model for customizations in which the reader's initial selections track that of an individual editor selected by the reader. We also continue to explore representations that will enable the semantically-consistent comparison of editions created by different editors, in order to support development of a reader's insight into the methodologies employed by the different editors.

We continue to find additional dimensions for customizations. The international appeal of *Don Quixote* means that we must plan to support Spanish-only readers and scholars, as well as bilingual Spanish/English readers and scholars. In this context, selection based on the language used in annotations becomes a useful customization option.

We also need to incorporate a flexible security model into the VERI. Although *Don Quixote* is not subject to copyright protection, our digitized page images are subject to licensing agreements with the edition's holders. Access allowed to the images will need to respect the differing conditions of those agreements.

4   Electronic Documentary Editions

No commonly-available commercial OCR program currently is capable of producing reliable machine-readable files for seventeenth century texts such as *Don Quixote*. To tackle an otherwise very laborious and time-consuming task, we have adopted a compromise approach to "reconstruct" the different editions by taking as our initial base text the Schevill and Bonilla's (Madrid, 1914-1941) electronic text, converted and edited by Jehle [10] and already in our Cervantes Digital Library. This initial text is then collated manually with the digitized images of the different copies and editions of *Don Quixote*, and variants are recorded and introduced into the text to produce multiple electronic documentary editions. Similarly, manual collation of the non-*princeps* editions with the electronic version produces electronic documentary editions for them as well.

Three set of manual collations are required: 1) the preliminary collation of the Spanish National Library's unique copy of the 1605 *princeps* edition; 2) the *princeps* collation, using the documentary edition developed in the first step along with five other *princeps* copies obtained in microfilm from libraries around the world; and 3) the collation of the *princeps* text produced by the previous collation with the other early editions published between 1605 and 1637 in order to produce documentary texts of each one of them.

The preliminary collation aims at producing an "old-spelling" documentary edition in electronic text format of the National Library of Spain's copy of the *princeps*, by removing all the changes and emendations introduced by Schevill and Bonilla. The results of this collation are then compared with Flores' text [2] as a control, and the final version is saved in electronic format to be used as the base text for the MVED, and to be manually collated against the other copies of the *princeps* to produce their electronic text representations. Finally, the MVED-produced unified text from the second collation is used as base text for MVED collation against other non-*princeps* editions

All manual collations are done chapter by chapter, and are checked at least thrice. Once the preliminary collation has produced an electronic documentary text for the National Library copy, we can easily reconstruct the other five copies by identifying the variants and, therefore, creating a documentary edition of all copies of the 1605 *princeps*. So far, this process has been completed for 42 of the 52 chapters of *Don Quixote*.

The final manual collation involves the production of multiple electronic texts of the significant editions identified earlier in this paper. The electronic texts resulting from these different sets of collations are introduced into the MVED and form the basis for the critical variorum edition, which can then be accessed through the reader's interface.

4.1   Observations about Source Materials

Many problems arise regarding spelling and other variants among the different copies. In the preliminary collation we are dealing with an old-spelling emended text in which Schevill and Bonilla also incorporated their own punctuation parameters. For example, they use different capitalization criteria and semicolons, a punctuation mark that was not in vogue in 1605 and 1615, when *Don Quixote* was originally published. Since our purpose is to produce a documentary edition—an edition that preserves all the characteristics and errors of the original, we must encode marks and symbols which are no longer used, such as the long intervocalic 's' and the abbreviation of certain vowels and consonants represented by a tilde '~'.

Another interesting observation is the presence of *press variants*. These are textual variants that arise during a press run, such as those caused by a stop press correction. For instance, it is not unusual to find letters that have been printed twice or upside down type.

Finally, difficulties arise concerning the use of accents, since three different kinds of accent marks were issued by the composers: the acute accent 'á', the grave accent 'à', and the circumflex accent 'â'. There are instances where such accents seem to appear, but are in fact caused when facsimile copies of microfilms were produced. In other words, the original text does not contain these accents, but imperfections in the reproduction process or subsequent aging of the microfilm made it seem that they were present. Apparent accents may also be caused if the type used during printing was broken, or worn, or if for some reason, the inking unit was not working properly.

5   Discussion and Conclusions

The past few years have seen a blossoming of research efforts devoted to producing state-of-the-art network-accessible digital libraries over humanities-based materials [7]. Just a few of the many notable examples include the Perseus Project[4], components of the Library of Congress' American Memory project[5], the Shakespeare Electronic Archive[6], and the Canterbury Tales Project[7]. These activities are historically-grounded in the much longer-lived decades-long activities directed towards humanities computing. Taken as a whole, these activities provide compelling evidence of the strength of humanities applications as foundation for novel research in digital libraries.

The Cervantes Project continues to teach us valuable lessons, both technical and organizational. From a technical perspective the topic domain of early modern Spanish texts frequently illustrates the design assumptions of the tools that we use. For example, searching utilities frequently are character-set neutral (we use the MG system [8, 11], but expect that these observations apply more generally). Because of our multilingual reader population, we are considering "folding" accented and non-accented characters together in search queries. This is firstly because English speakers often do not distinguish the accents and leave them out when typing. In addition, old Spanish includes accent marks and abbreviations unused, and consequently unexpected, by modern Spanish speakers, as suggested in the previous section's discussion. Often, the solution adopted here is to "modernize" the spelling, but this approach seems unattractive to us, as it discards information that may be of use to the serious scholar.

The world-wide popularity of Cervantes and of *Don Quixote* requires that we provide our materials in many forms and in multiple languages. Earlier we discussed

---

[4] http://www.perseus.tufts.edu/

[5] http://memory.loc.gov/

[6] http://shea.mit.edu/

[7] http://www.cta.dmu.ac.uk/projects/ctp/

a scheme for tracking changes in parallel versions of a Web site collection [4]. We also are investigating approaches towards specifying different "cuts" of our collection for different classes of readers (e.g., high school students, university students, university researchers, and the general public).

From an organizational standpoint, we continue to be interested in identifying ways to help achieve successful interdisciplinary collaboration. The easy observation is that a successful collaborative project requires an application that is meaningful and challenging to all participants when viewed from the context of their separate disciplines. Additionally, the participants must invest significant effort in understanding the others' areas and assumptions, and must remain open to reexamination of their own area's seemingly pre-established tenets.

The best methodology (perhaps the only successful methodology) we have been able to find for fostering cross-discipline understanding is a commitment to frequent and often lengthy whole-group meetings. Even so, after more than six years of collaboration we still encounter issues that we discover, after lengthy discussion, reflect differences in our own terminology and expectations, rather than fundamental differences in viewpoint. A recent multi-week discussion, for example, centered around differing definitions of terms such as "edition" and "annotation"—terms for which we had assumed we had a common understanding.

We continue to find rewards in the Cervantes Project. From the point of view of the Humanities, the materials that we are collecting and the tools that we are creating hold promise of making significantly broader resources available to scholars of Cervantes. This in turn has potential for modifying the ways in which research and education take place. From the point of view of Computer Science, the project provides a concrete testbed that supports the development and evaluation of tools and representations of a richly structured information collection. This provides the basis for investigation of Digital Libraries techniques with the potential for quite broad applicability.

Acknowledgements

We acknowledge Shueh-Cheng Hu's contributions to the project, completed in conjunction with his dissertation research [6]. This material is based upon work sponsored by the National Science Foundation under Grant No. IIS-0081420. Support for this work was provided (in part) by the Interdisciplinary Research Initiatives Program, administered by the Office of the Vice President for Research, Texas A&M University.

References

1.   Peter S. Donaldson, "Digital Archive as Expanded Text: Shakespeare and Electronic Textuality." In Katheryn Sutherland, editor, *Electronic text: Investigations in Method and Theory*. Oxford Clarendon Press, 1997, pp 173-197.

2. *Don Quixote de la Mancha. An old-spelling control edition based on the first editions of Parts I and II.* Prepared by R. M. Flores. Vancouver: University of British Columbia Press, 1988, 2 Vols.

3. Richard Furuta, Shueh-Cheng Hu, Siddarth Kalaspur, Rajiv Kochumman, Eduardo Urbina, and Ricardo Vivancos-Pérez, "Towards an Electronic Variorum Edition of Don Quixote", JCDL 2001: *The Joint ACM-IEEE Conference on Digital Libraries*, June 2001, to appear.

4. Shueh-Cheng Hu and Richard Furuta. "A Tool for Maintaining Multi-variant Hypertext Documents," in Roger D. Herch, Jacques André, and Heather Brown, editors, *Electronic Publishing, Artistic Imaging, and Digital Typography (7th International Conference on Electronic Publishing, EP'98, held jointly with the 4th International Conference on Raster Imaging and Digital Typography, RIDT'98)*, Springer 1998 (Lecture Notes in Computer Science #1375), pp. 525-536.

5. Shueh-Cheng Hu, Richard Furuta, and Eduardo Urbina, "An Electronic Edition of Don Quixote for Humanities Scholars". *Document Numérique*, 3(1–2), June 1999, pp. 75–91.

6. Shueh-Cheng Hu, *Towards an Electronic Variorum Edition Originating from Available-Quality Document Facsimiles*, Ph.D. dissertation, Texas A&M University, College Station, Texas, December 2000.

7. Cruz Yolanda Lugo Ibarra, *Don Quixote in the digital age: An analysis of traditional editorial practices and current electronic editions*, M.A. thesis, Texas A&M University, College Station, Texas, December 1999.

8. New Zealand Digital Library homepage at http://www.nzdl.org/

9. Francisco Rico, "Historia del texto," Prólogo, *Don Quijote de la Mancha*, Francisco Rico, dir., 2 vols. (Biblioteca Clásica 50, y Vol. Complementario). Barcelona: Instituto Cervantes-Crítica, 1998. 1: cxcii-ccxlii.

10. http://www.csdl.tamu.edu/cervantes/english/ctxt/sb/. Digital texts converted by Eduardo Urbina and Fred Jehle.

11. William Proctor Williams and Craig S. Abbott, *An Introduction to Bibliographical and Textual Studies*, Third Edition. Modern Language Association of America, 1999, pp. 69–125.

12. I. H. Witten, A. Moffat, and T.C. Bell, *Managing gigabytes: compressing and indexing documents and images*, Morgan Kaufmann, San Francisco, CA, 1999.

Fusion Approaches for Mappings between Heterogeneous Ontologies

Thomas Mandl, Christa Womser-Hacker

University of Hildesheim, Information Science, Marienburger Platz 22
D-31141 Hildesheim, Germany
{mandl, womser}@rz.uni-hildesheim.de

Abstract. Ordering principles of digital libraries expressed in ontologies may be highly heterogeneous even within a domain and especially over different cultures. Automatic methods for mappings between different ontologies are necessary to ensure successful retrieval of information stored in virtual digital libraries. Text categorization has discussed learning methods to map between full text terms and thesaurus descriptors. This article reports some experiments for the mapping between different ontologies and shows further that fusion methods which have been successfully applied to ad-hoc information retrieval can also be employed for text categorization.

1 Introduction

Ontologies are organized collections of concepts. Their structure expresses a certain view on the world or the domain. A considerable number of ontologies exists in many domains. This especially applies for different countries and cultures. Many ordering systems have concepts in common, however, because they arose within a certain context in response to special demands they may organize them differently. Although this situation is quite natural and not likely to change, it complicates or even prevents the successful communication between communities using different ontologies. The same is true for the exchange of documents between different groups within one digital library. The worldwide exchange of documents involves ontologies from different cultures which are sometimes organized extremely different. Due to the ever growing amount of knowledge available electronically, automated solutions need to be found for these mapping problems.

Text categorization between ontologies or terminologies seems to be the most appropriate technology for this task. Mostly, text categorization assign documents to predefined categories based on a full text analysis [27]. The text is indexed with standard information retrieval methods and represented by weights assigned to words or terms based on their frequency of occurrence. These terms can be regarded as features. In the same manner, terms from a controlled vocabulary like an ontology can serve as features for a text. Thus, the task for text categorization based on full text terms is equivalent to text categorization based on descriptors from ontologies. There are also applications for the second case [4].

P. Constantopoulos and I.T. Sølvberg (Eds.): ECDL 2001, LNCS 2163, pp. 83-94, 2001.
© Springer-Verlag Berlin Heidelberg 2001

Similarity thesauri for cross-lingual retrieval can also be viewed as an additional type of text categorization. In this case, the mapping leads from one set of free text terms to another set of free text terms [20]. Other applications of text categorization include recommender systems [18] and spam detection [6].

This article reviews some learning methods applied to text categorization in the following chapter. Chapter 3 shows how fusion methods are applied to ad-hoc retrieval. Chapter 4 discusses text categorization experiments for real world social science texts and applies fusion algorithms to these text categorization tasks.

2 Learning Methods in Text Categorization

Different learning methods have been applied to text categorization. Most often, statistical association measures like Naive Bayes map between pairs of terms. These learning algorithms derive the knowledge from examples provided as training data and do not rely on further human contribution.

In recent years neural networks and support vector machines have been employed as well [8, 11]. An overview is provided by Aas and Eikvil [1]. Many machine learning methods are available as JAVA code in the WEKA package for data mining [23].

Neural networks and in particular the multi-layer backpropagation network are learning schemes well suited for text categorization tasks [16]. Backpropagation networks are powerful learning systems which can learn complex functions such as non linear separable problems [10]. Neural networks can approximate intuitive expert knowledge which cannot be formalized in a rule based system. Calculations within a neural network are local. Each unit gathers its input from incoming connections and calculates its own activation and output. Signals travel along connections and are modified according to the connection strength. A typical backpropagation network consists of an input and an output layer and of one or more hidden layers. The input vector is propagated into the network which calculates the output [10].

Crestani and Rijsbergen present a backpropagation network for a mapping between different queries in which the representation schemes are equivalent. The same architecture can be modified for general transformations between heterogeneous representation schemes. A query was transformed into queries which achieved better results. Improved queries for training were found using relevance feedback. The transformed queries achieved similar retrieval quality compared to the original query [5]. The process can be seen as a query extension.

Other neural networks have been applied to text categorization tasks as well, e.g. a Hopfield style network to map between two thesauri. In one setting, descriptors from parts of the *ACM Computing Review Classification System* and the *Library of Congress Subject Headings* are represented as neurons in a Hopfield network [4]. However, the learning capabilities of Hopfield networks are restricted to unsupervised learning, therefore the knowledge in the examples typically available in text categorization is not fully exploited. The connections strengths are set according to user defined clusters which are also represented as neurons [4].

A similar approach is presented by Lee and Dubin [15]. Their neural network consists of separated layers for two thesauri. In this application, 4120 terms from the

Astrophysical Journal and 2305 terms from the *NASA* were mapped. A layer in between the term layers representing the common 15,000 documents defines the transformation. The connection strengths are set according to the co-occurrences of terms in the documents.

3 Fusion Methods

The basic idea behind fusion is to delegate a task to different algorithms and consider all the results returned. These single results are then combined into one final result. Obviously, this approach is especially promising, when the single results are very different.

As investigations on the results of the TREC conference have shown, the results of information retrieval systems performing similarly well are often different. This means, the systems find the same percentage of relevant documents, however, the overlap between their results is sometimes low [24].

For retrieval tasks a fusion system needs to integrate different probabilities for the relevance of a document whereas in text categorization fusion means the integration of various probabilities for the assignment of a term from an ontology.

3.1 Committee Machines in Machine Learning

In machine learning, the combination of various supervised learning algorithms for approximation, prognosis or classification is often called a committee machine. This metaphor suggests that these algorithms try to work like a committee of human experts who need to reach a decision based on their individual opinions. The following architectures are used [10]:

- Static methods: the input of single experts does not influence the fusion
    - Ensemble averaging: the output of different experts is combined linearly
    - Boosting: a weak learning algorithm is improved by retraining badly classified examples with another learning algorithm

- Dynamic methods: the input from the experts governs the integration process
    - Mixture of experts: the output of several experts is combined non-linearly
    - Hierarchical mixture of experts: the combination system is organized in a hierarchical manner

All these fusion methods do not need to be based on completely different experts. The results of a neural net usually depends on its random initialization. Thus, different initialization states of the same neural net can be considered as different experts. The same applies to other learning methods with different parameter settings.

3.2 Fusion in Information Retrieval

An overview of fusion methods in information retrieval is given by McCabe et al. [17]. Research concentrates on issues like which methods can be combined, how the retrieval status values of two or more systems can be combined and on which features of collections indicate that a fusion might lead to positive results.

Different retrieval methods can be defined according to various parameters. One possibility is using different indexing approaches, like word and phrase indexing [2]. Lee defines the single retrieval methods for his fusion approach according to their different term weighting schemes [14]. He investigates with cosine normalization which takes the varying length of documents into account, maximum normalization based on the maximal term weights and no normalization. Another parameter is the similarity function used [17].

The values are combined statically by taking the sum, the minimum or the maximum of the results from the individual systems [7]. Linear combinations assign a weight to each method which determines its influence on the final result. These weights may be optimized for example by heuristic optimization [21] or learning methods [22, 25].

In experimental systems, the methods to be fused are applied to the same collection. However, fusion has been applied to collections without overlap as well. A collection can be split into artificial sub-collections which are treated by an retrieval system [22]. In such a case, the goal of the fusion can be regarded as an attempt to derive knowledge about which collection leads to good results. For internet meta search engines, fusion often means elimination of documents returned by at least two search engines.

3.3 Fusion and Learning

The ideas from information retrieval and machine learning are combined in the algorithm RankBoost, which applies boosting to ranked result lists [13].

MIMOR represents a learning approach to the fusion task which is based on results of information retrieval research which shows that the overlap between different systems is often small [24]. On the other hand, relevance feedback is a very promising strategy for improving retrieval quality. As a consequence, the linear combination of different results is optimized through learning from relevance feedback. MIMOR integrates an information retrieval system managing poly-representation of queries and documents by selecting appropriate methods for indexing and matching. By learning from user feedback on the relevance of documents, the model adapts itself by assigning weights to the different retrieval methods. That way, MIMOR follows a long term learning strategy in which the relevance assessments are not just used for the current query. MIMOR is not limited to text documents but open to other data types such as structured data and multimedia objects. A formal model of MIMOR has been developed [25]. The conclusion of this paper will relate the MIMOR model to the fusion problem in text categorization.

4 Text Categorization Experiments

This chapter reviews experiments for text categorization for two corpora with a statistical approach and a neural network and analyzes the results.

The data used is part of a digital library for the social sciences [12] and some of it is part of the German collection for the cross language evaluation forum (CLEF), where cross lingual retrieval methods are tested in a way similar to the TREC evaluation studies [19].

The institutions providing the data are the Social Science Information Center, Bonn (IZ) and the library of the University of Cologne with its special collection for the social sciences (USB). Both institutions rely on intellectual indexing. The IZ represents the documents according to two representation schemes:

- the thesaurus: a collection of some 22.000 keywords and synonym relations
- the classification: a hierarchy of scientific disciplines from the perspective of the social sciences containing 157 entries

That way, the documents from the IZ can be used for text categorization. In this paper, a mapping from the thesaurus to the classification is presented.

The USB uses a different thesaurus for content analysis. Studies have shown, that there is a significant overlap between the collections and that therefore, many documents are indexed twice [12]. For these documents, text categorization tasks from the USB representations to the IZ schemes have been implemented. Within a digital library, these automatic transformations can support the user in dealing with the semantic heterogeneity. Terms defined differently by the information providers may cause low retrieval quality for users only familiar with one thesaurus, because they will find documents with unexpected usage of these terms. Users familiar with one representation scheme do not have to understand the other and may still access the documents provided only by one information provider. For such documents, an automatic text categorization system could implement a value added service and derive the relevant terms for the target thesaurus [12].

4.1 Categorization Tasks

As a first task, a mapping from the IZ thesaurus to the IZ classification was chosen. For this experiment, a subset of the IZ databases was selected which is part of CLEF and contains some 12.900 documents. In average each document is assigned 13 descriptors from the thesaurus and 2.3 classification entries. Especially for the number of thesaurus descriptors assigned to each document, the variance is high.

Because the subset did not contain all keywords and classification entries, the experiment was not set up as a direct transformation between thesaurus and classification. Only 5555 out of 22.000 thesaurus entries occurred in the 12.900 documents. Terms appearing at least four times were selected, which led to a representation scheme of 3800 terms. The data set contained 142 of all 157 classification categories. They were further accumulated intellectually to form 70 categories. That way, the task was to map a document described by a term vector of 3.800 elements into 70 categories. The training set contained 12,000 documents and the test set some 900.

The second task took advantage of the overlap between IZ and USB. Some 15,200 documents in common were identified. The second task is a mapping from the USB thesaurus with 3000 terms occurring in the set to 100 categories of the IZ thesaurus. The training set contained 13,000 and the test set some 2,200 documents. The IZ had assigned 11 thesaurus terms per document in average and the USB 2.9 terms.

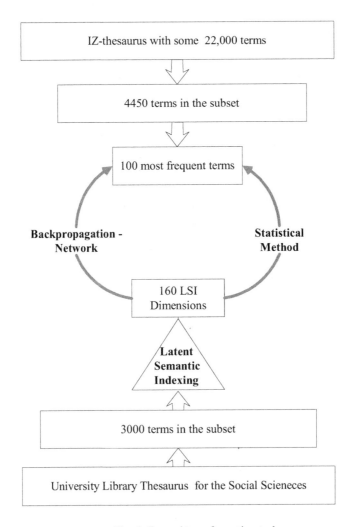

Fig. 1. Second transformation task.

The input spaces of the two tasks underwent a dimensionality reduction using latent semantic indexing [3]. A simple association based statistical method was employed as a first categorization method. It compares the frequency of a co-occurrence of term and category to the frequencies of the occurrence of term and category. As a second categorization method, a neural backpropagation network was applied to both tasks. Figure 1 shows the reduction of features in the second task.

4.2 Evaluation Method and Results

The performance of text categorization is commonly measured with recall and precision. The well known formulas used in information retrieval evaluation can be applied to text categorization. Relevant documents are replaced by relevant categories or correct assignments. In this case, correct assignments means the reproduction of the human classification. The identical formulas suggest that the measures express the same as in information retrieval evaluation. However, recall and precision in text categorization mean something different.

The number of relevant documents is usually determined considering the information need of a user and his relevance judgements. Often domain experts evaluate the documents, nevertheless, the basis for this assessment is still an information need. On the other hand, the assignment of relevant categories by a text categorization method merely shows how well an algorithm can approximate the categorization defined by a human. This categorization is carried out independently from any information need. It is unclear, how this relates to the success of a retrieval process. This needs to be considered when measuring the quality of text categorization methods with recall and precision.

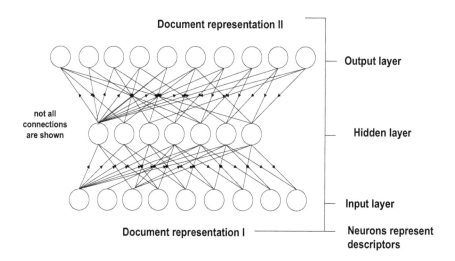

Fig. 2. Typical architecture of a backpropagation network for text categorization

For the first task, both methods performed almost equally well, while the overlap between the results was rather low. Therefore, a fusion of the results was considered in order to improve categorization. For the second task, the neural network performed better than the statistical method. This shows, that the performance depends much on the collection under consideration.

Table 1. Result overview

Task	Documents	Input dimensions	Target dimensions	Result
IZ-Thes. to IZ-Classific.	12,965	5555	70	Almost equal quality
USB-Thes. to IZ-Thes.	15,000	3000	100	Neural network much better

In order to estimate whether fusion methods could lead to a positive result, the overlap of the results for the first task were analyzed The analysis was done for the test set of the categorization task. The similarity between the corresponding results from both text categorization methods was analyzed in two ways. First, the correlation between the ranked lists was calculated. Secondly, the overlap of the result sets was measured, after considering a threshold in the ranked list.

The correlation between two ranked list may be calculated with rank correlation coefficients like the Spearman coefficient [9]. The Spearman correlation measure were calculated for each pair of result sets. The average was then calculated as the correlation between the results. The average correlation reaches only −0.05, which means that according to this coefficient, the results do not correlate and are very different.

Additionally, the overlap between result sets was determined. The ranked lists were cut off after n categories with the highest probability assigned to them by the categorization method. The number of common categories in both sets and the number of relevant or correct categories according to the test data was counted. Table 2 gives an overview of the overlap calculated.

Table 2. Overlap measures for result sets

	Categories found by both methods	in %	Relevant categories found by both methods	in %
First 20 categories	0.27	5.43	0.14	0.71
First 100 categories	4.92	4.92	0.83	0.83

The overlap of the results of the two methods for the categorization task is rather small. For all categories, it reaches some 5% for both thresholds and lies below 1% for the relevant categories only. The quality of the results is almost identical for all recall levels as table 3 shows. That means both methods find approximately the same number of relevant categories, but they find different ones.

5 Fusion Experiments for Text Categorization

The categorization results of both methods were fused using static approaches suggested in [7]. Since the results of the neural network depends much on the random initialization, two differently initialized networks were used for the fusion. Sum, minimum and maximum of both methods were tested.

For the first task, the fusion did not lead to a consistent improvement which would be reflected by the average precision. Only for some recall levels, the best fusion experiments led to an improvement compared to the best single categorization method. The improvement reaches up to 5 % as table 3 shows.

Table 3. Fusion results for the first categorization task

Recall	Neural network I	Neural network II	Statistics	Best Fusion Results:	Fusion stat + NN1 SUM	Fusion stat + NN1 MIN	Maximum improvement in %
0.1	0.306	0.306	0.313		0.321	0.298	+ 2.56
0.2	0.258	0.258	0.262		0.259	0.256	-
0.3	0.213	0.213	0.217		0.223	0.229	+ 5.53
0.4	0.197	0.197	0.201		0.199	0.205	+ 1.99
0.5	0.183	0.183	0.187		0.177	0.177	-
0.6	0.161	0.161	0.166		0.157	0.157	-
0.7	0.136	0.136	0.140		0.143	0.144	+ 2.86
0.8	0.119	0.119	0.123		0.118	0.121	-
0.9	0.102	0.102	0.106		0.092	0.097	-
Average Precision	**0.186**	**0.186**	**0.191**		**0.188**	**0.187**	

For the second task, the fusion leads to an improvement compared to the best single result. For this task, the difference between the single results are significant with the statistic approach performing much weaker than the neural network. However, this weak result still contributed to an improvement of 3 % to the maximum fusion method and of 0.4 % to the sum fusion method. The results of the fusion for the second task are shown in table 4.

The experiments show that fusion can lead to improvements in text categorization quality. The results differ very much between different corpora. Therefore, careful tests need to be carried out for each domain. The choice of individual and fusion methods has a great impact on the result as well. Furthermore, other fusion methods need to be tested.

Table 4. Fusion results for the second categorization task

Recall	Neural network	Statistic approach	Fusion: MAX	Fusion: SUM	Fusion: MIN
0.1	0.515	0.059	0.525	0.503	0.052
0.2	0.407	0.05	0.418	0.405	0.047
0.3	0.334	0.047	0.351	0.342	0.044
0.4	0.277	0.044	0.287	0.284	0.042
0.5	0.206	0.041	0.211	0.211	0.04
0.6	0.151	0.039	0.154	0.153	0.039
0.7	0.107	0.038	0.11	0.108	0.038
0.8	0.075	0.037	0.077	0.075	0.037
0.9	0.055	0.037	0.055	0.055	0.036
Average Precision	**0.236**	**0.044**	**0.243**	**0.237**	**0.042**

6 Conclusion

Different representation schemes express different views of the world or the domain. Varied approaches to the concepts of a domain may result in drastically different ontologies used for intellectual or automatic indexing. Concepts may be ordered differently and the hierarchical organization may be incomparable. Text categorization can be viewed as a transformation between heterogeneous representations for objects stored in digital libraries and there will be a growing demand for applications based on this technology.

The article reviews two text categorization experiments for collections from the social sciences using a neural network and a statistical approach. As the overlap between the results of the two methods is rather small, fusion for text categorization is introduced as a strategy to improve the overall result. For one of the two tasks, the average precision could be increased by 3 %.

Further research should investigate the effect of partitioning the learning space and the application of different learning methods for each partition. The partition can group features of clusters of documents. For example, an optimal learning scheme can be identified for a mapping from a group of terms to a another group of terms in the target ontology. The MIMOR-model provides a framework for such an approach. MIMOR can also be used to optimize a linear fusion based on user feedback [26].

References

1. Aas, K, Eikvil, L. (1999): Text Categorization: a Survey. Report No. 941, June, 1999 Norwegian Computing Center. http://citeseer.nj.nec.com/aas99text.html

2. Bartell, B, Cottrell, G, Belew, R (1994): Automatic Combination of Multiple Retrieval Systems. In 17th Annual Intl ACM SIGIR Conference on Research and Development in Information Retrieval (SIGIR '94).
3. Berry, M, Dumais, S., Letsche, T. (1995): Computational Methods for Intelligent Information Access. In ACM Supercomputing '95. San Diego, CA. pp. 1-38.
4. Chen, H. (1995): Machine Learning for Information Rerieval: Neural Networks, Symbolic Learning, and Genetic Algorithms. In Journal of the American Society for Information Science. JASIS 46 (3). pp. 194-216.
5. Crestani, F., Rijsbergen, K. van (1997): A Model for Adaptive Information Retrieval. In Journal of Intelligent Information Systems 8 (1). S. 29-56.
6. Drucker, H., Wu, D., Vapnik, V. (1999): Support Vector Machines for Spam Categorization. In IEEE Trans. on Neural Networks , vol 10 (5). pp. 1048-1054.
7. Fox, E., Shaw, J (1994): Combination of Multiple Searches. In Harman, D. (ed.): The Second Text Retrieval Conference. NIST Special Publication 500-215.
8. Goller, C., Löning, J., Will, T., Wolff, W. (2000): Automatic Document Classification: A thorough Evaluation of Various Methods. In Knorz, G., Kuhlen, R. (eds.): Informationskompetenz - Basiskompetenz in der Informationsgesellschaft. Proceedings 7. Intl Symposium für Informationswissenschaft. (ISI 2000) pp. 145-162.
9. Hartung, J. (1984): Lehr- und Handbuch der angewandten Statistik. München, Wien.
10. Haykin, S. (1999): Neural Networks: A Comprehensive Foundation.
11. Joachims, T. (1998): Text Categorization with Support Vector Machines: Learning with Many Relevant Features. In European Conference on Machine Learning (ECML). pp. 137-142.
12. Kluck, M., Krause, J., Müller, M., Schmiede, R., Wenzel, H., Winkler, S., Meier, W. (2000): Virtuelle Fachbibliothek Sozialwissenschaften. IZ technical report 19, Informationszentrum Sozialwissenschaften, Bonn. http://www.bonn.iz-soz.de/publications/series/working-papers
13. Iyer, R., Lewis, D., Schapire, R., Singer, Y., Singhal, A. (2000): Boosting for Document Routing. In Ninth ACM Conference on Information and Knowledge Management (CIKM).
14. Lee, J. H. (1995): Combining Multiple Evidence from Different Properties of Weighting Schemes. In: 18th Annual Intl ACM SIGIR Conference on Research and Development in Information Retrieval (SIGIR 95). pp. 180-188.
15. Lee, J., Dubin, D. (1999): Context-Sensitive Mapping with a Spreading Activation Network. In 22nd Annual Intl ACM SIGIR Conference on Research and Development in Information Retrieval (SIGIR '99). pp. 198-205.
16. Mandl, T. (1998): Vague Transformations in Information Retrieval. In Zimmermann, H., Schramm, V. (Eds.): Knowledge Management und Kommunikationssysteme: Workflow Management, Multimedia, Knowledge Transfer. 6. Intl Symposium für Informationswissenschaft. (ISI '98). pp. 312 – 325.
17. McCabe, M. Catherine, Chowdhury, A., Grossmann, D., Frieder, O. (1999): A Unified Framework for Fusion of Information Retrieval Appproaches. In Eigth ACM Conference on Information and Knowledge Management (CIKM). pp. 330-334.
18. Mooney, R., Roy, L. (2000): Content Based Book Recommending Using Learning for Text Categorization. In Fifth ACM Conference on Digital Libraries.
19. Peters, C. (ed.) (2001): Cross-Language Information Retrieval and Evaluation: Proceedings of the CLEF 2000 Workshop. Springer [LNCS 2069]
20. Sheridan, P., Ballerini, J.P. (1996): Experiments in Multilingual Information Retrieval using the SPIDER System. In 19th Annual Intl ACM SIGIR Conference on Research and Development in Information Retrieval (SIGIR '96). pp. 58-65.
21. Vogt, C., Cottrell, G.(1998): Predicting the Performance of Linearly Combined IR Systems. In 21th Annual Intl ACM SIGIR Conference on Research and Development in Information Retrieval (SIGIR '98). pp. 190-196.

22. Voorhees, E., Gupta, N., Johnon-Laird, B. (1995): Learning Collection Fusion Strategies. In 18th Annual Intl ACM SIGIR Conference on Research and Development in Information Retrieval (SIGIR '95). pp. 172-179.

23. Witten, I., Frank, E. (2000): Data Mining: Practical Machine Learning Tools and Techniques with JAVA Implementations.

24. Womser-Hacker, C. (1997): Das MIMOR-Modell. Mehrfachindexierung zur dynamischen Methoden-Objekt-Relationierung im Information Retrieval. Habilitationsschrift. Universität Regensburg, Informationswissenschaft.

25. Womser-Hacker, C., Mandl, T. (1999): Adapting Meta Information Retrieval to User Preferences and Document Features. In Bullinger, H-J., Ziegler, J. (eds.): Human-Computer Interaction: Communication, Cooperation and Application Design. HCI International '99, Munich, Germany, 22-27. August 1999. pp. 604-608.

26. Womser-Hacker, C., Mandl, T. (2000): Ein adaptives Information Retrieval Modell für Digitale Bibliotheken. In Knorz, G., Kuhlen, R. (eds.): Informationskompetenz - Basiskompetenz in der Informationsgesellschaft. Proceedings 7. Intl Symposium für Informationswissenschaft. (ISI 2000) pp. 1-16.

27. Yang, Y., Liu, X. (1999): A re-examination of text categorization methods. In 22nd Intl ACM SIGIR Conference on Research and Development in Information Retrieval. pp. 42-49.

Enhancing Digital Library Documents by A Posteriori Cross Linking Using XSLT

Michael G. Bauer[1] and Günther Specht[2]

[1] Institut für Informatik5 TU München
Orleansstraße Qy5 U YL~~8 München5 Germany
bauermi@in.tum.de
[2] Fakultät für Informatik5 TU Ilmenau
Postfach L00p~p5 U WYy Ilmenau5 Germany
gspecht@prakinf.tu-ilmenau.de

Abstract. In this paper we describe a way to enhance existing digital library documents by adding links without modifying the stored docu´ments themselves6 We show how to use a combination of XSLT and a host language to access a database with linking information and how to merge documents and links at run ´time (a posteriori cross linking)6 Our approach is already used in the system OMNIS/P5 which is an advanced meta system for existing digital library systems and enhances existing digital library systems or retrieval systems by additional storing and in´dexing of user ´defined multimedia documents5 automatic and personal linking concepts5 annotations5 filtering and personalization6

1 Introduction

With the growing amount of information that is available to the individual and the different media types, many different digital library systems were developed. These systems are established tools, but users still miss features that would improve their ability to work with documents in digital library systems as it is common with books printed on paper (i.e. adding references, marking pages and annotating text). This led to the development of the OMNIS/2 system which is a meta system for various existing digital libraries [7]. It equips users with a tool that enables them to search several systems at once and especially to benefit from links between documents of different digital library systems (cross linking of documents). Users are able to add links by themselves (with an authoring tool that is part of OMNIS/2) and we will soon offer links that are generated automatically whenever possible (e.g. for bibliographic references or keywords). Merging links and documents does not require a modification of the source documents and can even be done without harvesting, which would collect all documents and store the documents in a huge private database. This is achieved by the presented technique which adds the links at run-time using XSLT[9] right before the documents are presented to the user. In addition it is possible to annotate external documents without a write permission for the library systems which hold the annotated documents. The annotations are not limited to text and can

P. Constantopoulos and I.T. Sølvberg (Eds.): ECDL 2001, LNCS 2163, pp. 95–102, 2001.
© Springer-Verlag Berlin Heidelberg 2001

consist of multimedia documents. Users are able to use a personalization feature to create their own view on the documents and to "work" with digital library systems by themselves. In its current version the system has already access to some 80000 documents of the digital library system of the Faculty for Computer Science at TU München.

In the remaining parts of the paper we first discuss briefly the architecture of a meta system on the basis of OMNIS/2 which is necessary to understand the environment in which our a posteriori cross linking technique is implemented. We then explain details of the proposed technique and end with some hints on future developments and improvements.

2   Architecture of OMNIS/2

The meta system OMNIS/2 is separated basically into two layers (see Fig.1). We use established digital library systems as data providers and treat them as large containers with powerful query languages. We assume that the systems use XML to make their data available to the outside world as it is common for modern systems nowadays. It would also be possible to access the digital library systems through a tight coupling by using certain ports the systems provide, but we do not discuss this approach any further in this paper. Our system sits on top of the established digital library systems as a meta system and acts as a service provider to the users, who access OMNIS/2 through a common browser. We decided to implement the meta system as a Java servlet in the Apache webserver. The meta system stores and handles all of the linking information and also the annotations, i.e. multimedia documents that users can upload into the system, in its own relational database. With referential integrity dangling links are avoided within the OMNIS/2 system if referenced user-defined documents are removed. The system itself is not only a meta system for digital library systems, but it can also be used as a stand-alone multimedia digital library system as all features are available as well for user-defined documents.

3   A Posteriori Cross Linking

Of course the user has to access all documents through OMNIS/2 to benefit from the additional features. This can either be done by using the extended search facility of OMNIS/2 which itself searches in the underlying systems and annotates the result sets or by following links in documents which are presented (and therefore have been processed) by OMNIS/2. In any case retrieving new documents is processed as follows. The OMNIS/2 system first queries the local meta database to retrieve the information in which external system the requested documents reside. This requires of course that every document has a persistent unique identifier (UID) within the underlying system. For documents in the local database this can be easily achieved; for other digital library systems it is an requirement so that they can be utilized by OMNIS/2. After returning the answer the meta database is queried a second time to retrieve whether there are links

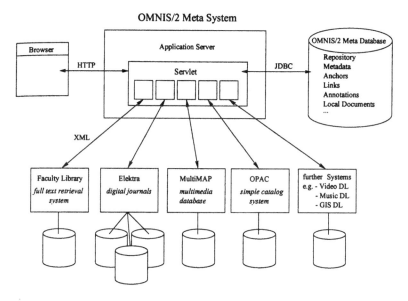

Fig. 1. Architecture of OMNIS/2

or annotations on the retrieved documents. If so we receive all corresponding anchor information. Anchors in this context follow the definition of the Dexter Hypertext Model [1] and in general are an abstraction of link sources and link destinations. Besides their exact position the anchors also need unique identifiers (AIDs) so that they can be associated with a document. After this second query the main part of our a posteriori cross linking is performed. We add the links to the documents and present them to the user.

Merging original XML documents and their linking information can be done with the help of XSLT. The W3C promotes XSLT as a language to transform XML documents into other XML documents, HTML documents or ASCII text. The manipulations of XML are performed by an XSLT processor using an XSLT stylesheet. XSLT processors are available for a variety of host languages (C++, Java, Perl, etc.). XSLT itself though does not provide a way to retrieve data (i.e. links) from a database. It is possible however to use the host language to perform this task and to exchange data with the XSLT style sheet by setting parameters. This combination is the central technique of our idea to utilize a posteriori cross linking in digital libraries. In our case the host language is Java and we chose Xalan[8] from the Apache project as the XSLT processor.

In the following sections we present our techniques using a short XML fragment of a document (in this case it is a simple metadata record) (Fig. 2). In the example we assume that a link to an annotation should be created which gives further information on the title of the XML document. For optimization reasons we combine two steps into one. Links are added to the documents, while the documents are transformed from XML into HTML for the users' browsers.

```
<item>
<dc>
  <identifier>omn:1</identifier>
  <creator> Guenther Specht, Michael G. Bauer </creator>
  <title>
     OMNIS/2 - A Multimedia Meta System for existing Digital Libraries
  </title>
  <subject/>
  <publisher>Springer Verlag, Berlin Heidelberg</publisher>
  <date>2000</date>
</dc>
</item>
```

Fig. 2. Sample XML document (fragment)

3.1   Simple Linking

At first we retrieve the link information (with UID being the key) from the meta database via JDBC (as we use Java as the host language). The next step is to build a complete URL which points to the linked document (which contains e.g. additional information). The information on the URL is available from the target anchor. This URL is the parameter which is passed on to the XSLT stylesheet. With the data provided by the parameters the XSLT stylesheet then creates a valid HTML link at the desired position. If the link includes the whole content of a tag then the content can be easily enclosed into the <A HREF>...</A> hyperlink statement of HTML. The following excerpt (Fig. 3) shows part of a simple XSLT stylesheet in detail.

```
 1 <xsl:param name="titlelink" select="''"/>
 2 <xsl:template match="title">
 3   <H3>Title:
 4      <xsl:if test="$titlelink!=''">
 5        <A><xsl:attribute name="HREF">
 6           <xsl:value-of select="$titlelink"/>
 7           </xsl:attribute>
 8        <xsl:apply-templates/></A>
 9      </xsl:if>
10      <xsl:if test="$titlelink=''">
11        <xsl:apply-templates/>
12      </xsl:if>
13   </H3>
14 </xsl:template>
```

Fig. 3. XSLT stylesheet for simple linking of tags (fragment)

It applies a posteriori cross linking on a <title> tag. The parameter which holds the target URL is called titlelink and it defaults to the empty string (no link). Its value is set by the Java part of OMNIS/2 at run-time. The resulting title string is enclosed in <H3> tags (Fig. 4).

```
<H3>Title:
<A HREF="http://www3.in.tum.de/servlet/omnis2?action=DisplayAnnotation&
id=anno:4">
OMNIS/2 - A Multimedia Meta System for existing Digital Libraries</A>
</H3>
```

Fig. 4. generated HTML code (fragment)

3.2   Linking Substrings within Tags

If only part of a tag is linked the technique becomes a bit more sophisticated (Fig. 5) and we have to address substrings of the tag and enclose those with the <A HREF>...</A> hyperlink statement (Fig. 6). The anchors have to carry information about the position of the substring within the tag content, but mostly simple integer identification is sufficient for this purpose. In the example below the parameters start and length, which are set by the Java part of OMNIS/2 at run-time, denote the postition of the link. For each anchor these values are stored in the meta database.

```
 1 <xsl:param name="titlelink" select="''"/>
 2 <xsl:template match="title">
 3  <H3>Title:
 4     <xsl:if test="$titlelink!=''">
 5       <xsl:value-of select="substring(., 1, $start - 1)"/>
 6       <A><xsl:attribute name="HREF">
 7          <xsl:value-of select="$titlelink"/>
 8          </xsl:attribute>
 9          <xsl:value-of select="substring(., $start, $length)"/>
10       </A>
11       <xsl:value-of select="substring(., $start + $length + 1)"/>
12     </xsl:if>
13     <xsl:if test="$titlelink=''">
14       <xsl:apply-templates/>
15     </xsl:if>
16  </H3>
17 </xsl:template>
```

Fig. 5. XSLT stylesheet for linking substrings (fragment)

```
<H3>Title: OMNIS/2 - A
<A HREF="http://www3.in.tum.de/servlet/omnis2?action=DisplayAnnotation&
id=anno:4">
Multimedia</A> Meta System for existing Digital Libraries
</H3>
```

Fig. 6. generated HTML code for linking substrings (fragment)

3.3 Advanced Linking Using Java Extensions within XSLT

The above presented techniques show very simple linking mechanisms. They link only exactly once in a tag and (without fundamental changes) work only for standalone documents. If a list of documents is returned (e.g. as a result of querying a digital library system) the single result items cannot be linked with the above presented methods. Each item can be uniquely identified but with the techniques so far it was not possible to transfer information from the XSLT stylesheet to the host language. (The above shown techniques use only the way from the host language to the XSLT stylesheet.) Another problem is that it is not possible to transform only part of an XML document and then update the variables for the remaining transformations with the XSLT stylesheets we have presented up to now. This is of course tightly linked to the above mentioned problem.

Most XSLT processors offer extensions, which enable the use of programming languages from within XSLT stylesheets. As mentioned above we use the Xalan XSLT processor, which offers Java extensions besides others. With a new namespace defined at the beginning of the stylesheet it is then possible to directly call Java methods in a way similar to XSLT functions. As the Java methods can be called with arbitrary parameters we can transfer parts of the XML data to the Java method, manipulate it (e.g. query a database) and return data to the XSLT stylesheet for further transformations. This gives us the flexibility to work beyond the functionality of simple XSLT stylesheets and to achieve the desired results. For the sake of readability we only provide a very short excerpt of a Java extended stylesheet omiting the source code of the Java classes (which carry the JDBC database calls, etc.). Line 9 in Fig. 7 shows the relevant call to the Java class.

4 Related Work

Some of the concepts of OMNIS/2 (section 2) and a posteriori cross linking have occurred in different forms in the scientific literature over the last years. The first project that we know of which describes shared annotations for webpages is ComMentor [5] from Stanford University. Commentor supports server side

```
 1 <?xml version="1.0"?>
 2 <xsl:stylesheet
 3     xmlns:xsl="http://www.w3.org/1999/XSL/Transform"
 4     version="1.0"
 5     xmlns:java="http://xml.apache.org/xslt/java"
 6     exclude-result-prefixes="java">
 7   <xsl:template match="title">
 8     <xsl:variable name="titlelink"
 9       select="java:Anchor.getLink(string(../identifier), string(.))"/>
10     <H3>Title: <xsl:value-of select="$titlelink"\> </H3>
11   </xsl:template>
12 </xsl:stylesheet>
```

Fig. 7. A Java call from an XSLT stylesheet (fragment)

annotations but the functionality is limited as the implementation is directly integrated into the source code of the browser.

The OSF Research Institute developed GrAnT (Group Annotation Transducer), which is a proxy based service and support annotations for the World Wide Web [6]. Annotations in GrAnT can only consist of texts and the system does not use a database system for managing annotations.

Project Clio of Grinnell College also deals with annotations on webpages and suggests user permissions and anchors similar to OMNIS/2. The available literature [3] though especially concentrates on user experiences with annotations.

Phelps and Wilensky have described the multivalent document model which supports multivalent annotations [4]. Their concept describes a solution where the annotations are stored on the client side and a special viewer is used to be able to benefit from the additional features.

5 Summary and Future Work

We have shown how to enhance existing digital library documents by adding links without modifying the source documents. We are using accepted standards like XML, XSLT and Java for this purpose which is an advance over solutions using proprietary implementations. The added links are stored separately from the source documents and can reference either documents within the same digital library, documents from other digital library systems or user-defined annotations. We call our presented technique a posteriori cross linking. Users can benefit from it because they can work with the digital library documents (add references and annotations) in a fashion that comes close to working with classic paper documents. Further improvements we want to implement in a later version target the transformation formats within the OMNIS/2 system. In our description above we have inserted the links directly while the XML source documents were transformed into HTML. The design of the transformation could be improved by creating XLink and XPointer from the stored link data. This would lead to an

XML only data format that can then be transformed with XSLT to HTML in a final step. This would result in a greater flexibility as XML shall replace HTML within the next years. In the future browsers will be able to display the XML format directly and OMNIS/2 could avoid the final step of transformation. We also plan to investigate the ability of OMNIS/2 to act as a service provider for the Open Archives Initiative [2], as the initiative proposes an XML based exchange format, which OMNIS/2 can work with as presented in this paper.

6   Acknowledgments

OMNIS/2 is funded by DFG (German Research Foundation) within the research initiative "V3D2" ("Distributed Processing and Delivery of Digital Documents") and is part of the Global Inventory Project (an initiative of the G7-countries).

References

1. Halasz F., Schwartz M., *The Dexter Hypertext Reference Model*, Comm. of the ACM, 37(2), Feb. 1994, pp. 30-39.
2. *Homepage of the Open Archives Initiative*, http://www.openarchives.org
3. Luebke S.M., Mason H.A., Rebelsky S.A., *Annotating the World-Wide-Web*, Proc. of ED-Media 99 World Conference on Educational Multimedia, Hypermedia and Telecommunications, June 1999, pp. 409-414.
4. Phelps T.A., Wilensky R., *Multivalent Annotations*, Proc. of the 1st European Conf. on Research and Advanced Technology for Digital Libraries (ECDL 1997), Springer, LNCS 1324, 1997, pp. 287-303.
5. Röscheisen M., Mogensen C., Winograd T., *Beyond Browsing: Shared Comments, SOAPs, Trails, and On-Line Communities*, Proc. of the 3rd World Wide Web Conference, April 10-14, 1995, Darmstadt, Germany.
6. Schickler M.A., Mazer M.S., Brooks C., *Pan-Browser Support for Annotations and Other Meta-Information on the World Wide Web*, Proc. of the 5th World Wide Web Conference, May 6-10, 1996, Paris, France.
7. Specht G., Bauer M.G., *OMNIS/2: A Multimedia Meta System for existing Digital Libraries*, Proc. of the 4th European Conf. on Research and Advanced Technology for Digital Libraries (ECDL 2000), Springer, LNCS 1923, 2000, pp. 180-189.
8. *The Apache XML Project*, http://xml.apache.org/
9. *XSL Transformations (XSLT), Version 1.0*, http://www.w3.org/TR/xslt

Using Copy-Detection and Text Comparison Algorithms for Cross-Referencing Multiple Editions of Literary Works

Arkady Zaslavsky[1], Alejandro Bia[2], and Krisztian Monostori[3]

[1] Monash University, Melbourne, Australia
a.zaslavsky@monash.edu.au
http://www.csse.monash.edu.au/~azaslavs/
[2] Miguel de Cervantes DL, University of Alicante, Alicante, Spain
abia@dlsi.ua.es
http://www.dlsi.ua.es/~abia/
[3] Monash University, Melbourne, Australia
Krisztian.Monostori@csse.monash.edu.au
http://www.ct.monash.edu.au/~kmonosto

Abstract. This article describes a joint research work between Monash University and the University of Alicante, where software originally meant for plagiarism and copy detection in academic works is successfully applied to perform comparative analysis of different editions of literary works. The experiments were performed with Spanish texts from the Miguel de Cervantes digital library. The results have proved useful for literary and linguistic research, automating part of the tedious task of comparative text analysis. Besides, other interesting uses were detected.

1 Copy-Detection, Plagiarism, and Comparative Literary Analysis

Digital libraries provide vast amounts of digitised information on-line. Preventing these documents from unauthorised copying and redistribution is a hard and challenging task, which often results in not putting valuable documents on-line [Garcia-Molina and Shivakumar, 1995b]. Copy-prevention mechanisms include distributing information on a separate disk, using special hardware or active documents [Garcia-Molina and Shivakumar, 1995a]. We believe that these approaches are very cumbersome for genuine users, therefore copy-detection approaches are more practical. Copy-detection does not try to hinder the distribution of documents but rather tries to identify illegal copies.

One of the most pressing areas of copy-detection applications is detecting plagiarism. With the enormous growth of the information available on the Internet users have a handy tool for writing research papers. With the numerous search engines users can easily find relevant articles and papers for their research. These documents are available in electronic form, which makes plagiarism achievable by cut-and-paste or drag-and-drop operations. Academic organizations as well

P. Constantopoulos and I.T. Sølvberg (Eds.): ECDL 2001, LNCS 2163, pp. 103–114, 2001.
© Springer-Verlag Berlin Heidelberg 2001

as research institutions are looking for a powerful tool for detecting plagiarism. Copy-detection tools aim to find whole and partial copies of documents either on the Internet or in local repositories. These tools can be used by digital libraries to find copies of their copyrighted documents redistributed on the Web or in newsgroups. The tools can also detect possible plagiarised documents, since textual overlap may prove to be plagiarism. Though there are more "sophisticated" ways to plagiarise, we believe that finding textual overlap would identify most cases of plagiarism.

Apart from the original purpose of plagiarism detection, it occurred to us that a very different use can be given to this kind of powerful comparison programs. Not only can we use such a system to detect illegal, or at least immoral, cases of text duplication but it may also help compare different documents for research purposes. In this paper we will present the result of a comparison among different editions of literary works like the famous Spanish masterpiece *El Ingenioso Hidalgo Don Quijote de la Mancha* of which there exists different versions. Librarians may also use this system to cross-reference different publications in some cases. Different problems of text comparison for DL professionals and linguists are discussed in the following section.

2   Applications of Text Comparison to DLs and Humanities Research

The idea of using the MDR (Match Detect Reveal) system with the purpose of establishing cross-references between literary works was born on a casual talk between members of Monash University and the Miguel de Cervantes DL project [Bia and Pedreño, 2001] at the DL'2000 conference in San Antonio, Texas, last year.

The Miguel de Cervantes DL, apart from being the biggest repository of digital literary texts in Spanish language, devotes part of its efforts to carry out multidisciplinary research projects where humanists and computer scientists can join their skills and experience on developing new tools and methods for DLs [Bia and Pedreño, 2001]. From this point of view, this initiative of applying advanced text comparison to literary texts promised to be not only an excellent case study and testing environment for MDR, but also the perspective of discovering a promising tool for digital libraries and humanities research.

We soon worked out the requirement specifications to fine tune MDR to this new kind of application. For preliminary tests, we first collected a set of texts making sure beforehand that some of them included overlapings (parts of text existent on other files of the sample). We also took note of the placement and kind of overlapings. With the help of some linguists from the Miguel de Cervantes DL we have chosen cases of cross-referred texts suitable for the tests. The results of the comparisons were amazing, no match was missed.

We have foreseen three potential applications for MDR on digital libraries and linguistic research, plus another we didn't think of. We will now describe them briefly.

2.1   Detecting Cross-References

The first application we thought of, was to automatically detect quotations or cross-references between different texts. In this case the quote could be hyperlinked to the original. We can imagine many research situations where automatic detection of similar sections of text can be useful. It could be a valuable aid in history research for instance.

2.2   Organizing Collections of Small Pieces of Text

Another use is to detect repeated poems in different poem collections (may also be tales, letters, etc.), where some of these textual units are repeated in different editions. Most often, when collections of poems are developed, it is difficult to keep track of which poems have been included and where, and which not. MDR proved to be a helpful tool for detecting and locating the corresponding pieces of text for verification purposes. One of our first experiments was to compare a couple of collections of poems from *Ramón de Campoamor y Campoosorio*. We could easily keep track of the poems that appeared in both collections. Figure 1 shows the cross-reference of one isolated poem that appears in two different poem selections.

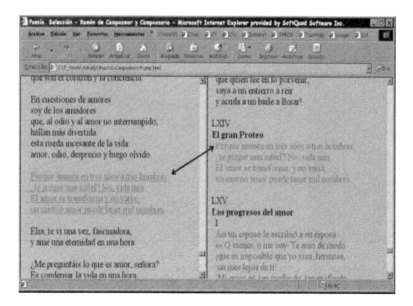

Fig. 1. A repeated poem in two different poem collections.

2.3 Comparative Analysis of Texts

The objective is to compare different editions of the same literary work. Philologists are usually interested in this kind of comparisons for research purposes. In ancient literature, there usually are different editions of the same work, with modifications performed some times by the author, some others by the editor. This comparative analysis is in itself an interesting but tedious field of study where any kind of automation is welcome. To cite an example, there are various ancient editions of the *Quijote de la Mancha*, all originals from Cervantes, but still different. This application differs from the previous ones, in the sense that here we have to find differences instead of matches. Although in this case the matching strings are usually in the same order in both sources, synchronization is not always possible since the sources may have long additions inserted in different places, apart from small differences in the matching zones. A conventional sequential comparison may also fail in this case.

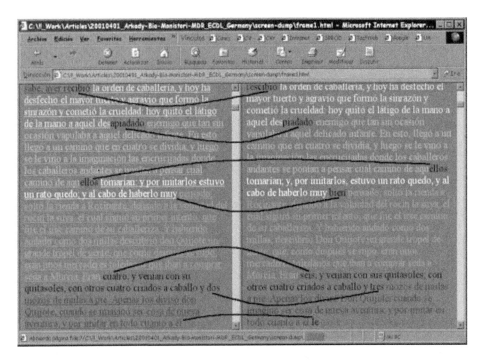

Fig. 2. Comparing two editions of *Don Quijote* (the real screen makes full use of colour to highlight the matches)

In the example of figure 2, we can see clear differences in two versions of Don Quijote: on the left frame we can read *"Eran cuatro, y venían con sus quitasoles, con otros cuatro criados a caballo y dos mozos de mulas a pie"*, while on the right one we see *"Eran seis, y venían con sus quitasoles, con otros cuatro criados a caballo y tres mozos de mulas a pie"*. The merchants from Toledo, in one case are six, in the other four, and their servants on foot are two on one side and three on the other. A little bit above there is another difference in meaning. On the left it says "muy pensado" (thoughtfully) and on the right "muy bien pensado" (very well thought). These are examples of changes introduced by editors through the centuries.

2.4   Detecting Variations and Mistypings

There are variations in spelling owed to ancient editor changes, which are not strictly errors since the Spanish language was not normalized until 1713, where the *Real Academia de la Lengua Española* was created and language spelling started to settle. Those variations, though legal, produce differences between editions. An example of ancient spelling variations can be seen in figure 2, where we can see *"recibió"* and *"rescibió"*, *"desapiadado"* and *"despiadado"*, and *"aquellos"* and *"aquéllos"*. None of these are errors, but ancient variations.

On the other hand, no matter how much care correctors put on freeing texts from digitization errors, there are always some errors that remain. So an unforeseen result of the application of MDR to comparative analysis was the detection of spelling errors or variations in DL texts, out of the comparison of different editions of the same work.

3   Existing Tools and Algorithms

Copy-detection schemes have two fundamental approaches: digital watermarking, and string comparison. The target of digital watermarking is to find illegal copies and track down the user who purchased the electronic document and redistributed it. This method cannot be used by librarians for the tasks discussed in the previous section. In watermarking methods, undetectable codewords are placed in documents similar to the method of placing watermarks in bank notes. These codewords can represent a unique document identifier and this identifier can be assigned to a given customer who purchased the document. Codewords can be hidden in the document by slightly altering the layout of the text. These alterations must be reliably decodable yet not perceptible to the user. In string-comparison based algorithms we can define the basic problem as with given two strings T and P with the length of m and n respectively, we have to divide T and P into substrings $T = t_1 s_1 t_2 s_2 t_3 s_3 ... t_k s_k t_{k+1}$ and $P = p_1 q_1 p_2 q_2 p_3 q_3 ... p_r q_r p_{r+1}$ where for each s_y there is an x so that $s_y = q_x$ and $S(|s_y|)$ is maximal. As an example compare $T = abcdbcadca$ and $P = aabaca$. One possible partition is $T = ()(ab)(cdb)(c)(adc)(a)()$ and $P = ()(a)()(ab)(a)(c)(a)$. T is partitioned into $t_1 = ()$, $s_1 = (ab)$, $t_2 = (cdb)$, $s_2 = (c)$, $t_3 = (adc)$, $s_3 = (a)$, $t_4 = ()$ and P is partitioned into $p_1 = ()$, $q_1 = (a)$, $p_2 = ()$, $q_2 = (ab)$, $p_3 = (a)$, $q_3 = (c)$, $p_4 = (a)$. $s_1 = q_2$, $s_2 = q_3$, $s_3 = q_1$. $S(|sx|) = 3$, which is not maximal in this case because the partition giving the maximum for $S(|sx|)$ is $T = ()(ab)()(c)()(b)()(ca)(d)(ca)()$ and $P = ()(a)()(ab)(a)(ca)()$. The maximum overlap is a single value, but different partitions can result in the same maximal overlap value, that is, the partition is not unique. We analysed four research prototypes that aim to solve the above-defined maximal overlap problem. These research prototypes include the SCAM (Stanford Copy Analysis Method) system [Garcia-Molina and Shivakumar, 1995a], the Koala system [Heintze, 1996], the "shingling approach" of [Broder et al.,], and the file system clustering method of the sif tool [Manber, 1994]. The general approach to define the maximal overlap is to split up the text into chunks, calculate some hash function on those chunks, select certain chunks from all the chunks to be stored in an index. When a document has to be compared to documents in the repository, the suspicious document, that we want to compare to others, has to be chunked using the same strategy as used in registration. The overlapping chunks then must be identified. Given these chunks, a decision function decides whether a given document is plagiarised, is a partial or exact copy of other documents depending on the objective of the system. If we want to use these methods for identifying the differences between e.g. two different versions of *Don Quijote* then this method is constrained by the chunking method and the selection strategy used. If we are using non-overlapping chunks of text of e.g. ten words then any difference between the texts will be at least ten words. As we will see in Section 5 sometimes there are only slight differences, such as different accents used, which are not easily picked up by the output of these systems. Our approach, which is discussed in the following section, uses a suffix tree structure, which is able to identify exact overlapping chunks by using the matching statitistics algorithm. The main advantage of this algorithm that it is able to pick up smaller differences, such as the above-mentioned differences in accents.

4   MDR Architecture

The procedure of processing documents is the following. Documents must undergo preprocessing in order to be indexed in the repository. This preprocessing converts documents in different formats into pure ASCII text and then they are further converted into a format that can be used by the matching-engine. This format also makes sure that simple modifications, i.e. using different punctuations, adding extra spaces, will not hinder detection.

Documents are then chunked and hashed and then recorded in the index. When a suspicious document is submitted to the system the search-engine identifies candidate documents in the index and candidate documents are compared using the matching-engine. The matching-engine builds a suffix tree for the suspicious document and compares the candidate documents to the suffix tree. A suffix tree is an index that represents all suffixes of a string, which means that all substrings are also represented. Suffix trees can be built in linear time, and our implementation uses Ukkonen's [Ukkonen, 1995] algorithm for the construction. Chang's matching statistics algorithm [Chang and Lawler, 1994] can be used to create an array of numbers that represents the longest overlapping chunk starting in each position in the suspicious document. Once this array is given it is easy to calculate overlap-percentage, the only thing we have to consider is that a matching statistic value of k at position i represents the same chunk as a matching statistic value of k-1 at position i+1.

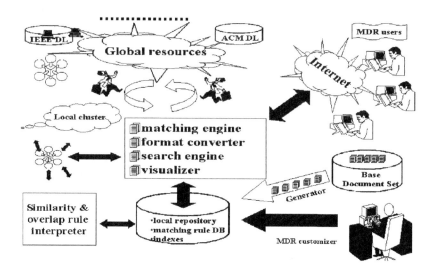

Fig. 3. This figure depicts the architecture of MDR. It is a general architecture that shows all potentials of the MDR system with different components.

Matching statistics can be calculated in linear time. The running time of the algorithm is proportional to the size of the string to be compared to the tree and independent from the size of the tree. Unfortunately suffix trees are too big to be used as an index, though the matching statistics algorithm runs fast (app. 1MB/sec) making it possible to be used in the second stage. The accuracy of the system is the highest possible because it identifies exact chunks and does not include any uncertainty, such as hashing. We consider this algorithm a method that could complement those methods used in other prototype systems and incorporated into our search-engine.

The MDR system also contains a submission system, whose scope is wider than the submission component of other prototype systems. It contains a complete system for submitting assignments for different courses. The similarity and rule interpreter component is under development. We would like to set up a set of rules for handling obvious modifications: changing the name of geographical names, changing numbers, adding or deleting extra whitespaces, etc. The document generator is a complementary component that can be used to generate documents that overlap with documents in the base document set. These documents then can be used to test our algorithms. Using the local cluster for the comparison is discussed in [Monostori et al., 1999]. Comparison jobs can be generated when a suspicious document is submitted and the local cluster can be used to compare documents in parallel.

This architecture of the MDR system is tailored for plagiarism-detection and copy-detection applications but core components may be used for other purposes including cross-referencing and comparison of different versions of the same document as mentioned in Section 2. If we have text versions of those documents we simply use the converter component to eliminate non-significant differences, i.e. multiple whitespaces, different punctuations. As soon as we have a canonical form of the document we can submit it to the matching engine, which provides us with positions and lengths of overlapping chunks. The Visualiser component is responsible for generating HTML files from these positions. Figure 2 depicts the output of the comparison of two versions of *Don Quijote*.

Identical colours depict identical chunks in both documents and black chunks are the differences between the documents. We could use a different colouring scheme that would use black for identical chunks and different colours for differences. The colouring scheme used stems from the colouring scheme of visualising plagiarised documents where similarity is more important than difference. The following subsection describes briefly how such comparison is done by the matching engine.

4.1   The Matching Engine

The matching engine component uses a suffix tree structure to compare documents. A suffix tree is a data structure that includes every suffix of a given string, thus every substring. Suffix trees can be built in linear time using different algorithms [Ukkonen, 1995, Gusfield, 1997]. We used Ukkonen's algorithm not only because of its relative simplicity but because it also stores suffix link information, which is heavily utilised by the matching statistics algorithm. The suffix tree of the string *abcdabca*$ is shown in figure 4. Chang et al. [Chang and Lawler, 1994]

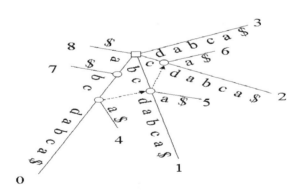

Fig. 4. Suffix tree of the string *abcdabca*$

describes an algorithm for finding so called matching statistics - $ms(i)$, which is the longest substring of T starting at position i that matches a substring somewhere in P. Having built a suffix tree for P, matching statistics of T can be found in $O(n)$ time where n is the length of T. The main idea of the algorithm is that starting from the first position in T we calculate the matching statistics $ms(0)$ by traversing the suffix tree of P. Then, in order to calculate $ms(i)$ while having calculated $ms(i-1)$ we have to back up to the node above our current position, follow the suffix link of that node and then traverse down from that node.

We have tailored both Ukkonen's building algorithm and Chang's matching statistics algorithm by taking into account that we only want to find overlaps starting at beginning of words. With this modification the space requirement can be reduced to approximately 20% of the original suffix tree and the matching statistics algorithm also benefits from this modification. This modification is similar to the one in Baeza-Yates et al. [Navarro et al., 1999] but they only suggest that substrings starting at the beginning of words are to be included and they do not consider how to build the tree in linear time. We analysed and modified Ukkonen's and Chang's algorithm to reflect these changes. We will also analyse the possibility of inserting only those suffixes that start at certain positions, e.g. every 30th, for further reducing the size of the suffix tree. Part of a modified suffix tree for the converted string "-they-were-the-last-to-arrive-but-they-were-not-late-" is depicted in figure 5. The character [-] depicts a space. If during the matching statistics algorithm we traverse down the route labelled

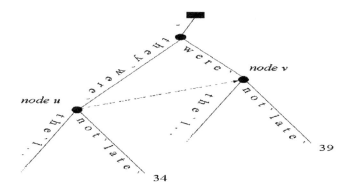

Fig. 5. Part of a Modified Suffix Tree

by "-they-were-not-" in the next step we do not have to start matching at the root rather we follow the suffix link between node u and node v (depicted by the dashed arrow) and continue traversing the tree from node v. This interpretation of the suffix link is different from the one in the original Ukkonen's algorithm and since we only insert suffixes starting at the beginning of words a suffix link points to the node with the label of the original node without the first word. In our example the label of node u is "-they-were-" and the label of node v is "-were-". Not only does this modified suffix tree require less space but the matching statistics algorithm can also benefit from it calculating the matching values only for positions where words start.

5   Results of Comparing Different Editions of Cervantes's Quijote with MDR

We compared three different editions of *El ingenioso hidalgo Don Quijote de la Mancha* by Miguel de Cervantes Saavedra. The first one, catalogued as #001270, is a digital edition based on the Madrid edition, published by Espasa-Calpe, 1911-1913. The second, catalogue #002035, is a digital edition based on the Barcelona edition, typography from F. Giró, 1888, 4th. ed., donated from the private library of Emma María Guijarro Hortelano, with a great number of engravings and reproduction of contemporary paintings. The third one, catalogue #002693, is a digital edition based on the Barcelona edition, A. López Robert, 1905, 3rd ed., with illustrations by the famous draftsman Don José Passos.

In spite of being both from the Barcelona branch of the Quijote family tree, editions #002035 and #002693 show phrases with opposite meanings:

- #002035: algunos que, no conteniéndose en los límites de su ignorancia
- #002693: algunos que, conteniéndose en los límites de su ignorancia

More surprising is to see that the number of silk merchants from Toledo that Don Quijote see in their way to Murcia were six, or just four?, and were accompanied by three or just two "mozos de mulas"?

- #001270: Eran seis, y venían con sus quitasoles, con otros cuatro criados a caballo y tres mozos de mulas a pie. (see figure 2)
- #002035: Eran cuatro, y venían con su quitasoles, con otros cuatro criados a caballo y dos mozos de mulas a pie.
- #002693: Eran seis, y venían con sus quitasoles, con otros cuatro criados a caballo y tres mozos de mulas a pie.

Below we read "Florimorte de Hircania", or is it "Florismarte de Hircania"?

- #001270: -Éste que se sigue es Florimorte de Hircania -dijo el Barbero. -Ahí está el señor Florimorte? -replicó el Cura-.
- #002035: Éste que se sigue es Florismarte de Hircania, dijo el barbero. Ahí está el señor Florismarte? replicó el cura;
- #002693: Éste que se sigue es Florismarte de Hircania dijo el barbero. Ahí está el señor Florismarte? replicó el cura.

These are examples of mismatches, easily detected by MDR. In these cases the differences are in meaning. In others we see that one version has been modernized: ancient forms of Spanish have been converted to modern, normalized Spanish.

The way traditional literature researchers like *Diaz y Diaz* did this job of comparative analysis was by filling tables by hand with the mismatches they found when reading two texts side by side. This method was slow and error prone. One important advantage of working with this kind of computerized tool is time saving. It takes only a few seconds to compare two versions of *El Quijote*, compared to weeks or months it may take without computer aid. Digital librarians and literary researchers also benefit from the friendly interface, that takes advantage of hyperlinks to match the coincidences and in this way revealing the differences with better accuracy and less mistakes than using traditional methods.

6   Conclusions

An interesting application of this technique is the development of critical editions. These are based on the comparative analysis of different editions of the same literary work, usually taking one that is considered the most faithful to the original work, and then annotating the differences between this text and the each of the others. During this process, misprints or editor changes will be detected. The research can focus either on ancient lexical usages or on the style of the author. A tool like MDR would save a considerable amount of time and effort.

Many differences between editions are related to punctuation and capitalization, since editors used to make this kinds of modifications at will. Ignoring them, as MDR does is desirable in most cases.

Conventional file comparison programs usually do sequential string comparison, which is a good approach when comparing similar texts in search of differences. Since sequential matching requires synchronization of the sources, this approach is useless when the matching strings appear in a different order and mixed with other text zones that do not match, i.e. when the texts are too different. MDR proved to be specially suitable for this task, since it does not require the matching zones of text to appear in any order.

MDR outperforms conventional sequential file comparison tools, being able to detect even small matches in texts which are highly different. These matches can appear in any place and any order and still be successfully detected. The format of the output, as cross-linked HTML files displayed on conventional browsers using frames is very convenient and practical.

Concerning digitisation processes, MDR can be used to compare the output of different OCR (optical character recognition) programs applied to the same book, or to compare two versions of the same text that have been corrected in parallel by different persons, or just to compare two versions of the same file to verify the changes performed to one to produce the other.

7   Future Work

MDR detects identical chunks of texts between two files, ignoring only punctuation and capitalization. Another interesting approach would be to detect similar but not identical strings. One possible approach could be to ignore a set of given stopwords, i.e. words that are generally meaningless, reducing the matching to compare meaningful words like nouns and verbs. The use of synonyms could be another attempt. This would be useful not only to detect plagiarism in the modern sense, but also to detect *imitatio*, the ancient practice of novel writers imitating the style and sometimes copying entire phrases of acclaimed writers. This is another interesting point in literary research.

Another possible improvement concerning the interface could be to use XML instead of HTML to mark up the output of MDR, indicating the matches and mismatches detected and the cross-linking between the chunks of texts of the compared files. Then we can use XSL transformations to produce different HTML renderings customized for different types of research: in this way we could highlight the differences, or otherwise the similarities, or produce bidirectional cross-links, or just customize the colors for ease of reading.

References

[Bia and Pedreño, 2001] Bia, A. and Pedreño, A. (2001). The Miguel de Cervantes Digital Library: The Hispanic Voice on the WEB. *LLC (Literary and Linguistic Computing) journal, Oxford University Press*, 16(2):161–177. Presented at ALLC/ACH 2000, The Joint International Conference of the Association for Literary and Linguistic Computing and the Association for Computers and the Humanities, 21/25 July 2000, University of Glasgow.

[Broder et al.,] Broder, A., Glassman, S., and Manasse, M. Syntatic Clustering of the Web. In *Sixth International Web Conference*, Santa Clara, California, USA. URL: http://decweb.ethz.ch/WWW6/Technical/Paper205/paper205.html.

[Chang and Lawler, 1994] Chang, W. and Lawler, E. (1994). Sublinear Approximate String Matching and Biological Applications. *Algorithmica*, 12:327–344.

[Garcia-Molina and Shivakumar, 1995a] Garcia-Molina, H. and Shivakumar, N. (1995a). SCAM: A Copy Detection Mechanism for Digital Documents. In *Proceedings of 2nd International Conference in Theory and Practice of Digital Libraries (DL'95)*, Austin, Texas.

[Garcia-Molina and Shivakumar, 1995b] Garcia-Molina, H. and Shivakumar, N. (1995b). The SCAM Approach To Copy Detection in Digital Libraries. *D-lib Magazine*.

[Gusfield, 1997] Gusfield, D. (1997). *Algorithms on Strings, Trees, and Sequences*. Cambridge University Press.

[Heintze, 1996] Heintze, N. (1996). Scalable Document Fingerprinting. In *Proceedings of the Second USENIX Workshop on Electronic Commerce*, Oakland, California. URL: http://www.cs.cmu.edu/afs/cs/user/nch/www/koala/main.html.

[Manber, 1994] Manber, U. (1994). Finding similar Files in a Large File System. In *Proceedings of the 1994 USENIX Conference*, pages 1–10. URL: http://www.cs.cmu.edu/afs/cs/user/nch/www/koala/main.html.

[Monostori et al., 1999] Monostori, K., Zaslavsky, A., and Schmidt, H. (1999). Parallel Overlap and Similarity Detection in Semi-Structured Document Collections. In *6th Annual Australasian Conference on Parallel And Real-Time Systems (PART '99)*.

[Navarro et al., 1999] Navarro, G., Baeza-Yates, R., and Ribeiro-Neto, B. (1999). Indexing and searching. In *Modern Information Retrieval*, chapter 8, pages 191–228. ACM press and Addison Wesley, Edinburgh Gate, Harlow, Essex CM20 2JE, England, 1st edition. See also http://www.dcc.ufmg.br/irbook or http://sunsite.dcc.uchile.cl/irbook.

[Ukkonen, 1995] Ukkonen, E. (1995). On-Line Construction of Suffix Trees. *Algorithmica*, 14:249–260.

An Architecture for Automatic Reference Linking

Donna Bergmark and Carl Lagoze

Cornell Digital Library Research Group⋆

Abstract. Along with the explosive growth of the Web has come a great increase in on-line scholarly literature, which is often more current than what appears in printed publications. The increasing proportion of on-line scholarly literature makes it possible to implement functionality desirable to all researchers – the ability to access cited documents immediately from the citing paper. Implementing this direct access is called "reference linking". The Cornell Digital Library Research Group employs *value-added surrogates* as a generalizable mechanism for providing reference-linking behavior in Web documents. This mechanism exposes reference linking data through a well-defined API, permitting the construction of reference linking services by external clients. We present two example reference linking applications buildable on this API. We also introduce a performance metric; currently we are (automatically) extracting reference linking information with more than 80% accuracy.

1 Background and Motivation

The variety of on-line scholarly literature has grown along with the web. Informal on-line archives are repositories for papers and technical reports. Proceedings are increasingly often published on the Web. The collection of on-line journals is growing. The increasing proportion of on-line scholarly literature (nearly 10,000 on-line journals in 1999 [11]) makes it possible to implement a function desirable to all researchers – the ability to access cited documents immediately from the citing paper. Implementing this direct access is called "reference linking".

Reference linking is actually an old idea. Classical reference linking arose from a desire to study citation patterns among scholarly articles. The Science Citation Index[5] founded by Eugene Garfield in the 60's was invented to do just that, and was a spectacular success. Staff captured a paper's bibliographic data, and then went to the reference section and did the same for each reference to a journal covered by the SCI.

As a result, one could look up the links and build a graph as shown in Fig. 1(a). The nodes in this graph represent scientific papers, and directional arcs have two contextual meanings. Outgoing arcs, with respect to a specific node, lead to *references* of that paper. Incoming arcs, with respect to a specific node, originate from that paper's *citations*. From the graph we can observe that Paper

---

⋆ NSF Digital Libraries Initiative, Grant # IIS-9907892

P. Constantopoulos and I.T. Sølvberg (Eds.): ECDL 2001, LNCS 2163, pp. 115–126, 2001.

C has 4 references and that Paper A has two citations. The links in the graph are *explicitly* contained in the SCI.

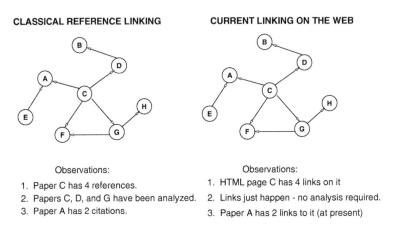

CLASSICAL REFERENCE LINKING

CURRENT LINKING ON THE WEB

Observations:
1. Paper C has 4 references.
2. Papers C, D, and G have been analyzed.
3. Paper A has 2 citations.

Observations:
1. HTML page C has 4 links on it
2. Links just happen - no analysis required.
3. Paper A has 2 links to it (at present)

Fig. 1. (a) Classical Reference Linking vs. (b) Current Linking on the Web

We then fast-forward some 40 years to the current time, where there is a growing amount of scholarly literature on-line. In many cases, the authors of this literature have inserted references to other works on the Web. These URLs allow efficient movement from the referencing to the cited work, but do nothing to help maintain an account of a paper's citations. Figure 1(b) shows a sub-graph of interlinked Web papers. From the fragment shown here, we can deduce that document C has four links in it to other Web documents and document A has at present two links to it.

Our reference linking project aims to bridge the classical view and what exists today on the Web. We wish to make the web graph explicit for selected repositories, as well as automatically supply additional links where possible. While a variety of uses exist for explicit hyperlink graphs in themselves [4, 6], we are aiming higher. We aim to create a *reference linking layer* on the Web that provides sufficient data for a variety of value-added *reference linking applications*. Some of these applications may be targeted at human use, consisting of a user interface for navigating the reference linked graph. Others may be *middleware*, massaging data for use by other applications, such as to provide a citation database. Our main objective is to provide this layer *automatically*, without the direct participation from authors or publishers.

Figure 2 is an example of a human-oriented reference linking application that exploits the data from a reference linking layer.

Implementing the functionality shown in Fig. 2 requires a number of steps. The *reference linking layer* must:

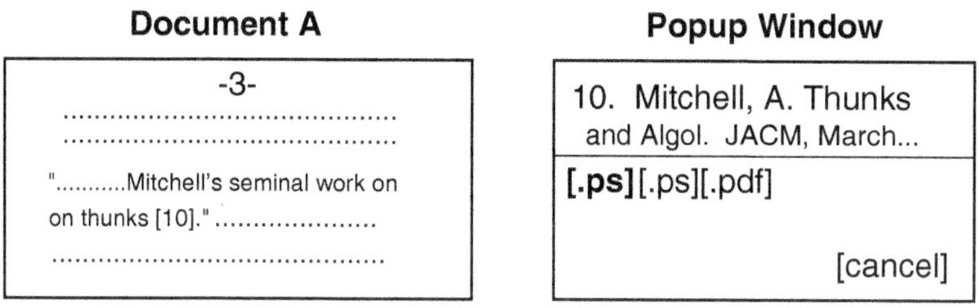

Document A	Popup Window
-3- .... " ....Mitchell's seminal work on on thunks [10]."	10. Mitchell, A. Thunks and Algol. JACM, March... **[.ps]**[.ps][.pdf] [cancel]

Fig. 2. A Reference Linking Application. User clicks on "[10]" while reading A. The popup window allows a copy of the reference to be retrieved.

1. Deduce that the string [10] in the text is a reference and that it matches the reference string, 10. `Mitchell, A. Thunks and Algol...`; in the reference section at the end of the paper.
2. Parse the reference string to decide what work it is, whether it is linkable, and whether it is something we've seen before so we can credit Mitchell with this paper as a citation.
3. Provide access to this reference linking data for use by applications.

The *reference linking application* must then:

4. Turn the "[10]" into a live link. In HTML and PDF this reference can be turned into a clickable anchor. For other formats an auxiliary display can provide clickable links.

From a data-flow perspective this process can be described as *analysis, data access*, and *presentation*. Our work has been concentrating on the first two. We describe an API that makes the data from this analysis available to client applications. In later work, we plan to examine the presentation layer.

1.1   Related Work

Reference linking is being implemented by a large group of publishers in the CrossRef project, which grew out of the DOI-X project described in [2]. This organization, consisting of professional journal publishers, is interlinking their on-line journals. Each publisher, using editorial input, generates its own metadata and shares it with the other publishers in the group.

Other systems, like ours, endeavor automatic metadata generation for Web items. For example, dc.dot <http://www.ukoln.ac.uk/metadata/dcdot/> extracts titles from <title> elements of HTML files, and keywords from headers and capitalized phrases. Jenkins [8] describes a system that automatically generates some Dublin Core metadata from specialized sources of data on the http server. Neither of these systems get their data by examining the body of the document itself, as we do. Also, our interest is only in bibliographic metadata, that which comprises citations and references. We do not collect keywords, nor do we attempt any classification of analyzed papers.

ResearchIndex[10] is a well-known reference linking application which seeks to build a large on-line database of computer science citation information, automatically. We have borrowed some of their techniques, including the retention of reference contexts [9]. Our work is distinguished from ResearchIndex by our clear architectural distinction between reference linking data and its presentation thus enabling a variety of reference linking services, while ResearchIndex's functionality is available only through their Web interface.

A related research project is context-sensitive reference linking, where the targets of clickable anchors depend upon the user's circumstances (e.g. which subscriptions the user owns, to what organization does the user belong). SFX[15], an advanced reference linking system that takes the user's context into account, was the first server for context-sensitive reference linking. Our effort could be used in conjunction with SFX.

Formally, our work is part of a larger project called OpCit based at Southampton University <http://opcit.eprints.org>. Funded jointly by JISC in the UK and the NSF in the US, OpCit's goal is to interlink online literature [7]. Code developed by Les Carr at Southampton plays a key role in the Java reference linking API described in this paper.

2   Definitions

In this section we present basic terms and definitions that will be used in the remainder of the paper.

2.1   Items and Works

There are two different types of entities contained in Fig. 2: there is Document A which the user is reading, and there is B, a work by Mitchell referenced by A. There is a subtle, but important, difference between A and B. A is an *Item*, something that has a specific format, is on-line,[1] and can be analyzed by a computer program. B is a *Work*, or an abstraction of a paper. In the example shown, B happens to exist in the form of several Items. In general, however, a Work need not be available on-line. Thus we say that Works exist in the form of zero or more on-line Items. In the rest of this report, we drop the capitalization of work and item, but continue to distinguish between them, because the distinction is important.

2.2   References and Citations

References and Citations (discussed with Fig. 1) both exist in the context of works, which may be on-line or not. In the remainder of this paper these two terms will be further qualified as follows:

---

[1] Our definition of Item deviates slightly from standard library usage in that it is limited to on-line copies. See [13, 14] for how the Work and Item distinction has played a role in traditional library cataloging theory.

- *linkable references* and *citations* are works for which copies can be found on-line.
- *reference anchor* is the reference in the paper's text, e.g. "[10]" in Fig. 2;
- *reference context* is the sentence containing that reference anchor;
- *reference string* is the complete description of the work as it occurs in the document (usually in a bibliography), e.g. "10. Mitchell. A. Thunks ...".

2.3 Repository

A *repository*, known sometimes as an *archive*, is any collection of on-line items, e.g. an on-line journal, a department's technical reports, or a personal collection.

3   The Reference Linking API

Our reference linking layer involves the notion of *item surrogates*. A surrogate is a digital object that encapsulates reference linking information relating to one single item on the Web. This is consistent with our overall architectural approach to digital library research: "value-added surrogates"[12] are a vehicle for endowing digital objects with a wide variety of extensible behaviors (e.g. preservation, access management).

The surrogate's knowledge of an item is accessed via a well-defined API, upon which a variety of reference linking services can be built. The API enables access to an on-line paper's metadata and that of its references. A typical use of the API would be to analyze all the papers in repository or other collection (e.g. somebody's Web site).

This architecture is depicted in Fig. 3. The central column represents a repository of network-accessible documents. The items listed in this column are linkable (they are on-line) and therefore analyzable (their bits are available). On

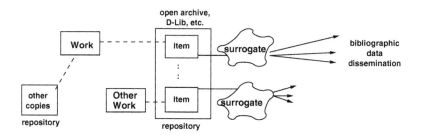

Fig. 3. An Architecture for Reference Analysis

the left are drawn the works that the items represent. Any work might have several copies spread across several repositories. All of these copies are "items" corresponding to that work. To the right of the archive items are the surrogates, shown as "blobs". Their job is to disseminate bibliographic data about the item, and indirectly, about the work.

The surrogates can be created on-demand to supply the data, or they can be stored and used later to supply the data. Thus the reference linking layer imposed on Web objects can be static or dynamic or some mixture of both.

The six methods in our reference linking API are:

- getLinkedText – returns the contents of the paper (as data) augmented with reference linking information. The application in Fig. 2 would use this method.
- getReferenceList – the references contained in this paper.
- getMyData - this returns that paper's own metadata.
- getCurrentCitationList – the list of works citing this paper to the best of the surrogate's knowledge.
- save and restore - handle persistent storage of surrogates.

Each one of these methods (except save and restore) returns an XML document. For illustrative purposes, we look at the output of getReferenceList and getLinkedText in more detail.

```
<? xml version="1.0" ?>
<api:reference_list xmlns:api="http://www.cs.cornell.edu/cdlrg/..."
      xmlns:dc="http://purl.org/dc/elements/1.1/" length="17" >
<api:reference ord="1">
          :
<api:reference ord="2">
  <dc:title>Smart Objects, Dumb Archives: A User-Centric Framework</dc:title>
  <dc:date>1999-03-01</dc:date>
  <dc:identifier>10.1045/march99-maly</dc:identifier>
  <dc:identifier>urn:maly1999smart object, dumb a</dc:identifier>
  <dc:creator>K Maly</dc:creator>
  <api:literal tag="2.">
     Maly K, "Smart Objects, Dumb Archives: A User-Centric Framework"
     in D-Lib Magazine, March 1999,
     &lt;http://www.dlib.org/dlib/march99-maly/03maly.html&gt;.
  </api:literal>
  <api:context-list>
    <api:context ord="9" anchor="[2]" normalization="[2]">
       The need for standards to support the interoperation of digital
       library systems has been reported on before in D-Lib[1],[2] ...
    </api:context>
  </api:context-list>
</api:reference>
          :
</api:reference_list>
```

Fig. 4. XML document from **getRerenceList**(), with reference 2 shown in full.

The data disseminated by `getReferenceList` (Fig. 4) contains elements in two XML namespaces: `dc` for the Dublin Core elements, and `api` for the elements specific to our API. The data is organized with one top level element, `<reference_list>`, which in turn consists of 0 or more `<reference>` elements. The `<reference>` element consists of:

1. Bibliographic data related to the reference work, expressed in Dublin Core format.
2. The reference string exactly as it appeared in the item (enclosed in a `<literal>` element and entified).
3. Zero or more contexts in which the work was cited in this item, listed as `<context>`s within a `<context_list>`.[2] This reference has one context.

Within the context, "[2]" is the reference anchor. Should the surrogate's `getLinkedText` method be invoked, this reference anchor is enclosed in a `<reflink>` element. The lower part of Fig. 5 shows an example `<reflink>`. Note that 0 or more `<url>` subelements are allowed within a `<reflink>`. The

```
Original Text:

    ... it was said [5] that ...
```
```
Linked Text with custom tag:

    ... it was said
    <api:reflink ord="5" author="last-name-of-first-author"
    title="title of this work"
    year="1999">
    <api:url>"http://www.some.org/..."</api:url>[5]</api:reflink>
    that ...
```

Fig. 5. A linked XML Item.

`<reflink>` elements can be translated (by a XSLT processor) into "actionable links", such as HREF's, XLinks, OpenURLS, or embedded JavaScripts.

3.1   A Java Implementation of the API

The API can be implemented in many languages. We implemented it as three JAVA packages: `Linkable.API`, `Linkable.Analysis`, and `Linkable.Utility`. Only the first is needed by reference linking applications.

---

[2] Zero contexts is a characteristic of papers that include gratuitous references.

One parameter is required for constructing a surrogate, the URL of the item to be parsed. The surrogate fetches the document at that URL and converts it to XHTML. Formatting hints (e.g. font size, line breaks) are retained to facilitate decomposition of the item into header, body, and reference sections.

After construction of the surrogate by the reference linking application, the item has been parsed and preliminary reference data has been stored into local data fields within the surrogate. Invoking one of the first four methods on the surrogate, e.g. `getLinkedText()`, causes further analysis of the reference data.

4   Experiments with the Architecture

The reference linking API can be used for a large variety of applications. This section briefly sketches two examples. The first example is an on-line application; the second is run off-line to produce stored data.

4.1   A Simple Display Application

The first example (Fig. 6) shows how on-demand surrogate creation can be used as part of a reference linked document viewer, a useful overlay to the Web.

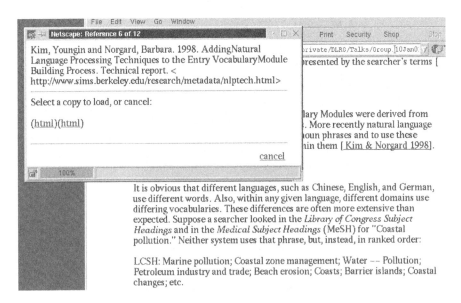

Fig. 6. A Simple Reference Linking Application: clicking on the [Kim & Norgard 1998] reference brings up a selection of this work's on-line items.

This application instantiates a surrogate object, passing it the URL of an on-line item. All further interactions with the reference linking API are via this surrogate. Here is a snippet of Java code from this sample application:

```
import Linkable.API.*;
   :

Surrogate s = new Surrogate ( url );
display ( s.getLinkedText() );
```

The linked text is an XML document containing <reflink> elements. The application's display routine converts the information in these elements into JavaScript code, which in turn presents a retrieval dialogue to the user.

4.2 Reference Linking the D-Lib Magazine

The second example gathers and stores reference linking information for future use. We used the reference linking API to analyze D-Lib articles. D-Lib is an on-line journal that has been appearing eleven times a year since July 1995; it makes an excellent analysis test bed because there is little editorial imposition of format on the papers published in the journal, and therefore provides a wide selection of paper layouts. All D-Lib articles are written in HTML.

The application runs from the command line. It reads in one URL at a time from a file of of D-Lib URLs. For each URL, it constructs a surrogate and stores it for later use. The Java code to perform this processing is:

```
import Linkable.API.*;
   :

Surrogate s = new Surrogate ( url );
s.save();
```

The application produces a repository of surrogates, which represents, and adds value to, the D-Lib on-line journal.

5 Evaluation of the Implementation

Because our approach extracts reference linking and bibliographic data *automatically* from widely variable sources, it cannot be expected that the data will be 100% accurate. Indeed, *automatic librarianship* inevitably means some trade-off in functionality and accuracy in exchange for its cost savings[1]. Examine, for example, the Web search engines that are immensely useful despite their "imperfect" behavior. The question is, how accurate are our methods?

There are two categories of parsing errors: incorrectly extracting bibliographic data about the item being analyzed; and incorrectly parsing the reference strings contained in the analyzed item. Since both of these must be minimized to attain an efficient reference linking layer, we devised a performance metric based on both of these inputs. For each item analyzed, the *item accuracy* is the number of elements parsed correctly, divided by the total number of elements in the item. Specifically, the elements used are: the item's title, the item's authors (each author counts as one element), the item's year of publication, the reference contexts (each context counts as one element) and the average reference accuracy times the number of reference strings.

The *reference accuracy* for one reference string is the per centage of correctly parsed elements, including title, authors, year, contexts, and URL (if present). The *average reference accuracy* is the average over all the references.

For evaluation purposes, we selected a random set of 70 D-Lib papers. Of this number, 4 were not able to be converted to XML (i.e. XHTML) and so were discarded.[3] For the remainder, item accuracies were determined by inspection of the data contained in stored surrogates; these are plotted in Fig. 7. Most accuracy points lie above 80%. Some of the items in Fig. 7 were very low for reasons such as the references being in a separate document, or the reference section of the paper not labeled as such, resulting in a zero "average reference parsing accuracy". For most items, however, the references were parsed.

Reference parsing accuracy is part of item accuracy. The first 66 items contained 504 references. Although reference strings occur in a wide variety of formats, they were parsed with an overall accuracy above 80% (see Fig. 8).

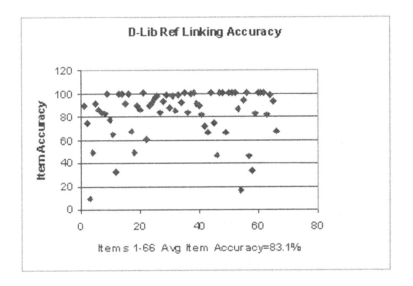

Fig. 7. Item accuracies for a set of 66 D-Lib papers

6   Conclusions and Further Research

Automatic extraction of reference linking information is difficult, but possible. It is good enough to allow a reference linking layer to be added to on-line technical literature. The flexible object-oriented API described in this paper makes it

---

[3] We use JTidy, a tool from W3C, to convert HTML items to their XML form, XHTML. JTidy finds some HTML documents insusceptible to conversion, due to ambiguities in the HTML. See [3] for examples of what can go wrong.

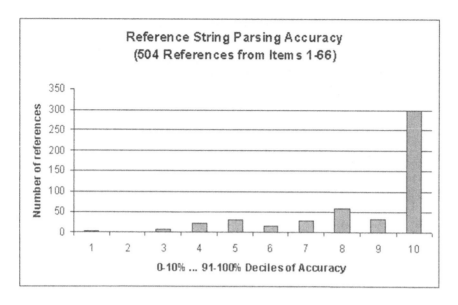

Fig. 8. Parsing accuracy for the 504 reference strings contained in a set of 66 D-Lib papers. More than half are in the 91–100% range.

exceptionally easy to build new reference linking applications and tools, and we are doing some of that now. We are also extending our automatic extraction to PDF files.

One area of interest, applicable to any automatic procedure, is how and how much to enhance machine processing with human effort. Using the API in batch mode, one could run an off-line "upgrade" procedure allowing human editing of surrogate encapsulated data. When an edited surrogate is resurrected, it will have the corrected information. The costs and benefits of this editing is one area of interesting research.

Another research area is data consistency. As more surrogates are instantiated, the same work could be encountered more than once (for example, as references in two different items). Slightly different data could exist for each instance. The problem then is to let the two surrogates pool their information so that both surrogates have a consistent world view. This requires either that the surrogates be able to find and communicate with each other, or to use a central database. Since central databases are best avoided, it would be preferable to have the surrogates communicate among themselves. This is for future research.

The extraction of reference linking data is difficult mainly because parsing text produced by many different authors with many different conventions is problematical. However, we have found that there are a relatively limited set of variations in format, and have developed grammars to handle most of them. A separate paper [3] discusses this problem in more detail, and presents the algorithms we use.

At this point we are analyzing papers, examining the errors, patching up the Java API, and then analyzing new papers. As each additional paper gets processed, the implementation improves a little. At the present time, our reference linking API returns results that are 80–85% accurate, indicating that its architecture and design are sound.

References

[1] Arms, W.: Automated digital libraries: How effectively can computers be used for the skill tasks of professional librarianship. *D-Lib Magazine* (July 2000).

[2] Atkins, H., Lyons, C., Ratner, H., Risher, C., Shillum, C., Sidman, D., and Stevens, A.: Reference linking with DOIs: A case study. *D-Lib Magazine 6*, 2 (Feb. 2000). <http://www.dlib.org/dlib/february00/02risher.html>

[3] Bergmark, D.: Automatic extraction of reference linking information from online documents. Tech. Rep. TR 2000-1821, Cornell Computer Science Department, Nov. 2000. in preparation.

[4] Chen, C., and Carr, L.: Trailablazing the literature of hypertext: Author co-citation analysis (1989–1998). In *ACM Hypertext '99* (Darmstadt, Germany, February 21-25 1999).

[5] Garfield, E.: SCIENCE CITATION INDEX - a new dimension in indexing. *Science 144*, 3619 (1964), 649.

[6] Henzinger, M. R.: Hyperlink analysis for the web. *IEEE Internet Computing 5*, 1 (January/February 2001), 45–50.

[7] Hitchcock, S., Carr, L., Jiao, Z., Bergmark, D., Hall, W., Lagoze, C., and Harnad, S.: Developing services for open eprint archives: Globalisation, integration and the impact of links. In *ACM Proceedings of Digital Libraries, 2000 (DL2000)* (San Antonio, Texas, 2000).

[8] Jenkins, C., and Inman, D.: Server-side automatic metadata generation using Qualified Dublin Core and RDF. In *IEEE Proc. Kyoto International Conference on Digital Libraries* (Kyoto, Japan, Nov. 2000).

[9] Lawrence, S., and Giles, C. L.: Context and page analysis for improved web search. *IEEE Internet Computing 2*, 4 (July/August 1998), 38–46.

[10] Lawrence, S., Giles, C. L., and Bollacker, K.: Digital libraries and autonomous citation indexing. *IEEE Computer 32*, 6 (1999), 67–71. <http://www.researchindex.com>

[11] MacLennan, B.: Presentation and access issues for electronic journals in a medium-sized academic institution. *The Journal of Electronic Publishing 5*, 1 (Sept. 1999). <http://www.press.umich.edu/jep/05-01/maclennan.h tml.

[12] Payette, S., and Lagoze, C.: Value-added surrogates for distributed content. *D-Lib Magazine 6*, 6 (June 2000).

[13] Saur, K. G.: Functional requirements for bibliographic records, 1998. UBCIM Publications - New Series Vol. 19.

[14] Svenonius, E.: *The Intellectual Foundation of Information Organization*. M.I.T. Press, 2000.

[15] van de Sompel, H., and Hochstenbach, P.: Reference linking in a hybrid libary environment, part 2: SFX, a generic linking solution. *D-Lib Magazine 5*, 4 (Apr. 1999).

Disambiguating Geographic Names in a Historical Digital Library*

David A. Smith and Gregory Crane

Perseus Project
Tufts University
Medford, MA, USA
{dasmith,gcrane}@perseus.tufts.edu

Abstract. Geographic interfaces provide natural, scalable visualizations for many digital library collections, but the wide range of data in digital libraries presents some particular problems for identifying and disambiguating place names. We describe the toponym-disambiguation system in the Perseus digital library and evaluate its performance. Name categorization varies significantly among different types of documents, but toponym disambiguation performs at a high level of precision and recall with a gazetteer an order of magnitude larger than most other applications.

1 Introduction

Geographic interfaces provide natural, scalable visualizations for many digital library collections. Although domain-specific ontologies or automatic clusterings of documents may produce productive browsing tools in many cases, real world maps, along with timelines, can situate a wide range of information in a consistent, familiar space. When the contents of digital library documents are georeferenced, users can get a sense of the scope and focus points of a collection or a document, plot geographic places mentioned on any page of text, or find information about the places mentioned on a map or in a region [4, 6]. At the Perseus Project, we have concentrated on representing historical data in the humanities from ancient Greece to nineteenth-century America [9]. With over one million identified toponym references, Perseus has built a rich digital library testbed and toolset that is available over the World Wide Web (http://www.perseus.tufts.edu; see Fig. 1, 2, and 3).

---

* This research was supported by a grant from the Digital Libraries Initiative, Phase 2, with primary funding from the National Science Foundation and National Endowment for the Humanities.

P. Constantopoulos and I.T. Sølvberg (Eds.): ECDL 2001, LNCS 2163, pp. 127–136, 2001.

Fig. 1. The scope and focus of the collection on the settlement of California. Note the fainter spread of sites across the U.S. and the concentration in northern California.

Fig. 2. Sites mentioned in Herodotus. Note the strong concentration in present-day Greece and western Turkey.

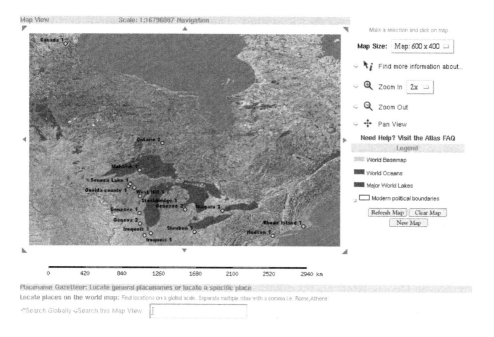

Fig. 3. Interactive map of the sites mentioned on one page of a diary of a voyage from Detroit to the source of the Mississippi, where the author is in Wisconsin but makes peripheral reference to the Naragansetts of Rhode Island. The user can zoom in on a particular region, such as the cluster in Oneida county, Wisconsin, or click on a site for more information.

In order to reap the benefits of geographic interfaces, digital librarians must identify geographic names and link them to information about their location, in most cases their type (e.g. river, mountain, populated place), and other useful information such as dates of occupation, population at various times, and relation to other places. For documents of highly central importance to a scholar's work, it might be worthwhile to spend the effort of manually tagging and disambiguating place names in a text, but manually tagging an entire corpus of any considerable size is impractical. Even at an optimistic ten seconds per toponym, it would take 28,000 person-hours to check the over one million toponyms in the Perseus DL of about 70 million words of English. We thus need automatic, or at least machine-assisted, methods for building georeferenced digital libraries.

2   Problem Description and Related Work

Linking strings in documents to locations on a map can be generally divided into two steps: name *identification and categorization* and *disambiguation* of those names classed as toponyms against a gazetteer with at least some coordinate information. In the past decade, many projects have devoted themselves to the first step and many fewer to the second. This concentration is not surprising; "named entity recognition", as the name categorization task is known, aims to classify entities as persons, organizations, dates, products, organisms, and so on, in addition to geographic entities, and has many applications in the fields of message understanding and information extraction as a whole. In addition, many named entity recognition systems operate without a list of known names. Although this is often necessary for the open-ended sets of personal and company names, it is not often that a text will record the coordinates of the places it mentions. We need a gazetteer not only as a list of possible toponyms but, in a georeferenced digital library, as a source of location information.

Two general strategies for named entity recognition can be represented by two widely known systems. BBN's Nymble [2] performs quite well with F-measures (see equation 1 below) at 90% or above, but requires at least 100,000 words of training data; IBM's Nominator [10] performs only slightly less well (F-measure approximately 88%) on Wall Street Journal documents with only simple heuristics, though the authors admit that the "heuristics are somewhat domain dependent". The Geo-Referenced Information Processing System (GIPSY) described by [11] and [6] matches geographic names in text to all possible spatial coordinates without disambiguation. When locations are aggregated over an entire text, the core area of discussion in a document becomes clear. Interestingly, this system also attempts to match such phrases as "south of Lake Tahoe" with fuzzy polygons. [8] describe a system to plot locations mentioned in transcripts of news broadcasts. Using a gazetteer of about 80,000 items, they report matching 269 out of 357 places (75%) in the test segments. Kanada reports 96% precision for geographic name disambiguation in Japanese text with a gazetteer of 55,000 Japanese and 41,000 foreign ones [5]. In an interesting parallel to our results below, he also reports significantly lower precision for Japanese toponyms than for foreign ones. Both these latter systems use modern political hierarchies to perform disambiguation: if an instance of "Springfield" is found in a text, the systems will search for instances of "Missouri" or "Massachusetts" or "United States" to resolve the ambiguity.

The documents in many digital libraries, however, present some particular problems for automatically identifying and disambiguating place names. Much work on proper names has dealt with news texts with useful discourse conventions for reducing ambiguity. A story mentioning Bill Clinton will use the full title "President Bill Clinton" on the first mention and "Mr. Clinton" or "Clinton" only afterwards. News stories also have relatively small scope, without long-distance anaphora. When a new story begins, President Bill Clinton is named in full all over again. Finally, place names themselves almost always have a disambiguating tag at their first mention, e.g. "London, Ontario" or "Clinton, New Jersey". Digital libraries, on the other hand, often contain documents of widely varying lengths written without benefit of journalistic style. Scholarly works often deal with several registers of time and place: a book on Shakespeare will talk not only about sixteenth-century Stratford (Warwickshire) but also about scholarship in nineteenth-century Cambridge (Massachusetts) and twentieth-century

Berkeley (California). A wide historical purview can also make some pieces of knowledge in a gazetteer useless or misleading. Although the city of Samos is now in Greece and Miletus is in Turkey, they were both founded by Ionian Greeks and are only about 30 kilometers apart. Actual distance on the earth tells more than modern political categories.

Finally, a heterogeneous digital library can benefit from large knowledge bases to deal with its diverse materials but must deal with the cost of clashes among items in these authority lists. We can explore some of these ambiguities *a priori* by looking at the distributions in a gazetteer (table 1). Although the proportions are dependent on the names and places selected for inclusion in this gazetteer, the relative rankings are suggestive. In long-settled areas—such as Asia, Africa, and Europe—a place may be called by many names over time, but individual names are often distinct. With the increasing tempo of settlement in modern times, however, many places may be called by the same name, particularly by nostalgic colonists in the New World. Other ambiguities arise when people and places share names. Very few Greek and Latin place names are also personal names. This is less true of Britain, where surnames (and surnames used as given names) are often taken from place names; in America, the confusion grows as numerous towns are named after prominent or obscure people. In practice, we can express the scope of the disambiguation problem as follows: not counting the other names that could be mistaken for place names, some 92% of the toponyms in the Perseus digital library refer, potentially, to more than one place.

Continent	% places w/multiple names	% names w/multiple places
North & Central America	11.5	57.1
Oceania	6.9	29.2
South America	11.6	25.0
Asia	32.7	20.3
Africa	27.0	18.2
Europe	18.2	16.6

Table 1. Places with multiple names and names applied to more than one place in the Getty *Thesaurus of Geographic Names*

3   Disambiguation Procedure

As mentioned above, toponym disambiguation consists of name identification and categorization and disambiguation of those names. Our methods for performing these tasks rely on evidence that is internal or external to the text. (Note the difference with the terminology and approach in [7], which uses evidence internal and external to the *name*.) Internal evidence includes the use of honorifics, generic geographic labels, or linguistic environment. External evidence includes gazetteers, biographical information, and general linguistic knowledge.

Before either identification or disambiguation could proceed, we gathered the knowledge sources used to make the categorization and disambiguation decisions. Perseus uses some knowledge sources, such as the Getty Thesaurus of Geographic Names or Cruchley's gazetteer of London, that were purpose-built for geocoding. We captured other information, such as lists of authors or the entries in the *Dictionary of National Biography*, as a by-product of constructing the digital library as a whole. In total, the gazetteer used for name identification and disambiguation contains over one million place names.

We then scan the documents in the digital library for possible proper names and assign the names, if possible, to broad categories such as person, place, or date. We chose to use simple heuristic methods like those used in Nominator [10] rather than learning systems, since we lacked training data for our types of documents, and since we were mostly interested in identifying geographic names and not in the broader task of named entity recognition and categorization. In English text, the Perseus system exploits generally used capitalization and punctuation conventions: initial candidate proper names are strings of capitalized words, and sentences are delimited with periods. Also at this stage, we exploit any markup that a document's editor has added, whether in tagging a string as a personal or place name, or in explicitly linking that name to an entry in a gazetteer. For initial categorization, the Perseus system uses language-specific honorifics (such as "Dr." or "Mrs.") as strong evidence that the following name is a personal name. In addition, once a "Col. Aldrich", for example, is seen in a document, further references to "Aldrich" are automatically classified a personal names. Generic topographic labels (such as "Rocky *Mountains*" or "Charles *River*") are taken as moderate evidence that the name is geographic. Standalone instances of the most common given names in Perseus' biographical dictionaries are labeled as personal names since a mere "John" is highly unlikely to refer to a town by that name in Louisiana or Virginia.

The system then attempts to match the names classed as geographic, as well as the uncertain names, against a gazetteer. As our aim is to allow for geographic browsing of a digital library, it is of little benefit if we identify a name that cannot be linked to spatial coordinates. As mentioned above, for the names in our corpus that have at least one match in the gazetteer, about 92% match more than one entity.

Disambiguating the possible place names then proceeds based on local context, document context, and general world knowledge. The simplest instances of local context are the explicit disambiguating tags that authors put after place names: e.g. "Lancaster, PA" or "Vienna, Austria". More generally, a place will more likely than not be near to other places mentioned around it. If "Philadelphia" and "Harrisburg" occur in the same paragraph, a reference to "Lancaster" is more likely to be to the town in Pennsylvania than to the one in England or Arizona. Document context can be characterized as the preponderance of geographic references in an entire document; for short documents, such as news articles, local and document context can be treated as the same. World knowledge may be captured from gazetteers or other reference works and comprises such facts about a place as its coordinates, political entities to which it belongs, and its size or relative importance.

The system begins by producing a simple characterization of the document context. All of the possible locations for all of the toponyms in the document are aggregated onto a one-by-one degree grid, with weights assigned for the number of mentions of each toponym. The system prunes some possibilities based on general world knowledge, so that only Spain the country, and not the town in Tennessee, will be counted. We compute the centroid of this weighted map and the standard deviation of the distance of the points from this centroid. We then discard points more than two standard deviations away from the centroid and calculate a new centroid from the remaining points, if any.

We then process the possible toponyms for final disambiguation. We represent the local context of a toponym's occurrence as a moving window of the four toponyms mentioned before it and the four after it. Only unambiguous or already disambiguated toponyms are taken into account, however, in constructing this context. Each possible location for a toponym is given a score based on (a) its proximity to other toponyms around it, (b) its proximity to the centroid for the document, and (c) its relative importance—e.g. all other things being equal, nations get a higher score than cities. Also at this stage, the system discards as probable false positives places that lack an explicit disambiguator, that receive a low importance score, and that are far away from the local and document centroids. If not thus eliminated, the candidate toponym identification with the highest score is declared the winner. Once the work of the disambiguation system is done, the resulting toponyms are loaded into a relational database for access by the runtime digital library system.

4   Evaluation

We evaluate the performance of the disambiguation system using standard precision and recall methods. Qualitatively, the system performs quite well at producing aggregate maps of the places mentioned in an entire document or corpus or in finding mentions of a particular place. For a more detailed look at the performance of the Perseus system on various texts, a human disambiguator worked through 20% of the output for a text from each of five representative corpora: ancient Greece, ancient Rome, the Bolles collection on the history and topography of London, and two Library of Congress collections on the settlement of California and the Upper Midwest. With a large gazetteer and conservative pruning rules, our system is biased towards more recall. In table 2, we show precision results for the system as a whole, which is what the end user actually experiences, and for the toponym disambiguation system independent of name categorization. We also show the F-measure for the whole system, a score that combines recall (R) and precision (P) with the recall/precision weighting factor β^2 usually valued at 1:

$$F = \frac{(\beta^2 + 1)RP}{(\beta^2 R) + P} \qquad (1)$$

Corpus	Precision	Perfect Categ.	Recall	F-measure
Greek	0.93	0.98	0.99	0.96
Roman	0.91	0.99	1.00	0.95
London	0.86	0.92	0.96	0.91
California	0.83	0.92	0.96	0.89
Upper Midwest	0.74	0.89	0.89	0.81

Table 2. Performance on five representative texts

From these figures, one can see that although our simple heuristic categorization algorithm was less adequate for certain tasks, the toponym disambiguator itself performed quite well. The evaluation of toponym disambiguation is, if anything, conservative since eliminating extraneous points from the local and document context should reduce the skew in the calculated centroids. Note also that the categorization performed better on the Greek and Roman history texts than on texts on the history of London, California, or the Upper Midwest. This reflects the degree to which toponyms are ambiguous with other names or non-names in the text (see table 1 above). This evaluation also turned up another linguistic issue: all of the mistaken toponym identifications in the Roman text—Caesar's *Gallic War*—were for the "Germans" whom Caesar is fighting. The ethnonym "German" is in the gazetteer in the record for Germany, but its plural is not. We could fill this deficiency by stemming the input, but proper names are not generally inflected in English, so on the whole stemming would do more harm than good. We can easily add these inflected geographic names to the gazetteer by hand. In general, the large gazetteer of over a million names probably depresses precision more than any other factor. In [5], for example, the gazetteer is an order of magnitude smaller (96,000) and precision reaches 96%.

5   Future Work

Although the Perseus toponym disambiguation system performs quite well, we will concentrate on improving the categorization system, especially for texts on North America. Many approaches to categorization require training data so that the system can learn context rules for the occurrence of various kinds of named entities. As noted above, important or canonical texts would in any case benefit from detailed hand markup, including name categorization and disambiguation, and systems such as Alembic [3] have demonstrated computer-assisted methods to optimize the tagging task.

Restricting the available toponyms at any point in the text by time period would also improve the system's performance. In a heterogeneous digital library of historical information, however, a mix of temporal references may occur in close proximity. We could, however, use the preponderance of temporal references, as we now use the weighted map of spatial references, to rank the possibilities. "Ovid" in a discussion of Roman poetry is unlikely to refer to Ovid,

Idaho. While the current system deduces this from the town's distance from Italy, where most of the other places in the document are located, the fact that the town was founded in the nineteenth century would also tend to exclude it from a document where most of the dates are in the first centuries B.C. and A.D.

As explained above, we characterize the document context or central "region of interest" of a document by the centroid of the most heavily referenced areas. There seems to be some lack of robustness in simply using the centroid, and we are experimenting with using a bounding rectangle or polygon to represent a document's region of interest.

Finally, we are compiling on a gazetteer of Greek and Latin toponyms to apply this work to the non-English texts in the Perseus digital library. Much of this information can be culled from digitized reference works such as the *Harper's Dictionary of Classical Antiquities* and Smith's *Dictionary of Greek and Roman Geography*. Although we note above that morphological stemming of the source text would be counterproductive for English, we will need to stem Greek and Latin texts with our existing tools in order to perform well with these highly inflected languages.

References

[1] Association for Computational Linguistics. *Proceedings of the Fifth Conference on Applied Natural Language Processing*, Washington, DC, April 1997.

[2] Daniel M. Bikel, Scott Miller, Richard Schwartz, and Ralph Weischedel. Nymble: A high-performance learning name-finder. In *Proceedings of the Fifth Conference on Applied Natural Language Processing* [1], pages 194–201.

[3] David Day, John Aberdeen, Lynette Hirschman, Robyn Kozierok, Patricia Robinson, and Marc Vilain. Mixed-initiative development of language processing systems. In *Proceedings of the Fifth Conference on Applied Natural Language Processing* [1], pages 348–355.

[4] Linda L. Hill, James Frew, and Qi Zheng. Geographic names: The implementation of a gazetteer in a georeferenced digital library. *D-Lib Magazine*, 5(1), January 1999. See http://www.dlib.org/dlib/january99/hill/01hill.html.

[5] Yasusi Kanada. A method of geographical name extraction from Japanese text for thematic geographical search. In *Proceedings of the Eighth International Conference on Information and Knowledge Management*, pages 46–54, Kansas City, Missouri, November 1999.

[6] Ray R. Larson. Geographic information retrieval and spatial browsing. In Linda C. Smith and Myke Gluck, editors, *Geographic Information Systems and Libraries: Patrons, Maps, and Spatial Information*, pages 81–123, April 1995. See http://sherlock.berkeley.edu/geo_ir/PART1.html.

[7] David D. McDonald. Internal and external evidence in the identification and semantic categorization of proper names. In Branimir Boguraev and James Pustejovsky, editors, *Corpus Processing for Lexical Acquisition*, pages 21–39. MIT Press, Cambridge, MA, 1996.

[8] Andreas M. Olligschlaeger and Alexander G. Hauptmann. Multimodal information systems and GIS: The Informedia digital video library. In *Proceedings of the ESRI User Conference*, San Diego, California, July 1999.

[9] David A. Smith, Jeffrey A. Rydberg-Cox, and Gregory R. Crane. The Perseus Project: A digital library for the humanities. *Literary and Linguistic Computing*, 15(1):15–25, 2000.

[10] Nina Wacholder, Yael Ravin, and Misook Choi. Disambiguation of proper names in text. In *Proceedings of the Fifth Conference on Applied Natural Language Processing* [1], pages 202–208.

[11] Allison G. Woodruff and Christian Plaunt. GIPSY: Automated geographic indexing of text documents. *Journal of the American Society for Information Science*, 45(9):645–655, 1994.

Greenstone: A Platform for Distributed Digital Library Applications

David Bainbridge, George Buchanan, John McPherson, Steve Jones,
Abdelaziz Mahoui, and Ian H. Witten

Waikato University, New Zealand & Middlesex University, UK
{d.bainbridge, jrm21, s.jones, am14, i.witten}@cs.waikato.ac.nz
g.buchanan@mdx.ac.uk

Abstract. This paper examines the issues surrounding distributed Digital Library protocols. First, it reviews three prominent digital library protocols: Z39.50, SDLIP, and Dienst, plus Greenstone's own protocol. Then, we summarise the implementation in the Greenstone Digital Libary of a number of different protocols for distributed digital libraries, and describe sample applications of the same: a digital library for children, a translator for Stanford's Simple Digital Library Interoperability Protocol, a Z39.50 client, and a bibliographic search tool. The paper concludes with a comparison of all four protocols, and a brief discussion of the impact of distributed protocols on the Greenstone system.

Keywords: Distributed protocol, Z39.50, CORBA, graphical user interface support

1   Introduction

Use of the open source Greenstone Digital Library software is gathering pace. By mid-2000, more than a dozen libraries and universities had arranged access to the software to help meet their digital library needs. Since its release on Source Forge (*www.sourceforge.net*) last October, there have been thousands of downloads per month—but the actual level of use is hard to determine. One project that uses Greenstone extensively is HumanInfo, a Belgian-based NGO that regularly produces humanitarian aid digital library collections on CD-ROM, and distributes upwards of 10,000 copies of each collection within developing countries.

As the user base expands, the collective needs of users expand too. To step outside the mind set indoctrinated by: generate a new Web page in response to a user clicking on a button or hyperlink—the classical form for a digital library, if you will—Greenstone, like other digital library projects [4, 7], provides a protocol for fine-grained interaction with other programs [5]. The protocol is implemented using CORBA [8] and has been extended to support both the SDLIP and Z39.50 protocols.

P. Constantopoulos and I.T. Sølvberg (Eds.): ECDL 2001, LNCS 2163, pp. 137–148, 2001.

The purpose of this paper is to demonstrate how distributed protocols promote a variety of distributed digital library applications. We select four applications, built within the Greenstone digital library framework, for discussion: a pilot digital library project for children, a translator for Stanford's Simple Digital Library Interoperability Protocol (SDLIP), a Z39.50 client, and a bibliographic search tool.

The digital library for children utilises a client (which in Greenstone is called a "receptionist") that provides a digital library environment specifically designed for primary school pupils. The receptionist supplies a different user interface from the standard Greenstone look and feel. Moreover, the protocol allows relevant collections served on other Greenstone sites to be seamlessly integrated into the children's work environment. The second example accepts requests from SDLIP clients and translates them into Greenstone protocol calls; data returned from Greenstone is then converted back to the appropriate SDLIP format.

The third illustration, a Z39.50 client, is another example of a receptionist, this time with the "standard" Greenstone look and feel. By incorporating into Greenstone the YAZ software package (*www.indexdata.dk*) the necessary protocol exchange can occur without changing any of the upper layers in the Greenstone code. This new "backend" can access any Z39.50 server; here we demonstrate its use with the Library of Congress's OPAC catalogue. In the final example we move to a Java client to support a rich dynamic graphical environment for user input and display, using the protocol to communicate with a Greenstone server.

The structure of the paper is as follows. We begin by reviewing three existing protocols used by digital library projects, followed by a summary of the Greenstone protocol (see [5] for a more detailed description). Next we describe the four selected applications that demonstrate different aspects of the Greenstone protocol and how it connects with other protocols. We conclude with a discussion that brings out the similarities and differences of all four protocols.

2   Existing Protocols

Three prominent protocols used in the digital library field are the ISO/ANSI/NISO approved Z39.50 protocol, Cornell University's Dienst protocol, and Stanford University's SDLIP.

2.1   Z39.50

Z39.50 specifies a wide-ranging protocol for information retrieval between a client and a database server [2]. Its origins stretch back to 1984, and three progressive versions of the specification were ratified by standards committees in 1988, 1992, and 1995. It is currently administered by the Library of Congress.

Defined as part of the application layer of the Open System Interconnection (OSI) Reference Model, message formats are specified using Abstract Syntax Notation One (ASN.1) and serialised for transmission over the OSI transport layer using Basic Encoding Rules (BER) [3]. The Transmission Control Protocol (TCP) is typically used for this.

Accessing and retrieving heterogeneous data through a protocol in a way that promotes interoperability is a challenging problem. To address the broad spectrum of different domains where it might be used—such as bibliographic data, museum collection information, and geospatial metadata—Z39.50 includes a set of classes, called "registries," that provide each domain with an agreed-upon structure and attributes. Registries cover query syntax, attribute fields, content retrieval formats, and diagnostic messages. For example, content retrieval formats include Simple Unstructured Text Record Syntax (SUTRS) and the various MARC formats.

The Z39.50 protocol is divided into eleven logical sections (called "facilities") that each provide a broad set of services. The protocol is predominantly client driven; that is to say, a client initiates requests, and the server responds. Only in a few places does the server demand information from the client—for example, the Access Control Facility might require the client to authenticate itself before a particular operation is performed. Any server that implements the protocol must retain information about the client's state, and apportion resources so it can respond sensibly to clients using the Initialization Facility. Mandatory search capabilities include fielded Boolean queries, which yields a result set that can be further processed by the Sort and Browse Facilities or cancelled by the Result-set-delete Facility. Results themselves are returned through the Retrieval Facility. At any stage, the response to a request might be an error diagnostic.

Establishing which of the many Z39.50 options, registries, and domain-specific attributes are supported by a particular server is accomplished through the Explain Facility. The Extended Services Facility is a mechanism to access server functionality that persists beyond the duration of a given client-server session— for example, periodic search schedules and updating the database. The client-server session can be canceled immediately by either side through the Termination Facility.

2.2   Dienst

Dienst is one of the longest-running DL projects in the research community: its origins stretch back to 1992 [4]. It has three facets: a conceptual architecture for distributed digital libraries, an open protocol for service communication, and a software system that implements the protocol.

The protocol supports search and retrieval of documents, browsing documents, adding new documents, and user registration. Each of these is an individual service (with version control), borne over HTTP. A digital library collection involves a combination of these services. There are six categories of service: *repository services* store digital documents and associated metadata; *index services* accept queries and returns lists of document identifiers; *query mediator services* dispatch queries to the relevant index servers; *info services* return information about the state of a server; *collection services* provide information on how a set of services interact; and *registry services* store user information.

2.3   Stanford Infobus

Interoperation between distributed objects has been central to Stanford University's digital library project, the "Infobus," where many Infobus objects are in fact proxies to established information sources and services [6]. The original CORBA-based Digital Library Interoperation Protocol (DLIOP) has recently been superseded by the Simple Digital Library Interoperability Protocol (SDLIP), designed in collaboration with other North American research projects [7].

Emphasis has been placed in SDLIP on a design that is scalable, permitting the development of digital library applications that run on hand-held devices such as PalmPilots, in addition to workstation- and mainframe-based systems. There are two transport options: one CORBA-based, the other borne over HTTP; applications can mix these freely.

The protocol supports both state-keeping and stateless exchanges on the server side, as well as synchronous and asynchronous interactions between client and server. However, servers need not implement all these parts. It is up to a client to establish—using the protocol—what functionality is supported.

There are four parts (called "interfaces") to the protocol: searching, result access, metadata, and delivery. The *search* interface initiates a search. In a synchronous, stateless exchange the client waits until all results are returned, but in a synchronous, state-keeping one only some of the results need be returned as part of the search—the rest can be accessed through the *result access* interface. A server that supports asynchronous searches must by nature also be state-keeping. When results to an asynchronous query become available, the server uses the *delivery* interface to notify the client. Finally, the *source metadata* interface provides a mechanism for clients to discover the functional capabilities of a server (including version number control), the collections stored there, and the metadata fields present in a particular collection.

3   The Greenstone Protocol

The Greenstone protocol is closely integrated with the digital library architecture, which supports full access to multimedia data: a text query to retrieve a book; a sung fragment of tune to retrieve a music score. Like the previous approaches the protocol adopts a client-server model, although the term "receptionist" is used instead of "client" to emphasise the role that this component plays in the architecture. The protocol is divided into three areas: General, Filtering and Documents. Since last reported [5], we have migrated from a Perl-based remote procedure call mechanism to the more general CORBA framework; the underlying functionality, however, remains essentially the same.

General operations available to a client include obtaining a list of collections offered by a server, testing to see whether a particular collection is running, and obtaining information specific to a collection—such as how many documents it contains, and when it was last updated. The filtering mechanism supports both

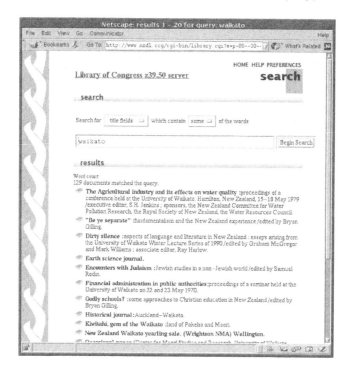

Fig. 1. Greenstone interface to the Library of Congress using protocol Z39.50.

searching and browsing. Filters provide an element of dynamic configurability to the protocol through an enumerated list of types that package together specific options. Finally, the Document support provides access to the content of individual documents.

The protocol is stateless, or—to be more accurate—designed for a stateless server. While this simplifies some matters, and meshes well with our digital library architecture, it imposes overheads elsewhere. We return to these in the final section, which compares the various protocols.

4   Applications

We now describe four applications that demonstrate the use of distributed digital library protocols in Greenstone.

4.1   Z39.50 Receptionist

Figure 1 shows the result of searching the Library of Congress's publicly available catalogue of bibliographic records for titles that include the word "Waikato" (the name of our university and geographical district). The interaction style follows the standard Greenstone interface. After selecting the field to search—from the choices *any fields*, *title*, and *author*—and whether *some* or *all* of the words must be included, a search is initiated by pressing the "Begin Search" button. This loads a new page (shown) that repeats the query settings for the given query at the top and includes matching entries below. Clicking on the "book" icon beside a matching entry produces a new page giving the full catalogue entry.

Due to the complexity of the Z39.50 bibliography registry, "title" metadata covers various different fields. However, for brevity, this system shows only one of these fields for each matching entry. Thus the display may not include the words in the query. For example, the second entry in Figure 1, "Be ye separate," does not specifically mention "Waikato" (although it is clearly related to New Zealand). However, the term does appear in the full citation, as will be revealed by clicking on the book icon.

The interaction between Greenstone and a Z39.50 server is a follows: using the freely available YAZ package, calls to the *General* part of the Greenstone protocol are translated into *Initialization* and *Explain Facility* calls; *Filtering* maps to the *Search*, *Sort* and *Browse* facilities (although presently we only use *Search*); and Greenstone *Document* requests use the *Retrieval* facility.

4.2   SDLIP Protocol Translator

The protocol translator maps Stanford's SDLIP protocol calls pertaining to stateless synchronous interaction to Greenstone protocol calls. The translator runs as a server in its own right, and Figure 2 shows it acts as an intermediary, accepting SDLIP requests transmitted either through CORBA or HTTP, and passing them on to Greenstone's CORBA-based protocol. Written in Java, the translator server implements the intersection of the Greenstone protocol and SDLIP's *search* and *source metadata* interfaces.

The *search* interface maps to Greenstone's Filter and Document operations, while *source metadata* maps to various calls from the General part of the Greenstone protocol. The remaining interfaces and services, such as the result access interface and the delivery interface, are set up to return trivial, default behavior, because they have no counterpart in a direct mapping to a synchronous stateless service.

Figure 3 shows the result of running the sample command-line driven SDLIP client available for download from the Infobus Web site. At the top we see diagnostic output from the SDLIP client; at the bottom is the diagnostic output from the SDLIP to Greenstone translator. We assume the existence of a Greenstone server (output not shown) whose location is specified when the translator server is started.

When the client program is run, it first connects to the SDLIP server specified on the command line (the translator, in our case) and then calls the *search* interface with the remaining command line arguments stored as the query. The translator server accepts these arguments and sets up a Filter call to emulate the call to SDLIP `search`. If the property list supplied by the SDLIP call specifies document text, a second call to Greenstone is made, this time using the

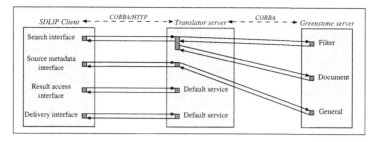

Fig. 2. How SDLIP protocol calls are mapped to the Greenstone protocol.

Document part of the protocol, to access the necessary information. The data obtained from these calls is then collated, and returned encoded as XML.

The translator example is intended for demonstration purposes only. A more sophisticated—and ultimately more desirable—approach is to enhance the translator with state keeping capabilities. Just because the Greenstone server does not keep state does not mean that state-based SDLIP interactions cannot be supported. For instance, when query results are returned from the CORBA call to Greenstone, the translator server can store the result locally and assign it a result set identifier. It can use this to support subsequent calls to the result access interface—including query refinement.

4.3   A Digital Library for Children

Figure 4 shows the home page of the Kids Digital Library, part of Middlesex University's digital library project. The vertical column in the center gives the collections available to the user. On the left are support services: a workspace for creative writing; a submission process for completed stories and poems; a bulletin board where selected works are discussed and annotated; and on-line training packages to help users learn about the digital library environment.

The receptionist asks the user to log in before reaching this page; in this case the user is Jamie, shown at the top of the page. There is also a special account for the class teacher, with extra functionality provided by the receptionist for updating collections with new stories and so forth. Authentication is not part of the protocol; instead it is built into the receptionist's software architecture.

From the home page a pupil can view the various collections on offer or access the support services mentioned above. *Poems* and *Short Stories* are collections of finished works by the pupils, vetted by the teacher. The collections are searchable by full text, author, and title; browsable by author and title. *Pictures & Images*, *Audio Sounds*, and *Ideas* are collections pulled together from various sources to provide resources and ideas for the pupils; they too have searchable and browsable structures. Finally, the *Personal Bookmarks* collection, which is specific to the particular user, is formed from the user's bookmarks file and includes the downloaded content of each Web page mentioned. The collection is fully indexed, and browsable by title and subject folder.

Client:

```
weka% java SimpleClient http://kiwi.cs.waikato.ac.nz:8282 "music style"
DOCUMENT: 1
        http://purl.org/metadata/dublin_core#Title
        = "Computer Graphic Aided Music Composition"
DOCUMENT: 2
        http://purl.org/metadata/dublin_core#Title
          = "Schenker s Theory of Tonal Music -- Its Explication ..."
DOCUMENT: 3
        http://purl.org/metadata/dublin_core#Title
          = "Andre Tchaikovsky Meets the Computer: A Concert ..."
DOCUMENT: 4
...
```

Server:

```
kiwi% java SdlipToGsdl http://www.nzdl.org hcibib 8282
GreenstoneCorba Init on www.nzdl.org OK
hcibib OK
hcibib is public? ... yes
Starting DASL/HTTP server transport on port: 8282

[SDLIP/DASL Server Transport] request from: weka.cs.waikato.ac.nz
Query is:
<a:basicsearch xmlns:a="DAV:">
        <a:select>
                <a:allprop/>
        </a:select>
        <a:where>
                <a:contains>music style</a:contains>
        </a:where>
        <a:limit>
                <a:nresults>10</a:nresults>
        </a:limit>
</a:basicsearch>

Query string = music style
Title: Computer Graphic Aided Music Composition
Title: Schenker s Theory of Tonal Music -- Its Explication ...
Title: Andre Tchaikovsky Meets the Computer: A Concert ...
Title: ...
```

Fig. 3. Example use of the SDLIP to Greenstone translator.

The idea behind the *Personal Bookmarks* collection is this. Pupils browse the Web using a variety of strategies for finding information pertinent to their work, bookmarking relevant pages. Upon activating "rebuild this collection" through a hyperlink on the Greenstone page for the Personal Bookmarks collection, new pages are downloaded and any existing pages that have changed are updated to form the latest version of their Personal Bookmarks collection.

Figure 5 shows the underlying structure of the Kids Digital Library environment. Unbeknownst to the user, collections are accessed from two servers: one local, the other remote. Small collections that are rebuilt frequently, such as personal bookmarks, short stories and the bulletin board, are served from the main site in Middlesex. The larger collections—intended as a source of inspiration—do not change so rapidly and are served remotely from the Waikato Greenstone site, which has more resources dedicated to supporting digital library collections. For example, in Figure 5 Jamie is accessing the *Sounds* and *Ideas* collections in Waikato as a basis for creative writing, and submitting the composition for the teacher's perusal.

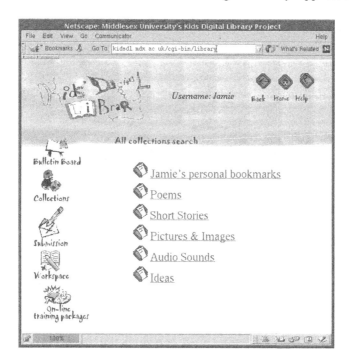

Fig. 4. The Middlesex University's Kids Digital Library environment.

4.4   A Java Application

We now turn to an interactive application written in Java. Figure 6 shows a bibliographic search tool that uses a citation's year and matching relevance score to graphically lay out the query result set. The result set is further enhanced through the use of colour: each word in the query is assigned a colour, and matching citations that include that word are displayed using that colour. In the case of a document containing more than one of the query terms, the box is divided into vertical coloured strips. The scroll bars adjacent to the graphics display area allow the user to zoom and pan around the search set; clicking on a particular document box pops up a new window that includes its full citation.

When the bibliographic tool is started, a Greenstone server is specified, along with the particular collection to use. The bibliographic tool requests year metadata, relevance score, and term frequency in addition to document identifier (which is included as standard) when a search is invoked through the protocol's Filter operation. This is sufficient information to generate the graphical display of the result set. When a user clicks on a document box, a new call over the protocol is made to request all metadata for the given document identifier. State information is kept client side.

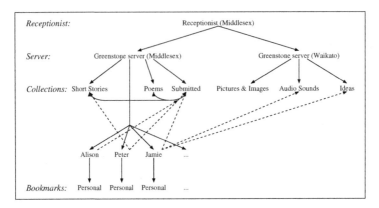

Fig. 5. How the Greenstone protocol is used to provide Middlesex University's Kids Digital Library environment.

5 Discussion

We have summarised the main features of four digital library protocols: Z39.50, Dienst, SDLIP, and Greenstone. Demonstrated by four examples, we have also discussed the distributed nature of the Greenstone digital library system, as supported by its protocol. Here we compare and comment on the similarities and differences of the protocols.

All support searching, browsing, and document retrieval. Text searching is relatively well understood—all four protocols support ranked and Boolean queries, with a rich array of options: fielded search, stemming, case matching, and so forth. The main detail for choice is the query syntax used; here Z39.50 and SDLIP are notable in their use of existing and/or emerging standards.

The role of browsing (normally closely associated with metadata) in a digital library is less clear, and support for this varies. Here, Greenstone's communication appears more general than the others, supporting, through its Filter mechanism, hierarchical browsing—it is not clear from the literature if the other protocols support this.

The final core service—document retrieval—is also well supported in the four protocols. Here we see protocols defining models of document structure, and enumerating document formats and types. Arguably, Dienst provides the richest functionality, with its ability to export logical structure in a variety of MIME types.

While not a core requirement of a digital library implementation (as defined, for example, in [1]) all four protocols include functionality to establish the services offered and options supported by a server. This enables more general clients to be written that configure themselves dynamically in response to different situations and, we believe, reflects a level of maturity in DL protocol design.

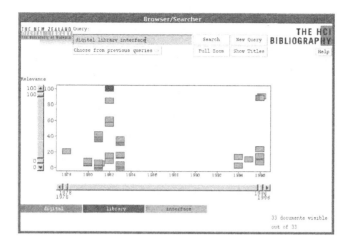

Fig. 6. A bibliographic search tool based on the Greenstone protocol.

Other important elements are version control and authentication. Version control is handled externally in Z39.50 by ratified standards. In SDLIP and Dienst it is built into the protocol: a more ambitious aim, with the onus on clients to resolve versioning conflicts. Time will tell how successful this approach is; however, current signs are encouraging. In Greenstone there is no explicit version control. With the protocol tied so closely to the software architecture, this is not as limiting as might first appear. Within the application program interface there is a certain latitude for backwards compatible extensions and the filtering mechanism—the main part of the protocol that is likely to change—has purposely been designed to be extensible. This is backed up by the Filter mechanism that includes calls to list the filter types supported and the options they take.

Although a framework for authentication is part of the Dienst protocol, how it is implemented is a detail left up to the service provider. In Z39.50, authentication is more rigorously defined by its Access Control Facility, which is in stark contrast to Greenstone, that has none. Here authentication is enforced through the receptionist, as seen in the Kids Digital Library example. In SDLIP, there is no mention of authentication [7]. Presumably a client end implementation, similar to Greenstone's, is feasible. Alternatively, a more encompassing security check might be imposed by the transport layer when a client connects to a server.

5.1   Considerations for DL Systems

As we have demonstrated, one digital library system is capable of supporting more than one protocol; at present, in the case of Greenstone, three different protocols are supported. Using the distributed protocols, we have also shown that they can be utilised not only to support *remote services* through one interface, but *novel interfaces* as well, in the form of graphical environments. The Kids' Digital Library shows the high degree of sophistication which can be achieved by utilising both benefits.

Greenstone is internally separated into two components; the "collection server" which provides *services* on one side, and a "receptionist" which accesses the services through an *interface* on the other. This has made it particularly adaptable to supporting both distributed traditional web-based access and more heavy-weight and richer graphical environments from one server program. Thus the component architecture already reported in [5] is further validated.

6   Conclusions

Digital library protocol design is at an interesting stage. While several alternative designs have emerged with varying degrees of complexity, from the elaborate Z39.50 to the simple but tightly prescribed Greenstone protocol, the different designs are not incompatible. As the SDLIP to Dienst proxy [7] and the SDLIP to Greenstone translator presented here both demonstrate, interoperability is alive and well. Furthermore, seemingly irreconcilable differences in protocol design, such as state-keeping and stateless, can often be overcome by appropriate programming support.

References

[1] R. M. Akscyn and I. H. Witten. *Report on the First Summit on International Cooperaton on Digital Libraries.* 1998. Available on-line at <ks.com/idla-wp-oct98>.

[2] ANSI/NISO. *Information Retrieval (Z39.50 version 3): Application Service Definition and Protocol Specification (ANSI/NISO Z39.50-1995).* NISO Press, Bethesda, MD, 1995. Available on-line at <lcweb.loc.gov/z3950/agency/document.html>.

[3] J. Larmouth. *ASN.1 Complete.* Morgan Kaufmann, 1999.

[4] C. Logoze and D. Fielding. Defining collections in distributed digital libraries. *D-Lib Magazine,* 4(11), Nov. 1998. Available on-line at <www.dlib.org/dlib/november98/lagoze/11lagoze.html>.

[5] R. McNab, I. Witten, and S. Boddie. A distributed digital library architecture incorporating different index styles. In *Proc. IEEE International Forum on Research and Technology Advances in Digital Libraries,* pages 36–45, Santa Barbara, California, 1998. IEEE Computer Society Press.

[6] A. Paepcke, M. Baldonado, C.-C. K. Chang, S. Cousins, and H. Garcia-Molina. Using distributed objects to build the stanford digital library infobus. *Computer,* 32(2):80–87, Feb. 1999.

[7] A. Paepcke, R. Brandriff, G. Janee, R. Larson, B. Ludaescher, S. Melnik, and S. Raghavan. Search middleware and the simple digital library interoperability protocol. *D-Lib Magazine,* 6(3), Mar. 2000. Available on-line at <www.dlib.org/dlib/march00/paepcke/03paepcke.html>.

[8] D. Slama, J. Garbis, and P. Russell. *Enterprise CORBA.* Prentice Hall, 1999.

Linking Information with Distributed Objects

Trond Aalberg

Norwegian University of Science and Technology,
Department of Computer and Information Science
Trond.Aalberg@idi.ntnu.no

Abstract. Digital libraries can be viewed as managed and organized information spaces. In building and using these information spaces there is a need for technology to express, navigate and manage relationships. This paper presents the DL-LinkService, an object-oriented solution for structuring information in digital libraries where the relationships are implemented as distributed objects. The service is inspired by the CORBA Relationship Service, but our contribution is more flexible because the typing of relationships is independent of the implementation of the service. This paper describes the DL-LinkService and its possible use in three scenarios. A prototype is developed and our experience with the DL-LinkService is that this is a promising solution for expressing and navigating the structural information of digital libraries.

1   Introduction

In this paper we emphasize a view on digital libraries as a managed and organized information space. A core element in this aspect of digital libraries is technology for expressing, navigating and managing relationships.

In traditional data storage systems relationships are usually predefined in static data models. In digital libraries this is often an insufficient approach due to the unpredictable types of relationships that may exist. A general trend is to use more dynamic solutions that allows relationships to be defined as the information space emerges. Specific metadata elements for describing relationships like the "relation" element of Dublin Core [7] may be used. RDF metadata [25] where the statements express a relationship is another possibility. The linking mechanisms of hypermedia are important technology as well, spanning from the simple embedded one-way linking of HTML [24] to the more advanced external linking constructs of XLink [26] and HyTime [13].

A major problem with relationships expressed as either metadata or external hypermedia links is that these are descriptive solutions. To process such relationship constructs, e.g. for navigational purposes, there is a need to both access the information by some protocol and interpret the returned information before taking action. In this paper we describe an object-oriented approach to relationships that allows for direct navigation. By encompassing both the processing and data level the resulting model represents a functional or operational approach rather than a descriptive approach.

P. Constantopoulos and I.T. Sølvberg (Eds.): ECDL 2001, LNCS 2163, pp. 149–160, 2001.

When using the DL-LinkService, information objects are related to each other in ways that are formally named and defined. The service allows for tracking these formal relationships as they are defined. This paper also focuses on relationship constraints. To enforce consistency on a body of information, it is often needed to constrain which relationships are allowed and how they can be configured. The proposed object-oriented approach allows for a constraint mechanism to be an integrated part of the relationships.

An information space may consist of information stored and maintained within one system, or it may be an open network of interrelated, but distributed information objects. To address the need for a relationship mechanism that easily can be used in a distributed environment, the DL-LinkService is based on the CORBA distributed object technology.

2   Relationships and Links

The terms *relationship* and *link* are frequently used in computer science to denote a variety of phenomena. In general a *relationship* represents a meaningful connection between two or more objects. Chen's article introducing the Entity-Relationship Model defines a *relationship* as an association among entities [5]. In the Unified Modelling Language (UML) a *relationship* is defined as a reified semantic connection between modelling elements [19], and a *link* is defined as the tuple of object references that is an instance of an association. In the hypermedia tradition a *link* can be defined as a traversable connections between the nodes of the hypertext [16], but a link is often considered to express or describe a relationship [27, 13, 3].

The view on relationships and links that is emphasized in this paper is that the relationship is an abstract type or concept while the link is the implementation counterpart. Both linking as we find it in hypermedia and the use of metadata to express relationships, can be characterized as *bottom-up* and *instance-oriented*, as opposed to the *top-down* and *model-oriented* approach of data modelling.

In the model-oriented approach to relationships we find that the implementation of relationships are diverse. The use of relations, key attributes, and foreign keys, are fundaments used in relational databases [8], while object-oriented databases rely on the use of references, object identifiers or by the use of a specific relationship property like in the Object Data Standard [4].

The instance-oriented approach to linking in hypermedia is diverse as well. Several different models of links exists e.g. the Dexter Hypertext Reference Model [12]. A more recent model supposed to be capable of representing the link models assumed by most existing hypertext systems, is defined by the Open Hypermedia Systems Working Group [6], but the XLink specification of W3C seems to be the most dominating at the present.

The solution proposed in this paper is based on the instance-oriented approach and the principle that a common generic data structure should be used to represent all kinds of relationships.

When using a generic construct to implement a relationship there is a need for a property describing the meaning or semantic role of the link. An example of this is the semantic attributes *role* and *arcrole* that can be used in XLink elements. A semantic type may be associated to the link as a whole, e.g. *Reference*, and/or a type may be associated to the participation role of the various entities, e.g. the corresponding roles *Is Referenced By* and *References*.

Developing a relationship taxonomy in advance for all the needs of a particular domain is a difficult task. Several taxonomies for hypermedia have been proposed and overviews are given by Kopak in [15] and by Verbyla in [23]. In the library domain there is a great interest in bibliographic relationships – the various relationships that may exist between bibliographic items [21, 20]. In this paper we do not assume a specific relationship taxonomy, but the DL-LinkService can be used with different taxonomies. The service also allows for new types to be easily added, and a relationship taxonomy can be developed as the information space emerges.

There is a need for a model that also allows for expressing constraints. Traditional relationship constraints are cardinality ratio and participation [8]. In data modelling the degree of a relationship is usually a static value, but when using a generic relationship construct there is also a need to specify the degree as a constraint. Other constraints to be considered are what relationship types to allow, what kind of information objects that can be related, and constraints on the navigation direction of relationships.

3   CORBA and the CORBA Relationship Service

The Common Object Request Broker Architecture (CORBA) is the Object Management Group's open architecture and infrastructure for distributed objects [11]. CORBA is object-oriented and CORBA objects are conceptually comparable to the objects of programming languages like Java and C++. A main difference is, however, that the CORBA middleware (the ORB – Object Request Broker) and the standardized protocol IIOP, allows for CORBA objects to interoperate over the network regardless of programming language, operating system or hardware.

What constitutes an object in CORBA is a design decision similar to the design of other object-oriented applications. A text document or an image can be modelled and implemented as an object as well as a search system for a bibliographic database. The DL-LinkService described in this paper is based on a model where both the entities and relationships are objects.

CORBA objects are typed by the use of OMGs Interface Definition Language (IDL) – a strongly typed declarative language. IDL is used to specify the interface of objects, which in essence is a formal description of the methods that can be called on an object. In practice IDL also serves other purposes. When developing a client application the IDL file is used as input for the automatic generation of the programming-language code that lets the client communicate with server objects as if they were local objects.

Although CORBA has been used as the infrastructure of several digital library projects [18, 1, 17, 2], the possible use of CORBA as the underlying infrastructure for digital libraries is not very well explored. CORBA is more than middleware that can be used for implementing monolithic applications. The overall architecture envisioned by OMG is an object-oriented environment covering all the aspects of distributed computing.

Cooperating information vendors want to integrate their information into a common information space. The intention of implementing the DL-LinkService by the use of CORBA distributed objects is to develop a service that can be used in such a distributed environments.

3.1   The CORBA Relationship Service

As a part of their object management architecture OMG has specified a set of generic services to support basic functions for the use and implementation of distributed objects. The Relationship Service [10] discussed in this section as well as the The Collection Service [9], are services that can be used to structure object systems. To our knowledge the possible use of these services has not been addressed very much in digital library research.

The Relationship Service of CORBA allows for relationships between objects to be explicitly represented. The specification defines three levels of service; *base*, *graph*, and *specific*.

The base level defines the interfaces for the role and relationship objects that implement a relationship[1]. Relationships are navigated by calling the methods of the role and relationship objects.

Role and relationship objects are created when needed by the use of factory objects. In the context of CORBA, a factory is an object responsible for the creation of object instances, e.g. a role object is instanciated by calling the create method on the role factory object.

A role object represents an entity in a relationship and is created by passing the reference of the entity object to a role factory. A relationship object, on the other hand, aggregates the participating roles of a relationship and is created by passing a set of roles to a relationship factory. Specific types of relationship and role objects are defined by the user of the service by inheriting these basic interfaces, and this also allows for domain or relationship specific methods and attributes to be implemented.

The Relationship Service allows for relationships of arbitrary degree. A relationship can contain two roles as in a binary relationship, or it can contain tree or more roles and thus support relationships of higher degree. A role can participate in any number of relationships only constrained by the minimum and maximum cardinality. Roles and relationships can further be constrained by the type of objects they each expect. The constraint mechanism is an integrated

---

[1] Note that the CORBA Relationship Service uses the term *relationship* to denote the association between two or more objects, but it also uses *relationship object* to denote a specific kind of objects used to aggregate role objects.

functionality of the object implementations and erroneous situations are handled by raising exceptions.

Since a role object only holds a reference to the entity object, it may represent a third-party object and in this way allow for relationships to be created without inferring with the related objects.

The graph level extends the base level by adding the concept of a node object as well as other interfaces for graph traversal. The purpose of the node is to tie the various relationships into a graph by aggregating the various roles of an entity object. The node interface may be inherited by entity objects or it may only contain a reference to the entity object it represents to allow for the graph to contain third party object.

Specific relationships are defined at the third level by the definition of interfaces for the two important relationships *containment* and *reference*.

3.2   Using the CORBA Relationship Service in Digital Libraries

The initial phase of this project was to evaluate the use of the CORBA Relationship Service. This was done by implementing the base level of the service and testing its usability on a collection of information objects. By doing this we got an understanding on how this service would work in a digital library environment. The conclusions are as following:

The positive aspect of this service is that it defines a generic object model that can support all kinds of relationships with respect to semantic types, structural features like degree, and constraints on cardinality and type. The service allows for relationships between third-party objects to be defined, and non-CORBA entities can be related by the use of intermediary objects holding URIs. This means that the object model of the service should be highly usable to represent and navigate relationships in digital libraries.

The negative aspect of the service is that it assumes a pre-defined and static information model where the different kinds of relationships have to be known in advance prior to implementing the service. For each kind of relationship there is a need to define and implement specific interfaces for both roles and relationship objects as well as their respective factories. The CORBA Relationship Service is thus more a toolkit for implementing relationships in specific applications. We believe that there is a need for a more generic and flexible solution in digital libraries. Relationship typing should be independent of the actual implementation of the relationship service. This would enable that the same implementation of the service could be used with different relationship taxonomies, and new relationships could easily be added without having to rebuild server and client applications. This would also enable different instances of the service to interoperate by sharing the same relationship taxonomy, e.g. using a common registry.

4   The DL-LinkService

Based on our experience from the initial evaluation of the CORBA Relationship Service, the chosen strategy for the further development of a relationship service

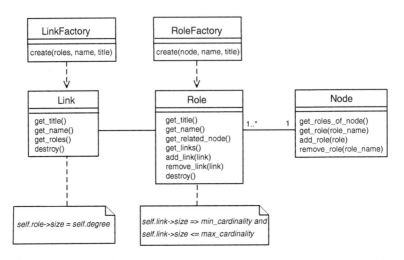

Fig. 1. A UML class diagram showing the object model of the DL-LinkService. The diagram is simplified for illustrative purposes and does not show the exceptions these functions raise or the private functions and variables of the classes.

was to define a new service. The DL-LinkService is inspired by the best parts of the CORBA Relationship Service, but implements a different mechanism for creating and typing relationships. A UML class diagram showing our object model is found in figure 1, and the service is summarized by the following:

The main types of objects are nodes, roles and links[2]. A node represents an entity participating in a relationship and aggregates the different roles of this entity, and in this way it enables graph traversal. The Node interface can be a common supertype that other objects inherit from regardless of what kind of entity they represent, e.g. by letting various kinds of information objects inherit this interface. To be able to support relationships between third-party objects or information units not implemented as CORBA objects, a node can also be an intermediary object that holds a CORBA reference or URI to another resource.

Role objects represent the endpoints of the relationship by holding a reference to the node of the related entity. A role participates in a relationship by holding a reference to the link object. Roles may be created and destroyed, and link objects may be added or removed during the lifetime of a role. Link objects aggregate the roles that represent the endpoints of the relationship. Link objects may be created and destroyed when needed, but may not be changed during their lifetime. Both the Link interface and the Role interface may be extended to include new attributes or methods if this is required to support specific applications.

---

[2] Rather than using the somewhat confusing terminology of the CORBA Relationship Service, we use "link object" to denote the interconnecting object.

Typing of the link and role objects in the DL-LinkService is based on the view that the *semantic type* of link and role objects should be independent of their *structural type*. An efficient way to implement this is to use a single IDL-type for respectively role and link objects and simply let the value of an attribute identify the semantics. In the DL-LinkService the semantic type of a link or role object is defined by the name that is given the object at creation time. An optional title attribute is defined to support additional labels or user defined descriptions.

The DL-LinkService is based on the use of two generic factory objects that are responsible for the creation of role and link objects. A link factory is responsible for the creation and configuration of the link objects the service supports, and a role factory is responsible for the creation and configuration of the role objects. The DL-LinkService is not concerned with the creation of node objects. This is an application-level decision. It is the responsibility of the node to ensure that the it only holds one role object for each role type. Nodes may constrain the role objects they are willing to hold, either by name or by interface type.

When links and roles are created they need to be initialised with the proper constraints for that particular semantic type. When a user calls the create method on a factory object, the factory uses the value of the name attribute to look up this information and initialise the object. Figure 2 shows a simplified example using an XML to structure this information. This information can be stored in a file or database and if needed it can be shared, e.g. using a registry.

The mechanisms for maintaining a consistent system is an internal part of the object implementations and erroneous situations are handled by the use of exceptions (not shown in the diagram).

4.1   The DL-LinkService Prototype System

A prototype system is implemented both as a means to guide the specification of the service and to demonstrate and evaluate the capabilities of the system.

The service is implemented in Java using Borland's Visibroker as the ORB. Link, role and node objects are persistent and the state of the objects are stored using a database. Objects are activated on request using the ServantLocator interface introduced in CORBA 2.3.

5   Three Usage Scenarios

This section discusses three usage scenarios, spanning quite different application areas of digital libraries. These scenarios do not describe the full complexity of these application domains, but illustrates the potential usage of the DL-LinkService and demonstrates how the service works.

The DL-LinkService can be used to structure compound information objects by the use of relationships as shown in figure 3. In this scenario the compound information object consists of different image files and metadata records that are related to each other. A node represents the image at the "work" level and aggregates the image files and the metadata record that are subparts of this

```
<LinkRules>
    <LinkType LinkID="Reference">
        <Degree>2</Degree>
        <LinkInterfaceID>IDL:LinkService/Link:1.0</LinkInterfaceID>
        <AllowedRoles>
            <RoleTypeRef RoleIdRef="References"/>
            <RoleTypeRef RoleIdRef="IsReferencedBy"/>
        </AllowedRoles>
    </LinkType>
    <RoleType RoleID="References">
        <RoleInterfaceID>IDL:LinkService/Role:1.0</RoleInterfaceID>
        <MaxCardinality>N</MaxCardinality>
        <MinCardinality>0</MinCardinality>
    </RoleType>
    <RoleType RoleID="IsReferencedBy">
        <RoleInterfaceID>IDL:LinkService/Role:1.0</RoleInterfaceID>
        <MaxCardinality>N</MaxCardinality>
        <MinCardinality>0</MinCardinality>
    </RoleType>
</LinkRules>
```

Fig. 2. An example on the template information for the binary and many-to-many relationship *Reference*.

object. Two different relationship types are used. *Description* is the relationship between the metadata record and the object that it describes. *Instance* is the relationship between the "work" and the different "items" of the work. Clients wanting to access the image have maybe encountered the reference of the node through the use of an Object Trading Service or by other means. By the methods of the node the client fetches a list of roles. If the client is interested in the metadata, it can navigate the *Description* relationship to fetch the metadata record. If this client is interested in particular image formats, it may iterate the *Instance* relationships, look up the associated metadata of each file and fetch the URI of the image file that it wants to access.

Subject-based hierarchical or network structures are often used to allow for navigation in large collections of information. Figure 4 shows how the DL-LinkService can be used as the basis of a navigational engine. In this case the example is based on the use of TopicMaps and XTM [14, 22]. The *Topic* element of XTM is implemented as a node and the *Association* and *Occurrence* elements are implemented by the use of relationships. This example is simplified, but we believe that it is possible to implement a complete TopicMap engine by extending the available interfaces and using the typing system of the DL-LinkService.

The last scenario illustrates how the DL-LinkService can be used in a distributed environment. The scenario is that of two publishers of electronic journals who cooperate to allow for automatic citation-based linking (figure 5). Here, the nodes represent the various articles, and the citations are implemented by the

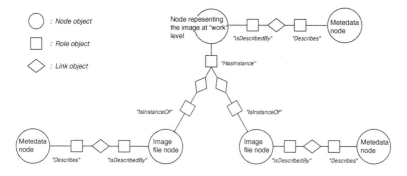

Fig. 3. Using relationships to structure a compound information object

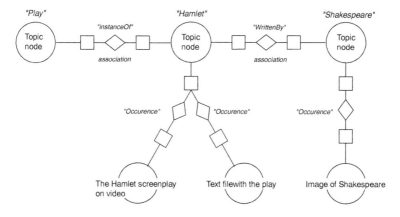

Fig. 4. Using the DL-LinkService to implement a simplified TopicMap engine.

use of *Reference* relationships. Both publishers run their own instance of the DL-LinkService, and the various relationship objects are distributed over two sites. A role and link may exist on site X, but the corresponding role at the opposite side of the relationship may exist on site Y. Due to the implemented constraint mechanisms the relationships structure will always be consistent.

6   Discussion

The DL-LinkService presented in this paper is a promising solution for implementing and managing relationships in digital library information spaces. The applicability of the service is illustrated by the three scenarios described and we believe the service could be of general use in digital libraries. The main application of this service is, however, in areas where there is a need to manage and control relationships, an area that is less covered by other solutions. A major contribution of this approach is the implementation of relationships using dis-

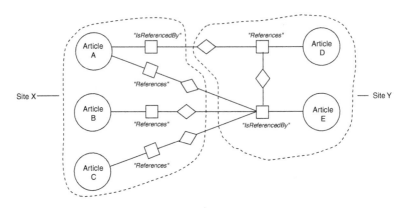

Fig. 5. A shared solution for reference linking, showing the partitioning of the objects over two sites.

tributed objects. We believe this is a promising approach due to the inherently distributed nature of the information in digital libraries.

Both RDF and extended XLinks are solutions relevant for information spaces. TopicMaps and XTM, another emerging solution, is also highly relevant. The focus on data structures that also can express relationships are common elements in all these solutions. How to manipulate or process these formats is, however, a separate issue. The DL-LinkService differs from these other solutions by the inherent encapsulation of data and processing. Relationships are dynamic units that easily can evolve and constraints are used to ensure that the relationship structure is consistent over time.

The nodes, roles and links of the DL-LinkService object model are based on a general model that frequently is found in modelling and other areas. This model is quite comparable to the extended linking construct of XLink and the associations of TopicMaps. The basic model of RDF is to some degree different, but by using compound RDF statements it should be possible to express this kind of relationship model. The main difference is not in the model used, but in the functional approach of the DL-LinkService compared to the descriptive approach of other solutions. If needed, it should be possible to convert to and from the text based representations of XLink, RDF or TopicMaps.

A new service based on the same object model as the CORBA Relationship Service is specified, but with a different mechanism for creating and typing the relationships. For CORBA-based applications this solution has both advantages and disadvantages. Not building on the CORBA Relationship Service means incompatibility with applications true to the specification and not having the possibility to use available implementations of the CORBA service. We do, however, believe this is necessary due to the need for a more flexible relationship service in digital library systems.

The DL-LinkSerice is depending on typed relations. This is a design choice to enable management of relationships. A service independent of type definitions could be implemented, e.g. by letting the users themselves initialise the objects when they are created. The disadvantage of such a solution is the loss of control and an inconsistent and less useful information space. The DL-LinkService can still support user-defined relationships e.g. using the title attribute to hold user-defined descriptions. The dynamic aspect of this service is that the same software can be used with different relationship taxonomies and that new types easily can be added as the information space emerges.

In this paper the first stage of a structuring service for digital libraries is presented. We have established a "stable" solution that can be the basis for further work in different directions. Related issues are how to present these relationships as links in user interfaces and the management of relationships in a distributed environment with respect to access management and security. A major element is the need for a query service, and we believe this can be achieved by creating a queryable "shadow" copy of the distributed graph e.g. using an object-oriented database and OQL.

References

[1] William Y. Arms, Christophe Blanchi, and Edward A. Overly. An architecture for information in digital libraries. *D-Lib Magazine*, 3(2), February 1997. Available at `http://www.dlib.org/dlib/february97/cnri/02arms1.html` (Last visited 18/6/2001).

[2] Michelle Baldonado, Chen-Chuan K. Chang, Luis Gravano, and Andreas Paepcke. Metadata for digital libraries: Architecture and design rationale. In *Proceedings of the 2nd ACM International Conference on Digital Libraries*, pages 23–26, Philadelphia, PA USA, July 1997. ACM.

[3] Leslie Carr, Wendy Hall, and David De Roure. The evolution of hypertext link services. *ACM Computing Surveys*, 31(4es), Dec. 1999.

[4] R. G. G. Cattell and Douglas K. Barry, editors. *The Object Data Standard : ODMG 3.0*. Morgan Kaufmann Publishers, 2000.

[5] Peter Pin-Shan Chen. The Entity Relationship Model : Towards a unified view of data. *ACM Transactions on Database Systems*, 1(1), March 1976.

[6] Hugh Charles Davis, Siegfried Reich, and David Millard. A proposal for a common navigational hypertext protocol. Technical report, Aarhus University, Dept. of Electronics and Computer Science, 1997. Presented at 3.5 Open Hypermedia System Working Group Meeting, Aarhus University, Denmark, September 8-11, 1997.

[7] The Dublin Core Metadata Initiative. Dublin Core metadata element set, version 1.1: Reference description, 1999. Available at `http://dublincore.org/documents/dces` (Last visited 18/6/2001).

[8] Ramez Elmasri and Shamkant B. Navathe. *Fundamentals of Database Systems*. Benjamin/Cummings publishing Company, 2000.

[9] Object Management Group. Object Collection Specification, 2000. Available at `ftp://ftp.omg.org/pub/docs/formal/00-06-13.pdf` (Last visited 18/6/2001).

[10] Object Management Group. Relationship Service Specification, 2000. Available at `ftp://ftp.omg.org/pub/docs/formal/00-06-24.pdf` (Last visited 18/6/2001).

[11] Object Management Group. The Common Object Request Broker : Architecture and Specification, 2001. Available at `ftp://ftp.omg.org/pub/docs/formal/01-02-33.pdf` (Last visited 18/6/2001).

[12] Frank Halasz and Mayer Schwartz. The Dexter hypertext reference model. *Communications of the ACM*, 37(2):30–39, 1994.

[13] The International Organization For Standardization. Hypermedia/Time-based Structuring Language (HyTime). International Standard ISO/IEC 10744:1977, ISO, 1997.

[14] The International Organization For Standardization. Topic Maps. International Standard ISO/IEC 13250:2000, ISO, 2000.

[15] Richard W. Kopak. Functional link typing in hypertext. *ACM Computing Surveys*, 31(4es), Dec. 1999.

[16] Steven R. Newcomb, Neill A. Kipp, and Victoria T. Newcomb. The HyTime hypermedia/time-based document structuring language. *Communications of the ACM*, 34(11):67–83, Nov. 1991.

[17] Andreas Paepcke, Michelle Q. Wang Baldonado, Chen-Chuan K. Chang, Steve Cousins, and Hector Garcia-Molina. Using distributed objects to build the Stanford Digital Library Infobus. *Computer*, 32(2):80–87, February 1999.

[18] Sandra Payette and Carl Lagoze. Flexible and extensible digital object and repository architecture. In *Research and Advanced Technology for Digital libraries : Second European Conference, ECDL 98*, volume 1513 of *Lecture notes in computer science*, Heraklion, Crete, Greece, September 1998. Springer.

[19] James Rumbaugh, Ivar Jacobsen, and Grady Booch. *The Unified Modelling Language Reference Manual*. Object Technology Series. Addison-Wesley, 1999.

[20] IFLA study group on the functional requirements for bibliographic records. Functional requirements for bibliographic records : Final report. Technical report, IFLA, 1998. Available at `http://www.ifla.org/VII/s13/frbr/frbr.pdf` (Last visited 18/6/2001).

[21] Barbara B. Tillett. A taxonomy of bibliographic relationships. *Library Resources & Technical Services*,, 35(2):150–158, April 1991.

[22] TopicMaps.Org. XML Topic Maps (XTM) 1.0, 2000. Available at `http://www.topicmaps.org/xtm/1.0` (Last visited 18/6/2001).

[23] Janet Verbyla. Unlinking the link. *ACM Computing Surveys*, 31(4es), Dec. 1999.

[24] W3C. HTML 4.01 specification. W3C Recommendation REC-html401-19991224, W3C, December 1999. Available at `http://www.w3.org/TR/1999/REC-html401-19991224/` (Last visited 18/6/2001).

[25] W3C. Resource Description Framework (RDF) : Model and syntax specification. W3C Recommendation REC-rdf-syntax-19990222, W3C, February 1999. Available at `http://www.w3.org/TR/REC-rdf-syntax/` (Last visited 18/6/2001).

[26] W3C. XML Linking Language (XLink) version 1.0. W3C Proposed Recommendation PR-xlink-20001220, W3C, December 2000. Available at `http://www.w3.org/TR/xlink/` (Last visited 18/6/2001).

[27] W3C Web Characterization Activity Working Group. Web characterization terminology and definitions sheet. W3C Working Draft 24-May-1999, W3C, May 1999. Available at `http://www.w3.org/1999/05/WCA-terms/` (Last visited 18/6/2001).

Metadata for Digital Preservation: A Review of Recent Developments

Michael Day

UKOLN: the UK Office for Library and Information Networking, University of Bath,
Bath BA2 7AY, United Kingdom
m.day@ukoln.ac.uk

Abstract. This paper is a review of recent developments relating to digital preservation metadata. It introduces the digital preservation problem and notes the importance of metadata for all proposed preservation strategies. The paper reviews some developments in the archives and records domain, describes the taxonomy of information object classes defined by the Reference Model for an Open Archival Information System (OAIS) and outlines some library-based projects.

1   Introduction

The long-term preservation of information in digital form is one of the most important problems faced by the cultural heritage professions in the early twenty-first century. Hedstrom [1] has defined digital preservation as "the planning, resource allocation, and application of preservation methods and technologies necessary to ensure that digital information of continuing value remains accessible and usable." Using this definition, it is clear that the digital preservation problem is not just a technical problem, but an organisational one as well. It may, in fact, be easier to solve many of the technical issues relating to the preservation of digital information than to create organisational and managerial structures to support their consistent application. Hedstrom's definition also stresses that preservation is about maintaining access to information - not just, for example, about the various technical options for long-term storage.

It has been clear for some time that the preservation of information in digital form will require more than just the preservation of the digital bits and bytes themselves. It has been widely assumed that if digital information to remain understandable over time, there will be a need to preserve information about the technological and other contexts of a digital object's creation and use. In the past, this was sometimes assumed to mean the concurrent preservation of all of the relevant documentation that might be associated with a digital object. At the present time, following other trends in digital library terminology, a more sophisticated understanding of this concept is now known under the name of 'preservation metadata.' This paper attempts to review some recent initiatives that relate to preservation metadata for digital objects.

P. Constantopoulos and I.T. Sølvberg (Eds.): ECDL 2001, LNCS 2163, pp. 161-172, 2001.

2   Digital Preservation Strategies and Metadata

In technical terms, the successful long-term preservation of digital information will be dependent upon organisations identifying and implementing suitable preservation strategies [2]. If one ignores strategies that involve converting digital information into non-digital forms (e.g. printouts or microforms), at the moment there are three main strategies: technology preservation, software emulation and data migration [3]. None of these options provides a single perfect solution and it is assumed that different digital information types may require different strategies to be adopted. In any case, whichever particular digital preservation strategy is adopted, preservation metadata is likely to be a key part of its implementation. Clifford Lynch [4] describes the function of some of this metadata:

> Within an archive, metadata accompanies and makes reference to each digital object and provides associated descriptive, structural, administrative, rights management, and other kinds of information.

Lynch's comments, however, give us a clue that preservation metadata must enable to do more than support the implementation of any particular preservation strategy. Day [5] has suggested, for example, that metadata could be used to help ensure the authenticity of digital objects, to manage user access based on intellectual property rights information as well as for more traditional metadata applications like resource description and discovery. This paper will now begin to look at some metadata developments in the archives and recordkeeping domain before proceeding to look at some recent library-based projects.

3   Metadata Formats for Recordkeeping

Some parts of the archives and records professions have been seriously considering digital preservation issues for some time. In the United States, for example, an awareness of the need for the preservation of economic data stored on punched cards and magnetic tape first became apparent in the early 1960s [6]. Shortly afterwards, some of the larger national archives had started to consider what were then generically known as machine-readable records, and a few set up separate divisions to deal with them.

Most of the first generation of machine-readable records were data sets stored on punched cards or magnetic tape. As a result, appraisal and custody regimes tended to follow a traditional pattern based on the physical records being transferred into the custody of an archival repository at the end of their active life cycle. Over time, however, a rapid growth in the use of computers and the ever-changing nature of the records that were being created, resulted in a widespread reassessment of archival theory and practice [7]. For example, in the new digital environment, it was no longer sufficient for archivists to make decisions about the retention or disposal of records at the end of their active life. By that time it may be too late to ensure their preservation in any useful form. O'Shea [8] has commented that the ideal time for archivists attention to be given to digital records, "is as part of the systems development process at the point systems are being established or upgraded, i.e. even before the records are created." The Australian archives community has in particular adopted a 'continuum' approach to records management. By the early 1990s, projects began to look at embedding recordkeeping requirements in the design of office systems. Examples of these are the National Archives of Canada's IMOSA (Information Management and Office Systems Advancement) project [9] and the Public Record Office's EROS (Electronic Records in Office Systems) Programme [10]. Examples of this type of activity can also be found in commercial contexts, most notably in the pharmaceutical industry [11].

The reassessment of archival theory and practice triggered by electronic records has also begun to influence archivists' understanding of archival description. Under the older model, archival description took place after the physical transfer of records to a repository. Traditional archival descriptions document the context of their creation as well as containing information on their accumulation, custodial history and arrangement. McKemmish and Parer [12] argue that these descriptions essentially act as cataloguing records, "surrogates whose primary purpose is to help researchers find relevant records." However, with a record continuum perspective, archival description can instead be envisaged "as part of a complex series of recordkeeping processes involving the attribution of authoritative metadata from the time of records creation." This metadata is commonly known as 'recordkeeping metadata', defined by McKemmish and Parer as "standardised information about the identity, authenticity, content, structure, context and essential management requirements of records." At least some of this data could be automatically captured at the time the record is created.

Since the 1990s, a variety of research projects and practically based initiatives have been concerned with the development of recordkeeping metadata schemes and standards. The most influential of these will be described here.

3.1   The Functional Requirements for Evidence in Recordkeeping Project

The first recordkeeping research project to develop a detailed concept of metadata for recordkeeping was the Functional Requirements for Evidence in Recordkeeping project. This was a project undertaken between 1994 and 1997 by the School of Information Sciences at the University of Pittsburgh and funded by the US National Historic Publications and Records Commission [13]. The core aim of the project was to "develop viable recordkeeping functional requirements through an analysis of the professional literature and via consultation with experts in the management of archives and records" [14]. What emerged was the idea of an electronic recordkeeping system that could support the capture, maintenance and continued usability of records.

One of the Pittsburgh Project's outcomes was the development of a 'Metadata Specification for Evidence' based on a model known as the Reference Model for Business Acceptable Communications (BAC). The BAC metadata specification proposed that digital records should carry a six-layer structure of metadata. These would contain a 'Handle Layer' that would include a unique identifier and basic resource discovery metadata. However, the specification also included other layers that would be able to store detailed information on terms and conditions of use, data structures, provenance, content, and the use of the record since its creation. This metadata would be directly linked to each record and would be able to describe the content and context of the record as well as enabling the decoding of its structure for future use [15]. The metadata was intended to carry all the necessary information that would allow the record to be used - even when the individuals, computer systems and information standards under which it was created no longer existed [16].

3.2 The Preservation of the Integrity of Electronic Records Project

At approximately the same time as the Pittsburgh Project was developing its functional requirements for recordkeeping, another project was looking at the 'Preservation of the Integrity of Electronic Records.' This project was funded by the Social Sciences and Humanities Research Council of Canada and was based at the School of Library, Archival and Information Studies at the University of British Columbia (UBC), in collaboration with the US Department of Defense. It ran from 1994 to 1997. The project was primarily concerned with the preservation of the completeness, reliability and authenticity of electronic records.

While the Pittsburgh Project was heavily influenced by the reappraisal of archival thinking occasioned by developments like the record continuum model [17], the UBC project looked to base their understanding of electronic records on more traditional archival concepts. The project adopted concepts of 'reliability' and 'authenticity' that had already been used within diplomatic theory and archival science. This resulted in a restatement of the importance of archival custody once records have become inactive. Duranti [18] noted that "the authenticity of inactive records traditionally has been protected by physically transferring them to an archival institution or programme and, once transferred, by arranging and describing them." The replacement of traditional archival description by the automated capture of contextual metadata (as proposed by the Pittsburgh Project) was therefore rejected [19]. Duranti [20] argued that automatically captured metadata are inadequate, because they "do not contain 'historical' context, but only the contextual data contemporary to records creation, and because they only record the limited contextual fabric that a document has within the electronic system in which it exists." The UBC project's research team developed a set of eight templates that were intended to help identify the necessary components of records in all recordkeeping environments. These templates may be seen as potentially forming the basis of a metadata scheme for records; but one that is more firmly based in the traditional custodial view of recordkeeping than the specification developed by the Pittsburgh Project.

3.3 The InterPARES Project

The InterPARES (International Research on Permanent Authentic Records in Electronic Systems) project is another project led by the School of Library, Archival and Information Studies at the University of British Columbia. The project is concerned with a wide range of issues relating to the reliability and authenticity of electronic records. Work has been undertaken by a series of task forces dealing with authenticity, preservation, appraisal and strategy. The project's task force on authenticity has the task of identifying the elements of electronic records that need to be preserved to ensure their authenticity. The task force first developed a template for analysing electronic records. Gilliland-Swetland and Eppard [21] note that the template "is a model of an ideal record that, based upon prior archival knowledge of record types, contains all the possible known elements that a record may contain." In common with the UBC Project (upon which the work is based), the identification of these elements has been guided by the general principles of diplomatic theory and archival science. It is accepted that no one single record would include all of the elements identified in the template. The project has also, therefore, developed a typology of electronic records to help to identify which 'core' elements would be applicable to all electronic records.

3.4 Australian Recordkeeping Metadata Standards

Since the Pittsburgh Project, it is the Australian archives and records community that has led the way in the development of metadata schemas for recordkeeping. A research project (the Recordkeeping Metadata Project) based in the School of Information Management and Systems at Monash University has developed a general framework known as the Australian Recordkeeping Metadata Schema (RKMS). The project, amongst other things, has attempted to specify and standardise the whole range of recordkeeping metadata that would be required to manage records in digital environments [22]. It has also been concerned with supporting interoperability with more generic metadata standards like the Dublin Core and relevant information locator schemes like the Australian Government Locator Service (AGLS) scheme. The RKMS defines a highly structured set of metadata elements that conforms to a data model based on that developed for the Resource Description Framework (RDF). The schema is designed to be extensible and can inherit metadata elements from other schemas.

In addition to the conceptual frameworks and elements developed as part of the RKMS, both the National Archives of Australia (NAA) and the State Records Authority of New South Wales have published metadata standards for recordkeeping. These are, respectively, the Recordkeeping Metadata Standard for Commonwealth Agencies [23] and the NSW Recordkeeping Metadata Standard [24]. The Victorian Electronic Records Strategy (VERS) has also defined a metadata scheme for self-documenting records. This scheme [25] is designed to be compatible with the Recordkeeping Metadata Standard developed by the NAA despite being based on a different conceptual model.

4 The OAIS Reference Model

Apart from the ongoing Australian efforts to define recordkeeping metadata frameworks and standards, the one other important development has been the development of the Reference Model for an Open Archival Information System (OAIS). This resulted from a request from the International Organization for Standardization (ISO) that the Consultative Committee for Space Data Systems (CCSDS) should co-ordinate the development of standards in support of the long-term preservation of digital information obtained from observations of the terrestrial and space environments. Although the OAIS model has been primarily developed by and for the space data community, its developers hope that the model has a much wider application.

The specification defines a high-level reference model for an OAIS, which is defined as an organisation of people and systems that have "accepted the responsibility to preserve information and make it available for a designated community" [26]. The OAIS model is not just concerned with metadata. It defines and provides a framework for a range of functions that are applicable to any archive - whether digital or not. These functions include those described within the OAIS specification as ingest, archival storage, data management, administration and access. Amongst other things, the OAIS model aims to provide a common framework that can be used to help understand archival challenges and especially those that relate to digital information. This is its real value: providing a common language that can facilitate discussion across the different communities interested in digital preservation. For example, one key concept in the OAIS model is that of an Archival Information Package (AIP) consisting of a digital object together with all of its associated metadata.

As part of this framework, the OAIS model identifies and distinguishes between the different types of metadata that will need to be exchanged and managed within an OAIS. Within the draft recommendation, the broad types of metadata that will be needed are defined as part of a 'Taxonomy of Information Object Classes.' Within this taxonomy, an AIP is perceived as encapsulating two different types of information, some Content Information and any associated Preservation Description Information (PDI) that will allow the understanding of the Content Information over an indefinite period of time. The Content Information is itself divided into the Data Object itself - which would typically be a sequence of bits - and the technical Representation Information that would give meaning to this sequence. Descriptive Information that can form the basis of finding aids (and other services) can be based on the information that is stored as part of the PDI, but is logically distinct.

The OAIS taxonomy also sub-divides the PDI into four distinct groups. These are based on general concepts described in the 1996 report of the Task Force on Archiving of Digital Information commissioned by the Commission on Preservation and Access (CPA) and the Research Libraries Group (RLG). The task force [27] wrote that "in the digital environment, the features that determine information integrity and deserve special attention for archival purposes include the following: content, fixity, reference, provenance and context." Accordingly, the OAIS taxonomy divides PDI into Reference Information, Context Information, Provenance Information and Fixity Information.

The OAIS model defines Reference Information as the information that "identifies, and if necessary describes, one or more mechanisms used to provide assigned identifiers for the Content Information." Reference Information, therefore, would be a logical place to record unique identifiers. It could also be used to store basic descriptive-type information that could be used as the basis for resource discovery, although that would not be its main purpose within the PDI.

Context Information is defined as information that "documents the relationships of the Content Environment to its environment." The CPA/RLG report suggests that 'context' should include information on the technical context of a digital object, e.g. to specify its hardware and software dependencies and to record things like hypertext links in a Web document. Context could also include information relating to the mode of distribution of a particular Digital Object (e.g. whether it is networked or provided on a particular storage device) and its wider societal context.

Within the OAIS taxonomy, Provenance Information refers generally to that information that "documents the history of the Content Information." The CPA/RLG report says that the "assumption underlying the principle of provenance is that the integrity of an information object is partly embodied in tracing from where it came. To preserve the integrity of an information object, digital archives must preserve a record of its origin and chain of custody." While Provenance Information is primarily concerned with supporting the integrity of a Data Object, the information that is recorded could also provide information that could be used to help the management and use of Digital Objects stored within a repository (e.g. administrative metadata). It could also store information about the ownership of intellectual property rights that could be used to manage access to the Content Information of which it forms a part.

Fixity Information - in OAIS terms - refers to any information that documents the particular authentication mechanisms in use within a particular repository. The CPA/RLG report comments that if the content of an object is "subject to change or withdrawal without notice, then its integrity may be compromised and its value as a cultural record would be severely diminished." Changes can either be deliberate or unintentional, but both will adversely effect the integrity of a Digital Object.

It is important to remember that the OAIS is a reference model and not a blueprint for an archive implementation. The OAIS model and its taxonomy, however, have begun to influence a number of projects that have been developed by the library community. In the last section we will, therefore, turn to look at these projects and some other digital preservation initiatives that have been undertaken by the library community.

5 Library-Based Projects

Like the archives and records domain, the library community has been aware of digital preservation issues for a long time [28]. The publication of the report of the CPA/RLG Task Force on Archiving of Digital Information was a catalyst for much recent work. A study of RLG member institutions (including libraries, archives and museums) revealed that by 1998 there was an strong awareness that institutions needed to assume responsibility for the preservation of information in digital form. However, this awareness was combined with a general lack of written policies, facilities and expertise [29]. One particular focus of libraries' interest in digital preservation issues has been preservation metadata.

Part of the motivation for looking at preservation metadata is related to the development of digitisation projects. For example, in May 1997 the RLG constituted a working group on the Preservation Issues of Metadata to help identify the kinds of information that would be required to manage a digital master file over time. The primary focus of the working group was the products of digital imaging technologies. The working group published its final report in May 1998 [30]. This defined sixteen metadata elements for digital image files. A more detailed technical metadata standard for digital images is currently under review as a draft NISO (National Information Standards Organization) standard [31].

Other preservation metadata implementations have been developed by national libraries and by research projects. The most influential of these will be reviewed in the following sections.

5.1   The National Library of Australia

The National Library of Australia (NLA) has long had a keen interest in digital preservation issues. This is demonstrated by its ongoing support for and hosting of the PADI (Preserving Access to Digital Information) service [32]. In 1996, the NLA established its PANDORA (Preserving and Accessing Networked DOcumentary Resources of Australia) archive as an operational 'proof-of-concept.' With regard to metadata, descriptive metadata for each object in the PANDORA archive was stored in the NLA's own library management system; individual items being identified by means of Persistent Uniform Resource Identifiers (PURLs). The project also developed a logical data model (based on entity-relationship modelling) to help identify the particular entities (metadata) that would need to be supported [33].

Later, the NLA also developed a specification entitled *Preservation Metadata for Digital Collections*, the exposure draft of which was published in October 1999 [34]. This was based on an 'data output model,' i.e. it defined the information that a digital storage system would need to generate in order to facilitate the preservation management of digital content. The NLA metadata element set defined 25 high level elements (some with sub-elements) at three distinct levels of granularity: the collection, the object and the sub-object (here called files). The metadata specification made no assumptions about the technological strategies that would need to be adopted to preserve the object, e.g. migration or emulation.

5.2   The Cedars Project

The Cedars (CURL Exemplars in Digital Archives) project was funded by the Joint Information Systems Committee as part of Phase III of the Electronic Libraries (eLib) Programme and was managed by the Consortium of University Research Libraries (CURL). The lead sites in the project were the universities of Cambridge, Leeds and Oxford, with expertise being drawn from both computing services and libraries within the three organisations. The project's aims were to address some of the strategic, methodological and practical issues relating to digital preservation. These issues were addressed in three main project strands; one looking at digital preservation strategies and techniques, another concerned with collection development and rights management issues and a third interested in defining the metadata that would be required to adequately preserve digital information objects [35].

The work on preservation metadata got underway in 1998 with a document that reviewed existing metadata initiatives [36]. The project then created a draft metadata specification that was broadly (and explicitly) structured according to the taxonomy of information object classes described in the OAIS reference model [37]. The draft metadata element set was developed both as a scheme that could be tested in the Cedars project's demonstrator archive and as a contribution to the wider international discussion about preservation metadata. The elements identified were defined at a relatively high-level (it was assumed that some elements could be sensibly subdivided into sub-elements) and were intended to be applicable to a wide range of digital objects at any granularity.

5.3 The NEDLIB Project

The NEDLIB (Networked European Deposit Library) project ran from 1998 to 2000 and was funded by the European Commission as part of its Telematics Applications Programme. The project was a consortium of national libraries, publishers, information technology organisations and a national archive. The project developed an architectural framework for what it called a deposit system for electronic publications (DSEP) - broadly based on the OAIS model. The project also attempted to define the minimum metadata elements that would be necessary for preservation management [38]. Like the Cedars element set, the NEDLIB schema explicitly adopts the OAIS model's terminology and structure. The schema, however, was much smaller (18 elements, 38 sub-elements) than the Cedars element set because it was focussed on only identifying 'core' (or mandatory) metadata elements. It was also primarily concerned with defining metadata that would address the problem of technological obsolescence and not with metadata for descriptive, administrative or legal purposes.

5.4 The OCLC/RLG Working Group on Preservation Metadata

The exposure draft of the NLA's *Preservation Metadata Specification* was published in 1999; the Cedars and NEDLIB element sets in 2000. It was an appropriate time for a collaborative attempt at synthesis and further development. In 2000, therefore, the OCLC Online Computer Library Center and the Research Libraries Group decided to co-operate on the formation of a Working Group on Preservation Metadata. The group has an international scope and has already produced a review of the state of the art in 'Preservation Metadata for Digital Objects' [39]. Future work will include the development of a metadata framework and the identification of the metadata elements that would be required to support it. The working group will also look at developing some form of test implementation and produce some recommendations on best practice.

6 Conclusions

This review of developments in digital preservation metadata has, of necessity, covered a wide range of initiatives, but not in great detail. Some trends can be seen. There is a tendency - at least among the library projects - to focus discussion on the terminology defined by the OAIS model. This has been one of the most important results of the development of the model. Another good outcome has been the identification of some weaknesses in the OAIS model that will hopefully inform its future development. The NEDLIB project noted, for example, that while the model had identified separate entities for things like ingest, administration and archival storage, it didn't actually say much about preservation itself. The NEDLIB project, therefore, included an explicit preservation entity in its OAIS based process model for a DSEP [40]. It might also be interesting for other communities to review the OAIS model with regard to their own needs, for example from the point of view of recordkeeping metadata requirements.

Other important issues have not yet been addressed. For example, more time and effort has been expended on developing conceptual metadata specifications than in testing them in meaningful applications. This is not intended as a criticism, but is just a reflection of how experimental the digital preservation area remains. There is also little published on the expertise and skills that would be required to generate preservation metadata and, therefore, its potential cost. This could be a fruitful area for future research, but again reflects a wider uncertainty about the precise economic and societal costs of the long-term preservation of digital information.

Acknowledgements

This paper is based on work undertaken for the Cedars project (funded by the Joint Information Systems Committee) and as part of the Metadata Watch activity of the SCHEMAS project (funded by the European Commission as part of its Information Societies Technology (IST) Programme - contract no. IST-1999-10010).

References

1. Hedstrom, M.: Digital Preservation: a Time Bomb for Digital Libraries. Computers and the Humanities **31** (1998) 189-202
2. Beagrie N., Greenstein, D.: A Strategic Policy Framework for Creating and Preserving Digital Collections. Library Information Technology Centre, London (1998)
3. Ross, S.: Consensus, Communication and Collaboration: Fostering Multidisciplinary Co-operation in Electronic Records. In: Proceedings of the DLM-Forum on Electronic Records, Brussels, 18-20 December 1996. INSAR: European Archives News, Supplement II. Office for Official Publications of the European Communities, Luxembourg (1997) 330-336
4. Lynch, C.: Canonicalization: a Fundamental Tool to Facilitate Preservation and Management of Digital Information D-Lib Magazine **5** (September 1999)
   http://www.dlib.org/dlib/september99/09lynch.html
5. Day, M.: Issues and Approaches to Preservation Metadata. In: Guidelines for Digital Imaging. National Preservation Office, London (1999) 73-84
6. Dollar, C.M.: Machine-Readable Records of the Federal Government and the National Archives. In: Geda, C.L., Austin, E.W., Blouin, F.X. (eds.): Archivists and Machine-Readable Records. Society of American Archivists, Chicago, Ill. (1980) 79-88
7. Bearman, D.: Electronic Evidence: Strategies for Managing Records in Contemporary Organizations. Archives and Museum Informatics, Pittsburgh, Pa. (1994)

8. O'Shea, G.: Keeping Electronic Records: Issues and Strategies. *Provenance* **1** (March 1996) http://www.netpac.com/provenance/vol1/no2/features/erecs1a.htm

9. McDonald, J.: Managing Information in an Office Systems Environment: the IMOSA Project. American Archivist **58** (1995) 142-153

10. Blake, R.: Overview of the Electronic Records in Office Systems (EROS) Programme. In: Electronic Access: Archives in the New Millennium. Public Record Office, London (1998) 52-58

11. Binns, S.E., Bowen, D.V., Murdock, A.: Migration Strategies Within an Electronic Archive: Practical Experience and Future Research. Archives and Museum Informatics **11** (1997) 301-306

12. McKemmish, S., Parer, D.: Towards Frameworks for Standardising Recordkeeping Metadata. Archives and Manuscripts **26** (1998) 24-45

13. Duff, W.: Ensuring the Preservation of Reliable Evidence: a Research Project Funded by the NHPRC. Archivaria **42** (1996) 28-45

14. Cox, R.J.: More than Diplomatic: Functional Requirements for Evidence in Recordkeeping. Records Management Journal **7** (1997) 21-30

15. Bearman, D., Duff, W.: Grounding Archival Description in the Functional Requirements for Evidence. Archivaria **41** (1996) 275-303

16. Bearman, D., Sochats, K.: Metadata Requirements for Evidence. University of Pittsburgh, School of Information Science, Pittsburgh, Pa. (1996) http://www.lis.pitt.edu/~nhprc/BACartic.html

17. Cunningham, A.: Journey to the End of the Night: Custody and the Dawning of a New Era on the Archival Threshold. Archives and Manuscripts **24** (1996) 312-321

18. Duranti, L.: The Preservation of the Integrity of Electronic Records. In: Proceedings of the DLM-Forum on Electronic Records, Brussels, 18-20 December 1996. INSAR: European Archives News, Supplement II. Office for Official Publications of the European Communities, Luxembourg (1997) 60-65

19. MacNeil, H.: Metadata Strategies and Archival Description: Comparing Apples to Oranges. *Archivaria* **39** (1995) 11-21

20. Duranti, L.: Reliability and Authenticity: the Concepts and their Implications. Archivaria **39** (1995) 5-10

21. Gilliland-Swetland, A.J., Eppard, P.B.: Preserving the Authenticity of Contingent Digital Objects: the InterPARES project. D-Lib Magazine, **6** (2000) http://www.dlib.org/dlib/july00/eppard/07eppard.html

22. McKemmish, S., Acland, G., Reed, B.: Towards a Framework for Standardising Recordkeeping Metadata: the Australian Recordkeeping Metadata Schema. Records Management Journal **9** (1999)

23. National Archives of Australia: Recordkeeping Metadata Standard for Commonwealth Agencies, version 1.0. National Archives of Australia, Canberra (1999) http://www.naa.gov.au/recordkeeping/control/rkms/summary.htm

24. State Records Authority of New South Wales: New South Wales Recordkeeping Metadata Standard (NRKMS). State Records Authority of New South Wales, Sydney (2000) http://www.records.nsw.gov.au/publicsector/erk/metadata/rkmetadata.htm

25. Public Record Office Victoria: Standard for the Management of Electronic Records, version 1.0. PROS 99/007. Public Record Office Victoria, Melbourne, (April 2000) http://www.prov.vic.gov.au/gservice/standard/pros9907.htm

26. Consultative Committee for Space Data Systems: Reference Model for an Open Archival Information System (OAIS), Red Book, Issue 1. CCSDS 650.0-R-1. CCSDS Secretariat, National Aeronautics and Space Administration, Washington, D.C. (1999) http://ssdoo.gsfc.nasa.gov/nost/isoas/ref_model.html

27. Garrett, J., Waters, D. (eds.): Preserving Digital Information: Report of the Task Force on Archiving of Digital Information. Commission on Preservation and Access, Washington, D.C. (1996) http://www.rlg.org/ArchTF/
28. Neavill, G.B.: Electronic Publishing, Libraries, and the Survival of Information. Library Resources and Technical Services **28** (1984) 76-89
29. Hedstrom, M., Montgomery, S.: Digital Preservation Needs and Requirements in RLG Member Institutions. Research Libraries Group, Mountain View, Calif. (1998) http://www.rlg.org/preserv/digpres.html
30. RLG Working Group on Preservation Issues of Metadata: Final Report. Research Libraries Group, Mountain View, Calif. (1998) http://www.rlg.org/preserv/presmeta.html
31. National Information Standards Organization: Data Dictionary: Technical Metadata for Digital Still Images. National Information Standards Organization, Bethesda, Md. (2000)
32. National Library of Australia: Preserving Access to Digital Information (PADI). National Library of Australia, Canberra http://www.nla.gov.au/padi/
33. National Library of Australia: PANDORA Logical Data Model, Version 2. National Library of Australia, Canberra (10 November 1997) http://www.nla.gov.au/pandora/ldmv2.html
34. Phillips, M., Woodyard, D., Bradley, K., Webb, C.: Preservation Metadata for Digital Collections: Exposure Draft. National Library of Australia, Canberra (1999) http://www.nla.gov.au/preserve/pmeta.html
35. Russell, K.: Digital Preservation and the Cedars Project Experience. New Review of Academic Librarianship **6** (2000) 139-154
36. Day, M.: Metadata for Preservation. UKOLN, the UK Office for Library and Information Networking, Bath (1998) http://www.ukoln.ac.uk/metadata/cedars/AIW01.html
37. Russell, K., Sergeant, D., Stone, A., Weinberger, E., Day, M.: Metadata for Digital Preservation. Cedars Project, Leeds (2000) http://www.leeds.ac.uk/cedars/metadata.html
38. Lupovici, C., Masanès, J.: Metadata for the Long Term Preservation of Electronic Publications. NEDLIB Report Series, 2. Koninklijke Bibliotheek, The Hague (2000)
39. OCLC/RLG Working Group on Preservation Metadata: Preservation Metadata for Digital Objects: a Review of the State of the Art. OCLC Online Computer Library Center, Dublin, Ohio (2000) http://www.oclc.org/digitalpreservation/wgdeliver.htm
40. Werf, T. van der: The Deposit System for Electronic Publications: a process model. NEDLIB Report Series, 6. Koninklijke Bibliotheek, The Hague (2000)

MARIAN: Flexible Interoperability for Federated Digital Libraries

Marcos André Gonçalves, Robert K. France and Edward A. Fox

Department of Computer Science
Virginia Tech
Blacksburg, VA 24061, USA
{mgoncalv,france,fox}@vt.edu

Abstract. Federated digital libraries are composed of distributed, autonomous, and often heterogeneous information services but provide users with a transparent, integrated view of collected information. In this paper we discuss a federated system for the Networked Digital Library of Theses and Dissertations (NDLTD), an international consortium of universities, libraries, and other supporting institutions focused on electronic theses and dissertations (ETDs). Federation requires dealing flexibly with differences among systems, ontologies, and data formats while respecting information sources' autonomy. Our solution involves adapting the object-oriented digital library system MARIAN to serve as mediation middleware for the federated NDLTD collection. Components of the solution include: 1) the use and integration of several harvesting techniques; 2) an architecture based on object-oriented ontologies of search modules and metadata; 3) reconciliation of diversity within the harvested data joined to a single collection view for the user; and 4) an integrated framework for addressing such questions as data quality, flexible and efficient search, and scalability.

Introduction

Networked or federated digital libraries are composed of autonomous, possibly heterogeneous information services, distributed across the Internet [14, 10]. The goal of federation is to provide users with a transparent, integrated view of such sources of information. Challenges faced include interoperability amongst different digital library systems/protocols [22], resource discovery (selection of the best sites to be searched) [12], and issues in data fusion (merging of results into a unique ranked list). In this paper we focus on the interoperability problem, one of the most challenging in the field of digital libraries. Heterogeneity occurs in both information representation and services, and must be addressed at four basic levels: system, structural, syntactic, and semantic [20].

One federated digital library where heterogeneity is a major problem is the Networked Digital Library of Theses and Dissertations [23], an international federation of universities, libraries, and other supporting institutions focused on efforts related to electronic theses and dissertations (ETDs). NDLTD has particular characteristics that complicate interoperability across member systems:

P. Constantopoulos and I.T. Sølvberg (Eds.): ECDL 2001, LNCS 2163, pp. 173-186, 2001.
© Springer-Verlag Berlin Heidelberg 2001

1. **Autonomy:** Members manage most services for their scholars.
2. **Decentralization:** Members are not (yet) asked to report either collection updates or changes in their metadata to central coordinators.
3. **Minimal interoperability:** Each source must provide unique URNs and metadata records for all stored works, but need not (yet) support the same standards or protocols.
4. **Heterogeneity:** Members differ in language, metadata, protocols, repository technologies, character coding, nature of data (structured, semi-structured and unstructured, multimedia), user characteristics, preferences, and capabilities.
5. **Massive amount of data and dynamism:** NDLTD already has over 100 members and eventually aims to support all those that will produce ETDs. New members are constantly added and there is a continuing flow of new data as theses and dissertations are submitted.

Due to the primary-source nature of ETD collections, the site selection process that is found in other systems (identifying a small number of candidate databases to search) is not always important here. For example, a query asking for new results in mathematics could retrieve information from almost every member university.

1. Federated Systems: Remote Search vs. Local Union

Transparent interoperability involves reconciling heterogeneity and integrating information sources at several levels [2]. A common architecture to deal with this problem uses mediators and wrappers [30]. Mediators export a common data model and provide a common query interface. Wrappers overcome some barriers of heterogeneity and produce source-specific queries. Wrappers also translate results between source and mediator data models. Within the mediated architecture there are two possible approaches to system integration [8]: 1) the union archive and 2) federated search.

In the union archive approach [26], information is periodically extracted from each source, processed, merged with information from other sources, and then loaded into a centralized data store – the union archive. Queries are posed against the local data without further interaction with the original sources. The main advantage of this approach is that adequate performance can be guaranteed at query time. On the other hand, union archives cannot guarantee delivery of the most current information to users. Concerns about data quality and consistency also must be addressed.

In the federated search solution, data remains at the sources and queries to the integrated system are decomposed at run time into queries to those sources. Data is not replicated and is guaranteed to be fresh at query time. On the other hand, more sophisticated query optimization and fusion techniques are required. Performance is also a drawback (see, e.g., [25]). Such factors must be considered as network latency and availability, amount of data to be transferred, etc. Overall performance is bounded by the worst-case situation.

In this paper we present MARIAN, an object-oriented digital library system, and demonstrate how we have used its modular architecture, flexible data model, and powerful search mechanism to create a federated system for NDLTD while addressing the problems described above. Due to poor and inconsistent network connectivities in the global NDLTD, variability in server load and administration, and the complexity of query translations in such a heterogeneous environment, we have chosen a union archive architecture for our integrated system. Components of our solution include: 1) the use and integration of several harvesting techniques; 2) a mediated union archive collection based on object-oriented ontologies of search modules and metadata; 3) a *collection view* mechanism for network representations comparable to database views; and 4) an integrated framework for addressing such questions as data quality, flexible and efficient search, and scalability. We use the unique characteristics of our system to build a common integrated solution for interoperability inside a unified framework.

2. The MARIAN Digital Library System

MARIAN is a search system for digital libraries [5, 7]. Originally designed for library catalogs, it has been used successfully for collections of varying sizes and structures, and has been enhanced to support digital library and semantic web [27] applications.

The MARIAN data model combines three powerful concepts. First, structure and relationships in MARIAN collections are captured in the form of an *information network* of explicit nodes and links. Similar graph-based models have proven effective in representing semi-structured data and Web documents [1], and for translating among different DL systems [17]. Second, MARIAN expands this model by insisting that the nodes and links of a collection graph be members of object-oriented *classes*. Classes are an organizing method similar to link labels in semi-structured graphs, but are strictly more powerful because they form a full lattice of subsets and can support inheritance. Furthermore, since nodes in the collection graph are instances of *information object* classes, they can support complex behaviors. In particular, they can support approximate matching of the sort pioneered in information retrieval (IR) systems. Third, nodes or links can be *weighted* to represent how well they suit some description or fulfill some role.

MARIAN is specialized for a universe where searching is distributed over a large graph of information objects. The output of a search operation is a *weighted set* of objects whose relationship to some external proposition is encoded in their (decreasing) weight within the set. Weights are used in IR, probabilistic reasoning systems, and fuzzy set theory. Our model grounds them firmly in a framework of weighted set operations [6] and extends them throughout the entire MARIAN system.

The use of object-oriented data and process abstractions in MARIAN helps to achieve physical and logical independence − common and useful concepts in the database field oft neglected in IR. Most current IR systems emphasize the physical level of term indexes and weight metrics, making it difficult to integrate systems at a conceptual level [11]. The flexibility of MARIAN's data model allows it to be used for object-oriented or semi-structured databases, knowledge representation, or IR. Its power comes from the smooth combination of a number of successful concepts from such fields and programming languages or artificial intelligence [9].

3. Harvesting Approaches

Any union archive approach includes: 1) mechanisms to gather or harvest data from the sources, and 2) some way of combining gathered data for use. This section covers harvesting approaches; Section 4 describes our architecture for combining harvested data.

Electronic theses and dissertations (ETDs) are large, sometimes archived in the form of several files. Many authors include multimedia material that would be difficult or impossible to include in printed publications. In response to this, a *de facto* standard has emerged at NDLTD sites of requiring a structured *title page* to serve both as directory to document files and as a convenient point for collecting and publishing metadata. Title page metadata are created by the author, usually with minimal oversight. At some sites additional metadata are added by trained catalogers. We choose to harvest all metadata – both controlled and uncontrolled – to create images of the sites in the union archive.

Much current work on federated DLs assumes a homogeneous structure or protocol (e.g., Dienst [14] or Z39.50 [16]) or a single means of harvesting (e.g., of HTML documents on the Web). In contrast, we work with several paradigms for harvesting data from heterogeneous sites, including the paradigms of the Open Archives Initiative and Harvest[TM]. In addition, a variety of data has been harvested using ad-hoc source-oriented approaches. The three approaches differ in the support they require from source archives.

The Open Archives Initiative (OAI) [15] is a multi-institutional project to address interoperability of archives and digital libraries by defining simple protocols for the exchange of metadata. The current OAI technical infrastructure is expressed by the Metadata Harvesting Protocol, which defines mechanisms for archives to expose and export their metadata. The OAI framework promotes an effective partial solution for interoperability, but particular archives must agree to implement the protocol and to export their metadata in a supported standard, which creates impedance to the solution. OAI emphasizes the distinction between data providers and service providers. The former manages a resource such as an e-print archive, acting on behalf of the authors who submit documents. The latter is a third party, creating end-user services based on data in archives.

The Harvest[TM] system [3] is a set of integrated tools for harvesting information from diverse repositories and building topic-specific content indexes. The architecture of the system is based on two main components: *gatherers* and *brokers*. Gatherers act as directed crawlers that collect and extract indexing and meta-information from repositories extracting summaries of content into a specific proprietary format (SOIF). Brokers provide the indexing and the query interface to the gathered information. They retrieve information from one or more Gatherers or other Brokers and incrementally update indexes. Although no metadata standard is enforced, external metadata standards (e.g., Dublin Core) can be incorporated.

We have faced situations where we cannot use any of these approaches, but where specific ways to gather data from sources exist. For example, in sources that use the Dienst protocol, specific combinations of services allow harvesting their data. The obvious drawback to ad hoc conversions is that they require development of specific solutions that are strongly dependent on the source.

4. The NDLTD Union Archive

In the prototype union collection described here, we have harvested metadata from four sources, each with its own formats. Table 1 summarizes the characteristics of each.

Collection	Harvesting Protocol	No. of records	Metadata format
PhysDis-ETD	Harvest	1256	SOIF – All DublinCore – 166
VT-ETD	OAI Z39.50	2427	ETD-MS – All MARC – All
MIT-ETD	Dienst	5000	RFC1807 – All

Table 1. Collections in the prototype union archive and their characteristics.

Just as there are many differences among institutions participating in NDLTD, there also are differences among the collections, especially regarding document format and access protocols. NDLTD did not specify standard formats or access protocols for documents or metadata. Although the adoption of standards is encouraged for NDLTD, it will be some time until a complete standardization takes place. Consequently our current union collection must cope with a multiplicity of formats, systems, protocols, etc.

Also, different collections support different document attributes and represent those attributes with different structures of data. Similar structures can be given different names by different sources, and structures with similar names may have very different semantics. For example, MARC records in the VT-ETD collection make a strong distinction between personal and corporate authors, while the *dc.creator* field of Dublin Core records may contain either. Again, some documents from the PhysDis collection are represented with Dublin Core metadata, including *dc.subject*, while others describe subjects with lists of automatically extracted keywords.

Thus, heterogeneity has several dimensions and induces four levels of interoperability concerns [20]: 1) system: which involves for example differences in harvesting protocols; 2) syntactic: including machine-dependable aspects of data representation; 3) structural: involving representational heterogeneity; and 4) semantic: with all the complexities related to meanings, significations, uncertainty, etc. In the following, we present how we use the unique characteristics of MARIAN to build an interoperability architecture that attacks each level of interoperability.

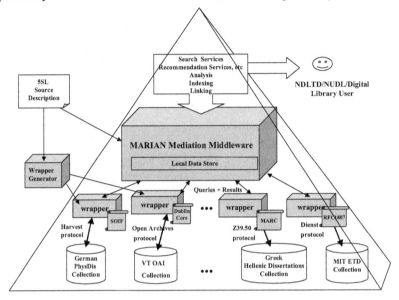

Fig. 1. The NDLTD Union Archive Architecture

4.1 MARIAN's Interoperability Architecture

The architecture of our system is presented in Fig. 1. The MARIAN Mediation Middleware provides the tools for structural and semantic interoperability. System and syntactic differences are addressed by wrapping sources with special software modules. Our 5SL language for declarative specification of digital libraries is used to describe capabilities of remote collections and their internal document structures. This information feeds data structures inside the mediator and allows semi-automatic generation of wrappers for harvested sources. Extended value-added services like searching, browsing, recommendation, personalization, and visualization are built on the top of the middleware.

4.2 System and Syntactic Interoperability

The harvesting process itself serves as a device to suppress some differences in source systems such as indexes and formatting, and helps towards systemic and syntactic homogenization. For example, textual information in different languages with different encodings can be locally homogenized to some standard like Unicode or UTF-8. Once we have harvested metadata from each remote collection and built local images for each, we can treat the local data with a unified set of text parsing, indexing and retrieval tools. Document (metadata) text fields such as *title, abstract,* or *body* are reduced to their individual terms using the same set of parsers, then matched to users' queries using the same search algorithms and ranking formula. This way we can ensure that the smallest atomic components, the text fields, will receive uniform treatment.

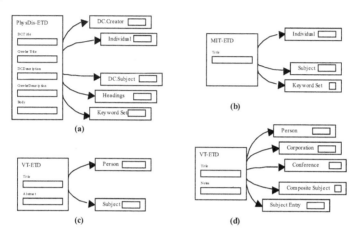

Figure 2. Images for (a) the SOIF PhysDis collection, (b) the RFC1807 MIT collection, (c) the ETD-MS VT collection, and (d) the MARC VT collection, all represented as class networks. Upward-curving links are (subclasses of) *HasAuthor* links; downward links, *HasSubject* links.

4.3 Structural Interoperability

Mediators map different representations of heterogeneous data sources to a common data model. Like many current approaches for data integration/mediation [4, 19], we use MARIAN's network representation to overcome structural heterogeneity, capturing the structure of the remote collections as faithfully as possible. Figure 2 represents the document structures in each of our experimental collections.

In contrast to other network approaches, MARIAN's nodes and links are associated with object-oriented classes, which give us three major advantages. First, instead of using a single global searcher for the entire network, nodes and links are partitioned among class managers for a marked decrease in search complexity. Second, indexing and search are regarded as functional aspects of the classes, and thus can capitalize on regularities of the class. Third, the hierarchy of classes and search mechanisms provide a basis for the next phase of resolution of semantic interoperability.

4.4 Semantic Interoperability

Semantic heterogeneity is solved by exploiting two further MARIAN mechanisms: 1) semantically "tuned" but functionally equivalent searchers, and 2) a *collection view* ontology.

Nodes in the MARIAN information network can be simple atomic or scalar objects, as in the semi-structured model, but also they can be complex information objects. Information objects support methods proper to their classes, and all information objects in MARIAN support the method of approximate match to a query. For instance, MARIAN treats title text as a special sort of natural language sequence, with various rules for capitalization, punctuation, and sentence formation, but treats person's names as sequences of atomic strings. Matching methods vary from class to class but all have the same functional profile: given an object description of the appropriate type, they calculate how closely they match the description and return that value as a weight. Class managers draw on these methods to provide class-level search functions that, given an object description, return a weighted set of objects in the class that match the description. MARIAN already has stock matching functions and searchers for a number of common information object classes, a sample of which are shown in Fig.3.

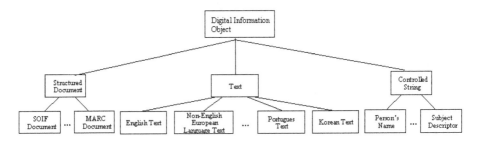

Figure 3. Part of the hierarchy of classes used in MARIAN.

Thus the first step in bringing a new document collection into semantic interoperability is to choose appropriate matching functions and searchers for the different objects in the collection. Since class managers and searchers are object-oriented, specialized versions can often be easily created through inheritance. For truly different information objects new matching functions sometimes need to be defined, but even in this case stock searcher algorithms can often be reused. All that is necessary is to provide methods that follow the API of taking an object description to a weight or weighted set of objects.

Once a local image has been defined for an NDLTD member collection a view can be constructed. This involves defining a mapping to the member collection classes from a supported view. Such a mapping may use any combination of linking, inheritance and weighting. In the remainder of this paper we concentrate on one mechanism that has proven powerful and useful in NDLTD: the creation of synthetic weighted superclasses.

In NDLTD we are fortunate that a complementary interoperability effort [http://www.ndltd.org/standards/metadata/] has developed a metadata standard for electronic theses and dissertations (ETD-MS). Mapped into an information network model, this standard provides a stable view to the outside world for the union collection. A subset of the ETD-MS view is presented in Figure 4; to keep things simple we show only the attributes *title, creator, subject*, and *description*. The view ontology consists of three classes of objects, *ThesisDissertation, Individual* and *Subject*, together with *HasAuthor* and *HasSubject* links. The *Individual* class subsumes both persons and corporate individuals, while the *Subject* class covers diverse treatments. Mappings between the view and the underlying structures can be modified seamlessly.

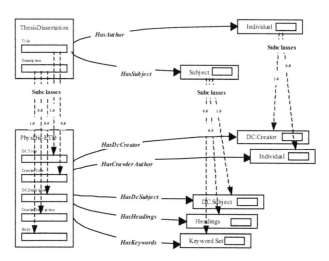

Figure 4. A collection view is abstracted from the PhysDis data to increase retrieval and usability.

In the case of the ETD-MS view of the PhysDis collection shown in Figure 4, all mappings make use of the weighted superclass construction. This construction asserts that all members of some specific class also are members of some view class, but that the extent to which they count as class members is different for different subclasses. In the case of PhysDis subject descriptions, subclass relationships are weighted to reflect the authority of the description. In the next section we discuss the use of weights to address data quality issues. These uses interact, and the simple construct of synthetic superclasses with weighted subclasses cannot handle every situation, but we have found it strikingly effective.

4.5. Combining Heterogeneous Collections and Merging Ontologies

A direct approach for combining collection images into a union collection is depicted in Figure 5. This solution involves a fair amount of redundancy. For instance, several source images include classes for *Individual* and *Subject.* Such redundancy raises a design issue: what should be the ontology for the overall union collection?

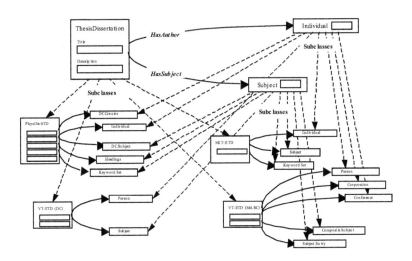

Figure 5. A direct approach for the union collection relates the views and images.

Figure 5 embodies one extreme where all the images are completely separate and only subclass-superclass relationships tie the object classes together. This approach has the disadvantage of data duplication: the same object (e.g., the subject heading "Computer Engineering") appears in several classes. Such redundancy wastes storage space in the class managers, and increases retrieval time when multiple classes are searched.

At the other extreme, we could immediately force all harvested data into our collection view by processing all incoming documents into structures with a single title and a single description field, all types of individuals into a single class, and all types of subjects and keyword lists into a class of subject strings. This would have the disadvantage of forcing us to combine fields as unlike as the PhysDis *Body* and *dc.description* fields into a single text, with corresponding losses to indexing specificity. It also would mean losing the information that sometimes we *do* know when an individual is a person, or when a subject heading comes from a controlled vocabulary.

Most importantly, however, pre-processing incoming data into the collection view ontology would mean giving up the ability to adjust to changing circumstances. Once our image of a remote collection has been cooked, we can no longer reconstruct it in its raw state. On the other hand, the more original structure we retain, the better we can react to changes in the original collection, to addition of new collections, and especially to changes in semantic requirements.

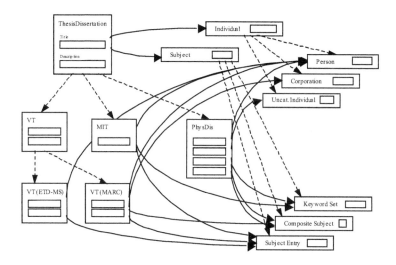

Figure 6. A more sensitive approach to the union catalog allows semantically similar object classes to overlap.

Between these two extremes lies a third alternative: merge image classes when these have sufficiently similar semantics, but keep classes separate when the semantics are different. Figure 6 shows this approach for the four images in the NDLTD union collection. The document hierarchy is as before. The *Individual* class has been analyzed into classes of (human) *Persons* and *Corporations*. SOIF, RFC1807 and Dublin Core author fields and MARC x00 fields, all of which require the name of a human person, are mapped to *HasAuthor* links to the *Person* class, while the MARC x10 fields produce links to the Corporation class. An *UncategorizedIndividual* class provides an image for those formats that make no such distinction, like the uncontrolled *author* field of the PhysDis collection. A similar breakdown of the *Subject* superclass into individual subject entries, composite strings with multiple entries, and sets of keywords provides image classes for all types of subject fields in the union collection. This approach simplifies the union collection ontology, with corresponding benefits in administration time and effort. It also saves string storage and retrieval time and adds functionality.

5. Solution Analysis

Combining weights, networks, and class structures enables us to both respect the data as it is harvested and provide simplified virtual collection views to users. It also makes it easy to change either the collection ontology or the underlying data without changing the view presented to the user, or to change the view presented to the user without restructuring the underlying representation or data. Moreover, it provides a unified framework to enhance retrieval effectiveness in the union archive system by providing the flexibility to use different configurations and priorities on the same underlying data. In this section, we consider some properties we consider essential in any solution for interoperability.

5.1 Data Quality Issues

Data quality issues arise when one wants to correct anomalies occurring inside the integrated union archive to improve effectiveness of services. Examples of anomalies include errors in data, imprecision, multiplicity of representations, etc. In our architecture, we use MARIAN's weighting scheme as a way to mitigate data quality discrepancies.

The PhysDis collection provides a good example of the use of weights to enhance data quality. Each text class in the view corresponds to two or three classes in the underlying collection: a Dublin Core class and at least one uncontrolled class (Fig. 5). Our observations of the data indicate that the Dublin Core texts are of better quality than the uncontrolled texts. The superclass searchers capitalize on this by giving more weight to DC subclasses. In addition, the *Description* superclass depends more heavily on the PhysDis *Body* attribute than on either DC or uncontrolled description attributes, because we have observed that *Body* text tends to be a better representation of document content. All of these weights can be tuned with the increasing of experience with the union collection and with empirical experiments.

5.2 Efficiency

As seen, each MARIAN class manager functions as a searcher for objects in that class. All the searchers needed for the union archive are of five standard types: superclass searchers, text and structured document searchers, and weighted and absolute link searchers. The searchers are designed for optimal efficiency using three rubrics:

1. *Use all available information about the inputs*: searching can be a costly operation. Under certain circumstances, however, we can use information about the incoming sets to achieve better performance
2. *Capitalize on the power-law distribution*: Our observations of links in text and among digital library objects indicate that like small-world networks [29] they follow power-law distributions. Whenever possible, the MARIAN searchers are designed to run most efficiently when their inputs follow this distribution.
3. *Be lazy*: All searchers in the MARIAN community are designed to do only the work required to return as many elements as are requested. By design and construction, the first elements developed by any searcher are those with the highest weight. Lazy evaluation has its greatest pay-off in simple searches authored by human users, few of whom are interested in digesting more than a few dozen objects.

MARIAN searchers have been used for collections of up to a million objects and tens of millions of links, most noticeably in a "shadow" of the Virginia Tech academic library [7]. Response times for simple queries on collections of this size are comparable to other Net searchers, and remain acceptable for more complex queries.

Research is currently under way to measure performance on collections of hundreds of millions of objects, and to verify the power-law model and its implications for searcher efficiency.

5.3 Scalability

Scalability, i.e., the ability to transparently and effectively grow a system, is a major concern in any platform based on integration of external sources. As important as large capacity are scalable query processing and the ability to incorporate new sources.

Just as analyzed objects are represented in MARIAN by graphs, queries are represented by relaxations of graphs and are processed following their structure. Elements of a MARIAN query are distributed to their governing class managers. Each class manager disassembles the portion of the query it receives; any parts it cannot handle are passed to others. Thus, an author / title search over the entire collection begins at the *Thesis-Dissertation* class. The title portion of the query is handled locally, but the author portion is passed to the link class manager for *HasAuthor* links, which passes the operation of finding matching people or corporations to the *Individual* class manager. Since query processing is distributed, it avoids evaluation bottlenecks and easily can be extended.

Easy incorporation of new sources is achieved by a mechanism for semi-automatically generating wrappers. Harvesting itself tremendously facilitates creating wrappers and communication with the mediator. In contrast to wrappers from other DL interoperation projects, which are *query processing oriented*, our wrappers are oriented towards *schema* and *ontological equivalence*. We have been using 5SL, a domain-specific language with a formal basis [13] designed for automatic generation of digital libraries, for describing external sources' capabilities for harvesting purposes. We describe external sources by their metadata structures and the correspondent harvesting protocols as scenarios (abstract sequences of events) that occur between the harvester/wrappers and the sources. Template wrappers can be configured (e.g., for periodicity of harvesting, additional mirrored repositories, or maximum number of harvesters acting at the same time). The wrappers currently in use in the union catalog, while originally crafted by hand, have since been successfully generated automatically from 5SL descriptions.

References

[1] Abiteboul, S., Buneman, P. Suciu, D., *Data on the Web: from relations to semistructured data and XML*. Morgan Kaufmann, 1999
[2] Adam, N., Atluri, V., Adiwijaya, I., "Systems Integration in Digital Libraries", *Communications of the ACM*, **43**(6), 2000, pp. 64-72
[3] Bowman, C. M., Danzig, P. B., Hardy, D. R., Manber, U., Schwartz, M. F., "The Harvest information discovery and access system", *Computer Networks and ISDN Systems*, **28**(1–2), 1995, pp. 119–126

[4] Fernandez, M. F., Florescu, D., Levy, A. Y., Suciu, D. "Declarative Specification of Web Sites with Strudel". *VLDB Journal* 9(1): 38-55 (2000)

[5] Fox, E.A., R.K. France, E. Sahle, A.M. Daoud, and B.E. Cline,"Development of a Modern OPAC: From REVTOLC to MARIAN". *Proc. 16th Int. ACM SIGIR Conf.*, 1993: pp. 248-259

[6]France, R.K.   "Weights and Measures: an Axiomatic Approach to Similarity Computations".   Internal   report,   Virginia   Tech,   1995; http://www.dlib.vt.edu/repors/WeightsMeasures.pdf

[7] France, R.K., L.T. Nowell, E.A. Fox, R.A. Saad, and J. Zhao: "Use and usability in a digital library search system." CoRR cs.DL/9902013:

[8] Florescu, D., Levy, A., Mendelzon, A. "Database techniques for the World-Wide Web: A Survey", *SIGMOD Record*. **27**(3) 1998, pp. 59-74

[9] Fuhr, N., Rolleke, T., "A Probabilistic Relational Algebra for the Integration of Information retrieval and Database Systems",.ACM Transactions on Information Systems, Vol. 15, No. 1, January, 1997, Pg. 32--66.

[10] Fuhr, N. "A Decision-Theoretic Approach to Database Selection in Networked IR". *ACM Transactions on Information Systems* 17(3): 229-249 (1999)

[11] Fuhr, N., "Towards Data Abstraction in Networked Information Retrieval Systems", *Information Processing and Management* 35(2): 101-119 (1999)

[12] Gravano, L., Garcia-Molina, H, "Merging Ranks from Heterogeneous Internet Sources", *Proc. of the 23rd International Conference on Very Large Databases, 1997*, pp. 196-205

[13] Gonçalves, M.A., Kipp, N.A., Fox, E.A., Watson,L.T., "Streams, Structures, Spaces, Scenarios and Societies(5S): A Formal Model for Digital Libraries",Tech. Rep.,Virginia Tech, 2001.

[14]Lagoze, C., Fielding, D., Payette, S., "Making Digital Libraries Work: Collection, Services, Connectivity Regions, and Collection Views",*Proc. 3rd ACM Digital Libraries*.1998, pp.134-143

[15] Lagoze. C., Sompel, H. V., "The Open Archives Initiative", Proc. of the First ACM-IEEE The Joint Conference on Digital Libraries, Roanoke, Virginia, 2001.

[16] Lynch, C., "The Z39.50 Information Retrieval Standard - Part I: A Strategic View of Its Past, Present and Future", *D-Lib Magazine*, April 1997.

[17] Melnik, S., H. Garcia-Molina and A. Paepcke, "A Mediation infrastructure for digital library services" *Proc. 5th ACM Digital Libraries, San Antonio, 2000* pp.123-132.

[19] McBrien, P., Poulovassilis, A., "Automatic Migration and Wrapping of Database Applications - A Schema Transformation Approach". ER 1999: 96-113

[20] Ouksel, A. M., Sheth, A. P., "Semantic Interoperability in Global Information Systems:A Brief Introduction to the Research Area" *SIGMOD Record* 28(1):5-12 1999

[22] Paepcke, A., Chang, C. K., Winograd, T., Garcia-Molina, H., "Interoperability for digital libraries worldwide." *Communications of the ACM* **41**(4), 1998, pp. 33–42.

[23] Phanouriou, C., Kipp, N. A., Sornil, O., Mather, P., Fox, E. A.,"A Digital Library for Authors: Recent Progress of the NDLTD", *Proc. 4th ACM Digital Libraries*, 1999, pp. 20-27

[25] Powell, A.L. and J.C. French, "Growth and server availability of the NCSTRL digital library." *Proc. 5th ACM Conf. On Digital Libraries (San Antonio, June 2-7, 2000)* pp. 264-265.

[26] Rundensteiner, E., Koeller, A., and Zhang, X., "Maintaining Data Warehouses over Changing Information Sources", *Communications of the ACM*, **43**(6), 2000, pp. 57-62

[27] Semantic Web Activity; http://www.w3.org/2001/sw/

[29] Watts,D. J.,"*Small Worlds:The Dynamics of Networks between Order and Randomness*", Princeton Univ. Press, 1999.

[30] Wiederhold,G.,"Mediators in the Architecture of Future Information Systems",*IEEE Computer*,**25**(3),1992, pg. 38-49.

Digital Libraries: A Generic Classification and Evaluation Scheme

Norbert Fuhr[1], Preben Hansen[2], Michael Mabe[3], Andras Micsik[4], and
Ingeborg Sølvberg[5]

[1] University of Dortmund, Germany.
`fuhr@cs.uni-dortmund.de`
[2] Swedish Institute of Computer Science, Kista, Sweden.
`preben@sics.se`
[3] Elsevier Science Ltd., Oxford, UK.
`m.mabe@elsevier.co.uk`
[4] MTA SZTAKI, Budapest, Hungary.
`micsik@sztaki.hu`
[5] Norwegian University of Science and Technology, Trondheim, Norway.
`Ingeborg.Solvberg@idi.ntnu.no`

Abstract. Evaluation of digital libraries (DLs) is essential for further development in this area. Whereas previous approaches were restricted to certain facets of the problem, we argue that evaluation of DLs should be based on a broad view of the subject area. For this purpose, we develop a new description scheme using four major dimensions: data/collection, system/technology, users, and usage. For each of these dimensions, we describe the major attributes. Using this scheme, existing DL test beds can be characterised. For this purpose, we have performed a survey by means of a questionnaire, which is now continued by setting up a DL meta-library.

1 Introduction and Background

"What is a digital library?" The answer depends upon whom you are asking. This is even truer if you ask, "What is a *good* digital library". Several research disciplines (e.g. library science, computer science, sociology) and groups of practitioners (e.g. publishers, librarians) are interested in and make contributions to digital libraries (DLs). Each of them has a different view on DLs, and is focusing on those aspects that are relevant from that specific viewpoint.

1.1 Digital Libraries and Evaluations

[1] identifies two "schools" which have different views and approaches towards DLs; the research community and the (traditional) library community.

The research community focuses upon the information content that are collected and organised in order to fulfil the needs of (selected) user groups; i.e. digital objects, architecture, and usage.

P. Constantopoulos and I.T. Sølvberg (Eds.): ECDL 2001, LNCS 2163, pp. 187–199, 2001.

Digital Libraries are concerned with the creation and management of information resources, the movement of information across global networks and the effective use of this information by a wide range of users. [From the introduction in the first issue of "International Journal on Digital Libraries", 1997]

The library community looks upon DLs as institutions or organisations that offer information services in digital form, and how existing structures can adapt to new technology and new challenges.

DLs are organisations that provide the resources, including the specialised staff, to select, structure, offer intellectual access to, interpret, distribute, preserve the integrity of, and ensure the persistence over time of collections of digital works so that they are readily and economically available for use by a defined community or set of communities. [Digital Library Federation (DLF), 1998]

The definition of a DL varies, and that is reflected in the questions on evaluation of DLs:

- What can be evaluated?
  For example, a librarian may focus on the collection, whereas a computer scientist may be interested in the technological aspects only, irrespective of the content of a DL. On the other hand, an institution wanting to subscribe to a DL may want to choose the best among several DLs with similar content, thus taking a user-oriented view on a DL.
- What and how to measure?
  Some system designers may focus on the efficiency of a DL system (i.e. usage of computational resources), whereas others are interested in effectiveness. For the latter, one could e.g. consider relevance only and apply the standard information retrieval measures of precision and recall; a broader view would look at typical tasks to be solved with the DL system and measure e.g. task time and completion rate.
- Who needs the results from the evaluation?
  In many cases, results are needed for decision-making: For example, the management of a library has to select a new DL software; a librarian managing subscriptions looks for DLs offering the content mostly needed by his clients; a system developer has to make design choices.
- When is it appropriate to evaluate?
  Evaluations may take place at any place in time: A system developer may have to choose between several methods for performing a certain function, for which a rather focused evaluation in a laboratory setting may suffice. Decisions for selecting a piece of software or subscribing to a DL should be based on the final product.

As stated in [13], any evaluation has to meet certain requirements. Hence, a set of important issues has to be considered, such as the construct for evaluation, the context of evaluation, the criteria, the measures and the methodology.

However, Saracevic and Covi [13] conclude that there are no clear agreements regarding the elements of criteria, measures, methodologies as well as of the larger "view" which involve the construct and context of evaluation. We therefore see our paper as a step in the direction of resolving some of these issues.

The US DLI test suite[1] is a group of six digital library test beds developed by the projects of the first phase of the US Digital Library Initiative. These test beds comprise different media; however, since the focus of most the projects spawning off the test beds was on technological aspects, users and usage as well as the content play a minor role in most of these test beds. Related to this effort, the D-Lib Working Group on Digital Library Metrics[2] was formed and was involved in the organisation of a workshop[3] in 1998, which addressed several aspects of DL evaluation. Unfortunately, this effort has not been continued.

The Digital Library Evaluation Forum of the DELOS Network of Excellence[4] aims at providing an infrastructure for the evaluation of performance related aspects in accessing digital libraries. Research into DLs needs large test beds to evaluate and demonstrate new concepts. In recent and coming years, several excellent collections have been/will be created with EU funding, and the collections will be integrated in new applications. For defining or describing a DL test suite, the dimensions of such a test bed have to be defined.

In this paper written by several members of the DELOS working group[5] "Digital Library Test Suite", we first give a brief survey on related work (section 2). Then we outline the general idea of our holistic approach to DL evaluation (section 3), followed by a more detailed presentation of our description scheme (section 4). Section 5 describes the results of the evaluation of the scheme and an ongoing effort for building a DL meta-library. Finally, we give an outlook on future work in this area.

2   Related Work

Methods and tools to evaluate computer systems have been investigated for several decades, with a special focus on basic parameters for measuring the performance of a system: effectiveness and efficiency. The cost factors can be calculated indirectly.

In the area of information retrieval (IR), evaluation plays a central role since many years. The TREC (Text retrieval Conference) initiative is an ongoing effort for developing standard benchmarks for IR methods and systems. In the different tracks of TREC [14], a variety of collections (Web documents, newspaper and newswire articles, spoken broadcast news) and uses (ad-hoc queries, interactive querying, filtering, question answering) are considered. As evaluation criterion, mainly retrieval effectiveness (in terms of recall and precision) is regarded. From

---

[1] http://www.dlib.org/test-suite/index.html
[2] http://www.dlib.org/metrics/public/index.html
[3] http://www.dlib.org/metrics/public/6-98-workshop/index.html
[4] http://www.ercim.org/DELOS
[5] http://www.sztaki.hu/delos_wg21

a DL point of view, the collections employed in TREC lack the rich structure and inter-document relationships that are typical for DL collections. Furthermore, involvement of real end-users is only marginal (in the interactive track).

Common approaches within the HCI research area are different usability evaluation methods ([10], [7]). Furthermore, in the process of assessment of users and their interaction with computers, HCI have used a diverse set of methods and techniques. These methods range from controlled laboratory-based settings, simulated situations with simulated tasks to longitudinal workplace studies (e.g. [12]). From a HCI point of view, techniques such as usability inspection methods, cognitive walk-through, task analysis methods, think aloud, ethnographic methods etc may be used in order to evaluate the use and usage of DLs. Usability studies (ease of operation) can be distinguished from usefulness (serving an intended purpose) even if the two are hard to separate in the context of evaluation [8].

Following these ideas, [9] describes a human-centred approach for designing DL systems. Here the focus is on assessing human information needs and corresponding tasks, thus evaluation deals with the effects of the DL on the subsequent human information behaviour. As a consequence, the authors claim that DL design should be process-oriented and iterative rather than product-oriented and summative.

A digital library has many similarities with a traditional, physical library, but it has also many differences. [2] distinguishes evaluation procedures in a physical library from those in a digital library. She reviews usability evaluation work within taxonomy of system design, development and deployment. In addition to an evaluation strategy where evaluation data are collected throughout the system life cycle, she includes a second strategy where the evaluation methods themselves are evaluated. This is the evaluation approach in the Alexandria Digital Library (ADL) [5]. In this study the user reactions to the ADL interface and to the functionality and content of ADL was evaluated, as well as the user characteristics used and the study approach itself.

With the current changes in the library area, the problems of library statistics and performance measurement have gained increasing attention[6]. [4] distinguishes five dimensions of evaluation: extensiveness, effectiveness, efficiency, costing and quality. [3] claims that the traditional notions of efficiency and effectiveness should be balanced with the benefit to customers ('value'), and describes a conceptual framework for measuring the latter. [11] presents lists of DL evaluation metrics (quantitative data) for two facets, namely users and data/services. In addition, so-called nuggets serve for collecting qualitative data relating to a variety of topics.

The different evaluation needs described above imply that both qualitative and quantitative data should be collected and analysed in order to contribute to our understanding of how DLs should to be designed in order to support different users and usages. Generally, we may say that from the level of system performance evaluation to the evaluation level of the situational and contextual

---

[6] See e.g. the bibliography at `http://web.syr.edu/~jryan/infopro/statgen.html`.

factors the different methods and techniques range from quantitative data collection methods (e.g. TREC-based performance measures) to qualitative data collection methods such as ethnographic Al observations.

This calls for building a collection of evaluation methods and techniques that may be used within the framework of DL evaluation. Different evaluation methods may be used for different purposes and levels of analysis.

3   A Holistic Approach to DL Evaluation

A DL is a special kind of an information system, and consists of several components such as a collection, a computer system (a technical system), persons, and the environment (or usage), for which the system is built. For DLs it is important to integrate systems, information/collection and humans, as well as support the viewpoints of the different shareholders in DL research. Thus, a librarian may focus on the collection, whereas a computer scientist may be interested in the technological aspects only, irrespective of the content of a DL. However, ignoring the other dimensions of the problem may lead to impractical solutions. For example, in the area of information retrieval, most technological-oriented research assumes a batch-like environment, whereas the few evaluations targeted towards interactive retrieval have not yet been able to show that technological differences really matter [14].

Important issues to be considered from a broader viewpoint of DL evaluation would include the following:

- The underlying system and its components (this involves e.g. classical information retrieval evaluation methods and techniques as well as overall systems performance).
- The interface and interaction level of the activities between the user and the system (this involves classical human-computer usability evaluation issues).
- Support for different access and usage strategies (e.g. analytical search, browsing, navigation, bibliographic search, collaboration, annotations).
- The work tasks should be supported. Often, only the task of searching is supported in the design of an access system.
- Situational and contextual factors of DLs are important, such as organisational and group issues.

When comparing these requirements with the outcomes of previous DL programmes, it becomes apparent that there is an imbalance in satisfying the different DL research domains, with a predominance of technology related initiatives.

In order to take a broader view on DL evaluation, our working group decided to focus on the development of test suites that satisfy the needs of all kinds of DL researchers. As a result of a brainstorming exercise, we developed the diagram shown in figure 1.

Our new approach uses a generic definition of a digital library as its starting point, and is illustrated by the small circles within the central circle labelled "DL DOMAIN". The model falls into three non-orthogonal components: the users, the

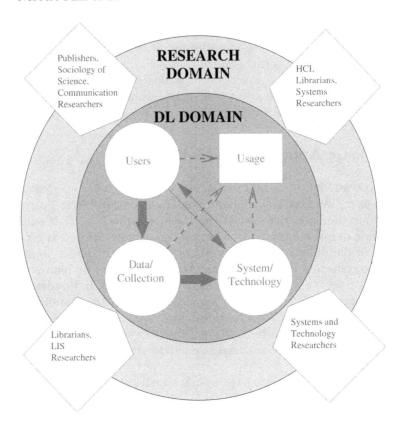

Fig. 1. A Generalised Schema for a Digital Library

data/collection, the technology used. Definition of the set of users predefines the appropriate range and content of the collection (block arrow connecting "users" to "collection"). The nature of the collection predefines the range of appropriate technologies that can be used (block arrow from "collection" to "technology"). Finally, the attractiveness of the collection to the users and, secondarily, the ease of use of the technologies by the user group, determine the extent of the usage of the digital library (thin arrows show the human-computer interactions, while the dotted arrows show the collective contribution of user, collection and technology interactions to observed overall usage).

From this starting point, it is possible to move outwards to the domain of the DL researchers (outer ring), and to use the non-orthogonal relationships between the principle research areas (users, usage, collection and technology) to create a set of researcher requirements for a DL test bed. Because "content is king", the nature, extent and form of the collection predetermine both the range of potential users and the required technology set.

Data/Collection:

- content: none/partial/full, audio, text, video, 2D, 3D
  diversity, age, size, quality (white/grey literature)
- meta-content: bibliographical, indexing / thesaurus / classification, citation
  media, level of detail
- management: rights, work-flow, user mgmt., maintenance
  document age, growth rate, immediacy, object completeness, maintenance intervals

Technology:

- user technology: document creation, disclosure, interface, browsing, search, printing, group/individual
- information access: retrieval, navigation, filtering, extraction, text mining
  efficiency, effectiveness
- systems structure technology: repository, transport model (protocols)
- document technology: document model, format

Users/Uses:

- user (who)
  - internal
  - general
  - education
  - professional
  - research
  number, distribution
- domain (what) = subject area
  distribution
- info seeking (how)
  - object seeking
  - browsing (rummagers, surfers)
  distribution
- purpose (why)
  - consume
  - analyse
  - synthesize
  distribution

Fig. 2. Description scheme and evaluation criteria for digital libraries

4   Evaluation Criteria and Metrics

4.1   Categories of Description Scheme for DLs

While many of the descriptive characteristics of DLs are interconnected and dependent (the nature of the user predefines the collection they will use, which in turn delimits the potential tool set they may adopt), it is possible to assign relatively independent criteria within the overall domain of data/collection, technology and users. Creating such a definition allows us then to select denumerable subsets as appropriate evaluation criteria.

As a refinement of the concepts developed in the previous section, we identified the major parameters characterising the three dimensions of the DL domain. These parameters are listed in figure 2. Most of these parameters are either binary (yes/no) valued or have a restricted set of values. A few additional parameters have numeric values, which are shown italics here. Below, we describe the parameters for the different dimensions in more detail.

4.2   Users and Uses

The uses and the user are intimately connected with the four basic questions that can be asked about any market. Who is the market? What are they interested in? How and why do they behave as they do?

The "who?" question is largely a matter of demographics and hierarchy within the information chain. In the first cut, users are either internal to the DL system or external. In the case of the external users, they correspond to different levels of the standard information pyramid: the mass market (general), primary, secondary and tertiary educational market, the industrial, manufacturing or professional users, the high level university, corporate or institutional research users. Following this classification of user demography we can evaluate in terms of the numbers of each user type and their distribution among the user classes.

The "what?" question concerns the subject area of interest to a user. That is the domain of their DL use. For evaluation we can use the distribution of subject areas as a metric.

The third dimension relates to the ways in which users seek information, the "how?" question. Users can adopt essentially two strategies. The first is direct object-seeking, that is the use of sophisticated tools (largely search engines) to identify specific, singular pieces of information that resolve closely defined questions. The second is the traditional wandering approach of library browsing. There may or may not be more systematic approaches contained within this strategy. A user may use a classification scheme or other labels to limit the domain of the browse. Alternatively they may randomly wander around the information lighting upon topics of interest serendipitously. For evaluation purposes, the distribution of users between these approaches can be used.

Lastly, we can consider the purpose behind a users information encounter, the answer to the "why?" question. For some users the encounter may simply be to consume the information for pleasure or interest. For others the information may be an object to analyse critically for educational, research or review purposes. For another group, the information will be crucial to synthesize new works via quotation, commentary, annotation or citation. Again for evaluation purposes, the distribution of uses between these categories can be a useful metric.

4.3 Data/Collection

The collections and the information objects in a Digital Library can be described using different axes: content description, quality/reliability qualifiers, and management and accessibility qualifiers.

The collections in a digital library contains information objects gathered according to some rules or ideas, on the basis of one or several attributes to be described collectively. It may be a thematic collection such as work by a specific author or composer (or "creator") (W. Shakespeare, J.S. Bach); or subject (mathematics, history); a collection based upon media types (paper, CDs, films, maps, a.o.); age (information objects 'produced after 1968'), or just a general collection for a wide audience where the collection may include a variety of media types. To describe quality in an objective manner is almost impossible. It is, however, feasible to give descriptors that may help to estimate quality and authenticity. In scientific domains it may be of importance to know if a collection contains 'grey' or reviewed literature, and if the collection's owner is well reputed, by giving the name of the owner.

The collections may contain primary objects like the text of Shakespeare's "Romeo and Juliet", or the film "Cinderella". Collections of secondary objects contain bibliographic descriptions; holdings; data to assist in authority control (thesauri, gazetteers, classification schemes, etc.), or may assist in the thematic information seeking process (collections of citations). The metadata scheme(s) used to describe the information objects gives the level of detail of the data (MARC format, Dublin Core, RFC1807, robot generated, none).

A collection needs maintenance. Redundant information objects have to be removed, errors have to be repaired, and the growth of a collection must be secured. A responsible organisation or body must be in charge of this work. Additional functions that need to be handled properly are user management, security and access control. Examples of possible qualifiers may be the name(s) of the body in charge; maintenance intervals; statistics of growth rate, accessibility, number of users, types of users, and others.

4.4 Technology

The technological issues can be subdivided into four areas, namely user technology, information access, systems structure and document technology.

User technology deals with the functions that the DL system offers to the user: Most basic, these functions have to be provided via an appropriate user interface. Documents are made accessible via searching and browsing; furthermore, there may be a disclosure mechanism that notifies the user about new documents that might be relevant for him. Once a relevant document is located, most users prefer to read it on paper; thus, a printing function is essential. Since users often work in teams, support for user groups also is an important function in DL systems, e.g. for collaborative filtering. Besides accessing existing documents, a DL system also may support the creation of new documents.

For information access, a DL system should implement a rich set of functions. Retrieval searches for documents in response to a query. Navigation follows (explicit or implicit) links between documents and/or metadata. Based on a profile specified by the user, filtering locates potentially relevant documents in a stream of incoming documents. Information extraction generates facts from text documents. Based on this input, text mining can discover correlations and trends in a document collection.

Systems structure technology deals with the architecture of the repository (e.g centralised/distributed database, relational/object-oriented database management system, middle-ware) and the transport model (protocols for communication between the system and the user interface or between system components).

Document technology addresses the issue of the representation of documents. The document model describes the abstract structure of documents such as the hierarchical/hyperlinked logical structure, content media, layout, semantic content and external attributes. The document format specifies the syntax of the internal document representation (e.g. postscript, PDF, RTF).

5 Evaluation of the Scheme: Questionnaires and Lessons Learned

The scheme described previously can serve as a basis of various evaluation and classification efforts. By attaching answers to the questions in the scheme, a specialised description of a digital library can be received. These descriptions can be used to compare digital libraries or to select some for a specific testing purpose. As a first trial of these ideas, a survey was done in the second half of 2000 with a questionnaire reflecting main ideas of the classification scheme.

5.1 First Survey

In order to gather a first set of information about Digital library collections and test collections, we designed a two-part questionnaire. The Questionnaire A (available digital libraries and test collections) concerned with the availability of existing digital libraries and test collections that could be used for research in the field of digital libraries. The Questionnaire B (desired digital library test collections) investigated future requirements of digital library test collections.

Questions in both questionnaires were put in a similar way, the wording was only changed to reflect the different target: existing DLs versus requirements and research needs. A set of questions corresponded to each of the three main categories of the scheme: Users/Uses, Data/Collection and Technology. Additionally, the gender and the work domain were asked about the person who responded. Answering questions was possible by selecting a single or multiple choices from a choice list and by optionally giving a comment. Naturally, respondents could abstain from answering some of the questions. Questionnaire A contained 31 questions and Questionnaire B contained 21 questions. (The reason why Questionnaire B had less questions is that some questions had no relevance to put for a not yet existing digital library.)

The survey was carried out by the open, Web-based survey tool of SZTAKI [6]. The survey was announced at various mailing lists with major audience of digital library researchers and developers, and our estimation is that roughly 3-4% of the targeted audience responded. Nearly 70% of the respondents were from the research domain, and the users of the evaluated digital libraries also had more than double weight in the research domain than in any other domain.

These surveys showed that while the proposed classification scheme seems to be appropriate for DL characterisation, the wording of the questions is rather problematic. Due to the holistic approach of the classification scheme, many different research areas are covered, and these areas have their different term sets and language usage, which makes it difficult to create questionnaires which are equally understandable by researchers of different areas. Naturally, creating questions about this lively and multidisciplinary research area is not an easy task. We received several suggestions either via comments in the survey or via e-mail, which showed that an additional problem is to guess a reasonable granularity of choices for questions, which on the other hand does not hide new or unorthodox approaches, as these have great importance in a research survey. The low response rate showed that the return of the investment was not clearly seen by research communities. The possibility that filling these surveys could be the starting point of research cooperations was not emphasised by the survey environment on the required level.

5.2   MetaLibrary

The DL MetaLibrary[7] is the current effort of the DELOS WG2.1 working group, where lessons learned from the survey and new ideas are taken into account. This is an extensible survey database, where each DL collection/test-bed can register and provide information about itself. Information provided here can be updated any time by the original submitters after a password-based authentication. Questions from the old survey were redesigned and more opportunity was given for answers in free text. Questions are mapped on a hierarchy suggested by the proposed classification scheme. Thus, nodes in this hierarchy represent a research area or a DL functionality. These are called slots and they are identified by a unique number sequence. Questions and answers are stored in their corresponding slots, thus new questions can be easily introduced into the existing survey database. Slots can also be used for enhanced searching and browsing of the contents of MetaLibrary. Users will be able to browse the hierarchy of slots, get summaries or statistics of available solutions in selected slots, or search for DLs having a certain solution in a selected slot. With a sufficient coverage of the activity in the area, MetaLibrary can help DL people to find systems, test-beds

---

[7] http://www.sztaki.hu/delos_wg21/metalib/

and research partners for their needs, and at the same time lacking features or holes in research can also be identified.

6   Conclusions and Outlook

In this paper, we have argued that evaluation of DLs should be based on a broad view of the subject area. For this purpose, we have developed a new description scheme using four major dimensions (collection, technology, users, usage) and we have described the major properties along each of these dimensions. Using this scheme, existing DL test beds can be characterised. For this purpose, we have performed a survey by means of a questionnaire, which is now continued by setting up a DL meta-library.

In order to ease the maintenance of this meta-library, we will investigate the possibility of switching to a harvesting scheme, where each provider of a DL test bed maintains a metadata record describing his/her test bed, and the harvester collects these records on a regular basis

Once we have metadata about a substantial number of existing test beds, we will relaunch our questionnaire on desired test collections: Given the existing test beds and the current interests of DL researchers, what types of test beds are still missing? The outcome of this poll may lead to an effort for building appropriate test collections, similar to the TREC and CLEF initiatives.

Acknowledgement This work was supported in part by the Network of Excellence DELOS funded by the European Commission.

References

1. C. Borgman. *From Gutenberg to the Global Information Infrastructure: Access to Information in the Networked World.* MIT Press, 2000.
2. B. Buttenfield. User evaluation for the alexandria digital library project. Allerton Inst. WS, `http://edfu.lis.uiuc.edu/allerton/95/s2/buttenfield`, 1995.
3. J. Cram. Six impossible things before breakfast: A multidimensional approach to measuring the value of libraries. In *Proc. 3rd Northumbria Intl. Conf. on Performance Measurement in Libraries and Information Services*, pages 19–29, Newcastle upon Tyne, 1999. Information North.
4. P. Hernon and E. Altman. *Service quality in academic libraries.* Ablex, Norwood, NJ, 1996.
5. L Hill, Ron Dolin, James Frew, R.B. Kemp, M. Larsgaard, D.R. Montello, Mary-Anna Rae, and J. Simpson. User evaluation: Summary of the methodologies and results for the alexandria digital library. In *Proc. ASIS*, pages 225–243, Medford, NJ, 1997. Information Today .
6. L. Kovacs and A. Micsik. A public service for surveys and decision polls. In *Proc. DEXA 2000*, pages 307–311, September 2000.
7. Roberta Lamb. Using online information resources: Reaching for the *.*'s. In *Digital Libraries '95 Conference Proceedings.*, New York, 1995. ACM.

8. T. K. Landauer. *The Trouble with Computers: Usefulness, Usability, and Productivity.* MIT Press, Cambridge, Mass., 1995.

9. G. Marchionini, C Plaisant, and A. Komlodi. The people in digital libraries: Multifaceted approaches to assessing needs and impact. In *Digital library use: Social practice in design and evaluation.* MIT Press, Cambridge, Mass., 2001. (in press).

10. J. Nielsen and R.L. Mack, editors. *Usability Inspection Methods.* John Wiley & Sons, New York, 1994.

11. Catherine Plaisant and Anita Komlodi. Evaluation challenges for a federation of heterogeneous information providers: The case of nasa's earth science information partnerships. In *Proc. WET ICE 2000, IEEE WS on Evaluating Collaborative Enterprises,* 2000.

12. J. Preece, Y. Rogers, H. Sharp, D. Benyon, S. Holland, and T. Carey. *Human-Computer Interaction.* Addison Wesley, Reading, Mass., 1994.

13. T. Saracevic and L. Covi. Challenges for digital library evaluation. In *Proceedings ASIS,* volume 37, pages 341–350, 2000.

14. E. Voorhees and D. Harman. Overview of the eighth text retrieval conference (trec-8). In *The Eighth Text REtrieval Conference (TREC-8),* pages 1–24. NIST, Gaithersburg, MD, USA, 2000.

A Deposit for Digital Collections

Norman Noronha[1], João P. Campos[1], Daniel Gomes[1], Mário J. Silva[1], and
José Borbinha[2]

[1] Faculdade de ffiências5 Universidade de Lisboa5 Portugal
{normann, jcampos, dcg, mjs}@di.fc.ul.pt
[2] ø iblioteca Nacional5 Portugal
jose.borbinha@bn.pt

Abstract. We present the architecture and requirements for a novel
system for managing the deposit of specific genres of digital publications
in a deposit library6 The system adopts a simple model for online pub´
lications and supports both harvesting and delivery models of deposit6
This paper describes that system5and presents an evaluation after a trial
period with the harvesting functions6

1 Introduction

Publications are changing from the traditional formats, like paper magazines, to
digital media, such as online news feeds. In addition, everyone with a connected
computer is now a potential publisher. This is increasing the number of new
publications, making the management of their deposit more complex.

The deposit and preservation of publications has a significant role in preserving the historical past. Publications in traditional media have been archived
since ancient times. However, archiving the Internet aiming for long term preservation is a non trivial task [3]. The tools used for building digital publications
have not been designed with preservation in mind and so do not meet most of
the preservation requirements. In addition, publishers on the Web do not have a
tradition of sending copies of their digital items to library deposits for archival.
However, the Internet makes it possible for librarians to harvest copies of publications on the Internet. There are efforts to archive the entire web [17]. These
are of marginal relevance to librarians, as most of the collected information has
no historical interest. Libraries need the tools to selectively choose the electronic
publications of great interest to collect and preserve [4]. Our research goal is to
evaluate how these publications could be collected for preservation.

The Networked European Deposit Library (NEDLIB) [5] is an intiative to
develop a common architecture and basic tools for building deposit systems
for electronic publications. Practical experiences, technical infrastructures and
organisational approaches taken by individual NEDLIB partners are gathered
and compiled in such a way that these experiences can be of use to other libraries
[6]. The National Library of Portugal is a one of the partners in NEDLIB.

We have developed an initial framework to select relevant publications from
the Internet, retrieve their contents over time and provide easy methods for accessing the collection to the general public. Access methods include a service to

P. Constantopoulos and I.T. Sølvberg (Eds.): ECDL 2001, LNCS 2163, pp. 200–212, 2001.
© Springer-Verlag Berlin Heidelberg 2001

resolve Universal Resource Names (URNs) [10, 7] into the individual collection items. This development is a part of DROP - Deposit of Online Digital Publications, a project for building a digital repository of all Portuguese Internet publications of historical interest jointly developed by the National Library of Portugal and the University of Lisbon. This paper presents the system we designed for retrieving copies of publications from the web, storing and accessing them from our repository.

Unlike Web Search engines, we do not intend to collect everything published on the net, but only those sites that librarians classify as historically relevant. The goal of DROP is to provide means for identifying, selecting and retrieving bounded and well defined publications.

Figure 1 illustrates the use cases of the system. Our framework consists of two subsystems:

Digital Deposit (DD) – registers publications, harvests, accepts the delivery, verifies and deposits items.

PURL.PT – registers and resolves URNs [7, 15] into URLs that represent the address of the collected publication. This is similar to the temporary solution taken by the PANDORA Project to resolve a permanent name [9, 8].

We support two methods for retrieving publication contents: delivery and harvesting. In the delivery case, someone, either a system operator or a publication editor, submits the contents of a publication directly to the system. In the harvesting case, a previously registered publication is copied from its home site on the Internet into the DD (possibly periodically).

The deposit of received items in our system starts after the harvesting or delivery of their elements. Before integrating these contents in the DD, an operator inspects the collected items; inspection may involve viewing the data or using some high level verification procedures. After evaluating the contents the operator may decide that it is not valuable, and discard it, or that it should be preserved, and accept it

Once an item is deposited, it may be accessed by the external readers of our collection. When a reader wants to access some publication referenced by a URN within the namespace controlled by the system, PURL.PT resolves the URN either into a reference to a publication within the deposit, or into a reference to the site on the Internet. If the reference points to the deposit, the reader will engage in the show publication use case.

We have an initial implementation of the DD and PURL.PT systems. This paper presents their design options, implementation approach and some of the statistics for the collection of Portuguese periodic publications that have been harvested with our system. It is organized as follows: section 2 explains the requirements for the various functions of the system; section 3 presents the architecture and documents the implementation options; section 4 presents some of the statistics for the collection of the periodic publications that have been harvested with our system. Finally, in section 5, we present our conclusions and directions for future work.

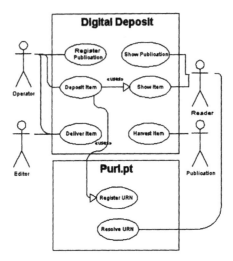

Fig. 1. Our framework for digital deposit and access to deposited copies of electronic publications is composed of two subsystems, Digital Deposit (DD) and PURL.PT. An *operator* registers *publications* with the DD system. Each of the *items* of a *publication* is either *harvested* by or *delivered* to the system. Collected items are then verified by an *operator* that either discards or accepts them in the *deposit* use case. A Universal Resource Name (URN) [7] is then assigned to each deposited item. Any user that later wants to access that item gives its URN to PURL.PT, which *resolves* it into an URL that references the storage location of the collected publicaton

2   Requirements

A deposit system for a digital collection must support multiple, sometimes conflicting requirements. We discuss the main requirements that we have identified for the digital deposit.

Persistency of the Entry Points - The system has to provide persistence of the entry points. As URNs [7] provide this kind of persistency, we assign URNs for resources following the National Library namespace draft proposal [1]. Each item stored within the DD has an assigned URN.

We support this as a general service that translates URNs in our namespace to their associated URLs on the Internet.

Publications Registry - Registering a publication needs to be a simple process, where a human operator, after identifying a publication to include in the collection creates a record indicating what URLs have to be collected and the retrieval method to use: harvesting or delivery.

DROP is part of a larger system within the National Library of Portugal. Publication records are not meant to overlap any existing data within bibliographic cataloging systems in use [11], but rather to specify meta data to be used when retrieving and processing items to be collected.

The publication title and the algorithm to be used to generate URNs for each of the items are attributes that must be specified in every record. If items are added to the collection through harvesting, additional information is necessary, such as where to start harvesting and the specification of the data formats to be transferred. Periodic publications have more specific attributes, including their periodicity and schedule for fetching new items.

DD operators also must be able to edit these records to make the necessary updates as the properties stored for harvested publications change.

Harvesting - The publications included in our collection are documents organized as sets of URLs that are available on the Internet. Some of these publications are published as Postscript or PDF files, some others as HTML documents linked to GIF or JPEG images.

The main focus in harvesting these publications is respecting restrictions imposed by the collection administrator on the contents to gather. Our harvester enables restrictions by domain name, depth of harvesting (number of links to follow), MIME types of the documents to retrieve and maximum size of the documents.

The harvester also can be programmed to collect every item of periodic publications and to retrieve their contents once published, before they are removed from the Web where they were originally published.

URN Assignments - The system generates an associated URN for every publication and item it manages. The URNs are generated by an algorithm that is specific of each publication.

The URN generation algorithm in DROP follows the policies defined by the National Library of Portugal [1].

Items of a periodic publication collected from the same space (same URL) but at different points in time will result in separate items with different URNs. A general URN can be used as a reference point to the last collected item of a periodic publication.

Publications Delivery - Delivery is another supported mode for importing contents into the system. In this mode, publishers or other agents push information into our repository. An operator, the publication editor or an author, manually collects all its files/URLs and submits them to the system. The delivery process associates the received data with the meta-data available for the publication (from the publication record).

Delivery can be partially automated by distributing software to editors for submitting new items. We have established initial contacts with some of the most prominent publishers in our culture for joint development of processes for automating the deposit of their digitally published materials. However, we fear that editors will show small interest in installing delivery software, as the only advantage they will get from doing it is the persistent depositing, which is of low business value in the short term.

Deposit - In our system, data collected from publications web sites is not stored permanently in the repository. Before deposit, data stored through harvest-

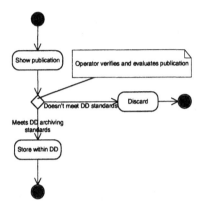

Fig. 2. Activity diagram for the deposit operation: deposit starts by showing the publication contents to the operator for verification. If it meets the depositing standards, it is then stored in the DD

ing or delivery is just candidate data. During deposit, this data can be either discarded (because it does not meet the requirements to be part of the collection), or stored permanently (figure 2).

Resolving a URN - The resolve operation is accomplished by the PURL.PT subsystem. When a reader calls the resolve operation, he is redirected either to our deposited copy of the item or to the original publishing site on the Internet. The decision of where to redirect the reader is based on the following criteria:
- permission to republish the resource
- location of the reader: local or remote

Redirection is supported directly by the HTTP protocol, and is used in our system so that readers can have their browsers point to the item intended when giving a URN to the PURL.PT server without intervention.

If the reader is redirected to a collected copy of the publication, it will ask the DD for the item requested. The copy displayed should look as similar as possible to the original. In particular, the reader should be able to browse collected items in the same way as he does with the original.

Storage - Persistent storage of digital contents is a complex problem with multiple perspectives and many pitfalls [12]. Our current work is on the building process of repositories for digital collections and providing easy access methods. Our assumption is that, in a production environment, our framework will operate upon a storage system that provides information preservation guarantees.

3   Architecture

DROP has been modeled as two main subsystems, to reflect the two different main functions:

Digital Deposit is the system that registers, collects and shows publications; **PURL.PT** is the system that registers and resolves URNs.

In this section, we present class and component models of our architecture.

3.1   Class Model

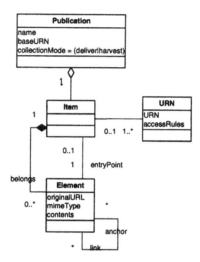

Fig. 3. Class diagram for the system. Publication objects represent publication records. Items represent collected editions of publications. Items are made of elements: elements are the objects that compose an item. Items are assigned URNs when deposited

The class model of our collection repository is represented in figure 3. A *publication* describes online publications in the digital deposit. Each publication has a *name*, a *baseURN*, specifying how to generate URNs for new items of the publication and the collection mode used to import it into the system.

Item represents the saved copies of monographs or issues of periodic publications in the collection. Each *publication* may have multiple associated items. The system assigns a URN to each item at deposit time. System operators may assign additional URNs to the same item.

Each *item* is composed of one or more *elements*. An *element* represents the contents of an URL downloaded from the Web or delivered to the system. *Original URLs* of elements are saved to enable the reconstruction of relative URLs linked from them. *MIME types* will indicate to the final user what interpreter to use when decoding the data. Links and anchors between documents are already embedded in the *contents* and need not be saved as meta-data.

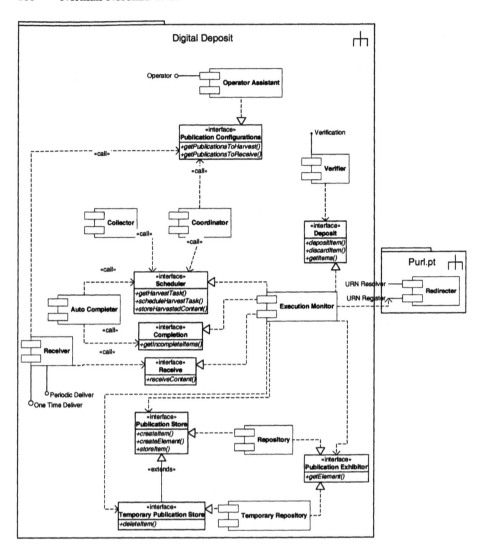

Fig. 4. Component diagram representing DD and PURL.PT subsystems. For the sake of simplicity only main operations are depicted. Component attributes are not represented

URNs reference resources. Each deposited item must be assigned a URN. URNs may reference several copies of the same resource to direct the user to the appropriate resource provider, according to some defined *access rules*.

3.2   Component Model

Our system architecture has the following main components (Figure 4 represents its component diagram):

Operator Assistant – saves publication records and provides an operator interface to register publications.

Coordinator – interprets publication records and schedules harvesting tasks.

Collector – gets harvesting work units from the execution monitor and retrieves the specified contents from the Web.

Auto Completer – is notified of possible incomplete items, and schedules a task to retrieve contents to complete the items.

Receiver – receives items from users through one of the two interfaces provided and inserts them in the system.

Verifier – provides a user interface to verify, evaluate and deposit or discard publications.

Repository – saves deposited items. Offers an interface to save items and an interface to retrieve them.

Temporary Repository – works like the repository but keeps temporary items, already delivered or harvested, but not yet deposited. The interface allows deletion of items.

Execution Monitor – orchestrates the concurrent execution of the other components. Provides interfaces for scheduling harvesting tasks, retrieve incomplete items, save delivered items, and deposit accepted items. Saves contents in the temporary repository and moves them to the repository (or deletes them). Registers URNs for deposited items.

Redirecter – saves URN resolving data. Offers interfaces for registering and resolving URNs.

The system components work together as follows:

– External operators register publications to collect with the *Operator Assistant*. Periodically, the *Coordinator* retrieves publication records to harvest from the *Operator Assistant* and schedules the tasks needed to gather them with the *Execution Monitor*.

– When the *Collector* is free to gather more data, it asks the *Execution Monitor* for work. It then gets the harvesting tasks, retrieves data from the Web and requests the *Execution Monitor* to store it. The *Collector* is designed for quick execution and does not try to recover from failures, it just logs them.

– The *Auto Completer* checks if all the retrieval tasks were successful. If not, and if items can be completed by retrieving the remainder of the contents from the Web, the *Auto Completer* re-schedules the appropriate tasks.

– The *Receiver* waits for a publisher to deposit contents through one of the provided interfaces or if this is a delivery of an item of a periodic publication, the receiver gets the publication meta-data from the *Operator assistant*. If a publication is delivered for the first time, the publisher must insert the data required to register the publication.

- The *Verifier* enables the evaluation of the items and provides an interface for depositing or discarding them. It calls the necessary interfaces on the *Execution Monitor* to complete these tasks.
- The *Execution Monitor* controls the contents flow within the system. It receives the contents from the *Collector* or from the *Receiver*, stores them in the *Temporary Repository*, guides the user to its evaluation and either moves it to the *Repository* or deletes it.
- The *Repository* saves items and allows access to them through the publication exhibitor interface.
- The *Redirecter* keeps all the data needed to reference users to the resources designated with the URNs presented for resolution. It collects this data when it is entered through the register URN interface, and uses it to resolve calls on the URN resolver interface.

The components are hosted in two separate subsystems so that one does not depend on the other: one might want to keep the PURL.PT and discontinue DD (if a better solution is offered on the market).

3.3   Implementation

In our implementation, we store items and elements in the file system of the server that hosts the DD: an item is a directory and all the elements that compose it are files within the directory. This structure may not reproduce the original file structure on the publications web site, as one element may be part of multiple items in the original site. However, it makes it easy to handle items as collections of files that can be detached from our file system and later accessed from a Web browser.

Additionally, publications harvested into the file system can be accessed from a *publication exhibitor* interface.

All the meta-data needed by the execution of our system is maintained in a PostgreSQL database[13].

The redirecter is implemented using the HTTP redirection mechanisms, on an Apache Web server[16] with the *mod_rewrite* and *mod_redirect* software.

4   Collection Statistics

We now present some statistical results from an initial crawl of a set of selected publications identified by our librarians. The selected publications contents varied in topic (general and specific) as well as in periodicity (daily, weekly, monthly, annual) and distribution (national and regional).

We limited our *collector* to retrieve only documents residing on the base server. The base server is the server that contains the entry point document for the publication. We also restricted our scan to collect URLs within a maximum depth of six from each entry point of a publication.

The *collector* made 60523 HTTP requests which retrieved successfully 72% of all documents of the list of publications (see Table 1). About 19% of the documents not collected resided on servers which were rejected because we chose to harvest only those documents available from the base server. We were surprised to find that less than 5% of all our HTTP requests were returned as non successful HTTP codes. HTTP response and *collector* error codes generated during the crawl of the Portuguese periodic publications collection are displayed in Table 1. Results from generic crawlers usually indicate higher percentages of broken links. Another interesting statistic is that only one publication excluded our crawler from harvesting it by the Robots Exclusion Protocol(REP)[14].

Table 1. HTTP response and *collector* error codes generated during the crawl of the Portuguese periodic publications collection

Code	Meaning	Number	Percent
200	OK	43322	72%
-5	Invalid server	11468	19%
-11	Exception	2743	5%
404	Not Found	2381	4%
-10	Exceeded document retrieval interval	103	0%
-2	Unnatural error	181	0%
-4	Exceeded size	129	0%

We also noticed that more than 83% of all documents varied in size in between 2KB and 32 KB (Figure 5).

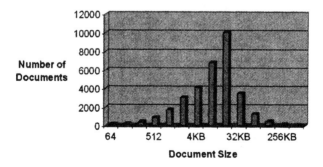

Fig. 5. Relation between documents retrieved and their size

Around 90% of all documents collected were either HTML documents, GIF images or JPEG images (see Table 2). Even though our *collector* was unable to determine the type of 9% of all documents, a more thorough study of their file extensions imply that most of them are HTML documents, GIF images and JPEG images.

Table 2. Distribution of MIME types

MIME type	Number	Percent
text/html	34424	70%
image/gif	5448	11%
unknown	4478	9%
image/jpeg	4400	9%
text/plain	238	0%
application/zip	64	0%
application/msword	57	0%
application/pdf	45	0%
	49256	100%

This means that 99% of all documents retrieved are small and easy to interpret. This shows a crawl restricted to those publications of historic interest could easily retrieve almost all their contents and that it can be easily reviewed with widely available tools.

The fact that the web publications that we harvested are much more easily handled (they only use the most widely adopted formats, have very few broken links, etc) may suggest that publishers in general strive to make their publications as easily accessible as possible to maximize their readership. This in turn makes our goal in harvesting for preservation easier to achieve. We believe that this trend will increase as the Internet matures as a publishing media.

5   Conclusions and Future Work

We have developed an information system for the deposit of digital items. Our approach separates the mechanisms for harvesting and accessing collected items from the policies that estabilish how they are performed. Hence, operators need to configure DROP and PURL.PT to behave as intended. However, policies are hard to estabilish, as we still face several open issues, such as respecting copyright policies and handling the merging and splitting of publications. Initial usage of the first prototype shows that it can handle those Internet publications of interest to our end-users.

We still face the problem of later being able to access harvested items. Many publications today use languages and programs such as JavaScript, Java Applets or ShockWave Flash to provide dynamic contents; our collector does not analyze these objects and may loose the harvesting of some of the URLs of a publication.

As a result, collected publications may not be properly harvested or may be hard to interpret.

These difficulties are just the unraveling of a bigger issue: it is very difficult to build a system made for preservation in a Web world with proprietary, incomplete, undefined, unclear, non followed, complex standards. Future work in this direction may provide the collector with a parser for interpreting scripts and collect all the referred documents. Additional future work in the harvesting process is also necessary, to automate ways of detecting faults and recovering from them. The study of techniques to optimize harvesting is currently a major work area [2].

References

[1] Jose Borbinha. A URN namespace for resources maintained by the National Library of Portugal – Internet Draft (submission in progress).

[2] Junghoo Cho and Hector Garcia-Molina. The evolution of the web and implications for an incremental crawler. In Amr El Abbadi, Michael L. Brodie, Sharma Chakravarthy, Umeshwar Dayal, Nabil Kamel, Gunter Schlageter, and Kyu-Young Whang, editors, *VLDB 2000, Proceedings of 26th International Conference on Very Large Data Bases, September 10-14, 2000, Cairo, Egypt*, pages 200–209, 2000.

[3] Working Group of the Conference of Directors of National Libraries. The legal deposit of electronic publications. Available at http://www.unesco.org/webworld/memory/legaldep.htm, December 1996.

[4] Library of Congress Must Improve Handling Of Digital Information. LC21: A Digital Strategy for the Library of Congress. Available at http://www4.nationalacademies.org/news.nsf/isbn/0309071445?OpenDocument Accessed on June 2001.

[5] Networked European Deposit Library Available at http://www.kb.nl/nedlib/. Accessed on June 2001.

[6] Long-term Preservation of Electronic Publications: The NEDLIB project Available at http://www.dlib.org/dlib/september99/vanderwerf/09vanderwerf.html. Accessed on June 2001.

[7] Naming and Addressing: URIs, URLs, ... Web Naming and Addressing Overview. Available at http://www.w3.org/Addressing/. Accessed on June 2001.

[8] Universal Resource identifiers in WWW Available at http://www.w3.org/Addressing/URL/uri-spec.html. Accessed on June 2001.

[9] The PANDORA Project: a summary of progress PANDORA Archive - Key Documents Available at http://pandora.nla.gov.au/documents.html. Accessed on June 2001.

[10] R. Moats. RFC 2141: URN syntax, 1997.

[11] National bibliographic database - Porbase. Available at http://portico.bl.uk/gabriel/en/countries/portugal-union-en.html, Porbase available at http://porbase.bn.pt/.

[12] Andrew Waugh, Ross Wilkinson, Brendan Hills, and Jon Dell'Oro. Preserving digital information forever. In *Proceedings of the Fifth ACM Conference on Digital Libraries, June 2-7, 2000, San Antonio, TX, USA*, pages 175–184. ACM, 2000.

[13] PostgreSQL. PostgreSQL - a sophisticated Object-Relational DBMS. Available at http://www.postgresql.org,

[14] Martijn Koster. A Standard for Robot Exclusion. Available at
http://info.webcrawler.com/mak/projects/robots/norobots.html,
The Robots pages at WebCrawler available at
http://info.webcrawler.com/mak/projects/robots/robots.html.

[15] OCLC PURL Service. Persistent URL at http://purl.oclc.org/

[16] The Apache Software Foundation. Available at http://www.apache.org

[17] Brewster Kahle Archiving the Internet Scientific American, March 1997.

Digital Libraries in a Clinical Setting: Friend or Foe?

Anne Adams and Ann Blandford

Middlesex University, Computer Science Dept, Bounds Green Road, London, N11 2NQ, U.K.
{A.Adams, A.Blandford}@mdx.ac.uk

Abstract. Clinical requirements for quick accessibility to reputable, up-to-date information have increased the importance of web accessible digital libraries for this user community. To understand the social and organisational impacts of ward-accessible digital libraries (DLs) for clinicians, we conducted a study of clinicians' perceptions of electronic information resources within a large London based hospital. The results highlight that although these resources appear to be a relatively innocuous means of information provision (i.e. no sensitive data) social and organisational issues can impede effective technology deployment. Clinical social structures, which produce information – and technology – hoarding behaviours can result from poor training, support and DL usability.

1   Introduction

The increased importance of evidenced based medicine for healthcare professionals necessitates the use of current best evidence in clinical decision-making. Within the clinical community there is, therefore, an escalating need to improve the accessibility of reputable information sources. Web accessible information resources present the potential to greatly advance learning capabilities regardless of users' location and time restrictions. In comparison with traditional libraries, digital libraries can provide specialized information in a format that is easily updated, with speedy searching and access facilities.

Wyatt [28] argues that poor use of computer databases and the Internet by clinicians to answer clinical questions is due to slow, inconvenient access to computer-based clinical knowledge resources. Digital Libraries offer the potential, as flexible information resources, to address these demands [19, 28, 15]. The National electronic Library for Health (NeLH) project is a proposed solution to resource problems within the UK. Wyatt [28] suggests that a predictor of the resource's success can be seen in the achievements of its pre-cursor, the Australian Clinical Information Access Project (CIAP). Since the launch of CIAP in 1997 [6] there has been a substantial increase in its use, as well as the development of a culture that is open to the sharing of clinical information within the New South Wales health system.

P. Constantopoulos and I.T. Sølvberg (Eds.): ECDL 2001, LNCS 2163, pp. 213-224, 2001.
© Springer-Verlag Berlin Heidelberg 2001

1.1 Background

Digital libraries (DLs) are major advances in information technology that frequently fall short of expectations [7, 28]. Covi & Kling [7] argue that understanding the wider context of technology use is essential to understanding digital library use and its implementation in different social worlds. Recent health informatics research also argues that social and organisational factors can determine the success or failure of healthcare IT developments [8, 11, 12]. Heathfield [11] suggests that this is due to the complex, autonomous nature of the medical discipline and the specialized (clinician or software engineer) approach to system development. Negative reactions to these systems is often due to inappropriate system design and poor implementation. However, there may be other less obvious social and political repercussions of information system design and deployment. Symon et al [26] have identified, within a hospital scenario, how social structures and work practices can be disrupted by technology implementation. Although these systems often deal with sensitive, personal information, other system design research has found that apparently innocuous data can be perceived as a threat to social and political stability [1,2,3]. To understand the impact of DLs within the medical profession, an in-depth evaluation is required of the introduction and later development of these applications within their specific social and organisational settings. However, as Covi & Kling [7] have highlighted, there are few high-level theories that aid designers in understanding the implication of these issues for DL design and implementation.

This 3 year project within a large London based hospital is evaluating the introduction of Internet and Intranet ward-accessible DLs (not containing any personal information) for all health care practitioners (from student nurses to surgeons). The research aims to identify current informal work practices, social structures (i.e. perceived roles and status) and technology perceptions, so as to inform system design, development and implementation. This study will therefore not be task and technology specific [26] or review patient / organisational interactions but assess psychosocial elements of clinicians' organization, information and technology perceptions. The work reported here focuses on the results of the first phase of the study – establishing a baseline from which to assess developments over time.

1.2 Hospital Library Scenario

Initially the hospital staff used a library within the hospital grounds. More recently, the library was positioned across the road from the hospital. The library repositioning meant that staff wishing to use the library and meet their own tight schedules found it increasingly difficult to get the information they required. The increased importance of up-to-date, relevant information on which to base clinical decisions and current practice necessitated a quick solution to this problem. To resolve this, computers were placed on the wards with access via the web to clinical digital libraries (e.g. Medline, Cochrane, NeLH).

1.3 Context of Use

DL Research increasingly focuses on the importance of directing DL design towards the work practices and communities they support [14, 7]. However, it is important to establish the differences between formal and informal work practices and the impact of social structures within those communities.

Formal procedures relay the correct way to conduct the work but do not allow for organisational dynamics, changing situations, evolution of task definitions, or social and political aspects (e.g. staff motivation, hierarchies) [9]. The distinction between formal and informal work practices can be even more important for health care systems. Symon et al [26] found that high status clinicians frequently deviated from formal procedures when a low value was placed on the work activity. Systems designed to support only formal work practices can be too inflexible. Adams & Sasse [4] found that systems which do not take into account informal work practices and are perceived to restrict these practices will be circumvented. DL designers must therefore design their systems around both formal and informal procedures, understanding both social and organisational norms.

An organisation's culture has a direct impact on informal practices that can develop into social and organisational norms [22]. When hospital information systems were first introduced, it was found that the greatest difficulties in the system's deployment lay not with technical issues but with the users, their reactions to its introduction and the acquisition of new skills [10]. Many of these issues related directly to social and organisational norms with regard to social structures.

The diverse organisational culture of hospital structures, made up of many different professions with their own specific social identifiers, can often produce conflicts between those professions [17, 27, 18]. Symon et al [26] identified conflicts within a clinical setting relating to social status and information procedures. Higher status professionals were identified as being more concerned with keeping their status as an expert than adhering to formal organisational norms. Schneider and Wagner [21] also highlighted the increased importance, within a clinical setting, of local knowledge, informal collaborative contexts and technology to support the sharing of information. However, the electronic dissemination of information within a clinical setting can be used and interpreted in politically sensitive ways. Digital libraries, in particular, can change the context of people's work-practices and can therefore restructure their relationships with both each other and the task in hand [26, 23]. The restructuring of these professional relationships can have far-reaching social and political consequences. Ultimately, system designers should be aware of social and political motivations within an organisation in order to develop and implement more sensitive design strategies.

2 Research Method

Focus groups and in-depth interview were used to gather data from 73 hospital clinicians. 50% of the respondents were nurses while the other 50% were senior and junior doctors, consultants, surgeons, Professions Allied to Medicine (PAMs) such as occupational therapists, managers and IT department members.

Four issues guided the focus of questions:

- Perceptions of what clinical information is currently required, available, and used to complete their job effectively.
- Perceptions of how this information is currently accessed, and how these processes accommodate current working practices
- The impact of organisational social structures on information perceptions, information accessibility and acceptability
- Technology perceptions (specifically of DLs) and how these affect other issues already identified.

An in-depth analysis of respondents' information and technology perceptions was conducted using the Grounded Theory method. A pre-defined concept for a 'Digital Library' was not employed so that users were allowed to explore what they perceived comprises a digital library. Respondents, however, also discussed specific digital libraries that they had used (e.g. Medline, Cochrane, NeLH).

Grounded Theory [25] is a social-science approach to data collection and analysis that combines systematic levels of abstraction into a framework about a phenomenon which is verified and expanded throughout the study. Once the data is collected it is analysed in a standard Grounded Theory format (i.e. open, axial and selective coding and identification of process effects). Unlike other social science methodologies, Grounded Theory provides a more focused, structured approach to research (closer in some ways to quantitative methods) [24]. The methodology's flexibility can cope with complex data and its continual cross-referencing allows for grounding of theory in the data thus uncovering previously unknown issues

3   Results

Users' current information needs, dissemination processes and the impact of newly introduced technology were identified in relation to organisational, social and political structures. It was found that perceptual problems associated with organisational hierarchies, technology misconceptions, the accessibility of the technology and its information impeded the introduction of digital library access via the Internet. These problems produced increased user resentment, decreasing the effectiveness of everyday working practices. Further analysis of data from high status users within the community found that reduced effectiveness of technology integration within the user community was directly related to poor usability, inadequate training and inappropriate task applicability. The main finding can be classified in terms of; 1 the perceived effectiveness of digital and traditional libraries as a clinical resource. 2 the relationships between control over, and access to, information according to perceived status of the clinician, 3 perceptions of the technology as tool or plaything, and 4 the different ways that various classes of clinicians access information.

3.1 Clinical Libraries (Traditional vs. Digital Libraries)

All the respondents noted that traditional libraries were perceived to have limited accessibility due to the physical location of the libraries. The poor usability of current library systems made it difficult to access specialized information and limited the use of information sources. Journal access, for example, was kept within the library with time-consuming, poor quality photocopying facilities limiting effective access to within the library confines. This meant that clinical users requiring high quality journal images to compare with samples under their microscope were unable to complete these tasks. These users proposed that digital libraries accessible from the laboratory, with reasonable multimedia representations and search facilities would be a major advance in library usability. Limited supply of source materials was also considered a major problem with traditional libraries, which the users perceived could be quickly and effectively solved via electronic supply of documents. However, many users noted that digital libraries were only now becoming useful because they now adequately covered their area of expertise.

3.2 Status Impacts on Current Information Dissemination Procedures

To fulfill nurses' and PAMs' information requirements two distribution procedures were identified: hard copy and verbal dissemination. Hard copy (e.g. paper guidelines, books) and verbal dissemination is hampered by poor accessibility due to priority access for those of a higher status. Verbal dissemination, due to the time restrictions and the status structure, was dealt with via a crisis management approach (i.e. information is released and passed onto the nurses as and when a crisis occurs or is imminent). Many nurses and PAMs perceived that accessibility problems were associated with senior staff's information hoarding behaviours. It was suggested that these procedures could be used to obscure senior staff's lack of up to date knowledge. These behaviours produced resentment in the nurses and feelings of social restricting pressures (i.e. putting them in their place, shutting them out). All the junior staff members (i.e. nurses, PAMs and doctors) considered digital libraries an essential tool in completing their jobs effectively. Nursing staff (especially student nurses) and PAMs perceived them as an 'empowering tool' providing them with the information and knowledge that they required.

All the senior staff members confirmed the current dissemination processes detailed above. However, senior staff members noted that status directed current information dissemination because:

- Higher status staff required more theoretical knowledge
- Lower status staff required more practical knowledge

Some senior staff expressed a concern that junior staff would not be able to interpret or fully understand some information sources. For example:

> "... you find that people will just go off and they will misunderstand the national guidelines because they come out in long documents which interpretation requires further study. So I think for junior doctors they can be misleading, harmful, damaging." (consultant)

Senior staff, therefore, do not perceive that digital libraries are required, or even desirable, for lower status staff.

3.3   Status Impacts on Technology Perceptions

The hospital's current information hierarchy (i.e. theoretical information only for those of a higher status) was identified as affects technology perceptions. Computers on the wards were identified as a threat to existing information dissemination procedures. Web-accessible digital libraries, in particular, disrupt these processes by increasing knowledge for those of lower status:

> *"they're going to be quoting text books at us and quoting policy notes*
> *but they need to go out there nursing patients."* (Nursing manager)

Some senior staff confirmed that they saw technology and specifically digital libraries as a benefit of status:

> *People lower down. Well they would resort to the actual standard*
> *text.'* (nursing manager)

Nurses and PAMs noted that information hoarding procedures by some senior staff also produced technology hoarding. Senior staff members often sought to retain their expert status by continuing to control information dissemination procedures via restricted access rights. Nurses' and PAMs' access to current technology within the hospital, is limited by either physical OR social restrictions (e.g. passwords, computer locks, location of computers). The hospital's current information hierarchy was also found to limit perceptions of future technology uses and locations for access. Access to digital libraries from the wards was particularly sensitive since higher status staff regarded this location as requiring practical rather than theoretical knowledge. Often the location of the computers on the wards within a specific territorial boundary caused friction between different user groups (e.g. doctors and nurses, senior and junior staff) who felt social pressure restricting their access.

Some senior staff argued that they would happily access information via the technology on behalf of junior staff. However, junior staff argued that security protocols would preclude a third party performing some information retrieval tasks.

Many senior staff members perceived digital libraries stored on an intranet and accessed by junior staff as less politically sensitive than web-accessible digital libraries. The Internet was seen as a threat to their status by providing open access to information sources while providing the potential for abuse (i.e. access for non-professional purposes). Intranet information provision, in contrast, was perceived as controlled by higher status staff members. Locally based DLs were also seen as advantageous for provision and effective updating of trust specific policies, protocols and standards. These were seen as not only increasing local accessibility to relevant documentation but also awareness.

3.4   DL Usability and Users' Perceptions of Technology

Many senior staff noted that poor usability meant that information access via computers was time-consuming. Computers were thought of as supporting research and not,

therefore, necessary on the wards. Some senior staff added that serious time constraints meant that clinicians sitting at computers on the wards would be viewed as a
wasting valuable time. Task specific libraries, however, were perceived far more as a
tool than a plaything:

> "I mean there are sort of Journals and manuals but they haven't got
> time to sit down and actually play per se." (nursing manager)

> "I'd like to think that as things are in the NHS with everybody so busy
> all day that there isn't a lot of time for all this sort of 'lets go and look
> at the computer screen and see what we can latch onto'." (consultant)

The usability of current medical digital libraries (e.g. Medline, Cochrane, NeLH),
in particular, was frequently noted as being so poor that clinicians would rather search
the Internet for the information they required. Using the Internet as one big digital
library was reported as quicker for picking up technology skills (e.g. browser usage)
than using specific DLs that employ varied and often complex searching mechanisms
– a finding that echoes those of a parallel study working with non-clinical users [5].
For a skilled clinician, the Internet was believed to be an important aid in accessing
reputable up-to-date information sources (e.g. academic sites, professional colleges).

Different routes for accessing digital libraries were noted as a key issue in the perceived usability of the system. Once the technology became less intrusive and more
familiar, the users' confidence in information retrieval greatly increased. Portals are
therefore an attractive proposition as long as they are appropriately designed to provide access to the right information.

Many senior clinicians, although able to navigate the web, did not perceive themselves as computer literate especially with regard to digital library usage. Recently
qualified staff members, in contrast, were perceived by their superiors as far more
computer literate. Of particular importance to all user groups was the subsequent
friction developing between recently qualified members of staff and those classed as
'old school professionals' who, in many cases, were techno-phobic.

> "the problem is that there is no formal help plan here and a lot of
> people feel 'well I should know about it but I don't and I feel silly go-
> ing to somebody that is much younger than I am saying explain it to
> me'." (surgeon)

> "because there are a lot of people in the department who haven't had
> any experience at all. You know who haven't been on training ses-
> sions and they're frightened of it." (PAM)

This generation gap was identified as a key factor in producing senior staff's perceptions of computers as a threat to their status as experts.

All the respondents noted the lack of support and training available with digital libraries. Effective on-line support was proposed as a major factor in changing negative
DL perceptions. However, some senior staff noted that current online training and
support facilities were not given at the right level for many clinicians needs.

> "Things either seem to be at the 'this is how you turn the computer
> on' level or very advanced and there doesn't seem to be much in be-
> tween." (surgeon)

3.5   DL Usability and Users' Perceptions of Technology

An important element of digital library perceptions is related to users' information management strategies. Digital libraries, while enabling users to develop some quicker, less stressful strategies, were restricted by the physicality of the medium and concepts of interaction styles.

Many of the clinicians proposed that digital libraries were a key element in enabling them to develop effective information management strategies. Previous hard copy management strategies required the user to frequently identify their current, imminent and future information needs for each journal they subscribed to. This meant frequent reading and re-reading of journals, sorting, cutting out and filing relevant sources. Electronic libraries enabled these users to dramatically simplify this process by speeding up the search, selection and filing procedures. However, many of the clinicians also noted that although DL mechanisms have speeded up these processes they do not support serendipitous skimming of information sources. Most senior clinicians, therefore, stated that they interwove their use of DLs with hard copy sources. Initially these users skim-read journals to identify potential articles of interest. This also supported their need for serendipitous interactions with articles not directly related to there area of expertise. These interactions were conducted with off-line sources because such resources are portable and staff are working to tight time constraints (e.g. they will read printed documents on their coffee break or while walking between meetings). Printed documents were also noted as being easier to interact with, digest and use as an interaction point with colleagues. Digital libraries were then used for later retrieval of previously identified articles or for directed searches to answer a current clinical query. Once these articles were found, however, the full documents (and frequently abridged versions) were always printed and read off-line. All the user groups, therefore, repeatedly noted the importance of adequate printing facilities. Key usability problems were also noted as relating to problems downloading and printing these documents.

Journals were noted as the major form of digital library information. International journals were highlighted as particularly important for obtaining up-to-date information on specialist areas of research.

> *"At a consultant level one tends to go less to text books and more and*
> *more to Journals."* (consultant)

However it was recognized that, because digital libraries were primarily used to store journals and related summaries, this constrained interpretations of future digital library uses. Restricted awareness of what digital libraries could store curbed perceptions of potential users (e.g. researchers, students, senior staff) and their tasks (e.g. research purposes, continued professional development and new developments).

Users' perceptions of the future relevance of digital libraries within a clinical setting related primarily to its interactivity. For example, current digital libraries simply represent mailed 'letters to the editor' electronically; this could be extended to online debates or reviews of articles. Similarly, the immediate benefits of updated, locally relevant day-to-day clinical information (e.g. policies, procedures, induction data, guidelines, and protocols), electronically stored and quickly retrievable, were recognized. Clinicians, however, require more than simple electronic representations of documents. These information sources would be invaluable if, subject to appropriate authentication, they could fulfill specific user needs, provide local knowledge and prompt updating requirements.

> *"... how to care for a wound point 6 ohhh yes I have to use this type of dressing and where are they kept ohhhh right they're kept under there"* (nursing manager)

Users also detailed the need for flexible libraries of organisational information (e.g. job title, role, contact details, schedules and diaries) that would then link into communication media such as email and ultimately the electronic patient record.

The IT department agreed that training was an issue within the organisation and that there was a need for more collaboration / communication with academic sites. However, the major problem identified with these developments was rapid organisational change with no apparent organisational body dealing with how these changes should occur.

The successful future deployment of this technology depends on collaboration and open mindedness towards technology uses as opposed to current information hoarding and technology misconceptions. Effective digital library design and use also depend on the provision of adequate digital library peripherals, usability and training with resources that meet research, practical and up-to-date information needs.

4 Discussion

The launch of CIAP (web-accessible DL) in Australia was accompanied by many stories of lives saved by clinicians who could quickly access relevant, specialised, up-to-date information. The publicity suggested that DLs were an instant success. However, as shown in this study, information is socially interpreted, and digital libraries can have significant effects on social relationships [23]. Within a clinical setting, information is negotiated and reinterpreted relative to experience and personal relationships [26]. This is especially relevant for those who regarded their status as an expert as being of paramount importance.

The findings detailed in this paper have also identified the importance of social structure and status in information dissemination processes. The majority of conflicts related to high status clinicians' information hoarding behaviours that led, in many cases, to technology hoarding. Increased information accessibility can provide users with knowledge which was previously inaccessible to them. Speedy, extensive information provision, as provided by digital libraries, was identified as a cause of conflicts and resentment within the organisational structure. However, the causes of information, and thus technology, hoarding can reveal potential solutions to these problems.

The main source of these behaviours was senior staffs' perception of their own inadequate technical abilities. With improved quality in IT training for subordinates there was a perceived increase in the gap between the knowledge acquisition abilities of junior and senior staff. Senior staff viewed the increased ability for junior staff to access information as a threat to perceptions of them as experts. As one participant noted:

> *"It's like being given a Rolls Royce and only knowing how to sound the horn."* (surgeon)

As noted by Levy et al [13], technology within the health profession is slowly eroding senior clinicians' sense of power. 'Smart' decision support tools and tele-health facilities are seen as re-directing the information power to lesser-trained providers or to the patients themselves. However, in reality, the nursing profession argue that technology is used to strengthen existing organisational cultures and status norms [20]. These findings identified, however, that nurses (specifically student nurses) were still very positive about digital libraries. Many nurses perceived DLs as not only an important information tool but also a device to liberate and empower them to complete their jobs more effectively.

Comparing the perceived success of CIAP [6] to our findings of conflicts from DL introduction, there are 3 main factors which have been suggested as being significant in the project's success [16]. Firstly CIAP was developed, deployed and managed by stakeholders in the system (i.e. all levels of clinicians and senior management): one of the major champions behind the system was a senior nurse. Secondly, usability was of primary importance in the system development and, finally, the system was deployed within a knowledge friendly culture where information sharing is encouraged.

The introduction of CIAP was hampered, however, by problems with access to PCs in clinical areas and resistance from IT managers who felt that their control on information and Internet access was being eroded. It was feared that clinicians would waste time 'playing' on the Internet. It is interesting to note that the IT department, within this study, were positive about computerised clinical information although they expressed a cautious approach to developments to ensure system usability while understanding the political sensitivity of any decisions they made.

5 Conclusion

Although DLs appear to be a relatively innocuous development in information provision (i.e. no sensitive data provision such as medical records), this research has highlighted how related social and organisational issues can impede effective technology deployment. To counteract these problems DL designers and implementers must first identify the social context prior to technology deployment. There is a need within this context to reduce perceived threats of DL technology amongst senior staff members by strongly supporting training. With increased usability and adequate technical support for senior clinicians, DLs would be perceived as support, rather than replacement, for their clinical expertise. Finally, to decrease the perception of DLs as irrelevant playthings (but work tools), increased general usability of the tools and task directed applicability are required. DLs must also be integrated appropriately into the workplace so that they aid all user groups in their work practices without being perceived as a tool to undermine senior clinicians' power. Increasing DL interactivity by blurring the divisions between supporting information, knowledge and communication tasks is a key issue in the development of applicable systems acceptable across the social structures.

Ultimately to design effective Digital Libraries we need to identify more than just effective mechanisms for storing and retrieving documents. There are further questions that should be asked with regard to the social repercussions of what is being stored, who will access it and for what purposes.

References

1. Adams, A.: Multimedia information changes the whole privacy ballgame. in proceedings of computers freedom and privacy 2000: challenging the assumptions. ACM Press CHI Conference Publications. (2000) 25 - 32
2. Adams, A. & Sasse, M. A.: Privacy issues in ubiquitous multimedia environments: Wake sleeping dogs, or let them lie? *In Proceedings of INTERACT' 99*, Edinburgh. (1999) 214-221
3. Adams, A. & Sasse, M. A.: Taming the wolf in sheep's clothing: privacy in multimedia communications. *In Proceedings of ACM multimedia' 99*, Orlando. (1999) 101-107
4. Adams, A. & Sasse, M. A.: The user is not the enemy. In Communications of ACM. (Dec. 1999) 40 – 46
5. Blandford, A., Stelmaszewska, H. & Bryan-Kinns, N.: Use of multiple digital libraries: a case study. To appear in Proc. JCDL 2001.
6. CIAP: www.clininfo.health.nsw.gov.au
7. Covi, L. & Kling, R.: Organisational dimensions of effective digital library use: Closed rational and open natural systems model. In *Kiesler, S* (ed) Culture of the Internet. Lawrence Erlbaum Associates, New Jersey (1997) 343-360
8. Gremy, F. and Bonnin, M.: Evaluation of automatic health information systems: what and how?, in Assessment and evaluation of information technologies. In *Gennip, E. and Talmon, J.L.* (eds.), "medicine van". Amsterdam: IOS Press (1995) 9-20
9. Grudin, J.: Groupware and social dynamics: Eight challengers for developers. Communications of the ACM, 37, (1994) 73-105.
10. Harrison, G. S.: The Winchester experience with the TDS hospital information system British Journal of Urology, 67(5). (May, 1991) 532-535
11. Heathfield, H.: The rise and fall of expert systems in medicine. In Expert Systems, Vol. 16, No.3. (August 1999) 183 – 188
12. Heathfield, H., Pitty, D. and Hanka, R.: Evaluating information technology in health care: barriers and challenges BMJ, 316, (1998) 1959 –1961
13. Levy, S., Bradley, M. J. M., Swanston, M. T. and Wilson, S.: Power as a concept in the evaluation of telehealth. In *Organisation development in health care: Strategies issues in health care management* Rushmer, R. K., Davies, H. T. O., Tavakoli, M. and Malek, M. (eds). (2001) Ashgate Publishing Ltd.
14. Marchionini, G. Nolet, V. Williams, H. Ding, W. Beale Jr., J. Rose, A. Gordon, A. Enomoto, E. and Harbinson, L.: Content + Connectivity => Community: Digital Resources for a learning community. In proceedings of ACM digital Libraries (DL'97), Philadelphia, ACM Press. (1997) 212-220
15. McColl, A. & Roland, M.: Clinical governance in primary care: Knowledge and information for clinical governance. BMJ, 321, (2000) 871-874.
16. Moody, D and Shanks, G.: Using knowledge management and the Internet to support evidence based practice. A medical case study, submitted to Australasian Conference on Information Systems. (1999)
17. Morgan, G.: Images of organization". London: Sage (1991)
18. Richman, J.: Medicine and Health. London: Longman(1987)
19. Sackett, D., Rosenberg, W., Gray, M., Haynes, B. & Richardson, S.: Evidence based medicine: what it is and what it isn't. BMJ, 312, (1996) 71-72

20. Sandellowski, M.: Culture, conceptive technology and nursing. *International Journal of nursing studies*, 36, (1999) 13-20
21. Schneider, K. & Wagner, I.: Constructing the 'Dossier Representatif': Computer-based information sharing in French hospitals. Computer Supported Cooperative Work, 1, (1993) 229-253.
22. Schein, E.: Organizational culture. American Psychologist, 45, (1990) 109-119
23. Schiff, L., Van House, N. & Butler, M.: Understanding complex information environments: a social analysis of watershed planning. In proceedings of ACM digital Libraries (DL'97), Philadelphia, ACM Press (1997) 161-168
24. Stevenson, C. & Cooper, N.: Qualitative and Quantitative research. *The Psychologist: Bulletin of the British Psychological Society*, April. (1997) 159-160
25. Strauss, A. & Corbin, J.: Basics of qualitative research: grounded theory procedures and techniques. Sage, Newbury Park. (1990)
26. Symon, G., Long, K & Ellis, J.: The Coordination of work activities: co-operation and conflict in a hospital context Computer supported cooperative work, 5 (1) (1996) 1-31
27. Turner, B.: Medical Power and Social Knowledge. London: Sage (1987)
28. Wyatt, J.: The clinical information access project, New South Wales: lessons from an NeLH precursor in proceedings of Advances in clinical knowledge management. Presented at ACKM 3 (2000)
www.ucl.ac.uk/kmc/kmc2/News/ACKM/ackm3/wyatt.html

Interactive, Domain-Independent Identification and Summarization of Topically Related News Articles

Dragomir R. Radev[1,2], Sasha Blair-Goldensohn[1], Zhu Zhang[1], and
Revathi Sundara Raghavan[2]

[1] School of Information, University of Michigan
Ann Arbor, MI 48109
{radev,sashabg,zhuzhang}@umich.edu
[2] Department of Electrical Engineering and Computer Science
University of Michigan, Ann Arbor, MI 48109
{radev, rsundara}@umich.edu

Abstract. In this paper[1] we present NewsInEssence, a fully deployed
digital news system. A user selects a current news story of interest which
is used as a seed article by NewsInEssence to find in real time other related stories from a large number of news sources. The output is a single
document summary presenting the most salient information gleaned from
the different sources. We discuss the algorithm used by NewsInEssence,
module interoperability, and conclude the paper with a number of empirical analyses.

1 Introduction

Text summarization[10] is used to provide concise versions of text documents to
a user who may not have the time to read the entire source material. A large
amount of research has been devoted to the automatic generation of summaries
of single documents. In this paper we extend the concept of a summary in three
ways - our input contains many sources, many documents, and many time points.

A news event is widely reported in the press. A large number of journalists
independently pick a newsworthy piece and turn it into a sequence of news
stories. We are concerned with the automatic generation of summaries of news
events as they occur. In the generic scenario for our system, NewsInEssence, a
user selects a single news story from a news Web site. Our system then searches
other live sources of news for other stories related to the same event and produces
summaries of a subset of the stories that it finds, as specified by the user.

In this paper, we will describe the functionality of NewsInEssence. We will
also discuss the particular challenges that a multi-source time-aware summarizer
has to surmount and the techniques that we used to address these challenges.
We conclude the paper with an evaluation of our approach, a discussion of its
scalability and portability, and with a glimpse into current work done at our
group to extend the functionality of NewsInEssence.

---

[1] Dragomir R. Radev is the correspondence author.

P. Constantopoulos and I.T. Sølvberg (Eds.): ECDL 2001, LNCS 2163, pp. 225–238, 2001.
© Springer-Verlag Berlin Heidelberg 2001

1.1   Related Work

Summarization of multiple documents originated with the SUMMONS system [5, 9]. In it, a series of related stories in a restricted domain were converted to a semantic representation using information extraction and then a summary was produced using natural language generation techniques. Later work on multi-document summarization includes the identification of similarities and difference among related articles [3, 4]. Maximal marginal relevance (MMR) was introduced in [2] as a measure for the amount of new information in an article. The summarizer used in NEWSINESSENCE makes use of relative utility, a metric similar to MMR.

Taxonomically, NEWSINESSENCE falls somewhere between FISHWRAP [1] and SUMMONS. As in FISHWRAP, it builds personalized view of news sources, and as in SUMMONS, it produces summaries of multiple documents. Unlike SUMMONS, NEWSINESSENCE is domain-independent and scalable to ten news sources and several dozen documents. In addition, our system automatically locates topically-related stories on a large number of real-time search engines.

2   The NewsInEssence System

2.1   Topic-Focused Search

Overview. Our system's topic-focused search is implemented by a web-crawling agent called NewsTroll. Beginning with a given news story's URL, NewsTroll attempts to gather a cluster of related stories from the Internet in real time.

The agent runs in two phases. In the primary phase, it looks for related articles by traversing links from the page containing the seed article. Using the seed article and any related articles it finds in this way, the agent then decides on a set of keywords. It does this using a modified TF*IDF technique to pick out words used often in this cluster but rarely in general.

Once it has settled on a set of keywords to use, it enters the secondary search phase. In this phase, it attempts to add to the cluster of related articles by going to the search engines of six news web sites and using the keywords which it found in the primary phase as search terms.

In both phases, NewsTroll selectively follows hyperlinks from its start page, i.e., the seed URL in the primary phase and the news site search pages in the secondary phase. In selecting which links to follow, NewsTroll aims to reach pages which contain related stories or further hyperlinks to such pages. In order to maximize the likelihood that a followed link is in one of these two categories, NewsTroll uses several levels of rule-based filtering.

Both general and site-specific rules help NewsTroll determine which URLs are likely to be useful. For example, its general rules tell it that a URL ending in ".jpg" should be screened out because it is unlikely to be a news story or contain links to news stories. A site-specific rule might say that on a given Web host, any link not pointing to the "news" directory is not of interest.

Only if NewsTroll determines a URL to be "interesting" according to these rules will it go to the Internet to fetch the pointed-to page. That page's hyperlinks are then extracted for review. A more stringent set of (mostly site-specific) rules are applied to determine whether the URL is likely to be a news story itself. If so, the similarity [7] of its text to that of the original seed page is computed. This similarity is measured as the cosine distance between IDF-weighted n-dimensional vector representations of the two documents. If the measured similarity is above a given threshold, the page is considered to contain a related news article and is saved and added to the cluster.

By using the logic of its rules and employing successively rigorous layers of filtering as described above, NewsTroll is able to screen out large numbers web pages quite inexpensively. The more intensive (and expensive) operation of testing lexical similarity is thus reserved for the much smaller number of pages which are likely to be related articles. Consequently, the agent can return useful results in real time.

Algorithm. The NewsTroll algorithm can be summarized as follows:

```
Input  : SeedUrl, SitesToSearch, ExitConditions
Output : Cluster

Cluster<-SeedUrl
WeightedKeywords<-get_common_keywords(SeedUrl, SeedUrl)
LinkedUrls<-get_links(SeedUrl)

//primary search
while UrlToTest<- next(LinkedUrls)
 && PrimaryExitCondition != true
   if follows_useful_rules(UrlToTest)
      LinkedUrls<- LinkedUrls + get_links(UrlToTest)
      if follows_article_rules(UrlToTest)
       && (similarity(SeedUrl, UrlToTest) > threshold)
         Cluster<- Cluster + UrlToTest
         WeightedKeyWords<- WeightedKeyWords +
          get_common_keywords(SeedUrl, UrlToTest)

SecSearchKeyWords<- max_n(WeightedKeyWords)

//secondary search
while SearchSite<-next(SitesToSearch)
 && SecondaryExitCondition != true
   SearchPage<- generate_search(SearchSite,
                      SecSearchKeyWords)
   LinkedUrls<- get_links(SearchPage)
   while UrlToTest<- next(LinkedUrls)
    && SecondaryExitCondition != true
      if follows_useful_rules(UrlToTest)
         LinkedUrls<- LinkedUrls + get_links(UrlToTest)
         if follows_article_rules(UrlToTest)
         && (similarity(SeedUrl,
                    UrlToTest) > threshold)
            Cluster<- Cluster + UrlToTest

Return Cluster
```

All input parameters to the NewsTroll algorithm, such as SeedUrl, SitesTo-Search, and ExitConditions, are modifiable by the user.

Annotated Sample Run. To illustrate the operation of the NewsTroll agent and its role the NewsInEssence, we will now explain the system's operation in a recent example run.

The example begins when we find a news article we would like to read more about. In this case we pick a story is about a breaking story regarding one of President-Elect Bush's cabinet nominees (see Figure 1).

Fig. 1. Sample Run - stage 1.

Now that we have found our seed story, we input its URL into the NewsInEssence system. We then, select our search timeout and other options, click 'Proceed' and wait for our results (see Figure 2).

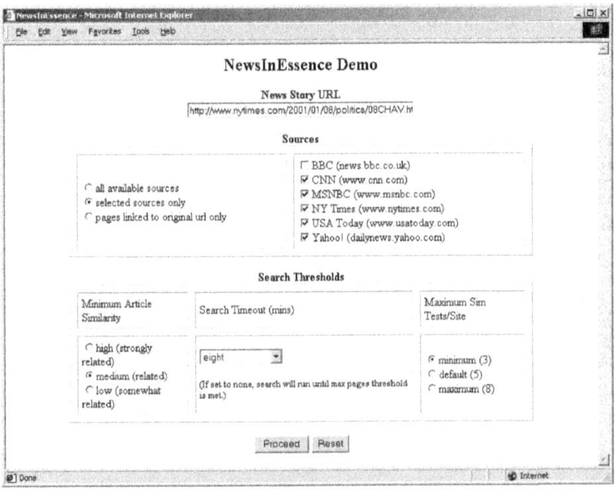

Fig. 2. Sample Run - stage 2.

NewsTroll begins its crawl at the start page we have selected. In a selection from the agent's output log in figure 3, we can see that it first extracts links from the page, and then decides to test one which look like news articles. We then see that it tests this article and determines it to be related. This article is added to the initial cluster, from which the list of top keywords is drawn (see Figure 3).

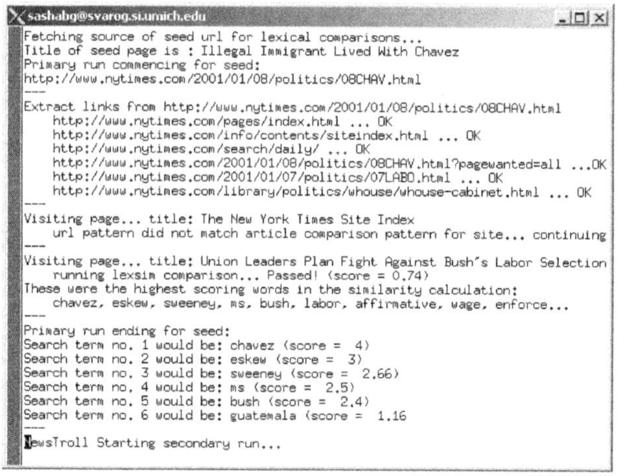

Fig. 3. Sample Run - stage 3.

In its secondary phase, NewsTroll uses these keywords to give the secondary search a targeted nature: it lets the search engines of the news sites do the work, and if we have selected good keywords (as we have in this case) most of the links seen by NewsTroll in the secondary search will indeed point to related articles (see Figure 4). In fact, the search terms are so successful in this case that only one of the 12 articles tested in the secondary phase turns out to be unrelated to the seed story. Upon exiting, NewsTroll reports the number of links it has seen, followed, tested/visited and retrieved (see Figure 4).

The agent reports its progress to the user and provides a link to the GUI for visualization of the cluster (Figure 5). Using the GUI, the user can visualize the cluster and select which of the articles to summarize (see Figures 6 and 7). Figures 8, and 9 show the interface to the summarizer.

2.2   Standardization of Document Formats

Processing the HTML files. Most language processing/summarization systems start with documents that may not share a common format. NEWSI-NESSENCE must address this problem in terms of handling news documents from web sources which format their documents very differently. In order to enable

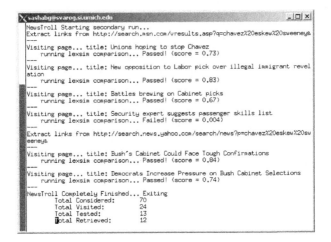

Fig. 4. Sample Run - stage 4.

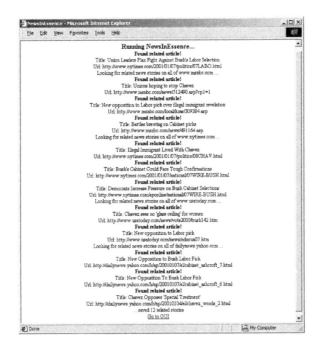

Fig. 5. Sample Run - stage 5.

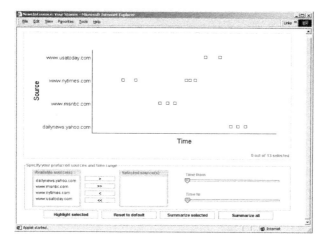

Fig. 6. Sample Run - stage 6.

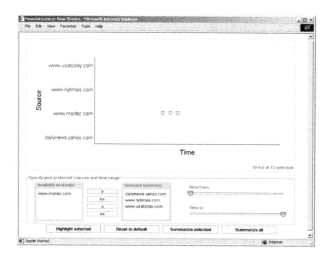

Fig. 7. Sample Run - stage 7.

our system to comprehend the information and use it effectively, it is hence essential to process the documents returned by the NewsTroll and represent them in a common format. Our system does this by translating the raw HTML data into an XML format with a fixed DTD.

Common News Format. The XML format used to represent all retrieved documents is illustrated below with an example of a conforming document. (Table 1 explains the individual tags and their purpose.)

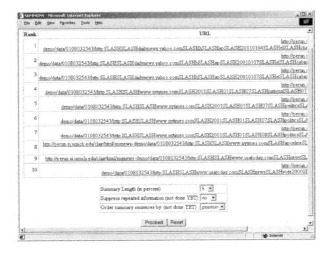

Fig. 8. Sample Run - stage 8.

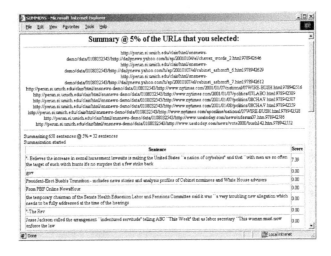

Fig. 9. Sample Run - stage 9.

```
<DOC>
  <HEAD>
    <FILENAME> /clair/afs/loaddir/index0212/a.xml </FILENAME>
    <SOURCE> www.cnn.com </SOURCE>
    <URL> www.cnn.com/news/index021200.html </URL>
    <HEADLINE> Were the voters confused  </HEADLINE>
    <DESCRIPTION>
       The U.S. media urges a swift resolution
       to the ongoing disputes over the outcome
```

```
      of the presidential election.
    </DESCRIPTION>
    <TITLE>
      bbc news | americas | were the voters confused?
    </TITLE>
    <KEYWORDS>
       bbc news world uk international foreign
       british online service
    </KEYWORDS>
    <RDATE> 979142176 </RDATE>
    <PDATE> 979142059 </PDATE>
  </HEAD>
  <BODY>
   <TEXT>
   Times have moved on from the days that voters
   simply needed to mark a cross next to their
   preferred candidates. Now, millions of Americans
   insert a card into the top of a machine known as
   a votomatic. They then use a pointed instrument
   or stylus to punch out a tiny rectangle of paper
   - the infamous Chad - from their ballot papers.
   </TEXT>
  </BODY>
</DOC>
```

Conversion. In order to achieve the conversion into this common format, we wrote software to process and translate documents from the raw HTML cluster which is retrieved and saved by the NewsTroll agent.

The first step in the conversion process involves cleaning the HTML to remove tags not of interest to our system, such as script tags, style tags, etc. Following this the HTML file is made well-formed with the aid of an open source program called TIDY. The well-formed HTML is then transformed into an XML file conforming to the DTD described above using an XSL style sheet. The current conversion is based on HTML formats observed from 6 supported news sources viz. CNN, BBC, MSNBC, NYTimes, Yahoo! and USAToday.

The XSL template must support the multiple formats used on these various sites in order to correctly extract meta-data into the set of tags used in our system's common article format. For example, our common format specifies that an article's publication date should be stored in the PDATE tag. However, one news site may store this data in an HTML meta-tag named "Original Publication Date", while another may store it under two separate meta-tags, "pubdate" and "pubtime". The XSL style sheet contains the rules for translation between these varying proprietary formats and our own common DTD. By encapsulating this knowledge in the XSL file, our approach makes it relatively easy to adapt to changes in source formats or support new sources.

TAGNAME	PURPOSE	TAG STATUS
DOC	This tag encloses the entire document	Required
HEAD	This tag contains information extracted from the meta data in the HTML files.	Required
FILENAME	This tag contains the local filename under which the document is stored	Required
SOURCE	This tag contains information about the source of the news article. E.g., BBC, CNN, etc.	Required
URL	This tag contains the exact url of the document	Required
HEADLINE	This tag contains the headline of the news story	Optional
DESCRIPTION	This tag contains a short description of the story.	Optional
TITLE	This tag contains the title of the webpage that the document corresponds to.	Optional
KEYWORDS	This tag contains some of the keywords in the news story.	Optional
RDATE	This tag contains the date on which the article was retrieved. The date is in an ASCII format that may be interpreted using existing Perl modules.	Required
PDATE	This tag contains the date that the article was published	Currently Optional
BODY	This tag currently only contains the text tags	Required
TEXT	This tag encloses the actual text or the news story.	Required

Table 1. Markup tags for XML documents in the common news article format.

Index files. Having retrieved a number of documents and processed them to conform to our own XML DTD we now require some way of indexing the documents so that some subset of them may be accessed for summarization. For example, the user may wish to summarize all the documents that have been retrieved from a given source or in a given time interval.

We achieve this indexing through another XSL-based translation. This second translation takes as input the XML documents produced by the above-described conversion of the cluster of HTML stories from the web. It then produces a single XML index file which contains index data for each of the articles in the cluster.

Index file Example. Figure 10 shows an example of the XML index file. The index is used to retrieve documents in the cluster by source, date of publication, etc.

2.3   User Interface

Once the news stories found by the NewsTroll agent are translated into XML and an index file generated, the user can use our systems GUI to visualize the cluster (See Figures 6 and 7).

```
<?xml version="1.0" standalone="yes" ?>
<INDEX>
  <DOC>
    <SOURCE>
      news.bbc.co.uk
    </SOURCE>
    <URL>
       http://news.bbc.co.uk/hi/english/business/newsid_1106000
       /1106035.stm
    </URL>
    <FILENAME>
      /clair/html/snsnews-demo/data/0110105404/http:SLASHSLASH
      news.bbc.co.ukSLASHhiSLASHenglishSLASHbusinessSLASH
      newsid_1106000SLASH1106035.stm.979142364
    </FILENAME>
    <PDATE>
      978956640
    </PDATE>
    <RDATE>
      979142364
    </RDATE>
  </DOC>
  <DOC>
    <SOURCE>
      www.msnbc.com
    </SOURCE>
    <URL>
      http://www.msnbc.com/news/513959.asp
    </URL>
    <FILENAME>
      /clair/html/snsnews-demo/data/0110105404/http:SLASHSLASH
      www.msnbc.comSLASHnewsSLASH513959.asp.979142059
    </FILENAME>
    <RDATE>
      979142059
    </RDATE>
  </DOC>
</INDEX>
```

Fig. 10. Sample Index File (abridged).

The GUI uses the document meta-data extracted in the conversion process described above to represent each article as a data point in a two-dimensional space. The horizontal axis is the time line while the vertical axis corresponds to various sources where the news articles come from. The coordinate system is scalable and can accommodate an arbitrary number of sources and arbitrary time range. The distance along the time axis between two data points is proportional to the actual difference between the two time points.

The GUI also gives users the flexibility to specify a time range and set of sources. The selected subset of data points can be highlighted in the 2D space and, using the cluster's index file, the GUI can then pass the corresponding articles' filenames to the summarizer. Using the local files which have been downloaded by the agent makes the summarization process extremely efficient.

The GUI is implemented as a Java Swing applet. IBM's XML4J parser is used to parse the index file in XML format. Portability of Java and XML technologies speaks for that of our system.

3   The Multi-document Summarization Backend

The multi-document summarization backend of NEWSINESSENCE is an improved version of the one used in NEWSINESSENCE's predecessor, ESSENSE [8, 6]. It is based on a technique, called *centroid-based summarization* which takes into account, among other things, salient terms from the entire cluster of related documents to pick what excerpts to select for the cluster summary.

4   Experiments

In order to test the current performance of the NewsTroll agent, the following experiment was carried out:

12 seed pages were selected, at least one each from the six news sites currently supported by NewsTroll's rules. The stories reported on these seed pages came from a range of topics, from the latest Middle East peace efforts, to the recent election of a new president in Ghana, and to power shortages in California.

For each story, two sample runs of the agent were performed. The only difference between the two runs was that the first would use a higher lexical similarity threshold (0.28), the second a lower one (0.18). The following parameters (all settable through the web interface in Figure 2) were used:

– Timeout for entire run = 8 minutes
– Maximum of 5 lexical similarity tests or 15 pages retrieved per source
– Use all sources if time permits

Results of the experiment are in Table 2.

| | Entire Search | | Primary Search | | | Secondary Search | | | | | | |
| | Links | | Pages | | | All Pages | | | Related Pages | | Sources | |
	Seen	Followed	Visit	Test	Save	Visit	Test	Save	Test	Save	Total	Fruitful
High	1700	293	74	40	23	228	123	71	75	70	37	25
Low	1399	267	75	40	23	193	115	80	81	77	32	21
Total	3099	560	149	80	46	421	238	151	156	147	69	46
Avg	129	23	6.2	3.3	1.9	17.5	9.9	6.2	6.5	6.1	2.9	1.9

Table 2. Results.

Note the following interesting results:

– An average of eight related pages returned per article, with 1.9 of these being found in the primary run.
– Approximately one-sixth of hyperlinks passed the first set of rules and were visited for link extraction. In turn, and approximately one-half of those pages were determined to be news articles and were tested for lexical similarity with the seed story.

- There was little correlation evident between the agent's results and whether the higher/lower similarity threshold was used. (Examination of the data showed that only 8 of 318 pages tested fell into the range in between the high and low thresholds used. These tended to be pages which were tangentially related to the seed article, i.e. news summaries which contained a small section about the story in question. Perhaps a larger or more diverse sample would yield more pages in this range. If so it might be useful to segregate these articles into a "background info" cluster)
- NewsTroll ran an average of 13.1 similarity tests in an entire run. On average, 6.5 of these 13.1 articles were judged by a human to be related, and of these NewsTroll correctly saved 6.1 on average. (The discrepancy of 6.5-6.1 = .4 articles/search is made up of articles which NewsTroll did not judge to be related, i.e. whose similarity to the seed page fell below the lexical similarity threshold used.)
- Although there are six news sources which the NewsTroll knows how to query in its secondary run, on average it only successfully reached three of these per run. This generally happened because the search timed out. Taken together with the result that 2/3 of sites visited in the secondary search yielded at least one related article, this indicates that with more tuning (or more time), the NewsTroll would very likely return a higher average number of stories per search.
- Only for one of twelve seed stories did the secondary search phase yield no related stories. This indicates that the primary search phase was extremely successful in choosing keywords for the secondary search from its initial cluster.

5   Conclusion

We presented a digital news system, NEWSINESSENCE which produces domain-independent multi-document summaries of clusters of related news articles that one of the system's modules, NewsTroll collects using lexical similarity from a user-specified seed story. A fully-functional system is available on the Web at `http://perun.si.umich.edu/clair/snsnews-demo/snsnews.cgi`.

5.1   Scalability and Portability Issues

The current implementation of NEWSINESSENCE works entirely through the web, and can be used by anyone with a Java-enabled browser. While our test usage required only the resources of a pedestrian web server, a larger-scale implementation would require a scaling up of certain system components. For instance, IDF data for lexical similarity tests is currently accessed from a flat file by each instance of the NewsTroll agent, where an online database would be more efficient for a larger number of concurrent users. Another scale issue is the addition of news sources to the agent's rule base. Although the system's modular design makes this fairly painless from our perspective, system administrators for commercial news sources might take a dim view of a large-scale robot slowing down their site.

5.2 Future Work

Aside from changes that would improve speed and efficiency of cluster gathering, a focus of future work on the system will be the summarization module. In particular, the increased reliability of our cluster gathering shifts the focus onto the task of multi-document summarization. That is, now that we can get a set of related stories, how best to produce a concise, non-redundant summary.

References

[1] W. Bender, P. Chesnais, S. Elo, A. Shaw, and M. Shaw. Enriching communities: Harbingers of news in the future. *IBM Systems Journal*, 35(3&4):369–380, 1996.

[2] J. Carbonell and J. Goldstein. The use of mmr, diversity-based reranking for reordering documents and producing summaries. In *Proceedings of SIGIR'98*, Melbourne, Australia, 1998.

[3] Inderjeet Mani and Eric Bloedorn. Multi-document summarization by graph search and matching. In *Proceedings of the Fourteenth National Conference on Artificial Intelligence (AAAI-97)*, pages 622–628, Providence, Rhode Island, 1997. American Association for Artificial Intelligence.

[4] Inderjeet Mani, Eric Bloedorn, and Barbara Gates. Using cohesion and coherence models for text summarization. In *Symposium on Intelligent Text Summarization*, pages 69–76, Stanford, California, March 1998. American Association for Artificial Intelligence.

[5] Kathleen R. McKeown and Dragomir R. Radev. Generating summaries of multiple news articles. In *Proceedings, 18th Annual International ACM SIGIR Conference on Research and Development in Information Retrieval*, pages 74–82, Seattle, Washington, July 1995.

[6] Dragomir Radev and Weiguo Fan. Automatic summarization of search engine hit lists. In *Proceedings, ACL Workshop on Recent Advances in NLP and IR*, Hong Kong, October 2000.

[7] Dragomir R. Radev, Vasileios Hatzivassiloglou, and Kathleen R. McKeown. A description of the CIDR system as used for TDT-2. In *DARPA Broadcast News Workshop*, Herndon, VA, February 1999.

[8] Dragomir R. Radev, Hongyan Jing, and Malgorzata Budzikowska. Summarization of multiple documents: clustering, sentence extraction, and evaluation. In *ANLP/NAACL Workshop on Summarization*, Seattle, WA, April 2000.

[9] Dragomir R. Radev and Kathleen R. McKeown. Generating natural language summaries from multiple on-line sources. *Computational Linguistics*, 24(3):469–500, September 1998.

[10] Karen Sparck-Jones. Automatic summarising: factors and directions. In Inderjeet Mani and Mark Maybury, editors, *Advances in Automatic Text Summarization*. MIT press, to appear, 1998.

Digital Work Environment (DWE): Using Tasks to Organize Digital Resources

Narayanan Meyyappan, Suliman Al-Hawamdeh and Schubert Foo

Division of Information Studies, Nanyang Technological University
Nanyang Avenue, Singapore 639798
assuliman@ntu.edu.sg; assfoo@ntu.edu.sg

Abstract. DWE is aimed at providing a one-stop access point to local and remote digital library collections, traditional in-house libraries, and most importantly, to the vast array of information resources that exists in the academic community's local Intranet. Due to vast amount of information available and the difficulty faced by students and staff in finding the relevant resources, there is a need for a better and logical organization of these resources. DWE uses tasks as a means of directing students and staff to the relevant resources. Tasks generally play an important role in system and user interface design. Identifying the user's tasks enables the designer to construct user interfaces reflecting the tasks' properties, including efficient usage patterns, easy-to-use interaction sequences, and powerful assistance features. The resources in DWE are organized according to specific tasks performed by the research students and staff in the division of information studies. The tasks and resources were elicited based on the needs of faculty and students through interviews and focus groups.

1 Introduction

Digital libraries, among its many roles, play an important part in assisting teaching and research activities. The traditional approach to libraries as a collection of material not longer holds true as a result of evolving technologies such as multimedia, voice recognition, intelligent agents and knowledge management practices. In the last few years, digital library (DL) research has drawn much attention not only in the developed countries but also in developing countries. Improvements in information technology and increased funding towards information infrastructure have led to the development of a wide range of DL collections and services [6,7]. In terms of DL, the academic community is possibly the largest and the most important group of users. User requirements from a digital library are influenced by their nature of work, affiliation, educational background, accessibility to technology, and so on [5,8]. The nature of work of faculty, staff, student and researcher vary according to their tasks in an academic setting. In order to perform these tasks, access and use of information from a variety of sources in both print and electronic forms, such as journals, CD-ROM databases, on-line databases, multimedia databases, Web pages will be required. In addition to that, other resources include course calendars, university statutes, various course offering, course registration, thesis and dissertation

P. Constantopoulos and I.T. Sølvberg (Eds.): ECDL 2001, LNCS 2163, pp. 239-250, 2001.

guidelines, style guides, laboratory facilities, availability of software, hardware, equipment, course materials, resource book/handout collections, local publication databases, locally produced theses and dissertations and so on. Almost all of the current digital libraries do not manage or provide access to these diverse buy yet extremely useful collections of information.

The problems faced by the users of a DL are many. First of all, they may not know which information source may be appropriate to accomplish a particular task or to resolve a particular problem. Secondly, even if users are aware of the existence of a particular information source, they may not know where and how to locate it, and finally how to retrieve the information. Current digital libraries along with systems on the World Wide Web, expect users to know what they want precisely and also expect them to formulate a query to represent their information needs, or to map their query onto the often unknown knowledge structure (subject directory). One of the biggest problems faced by students and faculty members in the academic community is that the needed resources are not organized efficiently and effectively. Rather, they are mostly scattered all over the place. The other problem is the number of resources is growing everyday at an astonishing rate, making it difficult to identify the needed resource. Building a DL environment using a task-based design provides one appropriate means to organize and group these resources according to the tasks and subtasks needed to accomplish different types of jobs.

Task based design and analysis is accepted within the Human Computer Interface community as an important tool in designing interactive applications. It has been recognized as an important factor in user interface design [1,2]. While task based design form the basis for software and system development, it is only recently, that we have seen methods which offer a tighter integration of task analysis activities with subsequent design activities, thereby supporting greater use of task information in creating user interface designs Task-based user interface design emphasise the importance of users and their tasks at the starting point of the design process. It emphasises the importance of designers developing an understanding of user' existing work tasks, the requirements of changing those tasks, and the consequences that new designs may have on tasks [3]. One of the important aspects of task based design is understanding users needs. This is normally done through observations, user studies, and interviews and from working experience with systems and people. The majority of today's systems use an interactive and event-driven paradigm. Events are messages the user, or the system, sends to the program. A keystroke is an event. So is a mouse-click. Interactive task based design systems place more emphasis on people and their needs to achieve a specific task. This allows people to work in the actual task domain rather than the computer domain [4].

Task-based design can help the user to locate the relevant resources at the right time by selecting the relevant task to be accomplished. The proposed Digital Work Environment (DWE) is aimed at assisting the academic users in carrying out various tasks, thereby eliminating some of the aforementioned problems

2   Task Oriented Research in Digital Libraries

Michelle and Wang [9] designed a user interface (SenseMaker) for information exploration in a heterogeneous digital library. SenseMaker facilitates both the contextual evolution of a user's interests and the moves between browsing and searching via structure-based searching and structure-based filtering. *MyLibrary* [10] is a Cornell University Library initiative to provide personalized library services to their students, faculty, and staff on the basis of a focus group study to gauge the feedback of library users. The *MyLibrary* project has two components, *MyLink* and *MyUpdate*. *MyLink* is used to facilitate their patrons to save useful information resource links that they found themselves or ones suggested by the librarians via a targeted notification in their personal space. Users can access this personal space from any place. *MyUpdate* periodically queries the on-line catalog and notifies the users when matches to the predefined needs of users are detected.

HeadLine [11] is one of the eLib programme's Phase 3 projects, developing a hybrid library system known as the HeadLine Personal Information Environment (PIE). This PIE uses portal-type technology to present an information environment that is personalized to the users' needs and support users' customization. PIE presents users with pages of resources relevant to their courses/department as well as an "All resources" page that contains all of the resources to which their library provides access. Both the MyLibrary and HeadLine projects are designed to provide users with direct links to information resources. Users can add the required information resources to their list and use the resources from any place, any time. However, in both of these systems, the users are still expected to browse through a lengthy list of resources and pick up the relevant ones, and organise them in such a way themselves in order to facilitate easy access in future.

In addition, a few other task oriented projects have been reported in the literature. The CORE project (involving the American Chemical Society and Chemical Abstracts Service, as well as Bellcore, Cornell, and OCLC) that deals with the chemical literature [12] uses a task-oriented approach to access information. This project was designed to access the chemical literature supporting the research, referencing and writing activities of staff in a university chemistry department.

Fox [13] designed a digital library, Envison, based on user needs. This project was built on nine principles as a "user centered databases from the computer science literature", using the publications of the Association of Computing Machinery (ACM). One of the principles is task-oriented access to electronic archives. This project has an interface designed on the basis of interview with users, experts in library, information and computer science. They conducted a usability evaluation of the developed interface and discussed various user needs on the basis of the interview and suggested for a task based digital library.

Cousins [14] developed the Digital Library Integrated Task Environment (DLITE) as part of the Stanford Digital Library project. This DLITE project is based on the concept of a workcenter, a place on the user interface that provides all the components necessary for the completion of a specific task. This interface is based on scenarios and published studies of library use. An important aspect of DLITE is its use of direct manipulation, and drag and drop style of interface.

The user needs explained earlier in this paper has been solved to some extent using profiles in digital library projects such as the PIE and MyLibrary projects. However, none of these projects have adequately resolved the users' problem of the need to have a one-stop environment that serves to aid the user to locate, access and use information directly, and to meet their information needs according to their tasks in totality. The proposed DWE aims to address this gap to provide a useful environment for the academic community.

3   Digital Work Environment

DWE is designed with the main objective of providing a one-stop access point to local and remote digital library collections, traditional in-house libraries, and most importantly, to the vast array of information resources that exists in the academic community's Intranet.   Additionally, it uses the task-based model to provide an efficient means of organising and facilitating access to these resources.   Many different tasks are accomplished by the three main user groups of faculty, students and staff in an academic community.

As an example, some of the tasks accomplished by graduate students in a Masters degree programme include those of course registration, course participation, examination, dissertation and other activities such as social, cultural and sports activities. Tasks accomplished by the corresponding faculty include preparing and delivering lectures, tutorials, research work, supervision of student dissertations, consultancy work, short courses, management activities and other activities such as social, cultural, and sports activities. Each of the main tasks can be broken down into a series of sub tasks, and sub-sub tasks as necessary until unit tasks can be specified uniquely. Differing resources and information are required at these differing levels for task accomplishment.

Many of these tasks, such as exam paper preparation, are in fact common between different departments and schools. However, due to the differing nature of disciplines within the academic environment, the process of writing a dissertation might vary from one school to another. However, one of the important issues here is that these tasks remain fairly stable and do not change that fast. After some time, a set of Best Practices will emerge to dictate how best to accomplish them and what are the corresponding information resources that are required for them. At the present day, most of the information related to guidelines, policies and procedures are generally available in the department or university's web-sites. Other information resources, such as databases, online public access catalogs, CD-ROMs, virtual and digital libraries are also available on the Web.

The DWE prototype focuses on the Dissertation task to illustrate the task-oriented concept for information access. The design is based on an underlying user needs study conducted at Division of Information Studies (DIS), School of Computer Engineering at Nanyang Technological University (NTU), Singapore. The Division conducts the Master of Science in Information Studies programme by coursework. It operates on a two-semester academic year system where each semester is divided equally into six months. The new academic year commences in the middle of July. The Division has an annual enrollment of approximately 90 students (both part-time and full-time) for its Master programme. The full time students typically require two semesters (1 year) to complete the programme while the part time students typically require four semesters (2 years). Apart from that, the Division has a small number of postgraduate students enrolled for research programmes leading to the Master of Applied Science and Doctor of Philosophy. The DWE prototype is developed in a web environment using the Tango Enterprises [15] application software that is coupled to the MS Access database.

3.1 Basic Architecture of the System

Figure 1 shows the basic architecture of the DWE. The system consists of a User Interface module that is linked to the User Authentication & Management module, Resource Maintenance module, Task/Sub-task module and Information Resource Organisation module. The environment is used by three main groups of users, namely, the *Information Resource Administrator, User Manager* and *the General Academic Users.*

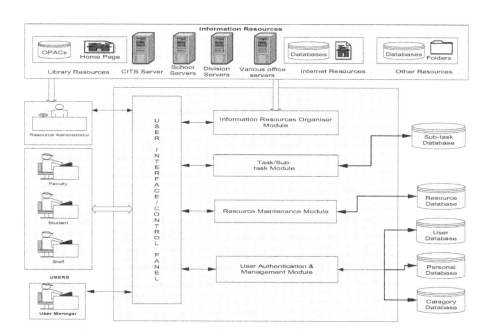

Figure 1: Basic Architecture of DWE

The *Information Resource Administrator* is responsible for collecting information about sub-tasks, information resources that are required to accomplish the task, creation and maintenance of the resource database. The *User Manager*, as the name implies, manages the overall collection of user-related information, creation of user accounts, maintenance of the User database and users personal space data in the personal database. The *General Academic Users* are the end users of the DWE. They include faculty, students and staff who uses the system to access the information resources to meet their information needs while accomplishing some tasks at hand.

The systems is composed of four main modules as follow:
The *User Authentication and Management Module* is used to identify a user during a user login process to ascertain the type of user by interacting with the user category database. With this information, it subsequently displays the corresponding lists of tasks that are related to that category of user. This module is used by the User Manager to append or update the respective user and category databases. The *Task/Sub-task Module* is used by the Resource Administrator to update the respective tasks and sub-tasks in the tasks database. This is used to define the relationships between main task, sub-task and sub-sub-tasks, thereby forming the hierarchy of parent-child tasks relationships.

The *Resource Maintenance Module* is maintained by the Resource Administrator for update of URL, resources password in resource database through the interface. The *Information Resources Organiser Module* responses to the users requests through the user interface and interacts with servers in the Intranet, library home page, databases, folders and Internet resources, and so on, to bring back the needed information resources to the users.

3.2   User Interface/Control Panel

The DWE interface is frame-based as shown in Figure 2. The interface shows the different types of tasks and subtasks that are performed in the Division by students. Some of these tasks are generic and similar to those performed in other divisions in the school. The interface is divided into three frames: *Welcome, Navigation tree, and Display*. In the *Navigation tree frame*, various tasks associated with each category of users in the DWE are organized in the form of a hierarchical tree structure starting with the general task and ending with the specific lowest level of sub-task.

The tree structure of DWE enables users to locate specific sub-tasks, sub-sub-tasks easily. It is to important to reiterate that this tree structure changes according to user categories since it is tailored to support different users of the system. Once the specific task is identified another level will be displayed in the tree structure to show the sub-tasks, and the next level shows the sub-sub-tasks and finally. The individual leaf of the tree structure shows the resource descriptor name, link and tools needed to perform the selected sub-task. Upon selecting an appropriate resource, the *Display frame* displays the content of the selected information resource. Users can expand and collapse the nodes in the tree structure to move to other resources.

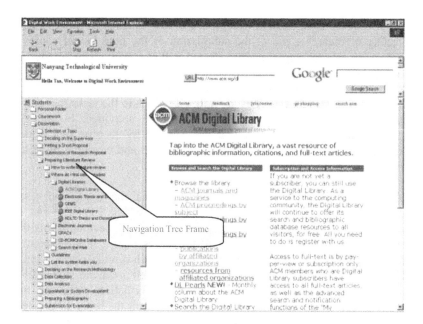

Figure 2: DWE Interface

As shown in the Navigation tree frame of Figure 2, the Dissertation task consists of a number of sub-tasks. These sub-tasks were identified based on a needs study of student and faculty users, the university and division policies and best practices derived in the past few years. The DWE is therefore serves as a gateway to digital resources, policies, guidelines and best practices of DIS. The DWE is not merely a collection of resources or a set of Web Links, but rather an intelligent platform that incorporates reference services such as questions and answers, search strategies, best practices and past experiences that can be captured and used to facilitate performing various tasks.

The use of DWE is simple and straightforward. A user enters the DWE URL on the web browser to be prompted to enter the user identification and password. Upon successful authentication, a personalised greeting message is displayed to the user. The user will navigate and activate the various frames of the DWE interface to select sub-tasks, sub-sub-tasks and information resources. The interface takes user information from the database and displays the appropriate navigation frame depending on the user category. For the Dissertation task, there may be some additional sub-task for faculty members that are not needed for students so that the navigation frame's tree nodes/sub-nodes are different for different categories of users.

3.3 Choosing a Representative Task

The Dissertation task that encompass the process of preparing and writing a dissertation is selected as a representative task in this prototype development due to the importance of the task, and knowledge of the well-established process that spans from selecting a research topic to the submission of the hard bound copies of the dissertation. The selected representative design will also be used to demonstrate the concept used in designing the DWE.

In task based system design, priorities are normally given to the tasks that are viewed important and critical to the users and organization activities. In an academic environment, there are many tasks that are viewed by faculty and students as important. Carrying out an independent research project and writing a dissertation is considered an important task in the course.

The techniques of user studies were used to define the associated tasks and information resources that are used in the Dissertation task. Faculty and student needs were elicited as well as best practices of the Division in accomplishing the task. Thus, the various sub-tasks, sub-sub-tasks of the representative task dissertation and the needed information resources were identified through discussions and interviews with three professors, three research students, and a few graduate students. These discussions formed the basis for providing the information resources that are subsequently stored in the resources database. It also forms the basis for the design of the DWE prototype for the academic community.

At the time of writing, the Division has accumulated over 400 dissertations, most of which are available in softcopy form. Students of this Division frequently refer to these dissertations for their dissertation work. Full time students normally start their project work at the end of the first semester and are expected to finish the dissertation by the end of the second semester. Part time students start their project at the beginning of the first semester of their second year and normally take two semesters to complete the project. The resources that are available in the DWE are therefore actively utilised during the whole course of the project. The system is expected to be augmented other additional tasks in future to create a fully functional DWE for the NTU academic community.

3.4 The Tasks of Writing a Master Dissertation

Students in the Division are required to undertake a research project and write a dissertation. This normally starts with selecting and deciding on a research project and a supervisor. Students normally are given the faculty profile and their research areas to facilitate the process of supervisor selection. The complete task of preparing for a dissertation can be broken into a number of sub-tasks that include:

- Familiarity with rules and regulations
- Familiarity with the guidelines to carry out the project
- Selecting a topic
- Finding faculty information and identifying potential supervisors
- Deciding on the supervisor
- Collecting information about necessary resources (e.g. computer and other equipment)

- Writing a short research proposal
- Submitting the topic and research proposal for approval
- Preparing and writing a literature review
- Deciding on the research methodology
- Presenting the proposal
- Data collection
- Data analysis
- Experiment or system development
- Familiarity of the style guide and standards for writing dissertation
- Preparing dissertation chapters
- Preparing a bibliography
- Submission of dissertation for examination
- Binding of amended dissertation
- Final submission

At each sub-task, students will require different types of information and resources. Some of these might involve resource discovery and access to digital libraries and resources over the Internet. For example, selecting a topic for dissertation involves many sub-tasks, such as knowing the specialisation of faculty members, knowing completed dissertations, on-going dissertations, equipment or facility available, number of students working under each faculty member in the division, and so on. Sometimes students may need help from other division faculty members for their projects. In that case, students will need information about other division's faculty specialisation and their availability. Such tasks will form the basis of the various sub tasks for the different aspect of the Dissertation task. The prototype designed therefore provides such a structure of tasks and sub-tasks, and the information resources that are appropriate for these different sub-tasks.

Taking another example, in preparing a literature review chapter, students need to tap into a wealth of resources to find similar studies and information related to their topic. These resources are not organized in any form and most of the time students find it hard to locate the right resources. Grouping these resources in one place for a specific task will facilitate the search process and shorten the time normally student spends in locating relevant resources. Providing merely links to resources might not be that effective in meeting the students needs. Therefore, providing additional tools such as intelligent agents, better search strategies, text and data mining will enable students to locate relevant resources and information in a more effective and efficient way.

Figure 2 shows some of the resources that students could use in locating relevant information to their project. The first part lists recommended resources such as the ACM digital library, Electronic Thesis and Dissertations (ETD), IEEE digital library, Networked Digital Library of Thesis and Dissertations (NDLTD) and NTU GEMS library. The second part is e-journals, third part is OPACs, the fourth part is CD-ROM/Online databases and the fifth part is web search engines. Beside that student could use the search engine to look up information on the Internet in the *Welcome frame*.

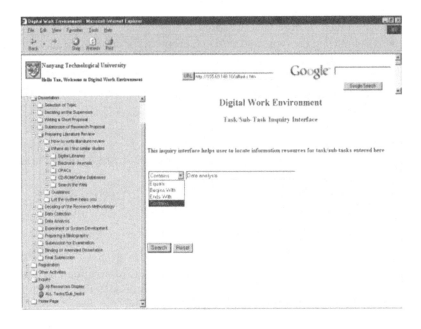

Figure 3: Task/Sub-task Inquiry Interface

The important aspect of the task-based design in DWE is that users are not bombarded with information, but rather presented with information as and when this information is needed. One of the biggest DL challenges today lies with organizing large number of documents and digital resources in a way that does not clutter the screen and yet provide an efficient and effective way of locating these resources. Figure 3 shows the interface in which the user can query the DWE stating the type of task or subtask they require information or help. Based on user keywords, the system will attempt to find the closest match and displays a list of tasks for user selection.

3.5 Personal Space

A personal space facility is provided and displayed as a first folder in the tree structure. The rest of the folders vary according to user categories. Personal space folder leaves provide hyperlinks to add/search favorite links, references/publications and notes. It also has links to display user information such as category of users, last visited date, year of study and so on. A personal space therefore contains references, URLs and notes added directly by users. The system also facilitates users to add his/her favourite or frequently visited information resource. Users can store/save references/publications with hyperlink in their personal space for future reference. If a user come across some important quotes or notes he/she can record those information in his/her personal space. The use of personal space is restricted to his/her personal account so that it is unavailable to other users.

4   Conclusion

The proposed DWE provides a means by which digital resources and critical information can be organized and presented to the users. The main advantage of this approach is in its ability to present information and resources according to the users needs. Most of the digital resources gateways tend to list resources according to subject headings or categories of information. While this approach is acceptable when we deal with generic application, the task-based design provides an effective approach in a specific domain. Likewise, designing a digital work environment using the concept of a long list of resources or links implies that the user must browse, judge and select the most appropriate resource for their use. Often, most users do not see the value of the listed resources unless they require them to perform a specific task. The DWE system provides needed information resources by filtering out unwanted or unrelated information resources. The system has facility to support searching of all its resources/task/sub-task though the inquiry interface. In addition, the all-resources option facilitates users to browse a complete listing of resources given in alphabetical order. Finally, DWE provides a personal space for each user to record and store frequently used information resources, references to information and personal notes.

References

1.   Gould, J., Lewis C.: Designing for Usability: Key Principles and What Designers Think. Communications of the ACM 28, (3) (1985) 300-311
2.   Lewis, C., Rieman J.: Task-centered User Interface Design – A Practical Introduction. University of Colorado, Boulder (1993)
3.   Wilson, S., Johnson P.: Bridging the Generation Gap: From Work Tasks to User Interface Design. In: J. Vanderdonckt (ed.): Computer-Aided Design of User Interfaces. Namur: Presses Universitaires de Manur (1996)
4.   Fischer, G., Lemke A.: Construction Kits and Design Environments: Steps Toward Human Problem-domain Communication, Human Computer Interaction, 3 (3) (1998) 179-222
5.   Oppenheim, C.: What is the Hybrid Library? Journal of Information Science, 25(2) (1999) 97-112
6.   Digital Library Federation(2000). Available at: http://www.clir.org/diglib/dlfhomepage.htm
7.   Borgman, C.L.: In: Fox, E A. (ed.), Source Book on Digital Libraries: Report for the National Science Foundation (TR-93-35-(439)) (VPI and SU Computer Science Department, Blacksburg, VA,) (1999). Available at: http://fox.cs.vt.edu/DLSB.html
8.   Meyyappan, N., Chowdhury, G., Foo, S. : A Review of the Status of 20 Working Digital Libraries. Journal of Information Science, 26(5) (2000) 337-55
9.   Michelle, Q., and Wang, B.: A User-Centered Interface for Information Exploration in a Heterogeneous Digital Library. Journal of the American Society for Information Science, 51(3) (2000) 297-310
10. Suzane, Cohen., John, Fereira., Angela, Horne., Bob, Kibbee., Holly, Mistlebauer and Adam, Smith: MyLibrary: Personalised Electronic Services in the Cornell University Library. D-Lib Magazine 6(4), (2000). Available at: http://www.dlib.org/dlib/pri100/mistlebauer/ 04mistlebauer.html
11. Anne Gambles.: Put Yourserlf in the PIE – The HeadLine Personal Information Environment. D-Lib magazine, 6(4) (2000)

12. Lesk, M.: The CORE Electronic Chemistry Library. In Proceedings of the 14th Annual International ACM/SIGIR Conference on R&D in Information Retrieval (1991) (pp 92-112), Chicago, IL
13. Fox, E.A., Hix, D., Nowell, L.T., Brunei, D.J., Wake, W.C., Heath, L.S., and Rao, D.: Users, User Interfaces, and Objects: Envison, a Digital Library. Journal of the American Society for Information Science, 44(8) (1993) 480-91
14. Cousins, S.: A Task-oriented Interface to a Digital Library. Proceedings of the CHI '96 Conference Companion on Human Factors in Computing Systems: Common Ground (1996), 103 – 104. Available at: http://www-diglib.stanford.edu/diglib/WP/PUBLIC/DOC44.html
15. EveryWare Development Inc.: Tango Enterprises 3:User's Guide (1999).

Learning Spaces in Digital Libraries

Anita S. Coleman, Terence R. Smith, Olha A. Buchel, and Richard E. Mayer

ₐlexandria Uigital Library Project5 Uepartment of ffomputer Science5
University of ffalifornia at Santa ø arbara5 Santa ø arbara5 ff ₐ WCLO⁻5 US ₐ 6
asc@acm.org

Abstract. The ₐlexandria Uigital Varth Prototype (ₐUVPT) Project
is developing services to support the construction and use of "learning
spaces" 5 or personalized ULs of geospatially referenced information and
services5 with applications in science education6 The project is focused
on helping students attain deep understanding (concept development)
and scientific reasoning skills (hypothesis development6 In relation to its
use of concepts and hypotheses for organizing and using collections and
services in ways that support such student learning activities5 we describe
four Project activities focused on developing: (L) use scenarios to inform
the ₐUVPT specification process; (P) both the concept of learning spaces
(LSs) and instances of LSs; (O) clients for LSs; and (y) meta information
environments5 including topic maps5 that support LSs6

1 Introduction

A general goal of the Alexandria Digital Earth Prototype [1] (ADEPT) Project
[1] is to build a distributed DL with services that support the construction and
use of "personalized" DLs of geospatially referenced information. A more specific goal of ADEPT is to investigate the potential value of such collections for
improving post-secondary science education and, in particular, for investigating
how they can be used in helping students develop deep understanding, which
we term concept development, and scientific reasoning skills, which we term hypothesis development. Hypothesis development involves constructing and testing
possible relationships between concepts. We employ the term *learning space* (LS)
to denote a personalized collection of georeferenced materials and an associated
set of services that support access to, and use of, the collection for purposes of
learning.

Collections and services facilitating the acquisition and improvement of cognitive skills for scientific reasoning are important components of digital libraries
(DLs) intended to support learning. In creating such collections and services
there is some risk of losing those attributes that mark a set of collections and
services as being part of a library, creating instead systems more akin to knowledge bases or intelligent tutoring systems.

---

[1] The work described herein was partially supported by the NSF U ₐ RP, N ₐ S ₐ
Uigital Libraries Initiative5 under cooperative agreements NSF IRW 7LLOO0 and NSF
IIS WIL8yOF6

P. Constantopoulos and I.T. Sølvberg (Eds.): ECDL 2001, LNCS 2163, pp. 251–262, 2001.

In seeking to create a true DL that supports such learning, we first note that the core characteristic of a DL that differentiate it from arbitrary collections of information objects, either on the Web or in general knowledge bases, is the meta-information that characterizes both collections and their individual items and that allows efficient access to relevant information. We further note that core characteristics differentiating scientific from less formal methods of knowledge acquisition and representation include deeper, and typically more rigorous, notions and uses of concepts and hypotheses. This suggests that, in combining basic DL functionality with support for learning, with a focus on scientific reasoning, both concepts and hypotheses be used as a basis for organizing, accessing, and using information in the collections of DLs.

We may, for example, construct an LS to support answering specific questions such as: "Why do the cross-sections of rivers have the shapes that we see in the real-world and what determines the variations in shapes?" (the "hydraulic geometry" problem.) We view an LS as characterized in terms of the appropriate set of concepts and hypotheses in addition to other meta-information. The LS for the hydraulic geometry problem, for example, may be organized in terms of such concepts as "river discharge" or "channel width" and such hypotheses as the idea that the width of a river is related to its discharge. An LS makes available to students a wide variety of sources of relevant information that the student not only learns how to retrieve, but also to use as a basis for reasoning and acquiring scientific understanding within the domain of interest. Thus, the learner must formulate testable hypotheses, seek relevant information, interpret the information with respect to the hypotheses, and draw conclusions.

ADEPT services for constructing and using LSs are being developed by extending the architecture and services of the Alexandria Digital Library (ADL) [1]. An ADEPT system may be viewed as a distributed set of nodes, each of which supports one or more collections of objects, subsets of which may be "published", or made visible, to other nodes. The collections are made available to a variety of clients through the ADEPT middleware services. We may view an arbitrary node as consisting of a three-layer architecture of multiple clients, middleware, and multiple collections, each characterized by possibly different meta-information schemas. The three features that underly the integration of the heterogeneous collections and objects into a uniform library, namely common collection-level metadata, the ADEPT bucket system (which is a common model for object-level metadata), and a central collection discovery service (see [2].)

Issues currently being resolved by the developers of ADEPT [2] include the design and development of various clients, middleware services, and collections that support the concept of an LS. In this paper we describe some of the associated development activities. We first discuss the notion that concepts and hypotheses provide an appropriate framework for organizing and constructing collections and services that help students to learn to reason in a scientific manner. We

---

[2] We acknowledge our close collaboration, on a variety of these issues, with the Digital Library for Earth Systems Education (DLESE) Project [3].

then briefly discuss four specific sets of ADEPT development activities relating to: (1) learning space use scenarios to inform the ADEPT specification process; (2) the concept of an LS and specific instances of LSs; (3) new clients with functionality that supports LSs; and (4) new meta-information environments that support LSs, including the use of concept and topic maps.

2   The Basis: Concepts, Hypotheses, and Scientific Reasoning

Research in cognitive science points to the domain-specificity of scientific reasoning, that is, the accepted modes of scientific inquiry and argument depend on the subject area (see [4], [5], [6]). In ADEPT, our initial focus is on geography as a target discipline because it offers a particularly rich venue for examining how students use georeferenced DLs. In geography, there are a variety of information sources including maps, diagrams, charts, illustrations, figures, photos, tables, animation, video, and text. In geography, it is possible to find interesting and authentic research questions that can be presented at a level appropriate for introductory students. Thus, specialized DLs can be used as educational tools to help introductory-level geography students gain experience in how to formulate and test hypotheses based on real geographic information.

There is growing consensus that science education should be a meaningful activity in which students learn to think like scientists rather than solely remember information. The National Science Education Standards [7] calls for students to engage in scientific reasoning in which they "become familiar with modes of scientific inquiry, rules of evidence, ways of formulating questions, and ways of proposing explanations" (p. 2). Similarly, The National Geography Standards [8] calls for teaching scientific reasoning skills systematically throughout each student's education so that they students learn to "think geographically." In particular, The National Geography Standards specify five fundamental skills in scientific reasoning in geography, which are fundamental in the design of LSs:

- **Asking geographic questions** which involves posing a question in such a way that it is searchable within a DL and appropriate for the discipline. This includes specifying problems, generating hypotheses, and identifying potential data sources. For the hydraulic geometry problem, some possible questions are: How can we determine the total discharge of a river?" and "How does the hydraulic geometry of a river change as we go downstream?"
- **Acquiring geographic information** which involves locating and gathering geographic information from a variety of sources, and assessing its value and relevance for the question at hand. In addressing the hydraulic geometry problem, the student might seek the the width and discharge of a specific set of rivers at various points along the them and at various points in time.
- **Organizing geographic information** which involves making connections across different information representations such as maps, graphs, tables, diagrams, prose, animation, and video. This includes designing representations

that are most appropriate for the question at hand. For the hydraulic geometry problem, the student might produce a graph showing how the width of a river varies as a function of the changes in discharge as one goes downstream.

- **Analyzing geographic information** which involves drawing conclusions and interpretations of from data representations. In the hydraulic geometry problem, the student might try fitting linear or logarithmic regression equations to the graphed data using elementary statistical packages.
- **Answering geographic questions** which involves inducing general theories or models and evaluating answers to the question at hand. For the hydraulic geometry problem, the student might develop some general principles about the ways in which rivers form their channels.

We are currently designing ADEPT modules that use specialized DLs to help students engage in scientific reasoning by supporting their attempts to formulate and test hypotheses about geography issues. Our target scenario is a college student or team of students working on a geography research question within the context of a lab or discussion section of their geography course. For example, in the lab or discussion section the students are given a problem such as the hydraulic geometry problem. They are also introduced to an on-line DL containing collections that are specifically related to the target problem.

In addition, we plan to compare versions of the interface that offer varying amounts of scaffolding. One version (nonscaffolded version) will provide no scaffolding so students will be free to explore as they would with currently available digital libraries. Another version (scaffolded version) will include prompts to engage in each of the five reasoning skills, so students will be asked to generate testable hypotheses, to specify the kinds of information needed for each hypothesis, to build representations such as graphs based on the information, to determine needed analyses, and to draw conclusions based on the analyzed information. We will evaluate the learning outcomes of students who learn with various versions of ADEPT as well students who receive conventional instruction in order to determine the cognitive consequences of experience in an ADEPT environment. In particular, we expect students who learn in the scaffolded ADEPT environment to show better understanding of the topic–such as fluvial process–as well as better skill in scientific reasoning in solving new geography problems.

Research in the cognitive science of learning and instruction suggests three principles that we incorporate into our ADEPT research (see [4], [5])

- **Domain-specific learning:** Students learn best when cognitive skills are taught within specific content areas rather than as general context-free principles. In ADEPT, we focus on helping students learn specific geography concepts and scientific reasoning skills appropriate for geography.
- **Case-based learning:** Students learn best when cognitive skills are learned in process of solving authentic problems rather than when pieces of information are presented as isolated facts to learn. In ADEPT, we begin each lesson with an authentic problem to solve, such as the hydraulic geometry problem, and allow students to learn within the context of solving the problem.

- **Scaffolded learning:** Students learn best when the task difficulty is adjusted to meet their capabilities. In ADEPT, we offer prompts and feedback designed to support learners as they develop skill in geographic reasoning.

Within the ADEPT project, DLs become instructional tools when they are organized as LSs based on their relevance for specific problems.

3   Towards an Operational ADEPT

We now describe four sets of ADEPT development activities whose ultimate goal is an operational ADEPT. These activities include: (1) constructing detailed use scenarios of ADEPT for generating specifications of ADEPT clients, middleware services, and collections; (2) developing the concept and instances of LSs; (3) designing and implementing a new generation of clients that support LSs; and (4) designing and implementing a meta-information framework adequate for describing LSs.

3.1   Scenarios for System Specification

LS scenarios are a valuable means of providing specifications for clients, middleware services, and collections. We are constructing scenarios with the help of instructors of specific undergraduate courses in various areas of physical, human, and cultural geography to specify collections and services that facilitate the learning of scientific reasoning. As an example of a scenario, we consider an LS design activity for Professor PG, who is creating a self-paced lab activity for a physical geography course for undergraduate students. PG's goal is to have students understand the concept of the *hydraulic geometry* (HG) of a river, as well as key related concepts, and to develop and test simple hypotheses about relationships among these concepts.

- PG first decides on a set of concepts she wants the students to learn, including width (w), depth (d), average velocity (v) and total discharge (Q) at a cross-section of a river channel. Using a concept mapping tool, she sketches a concept map in which a river is represented as a sequence of contiguous rectangles, each representing a cross-section of the river, with each cross-section in turn characterized by the concepts w, d, v, and Q.
- PG wishes to provide the students with data that can be used for constructing and testing hypotheses about relationships between the concepts, and in particular, to discover for themselves three well-known sets of relationships, characterizing: Q in terms of w,d, and v ($Q = wdv$); changes in w, d,and v in terms of Q as one goes downstream ($w = aQ^b$, etc., or *down-stream HG*); changes in w, d,and v in terms of Q as Q changes over time at a given cross-section ($w = cQ^d$, etc., *at-a-station HG.*)
- PG refines the query by choosing the grade level, the resource types of interest (data sets, images, maps), and the geographic area (Pennsylvania) for which datasets are desired. She searches across a preferred set of distributed

geoscience libraries and retrieves a famous dataset for the Brandywine Creek in Pennsylvania.
- PG notes 5 datasets, each with its own URL, for each of 5 cross-sections along the river channel and a sixth dataset of time variation at the third cross-section. She links these resources to the evolving concept map.
- PG adds a new node to the river channel node labelled "maps and images of Brandywine Creek" and executes a search for maps and images of Brandywine Creek that draws on both the network of concepts and the geospatial metadata associated with the previously chosen datasets to narrow the search.
- PG selects maps and images to include in the lab and gives this concept map to the students as a resource for a lab exercise, with instructions and hints for constructing and testing hypotheses.

This abbreviated scenario illustrates clearly how the use of concepts and hypotheses informs, for example, the design of clients that are based on concept mapping ideas. The middleware services that such scenarios may be used to specify include services for constructing personalized collections and semantic mapping services that enable mappings between different representations of semantically similar information to be used in support of search and analysis. The collections issues being informed include how concepts and hypotheses may be used to organize personalized learning collections, particular as a form of meta-information.

3.2 Developing the Concept of LSs and Instantiations

Traditional libraries typically provide educational collections through the use of the relatively passive and static reserve function and "readers". We are currently generalizing the concept of educational collections into that of learning spaces as multimedia collections, organized by concepts and hypotheses and useable through a broad range of services that support specific learning objectives.

As educational collections, LSs can be viewed as collaborative learning spaces. Instructors select materials useful for promoting learning while students use them to learn. For example, an LS for a lecture by Professor PG's on hydraulic geometric lesson would contain collections that foster student understanding of basic concepts (such as w, d, v, and Q) and enable hypothesis testing concerning relations among them. Furthermore, LSs can be customized by teachers or learners, and may include tools to promote learning.

LSs may contain textual resources that fulfill the information needs of learners engaged in reasoning including definitions, explanations, illustrations, elaborations, and facts. They may contain graphics including photos, maps, drawings, diagrams, charts, figures, video, and animation. They may include tools for engaging in each of the five components of scientific reasoning, including tools for prompting students to write specific hypotheses, representing data in various formats, making needed computations in available data, and creating concept maps.

Based on scenarios such as that provided above, we are developing conceptual models and experimental instantiations of LSs. ADEPT LSs currently under development involve educational collections of multimedia resources, organized in terms of geographic concepts and hypotheses, and useable in relation to a set of services. In particular, the collections involve a variety of resources for (1) concepts which the user specifies (e.g., a retrieval for the concept erosion shows context and relationship of erosion to another geographic process, fluvial processes), and (2) data sets that are relevant to a user's hypothesis about the relation between two concepts (e.g., a request for rainfall information in some river basin may return several sources represented in tables, figures, and even, text).

The use of concepts and their interrelationships provides a solution to the issue of how best to represent knowledge in a DL that supports learning. While the curriculum or course materials developed by one teacher only rarely are fully acceptable to another teacher, such curricula and materials are valuable resources from which other instructors can compose their own curricula and materials. The fact that the core of mathematics and the sciences is a large body of concepts and their interrelationships makes it highly plausible that concepts and their interrelationships provide possible the most useful level of granularity for organizing and re-organizing educational materials.

There are a variety of challenges in constructing an appropriate model of LSs that we are currently addressing, such as (1) the lack of a generally accepted and interoperable meta-information for educational elements that can be applied by catalogers and understood by users; (2) the granularity level for resource description which, to enable personal collections, makes the unit of analysis considerably smaller than that currently used by catalogers in traditional libraries; and (3) vocabulary control and conceptual (verbal subject) analysis problems for deep indexing, since traditional libraries do summarization level subject analysis as opposed to deep indexing of concepts.

Instantiating Learning Spaces for Use and Evaluation We are constructing a series of increasingly sophisticated LSs designed for use and evaluation for introductory classes in the areas of physical, human, and cultural geography at UCSB and UCLA. These LSs were designed for use in lecture/classroom contexts, and organized around specific sets of concepts selected by the instructors.

Concepts for the physical geography classes were related to the higher level concepts of river hydrology, river network structure and process, river and network evolution, and hillslope structure and process. Concepts for the human geography classes were related to the higher level concepts of settlement systems, spatial demography, diffusion processes, and spatial economics. Materials to support the teaching of these concepts and associated hypotheses in classroom settings involved the use of embedded PowerPoint presentations and embedded HTML presentations that incorporated a wide range of object types in different formats, including dynamic simulation models. Evaluations were made, using questionnaires, of the use of these materials in classroom settings [9].

3.3 Clients for ADEPT

The current ADL client, which enables users to search georeferenced collections using a direct manipulation interface with map display, was intended to support basic DL search for various classes of georeferenced materials. A new generation of clients is being developed to support the development and use of LSs. Our activities include: (1) evaluating various clients that are available from other sources and that support functionalities of value in learning environments; (2) designing clients from requirements obtained by our user evaluation and scenario building studies; (3) testing an implemented simulation of a client (the ADEPT Selector).

As examples of clients under evaluation, we are, examining:

- *concept mapping* clients that provide graphical representations of information fields that may be viewed in terms of nodes corresponding to concepts within a particular subject domain and lines delineating relationships between nodes (sometimes hypothetical). Generically, a concept map is a graphical representation of an information field that consists of nodes and lines, in which nodes correspond to concepts within a particular subject area or domain, and lines delineate the relationships between nodes (i.e., between concepts). We are investigating the use of the Visual Knowledge Builder (VKB), developed by Shipman [10], which enables users to collect, organize, and interpret information using visual and spatial properties to signify classification schemes and relationships. It uses look and layout, rather than explicit links, to infer relationships. Using VKB, users create visual interpretations that can evolve as the user's understanding changes. We are also exploring the use of the IHMC CMAP concept map software to create collaborative concept maps [11].
- Simulation clients enabling non-programmers to incrementally construct sophisticated models using graphical programming techniques. We believe that (dynamic) simulation models of processes in human and physical geography provide deep insights in many learning situations. In particular, we are examining the use of AgentSheets, developed by Repenning [12]. which provide a simulation environment enabling non-programmers, such as students and teachers, to incrementally construct sophisticated models using graphical programming techniques. Since AgentSheets is based on an underlying grid structure, it is useful for creating simulation models of processes studied in human and physical geography. To create a simulation, users develop a look and a set of behaviors for individual agents and place these agents in the grid. The simulation unfolds as agents react to each other based on their current, relative positions. AgentSheets provides rich media support for incorporating maps and images into a simulation backdrop, or even the look of an individual agent.

We have designed and implemented an experimental "client", the Adept Selector, that is intended to simulate a set of services corresponding to some of those in our current model of an LS, including:

- **View LS:** allows user to employ a web browser to access LSs. The user is able to enter a search term/concept phrase and the system responds with a map for the term/concept phrase. This is the learning space. Each node of this map has associated concepts with specific hierarchical, associative, and equivalence roles, that is concept maps that extend or narrow the role of geography topics as appropriate. They may also be linked to an individual resource. Roles, or concept relationships, may be varied as in entity-measure pairs where the relationship is between concepts and the unit of measure or entity/place pairs, where location is a contextual definition of the concept. Each node also has occurrence roles, the information resources associated with each concept. Resources may be aggregated by type of resource (for example, the number of models available for this concept) or may be a link to a single, individual resource.
- **Create LS:** allows the user to select objects to assemble collections for user-specified concepts.
- **Create Concept Maps:** supports users in saving existing concept maps, modifying them, or collaboratively creating new maps and saving them.
- **Select Models:** supports search by concepts and resource types to identify model builds of interest.
- **Dictionary service:** take user input in the form of concepts/terms and outputs definitions from related dictionaries via a concept map that has live links to dictionary definitions, thesaurus concept space, and the maps, images, datasets-models, visualizations, and multimedia formats available for this concept/term.
- **Concept mapping and thesaurus services:** takes user input in the form of concept maps and outputs the user concept map as well as the relevant concept map that is based on the ADEPT TopicThes (in-house thesaurus for geography)
- **Model service:** takes input in the form of concepts/terms/types and outputs the concept map with names and details of types (in this instance models) that are suitable for learning environments.

In conjunction with our evaluations of various clients, the Selector is providing us with input for the design of our own ADEPT clients.

3.4   Meta-information for Learning Spaces

Adequate meta-information structures lie at the core of DL technology. Many educational DLs, such as DLESE, ARIADNE, GEM, EdNA, SchoolNet, and VES, attempt to accommodate the needs of educators and learners through the use of meta-information important to educational applications [13]. ADEPT is currently engaged in three sets of activities in relation to meta-information. First, jointly with DLESE and NASA, ADEPT has established a metadata framework for geospatially-referenced learning resources. This meta-information standard integrates the DLESE standard (their current v2.1 is based upon v1.1 of the IMS metadata standard, which is in turn based on the IEEE-LOM v3.5) (see [3]), and the ADEPT Learning Object Metadata Model [14]. This standard is provisionally termed the ADEPT/DLESE/NASA (ADN) Joint Metadata Content Standard v1.0 [15]. Second, we are examing the use of concept and topic maps as important components of ADEPT meta-information environments. Third, we have developed a meta-information content [16] for representing software modules for simulation models that we believe will be an important component of many LSs, elements of which are being introduced into the ADN.

The ADN Joint Metadata Content Model In addition to metadata elements such as author, title, and subject, elements of ADN include descriptions of learning outcomes, educational objectives, ability to meet specified standards (such as the US National Science standards or US Geography standards), typical learning time, primary audience, audience level, semantic density of resource, and level of interactivity.

Metadata elements are grouped into the following logical categories based on the IEEE LOM:

1. General: context-independent features of the resource.
2. Lifecycle: features related to resource creation and publication.
3. Metametadata: cataloger information.
4. Technical: technical features.
5. Educational: educational or pedagogic features.
6. Rights: conditions of resource use.
7. Relation: relations to other resources.
8. Annotation: comments on educational use.
9. Geo-spatial/temporal: spatial and temporal information on coverage.
10. Discipline: place-holder for custom elements (e.g., concept maps).
11. Collection: collection level metadata.
12. Models/datasets: elements for specialized digital objects.

ADN educational and pedagogical elements, irrespective of the category into which they are fitted, include: (1) type of learning resource; (2) learning context; (3) audience; (4) educational objective; (5) function/use, (6) topic; (7) field of study; (8) geography standards, and (10) duration.

While ADEPT is now cataloging LS collections using this standard, unresolved issues remain. First, there is no educational metadata for the many resources that are created for non-education purposes. Second, users must be aware of instructional design principles in using educational metadata effectively. Third, there are issues of granularity (or the unit of analysis). This may be resolved with the use of analytical cataloging, although significant effort is required. Finally, there is the problem of the level of indexing, and associated vocabulary control problems, for concept-based cataloging, which requires deep indexing as opposed to the summarization level of traditional subject analysis in libraries. The use of ISO topic maps, together with the meta-information for learning spaces and the inclusion of a concept map, may provide a solution to these problems.

Topic Maps One may view concept maps, and the standardized version known as topic maps (TMs), as an extension of the meta-information environment of LSs that is focused on concepts and hypotheses. TMs have been shown to improve the organization of DLs with continuously growing collections. They provide "a standardized notation for interchangeably representing information about the structure of information resources used to define topics, and the relationships between topics" [17]. They add structure to data resources that otherwise can only be organized in simple ways because they may include references to both external and internal sources. TMs enable users to: (1) search by specific concept (phrase, term, etc.); (2) browse concept-related material; and (3) customize retrievals.

TMs maps provide the conceptual analysis framework and tools for promoting knowledge acquisition, scientific reasoning, and abstract thinking in students. Because the TM standard builds a structured semantic network over heterogeneous and topically diverse resources, it allows easy navigation to the requested information. Advantages of TMs are that, as definitions of LSs, they are kept separate from the actual information resources. Since they are expressed as DTDs they are available for customized application. The interface for TMs can be either conventional, with hyperlinks or graphical, the hyperbolic browser interface that represents concepts as the nodes in the hierarchies. Hyperbolic navigation, in which users may rearrange nodes and bring areas into focus with a mouse, has been shown to be a better interface for user understanding of large, complex data sets.

4   Summary

Our experiences in developing learning spaces as part of the ADEPT Project suggests strongly that structuring our client, middleware, and collections services around the notions of concepts and hypotheses leads to strong to support for students in their acquisition of scientific understanding and reasoning abilities. Furthermore, such an approach allows us to combine digital library and educational functions in a natural manner.

References

1. Alexandria Digital Library: www.alexandria.ucsb.edu
2. Smith, T.R., Janee, G., Frew, J., Coleman, A.: Towards the Alexandria Digital Earth Prototype System. Proceedings of the Joint Conference on Digital Libraries, Roanoke, Va (2001), ACM/IEEE.
3. Digital Library for Earth Systems Education: www.dlese.org
4. Bruer, J. T.: (1993). Schools for thought: A science of learning in the classroom (1993) Cambridge, MA: MIT Press.
5. Mayer, R. E.: The promise of educational psychology: Learning in the content areas. (1991) Upper Saddle River, NJ: Merrill Prentice Hall.
6. Mayer, R. E.: Teaching for meaningful learning. (2001) Upper Saddle River, NJ: Merrill Prentice Hall.

7. National Research Council: National science education standards. (1996) Washington, DC: National Academy Press.
8. Geography Education Standards Project: Geography for life: National geography standards. (1994) Washington, DC: National Geographic Research and Exploration.
9. Borgman, C.L., et al.: Evaluating Digital Libraries for Teaching and Learning in Undergraduate Education: A Case Study of the Alexandria Digital Earth Prototype (ADEPT). Library Trends 49(2) (2000), 228-250.
10. Shipman, F.: Visual Knowledge Builder. www.csdl.tamu.edu/ haowei/VKB/download.html (2000).
11. Novak, J.: The Theory Underlying Concept Maps and How to Construct Them. cmap.cogint.uwf.edu/info/printer.html (2001).
12. Repenning, A.: Agent Sheets. www.agentsheets.com (2000).
13. Ip, A., et al.: Managing Online Resources for Teaching and Learning. ausweb.scu.edu/aw2k/papers/ip/paper.html (2000).
14. ADEPT Learning Object Metadata Model. www.alexandria.ucsb.edu/ acoleman/alommv3.html (2001).
15. ADEPT: The ADN Joint metadata content model, v1.0. www.alexandria.ucsb.edu/metadata (2001).
16. Hill, L. L., Crosier, S. J., Smith, T. R., Goodchild, M. F.: A content standard for computational models. D-Lib Magazine, 7(6) (2001).
17. ISO/IEC 13250 Topic Maps: Information Technology – Document Description and Markup Languages. www.y12.doe.gov/sgml/sc34/document/0129.pdf (2000).

Ethnography, Evaluation, and Design as Integrated Strategies: A Case Study from WES

Michael Khoo

Department of Anthropology, CB 233
University of Colorado, Boulder, CO 80309-0233, U.S.A.
michael.khoo@colorado.edu

Abstract. The Water in the Earth System (WES) collection is a collection of the Digital Library for Earth SystemEducation. As WES relies on its user community to generate metadataresources; identification of robust user community features, and ofpotential user community problems, is thereforeimportant. This paper describes (a) how ethnography is being used to studythe WES community; (b) how technological frames theory and technology usemediation theory is being used to analyse this data; and (c) how researchoutcomes are being used to generate recommendations for supporting future WES development.

1   Introduction: DLESE and WES

The Digital Library for Earth System Education (DLESE: www.dlese.org) is aNational Science Foundation project that provides online access to earthsystem resources for a wide range of users, from schoolchildren touniversity professors. DLESE's development strategy emphasises the involvement of end-users in the design process.The aim is not just user-centred design, but sustainable user involvementin ongoing library operations; collections development, for instance, will rely upon libraryusers to contribute the metadata necessary to grow the collection. Userinvolvement is encouraged and supported in various ways; one strategyinvolves the development and support of user communities whose members meet in electronically mediated forums,and occasionally face-to-face.

The Water in the Earth System (WES) community isa prototype user community that has been given institutional identity andcoherence through the specification of a collection scope (water), and a constituency (primarily highschool educators). As a prototype, WES is 'road testing' a number offeatures, such as community-led collections development, that will underpinthe DLESE collection. The current WES community is not, however, thought to be representative of future WEScommunities. Future WES users will likely be less 'digital library'literate, and will articulate more diverse needs, than the presentcommunity [44]. On a practical note, the financial cost of meetings between participants currently flown around the countrywill not scale with WES's growth, and electronically mediated communitydevelopment will play an increasingly important role.

Future WES community growth will therefore be more distributed, andintegrate more people from more diverse backgrounds who are less familiarwith computational tools, than at present. As the participation of thiscommunity is central to WES's

P. Constantopoulos and I.T. Sølvberg (Eds.): ECDL 2001, LNCS 2163, pp. 263-274, 2001.
© Springer-Verlag Berlin Heidelberg 2001

growth, a major developmental question for WES lies in the identification of emergent features of this community suitable for strategicsupport once initial WES institutional scaffolding is (inevitably) scaledback. Ethnographic tracking of WES's growth offers an opportunity to tryand identify emergent features of the WES community within a longitudinal framework.

2   Science, Technology, and Ethnography

Ethnographic investigations of science and technologyrun the risk of falling between the stools of the various disciplines theyspeak to. Inquiries within anthropology,for instance, are infrequent, partly because of the perceived theoreticaldifficulty of constituting technical practice as a 'place' with anattendant 'culture' explicable through anthropological theory [10], partlybecause such accounts have been criticised for remaining on the level of theoretical speculation rather thanengaging with underlying technological realities [27]. Conversely,inquiries outside of anthropology can lack the contextual richness that theconsideration of human behaviour as cultural activity can provide. Some accounts [e.g. 1, 2, 5, 15, 16, 38, 39] havehowever transcended these boundaries, indicating that the locus ofinvestigation of science and technology lies between   disciplines.   Thissuggestion   is   supported   by   the   contributionsof heterogeneous fields of inquiry such as STS and theories such asActor-Network Theory [e.g. 9, 24].

Applying these observations to the question ofthe study of technology design and use, we again find that much researchelides cultural concerns, focusing instead on more traditional human factor and usability questions. Thisapproach overlooks what will be argued below is an important element ofuser-centred design: understanding the culturally located perceptions oftechnological artifacts, what the artifact 'means' to designers and the users.

This paper considers therefore not just thedigital library, but what a digital library can mean for designers andusers. In investigating these meanings, I am concerned particularly withthe difference between designers' and users' understandings of digital libraries, and theconsequences that these differences may have for library design anddevelopment,   including   (in   this   case)   the   development   of   sustainable usercommunities. Taking its interdisciplinary cue from science and technology studies, the investigation acknowledges a numberof disciplines, including (to greater or lesser degrees) anthropology,communication studies, computer science, and history. To address potentialproblems arising from the presence of divergent disciplinary methodologies, the research emphasises inductiverather than deductive methodologies and theoretical frameworks, such as:abductive inference [20]; actor-network theory [9]; adaptive structurationtheory [11]; applied anthropology[e.g. 4, 22, 29, 30]; grounded theory [14]; technology context schemes[19]; technological frames theory [36]; and technology structuring theory[1, 2].

The placement of these approaches in proximityis not intended to imply the existence of theoretical congruences; rather they are presented as a 'toolkit' to be pragmaticallyselected from according to circumstance. It is however possible to discerna common intention to capture the complexities of human activity, throughmethods that often are inductive and iterative. Grounded theory, for instance, looks for discontinuities inthe data, asks "What theory does this situation remind the researcher of?"and encourages the researcher to widen their theoretical remit to bring newperspectives to bear upon the data. Similarly, abductive inference—a strategy of working with themost economical guess of causes—allows for the development offurther inferences to be adopted if they prove more economical thanexisting ones.

In the following section, I will show how oneethnographic response to the question of "What might future requirements ofthe WES community be?" involves similar inductive cycles of inquiry.

3   An Ethnographic Research Cycle

The research carried out so far may be characterisedby although not confined to an iterative cycle of documentation andobservation, analysis, and outcome generation.

3.1 Documentation and Observation

First, the design process is being documented. DLESE and WES publicationsand ephemera (e-mails, meeting agendas, Powerpoint presentations, web sitepages, etc.) have been collected and archived. Unstructured interviews andother informal interactions arebeing recorded in order to obtain participants' understandings ofparticular situations. Away from the field site, archival and library workis researching the history of libraries and library technology.

Ethnography holds, however, that social process can not be discerned solelyfrom artifacts, or from participants' recollections of what they think theyhave done [17, 42]. What people think they do, and what they actually do,are often different things, and ethnography emphasises observing participants *insitu*. DLESE and WES meetings have thus been ethnographicallyobserved, with field notes recording both what is said, and also how it issaid—at what points meetings become contentious, off-topic, argumentative, aswell as points of general consensus and agreement.

A complementary strategy is that of microethnography, the minute analysison computer of digitised video clips of meetings, etc. Microethnographyexamines human interaction in order to identify repetitive patterns ofverbal and corporal behaviour that are held to embody communicative practices indicative of individuals' desiresto accomplish certain tasks (for instance the promotion of an agenda at ameeting) [e.g. 12, 28, 32].

3.2 Analysis

Second, the collected materials are being analysed. The theoreticalframework currently guiding this evaluation is derived from Weedman'sincentive theory of user-centred design [46], and the work of Orlikowskiand colleagues on technological frames theory and technology use mediation [33, 34, 35, 36, 37].

Weedman's case study describes the design ofcomputational tools for a global change research project (Sequoia 2000[40]). She identified a number of factors outside of the technological artifactitself that impacted the user-centred design process. These included therole of politics and power relationships in the institutions concerned, andthe fit of the technology with organisational processes. A third factor identified was that of the meaning ofthe artifact. Weedman found that the computer scientists saw the project asa revolutionary research challenge, while the geoscientists saw it as atool that would incrementally enhance their current research activities (making them faster, more efficient,etc.). The computer scientists were commited to extensive prototyping,which the geoscientists resisted, as it detracted from their research. Onthe other hand, the geoscientists wanted extensive debugging of the tools, which the computer scientistsopposed as it detracted from *their* research. At different stages in the project, therefore, geoscientists andcomputer scientists viewed the relevance of the project to their research in different ways, ways that produced varying levels of incentive to committo the project at any one time. These differences, Weedman holds, couldhave (although not necessarily would have) been alleviated by the presencein the project of 'boundary spanners,' individuals experienced in both geoscience and computer science whocould translate between the two communities.

The technological frames theory of Orlikowskiand colleagues analyses the shared frames of reference underlyingindividual and collectiveperceptions of technology, the "particular assumptions, expectations, andknowledge of the technology, which then serve to shape subsequent actionstoward it." In any situation of technology use, there is potential formultiple technological frames to be present. The relationships between these frames can be either 'congruent'and 'incongruent.' Congruent frames imply similar expectations of atechnology. Incongruent frames imply "important differences inexpectations, assumptions, or knowledge about some key aspects of technology ... We expect that where incongruent technologicalframes exist, organizations are likely to experience difficulties andconflicts around developing, implementing and using technologies" [37]. Ihave suggested elsewhere that in addition to congruent and incongruent frames, a third level of technologicalframe interaction exists termed, after Kuhn [23], 'incommensurate.' Whileonly a small proportion of a community might espouse incommensurateperspectives, the impact of that small group on the overall communicative efficiency might be out of proportion totheir size within the group.

Studies of the telephone call centres which dispatch emergency services,for instance, have found that callers who treat the service as a 'promptdelivery' service, akin to ordering a pizza, can become frustrated whentechnological and adminstrative constraints (including the need for dispatchers to collect and enter into adatabase certain information, and funding and staff shortages that resultin call triage) result in their concerns being addressed in an apparently tardyfashion [45]. These frustrations can generate arguments between callers anddispatchers that in rare cases have proved fatal [47].

As with Weedman's 'boundary spanners,'differences between technological frames may be bridged by mediators. In acase study of the introduction of a computer conferencing system in aninstitution, Okamura *et al* found that "the use of a computer conferencing system ... wassignificantly shaped by a set ofintervening actors-- mediators ... These mediators adapted the tchnology toits initial context and shaped user interaction with it; over time, theycontinued to modify the technology and influence use patterns to respond tochanging circumstances" [33]. In the case of incongruent technological frames, therefore, mediators canperform on an ongoing basis 'translation' between variant technologicalframes, bridging the gaps in understanding between technology users.

3.3 Outcome Generation

Third, ethnographic findings derived from thetheoretical analysis of data are used to evaluate and inform WES's development in a number of areas. This is occuring in a number ofareas, including: requirements for technical support; definitions of thefuture institutional relationships between the WES community and WES andDLESE project centres; and requirements for growth towards community self-sufficiency, such as induction andoutreach services for new community members.

4   Case Study of the WES Community

It must be emphasised that each of the above strategies forms part of an iterativeanalytical cycle that privileges no particular stage. All stages of theresearch inform, and are informed by, all other stages. To illustrate thecycle in practice, I will describe the stages in an ethnographic study of a WES meeting, as follows:

1. Description of research heuristicestablished in previous research cycle
2. Observation
3. Analysis
4. Evaluations and recommendations
5. Modifications to research heuristic
6. Application of modified heuristic to new research cycle

4.1 Description of Research HeuristicEstablished in Previous Research Cycle

I begin with a description of the research heuristic developedin prior analyses.

Early observations of DLESE meetings indicated the possible presence ofdivergent technological frames in DLESE discourse. The frames weretentatively outlined, evidence for them was then sought in analyses ofDLESE documentation, and a refined analysis was drawn up. The technological frames identified consisted of two alternate definitions of 'digital library': firstly as a librarythat is digitised, and secondly as a digital object with library-likefunctions [21]. This analysis was reapplied in a number of contexts, andfound to be an parsimonious explanation for a number of observable phenomena.

The first frame treats DLESE and WES aslibraries that are being digitised, essentially 'bricks-and-mortar'libraries made better and faster through the application of technology. Forinstance, in describing how library materials will be peer-reviewed and 'rigidly' catalogued,' DLESEpublications are referencing 'traditional' library practices. The secondframe treats DLESE as a digital object with library-like functions. In thisframe, DLESE is a 'portal,' a searchengine,' a 'network,' and a holder of 'digital artifacts.' Directlyreferencing Vannevar Bush's description of the Memex [8], the frameemphasises speed, seamlessness, hypertext, and fungible documents. A seriesof vignettes in DLESE's 'Community Report' describe how teachers and professors with approaching deadlines forcurriculum development turn to DLESE not just for resources but for ways tostructure diverse resources in systematic and meaningful ways. Acomputationally enhanced libary experience is seen as one way in which technology can render the vast amounts of earthscience data already accumulated more meaningful [26]. These two frames arecontrasted in Table 1. I suggest that these two frames correspond toWeedman's identified communities of interest in the Sequoia 2000 project, with the geoscientists being more alignedwith the left-hand column above, and the computer engineers being morealigned with the right-hand column.

Table 1. Technological frames andDLESE [21]

DLESE as a Library that is Digitised	DLESE as a Digital Artifact with Library-likeCharacteristics
Metaphor: The bricks and mortar library	Metaphor: The technology enabled community
Centralised, enclosed building	Decentralised, open network
Local holdings	Distributed resources
Repository	Portal
Catalogue	Search engines
Stable documents	Fungible/customisable documents

The presence of two definitions of 'digital library' in one institutionalcontext can affect the institutional efficiency of that context. In oneexample, confusion over the nature of electronic holdings impacteddiscussions of DLESE's collection review policies. In these discussions, academic publications and web sites areperceived as qualitatively different resources, with different reviewrequirements. Textual analysis of the e-mail list for DLESE's collections developmentgroup has indicated that discussion of collection review policy lacked aconsistent definition of what review should consist of, with a tensionbetween (a) the accession of stable resources assessed through expert peer review, and (b) the accession ofonline resources reused in various pedagogical contexts by thecommunity.

In another example, observation of meetingsnoted the presence of confusion amongst some community members (often newer community members) over the fact that DLESE and WES do not have'holdings' of their own (as bricks-and-mortar libraries might), but instead'hold' metadata records that point in the direction of resources elsewhereon the Internet (a function more in keeping with a digital object such as a portal site). Users' commentsreflected a feeling that while a bricks-and-mortar library's scope isrepresented in its catalogue and in the resources on its shelves and in itsstacks, and a web site's scope canbe represented through its search and discovery interfaces, precisely howDLESE's scope could be understood was unclear. In unstructured interviewscarried out at these meetings some community members, especially those newto DLESE or WES, expressed the desire for a way to get them 'up-to-speed' with what exactly DLESE or WESwere about.

These examples of alternate technologicalframings—meanings—of what a digital library is are the sortof differences potentially suitable for boundary spanning or mediation. Although detailed analysis of these roles in DLESE and WES has not yetbeen carried out, observation suggests that experienced community membersmay play an important role in this. These community members are able to seewhere WES (as a library) has come from, and also where WES (as a library) is going, and, importantly, areable to convey this information on an ongoing basis to other members of theWES community. They can mediate in discussions between experienced projectmembers and newcomers in whichmisunderstandings are occuring. While it may not be obvious either to theexperienced member or to the newcomer that they might mean different thingswhen they talk about a digital library, to the mediator these differencesare clearer. Thus they often intervene in the form of translation moves that can take the form of "Let metry and explain this ...," "I think what X is trying to say is ...," and soon. Awareness of the role that mediators play in DLESE and WES communitymeetings led to attention being payed to the points in DLESE and WES meetings where mediation appeared to beoccuring.

4.2 Observation at the WES Meeting

These analyses and theoretical speculations regarding technological framesand mediative practices, developed during previous ethnographic work, weresubsequently brought to bear on an analysis of a WES Working Group meeting.In January 2001, a number of WES members, including teachers and pedagogists, were flown into Boulder,Colorado, for a two day meeting. The second day of the meeting was observedby the author.

4.3 Analysis of the WES Meeting

Analysis of the WES meeting evidenced (a) the existence of competingtechnological frames along the lines outlined above, (b) the potential ofthese competing frames to impact the direction of the meeting, and (c) theexistence of various meeting strategies that were used to generate consensus amongst meeting members.

One example of technological frame incongruenceat the meeting has also (as has been pointed out) been observed in DLESE.It consists of a basic confusion over whether or not WES holds resources,or holds metadata records that *point to* resources held elsewhere. While the first morning session had awide-ranging agenda, most of the talk remained focused on what exactly adigital library resource was. Members voiced opinions of the advantages anddisadvantages of both 'traditional libraries,' and the Internet and hypertext. Traditional libraries were thought tobe limited in their holdings, but to hold items of a guaranteed 'quality.' Conversely, while the value of being able to link to any resourceinstantly was appreciated, members were wary of the undifferentiated massof information perceived to exist 'out there' on the Internet. The debateoften revolved around the question of whether it was better to link to a wide range of resources (WES as digitalartifact with library-like characteristics), or only to those that had beenrigorously reviewed (WES as library that is digitised). As illustrativeexamples of the discussion, one member asked, in a question that juxtaposed both sets of technological framesdiscussed above, "But are we going to have a jumble of categories that canbe searched, or a series of collections just like a normal library? Will webe searching by call number?Or will we be searching by [other standards of interest to high schoolteachers, such as] National Science Standards?" Another member stated: "Idon't want just another web site that I have to search through in order tofind a resource that's suitable." Athird member stated: "With a normal library you go and look at thecategories. So are we building an organised library, or a library organisedthrough searches?" The question appeared to remain unresolved. The secondmorning session, scheduled to discuss fundraising, had been in progress for about ten minutes before a communitymember ventured, "Finding resources is easy. The problem is the reviewprocess," a comment that effectively sidetracked the discussion back into adiscussion of two alternate reviewmodels for the rest of the morning. At this point, despite being providedwith a handout of a flowchart developed at earlier DLESE meetings thatrepresented a prototypical review procedure for DLESE, talk stilloscillated between whether peer review criteria should be narrow (the expert, traditional library model) or broad (thecommunity model).

Some of the differences in perception have beensummed in the following Table 2. While WES members appreciated thetechnological possibilities of WES, as teachersand pedagogists, they had to be sure that the advantages were not justtheoretical but real (again, this is a reading of the meeting that in manyways reflects Weedman's analysis of the feelings of geoscientists in theSequoia 2000 project).

Table 2. The WES Discussion

WES as Library that is Digitised	WES as Digital Artifact with Library-likeCharacteristics
Technologically unsophisticated but proven	Technologically sophisticated but unproven
Organisedlibrary	Jumble of resources
Organised by call number	Organised by searches and pedagogicalrequirement
Guaranteed quality	Just a list oflinks
Peer reviewer as expert gatekeeper	Peer reviewer as community colleague

The afternoon session moved from open discussion, to a brainstormingsession focused around a flip chart and a chalkboard, guided by the meetingfacilitator. In the brainstorming session, members constructed a 'conceptmap' that served as the focus of discussion. (A concept map is a graphical representation of an information field that consists of annotated nodes and lines, in which nodes correspond toconcepts within a particular subject area or domain, and lines delineatethe relationships between nodes, i.e., between concepts.) The meeting's useof the concept map involved the inscription on the chalk board of spatial arrangements of key concepts ofthe water cycle, an activity that generated large lists of points. Thesewere copied down by participants, several of whom volunteered to turn theselists into documents for later circulation. The discussion during the construction of the concept map wasfocused and productive; participants refered both to this session and tothe previous day's meeting, when concept mapping was also used, as usefuland constructive.

4.4 Evaluations and Recommendations for WES

This phase of the ethnographic cycle was concernedwith identification of opportunities for support for the WES community. Ashas been noted, during the meeting, participants made extensive use ofspatial modeling tools to make sense of the issues under discussion. A correlation was noted between theresolution of issues that were complex or time-consuming, and'brainstorming' sessions, with the issues addressed in this way includingthose affected by the presence of alternate technological frames, such as the design of a review policy for the WEScollection. As a corollary, it was felt that modeling tools and theirfacilitators fulfilled some of the requirements for boundary-spanning andtechnology use mediation.

Questions that arose from this observation were, therefore, How might the use of such toolsbe made available to the wider WES community? In what circumstances mightthey prove useful? Specific suggestions and recommendations arising fromthe analysis were therefore fed back to WES community members for comment, and were subsequentlyincorporated into WES grant proposals for further computational tools andsupport. As the field of user-sustained digital libraries is a relativelynew one, it is envisaged that these findings and proposal recommendations will also have relevance for similarcommunity development support programs to be developed by DLESE.

Besides being used to generate future funding, the findings are also beingapplied to a short- to mid-term project aimed at fulfilling a boundaryspanning or mediatory function within WES. The project will include thegeneration of interpretive materialsto present some of the findings so far, and the creation of on-lineresources available to community members that will discuss the differences between WES and DLESE considered as libraries that aredigitised, and digital artifacts with library-like characteristics.

4.5 Modifications to Research Heuristic

It should be noted that this is not the point at which the analysis stops.The research strategy outlined above emphasises the role that ongoinginvestigation of emergent phenomena can play in gaining furtherunderstanding of a situation. The next stage, therefore, involves feeding back observations and analyses into the researchheuristic.

From observation, it was realised that the concept maps of the WESbrainstorming sessions were being used as design tools. They surveyedmembers' perceptions of a knowledge field, and allowed those perceptions tobe folded back into the design process (of collection policy, review policy, etc.). They crystalised relationshipsinherent in the concept under discussion, and indicated where WES communitymembers placed their priorities. They also generated objects (the conceptmaps) that meeting members could then return to and re-discuss. Concept maps thereforeplayed a dual representational function: they represented the WEScollection to the WES community members present, but also represented theWES community needs to WES and DLESE. The useof concept maps and other brainstorming tools also appeared to beassociated with the emergence of mediator roles. Future research questionswill include, therefore: understanding what makes a community member becomea mediator; identifying the contexts in which successful mediation occurs; and identifying the tools that can helpmediators to be more effective. In pursuing these questions, a number of theoretical approaches suggest themselves, including 'situated learning,' 'boundary objects,' and 'boundary spanning.'

In Lave and Wenger's description of situated learning, initial 'legitimate peripheral participation' by newcomers can lead to a 'centrifugal' induction of new members into a community of knowledge [25]. One approach for WES might therefore be to ask how tools such as concept maps can mediate between new and experienced members, such that new members feel they have a stake in the design process that encourages them to become more deeply involved. Star and colleague's concept of 'boundary objects' examines objects at the boundaries of variant communities of perception that serve as orienting points for translational discourse [7, 43]. Again, one research direction might be to consider how mediators and the tools they use can function as boundary objects. A third approach, that of Weedman's analysis of incentives to participation in Sequoia 2000 [46], was suggested by an anonymous reviewer writing in response to a first draft of this paper, and subsequently incorporate into the final draft.

Note that in line with the methodologies outlined above, these new theoretical approaches are being treated as neither correct nor incorrect, but as heuristics aimed at gaining broader understanding of the processes involved in distributed collaborative collections building.

4.6 Application of Modified Heuristic to New Research Cycle

The next (future) stage in the ethnographic cycle will involve the application of the modified investigative toolkit to a new research situation. Currently, this is expected to be at a series of DLESE meetings, to be held in Arizona at the end of April 2001, and (again in Arizona) in August 2001.

5   Conclusion

The iterative ethnographic method outlined aims to produce descriptive and generative outcomes that will support the development of a sustainable WES user community. The method will produce archival material that document the growth of WES, and provide data for future research. It will be used to produce policy recommendations for WES in the areas of infrastructure, tools, outreach, library policy, etc. In order to address both these requirements, the methodology has drawn from various inductive theories to develop a series of iterative research cycles that aim to describe and reinforce emergent features of the community-led design process.

Acknowledgements

I wish to thank Ed Geary of WES for inviting my participation, and the anonymous reviewer who suggested Weedman's paper.

References

1. Barley, S.: Technology as anOccasion for Structuring: Evidence from Observations of CT Scanners and theSocial Order of Radiology Departments. Administrative Science Quarterly 31(1986) 78-108
2. Barley, S.: Images of Imaging:Notes on Doing Longitudinal Field Work. Organization Science 1(3) (August1990) 220-247
3. Barley, S., Orr, J. (Eds.): Between Craft and Science. TechnicalWork in U.S. Settings. Cornell University Press, Ithaca (1997)
4. Barth, F.: A Personal View of Present Tasks and Priorities inCultural and Social Anthropology. In: Borofsky, R. (ed.) (1994) 349-361
5. Born, G.: Rationalizing Culture. University of California Press,Berkeley CA (1995)
6. Borofsky, R.: Assessing Cultural Anthropology. McGraw-Hill, New York(1994)
7. Bowker, G., Star, S.: Sorting ThingsOut. MIT Press, Cambridge MA (1999)
   Bucciarelli, L.: Designing Engineers. MIT Press, Cambridge MA (1996)
8. Bush, V.: As We May Think. The Atlantic Monthly 176 (1945) 101-108.
9. Callon, M.: Society in theMaking. In: Bijker, W., Hughes, T., Pinch, T. (eds.): The SocialConstruction of Technological Systems. MIT Press, Cambridge MA (1987)83-103
10. Clifford, J. Routes. HarvardUniversity Press, Cambridge MA (1997)
11. DeSanctis, G., Poole, M.:Capturing the Complexity in Advanced Technology Use: Adaptive StructurationTheory. Organization Science 5(2) (1994) 121-147
12. Duranti, A.: Linguistic Anthropology. Cambridge University Press,Cambridge, 1997
13. Giddens, A.: Central Problems inSocial Theory. University of California Press, Berkeley CA (1979)
14. Glaser, B., Strauss, A.: TheDiscovery of Grounded Theory. Aldine Publishing, Chicago IL (1967)
15. Hakken, D,: Computing Myths, Class Realities. Westview Press,Boulder CO (1993)
16. Hakken, D.: Computing and Social Change: New Technology and theWorkplace Transformation, 1980-1990. Annual Review of Anthropology 22(1993) 107-132
17. Hakken, D.: Cyborgs@Cyberspace. An Ethnographer Looks to theFuture. Routledge, New York London (1999)
18. Hughes, J., King, V., Rodden, T., Andersen, H.: Moving Out of theControl Room: Ethnography in System Design. ACM CSCW (1994) 429-439
19. Jackson, M.: The Meaning of "Communication Technology": TheTechnology Context Scheme. Communication Yearbook 19 (1996) 229-267
20. Josephson, J. R., Josephson, S. G.: Abductive Inference.Computation, Philosophy, Technology. Cambridge University Press, Cambridge(1994)
21. Khoo, M.: Community Design of DLESE's Collections Review Policy: ATechnological Frames Analysis. ACM/IEEE JCDL (2001) (In press)
22. Kottack, C., Colson, E.: Multilevel Linkages: Longitudinal andComparative Studies. In: Borofsky, R. (ed.) (1994) 396-412
23. Kuhn, T: The Structure of Scientific Revolutions. 2nd edn. TheUniversity of Chicago Press, Chicago IL (1970)
24. Latour, B.: Science in Action.Harvard University Press, Cambridge MA (1987)
25. Lave, J., Wenger, E. SituatedLearning. Legitimate Peripheral Perception. Cambridge University Press,Cambridge (1991)
26. Manduca, C., Mogk, D.: DLESE: A Community Plan. DLESE ProgramCenter, Boulder CO (2000)
27. Martin, E.: Anthropology and the Cultural Study of Science.Science, Technology and Human Values 23(1) (1998) 24-44
28. Moerman, M.: Talking Culture: Ethnography and ConversationAnalysis. University of Philadelphia Press, Philadelphia PA (1988)

29. Moore, S.: Explaining the Present: Theoretical Dilemmas inProcessual Ethnography. American Ethnologist 14(4) (1987) 727-736
30. Moore, S.: The Ethnography of the Present and the Analysis ofProcess. In: Borofsky, R. (ed.) (1994) 362-376
31. Newman, M., Landay, J.: Sitemaps, Storyboards, and Specifications:A Sketch of Web Site Design Practices. ACM DIS (2000) 263-274
32. Nofsinger, R.: Everyday Conversation. Waveland Press, ProspectHeights IL (1999)
33. Okamura, K., Fujimoto, M.,Orlikowski, W., Yates, J.: Helping CSCW Applications Succeed: The Role ofMediators in the Context of Use. ACM CSCW (1994) 55-65
34. Orlikowski, W.: The Duality ofTechnology: Rethinking the Concept of Technology in Organizations.Organization Science 3(3) (1992) 398-427
35. Orlikowski, W.: Learning From Notes: Organizational Issues inGroupware Implementation. MIT Sloan School Working Paper #3428-92 (1992)
36. Orlikowski, W., Gash, C.:Technological Frames: Making Sense of Information Technology inOrganizations. ACM Transactions on Information Systems, 12 (April 1994),174-207
37. Orlikowski, W., Yates, J., Okamura, K., Fujimoto, M.: ShapingElectronic Communication: The Metastructuring of Technology in Use. MITSloan School Working Paper #3611-93 (1996)
38. Orr, J.: Talking About Machines.Cornell University Press, Ithaca (1996)
39. Rabinow, P.: French DNA: Troublein Purgatory. University of Chicago Press, Chicago IL (1999)
40. Sequoia 2000:http://s2k-ftp.cs.berkeley.edu:8000/
41. Shapiro, D.: The Limits ofEthnography: Combining Social Sciences for CSCW. ACM CSCW (1994)417-427
42. Simonsen, J., Kensing, F.: Using Ethnography in Contextual Design.Communications of the ACM 40 (7) (July 1997) 82-88
43. Star, S., Griesmer, J.: Institutional Ecology, "Translations" andBoundary Objects. Social Studies of Science 19 (1989) 387-420
44. Sumner, T., Dawe, M.: Looking at Digital Library Usability from aReuse Perspective. ACM/IEEE JCDL (2001) (In press)
45. Tracy, K.: Interactional Trouble in Emergency Service Requests: AProblem of Frames. Research on Language and Social Interaction 30(4) (1997)315–343
46. Weedman, J.: The Structure ofIncentive: Design and Client Roles in Application-Oriented Research.Science, Technology, and Human Values 23(3) (1998) 315–345
47. Whalen, J., Zimmerman., D., andWhalen M.: When Words Fail: A Single Case Analysis. Social Problems 35(4)(1988) 335–362

Dynamic Models of Expert Groups to Recommend Web Documents

DaeEun Kim[1] and Sea Woo Kim[2]

[1] Division of Informatics,
University of Edinburgh, 5 Forrest Hill
Edinburgh, EH1 2QL
United Kingdom
daeeun@dai.ed.ac.uk
[2] Manna Information System
Bangbae-dong 915-9, Seocho-gu
Seoul, 137-060, Korea
seawoo@unitel.co.kr

Abstract. Recently most recommender systems have been developed to recommend items or documents based on user preferences for a particular user, but they have difficulty in deriving user preferences for users who have not rated many documents. In this paper we use dynamic expert groups which are automatically formed to recommend domain-specific documents for unspecified users. The group members have dynamic authority weights depending on their performance of the ranking evaluations. Human evaluations over web pages are very effective to find relevant information in a specific domain. In addition, we have tested several effectiveness measures on rank order to determine if the current top-ranked lists recommended by experts are reliable. We show simulation results to check the possibility of dynamic expert group models for recommender systems.

1   Introduction

The development of recommender systems has emerged as an important issue in the Internet application, and have drawn attention in the academic and commercial fields. An example of this application is to recommend new products or items of interest to online customers, using customer preferences.

Recommender systems can be broadly categorized into content-based and collaborative filtering systems [6, 13, 16, 17]. Content-based filtering methods use textual descriptions of the documents or items to be recommended. A user's profile is associated with the content of the documents that the user has already rated. The features of documents are extracted from information retrieval, pattern recognition, or machine learning techniques. Then the content-based system recommends documents that match the user's profile or tendency [4, 17]. In contrast, collaborative filtering systems are based on user ratings rather than the features in the documents [1, 17, 16]. The systems predict the ratings of a user

P. Constantopoulos and I.T. Sølvberg (Eds.): ECDL 2001, LNCS 2163, pp. 275–286, 2001.
© Springer-Verlag Berlin Heidelberg 2001

over given documents or items, depending on ratings of other users with tastes similar to the user. Collaborating filtering systems, such as GroupLens [13, 9], can be a part of recommender systems for online shopping sites. They recommend items to users, with the history of products that similar users have ordered before or have been interested in.

Most recommender systems have focused on the recommendations for a particular user with the analysis of user preferences. Such systems require the user to judge many items in order to obtain the user's preferences. In general, many online customers or users are interested in other users' opinions or ratings about items that belong to a certain category, before they become used to searching for items of interest. For instance, customers in E-commerce like to see top-ranked lists of rating scores of many users for items that retailers provide, in order to purchase specific items. However, recommender systems still have the difficulty in providing relevant rating information before they receive a large number of user evaluations.

In this paper, we use a method to evaluate web documents by a representative board of human agents [7]; we call it an *expert* group. This is different from automatic recommender systems with software agents or feature extractions. We suggest dynamic expert groups among users should be automatically created to evaluate domain-specific documents for web page ranking and also the group members have dynamic authority weights depending on their performance of the ranking evaluations. This method is quite effective in recommending web documents or items that many users have not evaluated. A voting board of experts with expertise on a domain category is operated to evaluate the documents. In this kind of problem, it is not a feasible idea to replace human agents by intelligent soft agents.

Our recommender system with dynamic expert groups may be extended to challenge search engine designs and image retrieval problems. Many search engines find relevant information and its importance using automatic citation analysis to the general subject of queries. The connectivity of hypertext documents has been a good measure for automatic web citation. This method works on the assumption that a site which is cited many times is popular and important. Many automatic page ranking systems have used this citation metric to decide the relative importance of web documents. IBM HITS system maintains a hub and an authority score for every document [8]. A method called Page Rank is suggested to compute a ranking for every web document based on the web connectivity graph [2] with the random walk traversal. It also considers the relative importance by checking ranks of documents, which means that a document is ranked as highly important when the document has backlinks from documents with high authority, such as the Yahoo home page.

However, the automatic citation analysis has a limitation that it does not reflect well the importance in viewpoints of human evaluation. There are many cases where simple citation counting does not reflect our common sense concept of importance [2]. The method of developing a new ranking technique based on human interactions has been explored in this paper to handle the problems.

We run a pool of experts, human agents to evaluate web documents and their authorities are dynamically determined by their performance. Also we suggest several effectiveness measures based on rank order. We have simulation results of expert-selection process over users' random access to web documents.

2   Method

2.1   Dynamic Authority Weights of Experts

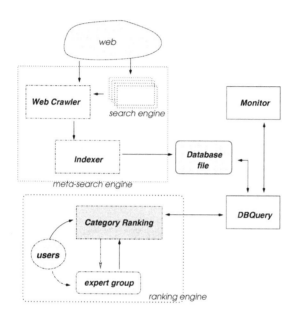

Fig. 1. Search engine diagram

We define a group of people with high authority and much expertise in a special field as an expert group. This expert group is automatically established to evaluate web documents on a specific category. We provide a framework for search engine with our recommender system in Fig.1. A meta-search engine is run to collect good web documents from conventional search engines(e.g. Yahoo, AltaVista, Excite, InfoSeek). Addresses of the documents cited in search engines are stored in the document DB. Each web document has the information of how many search engines in the meta-search engine are referring to the document, and keeps the record of how many times online users have accessed the web document using the search engine.

For every category there is a list of top ranked documents rated by an expert group, which are sorted by score. Authoritative web pages are determined by human expert members. The experts directly examine the content of candidate web pages, which are highly referenced among web documents or accessed by many users. The method of employing an expert group is based on the idea that for a given decision task requiring expert knowledge, many experts may be better than one if their individual judgments are properly combined. In our system, experts decide whether a web document should be classified into a recommended document for a given category. A simple way is the majority voting [11, 10], where each expert has a binary vote for a web document and then the document obtaining equal to or greater than half of the votes are classified into a top ranked list.

An alternative method we can consider is a weighted linear combination. A weighted linear sum of expert votings yields the collaborative net-effect ratings of documents. In this paper, we take the adaptive weighted linear combination method, where the individual contributions of members in the expert groups are weighted by their judgment performance. The evaluations of all the experts are summed with weighted linear combinations. The expert rating results will dynamically change depending on each expert's performance. Our approach of expert group decision is similar to a classifier committee concept in automatic text categorization [10, 15]. Their methods use classifiers based on various statistical or learning techniques instead of human interactions and decisions. This weighted measure is useful even when the number of experts is not fixed.

It will be an issue how to choose experts and decide authority weights. We define a rating score matrix $X = [\chi_{ij}]$ when the i-th expert rates a web document d_j with a score χ_{ij}. For each web document d_j, the voting score of an expert committee is given as follows :

$$V(d_j) = \sum_{i=1}^{N_e} r_i \chi_{ij} = \sum_{i=1}^{N_e} \frac{w_i}{\sum_{k=1}^{N_e} w_k} \chi_{ij}$$

where N_e is the number of experts for a given category and r_i is the relative authority for the i-th expert member in the expert pool, and w_i is the authority weight for the i-th expert member. We suppose w_i should be positive for all time. The weight w_i is a dynamic factor, and it represents each expert's authority to evaluate documents. The higher authority weight indicates the expert is more influential to make a voting decision.

We define the error measure E as a squared sum of differences between desired voting scores and actual voting scores as follows :

$$E = \frac{1}{2} \sum_{j=1}^{n} [V(d_j) - V'(d_j)]^2 = \frac{1}{2} \sum_{j=1}^{n} \{\sum_{i=1}^{N_e} \frac{w_i}{\sum_{k=1}^{N_e} w_k} \chi_{ij} - V'(d_j)\}^2$$

where n is the number of documents evaluated by users, $V'(d_j)$ is the users' voting score for an expert-voted document d_j. We assume $V'(d_j)$ is the average over all user scores, but in reality it is rarely possible to receive the feedback from all users. The authority weight for each expert is changed every session, which is a given period of time, and at the same time $V'(d_j)$ can be approximated by the central limit theorem with a set of $\widetilde{V'}(d_j)$, which is the average of user ratings during the given session.

We use a gradient-descent method over the error measure E with respect to a weight w_i and the gradient is given by

$$\frac{\partial E}{\partial w_i} = \frac{\partial}{\partial w_i}(\frac{1}{2}\sum_{j=1}^{n}[V(d_j) - \widetilde{V'}(d_j)]^2) = \sum_{j=1}^{n}[\chi_{ij} - V(d_j)]\frac{\Delta_j}{S}$$

where $S = \sum_{k=1}^{N_e} w_k$ is the sum of weights, and $\Delta_j = [V(d_j) - \widetilde{V'}(d_j)]$ is the difference between predicted voting score and users' rating score during a session for a document d_j.

We apply the similar scheme shown in error back-progation of multilayer perceptrons [5] to our approach. If we update weights of experts by feedback of users about a web document d_j, the weight is changed each session by the following dynamic equation :

$$w_i(t+1) = w_i(t) - \eta[\chi_{ij} - V(d_j)]\frac{\Delta_j}{S} + \alpha(w_i(t) - w_i(t-1))$$

where η is a learning rate proportional to the number of user ratings per session, and α is the momentum constant.

The above equation says how to reward or penalize authority weights for their share of the responsibility for any error. According to the equation, the weight change involves with the correlation between a voting score difference among experts and the error difference. For example, when both an expert-voted score and the desirable rank score are larger than the weighted average voting score, or both of them are smaller than the average score, the expert gets rewards, otherwise gets penalty. In this case some experts have rewards and others receive penalties depending on the weighted average voting score of the expert group.

2.2   Evaluation Effectiveness

When dynamic authority weights are assigned to experts for a category, the expert group ratings can form a ranking list in order. We need to determine if the given ranking list is reliable. Reliable ranking means that good experts are selected into a pool of expert group and they recommend relevant documents or items to general users. We evaluate the prediction performance of expert groups in terms of effectiveness, that is, a measure of the agreement between expert groups and users in ranking a test set of web documents. We assume there are many users to evaluate top-ranked lists in contrast to a small number of experts in a category group.

We suggest several effectiveness measures which are related to the agreement in rank order between expert ratings and user ratings. They are rank order window measure, rank function measure, Spearman's correlation measure and F_β measure with rank order partition.

Rank Order Window Measure Given a sample query or category, we can represent the effectiveness as the percentage of top-ranked lists that user ratings rank in the same or very close position as an expert group does. Given top-ranked web documents $D = \{d_1, d_2, ..., d_n\}$, we can define effectiveness Λ_{delta} with rank-order window $\delta(d_k)$ as

$$\Lambda_\delta = \frac{\sum_{k=1}^n S(d_k)}{n}$$

$$S(d_k) = 1 - \frac{1}{\delta(d_k)} \min(\delta(d_k), |\sum_{i=\mu(d_k)-\delta(d_k)}^{\mu(d_k)+\delta(d_k)} \frac{\mu(d_k) - Q(d_i)}{2\delta(d_k) + 1}|)$$

where d_k is the k-th web document from the test set for a given category, and $\delta(d_k)$ is the width of the window centered in the rank $\mu(d_k)$ assigned by the ratings of experts for d_k. $Q(d_i)$ is the rank position of the average rating score of users for a document d_i. $S(d_k)$ calculates the rate of the rank order difference in the window $[\mu(d_k) - \delta(d_k), \quad \mu(d_k) + \delta(d_k)]$.

Rank Function Measure Given web resources $D = \{d_1, d_2, ..., d_n\}$ and a set of all rank functions Φ over the set D, we suppose $d_1, d_2, ..., d_n$ is decreasingly ordered by their weighted rating values according to experts' judgements. We define a measure ρ to evaluate a ranking function $\phi \in \Phi$ over given ranked web documents D as follows :

$$\rho(\phi, d_k) = Card(\{d_i \in D | (1 \leq i < k) \wedge \phi(d_i) < \phi(d_k)\})$$

where $Card$ is a cardinality function to count the number of elements in a given set, and ϕ is a rank function over web resources D, which gives a sorting order.

We define a user satisfaction function Ψ over expert-voted ranked sites D as follows:

$$\Psi(\bar{\phi}) = \frac{\sum_{k=1}^n \rho(\bar{\phi}, d_k)}{(n-1)(n-2)/2}$$

where $\bar{\phi}$ is the rank function obtained from the result of all user ratings for n documents, and $0 \leq \Psi \leq 1$.

Spearman's Correlation Measure Spearman's rank-order correlation measure checks whether rank-ordered data is correlated. Let x_i be the rank of a document d_i in $D = \{d_1, d_2, ..., d_n\}$ by expert ratings, y_i be the rank of d_i by user ratings. The nonparametric correlation is defined to be the linear correlation coefficient of the ranks:

$$r_s = \frac{\sum_i (x_i - \bar{x})(y_i - \bar{y})}{\sqrt{\sum_i (x_i - \bar{x})^2} \sqrt{\sum_i (y_i - \bar{y})^2}}$$

where $\bar{x}, \bar{y}$ are the average of x_i, y_i, respectively. A value of $r_s = 1$ indicates complete positive correlation, which is a desirable state in our application, and $r_s = 0$ indicates no correlation of the data.

F_β Measure with Rank Order Partition Evaluation effectiveness also can be described in terms of precision and recall widely used in information retrieval. Precision is the conditional probability that when a document is predicted to be in a positive class, it truly belongs to this class. Recall is the conditional probability that a document belonging to positive class is truly classified into this class [12, 15]. We partition recommended documents by their rank order and make classes. We define a positive class i as top $[(i-1)*10+1 \sim i*10]$ ranked documents by expert voting and a negative class as the others. For example, class 2 documents are top $[11 \sim 20]$ ranked documents.

The precision probability P_i and recall probability R_i for ranking site class i may be estimated using the contingency relations between expert ratings and user ratings, and those probabilities in our application can be calculated with transition instances between classes. A transition instance p_{ij} is defined as the number of instances that are predicted to be in class i by expert ratings but belong to class j by user ratings.

$$P_i = \frac{p_{ii}}{\sum_{j=1}^{m} p_{ij} \cdot |i-j+1|}, \qquad R_i = \frac{p_{ii}}{\sum_{j=1}^{m} p_{ji} \cdot |i-j+1|}$$

$$\overline{P} = \frac{\sum_{i=1}^{m} P_i}{m}, \qquad \overline{R} = \frac{\sum_{i=1}^{m} R_i}{m}$$

where m is the number of classes, and $\overline{P}, \overline{R}$ are the average precision and recall probabilities, respectively. The distance between classes is considered to calculate P_i, R_i. Then effectiveness can be computed using the value of F_β for $0 \leq \beta \leq \infty$ [19, 3, 20].

$$F_\beta = \frac{(\beta^2+1) \cdot \overline{P} \cdot \overline{R}}{\beta^2 \cdot \overline{P} + \overline{R}}$$

To balance precision and recall, a value $\beta = 1$ is used in our experiments. If F_β is close to zero, then the current documents ranked in a class through expert voting results can be seen to have many false responses from feedback of general online users or many new documents positioned to the top ranks. If F_β is close to one, then top-ranked sites have good feedback from general users and little change occurs on the top ranked lists.

2.3   User Confidence Level

We maintain a rating record of each user. Many users evaluate web documents, but it is difficult to extract user preferences due to the lack of rating information. Before reflecting each user evaluation, we need to check if each user has rated a sufficient number of documents and the user evaluations are reliable. Thus, if we assume a rating score level from 1 to m, the confidence level C for a user u is defined as follows :

$$C(u) = -\sum_{i=1}^{m} p(i) \log p(i)$$

where $p(i)$ is the probability that the user u rates documents with score i, and it can be calculated by counting the number of documents with score i among all the documents that the user u has rated.

The confidence level of a user is an entropy measurement to check the distribution of score ratings. If it is more equally distributed, it is more likely that the user has given a sufficient number of ratings and also the user has unbiased criteria of evaluations. For example, if a user consistently puts only low scores or high scores on web documents, the user has a low confidence level. The rating information of users who keep low confidence levels for many sessions will not be considered for the database of rating scores as well as the analysis of user preferences.

3   Experiments

We simulated the dynamic process of web document ranking and creations of expert groups depending on their performance. The prediction performance of expert groups in reality will remain for future works. The purpose of the simulation test is to confirm that the dynamic expert groups reflect general users' opinions or ratings and has the potential to recommend documents that have not been rated yet. Also it will provide the results of effectiveness with several measures.

In the simulation, we assumed 10 categories to need expert groups, maximum 10 experts for each expert group, 10000 web documents $d_k, k = 1, .., 10000$ in the movie search engine, and also 500 random users logging into our search engine. We modeled random login patterns of online users as a Poisson process[14, 18]. Each user has an arrival rate, in other words, an access rate and a transaction processing time, thus we define the arrival rate λ_i for a user u_i, for $i = 1, ..., 500$. For a each user u_i, the probability that the user accesses the search engine document within time Δt is $P_i = 1 - e^{-\lambda_i \Delta t}$ where Δt is the basic time unit. Every session we have selected top-100 ranked documents recommended by an expert group for each category and applied our effectiveness measures to top-ranked lists. For rank order window measure, we used window size $\delta(d_k) = 4$. For F_β measure, we grouped the top-100 ranked documents into 10 classes each of which contains 10 documents.

Fig.2 shows the plots of effectiveness with four different measures, as the dynamic process of ranking evaluations continues. The expert group members and their knowledge levels are fixed for each category, and a random sequence of user ratings has been given. The results show the agreement level between expert groups and users in ranking documents according to the queries or categories. Simulation was run 10 times for each category, and only 2 category results are displayed among 10 categories. The figures show the average performance results with 95% confidence intervals. The results of rank order window measure are similar to those of rank function measure while the results of Spearman's correlation measure are similar to those of F_β measure. The rank order window and rank function measure can be seen as micro-view evaluations over rank order difference, and the others as macro-view.

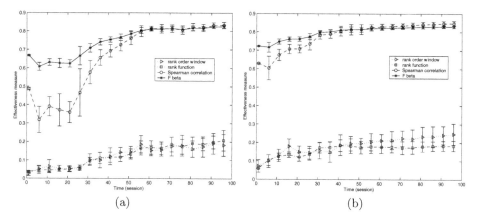

Fig. 2. Results of Effectiveness measures under different categories (a) category A (b) category B

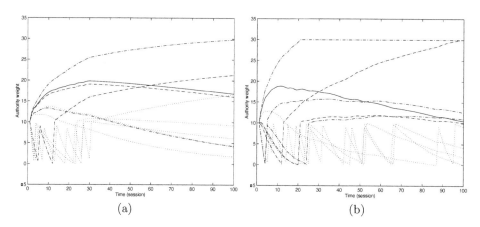

Fig. 3. An example of weight change for experts (a) category A (b) category B

Fig.3 shows the transitions of experts' authority weights according to their rating performance. Each expert has an initial weight 10 and maximum weight 30 is allowed to prevent too much authority over only a few experts. We assume that when one of the weights becomes negative, the corresponding expert is dropped from the committee. In simulation experiments it happened that some experts had high authority weights for a while and yielded their authority levels to other good experts. Many experts with bad performance have been dropped from the expert groups and then new members have been added; many oscillating curves of authority weights are seen between 0 and 10 in Fig.3. As a result, the above process plays a role on filtering out bad experts and keeping good experts as time passes. As the iteration of weight change continues for a long session, the authority weight may become stabilized as shown in Fig.4; there is no newcomer in the expert committee.

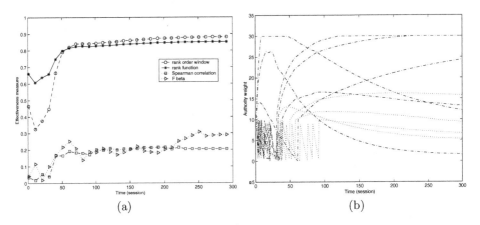

Fig. 4. An example of dynamic weights for expert committee members and their performance (a) effectiveness performance (b) weight change

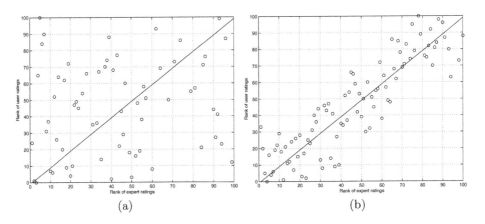

Fig. 5. An example of distribution of rank orders by expert group ratings and user ratings (a) before weight change (b) after weight change

Fig.5(b) shows an example of the agreement of rank order between the expert ratings and the user ratings in evaluating documents, while there is no regular pattern of the agreement at initial state as shown in Fig.5(a). After applying adaptive change of authority weights, the rank-order prediction of experts becomes close to the rank order of user ratings.

4   Discussion

We have used a simulation program to run expert groups for web page ranking. However, it is quite different from the real world in many respects. Some experts with good knowledge may have different opinions and views from general users. The access rate of each user is very irregular in reality. The behavior or access pattern of users will vary from category to category. In some categories, it may be difficult to assemble good experts.

Recommendation feedback process of users enables us to choose desirable experts for a given category. When users evaluate recommended documents, the system needs more evaluations for better performance, but users may be reluctant to provide feedbacks over a large number of documents. Also experts have their assignments to evaluate many documents. Score criteria of general users may be different from those of experts, which may make it difficult to compare numeric scores between expert groups and general users. Instead of numeric scores between expert groups and users, the rank order difference between two evaluators can be given in the weight change equation.

Our adaptive expert networks depending on user feedbacks can be applied to the combination model of classifiers instead of human agents. This will be useful in the field of text categorization or collaborative filtering. Also our effectiveness measures based on rank order can be possible evaluation criteria for collaborative filtering. After ratings of many users are obtained, it can be connected with collaborative filtering methods by analyzing user preferences.

5   Conclusion

In this paper we have shown dynamic expert groups for web page ranking through human interactions. Expert committee is automatically formed among users. Each expert has its own authority to evaluate web pages. This authority is dynamically changed using feedback of users.

As the user feedback or rating process continues, the dynamic change of authority weights increases weights for good experts and decreases weights for bad experts. It automatically chooses good experts for a given category and thus it improves the effectiveness measures that we suggest, which are rank order window measure, rank function measure, Spearman's rank-order correlation and F_β measure with rank order partition. Our effectiveness measures have a potential to select a pool of good experts. The system accumulates more user-feedback ratings of recommended documents as time passes, and it can improve the selection of experts as well as use collaborative filtering methods with the analysis of user preferences.

Currently we are applying this idea to design a meta-search engine for movie, music, and shopping mall sites. In many application, customers or users are interested in seeing the top ranked documents or products. The recommender system with dynamic expert groups will be a feasible solution to recommend items or documents for unspecified users in the field that automatic recommender systems cannot cover.

References

[1] J.S. Breese, D. Heckerman, and C. Kadie. Empirical analysis of predictive algorithms for collaborative filtering. In *Proceedings of the 14th Conference on Uncertainty in Artificial Intelligence*, pages 43–52, 1998.

[2] S. Brin and L. Page. The anatomy of a large-scale hypertextual web search engine. In *Proceedings of the Seventh International World Wide Web Conference*, 1998.

[3] W.W. Cohen and Y. Singer. Context-sensitive learning methods for text categorization. *ACM Transactions on Information Systems*, 17(2):141–173, 1999.

[4] J. Delgado, N. Ishii, and T. Ura. Content-based collaborative information filtering: Actively learning to classify and recommend documents. In *Proceedings of Cooperative Information Agents*, pages 206–215, 1998.

[5] S.S. Haykin. *Neural networks : a comprehensive foundation*. Prentice Hall, Upper Saddle River, N.J., 2nd edition, 1999.

[6] W. Hill, L. Stead, M. Rosenstein, and G. Furnas. Recommending and evaluating choices in a virtual community of use. In *Proceedings of ACM CHI'95*, pages 194–201, 1995.

[7] S.W. Kim and C.W. Chung. Web document ranking by differentiated expert group evaluation. In *Proceedings of the 9th International Conference on Human-Computer Interaction*, 2001.

[8] J. Kleinberg. Authoritative sources in a hyperlinked environment. In *Proceedings of the ACM-SIAM Symposium on Discrete Algorithms*, 1998.

[9] J. Konstan, B. Miller, D. Maltz, J. Herlocker, L. Gordon, and J. Riedl. Grouplense: Applying filtering to usenet news. *Communications of the ACM*, 40(3):77–87, March 1997.

[10] Y.H. Li and A.K. Jain. Classification of text documents. *The Computer Journal*, 41(8):537–546, 1998.

[11] R. Liere and P. Tadepalli. Active learning with committees for text categorization. In *Proceedings of the AAAI-97, 14th Conference of the American Association for Artificial Intelligence*, pages 591–596, 1997.

[12] V. Raghavan, P. Bollmann, and G. Jung. A critical investigatin of recall and precision as measures of retrieval system performance. *ACM transactions on Information Systems*, 7(3):205–229, 1989.

[13] P. Resnick, N. Iacovou, M. Sushak, P. Bergstrom, and J. Riedl. Grouplens: an open architecture for collaborative filtering of netnews. In *Proceedings of Computer Supported Cooperative Work Conference*, pages 175–186, 1994.

[14] S.M. Ross. *Introduction to Probability Models*. Academic Press, London, 7th edition, 2000.

[15] F. Sebastiani. Machine learning in automated text categorisation: a survey. Technical report, IEI-B4-31-1999, Istituto di Elaborazione dell'Informazione, C.N.R., Pisa, IT, 1999.

[16] U. Shardanand and P. Maes. Social information filtering: algorithms for automating 'word of mouth'. In *Proceedings of ACM CHI'95*, 1995.

[17] I. Soboroff, C. Nicholas, and M. Pazzani, editors. *Proceedings of the SIGIR-99 Workshop on Recommender Systems*. Berkeley,California, 1999.

[18] H.M. Taylor and S. Karlin. *An Introduction to Stochastic Modeling*. Academic Press, London, 3rd edition, 1998.

[19] C.J. van Rijsbergen. *Information Retrieval*. Butterworths, London, 1979.

[20] Y. Yang. An evaluation of statistical approaches to text categorization. *Information Retrieval*, 1(1-2):69–90, 2000.

Enhancing Information Retrieval in Federated Bibliographic Data Sources Using Author Network Based Stratagems

Peter Mutschke

Social Science Information Centre, Lennéstr. 30,
D-53113 Bonn, Germany
mutschke@bonn.iz-soz.de

Abstract. Despite the fact that many Digital Libraries (DLs) are available on the Internet, users cannot effectively use them because of inadequate functionality, deficient visualization and insufficient integration of different DLs. As part of the DAFFODIL[1] project we develop a user-oriented access system for DLs which overcomes these drawbacks. A major focus of the prototype concerns the implementation of search *stratagems* that exhaust the data structures stored in federated bibliographic DLs. The paper introduces stratagems taking into account information on the (social) status of scientific actors in author networks using network analysis methods. To make the propagation and analysis of actor networks more efficient an optimization strategy called main path analysis is employed.

1 Federated Digital Libraries and User Interface Issues

Digital libraries (DLs) offer a rich information structure. However, this wealth of information material implies that relevant information is mostly distributed over different information sources and services (bibliographic DLs, citation indices, categorized indices, full-text services). Moreover, DLs are structurally heterogeneous and only accessible via different retrieval languages. A further limitation of standard retrieval systems regards their strict document retrieval that does not allow to exploit the full complexity of information stored.

From a users point of view, DLs are therefore only meaningfully usable if effective search strategies and tactics can be used. Reducing the complexity of the search process by integrating different sources of information via a special wrapper technology is a necessary but not sufficient approach. It is moreover required to provide the user with high-level search functionality that exhausts the data structures in distributed DLs in various ways aiming at the aggregation of single distributed information objects. A typical example is an article where some meta data may be

---

[1] DAFFODIL is a joint project of the Department of Computer Science, University of Dortmund, and the Social Science Information Centre in Bonn. The project is sponsored by the German Research Foundation (DFG) as part of the strategic research initiative "Distributed Processing and Delivery of Digital Documents" (V3D2).

P. Constantopoulos and I.T. Sølvberg (Eds.): ECDL 2001, LNCS 2163, pp. 287-299, 2001.

found in DL A, its abstract in B, and its full text in C. This closely related data is to be combined and presented to the user as one integrated information object. A more sophisticated, knowledge discovery related scenario is to provide the user with generated meta information regarding, for instance, the structure of the research field studied, e.g. author networks and cliques, keyword clusters and so on. This suggests the development of "value-added" components that overcome the strict document orientation of standard indexing and retrieval methods by taking account of the analysis of *relationships* between single information objects. A further dimension of an integrated retrieval system for distributed, heterogeneous DLs regards its system support. Since DL users often need to control the granularity of system intelligence and strategic support this includes context-sensitive help, as well as adaptivity and pro-activity.

Due to these issues, Bates [1] categorized four conceptual levels of search activities which are based on each other. The lowest level represent "smallest units" in information searching (*moves*), such as "enter term A". The next higher level includes "strategic considerations ... with the purpose of improving or speeding search" (*tactics*). *Stratagems*, the third level, are complex methods "to exploit the file structure of a particular search domain". Finally, on the top, we have *strategies* which are „plan(s) for an entire search (that) may contain all of the previously mentioned types of search activity". Bates combined these types of search activities with different levels of system involvement, starting with "no system involvement", and ending with "executes automatically", to a matrix of twenty combinations. Bates strongly suggested that "more research and development attention (should) be paid to the central area of (the matrix)". This regards particularly the *stratagems* level.

In order to make a contribution to this issue, this paper focuses on stratagems exploiting co-author- and citation relationships between the actors of scientific work, i.e. stratagems operating on *author networks*. Those stratagems are essential tools in our DAFFODIL system that aims at applying Bates' matrix to a user-oriented access system for DLs to overcome the drawbacks sketched above. In Section 2 the architecture of DAFFODIL, particularly regarding its implementation of Bates' levels of search activities, is described. In Section 3 and 4 author networks and scenarios using them as search stratagems are discussed. Section 5 introduces an optimization strategy that makes the propagation and analysis of author networks more efficient. Section 6, finally, outlines the current status of implementation of author network based stratagems in DAFFODIL, as well as further project activities.

2   DAFFODIL: An Agent-Based Architecture for Supporting High-Level Search Activities in Federated DLs

Based on Bates' matrix the project DAFFODIL aims at the development of a scalable agent based architecture that supplies the user with search services on a conceptual higher level and hides the underlying heterogeneity of data sources by an integrating interface [6,7]. A key concept is the notion of *strategic support* by means of well-developed search *stratagems* and *strategies*. Strategic support implies, particularly as regards the occasional user, active system assistance that is scaled during the search process. Scaling is oriented towards the different levels of system involvement (here:

passive, context-sensitive help, adaptive, pro-active) and search activities (*moves, tactics, stratagems, strategies*) that are categorized by Bates.

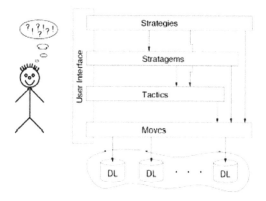

Fig. 1. Layer architecture of DAFFODIL[2]

The system is based on distributed agents that are arranged to each other as a layer architecture (see Fig. 1). The layers correspond to the four search activity categories of Bates' matrix: The lowest level consists of DLs which are addressed over wrappers (*moves* layer). The *tactics* layer aggregates single services of individual libraries to integrated services that represent simple functions which are used to adjust and push ahead the search, e.g. by widen the search with a broader term obtained from a thesaurus (*super term* tactic), or by searching for co-authors of a given author (*co-author search* tactic). The *stratagems* layer supplies services that represent strategic subprocesses of the search that exhaustively exploit the data structures of a single domain to communicate the full complexity of information. This is supplied by pursuing the implicit and explicit link structures within a DL and between a network of federated DLs. Stratagems are methods that apply one or more tactics iteratively on a certain domain and may implement sophisticated computations on the data structures found. A typical example is *citation search* that looks for other articles citing or cited by a document marked as relevant. *Strategies* finally, take the concrete situation of the user as the starting point. They are therefore complete search plans consisting of one or more stratagems or tactics suitable to the user's information needs. An example is a pre-search interview where the user is asked for known facts regarding his information needs, and depending on the answers one or more initial stratagems or tactics are fired. See [1] and [6] for further scenarios. The search activities at each level of the layer architecture of DAFFODIL are represented as tools on the interface according to the WOB[3] model for user interface design that is based on the tool metaphor [12,13,19]. Note that for the design of tactics, stratagems, and strategies empirical findings are used [1,6].

---

[2] The figure is taken from [7].
[3] „Auf der *W*erkzeugmetapher basierende strikt *o*bjektorientierte graphisch-direktmanipulative *B*enutzungsoberfläche"

Currently, twelve DLs have been wrapped into DAFFODIL so far [7]. Among them are ACM DL[4] as a data source of bibliographic information, citations, and full-text articles, DBLP[5] and Cora[6] that provide bibliographic information, and CiteSeer[7] as a full-text data source including citations, as well as NCSTRL[8].

As pointed out above, one of the substantial innovations of the prototype is the implementation of high-level search functionality that exhausts the information structures stored in federated bibliographic DLs. An approach to provide this is the use of information on cooperation and citation structures, i.e. (transitive) relationships between the actors of scientific work. The analysis of author networks supplies search stratagems that enable requests directed towards macro phenomena of the research field studied, like the question for the most central authors or researcher cliques of a scientific community.

As to this issue, we can fall back to outcomes of the AKCESS project where network analysis methods on the basis of author networks have been used for information retrieval purposes for the first time [14,16]. Actually, empirical tests using AKCESS and cognitive mapping methods have shown that central actors are most likely working on central subjects of the research field under study [15,17]. A further notion of centrality used in search engines is given by Kleinberg [9,10] and in Google[9] where the structural prominence of Web pages is determined by applying social network analysis.

In Section 3 we give an explanation of the concepts *author networks* and *author centrality*. In Section 4 appropriate author network based stratagems are introduced that are suitable to enrich or improve information retrieval in bibliographic DLs.

3   Author Networks and Author Centrality (in Bibliographic DLs)

An author network consists of a set of scientific actors who have one or more types of relations to others. As link types constructing author networks in DAFFODIL co-author- and citation relationships are used. Those relationships can be retrieved from the DLs connected. Since the methods introduced have been applied to co-authorships so far, the focus is on co-author networks in this paper.

Co-Author networks are propagated by recursively performing *co-author search* tactics, i.e. by pursuing the transitive closure of co-author relations. *Co-author search* retrieves documents of a given author and returns the set of co-authors found in these documents. As regards the DAFFODIL scenario where we are concerned with federated DLs, note that author networks might be distributed over several DLs (see Fig. 2). Operating on them is considered as *high-level* search functionality since it aggregates distributed but closely related information.

---

[4] http://www.acm.org/dl/
[5] http://dblp.uni-trier.de/
[6] http://cora.whizbang.com/
[7] http://www.csindex.com/
[8] http://www.ncstrl.org/
[9] http://www.google.com/

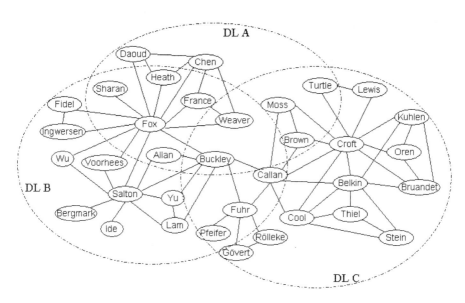

Fig. 2. An author network distributed over three DLs[10]

According to the notion of a *social network* [5,20], that is used in the social and behavioral science community to describe relationships among social actors, author networks[11] in DAFFODIL are described as a graph $G = (V, E)$, where the set V of vertices represents actors (here: authors), and the set E of edges represents links between them (here: co-author relations). In social network analysis, graph-theoretic concepts are used to explain social phenomena, particularly the social status (prominence) of an actor within a social structure. Attractive methods for the analysis of the social status of an actor in a network are *centrality* indices defined on the vertices of a graph [2,5]. Centrality is a structural attribute of an actor in a network that measures the contribution of a network position to the actor's prominence, influence or importance within a social structure. Apart from counting the number of ties leaving (resp. receiving) each node (*degree* centrality [5]), the most important centrality measures are based on shortest paths[12] counting like *closeness* centrality [5] $C_C(s)$, $s \in V$, that computes the sum of the shortest *distances* $d_G(s,t)$ between s and all $t \in V$ in G, $d_G(s,t)$ being the minimum length of any path connecting s and t in G. The actor with the highest closeness is therefore considered as the actor having the shortest distances to all other vertices in the graph. In contrast, *betweenness* centrality

---

[10] In order to reduce the complexity of the figure all edges in the graph appear only once. The graph displays a part of a network of 413 actors working on the subject "information retrieval" that have been found with DAFFODIL.

[11] Note that we are using *actor network* and *author network*, *actor centrality* and *author centrality* synonymously in the following.

[12] A *path* from $s \in V$ to $t \in V$ is considered as a sequence of linked pairs of edges, starting from s and ending in t, such that s and t are connected. The *shortest path* is the path with the minimum *length*, i.e. the minimal number of links connecting s and t in G (if edges are weighted the sum of the weights of the edges is taken).

[5] $C_B(v)$, $v \in V$, focuses on the ratio of shortest paths an actor lies on, i.e. the maximum number of shortest paths from all $s \in V$ to all $t \in V$ having v as one of the succeeding resp. preceding vertices on the shortest path connecting s and t in G. The actor having the highest betweenness is therefore a vertex connecting most of the actors in the network. Those actors may also serve as "bridges" between disparate partitions of the network. The normalized centrality scores for the actors from Figure 2 indicate evidently the structural prominence particularly of Fox, Salton, Buckley, Fuhr, Callan, Croft, and Belkin within this network (see Table 1).

Table 1. Normalized centrality scores of the actors from Figure 2 having more than three co-authorships, expressed as a percentage

Author	Degree[13]	Closeness[14]	Betweenness[15]
Fox	35.29	43.59	43.76
Salton	26.47	41.98	18.54
Buckley	20.59	50.00	54.10
Chen	14.71	31.78	0.36
Fuhr	14.71	41.46	16.93
Callan	20.59	46.58	47.77
Croft	29.41	37.78	21.98
Kuhlen	11.76	28.81	0.15
Belkin	20.59	36.56	10.25
Bruandet	11.76	28.81	0.15
Cool	14.71	35.79	5.08

In DAFFODIL betweenness is used as an appropriate filter to leave *hangers on*, i.e. actors having a strong closeness but a betweenness of zero (actors "hanging on" central actors), out of account. Since we have to reckon with an amount of data, the algorithm of Brandes [2] is implemented which provides an efficient mechanism to compute centrality in fairly large networks with thousands of actors. Note furthermore that author networks may be undirected and connected, thus they may have multiple edges and loops.

4   Author Network Based Stratagems

Founded on social network theory [5,20], the basic philosophy of author network based stratagems is to take advantage of knowledge about the (social) interaction among the actors of a scientifc community and the development of super-individual structures (networks, clusters, cliques) within a research field. Based on author

---

[13] The normalized degree centrality is the degree divided by $n-1$, where n is the number of vertices in the graph, expressed as a percentage.

[14] The normalized closeness centrality is the closeness divided by $n-1$, where n is the number of vertices in the graph, expressed as a percentage.

[15] The normalized betweenness centrality is the betweenness divided by the maximum possible betweenness expressed as a percentage.

networks and the centrality measures as described in Section 3, we suggest the following stratagems:

Central Author Search. An index of centrality in a communication structure might be desired for information retrieval purposes, as a clue to how much relevance an actor has for the domain in question because of his key position in the network. Accordingly, the basic hypothesis of this stratagem (and all other centrality based stratagems) is that central authors are relevant for the theme in question [15,17]. Therefore, information on the centrality of authors can be very useful to find relevant authors (experts). To achieve a ranked list of actors ordered by descending centrality three main scenarios are conceivable: (1) the user enters a term (e.g. a classification entry) and a list of central actors is returned; (2) central author search on the basis of a given (large enough) result set obtained from a subject search (in order see which authors are central within the document set retrieved); (3) central author search based upon a network that is propagated up to a designated depth cut-off starting with a given (known) author the user has either (3a) entered (i.e. network propagation independent of a special subject), or (3b) marked as relevant in a given result set. The basic idea of the latter approach, that might be called "*retrieval by connectedness*", is that further relevant entities can be found in the structural *neighborhood* of a relevant object. This application of *central author search* is suitable for a scenario where the user knows an actor and need to explore his personal network (in order to see whether the author is central within his "own" network or not, or to search for a more central actor in the neighborhood) [16].

As regards pro-activity, propagating author networks and computing author centrality could be done simultaneously during the retrieval process, and the list could be returned automatically when the search terminates. Once the list of central actors is generated, documents of these authors could be displayed and used as starting points for further search activities (*citation search, similarity search*). This might be particular interesting for documents of very central actors.

Author Network Browse. An author network (generated by one of the *central author search* methods described above) is displayed as a tree view or visualized as a graph. Author cliques are indicated. This stratagem is useful in a situation where a user needs to get an idea of how his research field is structured, or to explore the (social) neighborhood of an author by navigating through the network.

Query Expansion Using Central Authors. A query is expanded by (weighted) author lists obtained from a previous application of *central author search*. Documents of central authors are ranked higher within the result set.

Ranking a Document Result Set Using Author Centrality. Network information is furthermore useful to increase the precision of a subject based search for relevant documents. This is particular interesting when a user is confronted with a (too) large

---

[16] This application of *central author search* is only suitable for a network with a minimum depth of two.

result set, and he or she do not want or do not know how to narrow the search. Based on the hypothesis that documents of central actors are relevant, *central author search* (scenario (2)) is applied to the result set, i.e. the document set is ranked by descending centrality of the authors of these documents. The ranked document list starts with documents of the most central actors, including those publications of central authors that are not written in co-authorship.

Result Set Expansion Using Author Networks. In order to increase the recall of a subject search as well, this stratagem searches for documents in the *neighborhood* of relevant documents (resp. relevant authors) which were not found since those documents did not match with the search terms of the query but belong to authors who cooperate with (central) authors of relevant documents of the result set. Documents in the neighborhood of relevant authors that have been overlooked by the search engine, caused by a mismatch of indexing and search terms, are added to the result set. In order to avoid result set explosion, only documents are considered which do not fall below some minimum similarity to documents previously marked as relevant. Such application of the notion of *retrieval by connectedness* could be particularly interesting in a heterogeneous world (as it is the case in DAFFODIL) where a user performs searches in several DLs that are indexed by a different indexing vocabulary so that the user may succeed in DL A but not in B. In this situation relevant documents in B are possibly not found via term matching but by pursuing co-author links between the A- and B-actors. The result set is then expanded by documents of B-actors who are strongly connected to central A-actors, with no further regard to the query terms.

To illustrate the semantics of the layer architecture of DAFFODIL (see Fig. 1), particularly to give an idea of the role of *strategies*, let us finally sketch the following top-down scenario using author network based search activities (see Table 2):

Table 2. Levels of author network based search activities

Level	Example
Strategies	Expert Search
Stratagems	Central Author Search
Tactics	Co-Author Search
Moves	Enter Author

Assuming a user who needs to organize a hearing consisting of experts on a special subject, an adequate strategy might be *expert search*. A suitable method (stratagem) to achieve this goal is searching for the most central actors of the research field in question *(central author search*, based on, for instance, a previous plain search). The *central author search* stratagem itself is a composition of the recursive application of the *co-author search* tactic plus some computations on the networks propagated (centrality). *Co-author search*, finally, is traced back to a set of elementary actions (moves) on the level of the retrieval language. Note that a *strategy* in Daffodil is not a one-to-one representation of the user's information needs itself. It is rather one of possibly several general methods to achieve the user's goals.

5   Optimizing Network Propagation by Main Path Analysis

Propagating a co-author network by pursuing all link structures between authors starting with a given author (see *central author search*, scenario (3)) is done by performing a breadth-first search that considers all successor vertices of a given vertex first before expanding further. This is done by recursively firing *co-author search* tactics. In propagating a network this way we are concerned with the principle problem to define when searching should terminate. A possible solution, that is provided by Daffodil, is to let the user specify a depth cut-off, i.e. network propagation stops when a specified depth of the network is achieved. Given a cut-off of two, for instance, the network propagated includes all direct co-authors of the initial author (first order zone), as well as all co-authors of the actors within the first order zone, i.e. all actors who are two ties far away from the start author (second order zone). Setting a cut-off is sufficient in a situation where the user is only interested in examining the nearer social neighborhood of a particular author, in order to analyse, for instance, his or hers relationships to all co-authors (resp. co-co-authors) within the first and second order zone (see *author network browse*).

However, in the case of *central author search* (scenario (3)), where the user aims at searching for more central (more relevant) actors in the network of a particular author, the major conceptual problem of setting a cut-off is that more central actors might be located outside of the cut-off point. Here, specifying a maximum depth of the network is a completely arbitrary cut-off that might induce a misrepresentation of the social structure of the community studied. The latter issue is closely connected with the technical problem that breadth-first search within a large and distributed search space might be very time consuming, so that the user is forced to choose a low threshold. Note that even a cut-off of two may yield hundreds of actors.

In order to make the propagation and analysis of actor networks more efficient, an adaptation of a structural technique used in citation graph analysis called *main path analysis* (MPA) [3,8] is developed. In citation analysis this technique is used to evaluate the main stream literature by pursuing citation links that over time connect the most heavily cited publications, starting with a given paper. MPA can be therefore seen as a best-first search that reduces the number of paths to be pursued to the *best* ones by applying a particular evaluation function. In DAFFODIL the evaluation function is given by degree centrality measuring the number of co-authorships of a given actor, i.e. by MPA using degree centrality as evaluation criterion a path is traced through the valued network from node to node, always choosing as the next tie(s) that (those) edge(s) that connect(s) to (a) node(s) with the highest degree centrality score. But unlike MPA in citation graph analysis, and a little like hill-climbing, the propagation process in DAFFODIL terminates when a local maximum is achieved, i.e. the path terminates in a node that is locally the vertex that has a higher degree centrality score than all its neighbors. This yields a sequence of tie choices tracing a *main path* through the network that starts with a given vertex and terminates in a central one. This is either a central node in a subgraph or the global optimum, i.e. the most central node in the graph.

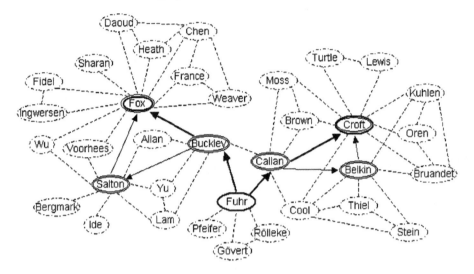

Fig. 3. "Primary" and "secondary" main paths starting with Fuhr

The notion of a "*main* path" emphasizes the idea that those paths represent cooperation structures that lead to the "centers of excellence" where the main research of a particular domain takes place (keeping in mind that all connecting actors on a main path might be particularly relevant as well). MPA is therefore a good method not only to drastically cut down the amount of search but also to reduce the number of paths to be followed to the most promising ones to find more relevant authors in the social neighborhood of a given start author. MPA in DAFFODIL yields a list of authors found on main paths ordered by descending degree centrality. As desired by the user the list can be reduced to terminal authors. Unlike pure hill-climbing, MPA in DAFFODIL uses a node list as in breadth-first search to allow backtracking, such that the method is able to record alternative ("secondary" etc.) main paths, i.e. MPA stepwise includes successors having the second (third etc.) highest degree centrality score and proceeds in propagating "primary" main paths emanating from those nodes[17].

Given the network from Figure 2 a main path starting with Fuhr, for instance (see Fig. 3), will terminate in Fox (via Buckley) and Croft (via Callan), who are the most central actors in this network by degree centrality (see Table 1). Suppose we are as well interested in examining "secondary" main paths emanating from Buckley and Callan we will moreover find Salton (via Buckley) and Belkin (via Callan). Thus, by applying MPA the final set of actors in the neighborhood of Fuhr will include Buckley, Fox, Salton, Callan, Belkin, and Croft, whereas applying breadth-first search

---

[17] Secondary main paths are useful to avoid the "plateau" effect known in hill-climbing where a whole set of neighboring nodes have the value so that it is not possible to determine the best direction in which to move.

with a depth cut-off of two, for instance, the network propagation process will exclude Fox and Croft.

None the less, setting a depth cut-off for the network propagation cannot be avoided since the DAFFODIL scenario is potentially concerned with a very large search space. However, introducing MPA into the network propagation process allows the user to choose a higher cut-off because the complexity of the graph propagated is reduced to main paths so that the search process can go deeper into the social structure to be analysed. A clue for a meaningful threshold might be given by the *small-world phenomenon* [11] saying that any two individuals in a network are likely to be connected through a sequence of at most six intermediate acquaintances, known as the "six degrees of separation" principle. On the assumption that a depth cut-off of six will accordingly produce networks that suitably represent the social structure of a scientific community, it is our intuition that all main paths will converge on actors who are actually central within the community[18].

6   Conclusion and Outlook

We introduced the notion of author networks in federated DLs and a set of suitable stratagems based on that data structure. Network information, particularly the concepts of centrality and connectedness introduced, might enrich the information seeking process immensely because it strongly emphasizes on information regarding the cooperation (communication) structure of a scientific community. Author network based stratagems are therefore useful tools for evaluating the (social) status of actors within a particular community (their centrality), their structural neighborhood, as well as to enhance the recall and precision of the retrieval process at all. Moreover, we introduced a structural technique (main path analysis) to optimize network propagation and the evaluation of actor centrality without imposing a low depth threshold.

As part of the DAFFODIL project basic methods propagating and operating on author networks are currently implemented as Java services, including the computation of author centrality, as well as most of the author network based stratagems introduced[19]. These services will be enhanced by the computation of author cliques, further developed measurements regarding centrality and connectivity, and heuristics for evaluating author identity. An ongoing main activity focuses on the visualization of author networks, in order to make browsing more comfortable and, more importantly, to provide the user with more insights into how a research field is structured. According to the main path analysis approach introduced, the complexity of a graph to be drawn could be restricted to main paths. In order to reduce latency time, caching mechanisms are going to be implemented so that the system can fall back on networks that have been already computed in previous sessions.

---

[18] This is consistent with an analysis of connectivity in a citation network using MPA (see [8], p. 55).

[19] The methods presented are likewise used within the GESINE prototype that supplies retrieval on the German social science databases SOLIS and FORIS [19].

Furthermore, usability and retrieval tests are still outstanding. Particularly the assumed improvement of recall and precision by considering author centrality and connectedness as well as the benefits of main path analysis in network propagation are to be proven by quantitative retrieval tests. At this point, we should like to emphasize that ranking mechanisms based on author centrality in networks might be only useful if the networks propagated provide an appropriate representation of the real communication structures of the particular domain under study. Therefore, more research attention should be paid to develop appropriate criteria for the use of author centrality for ranking. Those should take into consideration the completeness of the underlying data sources due to the information needs of the user, the number of the documents retrieved, the size of the networks found as well as their density. Particularly the internal coherence, given by the density of a network, is to be considered as a strong criterion of adequacy of the models proposed in this paper.

The methods introduced have been applied to co-authorships so far. We plan to apply them to citation networks (resp. co-citation networks) as well. Citation graph analysis (see for some recent examples [4,18,21]) provide a wide range of computational models that might enrich the information seeking process immensely if they are supplied to the user by well-developed tools. As an innovative future perspective (outside of the DAFFODIL project), we furthermore plan to integrate author network analysis with *cognitive mapping*, i.e. the analysis of relationships between actors, actor networks respectively, and keyword aggregations (*themes*) as it is outlined in [17].

References

1. Bates, M.: Where Should the Person Stop and the Information Search Interface Start? Information Processing and Management **26**(5) (1990) 575 591.
2. Brandes, U.: A Faster Algorithm for Betweenness Centrality. To appear in: Journal of Mathematical Sociology **25** (2001)
3. Carley, K.M., Hummon, N.P., Harty, M.: Scientific Influence. An Analysis of the Main Path Structure in the Journal of Conflict Resolution. Knowledge: Creation, Diffusion, Utilization **14**(4) (1993) 417-447
4. Chen, C.: Visualising semantic spaces and author co-citation networks in digital libraries. Information Processing and Management **35** (1999) 401-420
5. Freeman, L. C.: Centrality in social networks: Conceptual clarification. Social Networks **1** (1979) 215-239
6. Fuhr, N. Gövert, N. Klas, C.-P.: An Agent-Based Architecture for Supporting High-Level Search Activities in Federated Digital Libraries. In: Proceedings 3rd International Conference of Asian Digital Library. KAIST, Taejon, Korea (2000) 247-254
7. Gövert, N., Fuhr, N., Klas, C.-P.: Daffodil: Distributed Agents for User-Friendly Access of Digital Libraries. In: Research and Advanced Technology for Digital Libraries. Springer, Berlin et al. (2000) 352-355
8. Hummon, N.P., Doreian, P.: Connectivity in a Citation Network: The Development of DNA Theory. Social Networks **11** (1989) 39-63.
9. Kleinberg, J. M.: Authoritative sources in a hyperlinked environment. Journal of the Association for Computing Machinery **46**(5) (1999) 604-632
10. Kleinberg, J. M., Kumar, R., Raghavan, P., Rajagopalan, S., Tomkins, A. S.: The Web as a graph: Measurements, models, and methods. In: Asano, T., Imai, H., Lee, D. T., Nakano, S.,

Tokuyama, T. (eds.): Proceedings of the 5th International Conference on Computing and Combinatorics (COCOON '99). Lecture Notes in Computer Science, Vol. 1627. Springer-Verlag, Berlin Heidelberg New York (1999) 1-17

11. Kleinberg, J.: The Small-World Phenomenon: An Algorithmic Perspective. Cornell Computer Science Technical Report 99-1776 (October 1999)

12. Krause, J.: "Das WOB-Modell". In: Vages Information Retrieval und graphische Benutzungsoberflächen: Beispiel Werkstoffinformation. Universitätsverlag Konstanz (1997) 59-88

13. Krause, J., Schaefer, A.: Textrecherche-Oberfläche in ELVIRA II. ELVIRA Arbeitsbericht Nr. 16. Informationszentrum Sozialwissenschaften Bonn (1998)

14. Mutschke, P.: Processing Scientific Networks in Bibliographic Databases. In: Bock, H.H., et al. (eds.): Information Systems and Data Analysis. Prospects-Foundations-Applications. Proceedings 17th Annual Conference of the GfKl 1993. Springer-Verlag, Heidelberg Berlin (1994) 127-133

15. Mutschke, P., Renner, I.: Wissenschaftliche Akteure und Themen im Gewaltdiskurs. Eine Strukturanalyse der Forschungslandschaft. In: Mochmann, E., et al. (eds.): Gewalt in Deutschland. Soziale Befunde und Deutungslinien. Oldenbourg Verlag, München (1995) 147-192

16. Mutschke, P.: Uncertainty and Actor-Oriented Information Retrieval in μ-AKCESS. An Approach Based on Fuzzy Set Theory. In: Bock, H.-H. et al. (eds.): Data Analysis and Information Systems. Statistical and conceptual approaches. Springer-Verlag, Berlin-Heidelberg (1996) 126-138

17. Mutschke, P., Quan-Haase, A.: Cognitive and Social Structures in Social Science Research Fields and their Use in Information Systems. In: Blasius, J. et al. (eds.): The Fifth International Conference on Logic and Methodology. Cologne (2000) ISBN 90-801073-8-7

18. Perry, C.A., Rice, R.E.: Scholarly Communication in Developmental Dyslexia: Influence of Network Structur on Change in a Hybrid Problem Area. Journal of the American Society for Information Science **49**(2) (1998) 151-168

19. Schommler, M., Riege, U.: Integrated Retrieval on Heterogeneous Social Science Databases (Gesine). In: Blasius, J. et al. (eds.): The Fifth International Conference on Logic and Methodology. Cologne (2000) ISBN 90-801073-8-7

20. Wassermann, S.; Faust, K.: Social Network Analysis: Methods and Applications, Cambridge University Press, New York (1994)

21. White, H.D., McCain, K.W.: Visualizing a Discipline: An Author Co-Citation Analysis of Information Science, 1972-1995. Journal of the American Society for Information Science **49**(4) (1998) 327-355

Architecture for Event-Based Retrieval from Data Streams in Digital Libraries

Mohamed Kholief, Stewart Shen, Kurt Maly

Computer Science Department, Old Dominion Uinversity, Norfolk, VA 23529, USA
{kholief,shen,maly}@cs.odu.edu

Abstract. Data streams are very important sources of information for both researchers and other users. Data streams might be video or audio streams or streams of sensor readings or satellite images. Using digital libraries for archival, preservation, administration, and access control for this type of information greatly enhances the utility of data streams. For this specific type of digital libraries, our proposed event-based retrieval provides an alternate, yet a very natural way of retrieving information. People tend to remember or search by a specific event that occurred in the stream better than by the time at which this event occurred. In this paper we present the analysis and design of a digital library system that contains data streams and supports event-based retrieval.

Keywords: digital libraries, event-based retrieval, data streams, architecture.

1 Introduction

A data stream is a sequence of data units produced regularly over a period of time. Video and audio streams, sensor readings, and satellite images are all examples of data streams. Data streams are very important sources of information for many applications. Providing these streams in digital libraries allowing archival, preservation, administration, access control, etc would greatly enhance the value of this information and the utility of the digital libraries. Saving data streams in digital libraries is mostly limited to saving audio and video streams. Many digitized academic libraries now support the retrieval of video and audio files. These libraries may be identified as video/audio-on-demand systems as they mostly support playing back the whole file based on some bibliographic information. Other research projects in many universities are building video and audio digital libraries that support more sophisticated ways of retrieval such as content-based retrieval. Examples are the Informedia project [2], the VISION project [4], etc. The Image Information System Group at IBM is working on a project, SPIRE, which has a research agenda that involves producing progressive data representation for unstructured data (such as time series, image, video, and multidimensional data) [1], which illustrates the significance of saving data streams in digital libraries.

In this research the focus is on storing data streams in a digital library and on introducing a new means of retrieval from this kind of a digital library: event-based retrieval. In the context of data streams, this way of retrieval is more flexible and natural than the traditional retrieval methods such as content-based retrieval. This

P. Constantopoulos and I.T. Sølvberg (Eds.): ECDL 2001, LNCS 2163, pp. 300–311, 2001.

paper presents the analysis and design of a digital library system that illustrates this new approach. We also present our finding that this approach is feasible, natural, precise, and efficient.

2 Concepts for Event-Based Retrieval

In this section we present some of the definitions and concepts for event-based retrieval that we established during the course of our research.

A *data stream* is a sequence of data units produced regularly over a period of time. A data unit of a stream might be a video frame, an audio packet, a sensor reading, etc.

A set of streams that share the same characteristics are said to have the same *stream type*. Examples of a stream type would be a teacher audio, a weather sensor's readings, a TV news report, etc. A stream type is to be distinguished from a *stream format*. Many stream types can have the same format, e.g. audio format, but different in the way they are used depending on the application. The metadata set for a teacher audio stream would definitely be different from the metadata set for the audio stream of A TV news report. Many characteristics will be shared among streams of the same type such as the metadata fields associated with these streams, the criteria to be used to specify the events for this stream, the players to be used to play this stream, etc.

An *event* is literally a noteworthy occurrence that occurred during the stream. Searching data streams in a digital library by events besides other searching methods gives users extra flexibility and allows for faster and more precise retrieval. By faster retrieval we mean that users can get to the desired stream segment faster than just playing back the whole stream or even starting from a specific estimated time. In the context of a streams-based digital library, people would tend to be able to inquire more naturally by events rather than by time stamps on the streams. For example, in a digital library that contains the audio and video streams of a class session, a student might want to ask about what the teacher said when some other student asked a question rather than asking about what is on the audio stream after, say, 30 minutes from the start of the class. In a different context, consider weather data coming from different sources, a researcher might want to see the sensor readings, the satellite images, etc when a certain event instance, such as a hurricane upgrade, occurred. An ordinary user might want to retrieve the news aired that relate to this hurricane upgrade. In summary, this event-based retrieval approach can be useful for both ordinary and expert users of the library and is more natural for phrasing queries.

Events can be *atomic* or *composite*. An atomic event spans a discrete point in time, e.g. Netscape started or a hurricane degree upgraded. A composite event is an event that spans some duration, e.g. Netscape running or Mr. X talking. A composite event generally corresponds to an event-pair of two atomic events: a start and an end.

Events might occur many times during the course of one stream, e.g. a "Hurricane Upgrade" occurring two or three times in a wind velocities stream, or a "Student asking a question" occurring many times in the audio stream of one class session. We will always refer to these event occurrences as the *event instances*. A basic mathematical model for events and streams has been introduced in [6].

Event types are similar in concept to stream types. An *event class* will contain all events of the same type and will be used to browse through events, another way of retrieval in our library design. Event types and classes are detailed in section 5.2.

Users would normally use event instances not only to retrieve a segment of the stream at which this event occurred, but also to correlate this stream to other streams that relate to the same subject. We refer to other streams that the user might want to retrieve whenever he retrieves a stream as *related streams*. These streams might relate to other streams, to events that occurred during other streams, or to instances of events that occurred during other streams. We refer to these streams as *stream-related*, *event-related*, or *instance-related* respectively. Furthermore, related streams can be concurrent or non-concurrent. *Concurrent streams* can be synchronized while they are played back, e.g. the video and audio streams of the same class session.

A *domain expert* is needed to specify the related streams and the criteria to decide if a stream is related or not. The domain expert will also be responsible for specifying the event criteria to be applied to streams to generate event tables. An *event generator* software module will use these criteria to generate the event tables.

A *publisher* is responsible for inserting the stream data into the digital library. This publisher would specify the metadata of the stream and, usually, call the indexing services of the library to create the necessary indexes.

A *resource discovery user* is the end user who will search the digital library to retrieve and playback a stream or more based on the events that occurred during those streams as well as other stream metadata.

3 Potential Applications of the Proposed System

A digital library system that contains data streams and supports event-based retrieval in addition to other retrieval methods has many potential applications.

A stock market digital library: This library may contain the stock prices and index values, among other streams, and can be used to study the effects of different factors on the price fluctuations and the market behavior.

A digital library containing news-streams: Event-based retrieval from such a library would be useful in correlating the news coming from different sources. It is also possible to correlate those events to other streams such as the stock market streams or the weather streams.

A Weather-Related Digital Library: Over any specific area in the United States many weather streams can be stored in such a digital library, such as: the wind velocity over this area, the temperature, the humidity levels, the percentage of precipitation, the amount of rain or snow, and the satellite and radar maps. Furthermore, there are many streams that are indirectly related to weather that can also be saved in the digital library such as the TV and Radio weather reports.

An educational digital library: This library may contain data streams of an interactive distance-education system. A specific example is described here. IRI, *Interactive Remote Instruction*, is a distance education system that is being developed at Old Dominion University. IRI is an interactive multimedia collaboration system that provides a virtual classroom over a high speed Intranet in which individual computer workstations become each student's window into the virtual classroom. IRI is a multimedia, collaborative, integrated, learning environment that solves both learning paradigm and technical problems in a cost-effective way [8]. Many streams are used in IRI: teacher video stream, students video stream, teacher audio stream, students audio stream, a shared room view which is used to share the view of specific application windows among all the users, and a stream of all the buttons pressed during any session, e.g. a specific tool such as Netscape is started. These are basically the streams to be saved in the digital library. Examples of some of the events that could occur in these streams: class started, class session in progress, student X speaking, teacher started a specific application, someone joined the session, etc.

4 Design Considerations

We presented in the last section some example applications of the suggested digital library In order to design such a digital library; our approach was to think from the user viewpoint. We compiled a list of possible queries a user might want to use such a digital library to answer. We used these queries to specify what entities are needed in the library architecture and what software modules are needed to facilitate the usage of the library. These queries also showed the validation of using events as a means for retrieval. Some of the design considerations we concluded are presented here.

Multiple ways for retrieval: Users will need to search stored data stream segments in digital libraries by event instances that occurred during the generation of the corresponding stored streams and by other bibliographic data, e.g. title, creator, type, etc. For example, in the educational digital library described in section 3, the user can search by any event, e.g. "when the teacher started a certain tool, what did he say?" or by some bibliographic item, e.g. "return all classes taught by professor X".

An event occurs more than once: Multiple instances of an event may occur during the generation of a data stream. A user will need to be able to choose a specific event instance starting time to start playing some corresponding data stream segment. In the educational digital library example, the event of "a student asked a question" would normally happen many times in the span of a stream. A user would want to select a specific instance of such an event to playback the class streams.

Simultaneous playback: A user may choose to play several stream segments, which may be of different types, in a synchronous manner to be able to better understand the issue at hand by correlating them together. A clear example is the audio and video streams of the teacher in any class session. It would be very normal for any user to choose to playback both streams at the same time.

Related streams: A data stream might relate to another stream, to an event that occurs during another stream, or even to one instance of an event that occurs during another stream, based on some expert definition. An example of two streams related to each other would be the audio and video streams of a class session. An example of streams that relate to events is the video stream of a specific person whenever this person starts talking in a class session's audio stream. An example of a stream that relates to an event instance is the CNN broadcast when an upgrade occurred in a specific hurricane. The original stream would be a wind velocity stream and the general event would be just a "Hurricane upgrade".

Not all related streams are concurrent: Related streams might be concurrent or non-concurrent. *Concurrent streams* can be synchronized while they are played back, e.g. the video and audio streams of the same class session. *Non-concurrent* streams can still be played back simultaneously but obviously without synchronization. An example of a non-concurrent related stream that users might need to playback at the same time they play the original stream is the news broadcast about a hurricane upgrade. The news broadcast would, almost certainly, not happen at the same time of the hurricane upgrade, although still related. A controlling application will be needed to synchronize the playback of these streams.

Stream types: There are various stream types to be played back by users. Examples: video, audio, images, text, etc. There have to be a specific player for each.

Event generation: Domain or field experts are required to define and specify event instances. Software tools will be needed to help these experts to specify event criteria and apply these criteria to streams to create the event indexes for digital libraries.

Event criteria: Event criteria will depend on the event and stream types. The criteria will range from simple comparisons to, maybe, content-based retrieval algorithms. As every stream will have its own player application, it'll have its own modules to specify the event criteria.

5 The Digital Library Architecture

The architecture of the digital library is shown in Figure 1. A publisher will use a publishing tool to publish the streams into the digital library and to specify their metadata. The publishing tool will call indexing services to add any new stream metadata information to the current metadata of the system. A domain expert will use an event generation utility to generate the events of the streams in the digital library.

The scenario for the resource discovery user to retrieve a stream from the library and playback it is as follows:
1. The user will use a search form to specify the search criteria. These search criteria will be transferred via the Web to a search script. The script will contact the database server to search the system metadata and return the search results.
2. The search results, the hits, of the search will be presented to the end user and from which he will select a stream or an event to display.
3. The search script will get the user's selection and look for it in the object repositories (stream objects and event objects).
4. The selected object will be displayed to the user. A metadata list of that object will be presented followed by a playback form. If the selected object is a stream object then the playback form will include a list of all the events that occurred during the stream, a list of time instances of the selected event, and a list of the related streams. If the selected object is an event object then the playback form will include a list of time instances of that event and a list of the related streams.
5. The user will then specify the set of streams he wants to playback as well as the starting time from which these streams should start playing. This information will be passed to a control panel script that will start the stream servers and the stream player applets. The servers will then start streaming the stream data to the players.

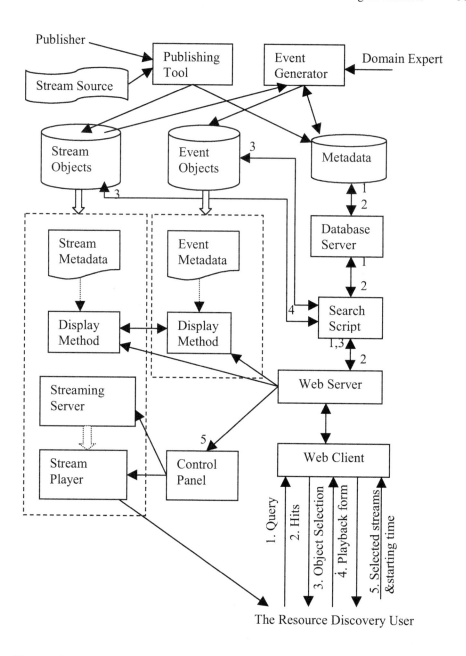

Fig. 1. The architecture of the digital library. The (*rectangular*) entities indicate software modules, the (*solid arrows*) indicate the data flow, the (*dashed rectangles*) indicate objects, the (*dashed thick arrow*) indicates streaming, and the (*numbers*) indicate the operations sequence

5.1 The Stream Object

A *stream object* is an object that encapsulates the stream data, the stream metadata, and the binaries that relate to this particular stream in only one physical object. The stream object contents, as seen in Figure 2, can be classified into three broad categories: data, metadata, and software tools.

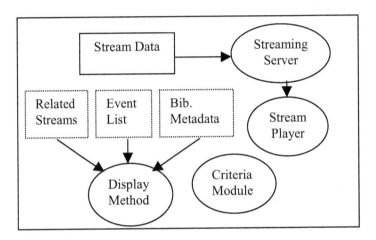

Fig. 2. The stream object. The (*solid rectangle*) indicates the stream data, the (*dashed rectangles*) indicate the stream metadata, and the (*ovals*) indicate software modules

The stream data: these are the stream data files. The stream object will either contain these files or contain references to their actual locations.

The stream metadata: these are the stream bibliographic information, the event list, and the related stream list. Examples of the stream bibliographic information are the stream title, creator, description, start time, end time, type, format, etc. The event list is a list of events that occurred during this stream. The event list will be a list of references to these events' corresponding objects. Please see the next section. The related streams are a list of the stream-related streams. Like the event list, the related-streams list will be a list of references to these streams' corresponding objects.

The stream-specific software modules:
- The stream display method: displays the bibliographic record of the stream as well as a playback form that lists the event list and the related streams list and allows the user to select an event instance to start playing back the stream, as well as selected related streams, from.
- The streaming server: sends the stream data to the stream player starting from a specific start time to an optional end time.
- The stream player: a client side applet that receives the stream data from the streaming server and displays it to the user.
- The criteria module: is used by the event generation application to create the events for this particular stream type. This module is needed because of the difference in specifying the event criteria from stream type to another. An example is a video stream where an event might be about a specific person appearing in the video for

the first time. In this example advanced content-based retrieval mechanisms are probably needed to specify this criteria of an event. Compare this to a text stream of wind velocities where the event might be that the wind velocities exceeded 50 miles per hour. In this example it is just a simple numeric comparison criteria. Having the criteria module in a stream means simply to let the stream specify how it will be queried.

The reason for using an object-oriented approach is that many streams that will need to be saved in this digital library are not from the same type. In the example of the educational library described above, video streams, audio streams, text streams, graphics streams are all saved in the same library. To playback any of these streams a different player will be needed. Separate modules will also be needed to query any of these stream types. It was more flexible to encapsulate the stream data files, metadata files, and all the software modules needed to access this stream in one stream object. The library can now be extended easily to accept new types with minimum changes in the code. The stream can be moved around, maybe to other libraries or for personal use, easily with all its required metadata and supportive code without a lot of hassle. Variations of this approach have been followed before in many prototypes and frameworks. The concept of aggregation is present in the *Kahn/Wilensky Framework* [5], and the Warwick Framework containers [7], the Flexible and Extensible Digital Object Repository Architecture (FEDORA) [3], and Buckets [9].

5.2 The Event Object

The object-oriented approach used for streams objects, as described in the last section, is taken a little further in our digital library design. Instead of implementing events as just sets of tables that include the event name and the set of times at which this event occurred, we implement the event as an object that contains the times of this event as well as references to all the streams that relate to it. Sometimes the event criteria might depend on information from more than one stream, thus associating it with only one stream would be inappropriate. Instead of repeating the event information in all the streams that relate to it, we chose to have the event represented as a separate object that contains its own criteria information, related streams, and the set of times at which this event occurred. We further allow the event to be part of the search results, besides the streams at which this event occurs. Further extensions to the system followed this idea.

An example would be that a student interrupted the teacher during the class session. This event would be part of the student's video stream as well as his audio stream. If there were a tool to get the teacher's attention in the distance-education system, the event would also be part of the tool stream (a stream of all the button clicks that occurred during the class session). The reaction to of the teacher to such an interruption might be important, for any reason, to some users so the event might as well be part of the teacher's audio and video streams. In conclusion, the event details may need to be inserted in the metadata of many stream objects. It was more flexible and more efficient to have the event represented as a separate object. Minimal information about this event object, e.g. the object ID and the event name, will need to be saved in the relevant streams' objects.

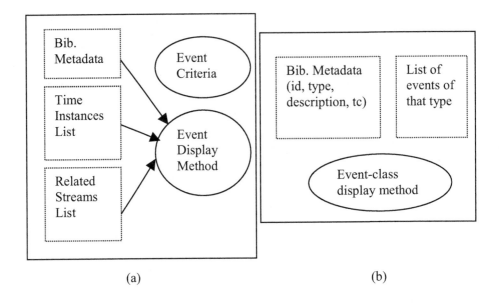

(a)   (b)

Fig. 3. (a) The event object. The (*dashed rectangles*) indicate the event metadata, and the (*ovals*) indicate software modules. (b) The event class object. The (*dashed rectangles*) indicate the event class metadata, and the (*oval*) indicates a software module

The structure of this event object is shown in Figure 3 (a). The contents of the event object can be described as follows:

- The bibliographic metadata of the event: that includes the event name, id, description, ...
- The time instances list: this list is either a list of times (in an atomic event object) or a list of time-pairs (in a composite event object).
- The related streams list: this is a list of the stream id's that relate to this particular event.
- The event criteria: is a software module that depends on the criteria modules in the stream objects involved in creating this event. This module contains the instructions to generate this event and would be used by the event generation tool.
- The event display method: displays the bibliographic record of the event as well as a playback form that lists the time instances and the related streams and allows the user to select an instance to start playing back the selected related streams from.

Events also have types just like streams. An event type would affect the event metadata and software modules, especially the criteria modules. An example of an event type is "a student interrupted the teacher to ask a question". An example of an event of this type would be "student X interrupted the teacher to ask a question".". A template object that depends on the event type and that contains all the common information and software modules of all the event objects of that type will be used to generate the event objects.

A simple generalization that would enhance the functionality of the system is by creating an object, the *event class*, which is retrievable itself. This event class object will contain some general descriptive information about this event type. It will also contain a list of all the events of that type. This object, as can be seen in Figure 3 (b), also contains its own display method which will list the bibliographic data of this event class object and then displays the list of event objects that have this type. The user can then select one of these event objects for further information.

6 Implementation Prototype

The search interface supports inquiring by bibliographic data as well as events, as shown in Figure 5. The search results can be stream objects, event objects, or event classes. By selecting any of these objects, the display method of this object will be executed. As seen in the previous sections, the display method will display the bibliographic metadata of the object and a form that depends on the object type. Figure 6 shows the stream object display. The user should select a time instance and a set of the related streams and then press a "playback" button to start the playback of the selected streams starting from the selected time instance.

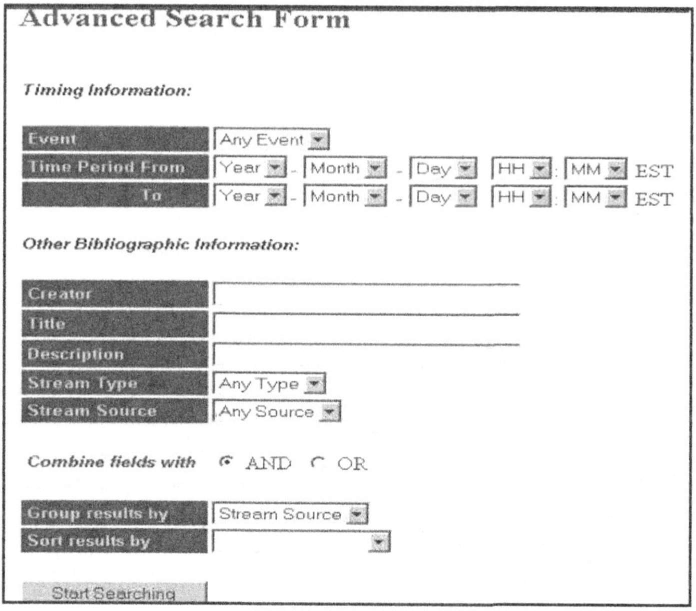

Fig. 5. The advanced search interface

When the user hits the "playback" button, a control panel that contains basic playback controls (play, stop, pause, rate control) would be displayed along with the player applets of each of the selected streams. For concurrent streams, one control panel will be used to control the players of these streams. For streams that are not concurrent with the original stream, a separate control panel will be used.

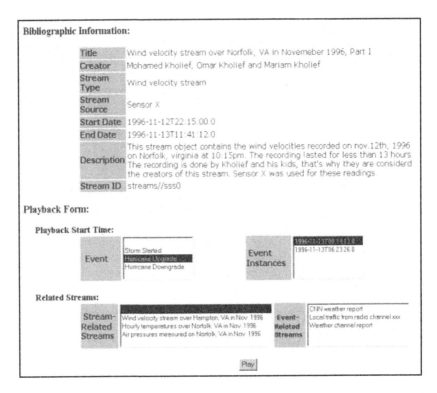

Fig. 6. The stream display method. The display is divided into (*bibliographic metadata*) display, and a (*playback form*)

7 Summary and Conclusions

This paper presents a new paradigm for resource discovery from digital libraries: event-based retrieval from stream-oriented digital libraries. We introduce the concepts of event-based retrieval, giving a detailed definition of the streams, events, related streams, and the different event classifications in addition to the different user roles regarding the suggested digital library. The main goal of this paper is the analysis and design of such a digital library. Our approach is first to consider the potential applications of such a digital library and the expectations of the intended users of some suggested applications. A list of the design considerations, which one should take into account while designing the digital library, was then formed. The paper then further deals with some of the most important design details. It presents the library architecture and the detailed aspects of the stream, event, and event class objects, justifying the use of an object-oriented approach in saving the streams and events data. This work defines the concept of event classes. It also presents some of the user scenarios explaining the implementation prototype.

One of the main conclusions of our research so far is that it is indeed feasible to build a digital library of streams and use events as the main mechanism to retrieve the desired streams and play them back at a specific event time. We have shown in our system design and the current implementation prototype that events can be defined by experts concisely, represented efficiently internally, and can be presented to users naturally in such a way that navigation among streams and playback of related segments is feasible.

Although all benefits of the system to end-users can only be shown when the final implementation and validation phases are complete, with our experience at this stage we strongly believe that storing streams and events in a digital library will be useful for a number of application domains such as distance learning and news dissemination. Our approach is clearly an extension of an already started and well-studied effort of saving video and audio information in a digital library. Using events to retrieve and playback stream segments is a natural and more precise way of retrieval from data streams. Our implementation shows that the resources needed to achieve quick response time in this approach are comparable to what are being used by other retrieval techniques.

References

1. Chung-Sheng Li: Scalable Content-Based Retrieval from Distributed Image/Video Databases. White paper. Available at:
   http://www.research.ibm.com/networked_data_systems/spire/whitepaper/paper.html.
2. Christel, M., et al: Informedia Digital Video Library, Communications of ACM, Vol. 38, No. 4 (1997) 57-58.
3. Daniel, R., Lagoze, C.: Distributed active relationships in the Warwick framework. Proceedings of the second IEEE metadata workshop, Silver Spring, MD. (1997)
4. Gauch, S., Li, W., Gauch, J.: The VISION Digital Video Library System, Information Processing & Management, 33(4) (1997) 413-426.
5. Kahn, R., Wilensky, R.: A framework for distributed digital object services. cnri.dlib/tn95-01. (1995) Available at http://www.cnri.reston.va.us/home/cstr/arch/k-w.html.
6. Kholief, M., Shen, S., Maly, K.: Event-Based Retrieval from Digital Libraries Containing Streamed Data. ITCC 2000, Las Vegas, Nevada (2000) 234-239.
7. Lagoze, C., Lynch C. A., Daniel, R.: The Warwick framework: a container architecture for aggregating sets of metadata. Cornell University Computer Science Technical Report TR-96-1593. (1996) Available at:
   http://ncstrl.cs.cornell.edu/Dienst/UI/1.0/Display/ncstrl.cornell/TR96-1593.
8. Maly K., Abdel-Wahab, H., Overstreet, C. M., Wild, C., Gupta, A., Youssef, A., Stoica E., El-Shaer, A.: Interactive distance learning over Intranets. J. IEEE Internet Computing, 1(1) (1997) 60-71.
9. Nelson, M.L, Maly, K.: "Smart Objects and Open Archives", D-Lib Magazine, February 2001, Volume 7 Issue 2

The Effects of the Relevance-Based Superimposition Model in Cross-Language Information Retrieval

Teruhito Kanazawa[1], Akiko Aizawa[2], Atsuhiro Takasu[2], and Jun Adachi[2]

[1] Graduate School of Engineering University of Tokyo
[2] National Institute of Informatics
{tkana, akiko, takasu, adachi}@nii.ac.jp

Abstract. We propose a cross-language information retrieval method that is based on document feature modification and query translation using a dictionary extracted from comparable corpora. In this paper, we show the language-independent effectiveness of our document feature modification model for dealing with semantic ambiguity, and demonstrate the practicality of the proposed method for extracting multilingual keyword clusters from digital libraries. The results of our experiments with multilingual corpora indicate that our document feature modification model avoid the difficulties of language-/domain-dependent parameters.

1 Introduction

Digital libraries provide broader accessibility to increasing varieties of digital documents. For the convenience of users, digital libraries should support access to those various resources by a unified interface. Because of language variation, users require retrieval by queries in one language of documents written in any of the languages. Most researchers in Cross-Language Information Retrieval (CLIR) focus on query translation, as translating documents is a very costly task for large-scale document sets.

In CLIR, using the query translation approach, the semantic ambiguity of a query can degrade the performance of retrieval. Current methods of solving this problem have difficulty in tuning parameters and handling terms that are not registered in a dictionary, when applied to large-scale and/or distributed digital libraries.

We proposed a method, named the Relevance-based Superimposition (RS) model, [1, 2, 3], in which document vectors are modified based on the relevance of the documents. In this model, relevant documents are organized into document sets when the index table is created, and supplementary index terms are chosen for each document set.

This paper presents the processes of extracting and using the relevance of documents and shows the superiority of the RS model in effectiveness of CLIR through experimental results. We compare its performance on Japanese queries/English documents (J-E) information retrieval (IR) in the cases of Japanese queries/Japanese documents (J-J) IR and English queries/English documents (E-E) IR. We prove that our method achieves a high cross-language performance without the complication of tuning parameters.

P. Constantopoulos and I.T. Sølvberg (Eds.): ECDL 2001, LNCS 2163, pp. 312–324, 2001.

2   The RS Model

2.1   Problems in Query Representation

When we use typical IR systems, a query is given in the form of a natural language sentence or by the specification of keywords. However, the query usually provides only a very restricted means to represent the user's intention. One expression may represent different concepts, such as 'ATM', which is the acronym for 'Asynchronous Transfer Mode' in telecommunication engineering, but stands for 'Automatic Teller Machine' in banking systems. Alternatively, one concept may be represented by various expressions, such as 'elevator' and 'lift'.

Therefore, it can be difficult to recognize the user's intention precisely from the query (or to salvage the latent semantics of the query).

This problem, called 'semantic ambiguity', is one of the most significant problems in IR studies and much work has been done on it. Those studies can be categorized into three groups: query modification (e.g., query expansion), document space modification (e.g., Latent Semantic Index(LSI)) and document feature modification.

Query expansion expands the query vector so that it includes index terms related to the original query expression. However, it is difficult to choose terms that represent the user's intention automatically and carefully. Therefore, the pragmatic effectiveness of retrieval cannot be achieved without adjusting many parameters to the database [4].

Reduction of the meaning space by multivariate analysis is another method of solving semantic ambiguity. The LSI model [5] is a typical method using reduction of the meaning space. In LSI, a 'term vs. document' index table is automatically transformed to a 'concept vs. document' index table by Singular Value Decomposition (SVD). However, there is no calculation method suitable for decomposition of large-scale databases (e.g., over 100,000 documents in a meaning space of over 10,000 dimensions). Thus, the cost of calculation is a crucial performance issue when applied to digital libraries.

Document feature vector modification is one of the methods that use information extracted from the documents. We believe it achieves higher recall without losing precision of retrieval, because documents usually have much more information than a query.

2.2   Model Overview

The proposed RS model is designed by the document vector modification approach, as described in Figure 1. This model partitions the documents so that the relevant documents fall into the same cluster. However, the idea is different from the traditional cluster-based methods, in which the document clusters are usually mutually exclusive. These methods assume that documents can be classified into orthogonal clusters by the frequencies of terms; however, it is natural to assume that a document belongs to several topics. This difference in assumptions will reflect on the retrieval.

Let us define the RS model formally. In the RS model, each document is represented by a feature vector. Term frequencies are often used as the feature. Suppose that a document database contains a set of documents $\{d_1, d_2, \cdots, d_n\}$ and their feature vectors are $\boldsymbol{d}_1, \boldsymbol{d}_2, \cdots, \boldsymbol{d}_n$.

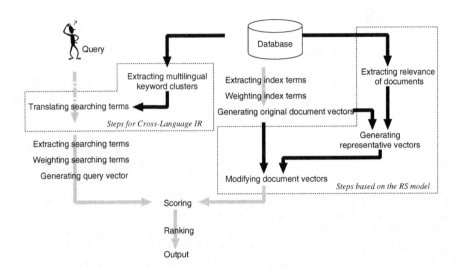

Fig. 1. The process flow of $R^2 D^2$

In the RS model, documents in the database form clusters $C_1, C_2, \cdots, C_m$. Note that a document may be contained in more than one cluster in the RS model, whereas clusters in other methods are often mutually exclusive. Figure 2 schematically depicts an example of document clusters in the RS model. At this point, we must decide what type of relevance we will use to make the clusters. The principle of the RS model is independent of the source of relevance information, and our choice will depend on the type of database and the types of elements in it. For instance, the following elements in the database can be candidates for the source of relevance information:

- keywords given by the authors,
- references, hyperlinks,
- bibliographic information, such as author name, publication date, and journal title.

In our experiments with the NTCIR test collection (see Section 4.1), as described in Figure 2 and the following section, we constructed the clusters based on the free keywords given by the authors of the documents. Suppose that there are two keywords A and B. Then there are two clusters corresponding to A and B, respectively. Cluster C_A consists of the documents that contain the keyword A, and the same relationship holds for C_B and B. For example, the document d_3 is in both C_A and C_B in Figure 2, because it contains both keywords A and B.

2.3   Representative Vector Generation

Using clusters the document feature vector is modified in two steps: (1) representative vector (RV) generation for each cluster, and then, (2) feature vector modification by RVs. The RV corresponds to the feature vector of document clusters and has the same dimension as the document feature vectors. RV r of cluster C is constructed

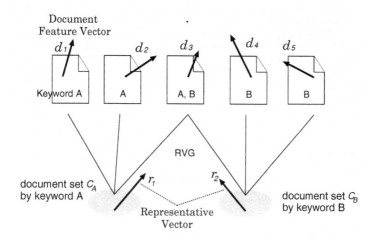

Fig. 2. Representative vector generation

from the feature vectors of the documents in C. Currently, we have tested five types of representative-vector-generator (RVG) functions, based on the α-family distributions [6], where the ith component of RV r is defined as follows:

$$r_i \equiv \left(\frac{1}{|C|} \sum_{d_j \in C} d_{j,i}^{\frac{1-\alpha_1}{2}} \right)^{\frac{2}{1-\alpha_1}} \tag{1}$$

where $d_{j,i}$ and $|C|$ denote the ith component of the feature vector of the document d_j and the number of documents contained in the cluster C, respectively. We empirically evaluated and selected the appropriate α_1 and identified $\alpha_1 = 0$ (root-mean-square) as the most effective parameter [2].

2.4 Document Vector Modification

The second step is modification of the document vector using the RVs of the clusters to which the document belongs. Figure 3 depicts this step schematically. In this case, the document vector d_1 is modified using r_1, because document d_1 belongs to cluster C_A, while the document vector d_3 is modified using both r_1 and r_2.

We assume that important index terms for a document d_j are any terms that occur frequently in any cluster to which d_j belongs, as well as terms occurring frequently in d_j itself. This characteristic is considered to be 'conjunctive'.

Currently, we propose the document-feature-vector-modifier (DVM) function. To define the DVM, we first define the vector of a cluster set D_j that consists of the clusters to which document d_j belongs. Let S_j denote the set of RVs that belong to the clusters belonging to D_j.

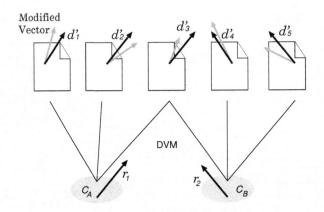

Fig. 3. Document vector modification

Then the ith component of the vector of D_j can be defined as follows:

$$s_{j,i} \equiv \left(\frac{1}{|S_j|} \sum_{r_k \in S_j} r_{k,i}^{\frac{1-\alpha_2}{2}} \right)^{\frac{2}{1-\alpha_2}} \tag{2}$$

Let $(d_{j,1}, d_{j,2}, \cdots, d_{j,I})$ represent the feature vector of a document d_j and let $(s_{j,1}, s_{j,2}, \cdots, s_{j,I})$ represent the vector of the cluster set D_j. The modified document feature vector d'_j is then defined as $(f_s(d_{j,1}, s_{j,1}), f_s(d_{j,2}, s_{j,2}), \cdots, f_s(d_{j,I}, s_{j,I}))$, where f_s is the superimposing function defined as:

$$f_s(x_1, x_2) \equiv \left\{ \frac{1}{2} \left(x_0^{\frac{1-\alpha_3}{2}} + x_1^{\frac{1-\alpha_3}{2}} \right) \right\}^{\frac{2}{1-\alpha_3}}. \tag{3}$$

We have evaluated some members of the α-family distributions for s_j and f_s, and identified $\alpha_2 = 0$(root-mean-square) and $\alpha_3 = \infty$(maximum) as the most effective parameters respectively [2].

3 Query Translation

3.1 Comparison of Methods

Methods for translation are categorized into three basic approaches: machine translation (MT), dictionary-based method, and corpus-based method. MT achieves higher quality translation when the topic domain can be obtained from the translating text; however, a query is short and tends not to have sufficient information for carefully estimating the semantic intention. From the CLIR viewpoint, MT is not regarded as a promising approach.

Some dictionary-based and corpus-based methods perform almost as well as monolingual retrieval [7, 8, 9]. In our experiments, we focused on the measurement of the

> **Japanese:** 遺伝アルゴリズム (*genetic algorithm*) / 最適探索 (*optimal search*) / 学習 (*learning*)[†]
> **English:** Genetic Algorithms / Optimization / Machine Learning [‡]

Fig. 4. An example of keyword lists given by the authors of documents

[†] English keywords in italics are added for the sake of explanation, and are not in the original data.
[‡] These English keywords are give by the authors of documents.

effectiveness of a dictionary-based query translation method in scientific document retrieval. Dictionary-based methods have a serious problem especially in scientific document retrieval in that there are many unregistered terms invented by the authors of the documents. Therefore, we expected that those methods extracting bilingual pairs, or multilingual sets, of scientific terms and keywords from comparable/parallel corpora would outperform static dictionary-based methods in scientific document retrieval. We generated the multilingual keyword clusters using the keyword lists assigned to the documents in the corpus.

3.2 Multilingual Keyword Clusters

Our approach for generating multilingual keyword clusters is graph-based [10, 11]. First, we extracted Japanese-English keyword pairs from the corpus. The NACPD collection (see Section 4.1) is a comparable corpus that contains bilingual keywords described in Figure 4. Although authors are not explicitly required to provide precise conceptual correspondence between the keywords in the two languages, it is likely that semantically corresponding bilingual keywords are listed in order. In our experiment [11], the accuracy was 93%. The initial graph expression of a bilingual keyword corpus is easily derived by representing Japanese and English keywords as nodes and their translation pairs as links. Figure 5 shows an example of the partitioning of the keyword cluster. The frequency of appearance of each keyword pair in the corpus is expressed as the capacity of the corresponding link.

The second step is partitioning keyword clusters. The initial graph contains two different types of errors to be considered, namely, totally irrelevant (e.g., '*keyword*' and '*information retrieval*' in Figure 5) and semantically associated (but non-corresponding) errors (e.g., '*text retrieval*' and '*information retrieval*'). While the first type of error should be eliminated whenever detected, the treatment of the second type depends on the application. For example, '*text retrieval*' and '*information retrieval*' may be an improper pair in view of a strict terminological definition, but not necessarily incorrect in IR. The detection of incorrectly generated links of the graph can be reduced to the minimum cut problem in graph theory. The following steps uses topological information from the graph as well as the frequencies of the links to control the degree of cluster partitioning.

1. Mark significant translation links which should not be eliminated.
2. Mark significant keywords which can support a separated new cluster.

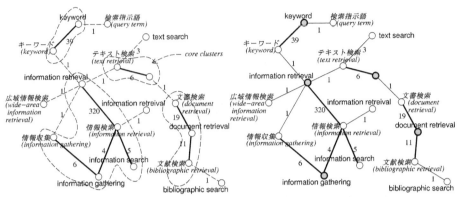

Step (1): Mark significant links with frequencies more than $N_\alpha(3)$.

Step (2): Mark significant keywords (only significant English keywords are highlighted in the figure).

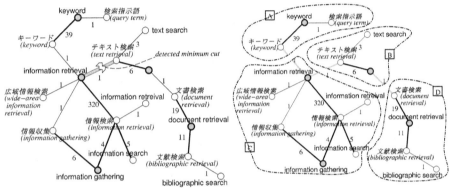

Step (3): Detect removable minimum cut between two significant keywords.

Final result of clustering.

Fig. 5. Cluster partitioning procedure

3. Detect the removable minimum cut between two significant keywords.
4. Remove the minimum cut from the graph.
5. Repeat steps (2)–(4) until no further partition is possible.

Steps (1), (2) and (3) are explained further below.

Step (1) Mark Significant Translation Links: First, links which should not be eliminated from the graph are checked. The *significant translation links* which we define here as non-removable are either (a) links whose Japanese and English notations are identical, or (b) links whose frequency is more than N_α.

Step (2) Mark Significant Keywords: In this step, nodes that occur frequently in the corpus are checked. The significant keywords are defined as keywords with (a) more than one translation link, and (b) at least one translation link whose frequency is more than N_β.

Here, condition (a) guarantees that every cluster generated contains at least one Japanese and one English keyword. In addition, increasing N_β has the effect of suppressing cluster partitioning. $N_\beta = 1$ means (a) is the only restriction preventing over-splitting.

Step (3) Detect Removable Minimum Cut: At this step, two significant keywords are selected to apply the minimum cut detection algorithm. If a minimum cut, which (a) has a total capacity equal to or less than N_ε and (b) generates clusters containing at least one Japanese and one English keyword, exists between the selected pairs (which do not include any significant links), the detected minimum cut can be eliminated from the graph. It is obvious that increasing N_β means more clusters are partitioned.

To summarize, N_α, N_β and N_ε are the three parameters used to control cluster partitioning. We are currently using the same parameter values for all the clusters. The values for N_β and N_ε are determined heuristically. In the following experiments, $N_\alpha = 3, N_\beta = 3$, and $N_\varepsilon = 10$ were used. Under those parameters, the total number of keyword clusters was 271,437.

3.3   Translation Using the Keyword Clusters

Using the generated keyword clusters, we translate the queries under the leftmost longest matching rule. The procedure of Japanese-to-English translation is described as follows:
1. Find the longest keyword matching to the leftmost expression in the translating Japanese sentence.
2. Select the keyword cluster which contains the keyword.
3. Translate to the English expression whose frequency is the highest in the keyword cluster.

4   Evaluation

4.1   Basic Characteristics of the Data

The corpora used in the following experiments are NII/NACSIS[1] Test Collection for IR (NTCIR)[12]. NTCIR is the name both of a multilingual IR evaluation project and of its test collections. The Japanese document corpus contains about 730,000 documents selected from the NACSIS Academic Conference Papers Database (NACPD) and the NACSIS Grant-in-Aid Scientific Research Database (NGSRD). NACPD is a collection of the summaries of papers presented at conferences hosted by 65 Japanese academic societies in various subject fields. NGSRD is a database of the collected summaries of scientific research results sponsored by the Ministry of Education, Science, Sports and CultureThe English document corpus contains about 320,000 documents selected from the NACPD and the NGSRD. Part of these are translations of the NTCIR Japanese documents and the information identifying which Japanese document corresponds to the

---

[1] National Institute of Informatics (NII), formerly known as National Center for Science Information Systems (NACSIS)

Table 1. Numbers of keywords

	# keywords	appear in ≥ 5 docs
NTCIR J	851,218	90,761
NTCIR E	632,930	46,418

English translation, i.e., they form a parallel corpus. All documents contain the same elements: titles, abstracts/summaries, and free keywords given by the authors. NTCIR contains 132 search topics (#1–83 and 101–149) and their relevance judgments. The relevance judgments of topics from #1 to #83 were done for a partial document set, therefore, we used them as the training topics for tuning the parameters of query expansion (QE). The search topics are described both in Japanese and in English. A topic consists of a title, description, detailed narrative, a list of concepts and topic categories. We use only the description, which is a sentence concisely describing the topic.

We developed an experimental retrieval system, named R^2D^2 that has indexing functions for the RS model as well as various tf·idf methods [3]. With this system, we evaluated the effects of the RS model in cross-language IR using the NTCIR test collections. NTCIR provides several IR evaluation tasks such as Japanese-English IR and Chinese-English IR. We evaluated the RS model on the NTCIR J-J, E-E and J-E tasks. J-J is a monolingual IR in which Japanese documents are retrieved by Japanese queries. E-E is a monolingual IR of English documents by English queries. J-E is a cross-language IR of English documents by Japanese queries.

4.2   Query Expansion

As we noted in Section 2.1, the RS model is designed as a document feature modification method. We examined it compared with QE. Moreover, QE and the RS model are not exclusive but are expected to cooperate and achieve higher performance.

We employed an automatic QE method via relevance feedback [13]. Expansion terms were chosen from the top D documents retrieved using the original query. T, the number of expansion terms was adjusted in our preliminary experiment with NTCIR queries from #31 to #83 and TREC 3. We found that most effective parameters are $D = 30, T = 10$ both for NTCIR and TREC 3 training topics, and D has considerable influence on the retrieval effectiveness. We then examined the improvements with other NTCIR queries from #101 to #149 obtained by QE when D changed.

4.3   Evaluation Method

The evaluation method is based on that used by NTCIR and TREC [14]. The evaluation is applied to the top 1,000 retrieved documents for each query.

Table 1 shows the number of keywords extracted from the NTCIR corpora. We did not use smaller clusters containing less than five documents because they tended to cause errors.

Table 2. Performance of the RS model and query expansion (average precisions)

QE	RS	training sets for QE		J-J	E-E	J-E	/relative to E-E
		J-J	TREC 3				
no	no	.3059	.2318	.2841	.2984	.2401	0.80
yes	no	.3270 (+7%)	.2578 (+11%)	.2886 (+2%)	.3044 (+2%)	.2441 (+2%)	0.80
no	yes			.3020 (+6%)	.3160 (+6%)	.2508 (+4%)	0.79
yes	yes			.3103 (+9%)	.3226 (+9%)	.2574 (+7%)	0.80

Table 3. Statistics of each method

QE	RS	mean	relative to QE	variance	relative to QE
yes	no	+0.0029	100%	0.0606	100%
no	yes	+0.0107	369%	0.0306	50%
yes	yes	+0.0176	607%	0.0686	113%

4.4 Results

Table 2 shows the effectiveness of the RS model and QE. The average precision of J-J baseline without RS nor QE is 0.2841. QE improves the performance by 2%, and RS by 6%. The most effective QE parameters are $D = 40, T = 10$; however, the difference between the average precisions using $D = 40$ (the best for NTCIR test topics) and $D = 30$ (the best for NTCIR and TREC 3 training topics) is only 0.3%. The average precision of the cross-lingual baseline is 0.2401. That is about 80% compared with the case of the E-E retrieval. The effectiveness of QE and RS is similar to monolingual results, and the J-E result for each method is 80% relative to E-E for the same method. In both monolingual and cross-lingual tasks, the combination of RS and QE achieves 7 to 9% improvement, which is more than the summation of their individual effectiveness.

Table 3 shows the statistics of the effectiveness of each method. The mean of difference for each query between the baseline and RS results is more than three times as great as that between the baseline and QE, while the variance of the difference between baseline and RS is about half of that between the baseline and QE. These prove that the RS model is robust for diversity of queries and overall achieves a higher performance. From the evidence that the effectiveness of QE with NTCIR test topics is less than that with NTCIR training topics or that with TREC training topics, it can be said that QE does not overcome the difficulties in tuning the parameters. Table 2 shows that the effectiveness of the RS model is independent of the language used both for the queries and for the documents.

Table 4 shows the numbers of each translation error type among the 49 queries. A, B and C are appropriate translation results. Overall, 54% of the query terms were translated exactly as the manual translations, 12% were translated to expressions similar to the manual translations (e.g., 'genomic mutation' and 'gene alteration') and 9% were translated to synonyms (e.g., 'implementation' and 'construction'). The total proportion of appropriate translations was about 75%. We note that most of the inappropriate translations (D, E, F and G) were insignificant terms for retrieval, e.g., 'various' in the sentence 'the effects of various antibiotics against MRSA', therefore their influence was small and the disadvantage of translation was about 20%, as shown at the last column of Table 2.

Table 4. Types of query translation using the automatically-generated keyword clusters

categories	# words	examples
A	149 (54%)	gravity, natural language processing
B	33 (12%)	genetic engineering techniques $\rightarrow$ genetic engineering
C	26 (9%)	heart disease $\rightarrow$ coronary artery disease
D	8 (3%)	tomography $\rightarrow$ imaging
E	21 (8%)	Historical materials on the Internet
		$\rightarrow$ historical materials, internet, electronics, database
F	37 (13%)	Distance education support system
G	4 (1%)	US $\rightarrow$ rice
total	278	

(A) The same expression as the manually-translated query.
(B) A similar expression that contains part of the manually-translated query.
(C) A relevant expression of the manually-translated query.
(D) A more abstract expression than the manually-translated query.
(E) An additional expression that does not appear in the manually-translated query.
(F) A lost expression, which appears in the manually-translated query but not in the automatic-translated query.
(G) An unfitted expression.

5   Discussion

With the rule of document clustering in this experiment, keywords appearing in fewer than five documents (about 90%) are unusable for modifying document vectors. We noticed that most of those keywords were misspelled, and we think that the keyword clusters extracted in our experiments may be helpful for obtaining more information from keywords, because our method classifies a misspelled keyword into the same cluster as that containing the correct one.

Furthermore, it is necessary to consider general circumstances where keywords are not given for documents in databases. Under the current implementation, both the multilingual keyword clustering and the RS model require well-maintained keyword lists. For query translation, we can apply the keyword clusters extracted from reliable corpora other than the database that we use for retrieval, while there are two possible answers for the RS model. One is automatic keyword extraction and the other is to give another source of relevance information. In both, the characteristics of document sets might be changed, and this may influence retrieval effectiveness.

6   Concluding Remarks

The results reported in this paper show the language-independent effectiveness of the proposed RS model and that graph-based automatic generation of multilingual keyword clusters is applicable to query translation.

The RS model, which is a document feature modification method based on mutual clustering of documents, achieved significant superiority over the baseline, independent of language. The combination of the RS model and QE seems to work well. Table 2 indicates that these two methods improve the performance complementarily; QE refines the query and that enhances the effectiveness of the RS model. In some cases, the combination achieves a larger gain in effectiveness than the summation of the individual RS and QE.

The query translation method using the keyword clusters extracted by graph theory achieves 80% retrieval effectiveness compared with monolingual IR. Without any fine tuning to the target database, the performance stands comparison with the best of the existing cross-language IR methods [15].

Acknowledgment

We participated in the NTCIR Workshop (March 2001), and used the NII/NACSIS Test Collection 2 (Preliminary version), constructed by NII. This research was supported by the 'Research for the Future' Program JSPS-RFTF96P00602 of the Japan Society for the Promotion of Science.

References

[1] T. Kanazawa, "R^2D^2 at NTCIR: Using the Relevance-based Superimposition Model," *NTCIR Workshop 1 Proc.*, pp. 83–88, Tokyo, Aug. 1999.

[2] T. Kanazawa, A. Takasu, and J. Adachi, "Effect of the Relevance-based Superimposition Model on Information Retrieval," *IPSJ Database workshop 2000 (IPSJ SIG Notes)*, Vol. 2000, No.69, 2000-DBS-122, pp. 57–64, Iwate, July 2000.

[3] T. Kanazawa, A. Takasu, and J. Adachi, "R^2D^2 at NTCIR 2 Ad-hoc Task: Relevance-based Superimposition Model for IR," *NTCIR Workshop 2 Proc.*, pp. 5–98–5–104, Tokyo, March 2001.

[4] M. Mitra, A. Singhal, and C. Buckley, "Improving Automatic Query Expansion," *SIGIR '98*, pp. 206–214, 1998.

[5] S. Deerwester, S. T. Dumais, T. K. Landauer, G. W. Furnas, and R. A. Harshman, "Indexing by latent semantic analysis," *J. American Society for Information Science*, Vol. 41, No.6, pp. 391–407, 1990.

[6] Y. Hayashi, "On a New Data Model suitable for Intellectual Accesses by Personal Preference," *IPSJ SIG Notes*, Vol. 98,No.58, 98-DBS-116(2), pp. 381–388, July 1998.

[7] A. Pirkola, "The Effects of Query Structure and Dictionary Setups in Dictionary-Based Cross-Language Information Retrieval," *SIGIR '98*, pp. 55–63, 1998.

[8] L. Ballesteros and W. Bruce Croft, "Resolving Ambiguity for Cross-Language Retrieval," *SIGIR '98*, pp. 64–71, 1998.

[9] S. Fujita, "Notes on the Limits of CLIR Effectiveness: NTCIR-2 Evaluation Experiments at Justsystem," *NTCIR Workshop 2 Proc.*, pp. 5–75–5–82, Tokyo, March 2001.

[10] A. Aizawa and K. Kageura, "An Approach to the Automatic Generation of Multilingual Keyword Clusters," *Proc. COMPTERM'98*, pp. 8–14, 1998.

[11] A. Aizawa and K. Kageura, "Automatic Generation of Clusters of Synonyms Utilizing Japanese-English Keyword Lists of Academic Papers," *J. Information Processing Society of Japan*, Vol. 41, No.4, pp. 1180–1191, 2000.

[12] NTCIR: http://research.nii.ac.jp/ntcir/.

[13] R. Baeza-Yates and B. Ribeiro-Neto, *Modern Information Retrieval*, Addison-Wesley, 1999.

[14] NTCIR staff, "Notes on Evaluation for Japanese & English IR Tasks," *NTCIR Workshop 2 Proc.*, pp. 6–117–6–120, March 2001.

[15] N. Kando, K. Kuriyama, M. Yoshioka, "Overview of Japanese and English Information Retrieval Tasks (JEIR) at the Second NTCIR Workshop," *NTCIR Workshop 2 Proc.*, pp. 4–37–4–59, March 2001.

An On-Line Document Clustering Method Based on Forgetting Factors

Yoshiharu Ishikawa[1], Yibing Chen[2]*, and Hiroyuki Kitagawa[1]

[1] Institute of Information Sciences and Electronics, University of Tsukuba
{ishikawa,kitagawa}@is.tsukuba.ac.jp
[2] Master's Program in Science and Engineering, University of Tsukuba

Abstract. With the rapid development of on-line information services, information technologies for on-line information processing have been receiving much attention recently. Clustering plays important roles in various on-line applications such as extraction of useful information from news feeding services and selection of relevant documents from the incoming scientific articles in digital libraries. In on-line environments, users generally have interests on newer documents than older ones and have no interests on obsolete old documents.
Based on this observation, we propose an on-line document clustering method F^2ICM (*Forgetting-Factor-based Incremental Clustering Method*) that incorporates the notion of a *forgetting factor* to calculate document similarities. The idea is that every document gradually losses its weight (or memory) as time passes according to this factor. Since F^2ICM generates clusters using a document similarity measure based on the forgetting factor, newer documents have much effects on the resulting cluster structure than older ones. In this paper, we present the fundamental idea of the F^2ICM method and describe its details such as the similarity measure and the clustering algorithm. Also, we show an efficient incremental statistics maintenance method of F^2ICM which is indispensable for on-line dynamic environments.
Keywords: clustering, on-line information processing, incremental algorithms, forgetting factors

1 Introduction

According to the recent information technology development such as the Internet and electronic documents, a huge number of on-line documents (e.g., on-line news articles and electronic journals) are delivered over the network and stored in digital libraries and electronic document archives. Since it is difficult for ordinal users to select required information from such huge document repositories, information filtering to select useful information from delivered new documents and summarization methods to extract important topics from documents have become important research areas. Additionally, topic detection and tracking (TDT) from on-line information sources has gained much attentions recently [10].

Document clustering is a method to collect similar documents to form document groups (*clusters*), and used as fundamental methods for information retrieval, information filtering, topic detection and tracking, and document categorization [2,5,7,8,9]. To

---

* Current affiliation: Yamatake Building Systems Co., Ltd.

P. Constantopoulos and I.T. Sølvberg (Eds.): ECDL 2001, LNCS 2163, pp. 325–339, 2001.
© Springer-Verlag Berlin Heidelberg 2001

summarize the trend of on-line documents incoming from various information sources (news wire services, Web pages, etc.) and to provide up-to-date information to users, we propose an on-line document clustering method F^2ICM (Forgetting-Factor-based Incremental Clustering Method) that can provide clustering results reflecting the novelty of documents; in this method, newer documents highly affect to the clustering results than older documents. The most characteristic feature of F^2ICM is that it incorporates the notion of a *forgetting factor*. In F^2ICM, we set an initial weight to every document when it is acquired from an information source. Document weights gradually decay as time passes according to the rate specified by the forgetting factor. Since the document similarity measure proposed in this paper is devised to reflect such document weights in computing similarity scores, F^2ICM based on the measure can generate clustering results by setting higher importance on recent documents and lower importance on obsolete old documents. Namely, we can say that F^2ICM continuously "forgets" old information and focuses mainly on "current" information to generate clusters.

The F^2ICM method is an extension of an existing seed-based clustering method C^2ICM proposed by Can [3]. When new documents are obtained, F^2ICM (also C^2ICM) incrementally updates the previous clustering result by computing new seeds and re-assigning documents into the seeds. Since F^2ICM uses a similarity measure based on the forgetting factor, we have to manage time-dependent statistics for the calculation of similarity scores and have to update these statistics when the document set is updated. In this paper, we show a sophisticated method to update such statistics incrementally with low overheads. Based on the algorithms, F^2ICM can adapt to on-line document clustering needs that require current "hot" information, and can be used as an underlying method to support on-line digital library tasks.

The following part of this paper is organized as follows. In Section 2, we briefly introduce the C^2ICM clustering method that is the basis of our proposed method F^2ICM. Then F^2ICM clustering method is described in Section 3. Section 4 focuses on the incremental update algorithm of statistics for the efficient update processing. In Section 5, we briefly mention the approaches for document expiration and parameter settings. Section 6 briefly reports the results of our experiments. Finally, Section 7 concludes the paper.

2   The C^2ICM Clustering Method

The clustering method F^2ICM proposed in this paper is partially based on the idea of *C^2ICM* (*Cover-Coefficient-based Incremental Clustering Methodology*) proposed by Can [3]. Before introducing F^2ICM in Section 3, we briefly describe the algorithms used in C^2ICM. For the differences between F^2ICM and C^2ICM, we mention them on appropriate points in the following discussion.

Suppose that a document set consists of m documents $d_1, \ldots, d_m$ and let all the terms appeared in these documents be $t_1, \ldots, t_n$. C^2ICM is a clustering method that is based on probabilistic modeling of document and term similarities[1]. In the method, two probabilities $\Pr(d_j|d_i)$ and $\Pr(t_l|t_k)$ play important roles: the former is the conditional

---

[1] Our notations are rather different from those in [3] to perform more clear probabilistic modeling of document similarities.

probability that the document d_j is obtained when a document d_i is given. Similarly, the latter is the conditional probability that the term t_l is obtained when a term t_k is given. These probabilities represent the degree of association between two documents or terms. In this section, we assume that these two probabilities are already given and present the clustering algorithms of C^2ICM. In Section 3, we describe the derivation of these two probabilities.

2.1 Seed Power

C^2ICM is a seed-based clustering method. In its clustering procedure, seed documents are initially selected from the document set then each remaining document is grouped with the most similar seed document and finally clusters are formulated. In this subsection, the notion of a *seed power*, an index used in the seed selection, is explained.

Decoupling Coefficient and Coupling Coefficient   First, two important notions used to calculate seed powers in C^2ICM are introduced. A probability $Pr(d_i|d_i)$ that the document d_i is obtained when a document d_i itself is given is called the *decoupling coefficient* δ_i for d_i [3]:

$$\delta_i \stackrel{\text{def}}{=} Pr(d_i|d_i). \tag{1}$$

Intuitively, δ_i is an index to indicate how d_i is independent (different) from other documents. On the other hand, the *coupling coefficient* φ_i for d_i, given by

$$\varphi_i \stackrel{\text{def}}{=} 1 - \delta_i, \tag{2}$$

is considered to be the degree of dependence of d_i.

Similar to the case of documents, the *decoupling coefficient* δ'_j and *coupling coefficient* φ'_j for a term t_j are defined as follows [3]:

$$\delta'_j \stackrel{\text{def}}{=} Pr(t_j|t_j) \quad \text{and} \quad \varphi'_j \stackrel{\text{def}}{=} 1 - \delta'_j. \tag{3}$$

Seed Power   In [3], document d_i's *seed power* sp_i that evaluates appropriateness of d_i as a cluster seed is given by the following formula:

$$sp_i \stackrel{\text{def}}{=} \delta_i \cdot \varphi_i \cdot \sum_{j=1}^{n} freq(d_i, t_j) \cdot \delta'_j \cdot \varphi'_j, \tag{4}$$

where $freq(d_i, t_j)$ is the occurrence frequency of term t_j within document d_i. The intuitive idea behind this formula is to select a document which has moderate dependency within the document set as a cluster seed document: the idea is represented by the part "$\delta_i \cdot \varphi_i$". The remaining summation of Eq. (4) is a normalized weighting by considering the occurrence frequency and the dependency/independency factors for each term.

2.2 Clustering Algorithms

The clustering algorithms of C^2ICM consist of the initial cluster generation algorithm and the incremental clustering algorithm that used in the update time.

Initial Clustering Algorithm

1. Calculate the seed power sp_i for each document d_i in the document set.
2. Select n_c documents which have the largest sp_i values as cluster seeds [2].
3. Each remaining document is appended to the cluster such that its cluster seed is the most similar one to the document. We can specify a threshold value for the assignment. A document that does not have a similarity score to any seeds that is larger than the threshold value is assigned to a special *ragbag cluster*.

Incremental Clustering Algorithm When documents are appended or deleted, the C^2ICM method maintains the clusters in an incremental manner:

1. Recompute the seed power of each document in the document set.
2. Select n_c documents which have the largest sp_i values as cluster seeds.
3. Examine each previous cluster: if its seed is re-selected at this time, the cluster is preserved. On the other hand, if the seed is not selected, we delete the cluster.
4. Perform reclustering: new documents, the documents contained in the clusters deleted in Step 3, and the documents in the ragbag cluster are assigned to the most similar clusters based on the similarity scores. As the initial clustering algorithm, a document that does not have a similarity score to any seeds that is larger than the threshold value is assigned to the ragbag cluster.

The point is not to recluster all the documents from scratch but to utilize partial results of the previous clustering because C^2ICM focuses on low update processing cost for on-line information processing. Although we did not mention the document deletion method above, we can easily incorporate the deletion phase into the update algorithm.

3   The F^2ICM Clustering Method

In this section, F^2ICM (Forgetting-Factor-based Incremental Clustering Method) is introduced. As mentioned before, this method is an extension of C^2ICM so that its algorithms are basically based on C^2ICM. The main difference between them is that F^2ICM assigns temporally decaying weights to documents and utilizes a document similarity measure that incorporates the notion of a forgetting factor. In this section, the document similarity measure used in F^2ICM is derived and some probabilities used in the algorithms, such as $\Pr(d_j|d_i)$ and $\Pr(t_l|t_k)$, are introduced.

3.1   Document Forgetting Model

The *document forgetting model* described in this subsection plays an important role in the F^2ICM method. The model is based on a simple intuition: the values of news articles delivered everyday and on-line journal articles maintained in digital libraries are

---

[2] Although the number of clusters n_c is automatically determined in the original C^2ICM method [3], this paper assumes that a user specifies n_c. This is for the simplification of the procedure.

considered to be gradually losing their values as time passes. The document forgetting model is based on a rough modeling of such behaviors.

Let the current time be $t = \tau$ and the acquisition time of each document d_i ($i = 1, \ldots, m$) be T_i ($T_i \leq \tau$); for example, we can use issue dates as the acquisition times for on-line news articles. We represent the *value* (also called *weight*) of d_i at time τ by $dw_i|_\tau$. The notation "$|_\tau$" is used to represent the value of a variable at time τ. If the context is clear, we omit "$|_\tau$".

Although we can consider various formulas to represent the decay of the information value of a document, we utilize the following exponential weighting formula:

$$dw_i|_\tau \stackrel{\text{def}}{=} \lambda^{\tau - T_i} \quad (0 < \lambda < 1), \tag{5}$$

where λ is a parameter tuned according to the target document set and the intended application. The smaller the value of λ is, the faster the value decay (forgetting) speed becomes. For this reason, we call λ a *forgetting factor*. The reasons to select this exponential forgetting model are summarized as follows:

1. The model that human memory will decrease as an exponential function depending on time appears as a behavioral law in procedural and declarative human memory modeling, and called the *power law of forgetting* [1][3]. Of course, such a cognitive human memory model and forgetting of document contents in our context do not have direct relationship, but we may be able to regard the human memory model as an informal background of our model.
2. If we use the exponential forgetting factor shown above, we can construct an efficient statistics maintenance method for our clustering method. The details of the maintenance method is described in Section 4.
3. The proposed document forgetting model simply uses one parameter λ to control the degree of weight decay. This means that the information value of every document decays with the same rate and works as a basis of efficient implementation of our cluster maintenance method. Although it is possible to set different λ values for different documents, the approach is not suited to on-line document clustering since its processing cost becomes much higher than that of our simple approach.

3.2 Derivation of the Document Similarity Measure

In this subsection, we derive the document similarity measure from a probabilistic perspective. For the derivation, we take the document forgetting model introduced above into account. In the following, we represent the documents in a document set by d_i ($i = 1, \ldots, m$) and all the index terms in the document set by t_k ($k = 1, \ldots, n$). The number of occurrences of term t_k within document d_i is represented by $freq(d_i, t_k)$. And we assume that the acquisition times of the documents $d_1, d_2, \ldots, d_m$ satisfy the relationship $T_1 \leq T_2 \leq \cdots \leq T_m$.

First we define the total weights of all the documents tdw by

$$tdw \stackrel{\text{def}}{=} \sum_{l=1}^{m} dw_l, \tag{6}$$

---

[3] But note that our document forgetting model (Eq. (5)) is too much simplified one for convenience; models used in the human cognition research area are more devised ones [1].

and define the probability $\Pr(d_i)$ that the document d_i is randomly selected from the document set by the following *subjective probability*:

$$\Pr(d_i) \stackrel{\text{def}}{=} \frac{dw_i}{tdw}. \tag{7}$$

Namely, we assume that old documents have smaller selection probability than newer ones.

Next, we derive the conditional probability $\Pr(t_k|d_i)$ that a term t_k is selected from a document d_i. We simply derive it based on the number of occurrences of terms in a document:

$$\Pr(t_k|d_i) \stackrel{\text{def}}{=} \frac{freq(d_i, t_k)}{\sum_{l=1}^{n} freq(d_i, t_l)}. \tag{8}$$

Since we can consider that the right hand of Eq. (8) gives the *term frequency* of t_k within d_i, we also denote it as

$$tf(d_i, t_k) \stackrel{\text{def}}{=} \Pr(t_k|d_i). \tag{9}$$

The occurrence probability of term t_k, $\Pr(t_k)$, can be derived by

$$\Pr(t_k) = \sum_{i=1}^{m} \Pr(t_k|d_i) \cdot \Pr(d_i). \tag{10}$$

Since we can consider that $\Pr(t_k)$ represents the *document frequency* of term t_k, we also denote $\Pr(t_k)$ as

$$df(t_k) \stackrel{\text{def}}{=} \Pr(t_k). \tag{11}$$

Also, since we can regard the reciprocal of $df(t_k)$ as the *inverse document frequency* (*IDF*) of t_k, we define

$$idf(t_k) \stackrel{\text{def}}{=} \frac{1}{df(t_k)}. \tag{12}$$

Using the above formulas and Bayes' theorem, we obtain

$$\Pr(d_j|t_k) = \frac{\Pr(t_k|d_j)\Pr(d_j)}{\Pr(t_k)} = \Pr(d_j) \cdot tf(d_j, t_k) \cdot idf(t_k). \tag{13}$$

Next, we consider the conditional probability $\Pr(d_j|d_i)$. It is defined as

$$\Pr(d_j|d_i) = \sum_{k=1}^{n} \Pr(d_j|d_i, t_k) \Pr(t_k|d_i). \tag{14}$$

Now we make an assumption that $\Pr(d_j|d_i, t_k) \simeq \Pr(d_j|t_k)$, then we get

$$\Pr(d_j|d_i) \simeq \sum_{k=1}^{n} \Pr(d_j|t_k) \Pr(t_k|d_i) = \Pr(d_j) \sum_{k=1}^{n} tf(d_i, t_k) \cdot tf(d_j, t_k) \cdot idf(t_k). \tag{15}$$

Based on the above formula, we also get

$$\Pr(d_i, d_j) = \Pr(d_j|d_i) \cdot \Pr(d_i) \simeq \Pr(d_i) \Pr(d_j) \sum_{k=1}^{n} tf(d_i, t_k) \cdot tf(d_j, t_k) \cdot idf(t_k). \tag{16}$$

In the following, we use $\Pr(d_i, d_j)$, the co-occurrence probability of documents d_i and d_j, as the similarity score for d_i and d_j, and define the document similarity measure as follows:

$$sim(d_i, d_j) \stackrel{\text{def}}{=} \Pr(d_i, d_j). \tag{17}$$

Based on the above definition, obsolete documents generally have small similarity scores with any other documents since their occurrence probabilities are quite small.

Similarly, if we make an assumption that $\Pr(t_i|d_k, t_j) \simeq \Pr(t_i|d_k)$, we get

$$
\begin{aligned}
\Pr(t_i|t_j) &= \sum_{k=1}^{m} \Pr(t_i|d_k, t_j) \cdot \Pr(d_k|t_j) \\
&\simeq \sum_{k=1}^{m} \Pr(t_i|d_k) \cdot \Pr(d_k|t_j) \\
&= idf(t_j) \cdot \sum_{k=1}^{m} \Pr(d_k) \cdot tf(d_k, t_i) \cdot tf(d_k, t_j)
\end{aligned}
\tag{18}
$$

and obtain

$$
\Pr(t_i, t_j) = \Pr(t_j)\Pr(t_i|t_j) \simeq \sum_{k=1}^{m} \Pr(d_k) \cdot tf(d_k, t_i) \cdot tf(d_k, t_j).
\tag{19}
$$

Now we briefly mention the relationship between two document similarity measures used in our F^2ICM method and the C^2ICM method [3]. In F^2ICM, we have revised the similarity measure used in C^2ICM from a more theoretical perspective and derived the similarity measure based on the probabilistic modeling. While the main difference of F^2ICM from C^2ICM is the incorporation of a forgetting factor into the probability calculation (e.g., $\Pr(d_i)$), even if we omit forgetting factors from our formulas, the formulas do not completely match the ones of C^2ICM. Another difference is that C^2ICM defines its document similarity measure by $\Pr(d_j|d_i)$ instead of $\Pr(d_i, d_j)$. However, $\Pr(d_i, d_j)$ and $\Pr(d_j|d_i)$ play almost equivalent roles as far as they are used in the clustering algorithms shown in Section 2.

4   Updating Statistics and Probabilities

We have already shown the basic clustering algorithm of the F^2ICM method in Section 2 and derived the document similarity measure in Section 3. Although we can generate and maintain document clusters based on them, we still have a room to improve the clustering method by devising the update procedure for statistics and probabilities used in the clustering. Since some of the statistics and probabilities used in our method (e.g., $\Pr(d_i)$ and $df(t_k)$) change their values when new documents are incorporated into the document set and when time has passed. Therefore, we have to recalculate their new values based on their definitions shown in Section 3. Since the recalculation becomes costly for large data sets, we devise the statistics update method which is based on incremental computation and fully utilizes previous statistics and probabilities to achieve efficient updates. In this section, we show such an incremental update method for statistics and probabilities.

Let the last update time of the given document set consisting of m documents $d_1, \ldots, d_m$ be $t = \tau$. Namely, the most recent documents are incorporated into the document set at $t = \tau$. Then suppose that m' new documents $d_{m+1}, \ldots, d_{m+m'}$ are appended at the time $t = \tau + \Delta\tau$. Therefore, their acquisition times are $T_{m+1} = \cdots = T_{m+m'} = \tau + \Delta\tau$. Let all the index terms contained in the document set at time $t = \tau$ be $t_1, \ldots, t_n$ and the additional terms incorporated by the insertion of documents $d_{m+1}, \ldots, d_{m+m'}$ be $t_{n+1}, \ldots, t_{n+n'}$. In the following discussion, we assume that $m \gg m'$ and $n \gg n'$ hold.

1. Updating of dw_i's: First we consider the update of document weights of documents $d_1, \ldots, d_m$. We have already assigned a weight $dw_i|_\tau$ to each document d_i ($1 \leq i \leq m$) at the last update time $t = \tau$. These weights have to be updated to $dw_i|_{\tau + \Delta \tau}$ in this update time. Since the relationship

$$dw_i|_{\tau + \Delta \tau} = \lambda^{\tau + \Delta \tau - T_i} = \lambda^{\Delta \tau} dw_i|_\tau \tag{20}$$

holds between $dw_i|_\tau$ and $dw_i|_{\tau + \Delta \tau}$, we can easily derive $dw_i|_{\tau + \Delta \tau}$ from $dw_i|_\tau$ by simply multiplying $\lambda^{\Delta \tau}$ to $dw_i|_\tau$. This property for the efficient update is due to the selection of the exponential forgetting factor in our document forgetting model. For the new incoming documents $d_{m+1}, \ldots, d_{m+m'}$, we simply set $dw_i|_{\tau + \Delta \tau} = 1$ ($m + 1 \leq i \leq m + m'$). The computational complexity of this step is estimated as $O(m + m') \approx O(m)$.

2. Updating of tdw: For the total weight of all the documents tdw, we can utilize the following update formula:

$$tdw|_{\tau + \Delta \tau} = \sum_{l=1}^{m+m'} \lambda^{\tau + \Delta \tau - T_i} = \lambda^{\Delta \tau} tdw|_\tau + m'. \tag{21}$$

The processing cost is $O(1)$.

3. Calculation of $\Pr(d_i)$'s: $\Pr(d_i)$, the occurrence probability of document d_i, is given by

$$\Pr(d_i)|_{\tau + \Delta \tau} = \frac{dw_i|_{\tau + \Delta \tau}}{tdw|_{\tau + \Delta \tau}}. \tag{22}$$

Since we have already obtained $dw_i|_{\tau + \Delta \tau}$ and $tdw|_{\tau + \Delta \tau}$ in Step 1 and 2, we can easily calculate $\Pr(d_i)$ when it is required.

4. Maintenance of $tf(d_i, t_k)$'s: For $tf(d_i, t_k)$, we decompose it into

$$tf(d_i, t_k) = \frac{freq(d_i, t_k)}{doclen_i}, \tag{23}$$

then maintain $freq(d_i, t_k)$ and $doclen_i$ instead of $tf(d_i, t_k)$[4], and calculate $tf(d_i, t_k)$ when it is required. Since $freq(d_i, t_k)$ and $doclen_i$ do not depend on time, we have to compute them only for the new documents $d_{m+1}, \ldots, d_{m+m'}$. If we roughly suppose that the number of terms contained in each document be a constant c, this step requires $O(cm') = O(m')$ computation time.

5. Updating of $df(t_k)$'s: The formula of $df(t_k)|_\tau$ can be transformed as

$$df(t_k)|_\tau = \sum_{i=1}^{m} \frac{dw_i|_\tau}{tdw|_\tau} \cdot tf(d_i, t_k) = \frac{1}{tdw|_\tau} \sum_{i=1}^{m} dw_i|_\tau \cdot tf(d_i, t_k). \tag{24}$$

Now we define $\widetilde{df}(t_k)|_\tau$ as

$$\widetilde{df}(t_k)|_\tau \stackrel{\text{def}}{=} \sum_{i=1}^{m} dw_i|_\tau \cdot tf(d_i, t_k), \tag{25}$$

then $df(t_k)|_\tau$ is given by

$$df(t_k)|_\tau = \frac{\widetilde{df}(t_k)|_\tau}{tdw|_\tau}. \tag{26}$$

---

[4] The reason to maintain $freq(d_i, t_k)$ and $doclen_i$ independently is that we need $freq(d_i, t_k)$ to calculate the seed power sp_i using Eq. (4).

By storing $\widetilde{df}(t_k)|_\tau$ instead of $df(t_k)|_\tau$, we can achieve the incremental update. When we need the new value $df(t_k)|_{\tau+\Delta\tau}$, we can compute it from $\widetilde{df}(t_k)|_{\tau+\Delta\tau}$ and $tdw|_{\tau+\Delta\tau}$ using the above formula.

As shown in [6], we can derive the update formula for $\widetilde{df}(t_k)$:

$$\widetilde{df}(t_k)|_{\tau+\Delta\tau} = \lambda^{\Delta\tau} \cdot \widetilde{df}(t_k)|_\tau + \Sigma_{i=m+1}^{m+m'} tf(d_i, t_k). \tag{27}$$

Now we define $\Delta t f_{\text{sum}}(t_k)$ as

$$\Delta t f_{\text{sum}}(t_k) \stackrel{\text{def}}{=} \Sigma_{i=m+1}^{m+m'} tf(d_i, t_k), \tag{28}$$

then we get a simplified update formula

$$\widetilde{df}(t_k)|_{\tau+\Delta\tau} = \lambda^{\Delta\tau} \cdot \widetilde{df}(t_k)|_\tau + \Delta t f_{\text{sum}}(t_k). \tag{29}$$

Since it takes $O(m')$ time to compute a $\Delta t f_{\text{sum}}(t_k)$ value, we need $O(m' \cdot (n+n')) \approx O(m'n)$ time for all the documents.

6. Calculation of δ_i's: Based on Eq. (14), we can transform the decoupling coefficient formula for documents as follows:

$$\delta_i|_\tau = \Pr(d_i|d_i)|_\tau = \Pr(d_i)|_\tau \Sigma_{k=1}^n tf(d_i, t_k)^2 \cdot idf(t_k)|_\tau. \tag{30}$$

For the documents $d_1 \ldots, d_m$, $\delta_i|_{\tau+\Delta\tau}$ is given by the following formula [6]:

$$\delta_i|_{\tau+\Delta\tau} = dw_i|_{\tau+\Delta\tau} \Sigma_{k=1}^n \frac{tf(d_i, t_k)^2}{df(t_k)|_{\tau+\Delta\tau}}. \tag{31}$$

Although we cannot derive $\delta_i|_{\tau+\Delta\tau}$ incrementally from $\delta_i|_\tau$, we can achieve $O(cm) = O(m)$ computation time using appropriate inverted index structures. For $d_{m+1}, \ldots, d_{m+m'}$, we can use the formula

$$\delta_i|_{\tau+\Delta\tau} = \Sigma_{k=1}^{n+n'} \frac{tf(d_i, t_k)^2}{\widetilde{df}(t_k)|_{\tau+\Delta\tau}}. \tag{32}$$

It takes $O(m')$ time. Therefore, the overall computation cost in this step is $O(m+m') \approx O(m)$.

7. Updating δ_i''s: The formula of $\delta_i'|_\tau$ is transformed as [6]:

$$\delta_i'|_\tau = \frac{1}{\widetilde{df}(t_i)|_\tau} \Sigma_{k=1}^m dw_k|_\tau \cdot tf(d_k, t_i)^2. \tag{33}$$

By defining $\widetilde{\delta_i'}|_\tau$ as

$$\widetilde{\delta_i'}|_\tau \stackrel{\text{def}}{=} \Sigma_{k=1}^m dw_k|_\tau \cdot tf(d_k, t_i)^2, \tag{34}$$

we get

$$\delta_i'|_\tau = \frac{\widetilde{\delta_i'}|_\tau}{\widetilde{df}(t_i)|_\tau}. \tag{35}$$

We store $\widetilde{\delta_i'}|_\tau$ instead of $\delta_i'|_\tau$ to enable the incremental update of δ_i'.

Since

$$\widetilde{\delta}'_i|_{\tau+\Delta\tau} = \lambda^{\Delta\tau} \cdot \widetilde{\delta}'_i|_\tau + \sum_{k=m+1}^{m+m'} tf(d_k, t_i)^2 \tag{36}$$

holds, by defining

$$\Delta t f_{\text{sqsum}}(t_i) \overset{\text{def}}{=} \sum_{k=m+1}^{m+m'} tf(d_k, t_i)^2, \tag{37}$$

we obtain the update formula

$$\widetilde{\delta}'_i|_{\tau+\Delta\tau} = \lambda^{\Delta\tau} \cdot \widetilde{\delta}'_i|_\tau + \Delta t f_{\text{sqsum}}(t_i). \tag{38}$$

As the computational cost for a $\Delta t f_{\text{sqsum}}(t_i)$ value is $O(m')$, the overall processing cost for the terms $t_1, \ldots, t_n$ becomes $O(m'n)$.

For the new terms $t_{n+1}, \ldots, t_{n+n'}$, we can use the formula

$$\widetilde{\delta}'_i|_{\tau+\Delta\tau} = \Delta t f_{\text{sqsum}}(t_i) \tag{39}$$

by setting $\widetilde{\delta}'_i|_\tau = 0$ in Eq. (38). The calculation cost is $O(m'n')$. Therefore, the overall cost of this step is $O(m'(n+n')) \approx O(m'n)$.

Based on the above discussion, the total cost to update statistics and probabilities in an incremental manner is given by

$$O(m) + O(1) + O(m') + O(m'n) + O(m) + O(m'n) \approx O(m+m'n). \tag{40}$$

On the other hand, the naive scheme that calculate statistics and probabilities on each update has $O((m+m') \cdot (n+n')) \approx O(mn)$ computation time [6] and is expensive for on-line document clustering applications.

Now we summarize the above ideas. We persistently store and incrementally maintain the following statistics: dw_i's, tdw, $freq(d_i, t_k)$'s, $doclen_i$'s, $\widetilde{df}(t_k)$'s, and $\widetilde{\delta}'_k$'s, and achieve the update cost $O(m+n)$. Other statistics and probabilities ($\Pr(d_i)$'s, $tf(d_i, t_k)$'s, $df(t_k)$'s, δ_i's, and δ'_i's) are computed when they are needed. Due to the limitation of the pages, we do not show the detailed description of the incremental statistics and probability update algorithm here. For the complete description, see [6].

5   Document Expiration and Parameter Setting Methods

5.1   Expiration of Old Documents

We have not mentioned deletion of old documents until now. Since the F^2ICM method weights each document according to the novelty of the document, old documents have small document weights (dw_i's) and do not have effects on the clustering results. Since F^2ICM is based on the philosophy to neglect obsolete documents, we can remove too old documents from the targets of the clustering. Such removal will improve the storage overhead and the update overhead of F^2ICM.

To remove obsolete documents from the clustering target documents, we take the following approaches:

1. First we consider the deletion condition of old documents. In this paper, we take a simple approach: if the document weight dw_i for a document d_i satisfies the condition

$$dw_i \leq \varepsilon \qquad (41)$$

   for a small positive constant ε, we delete the document d_i. In practice, we delete the document weight dw_i, maintained as described in the previous section, from a persistent storage.

2. When we delete dw_i of the deleted document d_i, we have to propagate the deletion to other statistics. For tdw, the total weight of all the documents, we have to modify it as $tdw = tdw - dw_i$ according to its original definition. However, since now $dw_i \approx 0$, $tdw - dw_i \approx tdw$ holds so that we do not have to modify tdw actually.

3. We also need to delete $freq(d_i, t_k)$'s, the term occurrence frequencies for d_i, to reduce the storage cost. Therefore, we simply delete $freq(d_i, t_k)$'s for all the term t_k's that satisfy $freq(d_i, t_k) > 0$.

4. Additionally, we have to delete $\widetilde{df}(t_k)$ and $\widetilde{\delta}'_k$ for each term t_k contained in d_i, but we should remind that the term t_k may be contained in other documents. In such a case, we should not delete these values because they are still active. To solve this problem, we simply use a reference counter for each term: when the reference counter becomes zero, we can safely delete the statistics values for the term.

For the details of the document deletion process, see [6].

5.2   Methods for Parameter Setting

The F^2ICM method uses two parameters in its algorithms:

- a forgetting factor λ $(0 < \lambda < 1)$ that specifies the speed of forgetting
- an expiration parameter ε $(0 < \varepsilon < 1)$, the threshold value for document deletion

To help the user's decision for the parameter settings, we use the following metaphors to give intuitive meanings to them.

To set the parameter λ, we assume that the user gives a *half-life span* value β. It specifies the period that a document loses half of its weight. Namely, β satisfies $\lambda^\beta = 1/2$. Therefore, λ can be derived as

$$\lambda = \exp(-\log 2/\beta). \qquad (42)$$

For the parameter ε, we assume that the user gives a *life span* value γ. The γ value specifies the period that a document is "active" as the target of clustering. Therefore the expiration parameter ε can be derived by

$$\varepsilon = \lambda^\gamma. \qquad (43)$$

These parameter setting methods are more intuitive than the direct setting of λ and ε and more easier for ordinal users.

6   Experimental Results

6.1   Dataset and Parameter Settings

In this section, we show two experimental results performed using F^2ICM. As the test dataset, we use an archive of Japanese newspaper articles of Mainichi Daily Newspaper for the year 1994. The archive is available as a CD-ROM format and articles in it are categorized by their issue dates and subject areas. A news article is typically assigned 50 to 150 keywords: we use such keywords as the index terms for an article. In the experiment, we mainly utilize articles on international affairs that issued in January and February in 1994. News articles are basically issued per-day basis and the number of news articles for each day is from 15 to 25.

In the experiments, we assume to perform the clustering procedure once in a day. The numbers of clusters n_c is fixed as $n_c = 10$ throughout the experiments. We set the half-life span parameter as $\beta = 7$. Namely, we assume that the value of an article reduces to $1/2$ in one week. Also, we set the life span parameter as $\gamma = 30$. Therefore, every document will be deleted from the clusters after 30 days from its incorporation.

6.2   Computational Cost for Clustering Sequences

First we show the experimental result on computation cost for daily clustering. Figure 1 plots the CPU time and the response time for each clustering performed everyday. The x-axis represents passed days from the start date (January 1st, 1994) and ends with 57th day (March 1st, 1994)[5].

As shown in this figure, the CPU and response times increase almost linearly until 30th day. This is because the size of the target document set increases almost linearly until 30th day and because F^2ICM has near-linear computational cost. After 30 days, the processing cost turns to be almost constant. This is because after 30 days, not only new articles are inserted into the target document set, but also old articles are deleted from it. Therefore, the size of the target document set becomes almost constant after 30 days. We can observe the abrupt increases of the processing cost at 33rd, 40th, and 42nd days. The reason would be because there are many articles particularly for these three days. Based on this experiment, we can say that F^2ICM has constant processing cost for continual clustering tasks which are required in on-line environments.

6.3   Overview of the Clustering Results

In this subsection, we show the experimental results of the clustering from the standpoint of their qualities. Unfortunately, for the target dataset, there are no relevance judgments or ideal clustering results to be used for the comparison purpose. Therefore, we briefly review the result of the manual observation of the clustering results.

As an example, we summarize the clusters obtained after the clustering process at January 31, 1994 (30th day).

---

[5] Although there are 60 days in this period, three no issue days exist in this dataset.

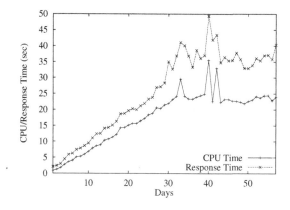

Fig. 1. CPU and Response Times of Clustering

1. East Europe, NATO, Russia, Ukraine
2. Clinton(White Water/politics), military issue(Korea/Myanmar/Mexico/Indonesia)
3. China(import and export/U.S.)
4. U.S. politics(economic sanctions on Vietnam/elections)
5. Clinton(Syria/South East issue/visiting Europe), Europe(France/Italy/Switzerland)
6. South Africa(ANC/human rights), East Europe(Boznia-Herzegovina, Croatia), Russia (Zhirinovsky/ruble/Ukraine)
7. Russia(economy/Moscow/U.S.), North Korea(IAEA/nuclear)
8. China(Patriot missiles/South Korea/Russia/Taiwan/economics)
9. Mexico(indigenous peoples/riot), Israel
10. South East Asia(Indonesia/Cambodia/Thailand), China(Taiwan/France), South Korea(politics),

Another example at March 1st, 1994 (57th day) is as follows:

1. Boznia-Herzegovina (NATO/PKO/UN/Serbia), China(diplomacy)
2. U.S. issue (Japan/economy/New Zealand/Boznia/Washington)
3. Myanmar, Russia, Mexico
4. Boznia-Herzegovina(Sarajevo/Serbia), U.S.(North Korea/economy/military)
5. North Korea(IAEA/U.S./nuclear)
6. East Asia(Hebron/random shooting/PLO), Myanmar, Boznia-Herzegovina
7. U.S.(society/crime/North Korea/IAEA)
8. U.N.(PKO/Boznia-Herzegovina/EU), China
9. Boznia-Herzegovina(U.N./PKO/Sarajevo), Russia(Moscow/Serbia)
10. Sarajevo(Boznia-Herzegovina), China(Taiwan/Tibet)

Based on the observation, we would be able to say that our method groups similar articles into a cluster as far as an appropriate article representing a specific topic is selected as a cluster seed, but a cluster obtained as the result of clustering usually contains multiple topics. This would partly due to the effect of the terms that commonly appear in news articles (e.g., U.S., China, military, president). To alleviate this problem, it would be beneficial to devise more sophisticated term weighting methods or to use thesauri to select effective index terms for document clustering.

As an another problem, we can observe that clustering results get worse in some cases because two or more articles belonging to the same topic are often selected as seed articles. This phenomenon is well observed in the result of March 1st, 1994 shown above. Since five seed articles are related to the topic "Boznia-Herzegovina issue", articles belonging to this topic are separately clustered in different clusters. This is because F^2ICM only uses seed powers in its seed selection step and does not consider similarities among the selected seed documents[6]. Based on this observation, we can say that we should devise a more sophisticated scheme for seed selection. As an another improvement, it may be useful to use two-step clustering approach (as in Scatter/Gather [4]) that consists of the first clustering step that clusters part of the documents with a costly, but high-quality clustering scheme, and the second clustering step that clusters remaining documents with a low-cost clustering scheme utilizing the result of the first clustering.

7   Conclusions and Future Work

In this paper, we have proposed an on-line document clustering method F^2ICM that is based on the notion of a forgetting factor to compute document similarities and to derive clustering results. The feature of F^2ICM is to "forget" past documents gradually and put high weights on newer documents than older documents to generate clusters. We have described the document similarity measure used in F^2ICM that incorporates the notion of a forgetting factor, the clustering algorithms, and the incremental statistics maintenance algorithm for the efficient update of clusters. We have briefly shown our experimental results performed on daily newspaper articles and analyzed the behaviors of F^2ICM.

As future work, we are planning to revise our clustering algorithms to improve the quality of the generated clusters. Also, we aim to devise an automatic estimation method of the number of clusters and a semi-automatic parameter setting method for the forgetting factor λ to achieve good clustering results. We are also planning to make more detailed experiments using other test data collections.

Acknowledgments

This research was supported in part by the Grant-in-Aid for Scientific Research from the Ministry of Education, Culture, Sports, Science and Technology, Japan.

---

[6] In the paper of C^2ICM [3], it is mentioned that selection of seeds belonging to a same topic can be avoided using a threshold value to evaluate their similarity. But it is not clear how to set this parameter appropriately.

References

1. J.R. Anderson (ed.), *Rules of the Mind*, Lawrence Erlbaum Associates, Hillsdale, NJ, 1993.
2. R. Baeza-Yates and B. Ribeiro-Neto. (eds.), *Modern Information Retrieval*, Addison-Wesley, 1999.
3. F. Can, "Incremental Clustering for Dynamic Information Processing", *ACM TOIS*, 11(2), pp. 143–164, 1993.
4. D.R. Cutting, D.R. Karger, J.O. Pedersen, "Constraint Interaction-Time Scatter/Gather Browsing of Very Large Document Collections", *Proc. ACM SIGIR*, pp. 126-134, 1993.
5. W.B. Frakes and R. Baeza-Yates, *Information Retrieval: Data Structure & Algorithms*, Prentice-Hall, 1992.
6. Y. Ishikawa, Y. Chen, and H. Kitagawa, "An Online Document Clustering Method Based on Forgetting Factors (long version)", available from
   `http://www.kde.is.tsukuba.ac.jp/~ishikawa/ecd101-long.pdf`.
7. A.K. Jain, M.N. Murty, P.J. Flynn, "Data Clustering: A Review", *ACM Computing Surveys*, 31(3), 1999.
8. G. Salton and M.J. McGill, *Introduction to Modern Information Retrieval*, McGraw-Hill, 1983.
9. C.J. van Rijsbergen, *Information Retrieval* (2nd ed.), Butterworth, 1979.
10. Y. Yang, J.G. Carbonell, R.D. Brown, T. Pierce, B.T. Archibald, X. Liu, "Learning Approaches for Detecting and Tracking News Events", *IEEE Intelligent Systems*, 14(4), 1999.

Towards a Theory of Information Preservation

James Cheney[1], Carl Lagoze[1], and Peter Botticelli[2]

[1] Computer Science Department
Cornell University
Ithaca, NY 14850
{jcheney,lagoze}@cs.cornell.edu
[2] Cornell University Library
Cornell University
Ithaca, NY 14850
pkb4@cornell.edu

Abstract. Digital preservation is a pressing challenge to the library community. In this paper, we describe the initial results of our efforts towards understanding digital (as well as traditional) preservation problems from first principles. Our approach is to use the language of mathematics to formalize the concepts that are relevant to preservation. Our theory of *preservation spaces* draws upon ideas from logic and programming language semantics to describe the relationship between concrete objects and their information contents. We also draw on game theory to show how objects change over time as a result of uncontrollable environment effects and directed preservation actions. In the second half of this paper, we show how to use the mathematics of universal algebra as a language for objects whose information content depends on many components. We use this language to describe both migration and emulation strategies for digital preservation.
[*Due to space constraints, the second part of the paper has been omitted. The full paper is available at [1].*]

1 Introduction

Preservation is essential to the mission of libraries and archives. For print materials, we have well-established techniques for protecting and conserving physical artifacts and for reformatting content onto highly durable media (e.g., microfilm). In recent years, however, the growth of digital content has made preservation a critical and vexing problem, one that violates many of the assumptions that govern established preservation programs. Since we do not yet have proven methods or strategies for preserving "born digital" files with no print analogues, there is an urgent need to explore new approaches and to closely examine all potential solutions.

Many in the archives community have begun to tackle digital preservation by returning to first principles, by first asking what essential attributes of digital records ought to be preserved, before considering the technical possibilities for preserving digital objects. It is often argued that digital preservation depends

P. Constantopoulos and I.T. Sølvberg (Eds.): ECDL 2001, LNCS 2163, pp. 340–351, 2001.

on our ability to preserve not a set of file structures so much as information of enduring value, or the content contained in digital files [17, 9]. In the digital library community, Clifford Lynch has developed this idea by arguing that digital preservation should focus on a "canonicalization" of the content rather than the bits themselves [12]. In essence, Lynch and others have called for the development of a theoretical approach to managing information in an abstract form that can be isolated from particular file formats and display technologies[1].

Nonetheless, many archivists are justifiably skeptical on the question of whether we can preserve digital content in an unstable and rapidly evolving computing environment. Indeed, in the print world, the concreteness and the relative stability of artifacts has enabled us to effectively preserve information by simply preserving its physical container. In other words, the information contained in traditional document formats (e.g. paper with ink, vinyl with groove patterns) is tightly coupled with the physical characteristics of the medium[2]. This is also true of digital formats, which represent the interaction between data (stored as bits) and a finite set of hardware and software artifacts[3]. However, the complexity of the "physical characteristics" of the digital medium—hardware plus software plus data—makes it potentially very costly to preserve information by preserving that complete set of characteristics. Thus, from a theoretical perspective, we argue that practical strategies for preservation depend on our ability to understand and manage the changing relationship between information—the canonical values we ultimately wish to preserve—and the physical environment in which documents are produced and stored.

This paper describes our initial steps toward the development of a mathematical approach to preserving information, one that we hope will eventually enable us to model the behavior of both print and digital documents as information carriers. Our main goal at this stage is to demonstrate the utility of using mathematical models to analyze the outcome of preservation strategies in practical situations. Our modeling approach draws on a number of theoretical bases, including game theory [10, 15], programming language semantics [14], and universal algebra [19].

---

[1] Archivists in Australia, in particular, and also Canada have made considerable progress in exploring the relationship between the record, as a physical or digital object, and the web of contextual information needed to make sense of records—and which in many instances cannot be contained in the artifact itself. See [13, 2, 18]. For a general discussion of archival approaches to preserving the authenticity of digital records, see [7].

[2] This view is strongly reflected in the practice of archival diplomatics, which analyzes the physical structure of documents to determine their authenticity. See [6]. Duranti is also the leading contemporary advocate for a "custodial" approach to digital archives, as a way to maintain control of records by physically controlling the bits used to encode them.

[3] We should note that Jeff Rothenberg has been influential in arguing for emulation as a preservation strategy, though it remains to be seen whether the functionality of computing environments can be effectively preserved over long periods of time. See [16]

In applying modeling techniques to the problem of preserving information, we first had to devise a formal way to represent information as a set of relative, and not absolute, values. We thus developed the notion of an *interpretation*, which we define as a mathematical function that describes the complex relationship between the physical manifestation of a document and its accompanying information content.

People naturally form an interpretation whenever they use a document. In most cases, interpretations are expressed only in tacit, informal ways, and yet they have important consequences for preservation. A web page, for example, can have several interpretations, depending on how we use them. A single page can be interpreted as an HTML source text, as a page image displayed on a monitor, or as a browsing experience mediated by a variety of applications and data sources. Different preservation strategies will obviously be needed to preserve the information represented by these different interpretations. We also need to account for the fact that individual interpretations will differ in granularity; i.e., a page-image interpretation might specify a color model to be used for rendering an exact shade of red, while another interpretation might allow for any shade of "red" to be used. In this case, there are two different strategies, with significant differences in cost, for preserving a single web page; the choice of strategy depends upon which interpretation is more appropriate. Thus, our approach to preservation demands that we first transform our otherwise tacit observations into some kind of formal statement about the relationship between physical objects (including software) and the information values we wish to preserve.

By allowing for variable interpretations, our goal is to develop mathematical models that will enable us to test the broadest possible range of preservation strategies for both physical and digital objects. To model the effects of particular strategies, we have begun to develop a mathematical structure that we call a *preservation space*. In broad terms, this structure consists of:

1. Physical objects that can represent information.
2. Information content representable by physical objects.
3. Interpretations that link physical objects to information content.
4. Environmental factors that may cause changes to physical objects (and, indirectly, the information they represent) over time.
5. Actions that preservation agents (e.g., individuals, libraries, archives, museums) can take in response to environmental factors.
6. Effects of the interaction of environment and agent actions on physical objects.

Our goal is to use the concept of a preservation space to understand and mathematically model:

- Preservation policies that formally express what information (what interpretation of the physical space) should be preserved over time.
- Preservation plans that define a program-like series of steps that absolutely or probabilistically accomplish a preservation policy.
- Preservation costs that determine the feasibility of policies and plans.

Our theoretical approach to digital preservation co-exists with a number of ongoing research projects. For instance, researchers at the San Diego Supercomputer Center are seeking to design a digital archives as a stable technical environment in which documents can be preserved and used for long periods of time [11]. Work at Stanford focuses on the preservation of documents as bits, and is examining ways to preserve information in spite of hardware failures [4, 5, 3]. The CAMiLEON project is investigating the outcomes of different emulation strategies in preserving digital objects [8]. All of these approaches have distinct merits, and our work is not meant to stand in contrast to them. Rather, our work is intended to provide a framework for understanding these various approaches and evaluating their effectiveness in addressing particular preservation issues.

In the remainder of this paper, we explain our initial theory-building efforts. We begin by developing the basic elements of the preservation space. Next, we use these building blocks to analyze first the preservation of single, self-contained objects, then collections of objects, and finally complex, context-dependent objects. We close by describing some possible future paths for this work.

2   Preservation Spaces

In this section we will define the *preservation spaces* that were introduced in the previous section. A preservation space consists of two basic components: a *semantics*, or a way of interpreting objects as information, and a *dynamics*, that is, a description of how objects change over time. Using this framework, we define information preservation as preservation of information content subject to some interpretation, despite changes in representation. We then develop the notions of *plans* and *policies* for preservation.

2.1   Semantics

Our theory distinguishes between an *object state space* S and an *information content space* C. The object state space consists of all the possible states that objects representing information might assume, and the information space contains the information content representable in the object state space. A partial function $I : S \rightharpoonup C$ mapping states to their information content is called an *interpretation*. The structure (S, C, I) is a *semantics*.

For example, the object states might be eight-bit character sequences and the information content might be English text. One interpretation is the standard ASCII code, while others include EBCDIC and UNICODE. Another somewhat fuzzier example consists of everyday physical objects whose information content can consist of perceivable properties such as color, shape, size, and so on. Interpretations in this example include "approximate color" (group objects together as being "red", "blue", "green", etc.) and "exact color" (the exact visible light component of the color of an object).

Any interpretation I induces a *partial equivalence relation* $\equiv_I$ over S, namely $x \equiv_I y \iff I(x) = I(y)$. That is to say, given an interpretation I, we can

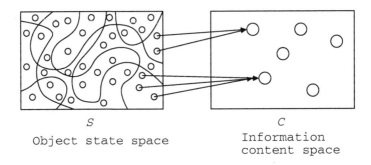

S
Object state space

C
Information
content space

Fig. 1. Object state and information content spaces and interpretation

partition the state space into classes that represent the same information. Figure 1 diagrams a simple object state space and information space. The arrows show part of an interpretation $I : S \rightharpoonup C$. The object state space S is divided into cells of $\equiv_I$-equivalence classes.

The choice of semantics depends on the problem domain. In the case of Web pages, the object state space is the set of all ASCII text files. The corresponding forms of information content include "HTML source", "page image", and "total page interaction experience". The correspondences between the object states and these information content forms are interpretations. For example, two text files are equivalent from the "HTML source" perspective only if they are literally the same text document. However, two source files are equivalent from the "page image" perspective if they render the same (but they may have different markup). Finally, equivalence from the "total page interaction experience" perspective means pages are indistinguishable based on the user's browsing experience. These interpretations are partial functions, since some text files are not legal HTML and thus have no information content in any of the above senses.

Our use of the word *semantics* to describe the relationship between objects and their content is close to the that in programming language theory. A program's semantics is an abstract description of its behavior when run (such as the value or function it computes), and a language's semantics is a way of calculating the semantics of programs in the language. Two programs that have the same semantics are considered to be equivalent, even though they might be different in other ways, for example, size or running time. In programming language theory, the choice of semantics implicitly determines what properties of programs (such as running time, storage usage, and long-term behavior) are considered important. Programming language semantics are a special case of preservation semantics, but an important one, especially for digital preservation problems in which the objects of interest include programs.

2.2 Dynamics

Objects are physical entities and so are subject to change over time. In our theory, changes result either from actions taken by the preservation agent, or from interactions with the "environment", that is, circumstances not under the agent's control. We will model this state of affairs as a two-player game, or a graph whose vertices are game states and edges are moves made by the preservation agent or by the environment. In this view, we want to know whether there is some strategy by which the preservation agent can "win" playing against the environment, where winning means preserving the information.

For example, in a preservation space model for a digital preservation problem, the environmental factors would include both media decay, in which bits on magnetic or optical media are no longer readable, and technological obsolescence, in which readers for the media no longer exist. The actions available to a preservation agent would include making duplicate copies of media, refreshing data onto more long-lasting media, migrating data from obsolete media formats to state-of-the-art ones, as well as other, domain-dependent actions. However, in a general preservation space, there are no *a priori* assumptions on the nature of the environment effects and agent actions.

Formally, let $\mathcal{E}$ be a set of *environment moves*, and let $\mathcal{A}$ be a set of *agent actions*. Each object state $s \in \mathcal{S}$ is a game state and the rules of the game are described by $\mathcal{E}$ or $\mathcal{A}$-labeled edges $s \to_e t$, $s \to_a t$ between states. An edge $s \to_a t$ means "in state s, action a results in state t", and similarly for $s \to_e t$. The game is deterministic, so from any state s, there can be at most one edge $s \to_a t$ labeled with a given move a (and similarly for environment moves). The environment and agent take turns making moves; the environment makes its moves randomly, while the agent can decide what moves to make. This is a simplification of a more general form of game in which the players can move simultaneously; the alternating-move game seems adequate for most purposes.

We regard one turn of the game as one time step. Thus, in each time step the environment has some effect on the state and then the agent takes some action that may also change the state. We define a *game sequence* to be a sequence $\omega = s_0 e_1 a_1 s_1 \cdots e_k a_k s_k$ where s_0 is the initial state of the game, each e_i and a_i is the ith move made by the environment or agent, and s_{i+1} is the state after the $i + 1$th turn (that is, $s_i \to_{e_i} t \to_{a_i} s_{i+1}$ for some t).

So far we have been using the term "object" informally. In formalizing the concept of object, the central issue is how to model *identity*, that is, whatever it is that makes us believe that *different states* are instantiations of the *same object* at *different times*. It is tempting to regard an object as a sequence $s_1 \ldots s_k$ of object states assumed over time. In this approach, two states in this sequence are aspects of the same object. However, this definition is too broad. It requires us to consider too many possible object behaviors, including those which violate the rules of the game. We wish to exclude those state sequences that can never be actual sequences of game states.

Thus, we could instead define an object to be a state sequence $s_1 \ldots s_k$ for which a game sequence $s_0 e_1 a_1 s_1 \cdots e_k a_k s_k$ that runs through its states exists. It would also be adequate to define an object simply as a game sequence. Defining objects as game sequences has two advantages over the state-sequence approach. First, it is notationally simpler. Second, it makes analyzing specific objects easier since we need only consider one game sequence at a time, not all game sequences generating a state sequence. It is this approach that we prefer: formally, an *object* is a game sequence ω.

Games are usually characterized as either competitive or cooperative. We might ask which best describes a preservation game. In a competitive game, the environment should always make moves that threaten the integrity of the information, since the preservation agent's goal is to preserve it. In a cooperative game, the environment and agent would share the goal of preservation, and so a trivial winning strategy would be for both to do nothing. Neither of these descriptions matches our intuition about the environment. The environment can be either harmful or helpful, but is not motivated by malice, benevolence, or indeed, in our view, any will at all. Thus, it seems more appropriate to think of the environment as an indifferent player whose moves are chosen according to some unpredictable process that we can describe using some probability distribution P. Nevertheless, cooperation and competition are likely to be useful concepts in situations with several independent preservation agents.

To summarize, a *preservation space* is a structure with the following components:

Semantics	$\mathcal{S}$	object state space
	$\mathcal{C}$	information content space
	$I_1, I_2, \ldots : \mathcal{S} \rightharpoonup \mathcal{C}$	interpretations
Dynamics	$\mathcal{E}$	environment effects
	$\mathcal{A}$	agent actions
	$s \rightarrow_e t, s \rightarrow_a t$	results of actions and effects
	P	probability distribution of environment effects

2.3   Preservation, Plans, and Policies

In this section we employ preservation spaces to analyze relatively simple preservation scenarios. We begin by modeling preservation of single objects; for example, books, web pages, and the like. In reality, information brokers such as libraries and archives are responsible for collections of similar objects or for interdependent objects. Later in the section, we therefore extend our modeling principles to the collection level. This provides the tools for analyzing more complex preservation scenarios in the following section.

Single Objects We say that the information of an object $\omega = s_0 e_1 a_1 \cdots s_k$ is *preserved* if the object's state always represents the same information over its lifetime. Formally, preserving ω with respect to an interpretation I means that for each $t, 0 \leq t \leq k$, we have $I(s_t) = I(s_0)$. Schematically, preservation means that the state of ω stays within the same $\equiv_I$-equivalence class. We can visualize this by thinking of the states of ω as a path wandering through $\mathcal{S}$ but never crossing a $\equiv_I$-border (see Figure 2).

The simplest kind of preservation goal, or *policy*, is to preserve an object for n time steps with respect to an interpretation I_i. This policy is written

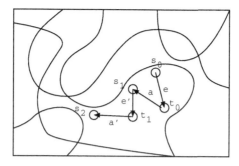

Fig. 2. Object whose information is preserved

preserve(i, n). If ω is a object whose I_i-information is preserved for n steps, then we write $\omega \models$ preserve(i, n) (read "ω satisfies policy preserve(i, n)").

Now, suppose we are given a policy A and an initial state s_0, and we want to know if we can accomplish the policy. One might guess that this means determining whether there is an ω starting at s_0 such that $\omega \models A$. This is not the case, because there is no guarantee that the indifferent environment will cooperate in having the effects necessary to construct ω. Also, there may be no way for the agent to determine which actions to take without knowledge of the the future. Consequently, it is not enough to know that it is possible for the information to be preserved; instead, we need something stronger. In game-theoretic terms, we seek a *strategy* that ensures that the information is preserved with high probability.

In game theory, a strategy is a method for deciding what move to make next, given the current game state. The question of interest in cooperative and competitive games is what strategies players should follow to maximize the expected payoff. In an indifferent-environment game, the environment has no payoff and its "strategy" (a random process) is already set. So in an indifferent game, the question of interest is what strategy the preservation agent should follow to maximize the likelihood of accomplishing its policy. We will call strategies for preserving information *preservation plans* (or just *plans*).

Formally, a plan is a function $\varphi : \mathcal{S} \to \mathcal{A}$ that picks an action $\varphi(s)$ to perform if the object is in state s. For example, a reasonable plan might be to attempt emergency recovery if s is an unstable state with a high likelihood of disastrous decay, and otherwise do nothing. An equally valid (but less reasonable) plan might be to do nothing in every state. Plans may or may not be likely to accomplish preservation goals.

If a preservation agent follows a plan φ starting from state s_0, and the environment has effects $e_1 \cdots e_k$, then the resulting object is uniquely determined. This object is denoted $\varphi(s_0, e_1 \cdots e_k) = s_0 e_1 a_1 s_1 \cdots e_k a_k s_k$ such that $s_{i-1} \to_e t_i$, $a_i = \varphi(t_i)$, and $t_i \to_{a_i} s_i$ for each i from 1 to n.

The environment's effects are, of course, not known in advance, but generated at random. Consequently, the actual effects of following plans are probabilistic in nature. Suppose that the agent follows plan φ for s_0, and $E_1 \cdots E_k$ is a sequence of $\mathcal{E}$-valued random variables distributed according to P. Then there is a unique random object (that is, an object-valued random variable) determined by these conditions. This random object is $\varphi(s_0, E_1 \cdots E_k) = s_0 E_1 A_1 S_1 \cdots E_k A_k S_k$.

Put simply, in our theory, being able to preserve information means finding a plan φ for a given state s that maximizes the probability that the resulting random object preserves its information. A *simple preservation problem* $\langle s, \mathsf{preserve}(i, n) \rangle$ consists of an initial state s and a policy $\mathsf{preserve}(i, n)$. A plan φ solves a simple preservation problem $\langle s, \mathsf{preserve}(i, n) \rangle$ with probability p if $p = P(\varphi(s_0, E_1 \cdots E_k) \models \mathsf{preserve}(i, n))$. A problem with only probability-0 solutions is *impossible*. A plan which is a probability-1 solution to a problem is an *absolute solution*.

Multiple Objects In the real world situations we would like to model, preservation agents are responsible for large, interdependent collections of objects, not just single, self-contained ones. A simplistic solution to this problem would be to consider collections of object states to be indexed sets $S = \{s_1, \ldots, s_k\}$, collection policies to be sets $\{A_1, \ldots, A_k\}$ of statements $A_j = \mathsf{preserve}(i_j, t_j)$, and collection plans to be sets $\Phi = \{\varphi_1, \ldots, \varphi_k\}$. In this approach, a preservation problem is a pair $\langle S, A \rangle$ of a state collection and collection policy, and a probability-p solution is a collection plan Φ such that the probability that each φ_i solves each subproblem $\langle s_i, A_i \rangle$ is p.

There are two reasons why this approach is too simplistic. First, it requires considering each object in a collection on its own, which makes reasoning about large collections very complex. For example, in a million-object collection of very similar objects, we would like to be able to treat the many similar objects the same way rather than on a case-by-case basis. If all the objects are essentially the same from a preservation point of view, then it suffices to find a solution for the single-object model and apply it to all the objects. If instead there are many different kinds of objects, then we can represent each kind as a distinct object in the simple manner described above. In the million-object collection, suppose 50% of the items are images, 25% are text documents, and 25% are binary data files in the same format. Instead of naively considering each of the million objects, policies, and plans separately, we can get away with only three, representing generic text, image, and binary documents. The document kind representatives can be either a single typical document, or a representative sample.

Second, the simplistic approach does not make any allowance for preservation dependences among objects. It only allows preservation policies that are logical conjunctions of single-object policies. Real-world policies can be more complex. For example, it might be acceptable to preserve at least one of several duplicates of a document rather than all of them. Also, the question of whether one object is worth preserving may depend on whether another has been successfully preserved; thus, we might only want to bother with policy B if policy A succeeded. Finally, in some situations it is important to ensure that information is *not* been preserved; this is why offices have paper shredders.

To address this problem, instead of collection policies $\{A_1, \ldots, A_k\}$, policies are logical formulas A, B of the form j : preserve(i, n) (where $1 \leq j \leq k$), A AND B, A OR B, IF A THEN B, and NOTA. The collection policy

$$\{\text{preserve}(i_1, t_1), \ldots, \text{preserve}(i_k, t_k)\}$$

is equivalent to

$$1 : \text{preserve}(i_1, t_1) \text{ AND } \cdots \text{ AND } k : \text{preserve}(i_k, t_k)$$

The other policy forms OR , IF THEN , and NOT correspond to the "preserve at least one", "conditionally preserve", and "ensure not preserved" policies.

Suppose $\Omega = \{\omega_1, \ldots, \omega_k\}$ is a collection of objects. The j in the basic policy j : preserve(i, n) refers to the object of Ω that is to be preserved; that is, j : preserve(i, n) says that ω_j is to be preserved under interpretation I_i for t time steps. In that case, we write $\Omega \models j$: preserve(i, n). The meanings of the other forms of policies are the standard meanings defined in propositional logic. For example, $\Omega \models A$ AND B means that $\Omega \models A$ and $\Omega \models B$.

Suppose $S = \{s_1, \ldots, s_k\}$ is the set of initial states of the objects under consideration, and A is a policy expressed as a logical formula. A *preservation problem* is a pair $\langle S, A \rangle$. A collection plan Φ is a probability-p solution to $\langle S, A \rangle$ if the object collection Ω constructed by following the plans in Φ starting with the states in S satisfies A with probability p.

3   Compound Object Preservation Spaces

[Due to space constraints, this section has been omitted. The full paper is available at [1].]

4   Future Directions

There are many important issues in preservation that our theory, as presented, does not yet address. In real situations, agents have limited resources with which to enforce preservation policies. We believe our theory can readily include preservation costs, and should therefore be useful for analyzing preservation problems involving constrained resources. Another issue is that the value (or utility, as in economics) of different kinds of information varies and can change over time. As with cost, we believe that it is possible to add information utility to our theory and to consider preservation as a utility-maximization problem. By adding these factors to our theory, we should be able to formulate optimal preservation strategies in which agents seek the best tradeoff between cost and utility.

A third issue is that all our interpretations are discrete, in the sense that information content must be preserved exactly. There are many situations (e.g. image preservation using lossy compression) in which this view is too strict; instead information degrades gradually and continuously until the distortion is no longer acceptable. We believe that it is possible to enrich our theory to handle gradual degradation gracefully, possibly using many interpretations I_α, $0 \leq \alpha \leq 1$, that capture information equivalence up to distortion level α, or a "distortion function" $d : \mathcal{C} \times \mathcal{C} \to [0,1]$, that indicates how acceptable a substitute one informational entity is for another.

A fourth issue is that of multiple agents. In the real world, there are many independent organizations and individuals, each with different preservation goals (as well as other goals, such as security). These agents may cooperate, compete, or behave indifferently towards one another. Again, we believe that it is possible to augment our theory to describe multi-agent situations and to formulate and solve preservation problems involving many agents.

5   Conclusions

We have presented a mathematical framework for analyzing preservation problems involving print and digital media. We also showed how to enrich this framework using universal algebra in order to reason about preserving information carried by composing objects together.

Our approach develops the concept of a preservation space, in which we can apply modeling techniques in ways that are general enough to help us understand a wide variety of preservation problems and potential strategies. We are seeking a preservation theory that will unify the seemingly incompatible views of information as either analog or digital, by abstracting out the commonalities and showing where the differences arise. Our eventual goal is to provide a firm theoretical basis on which we can evaluate the effectiveness of technical solutions to preserving information, and to contribute to our understanding of how information can be preserved in highly complex forms where purely intuitive approaches to preservation are unlikely to succeed.

Acknowldegements We thank Bill Arms for many thoughtful discussions and criticisms of this paper. The work described in this paper is supported by the National Science Foundation (Grant No. IIS-9905955, The PRISM Project).

References

[1] James Cheney, Carl Lagoze, and Peter Botticelli. Towards a theory of information preservation (Complete Version). Technical Report TR2001-1841, Cornell University, 2001. http://cs-tr.cs.cornell.edu:80/Dienst/UI/1.0/Display/ ncstrl.cornell/TR2001-1841.

[2] Terry Cook. Electronic records, paper minds: The revolution in information management and archvies in the post-custodial and post-modernist era. *Archives and Manuscripts*, 22(2), November 1992.

[3] Brian Cooper, Arturo Crespo, and Hector Garcia-Molina. Implementing a reliable digital object archive. In *Fourth European Conference on Digital Libraries*, 2000.

[4] Arturo Crespo and Hector Garcia-Molina. Archival storage for digital libraries. In *Third ACM Conference on Digital Libraries*, 1998.

[5] Arturo Crespo and Hector Garcia-Molina. Modeling archival repositories. In *Fourth European Conference on Digital Libraries*, 2000.

[6] Luciana Duranti. *Diplomatics: New Uses for an Old Science*. Scarecrow Press, 1998.

[7] Anne J. Gilliland-Swetland. Enduring paradigm, new opportunities: The value of the archival perspective in the digital environment. Technical Report 89, Council on Library and Information Resources, 2000.
http://www.clir.org/pubs/reports/pub89/contents.html.

[8] Stewart Granger. Digital preservation and the CAMiLEON project.
http://ds.dial.pipex.com/stewartg/cam-london.html.

[9] Margaret Hedstrom. Digital preservation: A time bomb for digital libraries.
http://www.uky.edu/~kiernan/DL/hedstrom.html, 1997.

[10] A. J. Jones. *Game Theory: Mathematical Models of Conflict*. Ellis Horwood, 1980.

[11] Bertram Ludascher, Richard Marciano, and Reagan Moore. Towards self-validating knowledge-based archives.
http://www.sdsc.edu/~ludaesch/Paper/ride01.html, 2001.

[12] Clifford Lynch. Canonicalization: A fundamental tool to facilitate preservation and management of digital information. *D-LIb Magazine*, 5(9), September 1999.
http://www.dlib.org/dlib/september99/09lynch.html.

[13] Sue McKemmish. Are records ever actual. Technical report, Monash University, 1998.

[14] John C. Mitchell. *Foundations for Programming Languages*. MIT Press, 1996.

[15] Peter Morris. *Introduction to Game Theory*. Springer-Verlag, 1994.

[16] Jeff Rothenberg. Ensuring the longevity of digital documents. *Scientific American*, 272(1):42–7, January 1995.

[17] Donald Waters and John Garrett. Preserving digital information, report of the task force on archiving of digital information. Technical Report 63, Council on Library and Information Resources, 1996.
http://www.clir.org/pubs/reports/pub63/contents.html.

[18] Andrew Waugh, Ross Wilkinson, Brendan Hills, and Jon Dell'oro. Preserving digital information forever. In *Proceedings of the Fifth ACM International Conference on Digital Libraries*, 2000.

[19] Wolfgang Wechler. *Universal Algebra for Computer Scientists*. Springer, Berlin, 1992.

C-Merge: A Tool for Policy-Based Merging of Resource Classifications

Florian Matthes, Claudia Niederée, and Ulrike Steffens

Software Systems Institute,
Technical University Hamburg-Harburg, Hamburg, Germany
{f.matthes,c.niederee,ul.steffens}@tu-harburg.de
www.sts.tu-harburg.de

Abstract. In this paper we present an interactive tool for policy-based merging of resource-classifying networks (RCNs). We motivate our approach by identifying several merge scenarios within organizations and discuss their individual requirements on RCN merge support. The quality-controlled merging of RCNs integrates the contributions from different authors, fostering synergies and the achievement of common goals.

The *C-Merge* tool design is based on a generalized view of the merge process and a simple but flexible model of RCNs. The tool is policy-driven and supports a variable degree of automation. Powerful options for user interaction and expressive change visualization enable substantial user support as well as effective quality control for the merge process.

Keywords: Categorization, Taxonomy, Merging, CSCW, Knowledge Management, Knowledge Visualization, Quality Control

1 Introduction

Effective cooperative construction, structuring, and handling of digital content is a crucial factor in the information society. Beyond the use of digital documents cooperative work with content also involves information resources like personal interests, special expertise etc. Effective discovery and use of, as well as communication about all these resources can be improved by imposing a common classification scheme.

The materialization and adequate visualization of classification hierarchies leads to *resource-classifying networks* (RCN) that use enriched classification hierarchies as an access structure improving information discovery, navigation and exploration. Innovative graphical user interfaces further enhance the usability of such networks.

The construction of RCNs is often a cooperative, long-term effort which includes extension, correction, refocusing as well as restructuring and reacts to new developments and insights assuring a high quality of the classified collection. The construction process is a mix of autonomous efforts, close and loose cooperation as well as online and offline work. This leads to separate, partly competing,

P. Constantopoulos and I.T. Sølvberg (Eds.): ECDL 2001, LNCS 2163, pp. 352–365, 2001.

partly complementing artifacts that have to be reintegrated to gain a common overall result. RCN merging, thus, is an integral part of the construction process and is required

- to achieve consensus between cooperation partners,
- to benefit from co-workers contributions, and
- to exploit independent, but semantically related evolution.

The potential size and complexity of RCNs makes manual merging a tedious task. Hence, semi-automatic merge support is crucial. This paper presents *C-Merge*, a prototype tool that implements a proposal-oriented approach for merging RCNs. It combines powerful merge support with a user-defined degree of automation and effective options for user intervention.

Flexible RCN merge support is motivated in the next section by considering various cooperative merge scenarios. Section 3 discusses the RCN merge process requirements together with the solutions employed in our approach. The *C-Merge* service architecture and functionality is summarized in section 4. The paper concludes with a discussion of related work and future research directions.

2   Motivation: Merging RCNs

Resource classifying networks play an important role in the cooperative work with information. This section starts with a description of our model of RCNs and identifies several merge scenarios which require flexible RCN merge support.

2.1   A Model for Resource-Classifying Networks

The classification of information objects according to a predefined hierarchy of concepts is an important contribution to their description and discovery. Resources that are structured this way include documents in traditional and digital libraries, co-workers expertise as found in knowledge management, physical facilities like rooms, and events like conferences. If classification hierarchies are materialized they can be used for the structuring and navigation of an information space and contribute to communication and a common domain understanding inside a community [10].

For the merge process we consider a simple but flexible model of such materialized classification structures termed *resource-classifying networks* (RCNs) in what follows. They consist of three integral parts:

- *Classifier nodes* represent classification categories. They comprise the name of the category, an optional ID, a description of the category and further properties.
- *Content nodes* represent the classified resources, which may be local or remote. It is assumed here that resources are identified by a URL. The information resources themselves are not considered part of the RCN.

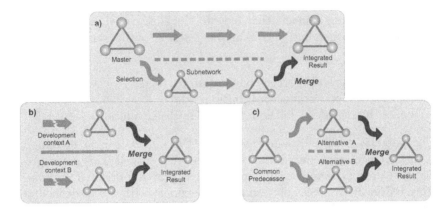

Fig. 1. a) Re-integration of subproject results; b) Merging independent developments; c) Integrating parallel versions

- Three types of links can exist between the nodes. *Parent links* between classification nodes build up the classification hierarchy, multiple inheritance inclusive. *Classification links* connect content nodes with classification nodes and *jump links* connect arbitrary nodes to represent general associations.

In contrast to formal approaches like ontologies known from AI [5] we consider a restricted set of link types and do not assume a formal description of semantics. Hence, our approach is applicable to more simple, ad-hoc hierarchies as they emerge in many domains and organizations. RCN example applications are traditional classification hierarchies, Web catalogs [7], and knowledge portals [9].

2.2   Merge Scenarios

When developing RCNs the need for merging arises in several cooperative situations:

- A work group is asked to autonomously revise and extend a part of an organization's RCN. The use of autonomous subnetworks resolves the conflict between organizational and work group view [3]: The organization's view is focussed on long-term usability and consensus with the organization's objectives whereas work groups creatively change the RCN according to their task. The revised subnetwork is later re-integrated into the organization's network (see Fig. 1 a)).
- An author discovers an RCN of another domain expert in the Web, which has a focus similar to his own network (see Fig. 1 b)). A controlled integration of the overlapping areas allows the author to benefit from this expert's contributions.
- Two independent project teams work on alternative proposals for the restructuring of an organization's intranet developing two RCNs. The intranet's

acceptance can be improved by carefully merging both proposals (see Fig. 1 c)).

These situations differ in their requirements. Adequate merge support depends on factors like the relationship between authors or the importance of the respective RCNs, which influence the degree of automation and the quality control requirements. Confidence in an author's expertise, for example, enables a higher degree of automation whereas integrating developments from an unknown author opts for more quality control. In each case system support has to enable the user to understand the consequences of integrating contributions. A user-friendly visualization, as implemented in the *C-Merge* tool (see Fig. 2), is a major step in this direction.

3   System Analysis and Design

The characteristics of RCNs as well as their crucial role for information structuring and discovery impose special requirements on a process for merging this kind of information objects. This section starts with a general overview of the process of merging which in the second part is adapted to the requirements of our RCN model.

3.1   Overview of the Merge Process

Considered on a general level four phases can be identified for a merge process:

1. *Merge configuration:* The definition of a merge configuration fixes the number and the roles of the information objects involved in the merge process.
2. *Matching:* The computation of a matching identifies the corresponding components of the information objects to be merged.
3. *Change detection:* The differences between the considered information objects are determined by a change detection algorithm.
4. *Change integration:* The contributions are combined into one result object.

Manual merging provides the user with full process control but may be tedious, especially for larger information structures like RCNs. Fully automated merging, on the other hand, is the most comfortable solution, but quality control and conflict resolution completely steered by the system are not always acceptable. Semi-automatic solutions provide a compromise between user-driven control and user comfort.

Merge Configuration This phase assigns roles to the involved information objects, the *merge candidates*: Candidates which contain the contributions to be merged appear in the role of *change sources*. Furthermore, a *change target* is chosen, i.e. a candidate into which the contributions are to be integrated. *Change reference* is the third possible role. A merge candidate in this role is compared with the change source(s) to compute relevant differences. The roles change reference and change target often coincide, but there are other conceivable options, too.

Matching A prerequisite for change detection is the computation of a *matching* identifying corresponding parts in the considered merge candidates. For the matching the merge candidates have to be divided into *components* where a component can e.g. be a sentence in a text file, an element of a collection, or a leaf element in an XML document. The similarity of components depends on different factors:

Component content: Equality or similarity of content is the most obvious evidence for the similarity of two components.

Component context: The similarity of two components may also depend on their environment or context. In a tree, for example, the similarity of two nodes is influenced by the similarity of their children and/or parents.

Component properties: Meta information like size, author or creation date may also be taken into account when computing the similarity of two components.

Component type: In many cases components that are not of the same type are not compared at all. In contrast, some component types may be considerably similar for the respective components to be compared.

Comparing each component of the change source with each component of the change reference results in a large number of comparisons and makes matching inefficient. In many cases it is possible to either exclude components of the change reference from the set of potentially matching candidates or to identify the most promising candidates with little effort. For the computation of the actual matching one or more of the above mentioned similarity factors can be chosen and combined.

Change Detection The purpose of this phase is to determine the change source's contributions to be integrated into the change target. They are represented by a so called Δ-*collection*, a partially ordered collection of change operations from an *operation repertoire*, which, when applied to the change target, adopt the change source's contributions. The Δ-collection is either computed by comparing change source and reference or extracted from a change history. The change detection process is characterized by the chosen operation repertoire and the granularity of considered changes.

Change Integration This phase integrates the identified changes into the change target. An uncontrolled application of the operations from the Δ-collection may reduce the result quality. Therefore, the operations are filtered before they are applied to the change target. The filter process may depend upon user interaction, a merge strategy, consistency rules, or the state of the change target.

Depending on the considered merge scenario and the type of information objects different degrees of automation are adequate for change integration. Semi-automatic merging may support automatic detection and visualization of changes which are manually accepted or rejected by the user (e.g. [14]). An adequate change visualization enables comprehension and reliable integration decisions. A flexible degree of automation is achieved by policy-based merging as discussed in [11] where a merge policy determines what kind of changes are automatically integrated or rejected and what kind of changes require interactive approval.

3.2   Design of the RCN Merge Process

The RCN merge process is influenced by two competing requirements: The complexity of the networks calls for a high degree of process automation to make it feasible. Yet, RCNs are often high investment structures intended for the long-term use making strict quality control crucial. In our approach matching and change detection are automated but also augmented with options for user intervention. This is combined with a flexible degree of automation in the change integration phase, which is of special importance for quality control.

Another issue for semi-automatic RCN merging is the sequence of components to be merged. During the RCN merge process the user must be guided through the network in a way that preserves his orientation to support meaningful integration decisions. Proceeding along the classification hierarchy seems intuitive here.

Our work focusses on the merging of the network structure. For the node content we rely on existing approaches for document merging (e.g. [8]).

Merge Configuration Although merging of more than two networks might be desirable in some organizational contexts (see Sect. 2) and is also technically possible, keeping track of the changes in all the networks would probably overstrain the user. We therefore restricted ourselves to two merge candidates at a time, where one appears as change source and the other as both, change target and reference. This corresponds to the scenario in which an author integrates contributions from another RCN (change source) into his own one (change target and reference).

The coverage of the two networks to be merged may differ substantially. One network may for example structure the entire area of digital library research whereas the second network may be restricted to IR issues. This situation is handled by providing support for the merging of user-defined subnetworks.

RCN Matching The nodes within RCNs carry an elaborate and often also stable part of the network's semantics. Using RCN nodes as matching components is therefore a straightforward approach.

Content and classifier nodes represent different types of RCN components. As they perform different tasks within the RCN, instances of different types are disregarded for matching. Considering node content, the matching of classifier nodes mainly relies on the name of the corresponding concept and can also involve the ID or description if present. Content nodes are matched by comparing the referenced resources. The matching result is further refined by taking into account the nodes' context, mainly focussing on the comparison of parent and classification links.

To achieve a tolerable efficiency for the RCN matching process, it is subdivided into two phases. Initial matching candidates are computed making use of indexes over the node names and the resource's URLs, respectively. The intermediate result set is then further narrowed by comparing the nodes' context.

A comparison of the computed similarities with two customizable threshold values subdivides the matching pairs into proposed and confirmed pairs. Pairs with a similarity below the smaller threshold are not considered as a matching at all.

Change Detection in RCNs Taking a node-centered approach change detection and change integration are realized as alternating phases within the merge process.

The operation repertoire for networks consists of operations on nodes and links. Our approach supports a restricted repertoire that is manageable for the user. It includes operations for node insertion, update, and deletion as well as for link creation and removal. Additionally, we consider two operations for link update: *re-parent*, redirecting a parent link to a different parent node, which corresponds to moving a subtree, and *changeType*, turning a parent link into a jump link or vice versa.

A precomputation of the complete Δ-collection in a separate pass is inadequate for RCNs. It does not take dynamic changes during merging into account (see Sect. 4.2). Instead our approach locally determines the differences node by node, just in time for change integration. Change detection and integration rely on the notion of a *focus node* which is the node currently processed. In succession, each node becomes a focus node in a variant of a breadth-first processing order along the hierarchy.

For change detection the focus node environment is compared with the environment of its matching partner. The environment of a node includes all direct neighbors of a node and the connecting links. Links that differ within the two environments are matched with a set of possible difference situations in order to identify the operations for the Δ-collection. Single nodes, i.e. nodes that have no matching partner, get special treatment.

Change Integration in RCNs The automation of the change integration phase is a challenging task. For RCNs this is further tightened by the complexity of the information structure to be merged. To achieve a variable degree of interactivity we decided to employ merge policies as proposed in [11].

A merge policy customizes the merge process by defining rules for handling occurring changes. Since we have only one change source, the policies can be implemented by simplified, single-column merge matrices that provide an entry for each possible change operation. This entry specifies if the operation is automatically applied, ignored or if the user is asked for a decision. The matrices are used to look up the further proceeding for the operations found in the Δ-collection. Flexibility is increased by enabling users to define their own merge policies.

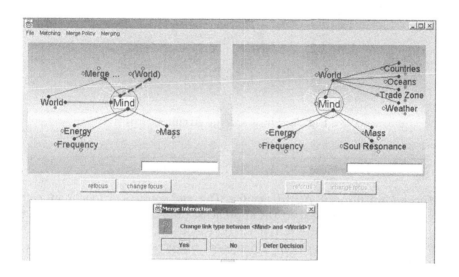

Fig. 2. Proposal of Changing a Link Type

Most policies chosen for RCN merging will not be fully automatic: A change will be proposed to the user and he decides about its integration. The visualization must enable the user to understand the proposed change as well as the consequences of its acceptance or rejection. For this purpose the change is presented as part of the focus node context: The change under consideration is entered into the focus node environment and highlighted according to the type of change. As an example figure 2 shows the proposal of changing a link type. Via a dialog box the user can accept or reject the change. In addition we enable intermediate browsing through the RCN during change integration so that the user can gain more context information.

4   The *C-Merge* Prototype

This section presents *C-Merge*, a flexible Java prototype tool for the merging of RCNs implemented at our department. The implementation relies on existing components and libraries and uses a commercially available RCN format. The prototype is characterized by a proposal-based change integration and offers several options for user interaction and intervention enabling a flexible process control.

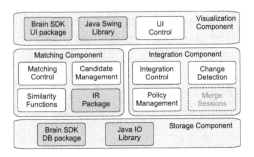

Fig. 3. The *C-Merge* Architecture

4.1   System Overview

***C-Merge* Component Architecture** The tool consists of four main compo-
nents (see Fig. 3) implementing the approaches presented in the previous section:

The **integration component** implements the presented approach for change
detection, provides support for the definition, management and application
of merge policies and controls the change integration process according to
the chosen policy. Advanced merge session support is planned for a future
version.

The **matching component** computes the RCN matching. It includes a component for the management of matching candidates, matching pairs and
single lists as well as a component for the control of the matching process.
An existing Java IR package is employed to compute the similarity of text
properties.

The **visualization component** relies on the Java Swing library and the UI
package of the *BrainSDK*, a Java library that comes with the RCN format
employed in the prototype. This imported functionality is integrated and
controlled by a set of application specific user interface classes.

The **storage component** uses the *BrainSDK* DB package functionality for
the persistent storage of the employed RCN format. Further merge-related
information like merge policies are stored using the classes of the Java IO
library.

Processing Sequence The UML activity diagram in figure 4 shows a pass
through a typical merge session with the *C-Merge* prototype. During the process
intermediate merge results can be stored.

The *Brain* RCN Format The prototype uses a commercially available RCN
format, namely the *Brain* format from *Natrificial* (www.thebrain.com). The
metaphor behind this format is a brain consisting of a set of associated thoughts.
The *thoughts*, which are the nodes of the *Brain* RCNs, are connected by two types

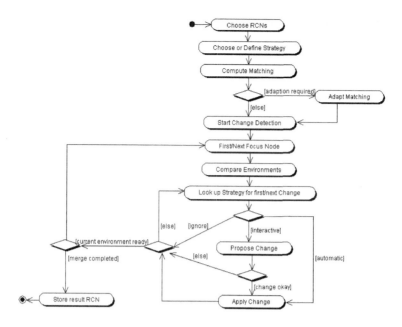

Fig. 4. A typical *C-Merge* session

of links: *parent links* create a hierarchy and *jump links* express general references between thoughts.

The *BrainSDK*, a development kit provided by Natrificial, includes Java class libraries for the visualization, manipulation, and storage of the Brain RCNs and provided a good starting point for the implementation of our tool.

4.2 User Interaction and User Intervention

A challenging issue in tool design is the coordination of user interaction with the automatic steps of the merge process. In addition to *user input* at well-defined points like merge policy definition and integration decisions as required by the policy there is another kind of user interaction: Task-driven *user intervention* spontaneously manipulating and redirecting the process flow. Possible user interventions are:

- Update of the matching
- Change of the focus node
- Update of the RCN

The increased complexity of the control flow requires additional book-keeping. Node processing states are used for this purpose. The states *unprocessed, in work,* and *ready* are distinguished. An additional state, *modified,* marks nodes that have already been processed but need reconsideration because of some user intervention.

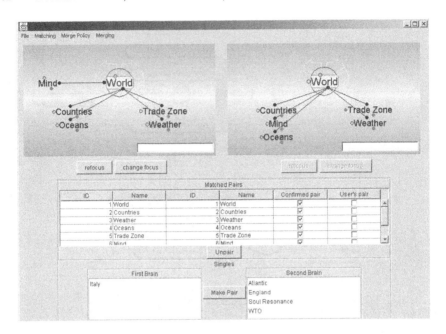

Fig. 5. *C-Merge* User Interface

Change of Focus Node The predefined processing order for change detection and integration may be changed by manually choosing a new focus node. The user may decide interactively if he wants only this node processed or the entire subtree rooted at the new focus node. For the subtree option the processing of the actual focus node f_{act} is considered completed. The node processing state changes from *in work* to *ready*. The chosen node f_{new} becomes the new focus node and is processed next. Subsequently, the subtree of which f_{new} is the root is processed. Finally, processing returns to the normal order. A nested change of focus node is possible.

During the merge process the user can browse both RCNs to get more context information. Pressing a button he can return to the current focus node.

Update of Matching The computed matching results in a list of matched nodes presented side by side, where some pairs are marked as confirmed matchings. In addition there is a list of single nodes for each involved RCN (see Fig. 5). The matching can be modified manually by the user which can have implications for the rest of the matching as well as for the change detection process.

The effects on change detection are handled through the node states. If a matching is changed all involved nodes in state *ready* are changed to the state *modified* and change detection re-starts at the top. Only nodes that are in the state *in work, unprocessed* or *modified* are considered in this pass through the RCN.

No automatic re-matching is performed as an effect of a manual change, unless explicitly triggered by the user, because, although useful in some settings, it may effect large parts of the network and complicate the running merge process.

Update of the RCN Merging RCNs implicitly involves rethinking of the networks' semantics. To directly integrate new ideas the user is allowed to change the RCN acting as change target in the course of the merge process.

RCN modifications influence the merge process, especially change detection. The consequences of such changes depend on the operation type and the states of the involved nodes. For an *unprocessed* node a modification of it or its environment will be handled as part of the normal processing. For a node that is in state *ready* a modification is considered as a post-merging operation that requires no further processing. For a node that is currently *in work* change detection is reconsidered taking into account the integration decisions already made by the user.

5   Related Work

Like RCNs, topic maps [2] are materialized classification structures, but exhibit a richer meta level with typed nodes and links as well as scopes for topics. Ontologies [5] used for the conceptualization and representation of knowledge are based on a more formal approach. RCNs can be considered as weakly structured ontologies [6] that exhibit a restricted set of link types and do not formalize the semantics.

The need for merging comes up in cooperation situations where stronger forms of synchronization are not possible. Examples are offline work, parallel work due to time constraints and loose cooperation with high autonomy for the cooperation partners. These forms of so-called *autonomous collaboration* are motivated and discussed in more detail in [4]. Further mechanisms relevant in such cooperation contexts are change notification (e.g. [12]) and advanced link management [13].

Merging support mainly exists in multi-version working contexts like cooperative software development and information artifact authoring. Hence, typical merge candidate formats are pure text files [8], other document formats like Microsoft Word, and source code files [15]. The merge candidates considered in our tool are often high-investment structures whose correctness and adequateness plays an important role for an organization. This imposes additional requirements on merge support.

All existing merge tools are semi-automatic where a frequent solution is automatic change detection and visualization combined with interactive change integration (e.g. [8]). Our tool is based on a more flexible approach proposed in [11], where the degree of automation can be gradually adapted via merge policies. A somewhat different approach to merging is taken in the GINA framework [1], which is based on protocolled changes managed in operation histories. Special redo operations enable operation re-application in a modified object state during merging.

6   Conclusions and Future Work

In this report we presented *C-Merge*, a flexible tool for the semi-automatic merging of resource-classifying networks. First experiments with the tool at our department showed that it enables comfortable and quality-preserving merging of RCNs. Especially the enhanced change proposal visualization and the customizable merge policies contributed to user satisfaction.

Merging larger RCNs can be a time-consuming task even with semi-automatic merge support as provided by our tool. Thus, it is desirable to have persistent merge sessions that can be interrupted and resumed later without losing the effort already invested. In addition to the current state of the change target RCN further process information has to be made persistent for this purpose. We plan to integrate a merge session management into the prototype.

In the current prototype we restricted ourselves to a simple operation repertoire avoiding information overload in the visualization. In a future version we will experiment with the detection and visualization of important more complex change operations, which are typical for RCN restructuring, like the splitting of a node or the merging of two nodes. We expect that a carefully tuned operation repertoire provides the user with valuable additional information for his integration decisions.

Some merge scenarios, as e.g. the integration of parallel versions of a common predecessor, are more adequately mapped by a three-way merge. For this reason we intend to examine options for three network merge configurations although the danger of information overload is rather high. A careful user interface design and conflict management are crucial in this context.

Acknowledgments: The described research was partly supported by the HSPIII Project WEL and the DFG Project KOLIBRI (DFG Schm450/7-1, MA2005/1-2).
We would like to thank Siripong Treetasanatavorn and Hendry Chandra for their help in implementing the prototype.

References

[1] Thomas Berlage and Andreas Genau. A Framework for Shared Applications with a Replicated Architecture. In *Proceedings of the ACM Symposium on User Interface Software and Technology, Atlanta, GA*, pages 249–257, November 1993.

[2] Michel Biezunski, Martin Bryan, and Steve Newcomb. ISO/IEC FCD 13250:1999 - Topic Maps, April 1999. http://www.ornl.gov/sgml/sc34/document/0058.htm.

[3] Giorgio De Michelis, Eric Dubois, Matthias Jarke, Florian Matthes, John Mylopoulos, Joachim W. Schmidt, Carson Woo, and Eric Yu. A Three-Faceted View of Information Systems. *Communications of the ACM*, 41(12):64–70, December 1998.

[4] W. Keith Edwards and Elizabeth D. Mynatt. Timewarp: Techniques for Autonomous Collaboration. In *Proceedings of the Conference on Human Factors in Computing Systems (CHI'97), Atlanta, GA*, pages 218–225, March 1997.

[5] T. R. Gruber. A translation approach to portable ontology specifications. Technical Report KSL 92-71, Computer Science Department, Stanford University, CA, 1993.

[6] Michiaki Iwazume, Kengo Shirakami, Kazuaki Hatadani, Hideaki Takeda, and Toyoaki Nishida. IICA: An Ontology-based Internet Navigation System. In *AAAI Workshop Internet-Based Information Systems, Portland, OR*, pages 65 – 78, August 1996.

[7] Yannis Labrou and Tim Finin. Yahoo! As an Ontology: Using Yahoo! Categories to Describe Documents. In *Proceedings of the 8th International Conference on Information Knowledgement (CIKM-99)*, pages 180–187, N.Y., November 2000.

[8] David MacKenzie, Paul Eggert, and Richard Stallman. Comparing and Merging Files. http://www.gnu.org/manual/diffutils-2.7/html_mono/diff.html, September 1993.

[9] F. Matthes and U. Steffens. Establishing a Cooperative Digital Library for Teaching Materials - A Case Study. Technical report, Software Systems Group, Hamburg University of Technology, Germany, August 2000.

[10] Rainer Müller, Claudia Niederée, and Joachim W. Schmidt. Design Principles for Internet Community Information Gateways: MARINFO - A Case Study for a Maritime Information Infrastructure. In *Proceedings of the 1st International Conference on Computer Applications and Information Technology in the Maritime Industries (COMPIT 2000), Potsdam/Berlin, Germany*, pages 302–322, April 2000.

[11] J. Munson and P. Dewan. A Flexible Object Merging Framework. In *Proceedings of the ACM CSCW'94 Conference on Computer Supported Cooperative Work, Chapel Hill, NC*, pages 231 – 242, October 1994.

[12] NetMind. Mind-It Notification Service. http://www.netmind.com/.

[13] Claudia Niederée, Ulrike Steffens, Joachim W. Schmidt, and Florian Matthes. Aging Links. In *Research and Advanced Technology for Digital Libraries, Proceedings of the 3rd Europ. Conf., ECDL2000, Lisbon, Portugal*, pages 269 – 279, September 2000.

[14] Presto Soft. Exam Diff Pro. http://www.nisnevich.com/examdiff/examdiffpro.htm.

[15] Bernhard Westfechtel. Structure-Oriented Merging of Revisions of Software Documents. In *Proceedings of the 3rd International Workshop on Software Configuration Management*, pages 68 – 80, 1991.

Truth in the Digital Library: From Ontological to Hermeneutical Systems[*]

Aurélien Bénel[†‡], Elöd Egyed-Zsigmond[†§], Yannick Prié[§], Sylvie Calabretto[†],
Alain Mille[§], Andréa Iacovella[‡], Jean-Marie Pinon[†]

(†) LISI – INSA Lyon
Bâtiment Blaise Pascal, 69621 Villeurbanne CEDEX, France
`Firstname.Surname@lisi.insa-lyon.fr`

(‡) French School of Archaeology (EFA)
6 Didotou street, 10680 Athens, Greece
`Firstname.Surname@efa.gr`

(§) LISI – Université Lyon 1
Bâtiment Nautibus, 69622 Villeurbanne CEDEX, France
`{eegyed, yprie, amille}@lisi.univ-lyon1.fr`

Abstract. This paper deals with the conceptual structures which describe document contents in a digital library. Indeed, the underlying question is about the truth of a description: obvious (ontological), by convention (normative) or based on interpretation (hermeneutical). In the first part, we examine the differences between these three points of view and choose the hermeneutical one. Then in the second and third part, we present two "assisted interpretation systems" (AIS) for digital libraries (audiovisual documents and scholarly publications). Both provide a dynamic annotation framework for readers' augmentations and social interactions. In the fourth part, a few synthetic guidelines are given to design such "assisted interpretation systems" in other digital libraries.

Keywords. Interpretation, collaboration, annotation, ontology, graphs, interactive information retrieval, assisted interpretation systems.

Introduction

How can we solve in digital libraries the problems of structuring, interoperability and reuse? The current approach is to consider *Ontology*, a concept borrowed from philosophy, as the panacea. This borrowing seems so legitimate that researchers have only discussed related topics like cost [17]. But there are other metaphysics of Truth (*Conventionalism* and especially *Hermeneutics*) that could be more useful to the creators and users of digital libraries.

One can argue that Ontology and its metaphysical aspects are not to be confused with the ontologies which are proposed by computer scientists. But, as we will see,

[*] The authors are truly indebted to Phyllis Graham for her help with the English manuscript.

P. Constantopoulos and I.T. Sølvberg (Eds.): ECDL 2001, LNCS 2163, pp. 366–377, 2001.

the simple use of the term "ontology" implies the admission of its *a priori* understanding of reality.

In the first part, we will discuss the postulates and consequences of the ontological approach and introduce the conventional and hermeneutical ones. We firmly support the hermeneutical approach (i.e. based on interpretation) and its interactive and collaborative aspects. In the next two parts, we will present two assisted interpretation systems (AIS) for digital libraries: *E-SIA* and *Porphyry 2000*. In the last part, we will propose some general criteria for building hermeneutical digital library systems.

Ontology and Hermeneutics

The particular concern of computer science in "ontologies" comes from its original relationship to reality. On the one hand, computer science derives from modern mathematics which are based on *conventionalism*. In this approach, there is no concern with the conformity to the real world. Only the internal coherence of a *conventionally true* ("axiomatic") system matters. On the other hand, computer science as a support for human practices is an applied science and should keep a connection between its formal results and the "real world".

The ontological approach dates from Aristotle [2]. By definition, it is the metaphysical study of *being* or, more pragmatically, the *a priori* structure of reality. It is based on the utterance of *obviously true* principles ("true" means "complying with reality"). This way, every deduced proposition complies with reality. Much discussions has concerned Ontology, but nobody has yet managed to get it. We know several "local ontologies". However they are often mutually contradictory and hard to reuse in different applications [6]. There are also many great philosophers, logicians and computer scientists who have tried to find the "top-level ontology" [11]: starting from Aristotle's categories, to Ontolingua [13], and passing through Pierce's categories. But we can't help questioning the ontological approach itself when we read the lengthy catalogue [16] of these works.

The "apriorism" of the ontological approach does not correspond to the practice of those who take part in the consensual elaboration of thesauri or domain models. And in fact, the "ontology" concept, in its postmodern meaning, is a mix of *a priori* truth, *conventional truth* and *consensual truth*. It is often referred as a "common ground" for communication within a group [18] or as capturing consensual knowledge as accepted by a group [13] [6]. Indeed experts know that constructing a model is a slow, difficult, collective and regularly repeated process. Even in well defined and formalized domains (medicine, zoology), experts seldom agree on well established concepts [17]. As a matter of fact, the knowledge modeler has had to abandon the ontological "apriorism" in order to continue working. "Apriorism" did not provide many guidelines on how to handle models through their creation, evolution, shared use, learning by a human, fusion, and dependence on practices.

On the contrary, these aspects of collaborative construction are well represented in the *hermeneutic* approach. Traditionally, hermeneutics deals with the production and interpretation of text and speech. "Interpretation" is used in the sense of a "trail" [23] in a text or a system of signs. This requires an interpreted subject situated in an action, a social practice, a history and a culture.

Whereas the ontological approach stresses representation, the hermeneutic one gives priority to communication. While, for the former, properties of an *occurrence* are inferred from relations between *types*, for the latter there are only *source occurrences* and *revisited occurrences* influencing each other. In addition, the first approach assumes a knowledge "revelation" while the second proposes a *hypothetical, transitory*, and *debate-based* knowledge construction.

In a few words, two communicating people must adapt their own vision of the world, learn from each other, discover the other's subjectivity, understand the other's interpretations, and resolve misunderstandings. In the next sections we will illustrate this theoretical approach with two systems we have designed.

Illustration #1 : *E-SIA*

Context and Motivation

The E-SIA (Extended Annotation Interconnected Strata) model is developed in a project supervised by the French National Telecommunication Research Network (RNRT), in collaboration with France Télécom[1] and INRIA[2].

The objective of this project is to study and develop tools that enrich access and research services to multimedia information.

Our team focuses mainly on document description. In fact both the search and the annotation pass through a description process. In the first case we describe what we would like to find, in the second the description concerns what we perceive and interpret. In our case the description is done by annotating the documents. As the description is done by different users in different circumstances, it is important to provide tools making possible a homogeneous annotation. For example in the case of a sport TV program it is annoying if the participants of a cycle race are designated at different times as *runners, cyclists,* or *competitors*.

Annotation is controlled by a vocabulary. This means that every term used to annotate has to be added to a sort of thesaurus. Once a term is in the vocabulary it can be reused to annotate documents. We have developed a document description model, to organize and exploit annotations. For the moment, this model concerns audiovisual documents and provides thesaurus management, query construction and refinement of queries. We have created a prototype application enabling document annotation and exploitation [10], managing these annotations as XML documents.

In our system both the documents and the annotations are distributed over a network. We want to make it possible for users to exploit and over-annotate the descriptions created by others. It is in the collaborative use of the vocabulary that one of the major difficulties of the project resides. Several persons (with different cultural and professional backgrounds) modify the vocabulary annotating and over-annotating documents ("using knowledge changes knowledge" [17]). We insist on the fact that annotations are freely added by individual users, but can be controlled (in the case of institutions, like TV channels archiving their programs according to precise

---

[1] France Telecom Recherche et Développement (http://www.rd.francetelecom.fr/)

[2] Institut National de Recherche en Informatique et Automatique (http://www-rocq.inria.fr/imedia/)

guidelines). As these guidelines are documented their interpretation and comprehension should be easy.

System Overview

The E-SIA system relays on a graph based document description model [22]. The annotations and the documents are distributed, the system is used by a large number of users.

In E-SIA, documents are described by annotations (AE) taken from a "knowledge base" defining the vocabulary (abstract annotation elements (AAE)) to be used for annotation. These terms can be grouped in analysis dimensions (AD). This way, they form smaller sets useful for a given annotation task. The annotation elements (AE) describe document fragments represented in the graph by audiovisual units (AVU). All these elements make up a connected, labeled graph.

We propose also the formalization of annotation results. This is done by a structure called description scheme (DS). It specifies which analysis dimensions (AD) are to be used, and which relations are to be created between the descriptors. We say that the annotation is done following a DS. Relations defined in description schemes and instanced across annotation elements, define contexts between these AE-s. Elements are contextualized by other elements with which they have explicit or temporal relations. For example in Fig. 1 *AE:Lt.Tonton* is in the context of *AE:Freeing*, because there is an direct relation between them. Generally, we consider any sub-graph as a context.

Fig. 1 illustrates the layers composing the annotation graph. Some terms of the thesaurus are structured in 3 analysis dimensions, in order to annotate videos presenting first aid techniques in accidents. The description scheme *DS:Accident* specifies that a *Fireman* carries out *Operations* on *Victims*. We note that an other description has been done, assigning the term *Fire* to an audiovisual unit. This annotation was carried out following another description scheme.

A description scheme provides information on the structure of created annotations. It is possible for the same document to be described more than once, in which case we could say that it is annotated following more than one description scheme. The description schemes (SD) as well as audiovisual units (AVU), annotation elements (AE), abstract annotation elements (AAE) and analysis dimensions (AD) are nodes of the global annotation graph

In practice the annotation begins by the selection of a description scheme (it can be a very loose one). Then the user examines the document to be described and describes the user-defined parts with the AAE-s (terms) taken from the analysis dimensions of the description scheme. The user has to create the relations defined by the description scheme.

After this short presentation of the E-SIA system, we concentrate now on the creation, structuring, sharing, and reuse aspects of the thesaurus.

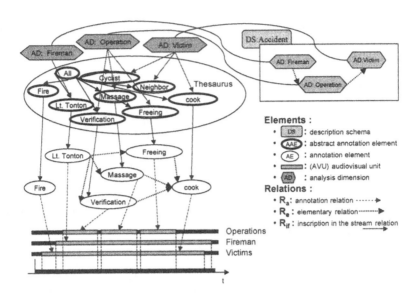

Fig. 1. The several layers composing the annotation graph in E-SIA.

Thesaurus Creation and Structuring

Even for one user, the creation and management of a structured annotation vocabulary is a difficult task. The user looks for terms he wants to use to annotate. If he doesn't find them he can create them. He groups the terms in analysis dimensions, organizes the analysis dimensions in description schemes and begins the annotation. While annotating he reiterates the thesaurus management operations. When creating a new term, some analysis dimensions may have to be updated. When a new type of document is being described for the first time, new analysis dimensions and description schemes may need to be created.

When the system is used by several users the vocabulary management becomes much more complex. In this case the diffusion of single user's structures, and their comprehension and adaptation by others is to be considered.

By grouping the terms (AAE) of the thesaurus in sets (expressed by analysis dimensions) we avoid the structuring of the vocabulary in a class hierarchy. A term can be part of several analysis dimensions. An analysis dimension is always created for a precise task, terms can be added one by one, but it can be completed by other analysis dimensions. We preserve a "trace", that is to say a record, of operations made on an analysis dimension to be able to follow its evolution.

In E-SIA it is impossible to delete an element after it has been used for annotation. This way we prevent incoherence and updating problems, every created element remains coherent with its "origins". If the user wants to restrict an analysis dimension he has to create a new one.

Thesaurus Sharing and Reuse

In this section we present some tools allowing us to *a priori* document and constrain annotation structures and other tools which permit us to analyze existing annotations *a posteriori* in order to discover the methods and structures used by those who created these annotations. These tools "upstream" and "downstream" of the annotation will both serve the users in their describing and searching tasks.

As we said before, we suppose that annotation is done by different people, possibly clustered in groups. Each group has its own analysis dimensions and description schemes. In order to exploit the annotations created by a group, an external user can consult their analysis dimensions and description schemes (*a priori* tools) in order to build more precise queries. For the research and exploitation of annotations (*a posteriori* tools) we set up methods based on the navigation in the annotation graph, we created a tool based on the graph structure to represent queries and we studied statistical views (inspired by the self organizing maps of Kohonen [14]) permitting the emergence of existing annotation structures. In this way the system enables a user to exploit, understand, adapt, and reuse the annotations and structures of other users. These *a posteriori* tools help users and groups to improve their own structures and annotations. They allow the emergence of practical usage information making it possible to update and adapt existing description schemes and analysis dimensions. We study these tools to "warehouse" user experience for later reuse. This retention is based on the Case Based Reasoning paradigm [1].

Having these two kinds of tools (*a priori* and *a posteriori*) and using them in a loop, we enable a considerable freedom in organizing and using the annotation vocabulary and the annotation methods. At the same time we enable easy discovery and comprehension of preexisting structures and terms. We do not constrain annotation but enable the documentation of eventual description canons.

Illustration #2 : *Porphyry 2000*

Context and Motivation

Our study is related to a digitization project by the French School of Archaeology in Athens[3]. This project will provide online access to one of the main periodicals: "La Chronique des fouilles", an annual survey of archeological excavations and discoveries. This corpus has been chosen since although its size is reasonable (about 12,000 pages), it is nearly exhaustive in regard to the past 80 years of archaeological activity in Greece and Cyprus. In addition, the "Chronique" is read daily in libraries throughout the world.

We must stress that the information retrieval problem is not new concerning the "Chronique". Publishers have tried for 80 years to make it easier to consult. It is comprised of small independent parts (about 50,000) which are hierarchically structured and indexed according to artifact location, dating and typology.

---

[3] Ecole française d'Athènes (http://www.efa.gr)

Archaeologists who have tried retrieval systems based on automatic indexing or manual indexing using thesauri have found neither satisfactory. The former is considered inadequate because it deals with out-of-context terms. The latter is hard to manage over time by the indexing team since it needs periodic updates of both thesauri and indexes in order to reflect scientific progress.

As an example, there was several years ago a disagreement between two archaeologists about whether mosaic borders with the meander design was black or white (often ambiguous). An automatic indexing system would have extracted only the point of view in the text. Moreover, without knowing whose point of view it is, the index could not have been interpreted. As a second example, when the Copper Age was inserted in the chronology between the Neolithic Period and the Bronze Age, the thesaurus-based systems required that many documents be reinterpreted and re-indexed.

System Overview

Porphyry 2000 is a client-server system designed to create, retrieve, and share documents and annotations (see Fig. 2). The annotation structure is an acyclic graph of descriptors, which formally signifies that if, for two descriptors D_1 and D_2, $D_1 \rightarrow D_2$, then any document described by D_2 is described by D_1 too. It is worth mentioning that only edges and nodes have significance for the system. But, so that users can interpret the graph, we store labels too. Node labels contain short descriptions and edge labels contain information (see the edge popup label in Fig. 2 at the center) about their creation (user, date) and publication (group, date). As long as the formal signification of this framework is observed, users are free to use it in order to represent: specialization, composition, attributes, attribute values, relations, etc (see Fig. 3).

Formally, the annotation structure looks like what is misleadingly called an "ontology". But, as we will see in the next three parts, its use is radically different. And this is sufficient partially to solve problems concerning creation, evolution, fusion, diffusion, and learning of this structure.

Model Creation and Evolution

Usually, describing a document is considered a question of "metadata" chosen by authors, editors or librarians. Therefore, we have given the system the ability to reuse the indexes and title hierarchies contained in documents. However this type of information is necessary but definitely not sufficient. Indeed, even if indexing were perfectly done, this would result in impoverishment of meaning. A document is an *open work* (see Umberto Eco [9]). Its meaning is given not only by the author or by the indexing professional but also by the whole of its readership.

We should note that this approach is particularly adapted to the scientists that our system is designed for. Indeed, for modern science there is no definitive knowledge but only testable theories [21]. Conformity to reality is set in a new way. The scientific tool is refutation: it is by refuting hypotheses that science progresses.

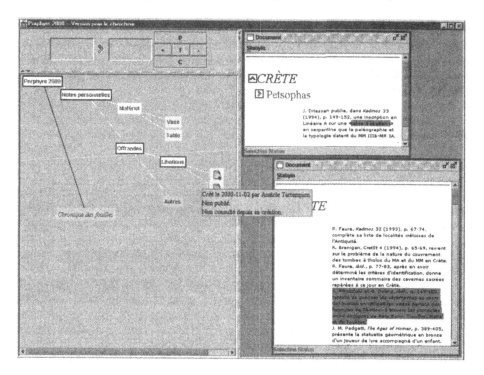

Fig. 2. *Porphyry 2000* screenshot: annotations and documents.

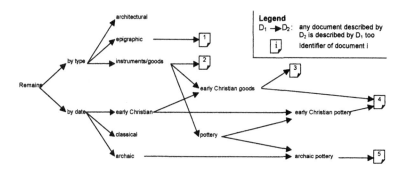

Fig. 3. Sample personal annotations.

Reader augmentation in digital libraries (as in *Synchrony* [12]) is the subject of a recent user study by Kenton O'Hara *et al.* [19]. This study concerned the document–related research activities of Ph.D. students during a working day. It appears that their tasks go beyond the traditional searching and retrieving of information. They also take notes, photocopy, read, annotate, review information, and write documents. In short, they are not only knowledge "consumers" but also knowledge "producers".

In our system, the metaphor used to represent user augmentations is "annotation" (as in *Yawas* [8]) pointing at explicit document parts (chapters, sections…) or zones highlighted by the user (see Fig. 2). Owing to the annotation structure, annotations can be collected or distinguished just as in a thematic bibliography or in the contents of an article. One of the main benefits of these personal descriptions over institutional ones is their flexibility. In fact, like draft pages, they have to "reflect" at any moment the "mind trail" of the reader.

Model Diffusion and Fusion

Because a library is not a document warehouse but a place for social interactions (see Klaus Tochtermann [24] and Andreas Paepcke [20]), the digital library must provide ways to share ideas. In our system, we do so by disseminating personal annotations and documents. But, given the knowledge of each individual, what is the knowledge of the group? Expressed in a different way: "How do we get a syntactic and semantic coherence from these different (and even contradictory) models?" If these questions are raised for Knowledge Managing in general, they find a traditional answer in the scientific praxis: *publication.*

Indeed "publication" (making public) is the key of scientific knowledge construction. Owing to pair critics (from working groups to colloquiums), scientific theories are either refuted or corroborated. In the traditional publication process, the "publishers" (real publishers, reviewers, committees...) check submitted papers regarding form and contents in order to ensure their validity for the group.

As a result we propose that in our system scientists can choose to join groups headed by "publishers" they regard as authorities. Then their annotation graph and/or documents can be "published" through the reviewing process chosen by the group.

One should note that "auto-publication" (such as a "home page" on the web) can be supported by the system as a borderline case. This is a publication in a group of limited authority, with no editorial constraints, which will have probably very few "subscribers".

Of course, the reviewing process will not resolve all the contradictions within a group. Moreover it will have little effect on the contradictions between groups. But we should emphasize that every annotation or document is situated (by its author, group, writing date, publication date). Therefore each point of view can be interpreted, and even the conflicts "make sense". The progress of science is a history of polemics within and among scientific communities (see Thomas S. Kühn [15]).

Model Learning & Practice Emergence

One of the challenge of our system is to assist the researcher in learning others' theoretic models. By showing current practices, the system should help the researcher to reuse those models with which he/she agrees.

Our model consists in filtering the annotation graph during the navigation between document corpora. The principles we use are described in depth in our prior works [3][4]. In a few words, this principle can be compared with the "auto-completion" featured by some shells or browsers. But the structure it deals with is not hierarchical but acyclic (a "child" can have several "fathers"). Given a selection of descriptors, it consists in inducing some descriptors, in interdicting others, and in suggesting others.

Therefore, from selection to selection, the user navigates through corpora until he/she finds the most pertinent one.

Owing to our system's ability to give a synthetic view of the annotation graph, we can go without thesauri. By letting practices emerge, the system can guide the user in reading (retrieval) and writing (indexing) phases. However this kind of approach, because it is *inductive*, could raise logicians' suspicion. In fact, it only consists in summing up (by classifying) known cases. The user is free to reuse the inducted rules for new cases or to amplify them in a theoretic model.

Synthesis: Hermeneutical Guidelines for Digital Libraries

In the preceding parts, we have shown two digital library systems in which it has been possible to do away with Ontological assumptions. It is time to propose a few general guidelines to apply hermeneutics to digital libraries. We claim that, as in any complex activity, library use is composed of "methodic" tasks and "creative" ones. The former are "conventional" and can be modeled through a *normative* process. The latter are a "matter of discussion" and should be modeled through a *hermeneutic* process. To computerize such a process is quite delicate. On the one hand, if we formalize it too much, we make it "normalized". On the other hand, if we formalize it too little, we cannot provide utilities. Since we want to build an "Assisted Interpretation System", the only aspects we should fix are those concerning the hermeneutical process itself.

First, the system must deal with interpretable artifacts (called "document contents" in a broad sense) and not with signs whose signification is given. Therefore, it is a *documentary system* and not a factual nor a data system ("data" means "given things" in Latin). Moreover, one way for a reader to "make sense" consists in comparing various sources. As a matter of fact, documents "select" sense in each other by being read together (see Rastier). So, the system must provide the ability to compare documents (as with the "viewing positions" in the "Memex" [5]). and to gather them in perennial corpora (as in PreSS [7]). Furthermore, the system must offer not only *sources* but also supplementary readings provided as a basis for their critical study (*apparatus criticus*). In addition, the system must be able to show the source either in its original integrity or enriched with its *apparatus.* We should note that the *apparatus* can be considered as documents too and so can be interpreted and criticized.

Second, the system must store and process *interpretation traces.* Although *interpretation trails* are mental and probably unknowable, a system can capture "traces" which, once interpreted by a human, call to mind the original trails or other ones. These reading "traces" can be navigation log files, annotations, links between corpora, new documents, mediated social interactions… We must stress that in order to be interpreted the traces must be both *contextualized* and *situated.* By "context" (etymologically, "woven together") we mean the traces which are linked to one another. By "situation" we mean not only the "here and now" from linguistic pragmatics but also the persons involved, their practice and culture.

Third, the system must provide users the ability to share their personal interpretation traces. Through the conflicts of interpretation that will arise, users can go beyond subjectivity towards *intersubjectivity.* Also, any assisted interpretation system should allow storage of conflicts (An interesting research direction could also be to provide utilities to assist users and groups in identifying and/or solving some of them). Last but not least, we saw that there is no constraint by default on how to describe a document. But, in order to support group practices, it is recommended that groups be able to add their own rules to the system (like DTDs in XML).

Conclusion

In this paper we have discussed the ontological and hermeneutical approach to digital libraries. Digital libraries are *par excellence* information universes used by many people. We have seen that there can not be a universal consensus between all these people from an ontological point of view, so other techniques must be used in order to make the system optimal. We argued that the key issue of *truth* in digital libraries is related to the point of view, the way people interpret terms.

In order to formulate some guidelines for "Assisted Interpretation Systems", we presented two projects related to digital libraries produced by our teams. We discussed creation, structuring, evolution, diffusion, fusion, learning, and reuse questions of *thesauri* and models. We reached the conclusion that AIS should be *human centered*, should enable the clarification of personal points of view and metaphors. It has to tolerate conflicts between humans and help them to overcome these conflicts by communication. It should be a mediation tool permitting the emergence of common practices. In practice, we argue that the system must deal with interpretable artifacts ("document contents" in a broad sense), must store *interpretation traces* and enable their shared use.

We plan to continue developing systems enabling the retention and reuse of collective experience. Beyond this goal, we also intend to study computer-assisted detection of conflict of interpretation.

References

[1] AAMODT A. & PLAZA E. (1994). Case-based reasoning: Foundational issues, methodological variations, and system approaches. In *Artificial Intelligence Communications. Volume 7, Issue 1.* IOS Press. pp.39-59.

[2] ARISTOTLE (4th century BC). *Organon: Categories and Interpretation.*

[3] BENEL A., CALABRETTO S., PINON J.-M. & IACOVELLA A. (2000a). Vers un outil documentaire unifié pour les chercheurs en archéologie. In *Proceedings of the 17th Congress on Informatics and Organizations (INFORSID).* In French. INFORSID Editions, Toulouse (France). pp.133-145. ISBN 2-906855-16-2.

[4] BENEL A., CALABRETTO S., PINON J.-M. & IACOVELLA A. (2000b). Consultation de documents et sémantique : Application à des publications savantes. In *Proceedings of the 2nd International French Speaking Colloquium on Writing and Document (CIFED).* In French. PPUR Editions, Lausanne (Switzerland). pp.271-280. ISBN 2-88074-460-1.

[5] BUSH V. (1945) As we may think. In: *The Atlantic Monthly. July 1945.*

[6] BOUAUD J., BACHIMONT B., CHARLET J. & ZWEIGENBAUM P. (1994). Acquisition and structuring of an ontology within conceptual graphs. In *Proceedings of ICCS'94 Workshop on Knowledge Acquisition using Conceptual Graph Theory.* pp.1-25.

[7] COX D. & GREENBERG S. (2000). Supporting collaborative interpretation in distributed groupware. In *Proceedings on the ACM CSCW'2000 Conference on Computer Supported Cooperative Work.* pp.289-298.

[8] DENOUE L. & VIGNOLLET L. (2000). An annotation tool for web browsers and its applications to information retrieval. In *RIAO'2000 Conference Proceedings. "Content-based multimedia information access".* CID-CASIS. pp.180-195.

[9] ECO U. (1962). *The Open Work.* 4th revised edition and English translation. Harvard University Publishing, 1989.

[10] EGYED-ZS. E., PRIE Y., MILLE A. & PINON J.-M. (2000). A graph based audio-visual document annotation and browsing system. In *RIAO'2000 Conference Proceedings. "Content-based multimedia information access".* CID-CASIS. pp.1381-1389. ISBN 2-905450-07-X

[11] GUARINO N. (1997). Some organizing principles for a unified top-level ontology. In *Proceedings of AAAI 1997 Spring Symposium on Ontological Engineering.* AAAI Press.

[12] GOH D. & LEGGETT J. (2000). Patron-augmented digital libraries. In *Proceedings of the Fifth ACM Conference on Digital Libraries.* pp.153-163.

[13] GRUBER T.R. (1993). A translation approach to portable ontology specifications. In *Knowledge Acquisition. Volume 5, Issue 2.* pp.199-220.

[14] KOHONEN T. & KASKI S. (2000). Self Organization of a Massive Document Collection. In *IEEE Transactions on Neural Networks, Volume 11, Issue 3.* pp.574-585

[15] KÜHN T.S. (1962). *The Structure of Scientific Revolutions.* University of Chicago Press.

[16] LEHMANN P. (1994). CCAT: The current status of the conceptual catalogue (Ontology) group with proposals. In *Proceedings of the Fourth International Workshop on Peirce, "A conceptual Graph Workbench".*

[17] MENZIES T. (1999). Cost benefits of ontologies. In *ACM Magazine on Intelligence : New Visions of AI in Practice. Volume 10, Issue 3.* pp.26-32.

[18] MITRA P. & WIEDERHOLD G. (2000). A Graph-Oriented Model for Articulation of Ontology Interdependencies. *Proceedings of the EDBT'2000 Conference on Extending Database Technology.* Springer. 15p.

[19] O'HARA K., SMITH F., NEWMAN W. & SELLEN A. (1998). Student readers' use of library documents: implications for library technologies. In *ACM CHI'98 Conference Proceedings on Human Factors in Computing Systems.* pp.233-240.

[20] PAEPCKE A. (1996). Digital libraries: Searching is not Enough. What we learned on-site. In *D-Lib Magazine. May 1996.*

[21] POPPER K.R. (1972). *Objective Knowledge: an Evolutionary Approach.* Clarendon Press.

[22] PRIE Y., MILLE A. & PINON J.-M. (1999). A Context-Based Audiovisual Representation Model for Audiovisual Information Systems. In *Context'99, Second International and Interdisciplinary Conference on Modeling and using Context, Trento (Italy).* pp.296-309.

[23] RASTIER F. (1995). Le terme : entre ontologie et linguistique. In *La banque des mots, n°7.*

[24] TOCHTERMANN K. (1994). A first step toward communication in virtual libraries. In *First Annual Conference on the Theory and Practice of Digital Libraries. College Station (Texas). June 19-21 1994.*

XSL-based Content Management for Multi-presentation Digital Museum Exhibitions

Jen-Shin Hong, Bai-Hsuen Chen, Jieh Hsiang

Dept. of Computer Science and Information Engineering
National ChiNan University, Taiwan
{jshong,hsiang}@csie.ncnu.edu.tw

Abstract. Similar to a conventional museum, a digital museum draws a set of objects from its collection of digital artifacts to produce exhibitions about a specific topic. Online exhibitions often consist of a variety of multimedia objects such as webpages, animation, and video clips. In a physical museum, the exhibition is confined by the physical limitation of the artifacts. That is, there can only be *one* exhibition using the same set of artifacts. Thus, if one wishes to design different exhibitions about the same topic for different user groups, one has to use different sets of artifacts, and exhibit them in different physical locations.

A digital museum does not have such physical restrictions. One can design different exhibitions about the same topic for adults, children, experts, novices, high bandwidth users, and low bandwidth users, all using the same set of digital artifacts. A user can simply click and choose the specific style of exhibition that she wants to explore. The difficulty here is that it is time-consuming to produce illustrative and intriguing online exhibitions. One can spend hours designing webpages for just one exhibition alone, not to mention several. In this paper, we present the design of an XSL-based Multi-Presentation Content Management System (XMP-CMS). This framework is a novel approach for organizing digital collections, and for quickly selecting, integrating, and composing objects from the collection to produce exhibitions of different presentation styles, one for each user group. A prototype based on our framework has been implemented and successfully used in the production of a Lanyu digital museum. Using our method, the Lanyu Digital Museum online exhibition has several features: (1) It provides an easy way to compose artifacts extracted from the digital collection into exhibitions. (2) It provides an easy way to create different presentations of the same exhibition content that are catered to users with different needs. (3) It provides easy-to-use film-editing capability to re-arrange an exhibition and to produce new exhibitions from existing ones.

1 Introduction

While a digital library focuses on conserving, cataloging, accessing, and tracking the usage of digitized material [1], a digital museum also emphasizes on providing users with highly educational and motivating exhibitions [2,3]. To this end, the system architecture developed for digital museum goes beyond a simple "query-and-answer" approach that is typical for most digital library systems.

P. Constantopoulos and I.T. Sølvberg (Eds.): ECDL 2001, LNCS 2163, pp. 378-389, 2001.

The workflow of creating an exhibition in a museum roughly works as follow. First, the topic of the exhibition is decided. Then a scenario is designed, according to which the artifacts necessary for the exhibition are selected from the museum collections. The exhibition is then implemented. If an accompanying exhibition about the same topic, say specifically designed for children, is to be presented at the same time, the same process pretty much needs to be done again. At this level, the main difference between a physical museum and a digital one is only on the type of material with which the designer is working.

While a person working in a physical museum needs to deal with real artifacts and space limitation, a digital museum designer implements the virtual exhibitions using digital images, webpages, animation, video clips, and other multimedia gadgets [4]. Although there is no space and related limitations in the cyber world, there are other factors that a digital designer needs to consider. For instance, the bandwidth that is available to different users can vary tremendously. Attention span is another factor. While an adult may be willing to go through long explanations in text, a child may prefer graphic-intensive slideshows. Furthermore, the sophistication of users should also be considered. An expert and a novice apparently will expect different experiences when browsing through a digital museum. With the flexibility allowed to the digital form of media presentation, a digital museum should try to accommodate as many different user needs as possible. And a user, when browsing through an exhibition, can simply click and choose the style most suitable.

While most people might agree that such a multi-style exhibition scheme for different users is desirable, there are not so many such exhibitions on the Web today. The reason is that using current techniques, each style of the same exhibition needs to be constructed separately. For online exhibitions involving video, animation, or SMIL-based shows, the realization of an exhibition scenario usually requires tedious multimedia composing, and is thereby very time-consuming. It is also quite cumbersome to modify the information content afterwards. If an online exhibition uses mainly HTML-based webpages, the resulting pages are relatively easy to compose, but they are also tight up with the visual art design and are thereby difficult to be modified by the content-provider alone. Furthermore, once the information content grows to a significant amount, the "hyperlinks" between associated exhibition webpages are difficult to track and maintain.

The second problem with the hand-crafted online exhibition approach is that the content can only be presented to the user in a fixed presentation style. Since the Web users may have different multimedia and bandwidth capacities, it is difficult to design a one-size-fit-all exhibition. This indeed hinders the educational functions of the digital museum.

Our goal is to design an optimal solution for building online digital museum exhibitions. In the literature, while large and coordinated efforts have focused on standardizing media formats, providing shared access to museum databases, and developing search mechanisms for data retrieval [1], little emphasis is placed on designing mechanisms for turning the digitized museum collection into educational experiences for users. In this paper, we will present the design of an XSL-based Multi-Presentation Content Management System (XMP-CMS) that provides a novel approach for organizing, integrating, and composing the digital museum collection into multi-style exhibitions to accommodate different user needs. In the following sections, we will introduce the design issues and the framework of the XMP-CMS. A testbed system implemented for the Lanyu Digital Museum will then be addressed to demonstrate the performance of the proposed framework.

2 Design Issues of Digital Museum Exhibitions

In this section we describe some design issues that our framework for constructing online exhibitions needs to address.

An exhibition can be regarded as a choreographed presentation of a certain topic using artifacts from a museum. We call the choreography the script of the exhibition. An online exhibition, from the user's viewpoint, can be treated as a sequence of webpages. (A webpage can, of course, contain complex objects such as a video clip.) We call each of these webpages an exhibition element. In our methodology, we address three issues which we consider central to producing flexible and easy to use exhibitions.

1. There should be an easy way to produce exhibition elements from the digital archive of the digital museum.
2. Once an exhibition is produced, there should be an easy way to create different presentation styles suitable for different users.
3. There should be an easy way to re-arrange an existing exhibition to accommodate different user need and to make new exhibitions from existing ones.

In the following we address our solution to these three issues.

The digital artifacts of the museum are stored in a multimedia database. Our approach treats each of them as a building block and provides a mechanism for drawing them easily to form XML documents. Each XML document is then an exhibition element.

For the second point, we note that an exhibition should accommodate users of different interests, backgrounds, sophistication, and computer/network capacity. Conventional online exhibitions often only provide a single presentation for all the users. If one must convey the same message to all the users, one is faced with the problem of choosing a single representational form that is deemed most suitable for the largest user population. The outcome is usually a compromise. This certainly is not an optimal solution.

In our approach we provide an easy way to generate multi-style exhibitions with the same exhibition elements. This means that the same exhibition may appear in different ways to different users, with different multimedia styles and levels of detail. The deciding factors include (1) the user's network bandwidth, (2) the user's Web browser, and (3) the user profile. For example, when interacting with school children with multimedia-capable computers and high bandwidth network, the system can provide high-resolution graphics and slide shows overlaid with narrative audio data.

On the other extreme, for a domain expert keen on information content, the system may only provide static pages with loads of text information but little visual fanfare to reduce the data transmission. This is done by designing different style sheets (XSL) for different purposes. Coupling the exhibition elements with a specific style sheet produces an exhibition for a user group. Note, for instance, that a style sheet for "lower bandwidth" consumers will automatically drop all the audio and video.

The third issue also has to do with different user needs. An exhibition designed according to a script may be suitable for adults but too long for children. The designer may want to re-organize the order of the exhibition elements in the sequence for different people. She may also want to combine several exhibitions and make a more extensive one. Our method provides an easy way to make such "film-editing".

It is also desirable to make an exhibition into a slide show, which automatically runs through all the exhibition elements. We call this *auto-navigation*, and is also provided in our method.

3 Framework

In this section we describe our method, an XSL-based Multi-Presentation Content Management System (XMP-CMS) framework (Figure 1) for the resource organizing of the digital museum exhibition, in detail. An XML-based exhibition element can be presented in multi-styles using different XSL documents. We hope the system can present the collections in a more vivid and rich manner.

Our system takes a realistic approach to construct digital museum exhibitions based on XML and XSL techniques [5,6,7], which is more suitable for description and presentation of hierarchical media structures and operations than a traditional relational database. The Data Type Definition (DTD) of XML imposes less restrictive and permits more variation in the data than conventional database schemes do. In this stage, both Microsoft and Netscape have announced that new version of their respective browsers will contain XML processors, which can parse XML documents and make the resulting tree structures available for subsequent data manipulation. Also, XML has gradually becomes the emerging standard for information exchange on Internet. On the other hand, to facilitate the presentation of XML documents on WWW, the W3C has specified and Extensible Style Sheet Language (XSL) for convenient presentation and display of XML documents over WWW. XSL can rearrange document structure, making it strictly more powerful than Cascading Style Sheets. Based on the abovementioned features of XML and XSL, we believe that an XML/XSL-based framework is capable to fulfill the system requirements of multi-style presentation digital museum exhibitions.

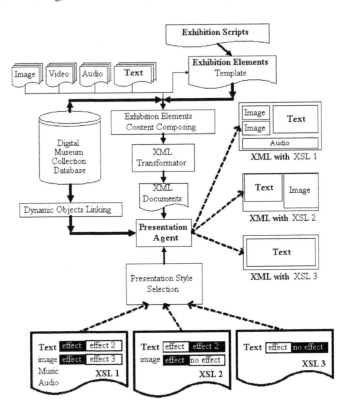

Fig. 1. The framework of the XSL-based Multi-Presentation Content Management System. An XML-based exhibition element can be presented in multi-styles using different XSL documents.

In the framework, the exhibition scripts of the digital museum are differentiated to a sequence of "exhibition elements" based on an XML-based conceptual hypermedia document model. The conceptual representation of the exhibition elements is composed from several concrete digital objects managed by museum database. Using the XSL to present the XML documents, the system is able to select in a more or less automatic way the set of suitable presentations according to the user needs.

The main components of the XMP-CMS framework are the following:

- An XML-based conceptual document model, able to express a unique, formal representation of the content of a typical hypermedia document in digital museum exhibitions. The document content should include different types of information: text, data, table, graphics, images, hyperlinks, and so on.
- An authoring environment for editing the layouts and media presentation effects of XSL documents which provide different presentation styles for the XML documents of exhibition elements.
- An database management system providing operational environment for creating, viewing, editing, storing, and retrieving documents, through a set of tools for manipulating texts, table, graphic and images.

- A user-interface for selecting the suitable mappings between the contents and the presentations both during the initial document authoring activity, and during its successive reading.

3.1 XML-based Hypermedia Document Model for Exhibition Elements

Generally speaking, the common document component types [8] in a typical multimedia document could include the structural text, data series (e.g., spreadsheet-like tables), graphic representations of functions and tabular data, geometric drawing, animations, video, etc. Yet, in this stage, our XMP-CMS considers the following simplified hypermedia documents component types for the digital museum exhibition elements:

- Description text that are classified in three subclasses: (1) the title, (2) the main description of an exhibition element, and (3) the hyperlink address representing the ancestor nodes, descendants nodes, collateral nodes, and media objects.
- Images: including the information images and background images.
- Audios: including content narration of the exhibition element and background music.

In the future we plan to define more robust XML-based conceptual document model for representing the exhibition elements XML documents.

3.2 XSL-based Multi-style Presentation

The Extensible Style sheet Language (XSL) is used for versatile/convenient presentation of the exhibition element XML documents over WWW. The XSL documents specify the layout and presentation style of the title, main description text, image, audio, and hyperlinks in an exhibition element. Furthermore, to give the users a vivid and rich presentation of the museum collections, numerous presentation and transition effects of the texts, images are incorporated into the XSL documents using sophisticated Java-Script technology.

In our design, a XSL document contains three major functional blocks (1) XML Parser: to analyze and extract the tags in the XML documents representing exhibition elements. (2) Layout Modules: for organizing the layout of the textual/multimedia objects appears in an exhibition element. (3) Media Effect Modules: for incorporating various special effects for the media presentation using Java-Script techniques.

3.3 Digital Museum Resource Management System

Figure 2 shows the major components of the digital museum resource management system. The digital museum management system supports the efficient execution of the essential administrative and documents organization/presentation related activities, and is characterized by the following features:

1. Input of multimedia digital objects, including the text, images, audio, video.

2. Organizing, composing, and integration of the XML-based multimedia exhibition element documents.

3. Management of the XSL documents for presentation.

4. Definition and management of user profiles.

5. Management of the document presentations according the user needs and profiles.

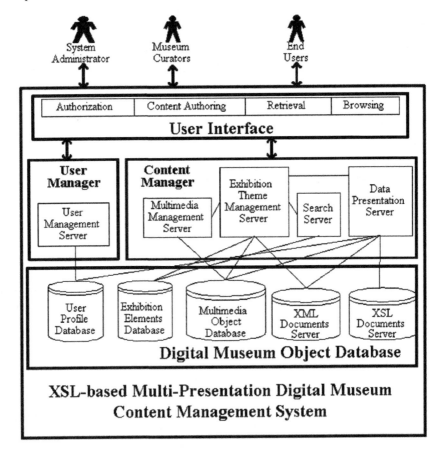

Fig. 2. The major components of the digital museum resource management system.

4 System Implementation - A Case Study in the Lanyu Digital Museum

Based on the aforementioned XSL-based Multi-Presentation Content Management System (XMP-CMS) framework, we have built a digital museum for the Lanyu Island

and its inhabitants, the Yami people. Lanyu is an island off the coast of southeastern Taiwan, and the Yami are a part of the Austronesian group. Lanyu has many unique species of plants and animals not found anywhere in the world. Unlike the other indigenous groups of Taiwan, the Yami people, also called Dao, were originated from the Batan Islands of the Philippines. By providing a digital museum incorporating the cultural, geographical, and biological aspects of Lanyu, we hope to present Lanyu in its entirety.

The project is sponsored by the National Science Council of the Republic of China, and is jointly developed by the National Chi-Nan University and the National Museum of Natural Science. The Lanyu Digital Museum is accessible through the Web at http://dlm.ncnu.edu.tw. The digital museum indeed provides an interactive educational environment for the general public on the cultural/biological diversities of the Lanyu, as well as a modern research environment for academic institutions. The Lanyu digital museum contains four modules: (1) the Lanyu Virtual Exhibition Hall: for introducing the essential cultural, geographical, and biological issues regarding the Lanyu Island and Yami. (2) Digital Collection Archives- for organizing and depositing the digital objects of Lanyu in a systematical and efficient manner. (3) Information Discovery Interfaces- for providing multi-facet information retrieval interfaces to meet the need of different users. (4) Personalization Server- for managing the user profiles and logging the user behavior to provide user-dependent presentations of the virtual collections/exhibitions.

The diversity of the digital subjects in the Lanyu Digital Museum indeed presented a challenge to the overall design of the digital museum system. The most unique technical feature in the Lanyu Digital Museum is the XML/XSL-based Lanyu Virtual Exhibition Hall. Conventionally, the virtual exhibitions in a digital museum are constructed using massive cross-linked HTML documents or graphic-intensive animations to present the content, and are extremely time-consuming to construct and maintain. And, based on the conventional approach, it is not probable for the digital museum exhibition to present the contents differently, to accommodate the users' personal preferences and different network bandwidths.

Based on the XMP-CMS framework proposed, we have implemented a Digital Museum Resource Management System for constructing the Lanyu Virtual Exhibition Hall. The exhibition scripts provided by the content expert, are first partitioned into a sequence of exhibition elements, and are organized using a relational database. The information contents in the database are also transformed into a groups of XML documents representing the respective scenes in the exhibition scripts. The cross-linkages between the associated XML documents act as the dynamic hyperlinks in the resulting webpages presented to the users.

To present the XML documents in different fashions for users of different interests, backgrounds, sophistication, and computer/network capacity, several groups of XSL documents are used for multi-style presentation. Various web-based Java-scripting codes are inserted into the XSL documents to provide more intriguing multimedia presentation of the exhibitions elements.

4.1 Content Authoring Interface of the Lanyu Digital Museum

The content authoring interfaces provide the content experts a user-friendly tool to input/organize the multimedia objects and the exhibition elements. Through the interface, the context experts first create the fundamental hierarchical structure of the exhibition based on the exhibition scripts designed. The textual content of each exhibition elements is then input through the content authoring interface using simple "fill-the-blank" method. In our system, the museum curators can easily compose the online exhibition without any technical backgrounds for the HTML pages composition.   Figure 3 shows the user interface for the authoring of exhibiton elements and hierarchical structure of exhibition scripts.

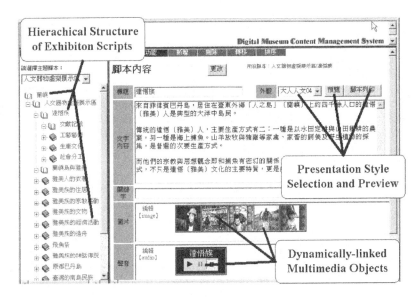

Fig. 3. The user interface for the authoring of exhibition elements and hierarchical structures of exhibition scripts.

In the XMP-CMS framework, all the texts, images, audio clips of the exhibition elements are deposited separately in the multimedia object database. The content expert can browse or search the multimedia database to locate specific media object to link to an exhibition element. The information contents of all exhibition elements are managed using a relational database. These information content are also translated into XML documents for XSL-based multi-style presentations. For each exhibition element, a keyword is provided for the purpose of fine-grained content retrieval of the museum exhibitions. Furthermore, the system provides easy-to-use "film-editing" functions for the content author to re-organize the hierarchical structures of the exhibition scripts for different user groups.   Figure 3 shows the content authoring interface in the Lany Digital Museum.

4.2 Multi-style Content Presentations

In the current stage, the Lany Digital Museum provides hundreds of XSL documents that present the exhibition elements in various multimedia styles. These XSL documents specify the layout and presentation style of the title, main textual description, image, audio, and hyperlinks in an exhibition element. To provide vivid multimedia presentations other than static pages, numerous transition effects of the texts, images are also encoded into the XSL documents using Java-Script. In certain cases, to give the end-user more "virtual" feeling of an online slide shows, the "skin" of the presentation windows are designed to "frame" the presentation (Figure 4).

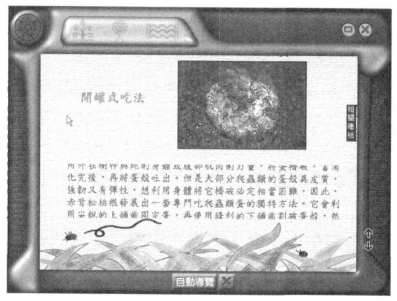

Fig. 4. A snapshot of an exhibition element presented using the "High-bandwidth children version". The presentation is framed by a toy-like "browser skin" to create a more entertaining browsing environment for the children. The text is presented with larger fonts.

The style sheets XSL of the Lanyu virtual exhibition are classified into three major categories: the "high-bandwidth adult version", "high-bandwidth child version", and "low-bandwidth version". The adult and child version present the exhibition elements using narrated multimedia online slide shows style. This usually requires high network bandwidth for the user to experience vivid multimedia presentations. The presentations in the children version is decorated with interesting interface with larger fonts and more amusing narration. Both the adult and child versions provide the "auto-navigation" functions, which automatically run through the exhibition elements based on the sequence specified in the XMP-CMS. On the other hand, for a domain expert keen on the information content, or users with low bandwidth network connections, the low bandwidth version provides static pages with little visual fanfare to reduce the data transmission.

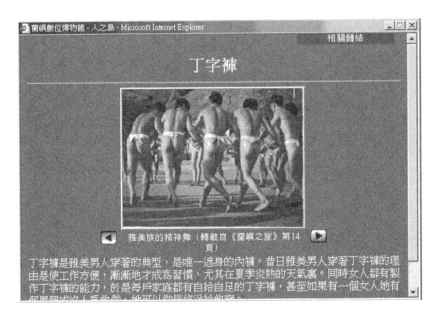

Fig. 5. A snapshot of an exhibition element presented in the "Low-bandwidth version". The presentation provides static pages with little visual fanfare for users print easily the content.

5 Conclusions

In this paper we present the design of an XSL-based Multi-Presentation Content Management System (XMP-CMS). The framework provides mechanism for quickly producing multi-style exhibitions from a digital collection. The effectiveness of the methodology is amply demonstrated in the Lanyu Digital Museum. Based on XMP-CMS, the Lanyu Digital Museum exhibition contains several novel features which seem superior to the conventional approaches: (1) It provides an easy way to compose artifacts extracted from the digital collection into exhibitions. (2) It provides an easy way to create different presentations of the same exhibition content that are catered to users with different needs. (3) It provides easy-to-use film-editing capability to re-arrange an exhibition and to produce new exhibitions from existing ones. (4) It provides *auto-navigation* functions which automatically runs through all the exhibition elements.

In the future we plan to define more robust XML-based conceptual document model for representing the exhibition element. The model should include more detail specifications of the textual and media objects that may appear in the digital museum exhibition. Also, the synchronization issues for the concurrent presentation of heterogeneous media objects [10,11] will be explored in depth in our feature work.

Acknowledgment

The project is sponsored by the National Science Council of Republic of China, numbered NSC-89-2750-P-260-001. The Lanyu Digital Museum Project is a joint effort of the National Chi-Nan University and the National Museum of Natural Science. It would not have been possible without the active participation of many colleagues, assistants, and students. We would especially like to thank the support of the NMNS Museum Curator, Dr. Yien-Shing Chou and his staff.

References

1.   Su-Shing Chen, Digital Libraries- The Life Cycle of Information, BE Publisher, Columbia, USA, 1998.
2.   Junichi Takahashi, et al. Global Digital Museum, Multimedia information access and creation in the Internet; Proceedings of the third ACM Conference on Digital libraries, 1998, pp. 244 – 253.
3.   Jen-Shin Hong, Herng-Yow Chen and Jieh Hsiang; A digital museum of Taiwanese butterflies, in Proc. of the fifth ACM conference on ACM 2000 digital libraries, 2000, pp. 260 – 261.
4.   Rutledge L., et al., Practical application of existing hypermedia standards and tools, in Proc. Of the 3rd ACM Conference on Digital Libraries (Pittsburgh, June 23-26,1998), ACM Press, pp. 191-199.
5.   Royappa, Andrew V. Implementing catalog clearinghouses with XML and XSL. In Proceedings of the 1999 ACM symposium on Applied computing 1999, pp. 616 – 621.
6.   XSL, http://www.w3.org/Style/XSL/.
7.   XML, http://www.w3.org/XML/.
8.   Augusto Celentano, SilvanoPozzi, and Donato Toppeta. A Multiple Presentation Document Management System. In Proceedings of the 10th ACM annual international conference on Systems documentation 1992, pp. 63-71.
9.   Marshall, C. C. Making metadata a study of metadata creation for a mixed physical-digital collection, in Proc. Of the 3rd ACM Conference on Digital Libraries (Pittsburgh, June 23-26,1998), pp. 162 – 171.
10.   Tomas D.C. Little, Arif Ghafoor, and C.Y Roger Chen, Conceptual Data Models for Time-Dependent Multimedia Data. In Proc. Of Multimedia Informations systems Workshop. Temple, Arizona, Feb. 1992, pp. 86-110.
11.   Hardman, L., Bulterman, D.C.A. & Van Rossum, G., "The Amsterdam Hypermedia Model: Adding Time and Context to the Dexter Model", Communications of the *ACM* 37(2), Feb 94, pp 50-62.

Iterative Design and Evaluation of a Geographic Digital Library for University Students: A Case Study of the Alexandria Digital Earth Prototype (ADEPT)

Christine L. Borgman, Gregory H. Leazer, Anne J. Gilliland-Swetland, Rich Gazan

Dept. of Information Studies, GSE&IS Bldg., University of California, Los Angeles
Los Angeles, CA 90095-1520
{cborgman, gleazer, swetland, richg}@ucla.edu

Abstract. We report on the first two years of a five-year project to design and evaluate the Alexandria Digital Earth ProtoType (ADEPT), a digital library of geo-referenced information resources, for use in undergraduate education. To date, we have established design principles, observed classroom activities, gathered baseline data from instructors and students, and evaluated early prototypes. While students and instructors are generally enthusiastic about ADEPT, they have concerns about the effort required and the effectiveness of computer-based technologies in the classroom. Instructors vary widely in their use of instructional materials and technologies, teaching styles, and areas of expertise. Results of our work are being incorporated in an iterative cycle of design and evaluation. The paper concludes by presenting research and evaluation methods, design principles, and requirements for educational applications of digital libraries.

1 Introduction

Digital libraries have the potential to improve access to information, learning, and worker productivity. Our project is one of few that evaluates digital libraries in active use. We report on the first two years of a five-year educational evaluation study (1999-2004) of a geographic digital library in undergraduate education at the University of California, Los Angeles (UCLA) and the University of California, Santa Barbara (UCSB) [1], [2], [3], [4]. This study is part of the Alexandria Digital Earth ProtoType (ADEPT) project funded by the U.S. Digital Libraries Initiative, Phase 2 (http://www.dli2.nsf.gov). ADEPT seeks to provide instructors, teaching assistants, and students with the means to discover, manipulate, and display geographical content.

2 Evaluating Digital Libraries

Digital libraries can improve access to information resources in support of both "traditional" on-campus instruction and distance-independent learning [5], [6]. However,

P. Constantopoulos and I.T. Sølvberg (Eds.): ECDL 2001, LNCS 2163, pp. 390-401, 2001.

they are difficult to evaluate due to their technological complexity, variety of content, uses, and users, and the lack of evaluation methods and metrics. Many general criteria for usability exist, but they must be adapted intelligently to the application and the user community. Moreover, "usability" often fails to include other salient factors such as learning outcomes. While a significant body of usability studies that focus on libraries and other information systems exists, little of this work is applicable to digital libraries. Most are summative evaluation of final systems. Formative evaluation is an iterative process, designed to inform ongoing system development [7]. This approach is particularly valuable because user needs and requirements can be studied in parallel with initial stages of system design [8]. For example, the Digital Library for Earth Sciences Education (DLESE) project (http://www.dlese.org), with which ADEPT is a cooperating partner, is conducting formative evaluation by gathering scenarios from their user community of K-12 teachers. The DLESE requirements are a moving target, however, because as the community's sophistication grows, so does the number and sophistication of their requests [9]. Identifying outcomes from the use of digital libraries is best accomplished by integrating multiple forms of data collection such as observations, interviews, and document analysis, with the results iteratively applied to ongoing system design [10], [11].

Geography is a particularly fruitful area for studying the role of digital libraries in scientific thinking. Geographic information systems are widely available and geographic learning is relatively well-documented. Consensus exists that students need to learn five skill sets in order to engage in scientific thinking in geography, all of which can be aided by digital libraries: (1) asking geographic questions, (2) acquiring geographic information, (3) organizing geographic information, (4) analyzing geographic information, and (5) answering geographic questions [12]. Similarly, the U.S. National Science Education Standards [13] emphasizes "inquiry into authentic questions generated from student experiences." Although we focus on promoting geographic thinking in our project, the same kinds of skills that support geographic thinking also apply to other disciplines. The five skills can be used in inductive (or data-driven) reasoning, such as looking for trends in data that lead to a theory, or in deductive (or theory-driven) reasoning, such as testing two competing theories through dynamic modeling.

3   ADEPT for Undergraduate Learning

ADEPT is an extension and enhancement of the Alexandria Digital Library (ADL), which was developed at UCSB under the first Digital Libraries Initiative (1994-1998). ADL is an operational digital library, providing access to collections of maps, images, and other geo-referenced materials the UCSB Map and Imagery Laboratory (http://www.alexandria.ucsb.edu). ADL is now online as part of the California Digital Library (http://www.cdlib.edu). Formative evaluation of ADL focused on earth scientists, information specialists, and educators, and research methods included online surveys, ethnographic studies, a classroom study [14], and transaction logs [15]. The ADEPT project, also centered at UCSB, is applying a digital earth metaphor to the organization, use, and presentation of information at various levels of spatial and temporal resolution. A central aspect of ADEPT is the development of I-Scapes (information landscapes). I-Scapes are a means of expressing, visualizing, and manipulating geo-spatial concepts and processes for research, instruction, and learning. Our working scenario for the use of ADEPT I-Scapes is as follows:

> The course instructor identifies a topic and the associated set of concepts to be taught. Using ADEPT tools, the instructor assembles a collection of information resources on the topic to create one or more I-Scapes. I-Scape content can be drawn from the ADEPT collection and from outside sources. The instructor uses these I-Scapes to present the topic in class lecture sessions. Teaching assistants later use the I-Scapes to discuss and demonstrate the topic in laboratory sessions. Students perform exercises in lab sessions and outside class using I-Scapes to test hypotheses in the pre-selected collection of resources. Students also use ADEPT for exploratory learning. ADEPT continues to be available after the course ends, allowing students to use it in support of future courses or projects.

We are developing more specific I-Scape scenarios that detail activities on individual course topics from the perspectives of instructors, teaching assistants, and students. The scenarios and other data from the education and evaluation team are being incorporated into the design of the ADEPT system by multiple teams in this large, collaborative project. The implementation team is responsible for evolving the ADL testbed architecture and services into ADEPT, such as interface specifications, service prototypes, interoperability, and collection growth and diversity. The collections team is establishing criteria for selecting, collecting, and organizing geographic content and learning objects. Similarly, the metadata team is developing requirements for collections and services. The education and evaluation team, whose work is reported in this paper, is responsible for needs assessment, evaluating prototypes in active use, and studying scientific thinking, for the purpose of integrating evaluation in design.

3.1 Research Questions

Our over-arching research question is whether digital library services that provide instructors, teaching assistants, and students with the means to discover, manipulate, and display dynamic geographical processes will contribute positively to undergraduate instruction and to the development of scientific and other discipline-specific reasoning skills. Specific research questions include the following:

– How are geography courses presently being taught? How can knowledge of current pedagogy best be applied in the design of ADEPT?
– How can ADEPT I-Scapes and services assist students in geographic thinking?
– How can ADEPT accommodate users with different skills, knowledge, cognitive styles, and pedagogical styles?
– How can ADEPT provide the range of heterogeneous resources and metadata necessary for learning applications?

We have explored these research questions via a range of "top down" and "bottom up" evaluation methods during the first two years of the project. In years three through five we will continue the integrated usability and evaluation studies with subsequent iterations of I-Scapes in multiple classrooms in multiple disciplines.

3.2 Top-Down Approaches to Digital Library Design

We devoted the first year of the project to framing general principles and models of ADEPT use, which we deemed a "top down" approach. Activities included developing the scenario for use by faculty, teaching assistants, and students outlined above and identifying conceptual design principles that followed from the scenario and from other studies of user behavior with digital libraries and information systems [1], [2], [3], [4]. Our proposed design principles include the following:

- Usability and transparency: Beginning ADEPT users should be able to learn basic skills of ADEPT module functions and features in less than 30 minutes. Learning should focus on scientific concepts rather than on the technology of ADEPT.
- Parameter variation: I-Scapes can support interactive models of dynamic processes and hypothetical scenarios. Users can vary parameters and display results.
- Diversity and extensibility of metadata: Creators of I-Scapes should be able to integrate new resources and associated metadata and create metadata for extant resources specific to their instructional or learning activities.
- Support of disciplinary conventions: I-Scapes adhere to disciplinary conventions for concept representation such as labeling, use of color, and visual perspectives.
- Collaboration: I-Scapes should facilitate group work through collaboration tools.

3.3 Bottom-Up Approaches to Digital Library Design

While the top-down approaches are essential to providing a framework for design, they do not lead directly to programmable specifications. Our bottom-up approaches develop exemplar cases from which we can generalize design. We selected cases suggested by instructors of physical geography (erosion/fluvial processes and subduction/plate tectonics) and human geography (disease vectors). The requirements for these cases are being derived from the baseline data collection and analysis.

3.3.1 Baseline Data on Geography Instruction

Data on current instruction serves two purposes: (1) They assist us in designing I-Scape tools and services appropriate to the educational context, and (2) they provide a baseline for later comparison with ADEPT-based instruction.

One of our first steps was to consult with the chairs of the geography departments at UCSB and UCLA to identify the most appropriate courses and instructors to participate in ADEPT. The introductory courses in physical geography at both campuses were deemed best suited for initial studies. These are lower division courses (fresh-man-sophomore) that satisfy general education requirements for the bachelor's degree, so they draw students from all disciplines. UCLA offers the course three times per year (fall, winter, and spring terms). The equivalent course is taught once per year at UCSB, which is a smaller campus. All four instructors for the 1999-2000 academic year agreed to participate in the evaluation study and all four courses were observed on a regular basis by members of the ADEPT education and evaluation team. The instructors also provided copies of laboratory assignments and exams used to assess students. Observations of these courses continued in the 2000-2001 academic year.

We recognized early in the project that ADEPT modules would have to be flexible, adaptable, and relatively small in scope in order to be integrated smoothly into existing instruction. Our observations of lectures and discussion sections were guided by questions such as: At what level of detail or granularity should I-Scapes be created? How detailed can or should modules be, if they are to be useful for multiple instructors? What are the implications for metadata to describe and represent the concepts? What are the collection requirements for ADEPT?

We developed and deployed surveys, structured interviews, and classroom observation instruments. Student interviews focused on their knowledge of geographic principles and their evaluation of instructional methods, alternative models of instruction, and ADEPT prototypes. Faculty interviews focused on their perceptions of the field, pedagogical goals, uses of information technology in instruction, uses of geographic information resources, and evaluation of ADEPT prototypes. We are also conducting a modified concept mapping exercise to study the impact of the ADEPT system.

3.3.2 Evaluation of ADEPT Prototypes

We wanted to test our evaluation methods for prototypes early in the project, while the ADEPT implementation team was still building core system architecture. To do so, we developed simulated I-Scapes using Microsoft PowerPoint and deployed them in one section of the physical geography courses at UCSB and UCLA. The I-Scape topic selected in consultation with the instructors was hydrology and fluvial processes. Graduate student researchers at each campus worked closely with instructors to gather static and moving images, diagrams, simulations, and other geographic content that served the instructors' pedagogical goals. At UCSB, the four I-Scape lectures were given by a guest faculty member who is part of the ADEPT team. At UCLA, the regular course instructor used our simulated I-Scape in one class session.

These simulations were evaluated using classroom observations and pre- and post-implementation interviews with students and instructors. We are now conducting structured interviews with participating instructors other than those who used the ADEPT prototype in their classrooms. These instructors are being asked to assess which components of the simulation would be useful to them and how those components might be extended to more fully developed I-Scapes that would suit these instructors' pedagogical goals and approaches.

3.3.3 Assessing Learning Outcomes

We will employ performance assessments to evaluate learning outcomes in the third year of the project, after more fully functional I-Scapes are available for deployment in instruction [3]. These metrics are being developed by members of the ADEPT Education and Evaluation team in the Department of Psychology at UCSB. Students will be given realistic scientific tasks and then will be observed as they engage in scientific problem solving, using performance assessment methods. We will assess the cognitive consequences of participation in the ADEPT program by testing an ADEPT group and a comparison group on a series of tasks, each tapping one of the five target skills in geographical thinking.

4 Results and Discussion

In an exploratory project such as this, it is difficult to separate methods from results, and evaluation from design. The conceptual design principles followed from the initial scenario in the ADEPT grant proposal and from related research on digital libraries. In turn, the scenario and design principles led to the choice of courses, instructors and students, which informed the choices of cases to develop into I-Scape prototypes.

4.1 Classroom Observations

Faculty and graduate student researchers from the ADEPT education and evaluation team observed a sampling of class sessions before, during, and after the implementation of the I-Scape prototypes. These observations form baseline data to determine what is in common and what varies across the multiple offerings of the same and similar courses, what aspects of the courses might be incorporated in I-Scapes, and what aspects are independent of I-Scapes.

We found that topic emphasis varied considerably between courses, due to differences in texts and in instructors' interests, expertise, experience, and teaching styles. The five instructors observed (four regular classroom instructors plus the instructor who gave guest lectures at UCSB using the prototype I-Scapes) were experts in climatology, geomorphology, remote sensing, river systems, pedology, and soil evolution. Although all the instructors covered all the requisite topics, the proportional amount of time devoted to each topic reflected their respective research areas. They also varied in their use of instructional technology, employing chalk, overheads, slides, maps, objects such as rock samples, and computer-based tools other than ADEPT [3].

Observational data also are being employed to develop "course topographies" that represent relationships between topics taught in a course [16]. This approach will uncover the principal concepts in introductory geography courses, helping us gather appropriate instructional materials in ADEPT. The resultant maps provide a conceptual framework that will integrate with other efforts to enhance the discovery and utilization of resources in large repositories of learning materials. The concept maps will also lead to the development of topic maps [17] which can be used to organize materials and navigate among concepts. Finally, each instance of an object in the concept map can be further characterized by a set of descriptive attributes or metadata to aid in their discovery and retrieval.

4.2 Classroom Implementation of ADEPT I-Scape Prototypes

The simple ADEPT prototypes tested at UCLA and UCSB in the 2000-2001 academic year incorporated text, photographs, diagrams, images, and moving images that illustrated fluvial processes. Instructors could add comments and annotations in real time. The UCLA prototype was constructed for a single lecture on fluvial processes. We combined graphics, simulations, and the lecture outline in one file and used one computer and projector. The UCSB guest instructor developed four lectures on fluvial processes using a two-screen projection method (one for graphics and simulations and one for the lecture outline). We revised the UCLA I-Scape for use the following academic year, at the instructor's request, as a two-screen presentation, with an overhead projector on the second screen.

For the purposes of the early prototype, we collected instructors' content, such as lecture outlines and notes, diagrams, or personal slide collections, and other materials of interest. Sources included textbooks, CD-ROMs, and online resources, or other sources for which they did not necessarily hold intellectual property rights. Intellectual property issues are problematic because of instructors' desires to incorporate whatever materials in their lectures that they find relevant. However, we cannot post materials for use by students and others without prior copyright permission.

We found that display, layout, and other presentation features are essential considerations for ADEPT content. Instructors often selected illustrations based on graphical qualities over relevance and familiarity (e.g., an image of a river in Africa was visually more striking than an available image of a local river). Clear labeling, zooming, and use of recognizable geographic features are needed to provide visual context [3].

4.3 Interviews with Students and Faculty

We interviewed students and participating faculty before and after the deployment of the initial ADEPT I-Scape simulations. Students (n=109) were recruited in discussion sections led by teaching assistants and appointments were made for private interviews. The interviews were audiotaped. Six UCLA students participated in pre-

ADEPT implementation interviews and 3 UCLA and 8 UCSB students participated in post-ADEPT interviews. The two faculty who deployed the ADEPT I-Scape prototypes were interviewed before and after deployment. Early in the project, we conducted informal interviews (taking notes but not audiotaping) with other faculty whose classrooms were observed. One of them was later interviewed using a combination of the pre- and post-ADEPT questions. Other faculty will be interviewed in more depth at the time they are teaching the courses that ADEPT is studying.

Interviews to date indicate that both faculty and students feel that primary scientific evidence can play a more significant role in geography education. Several professors commented that collections of observational data should be incorporated in geography instruction, because scientific knowledge in geography is obtained through observation. According to one professor, introductory geography involves large- and small-scale earth processes and their interactions over time, and these processes are particularly good candidates for computer-based visualization and simulations based on scientific evidence. Most students said they understand concepts better if they can "see it happening." One professor noted that the potential for the ADEPT system to provide real-time, local data would assist instructors in demonstrating concepts with local examples, which is viewed as a means to increase student interest.

Our conversations with students about the design of the ADEPT service revealed concerns about the use of technology in instruction. Students fretted about having to learn a technical system in addition to the primary geography course content. Some students observed that instructors already seemed hindered by information technology in the classroom, to the overall detriment of the lecture. Others commented that the high rate of information presented in the ADEPT prototype sometimes led to overload. Students occasionally found themselves inundated, as professors that previously lectured with few visual aids (overheads, slides, or schematic chalk drawings) suddenly had dozens of photographs and satellite images to illustrate concepts, which they might rush through in the course of a 60- to 75-minute lecture.

Instructors had similar concerns about deploying ADEPT in their classrooms. Some professors worried about the investment of time required to learn ADEPT, to build personalized collections, and to create I-Scape presentations. These faculty rely on graduate teaching assistants to gather course materials and lead laboratory exercises; the teaching assistants may become the primary users of ADEPT. The geography faculty in our study are sophisticated computer users who employ scientific workstations and even supercomputers in their research work. They are familiar with the problems of using information technology in lecture settings, having experienced technical difficulties and breakdowns. One common sentiment was "transparencies don't crash." Faculty tend to develop their own teaching styles and become comfortable with them, as some of our participating faculty acknowledged. One goal of ADEPT is to assist professors in developing a pedagogical style that will inculcate scientific behaviors in students. Another concern was that a visual system like ADEPT might encourage students to view simulations passively, like they do with television, rather than engage in active scientific thinking.

One participating instructor in whose classroom we did not implement ADEPT provided comments on our ADEPT prototype on fluvial processes. This interview and others planned attempt to determine how to construct ADEPT capabilities that will be useful for multiple instructors. This instructor was very selective about the images that would be chosen for re-use (roughly 10% of the images, most of which would require changes). A principal complaint was that illustrations and photographs should be at a high resolution, with contrasting colors for demonstration in lecture. Even then, graphics should have annotations that are readable from the back rows of a large lecture hall and an accompanying graphic that shows the picture in geomorphological context.

Despite their concerns, professors remained generally enthusiastic about the ADEPT system. A scenario that particularly excited several of them was a simulation in which images of a river are accompanied by actual streamflow data, levee heights, and other variables. Each of these variables could be altered by the instructor to illustrate the effects of each variable, and students could perform the experiment as a lab exercise.

4.4   User Groups and Tasks

Our initial scenario focused on the activities of instructors and students. After our first rounds of classroom observations and interviews, it became apparent that teaching assistants play a larger role in instruction than was represented in our initial research design. The teaching practices of professors appear to vary more widely than do the practices of the teaching assistants who manage the weekly class discussion sections. Much of the learning of scientific processes may take place in these discussion sections, where students perform exercises and get answers to most of their questions about course content.

We have refined the scenario to recognize four user groups for study: faculty (in their role as course instructors), teaching assistants, students in the courses where ADEPT is implemented, and students continuing to study the discipline after the completion of the course. These groups differ in needs, activities, and levels of domain knowledge and thus generate different requirements for ADEPT. We have identified the following list of candidate tasks that ADEPT I-Scapes should support:

- Highly directed uses such as lab exercises to reinforce disciplinary concepts
- Instructional modules that introduce concepts in an incremental manner and can be customized and extended by faculty for use in lectures
- Free-form exploration conducted by students preparing term papers or by faculty putting together a lecture. These may include manipulation and visualization of data sets and the integration of new information to augment existing content.
- Collaborative applications that can be used by students doing team projects or by faculty and teaching assistants who are team teaching

- Discipline or domain-specific methods of building knowledge that support information seeking and use

4.5 Requirements for I-Scape Cases

Based on our work to date, we are developing requirements for the three I-Scape cases (fluvial processes, plate tectonics, disease vectors) such as these:

- Appropriate metadata and representation of content
- Appropriate searching capabilities to select content within I-Scapes
- Parameters that can be manipulated to demonstrate processes and test hypotheses
- Visualization features to demonstrate processes and test hypotheses
- Ability for individual students and instructors to save their work for reuse
- Instrumentation to capture user-system interactions

5 Summary and Conclusions

Digital libraries offer many opportunities to support the teaching and learning of geography and other subjects that employ geospatial content. They can provide access to primary sources, including data about local places, in forms that instructors can use to present dynamic processes such as river erosion, earthquakes, and the vectors by which diseases are spread through populations. Our goals in the ADEPT project are to design, develop, and deploy digital libraries of geospatial resources for use in undergraduate instruction.

Ours is an exploratory project, as little is known about the use of digital libraries for these purposes. We are conducting formative evaluation as part of the iterative design of ADEPT. In the first two years of a five-year project, we established general conceptual principles for design, observed classroom activities, gathered baseline data from instructors and students on how courses are currently being taught, and evaluated early prototypes. Instructors vary widely in their use of instructional materials and technologies, teaching styles, and areas of expertise. While students and instructors are generally enthusiastic about ADEPT, they have concerns about the effort required and the effectiveness of computer-based technologies in the classroom. We are continuing to gather baseline data on how courses are being taught, as it is essential to understand the present approaches, so that we can design a system that is effective in context and so that we have a basis for comparison following system implementation.

The next phases of research and evaluation are on the course topographies and on assessing scientific learning. Mapping course topographies will help us to understand how instructors construct relationships between topics and how these can be represented as scientific models. Performance assessments can be done when we have ADEPT I-Scapes that support these scientific models.

The ADEPT web sites at UCLA (http://is.gseis.ucla.edu/adept/) and UCSB (http://www.alexandria.ucsb.edu/adept/) will provide links to continuing reports of ADEPT research.

6 Acknowledgments

This article is based upon work supported by the National Science Foundation under grant no. IIS-9817432, Terence R. Smith, University of California, Santa Barbara, Principal Investigator. Our thanks go to our colleagues at UCSB and DLESE and to the faculty and students at UCLA and UCSB who are participating in the ADEPT project. The education and evaluation effort relies heavily on our excellent research assistants at UCLA: Rich Gazan, David Gwynn, Jason Finley, Laura Smart, and Annie Zeidman, and at UCSB: Tricia Mautone and Rachel Michael Nilsson.

References

1. Leazer, G.H., Gilliland-Swetland, A.J., Borgman, C.L.: Evaluating the Use of a Geographic Digital Library in Undergraduate Classrooms: The Alexandria Digital Earth Prototype (ADEPT). Proceedings of the Fifth ACM Conference on Digital Libraries, (2000) 248-249
2. Leazer, G.H., Gilliland-Swetland, A.J., Borgman, C.L., Mayer, R.: Classroom Evaluation of the Alexandria Digital Earth Prototype (ADEPT). Proceedings of the American Society for Information Science Annual Meeting (2000) 334-340
3. Borgman, C.L., Gilliland-Swetland, A.J., Leazer, G.H., Mayer, R., Gwynn, D., Gazan, R., Mautone, P.: Evaluating Digital Libraries for Teaching and Learning in Undergraduate Education: A Case Study of the Alexandria Digital Earth Prototype (ADEPT). Libr. Trends 49 (2000) 228-250
4. Gilliland-Swetland, A.J., Leazer, G.H.: Iscapes: Digital Library Environments to Promote Scientific Thinking by Undergraduates in Geography. Proceedings of the First ACM/IEEE Joint Conference on Digital Libraries (2001; in press)
5. Borgman, C.L.: From Gutenberg to the Global Information Infrastructure: Access to Information in the Networked World. Cambridge, MA: MIT Press (2000)
6. Borgman, C.L.: Digital Libraries and Virtual Universities. In: Della Senta, T., Tschang, T. (eds.): Access to Knowledge: New Information Technologies and the Emergence of the Virtual University. International Association of Universities Press, Paris, and Pergamon, Oxford (2000)
7. Fitz-Gibbon, C.T., Morris, L.L.: How to Design a Program Evaluation. Sage, Newbury Park, CA (1987)
8. Gilliland-Swetland, A.J.: Evaluation Design for Large-Scale, Collaborative Online Archives: Interim Report of the Online Archive of California Evaluation Project. Arch. Museum Informatics 12 (1998) 177-203
9. Khoo, M.: Community Design of DLESE's Collections Review Policy: A Technological Frames Analysis. Proceedings of the First ACM/IEEE Joint Conference on Digital Libraries (2001; in press)
10. Marchionini, G., Crane, G.: Evaluating Hypermedia and Learning: Methods and Results from the Perseus Project. ACM T. Inform. Sys. 12 (1994) 5-34

11. Bishop, A.P., Buttenfield, B.P., Van House, N. (eds.): Digital Library Use: Social Practice in Design and Evaluation. MIT Press, Cambridge, MA (2001; in press)
12. Geography Education Standards Project: Geography for Life: National Geography Standards. National Geographic Society, Washington, DC (1994)
13. National Research Council: National Science Education Standards. National Academy Press, Washington, DC (1996)
14. Hill, L.L., Carver, L., Larsgaard, M., Dolin, R., Smith, T.R., Frew, J., Rae, M.A.: Alexandria Digital Library: User Evaluation Studies and System Design. J. Am. Soc. Inform. Sci. 51 (2000) 246-259.
15. Buttenfield, B.P., Kumler, M.P.: Tools for Browsing Environmental Data: The Alexandria Digital Library Interface. Proceedings of the Third International Conference on Integrating Geographic Information Systems and Environmental Modeling. Santa Fe, NM, January 21-25. http://www.ncgia.ucsb.edu/conf/SANTA_FE_CD-ROM/sd_papers/buttenfield_babs/babs_paper.html (1996)
16. Novak, J.D.: Learning, Creating, and Using Knowledge: Concept Maps as Facilitative Tools in Schools and Corporations. L. Erlbaum Associates, Mahwah, N.J. (1998)
17. International Organization for Standardization: Topic Maps (ISO/IEC 13250:2000) (2000)

Automatically Analyzing and Organizing Music Archives

Andreas Rauber and Markus Frühwirth

Department of Software Technology, Vienna University of Technology
Favoritenstr. 9 - 11 / 188, A–1040 Wien, Austria
http://www.ifs.tuwien.ac.at

Abstract. We are experiencing a tremendous increase in the amount of music being made available in digital form. With the creation of large multimedia collections, however, we need to devise ways to make those collections accessible to the users. While music repositories exist today, they mostly limit access to their content to query-based retrieval of their items based on textual meta-information, with some advanced systems supporting acoustic queries. What we would like to have additionally, is a way to facilitate exploration of musical libraries. We thus need to automatically organize music according to its sound characteristics in such a way that we find similar pieces of music grouped together, allowing us to find a classical section, or a hard-rock section etc. in a music repository. In this paper we present an approach to obtain such an organization of music data based on an extension to our *SOMLib* digital library system for text documents. Particularly, we employ the *Self-Organizing Map* to create a map of a musical archive, where pieces of music with similar sound characteristics are organized next to each other on the two-dimensional map display. Locating a piece of music on the map then leaves you with related music next to it, allowing intuitive exploration of a music archive.
Keywords: Multimedia, Music Library, Self-Organizing Map (SOM), Exploration of Information Spaces, User Interface, MP3

1 Introduction

Currently, we are experiencing a tremendous increase in the amount of music being made available in digital form. Following the sweeping success of music swapping systems such as Napster, a further rise in the amount of music distributed via electronic archives is to be expected due to the current move of music industry towards electronic distribution of their products. As a consequence we may expect to find even larger archives containing innumerable pieces of music from a variety of genres. With the creation of large audio collections, however, we need to devise ways to make those collections accessible to the users. When talking about multimedia content we have to differentiate between the different forms in which content is made available, i.e. textual form, audio, video, animations, etc. While automatic handling and analysis of textual data has a long

P. Constantopoulos and I.T. Sølvberg (Eds.): ECDL 2001, LNCS 2163, pp. 402–414, 2001.

history in (textual) information retrieval, the more prominent types of multimedia information still rely heavily on manual indexing and description to facilitate automatic content-based access later on. We thus find these kinds of metadata descriptors to form one of the core entities in the MPEG-7 standard [16]. However, due to the diversity and complexity of multimedia data we will, for the work described in this paper, limit our discussion to audio data.

When talking about interfaces to electronic music archives we may basically distinguish between four primary modes of access, which can be summarized as (1) database-oriented access allowing search via metadata; (2) text-based access searching the text of songs for particular phrases; (3) searching for a particular melody or tune; or (4) looking for a particular type of music, i.e. for titles within a specific musical genre.

Most music repositories existing today limit access to their content to the first approach, allowing query-based retrieval of their documents based on textual information, i.e. mainly via metadata about the documents, such as title, composer, artist, or band information, the label, and so on. This allows users to conveniently locate a particular piece of music when the necessary meta-information is available, satisfying a large percentage of users requests.

Slightly more challenging is the task of finding a particular piece of music based on the lyrics. This means of access requires the transcripts of texts to be available in electronic form, which has to be created mostly manually, with only limited support from speech recognition programs possible in the given setting.

The third way of searching music archives is based on melodies, which form a very natural approach to such collections. In this case, the input to the system is formed by a melody taken from a recording or hummed by a user, with the system trying to extract melody scores and matching those with the tunes in the collection.

Yet, all of these approaches address searches for a particular title, i.e. situations where a users knows more or less exactly what he or she is looking for. None of the three approaches naturally supports browsing of a collection, searching for a certain type of music, rather than for a specific title. Still, this approach to exploring music archives is one of the most prominent in conventional record stores, where customers find titles organized primarily by genre, with only subsequent alphabetical sorting by artists within the various sections. This allows users to browser through their sections of interest to find new pieces of music, reflecting an exploratory approach of music search as opposed to a direct search for a particular title. A similar form of organization is found with most people's private record collections, which commonly are organized by types of music as well, making it easier to pick the kind of music one would like to hear in a particular situation.

The need to support this kind of interaction resulted in the creation of manually tendered groupings of music files in most electronic music repositories, where artists file their music according to certain genres, such as Pop, Classic, Jazz, Punk, Blues, etc., mimicking the way music is organized in conventional music stores or libraries. Yet, when analyzing these genres we find them to be both rather subjective, and sometimes hard to interpret, as the variations within each genre are considerably large and sometimes not too well defined. The music archive *mp3.com* [14] for example, list its titles under 350 different genres, organized in up to four hierarchical layers. Since titles are commonly filed into such a hierarchy by different people, the sound characteristics of titles of the same genre often vary a lot, making the classification a rather weak guideline to match to ones own musical taste. Furthermore, the manual classification task involved renders this approach difficult to support by many large archives with frequently changing collections.

What we would like to have, in this context, is a way to automatically organize music according to its sound characteristics in such a way, that we find similar pieces of music grouped together. This would allow us to find, e.g., a classical section, or a hard-rock section in a music repository, supporting an exploratory interface to audio collections. In this paper we present an approach to obtain such an organization of music data using a neural network approach which creates a map of the titles in a music archive. The task is comparable to content-based organization of textual documents, i.e. the grouping of texts according to the subject they deal with. We thus adapted the concepts of our *SOMLib* digital library system [19], a system providing content-based organization of text documents, to include audio data. We employ the *Self-Organizing Map (SOM)* [9] to create a map of a musical archive, where pieces of music sounding similar are organized next to each other on the two-dimensional map display. Locating a piece of music on the map then leaves you with similar music next to it, allowing intuitive exploration of a music archive.

The remainder of this paper is organized as follows: Section 2 provides an overview of related work in the field of music retrieval. This is followed by a presentation of our approach to automatic organization of music archives by sound similarity in Section 3, covering feature extraction, the principles of the *Self-Organizing Map*, and the two-layered architecture used to organize music. Experimental results organizing an archive of MP3 music are presented in Section 4, followed by some conclusions as well as an outlook on future work in Section 5.

2   Related Work

Analysis of audio data has a long history, with the focus of work in this area ranging from spectra identification of certain instruments, via voice recognition, to fault detection in electric drives. With respect to music classification, we can distinguish between two main approaches, relying on frequency spectra analysis, or on melody analysis, respectively. Most melody-based approaches may be seen as an analogy to information-retrieval in text-based systems. Queries are either sung, or hummed, with the system extracting characteristic melody features and trying to match those with the audio files in the archive. In this setting, most works rely on the Musical Instruments Digital Interface (MIDI) file format [13], representing the scores for a series of instruments, rather than the sound itself.

The scores have to be interpreted to synthesize the sound as such, making it a descriptive format for how to produce sound, rather than an audio file format itself. Yet, it has huge benefits in terms of melody retrieval, as it reduces the complexity of melody-based retrieval somewhat to the problem of matching symbolic musical notes. Hawley [8] developed a system that allows a note sequence being entered via a MIDI keyboard. It then searches the tunes whose beginnings exactly match the input.

To facilitate acoustic querying of MIDI data, the transcription of acoustic input into symbolic musical notes is highly challenging, as it requires the system to make up for all kinds of impreciseness, such as badly sung queries, rhythmic and melodic differences between various versions of the same melody, etc. Ghias [7] transforms a hummed query into a series of strings of tokens *U, D,* and *S*, representing up, down, and the same musical note as the previous one, using subsequent approximate string-matching for retrieval. One of the most prominent representatives of this kind of systems is the New Zealand Musical Digital Library [1,12]. Apart from a variety of text-based searches within metadata records or the lyrics of songs, this system also allows the retrieval of tunes based on hummed queries. Users can specify their trust in their own capabilities of maintaining the right pitch, or rhythm, with the system then trying to match the hummed melody with the tunes in the collection. A similar system is reported in [21].

Yet, all of these systems focus on the retrieval of music data based on searches. We thus find a separate stream of research addressing analysis and classification of musical data. These mostly concentrate on the extraction of characteristic features, such as loudness, pitch, dynamics, and other sound characteristics. These are compared with reference vectors in a database to provide corresponding classification, allowing, for example, the distinction between different kinds of sounds such as applause or laughter. As one of the seminal works in this field we find the works by Wold et al. [22], as well as a similar system described by Foote [6], which uses a tree-structured vector quantizer, identifying, e.g. different types of speakers. Pfeiffer describes a system capable of violence detection in video soundtracks [17]. Other systems working directly on acoustic audio data in this context concentrate on beat tracking, trying to identify regular rhythmic structures. Works in this direction are reported in [4,15].

In the same spirit we find works addressing instrument detection based on frequency analysis. Special filters are being applied to extract and put more weight on frequencies characteristics for a specific instrument. Cosi et al. [2] describe a system for timbre classification to identify 12 instruments in both clean and degraded conditions. Similar to the works described in this paper, a *Self-Organizing Map* is used to cluster the resulting feature vectors. A similar approach, yet incorporating psycho-acoustic models for frequency transformation are described by Feiten [5], again using *SOMs* for clustering the data.

3 The SOMeJukebox

3.1 Basic Principles

What we would like to have is a digital library system capable of automatically organizing musical data based on its sound characteristics. We have thus extended our *SOMLib* digital library system [19,20] to incorporate audio data, resulting in the *SOMeJB*, i.e. the *SOM-extended Jukebox* system. The *SOMLib* system is capable of automatically organizing a collection of text documents according to their content. The *Self-Organizing Map (SOM)*, a popular unsupervised neural network model, is used to provide a topically sorted map of the various documents, using word histogram representations during an unsupervised training process.

By including a special feature extraction process we can apply the systems principles to the automatic organization of musical data. Figure 1 provides an overview of the resulting *SOMeJB* system. As the characteristics of a piece of music vary, a two-layered clustering procedure is used to first create a cluster of music segments of about 3 to 5 seconds length. In a second step, the clustering results of the various musical segments are used to analyze and cluster pieces of music according to their overall similarity.

In a nutshell, the principles of the system can be described as follows. We use *XMMS*, a popular open source media player, to extract frequency spectra from music data such as MP3 or Wave files. As these frequency spectra are not provided in evenly spaced time intervals, we use Lagrange transformation to obtain timed snapshots. This is followed by a Fast Fourier Transformation (FFT) across the segments for a selected set of frequency spectra to obtain Fourier coefficients modeling the dynamics. These feature vectors are used to train a *SOM* of music segments. Segments with similar sound characteristics are located next to each other on the map, while highly differently sounding segments are found in sections far apart on the map. Quite frequently we also find pieces of music to show two very distinct sound characteristics in their verses and chorus parts, thus having their segments spread across different parts of the map. In a second step, a unique feature vector is created for each piece of music based on the cluster distribution of its segments. These vectors are again fed into a *SOM* to create a map of the music. The individual steps are described in more detail in the following subsections.

3.2 Feature Extraction and Preprocessing

Music comes in a variety of file formats such as MP3, WAV, AU, etc., all of which basically store the sound information in the form of pulse code modulation (PCM) using a sampling rate of 44.1 kHz. The analog sound signal is thus represented by 44.100 16 bit integer numbers per second, which are interpreted by media players to reproduce the sound signal. In order to be able to compute similarity scores between musical tunes, a feature vector representation of the

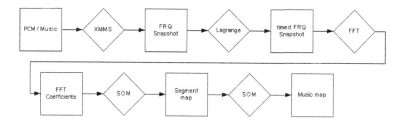

Fig. 1. SOMeJukeBox System: feature extraction, conversion, and 2-level SOM training

various pieces of music needs to be created, which can further be analyzed by the *SOM*.

Starting with any popular music file format, most media players, such as the open source X Multimedia System (XMMS) are capable of splitting this data stream into several frequency bands. Using XMMS, the signal is split into 256 frequency bands, with approximately one sample value every 20 to 25 ms each. Since not all frequency bands are necessary for evaluating sound similarity, and in order to reduce the amount of data to be processed, a subset of 17 frequency bands (i.e. every 15th frequency band) is selected for further analysis, covering the whole spectrum available. In order to capture musical variations of a tune, the music stream is split into sections of 5 seconds length, which are further treated as the single musical entities to be analyzed. While basically all 5-second sequences could be used for further analysis, or even overlapping segments might be chosen, experimental results have shown that appropriate clustering results can be obtained by the *SOM* using only a subset of all available segments. Especially segments at the beginning as well as at the end of a specific piece of music can be eliminated to ignore fade-in and fade-out effects. Furthermore, our results show that choosing every second to third segment, i.e. a 5-second interval every 10 to 15 seconds, provides sufficient quality of data analysis.

The intervals between the frequency snapshots provided by the player varies with the system load and can thus not be guaranteed to occur at specified time intervals. We thus have a set of amplitude/timestamp values about every 20 to 25 ms in each of the 17 selected frequency bands. In order to obtain equi-distant data points, a Lagrange interpolation is performed on these values as provided in Expression 1, where $f(z_k)$ represents the amplitude of the sample point at time stamp z_k for $n + 1$ sample points.

$$P_n(z) = \sum_{k=0}^{n} \left(\prod_{l=0,l\neq k}^{n} \frac{z - z_l}{z_k - z_l} \right) f(z_k) \tag{1}$$

As a result of this transformation we now have equi-distant data samples in each frequency band. The resulting function can be approximated by a linear combination of sine and cosine waves with different frequencies. We can thus obtain a closed representation for each frequency band by performing a Fast Fourier Transformation (FFT), resulting in a set of 256 coefficients for the respective sine and cosine parts. Combining the 256 coefficients for the 17 frequency bands results in a 4352-dimensional vector representing a 5-second segment of music. These feature vectors are further used for training a *Self-Organizing Map*.

3.3 Self-Organizing Maps

The *Self-Organizing Map* (*SOM*) [9] is an unsupervised neural network providing a mapping from a high-dimensional input space to a usually two-dimensional output space while preserving topological relations as faithfully as possible. The *SOM* consists of a set of i units arranged in a two-dimensional grid, with a weight vector $m_i \in \Re^n$ attached to each unit. Elements from the high dimensional input space, referred to as input vectors $x \in \Re^n$, are presented to the *SOM*, and the activation of each unit for the presented input vector is calculated. Commonly, the Euclidean distance between the weight vector of the unit and the input vector serves as the activation function. In the next step the weight vector of the unit showing the highest activation (i.e. the smallest Euclidean distance) is selected as the 'winner' and is modified as to more closely resemble the presented input vector. Pragmatically speaking, the weight vector of the winner is moved towards the presented input signal by a certain fraction of the Euclidean distance as indicated by a time-decreasing learning rate α. Thus, this unit's activation will be even higher the next time the same input signal is presented. Furthermore, the weight vectors of units in the neighborhood of the winner as described by a time-decreasing neighborhood function ϵ are modified accordingly, yet to a less strong amount than the winner.

This learning procedure finally leads to a topologically ordered mapping of the presented input signals. The weight vectors of a trained map serve as prototype vectors, or cluster centroids. Similar input data is mapped onto neighboring regions on the map. While each feature vector is mapped onto its most similar unit, we may further use the mapping distance, i.e. the Euclidean distance between the feature vector and the unit's weight vector, as an indicator of how well the feature vector corresponds to the characteristics of the cluster.

SOM based architectures found wide appreciation in the field of text clustering [10,11] due to their capabilities of handling very high-dimensional feature spaces as well as being able to cope with the inherent noise in the data representation. These characteristics also make the *SOM* a particularly suitable tool for music data clustering [2,5], where we find rather similar situations. The *GHSOM* [3], an extension to the basic *SOM* algorithm furthermore allows the detection of hierarchical clusters, making it a suitable interface to explore large data collections [18]. For the given experimental setting, however, we will rely on the standard *SOM*.

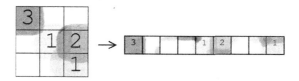

Fig. 2. Creating 2nd-level vectors based on segment distribution

3.4   Music Clustering: Segments and Pieces of Music

The feature vectors representing music segments can be thought of as data points in a 4352-dimensional space, with similar pieces of music, i.e. segments exhibiting similar frequency spectra and thus similar FFT coefficients, being located close to each other. Using the *SOM* to cluster these feature vectors, we may expect similar music segments to be located close to each other in the resulting map display.

On the resulting segment *SOM* the various segments are scattered across the map according to their mutual similarity. This allows, for example, pieces of music touching on different musical genres to be located in two or more different clusters, whereas rather homogeneous pieces of music are usually located within one rather confined cluster on the map. While this already provides a very intuitive interface to a musical collection, a second clustering may be built on top of the segment map to obtain a grouping of pieces of music according to their overall characteristics.

To obtain such a clustering, we use the mapping positions of the segments of a piece of music. We create a feature vector representation for each piece of music using the location of its segments as descriptive attributes. Given an $x \times y$ *SOM* we create an $x \cdot y$ dimensional weight vector, where the attributes are the (coordinates of) the units of the segment *SOM*. Each vector attribute represents the number of segments of a particular piece of music mapped onto the respective unit in the *SOM*. Consider a piece of music A consisting of 7 segments, three of which are mapped onto unit $(0/0)$[1] in the upper left corner of a 3×3 map, two segments on unit $(2/1)$, and one segment on the neighboring units $(1/1)$ and $(2/2)$, respectively, as depicted in Figure 2. The attributes of the resulting 9-dimensional feature vector of the song are basically set to the according values $(3\ 0\ 0\ 0\ 1\ 2\ 0\ 0\ 1)^T$. Subsequent norming to unit length makes up for length differences of songs.

Instead of directly using the number of segments mapped onto a specific unit as the attribute of the newly created input vector for a given piece of music, we may improve data representation by incorporating information about the similarity of a given segment with the weight vector of the unit it is mapped

---

[1] We use the notation (x/y) to refer to the unit in column x, row y, starting with $(0/0)$ in the upper left corner

onto. As the weight vector serves as a cluster prototype, we can use the mapping distance between a segments feature vector and the unit's weight vector to give higher weights to segments that are very similar to the cluster centroid, whereas we may give lower weights to segments that are not mapped as well onto this unit. Furthermore, we may distribute the contribution of a segment being mapped onto a specific unit also across units in the neighborhood, utilizing the topology-preserving characteristics of the *SOM*. This allows for a more stable representation of the segments distribution across the segment map. A Gaussian centered at the winner can thus be used to model the contribution of each segment's location onto the neighboring units, and thus onto the attributes of the feature vector for the music *SOM*, as indicated by the shadings in Figure 2.

We thus create a feature vector for each particular piece of music based on the distribution of its segments on the segment *SOM*. Training a second *SOM* using these feature vectors we obtain a clustering where each piece of music is mapped onto one single location on the resulting map, with similar pieces of music being mapped close to each other.

4   Experiments

For the following experiments we use a collection of 230 pieces of music, ranging from classical music, such as *Mozart's "Kleine Nachtmusik"*, via some hits from the 1960's such as *Cat Steven's "Father and Son"* or *Queen's "I want to break free"*, to modern titles, e.g. *Tom Jones' "Sexbomb"*.

These songs were segmented into 5-second-intervals, of which every second segment was used for further processing, with a total of 17 frequency bands being selected. Following the Lagrange interpolations and FFT we thus end up with 5022 feature vectors representing the 5022 5-second segments of the 230 songs in a 4352-dimensional feature space. These feature vectors were further used to train a 22×22 dimensional segment *SOM*. Due to space restrictions we cannot provide a representation of the resulting map, yet we will use some examples for discussion.

For most songs the individual segments are mapped onto a rather small number of neighboring units. For example, we find most segments from classical titles mapped onto the lower right area of the segment *SOM*. To provide just one example of the segment *SOM* we find unit (13/21) to represent mostly classical segments mapped onto it, such as *Adagio, Air, Ave Maria, Beethoven's 5th Symphony, Brandenburg Concerts, Kleine Nachtmusik, Nocturne*, and many more. However, we also find the third segment of *Crash Boom Bang* by *Roxette* on this unit, which is definitely not a classical piece of music. Yet in this particular segment we find the music to be rather calm and "classic-like", resulting in the mapping of this particular segment onto this cluster. Furthermore, we find many intros as well as fade-out passages of songs to be mapped into the classic cluster on the segment *SOM*, as in those passages we quite frequently find violin or guitar music, independent of the instrumentation of the rest of the song. Some titles, such as *"Ironic"* by *Alanis Morissette* contain both rather soft and very

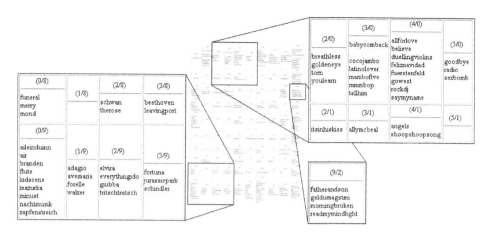

Fig. 3. SOM representing 230 pieces of music

dynamic passages and thus have their segments spread across several clusters co-located with segments from other songs of similar characteristics. However, the characteristics of some songs are too diverse to allow precise mapping of their segments and are thus spread across larger areas on the segment map.

In order to obtain a more compact representation of the musical archive, we create new feature vectors for each song based on the location of their segments. This results in a $22 \cdot 22$, i.e. 484-dimensional feature vector for each of the 230 songs. These feature vectors are used to train the 10×10 *SOM* represented in Figure 3.

Each song is now mapped onto one single position according to its musical characteristics. Taking a look at the Classic cluster in the lower left corner of the map, we find unit (0/8) to represent the *Funeral March (Chopin)* as well as the *Moonlight Sonata (Beethoven)* and the *Merry Peasant (Schuhmann)*. All three pieces consist of rather calm piano music, and have their segments mapped mostly in the classic cluster on the segment map. Unit (0/9) also represents almost solely classical music, such as *Air* or the *Brandenburg Concerts* by *Bach*, as well as, again, pieces by *Schuhmann, Chopin* and *Mozart (Fremde Länder und Menschen (Schuhmann), Mazurka (Chopin),* and *Kleine Nachtmusik (Mozart))*. The song *Ailein Duinn* is a Scottish folk song and thus at first glance does not seem to fit into this cluster. Yet, when listening to it we find it to be a ballad sung by a woman and accompanied only by violin and harp, thus making it sound-wise fit perfectly into the classic cluster, even though it would be organized into the folk cluster by strict musical genre. On the neighboring unit (1/9) we find two pieces by *Schubert*, namely *Ave Maria, Themen und Variationen der Forelle*, as well as a piece by *Mozart*, i.e. the *Adagio* of his *Clarinet Concert*.

It is important to note, that the *SOM* does not organize the songs according to their melody, but rather according to their sound characteristics. If we move on to unit (2/9) we find it to represent some more dynamic pieces of classic music, such as the *Tritsch Tratsch Polka* by *Strauß* or again compositions by

Mozart. We also find two vocal pieces on this unit, namely *Vesti la Giubba (Domingo)* and *Everything I do* by *Bryan Adams.* Obviously, *Everything I do* is not a classical piece of music in the strict sense, yet in terms of its music we find it very calm and to be accompanied by an orchestra most of the time. Even more interesting, we find unit (3/9) further to the right, and still more dynamic, to represent two pieces by *John Williams,* i.e. the main theme of the movies *Jurassic Park* and *Schindler's List.* We also find mapped onto the same unit both *Tchaikovsky's "Schwanensee"* as well as *Bette Midler's "The Rose",* a very soft love song with mostly piano and violin passages, both on unit (2/8). This cluster also nicely demonstrates the topology preservation capabilities of the *SOM*, with the dynamics and intensity of the various pieces of music increasing from left to the right.

To pick just one further example from a different section of the map, we find *Cher's "Believe", Robbie Williams' "Rock DJ", The Pet Shop Boys' "Go West"* mapped together on unit (4/0) next to *Lou Bega's "Mambo No. 5"* and *Tom Jones' "Sexbomb"* on units (3/0), and (5/0), respectively. Another special mapping worth mentioning in this cluster is the co-location of three songs by a single singer. *Ally McBeal - Searching My Soul, Tell Him* and *It's in his Kiss* on the neighboring units (2/1),(3/0) and (3/1) respectively, are all sung by *Vonda Shepard* and were taken from the same CD, played by the same group with the same set of accompanying instruments. Furthermore, the title *It's in his Kiss* is a cover version of *Cher's Shoop Shoop Song,* which is also located in this cluster on unit (4/1).

5   Conclusions

Access to digital libraries requires, apart from query-and-retrieval based approaches, a means to explore and browse the available collections in order to get an understanding of the information available. While many approaches exist for the exploration of textual libraries, access to multimedia collections has mainly been limited to retrieving items based on queries, be it textual or acoustic-based queries. Exploration of multimedia collections has only found limited support, with content-based browsing facilities mostly relying on preceding manual categorization of the items.

In this paper we presented an approach to create a content-based organization of music archives. The acoustic characteristics of pieces of music are analyzed, and the *Self-Organizing Map*, an unsupervised neural network, is used to create a mapping according to their similarity. Following the extraction of frequency spectra, segments of 5 seconds length are clustered, such that segments with similar sound characteristics are mapped physically close together on the resulting segment *SOM*. In this first step, music segments are organized to obtain a fine-grained representation of segment-wise similarities, based upon which a clustering of the complete songs can be obtained. In a second level clustering process, the distribution across the segment *SOM* is used to create a feature vector for each piece of music, which is fed into another *Self-Organizing Map.*

On the second level map we thus obtain an organization of an archive of music according to sound similarities. We find, for example, classical pieces of music to be grouped closely together, set well-apart from hard-rock or pop music. On the other hand, we find rather "soft" pop titles with mainly classical instruments mapped closer to the classical sector on the map.

The presented approach supports browsing and exploration of music archives by automatically grouping titles by sound characteristics, creating a kind of genre-based organization. It thus nicely combines with and complements more traditional interfaces to music archives, such as conventional database queries for music metadata, or advanced retrieval methods based on, e.g., melody.

In order to further improve the quality of the clustering, additional features will be incorporated. Apart from mere frequency spectra and their dynamics we are currently investigating the addition of beat information. Furthermore, modeling psycho-acoustic features should provide a better separation according to the perceived similarity of sounds.

References

1. D. Bainbridge, C. Nevill-Manning, H. Witten, L. Smith, and R. McNab. Towards a digital library of popular music. In E. Fox and N. Rowe, editors, *Proc of the ACM Conf on Digital Libraries (ACMDL'99)*, pages 161–169, Berkeley, CA, August 11-14 1999. ACM. http://www.acm.org/dl.
2. P. Cosi, G. De Poli, and G. Lauzzana. Auditory modeling and self organizing neural networks for timbre classification. *Journal of New Music Research*, 1994.
3. M. Dittenbach, D. Merkl, and A. Rauber. The growing hierarchical self-organizing map. In S. Amari, C. L. Giles, M. Gori, and V. Puri, editors, *Proc of the Intern. Joint Conf on Neural Networks (IJCNN 2000)*, volume VI, pages 15 – 19, Como, Italy, July 24-27 2000. IEEE Computer Society. http://www.ifs.tuwien.ac.at/ifs/research/publications.html.
4. S. Dixon and E. Cambouropoulos. Beat tracking with musical knowledge. In W. Horn, editor, *Proc of the 14th European Conf on Artificial Intelligence*, pages 626–630, Amsterdam, Netherlands, 2000. IOS Press. http://www.ai.univie.ac.at/~simon/.
5. B. Feiten and S. Günzel. Automatic indexing of a sound database using self-organizing neural nets. *Computer Music Journal*, 18(3):53–65, 1994.
6. J. Foote. Content-based retrieval of music and audio. In C. Kuo, editor, *Proc of SPIE Multimedia Storage and Archiving Systems II*, volume 3229, pages 138–147, 1997. http://www.fxpal.xerox.com/people/foote/papers/spie97-abs.html.
7. A. Ghias, J. Logan, D. Chamberlin, and S. B.C. Query by humming: Musical information retrieval in an audio database. In *Proc of the Third ACM Intern. Conf on Multimedia*, pages 231–236, San Francisco, CA, November 5 - 9 1995. ACM. http://www.acm.org/dl.
8. M. Hawley. The personal orchestra. *Computing Systems*, 3(2):289–329, 1990.
9. T. Kohonen. *Self-organizing maps*. Springer-Verlag, Berlin, 1995.
10. T. Kohonen, S. Kaski, K. Lagus, J. Salojärvi, J. Honkela, V. Paatero, and A. Saarela. Self-organization of a massive document collection. *IEEE Transactions on Neural Networks*, 11(3):574–585, May 2000. http://ieeexplore.ieee.org/.

11. X. Lin. A self-organizing semantic map for information retrieval. In *Proc of the 14. Annual Intern. ACM SIGIR Conf on Research and Development in Information Retrieval (SIGIR91)*, pages 262–269, Chicago, IL, October 13 - 16 1991. ACM. http://www.acm.org/dl.

12. R. McNab, L. Smith, J. Witten, C. Henderson, and S. Cunningham. Towards the digital music library: Tune retrieval from acoustic input. In *Proc of the 1st ACM Intern. Conf on Digital Libraries*, pages 11–18, Bethesda, MD, USA, March 20 - 23 1996. ACM. http://www.acm.org/dl.

13. M. (MMA). MIDI 1.0 Specification, V 96.1. online, March 1996. http://www.midi.org.

14. mp3. mp3.com. Website, May 2001. http://www.mp3.com as of May 2001.

15. Y. Muraoka and M. Goto. Real-time rhythm tracking for drumless audio signals - chord change detection for musical decisions. In *Proc of the IJCAI97 Workshop on Computational Auditory Scene Analysis*, Nagoya, Japan, August 23-29 1997. http://www.etl.go.jp/~goto/PROJ/bts-j.html.

16. F. Nack and A. Lindsay. Everything you wanted to know about MPEG7 - part 1. *IEEE MultiMedia*, pages 65– 77, July-September 1999.

17. S. Pfeiffer, S. Fischer, and W. Effelsber. Automatic audio content analysis. In *Proc of the Fourth ACM Conf on Multimedia*, pages 21–30, Boston, USA, November 18 - 22 1996. http://www.acm.org/dl.

18. A. Rauber, M. Dittenbach, and D. Merkl. Automatically detecting and organizing documents into topic hierarchies: A neural-network based approach to bookshelf creation and arrangement. In J. Borbinha and T. Baker, editors, *Proc of the 4. European Conf on Research and Advanced Technologies for Digital Libraries (ECDL2000)*, number 1923 in Lecture Notes in Computer Science, pages 348–351, Lisboa, Portugal, September 18-20 2000. Springer. http://www.ifs.tuwien.ac.at/ifs/research/publications.html.

19. A. Rauber and D. Merkl. The SOMLib Digital Library System. In S. Abiteboul and A. Vercoustre, editors, *Proc of the 3. European Conf on Research and Advanced Technology for Digital Libraries (ECDL99)*, number LNCS 1696 in Lecture Notes in Computer Science, pages 323–342, Paris, France, September 22-24 1999. Springer. http://www.ifs.tuwien.ac.at/ifs/research/publications.html.

20. A. Rauber and A. Müller-Kögler. Integrating automatic genre analysis into digital libraries. In *Proc of the First ACM-IEEE Joint Conf on Digital Libraries*, Roanoke, VA, June 24-28 2001. ACM.

21. Y. Tseng. Content-based retrieval for music collections. In *Proc of the 22. Annual Intern. ACM SIGIR Conf on Research and Development in Information Retrieval*, pages 176–182, Berkeley, CA, August 15 - 19 1999. ACM. http://www.acm.org/dl.

22. E. Wold, T. Blum, D. Keislar, and J. Wheaton. Content-based classification search and retrieval of audio. *IEEE Multimedia*, 3(3):27–36, Fall 1996.

Building and Indexing a Distributed Multimedia Presentation Archive Using SMIL

Jane Hunter, Suzanne Little

DSTC Pty Ltd, Level 7, GP South, University of Queensland,
St Lucia, Queensland, Australia 4072
{jane, s.little}@dstc.edu.au

Abstract. This paper proposes an approach to the problem of generating meta-data for composite mixed-media digital objects by appropriately combining and exploiting existing knowledge or metadata associated with the individual atomic components which comprise the composite object. Using a distributed collection of multimedia learning objects, we test this proposal by investigating mechanisms for capturing, indexing, searching and delivering digital online presentations using SMIL (Synchronized Multimedia Integration Language). A set of tools have been developed to automate and streamline the construction and fine-grained indexing of a distributed library of digital multimedia presentation objects by applying SMIL to lecture content from both the University of Qld and Cornell University. Using temporal information which is captured automatically at the time of lecture delivery, the system can automatically synchronize the video of a lecture with the corresponding Powerpoint slides to generate a finely-indexed presentation at minimum cost and effort. This approach enables users to search and retrieve relevant streaming video segments of the lecture based on keyword or free text searches within the slide content. The underlying metadata schema, the metadata processing/generation tools, distributed archive, backend database and the search, browse and playback interfaces which comprise the system are also described in this paper. We believe that the relatively low cost and high speed of development of this apparently sophisticated multimedia archive with rich search capabilities, provides evidence to support the validity of our initial proposal.

1 Introduction

The future will lead to many more compound multimedia documents on the web which combine text, image, audio and video in rich complex structured documents in which temporal, spatial, structural and semantic relationships exist between the components. The problems associated with indexing, archiving, searching, browsing and retrieving these kinds of structured dynamic documents initially appear to be infinitely more complex than the resource discovery of simple atomic textual documents. However we propose that by exploiting the complementary and rich nature of the existing knowledge or metadata provided by each of the separate atomic components, it may actually be relatively easy to generate high quality fine-grained metadata for the composite mixed-media objects. Figure 1 demonstrates the theory underlying the work

P. Constantopoulos and I.T. Sølvberg (Eds.): ECDL 2001, LNCS 2163, pp. 415-428, 2001.
© Springer-Verlag Berlin Heidelberg 2001

described in this paper - that high quality metadata for a composite object can be derived by exploiting the existing metadata associated with the individual components together with the knowledge of the spatio-temporal relationships between them. We believe that the combined effect of the metadata provided by each of the atomic objects may in some scenarios, be greater than the sum of their parts.

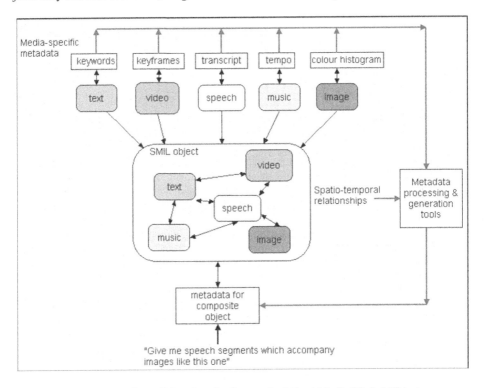

Fig. 1. Generation of Metadata for Composite Mixed-Media Digital Objects

To test this proposal, we developed a test bed of multimedia learning objects which use the W3C Recommendation SMIL 1.0 (Synchronised Multimedia Integration Language) [1] to combine video, PowerPoint images and text from actual university lectures from the University of Queensland and Cornell University. This paper describes the complete system - from the filming of lectures, to the automatic SMIL object generation and archival, the metadata processing and generation tools and the search, browse and retrieval interface.

In addition to being a testbed for our multimedia metadata research, this distributed collection could be further developed into a valuable distance learning resource. Universities and other educational organizations, are finding that both students and lecturers are demanding more flexible delivery mechanisms which allow them to peruse and deliver digital multimedia educational resources at any time and from any place. There are also growing markets for course material which can be packaged and sold to overseas universities or other educational organizations. Consequently there is huge potential commercial benefit for those universities and organizations who are able to cost-effectively provide such flexible learning/teaching environments through the internet.

However, a fundamental requirement of distance learning systems is that they must be as platform and network independent as possible to allow access and dissemination to as wide an audience as possible. Access to high quality information and knowledge should not be dependent on expensive high bandwidth networks or proprietary software or hardware, which is beyond the price range of students. For an archive of presentations to be an effective learning tool, it also requires fast, efficient, precise search facilities at various levels - across distributed collections as well as within individual presentations. In order to provide these services, standardized and well-modeled multi-level metadata is required. Metadata descriptions are required at the collection, presentation and slide/segment level. Segment-level metadata enables students to search on particular keywords and to find the individual slide or corresponding segment of the lecture video in which this topic was discussed. The high cost of manual transcription and the limitations of automatic speech recognition systems, make indexing of lectures via transcript unviable. However the textual content of the PowerPoint slides provides almost as powerful a resource as the transcript.

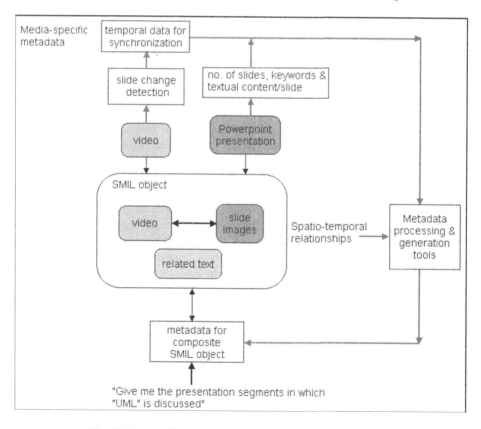

Fig. 2. Metadata Processing Steps for this Presentation Archive

In this project, we provide mechanisms for automating the temporal alignment of the PowerPoint slide content with the video of the lecture. We also provide metadata input tools to streamline the additional manual entry of descriptive or administrative metadata such as the lecturer, department, subject, date/time, place etc.

A web-based search interface has been built which enables users to search and browse the archive both across the distributed collections as well as within individual presentations and to retrieve and play the matching streaming segment of the relevant SMIL file. Figure 2 illustrates the metadata processing and generation components for this application.

The remainder of the paper is as follows. In Section 2 we describe related work and the particular objectives and features of our system which differentiate it from other systems. Section 3 provides an overview of SMIL and a simple example to demonstrate the basic concepts. Section 4 describes the individual components of the system architecture, including the presentation capture process, the indexing and archival tools and the search, browse and retrieval interface. The paper concludes in Section 5 with an assessment of our ability to meet our objectives, an evaluation of our original proposal in the context of this digital multimedia collection and anticipated future work directions.

2   Evaluation of Related Work and Objectives

Early approaches to online learning involving digital video and audio primarily used CD-ROM or the internet to provide video or audio clips as a supplementary resource to written text. Typically the multimedia content was not integrated or synchronised with the textual resources and the indexing and search capabilities were very coarse.

A number of commercial products have recently appeared which enable the online publishing of lecture videos synchronised with PowerPoint presentations. These include Presenter.com [2], EZPresenter [3], Real Presenter Plus [4] and StreamAuthor [5]. These systems are typically expensive and depend on proprietary platform-dependent or application-dependent software to perform the synchronization or the replay. Presenter.com and EZPresenter lack the ability to automatically capture the synchronisation details and (apart from high-level browse interfaces) their indexing and search capabilities are negligible. They are also expensive which makes them inaccessible to many university departments. StreamAuthor does enable the video of the presentation to be synchronized with the PowerPoint presentation at the time of capture but does not support any search facilities other than high-level browsing across a single presentation. Real Presenter does provide an integrated table of contents for each presentation so viewers can jump ahead to a particular slide but it doesn't provide keyword or text searches across multiple presentations.

None of the systems utilize metadata standards to enable search and retrieval via a web search interface, across institutions, collections or within presentations. Hence the objectives of the work described in this paper, which differentiate it from other similar systems, were as follows:

- To investigate mechanisms for automatically generating metadata for composite multimedia objects by utilizing existing metadata or knowledge associated with or extracted from the individual atomic digital objects;
- To build low-cost tools to streamline and automate the internet publishing of synchronised lectures and PowerPoint slides with links to other related course resources;
- To evaluate SMIL as a tool for marking-up and coordinating synchronized presentations of multimedia components;
- To build an online distributed collection of SMIL presentations using lecture content from the Uni. Of Qld and Cornell University, which is platform and network independent;
- To provide a search, browse and retrieval interface across the distributed archive at the collection, presentation and slide level, which supports keyword and text searches;
- To investigate the application of existing relevant metadata standards such as Dublin Core [6] (for resource discovery), IMS [7] (for educational resources) and MPEG-7 [8] (for multimedia content description), to satisfy the search and indexing requirements of this collection.

3 Overview of SMIL

Synchronized Multimedia Integration Language (SMIL 1.0) is a W3C Recommendation designed for choreographing web-based multimedia presentations which combine audio, video, text and graphics in real-time. It uses a simple XML-based markup language, similar to HTML, which enables an author to describe the temporal behavior of a multimedia presentation, associate hyperlinks with media objects and describe the layout of the presentation on a screen. The W3C SYMM (Synchronised Multimedia) Working Group recently released the SMIL 2.0 Proposed Recommendation [9] which extends the functionality contained in SMIL 1.0 by enabling interactivity in multimedia presentations, advancing the timing model and improving the accessibility features. In the work described here we have used SMIL 1.0 but when SMIL 2.0 moves to Recommendation stage and more SMIL 2.0 players become available then we plan to upgrade the system to SMIL 2.0.

SMIL has the following advantages to offer in the context of the application described in this paper:

- Human-readability and similarity to HTML make SMIL easy to understand and use. Authoring can be done very cheaply and easily using simple text editors;
- Platform independence - as a W3C recommendation, SMIL is not a proprietary technology and hence does not tie the implementation to particular platforms or programming languages;
- Network and client adaptability - SMIL provides a switch tag which can be used to dynamically choose the most appropriate media object to stream, depending on client display capabilities or connection speed e.g., use audio instead of video for low bandwidths;

- Ready availability of SMIL players - there are nine SMIL 1.0 players available covering a wide range of platforms [10]. The most popular of these are Apple's QuickTime 4.1, Microsoft's Internet Explorer 5.5 Preview Browser and RealNetworks' RealPlayer 8.

3.1 Basic Concepts and a Simple Example

Generating a SMIL presentation consists of three basic steps: defining the regions for your media; linking media objects to those regions and determining the order, in which to play them (in sequence, parallel or some combination of both). The code below illustrates the skeleton for a simple SMIL example.

```
<smil>
    <head>
        <meta name="publisher" content="DSTC Pty Ltd"/>
        <meta name="date" content="2001-03-21"/>
        <layout>
            <!-- layout tags -->
        </layout>
    </head>
    <body>
        <!-- media and synchronization tags -->
    </body>
</smil>
```

The *layout*, *root-layout* and *region* tags can be used to define spatial regions within a presentation (e.g., a video region, a slide region, a text region...). One can specify locations in pixels, relative to the top left hand corner or some other specified position. Figure 3 illustrates the SMIL code and the corresponding layout for a simple example which is very similar to our SMIL presentation replayer, shown in Figure 4 and described in Section 4.3.

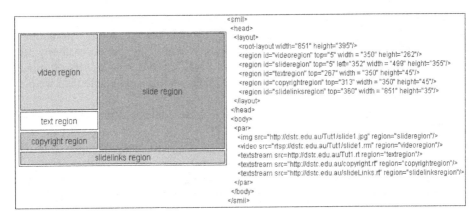

Fig. 3. Spatial Layout for a Simple SMIL Example

The media and synchronization information is defined inside the *body* tag. Coarse-grained temporal structuring can be specified using the *seq* and *par* tags. The *seq* tag defines a sequence - its children are executed one after the other. The *par* tag specifies that its children must be executed in parallel. Fine grained synchronization is specified using the *dur* and *begin* tags. In the body section of our example in Figure 3, all of the media components are contained within a *par* tag because they are synchronized to replay in parallel, starting at the same time. The media type and a URL to the media object associated with each region ID are specified inside the temporal structuring tags.

Figure 4 below illustrates the replay interface for the SMIL presentations generated by our system and replayed using RealNetworks RealPlayer 8. It shows the first slide from a lecture by Prof. Simon Kaplan from the Computer Science Department at the University of Qld.

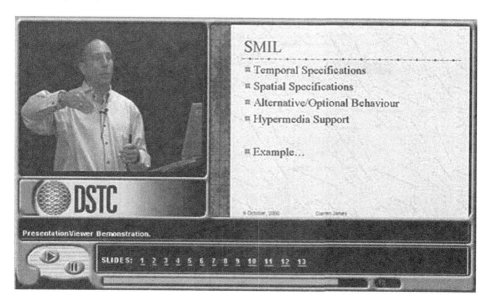

Fig. 4. Replay Interface for a SMIL Presentation

4 The System Components

This section describes the separate components of the system and how they fit into the overall process of building a searchable online presentation archive. Figure 5 provides an overview of the various components and the processes involved.

4.1 Presentation Capture

The presentation capture process involves the following steps:
- Filming a lecturer giving a PowerPoint presentation;
- Digitizing and encoding the video footage to MPEG format (for analysis) and RealMedia format (for streaming);

- Analysing the digitized footage or logging data to determine the times at which slide changes occur;
- Using the temporal information to generate a SMIL presentation which integrates synchronized digital video and PowerPoint slides with a timeline for browsing and jumping directly to a particular slide.

Cornell University and the University of Queensland/DSTC systems adopt different approaches to the filming and segmentation/synchronization processes. Cornell uses two cameras set up in the lecture hall to capture the video footage. The overview camera captures the entire lecture dais from which the presenter lectures.

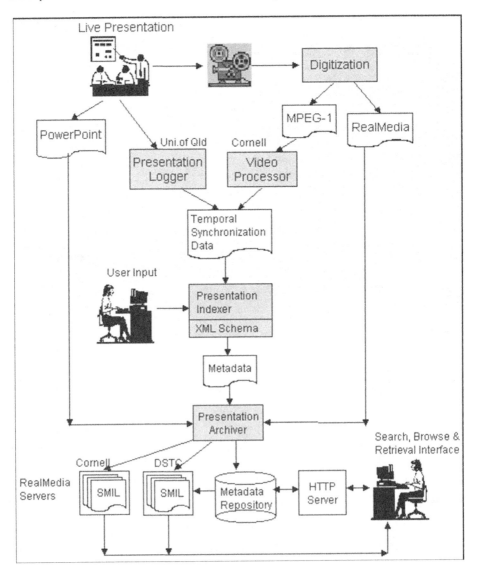

Fig. 5. Overview of System Components and Process Flow

The tracking camera, which contains a built-in hardware tracker to follow the speaker, captures a head-and-shoulders shot of the presenter. At the end of the lecture, the footage is transmitted over a network to a processing server. The lecturer also uploads the PowerPoint slides to this server. The processing server then uses image recognition techniques to match the PowerPoint slides to the sequences of video frames and to determine the times at which slide changes occur. Details of Cornell's Lecture-Browser system are described in [11]. Our system takes the video footage, PowerPoint slides and timing information generated by the Cornell processing server and generates a log file consistent with the output from the PresentationLogger.

DSTC, on the other hand, uses a PresentationLogger (Windows) application which runs in the background during the presentation recording the time at which PowerPoint slide changes occur. The application logs the slide number, the time it appeared, the keywords of the slide (extracted from the title), and the full text of the slide (extracted from the text boxes on the slide). It also records the PowerPoint file location, the duration of the entire presentation and the date of the presentation (from the system time of the machine the presentation was given on). The advantage of DSTC's approach is that the system can run in any lecture room, as long as the PresentationLogger software has been installed on the PC or laptop being used to give the presentation. The disadvantage is that only one manually-operated camera is used. Although manning the camera is labor-intensive, it also means better video quality since the camera settings can be adjusted to suit variations in lighting, rapid lecturer movement etc. This is supported by the conspicuous difference in video quality between Cornell University content (which uses unmanned cameras) and the University of Qld. lectures (which have been manually filmed).

4.2 Presentation Indexing and Archival

The PresentationIndexer is a Visual Basic application which provides a user interface for the manual entry of additional descriptive and administrative metadata which cannot be extracted or inferred from the component media objects. Metadata input includes the location of the log file generated by the PresentationLogger plus details such as the presentation location, lecturer, department, institution, the presentation description, and metadata for the collection that this presentation belongs to (if this hasn't already been entered). To speed up metadata entry, a behind-the-scenes database is using default values and previously entered data to populate fields ahead of the user.

A metadata model was developed which enables the resource discovery of three entity types, corresponding to three levels of granularity:

- Collections;
- Presentations;
- Segments.

The properties associated with each of the entities are based on the Dublin Core Element Set [12] but with additional properties to cover the educational and multimedia aspects of the content. An XML Schema [13] corresponding to the metadata model was developed and is available at [19]. Figure 6 below is a screen dump of some of the metadata input forms which comprise the PresentationIndexer application.

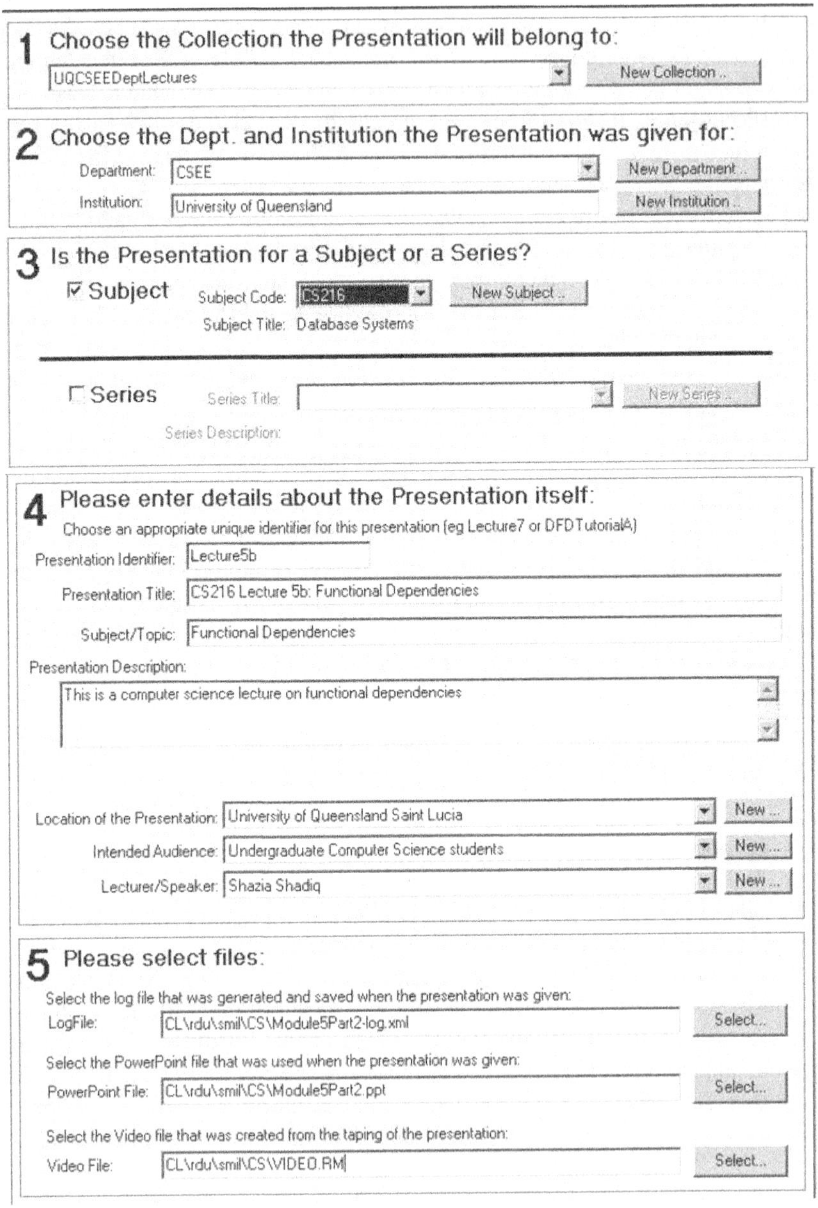

1 Choose the Collection the Presentation will belong to:

UQCSEEDeptLectures ▾   New Collection ..

2 Choose the Dept. and Institution the Presentation was given for:

Department: CSEE ▾   New Department ...

Institution: University of Queensland   New Institution ..

3 Is the Presentation for a Subject or a Series?

☑ Subject   Subject Code: CS216 ▾   New Subject ..

Subject Title: Database Systems

☐ Series   Series Title: ▾   New Series ..

Series Description:

4 Please enter details about the Presentation itself:

Choose an appropriate unique identifier for this presentation (eg Lecture7 or DFDTutorialA)

Presentation Identifier: Lecture5b

Presentation Title: CS216 Lecture 5b: Functional Dependencies

Subject/Topic: Functional Dependencies

Presentation Description:

This is a computer science lecture on functional dependencies

Location of the Presentation: University of Queensland Saint Lucia ▾   New ...

Intended Audience: Undergraduate Computer Science students ▾   New ...

Lecturer/Speaker: Shazia Shadiq ▾   New ...

5 Please select files:

Select the log file that was generated and saved when the presentation was given:

LogFile: CL\rdu\smil\CS\Module5Part2-log.xml   Select...

Select the PowerPoint file that was used when the presentation was given:

PowerPoint File: CL\rdu\smil\CS\Module5Part2.ppt   Select...

Select the Video file that was created from the taping of the presentation:

Video File: CL\rdu\smil\CS\VIDEO.RM   Select...

Fig. 6. Presentation Indexer Application User Interface

Before the description is saved to an XML file, XML Spy [14] is used to check that the metadata input conforms to the XML Schema. If the metadata description does not conform, appropriate error messages are generated. An example of a metadata description which conforms to this schema is available at [20]. The PresentationArchiver program takes the validated XML output from the PresentationIndexer, together with the associated PowerPoint and RealMedia files and generates a synchronised SMIL presentation. The SMIL files are saved to specified server locations at either DSTC or Cornell (or to CD-ROM for distribution). Alternatively web server scripts can regenerate the SMIL presentations dynamically from the metadata (which is stored in a database) and serve them across the web.

The associated metadata descriptions are saved to a database with links to the associated SMIL file and component objects. Alternatively the metadata could be embedded within the header of the SMIL file using the meta tag, as illustrated in the skeleton SMIL example in Section 3.1. SMIL 2.0 provides a metadata tag [15] which is capable of supporting more complex structured multimedia metadata descriptions (e.g., MPEG-7 descriptions) embedded within the SMIL file header.

4.3 The Search, Browse, and Retrieval Interface

The Web search, browse and retrieval interface to the distributed presentation archive can be accessed at [16]. In order to replay retrieved presentations or presentation segments, users need to have the RealPlayer plugin [17] installed on their workstation. The Web interface enables users to browse the complete list of presentations [18], or to perform free text or keyword searches:

- over the complete distributed archive (both Cornell and DSTC),
- within individual collections (either Cornell or DSTC), or
- within particular presentations.

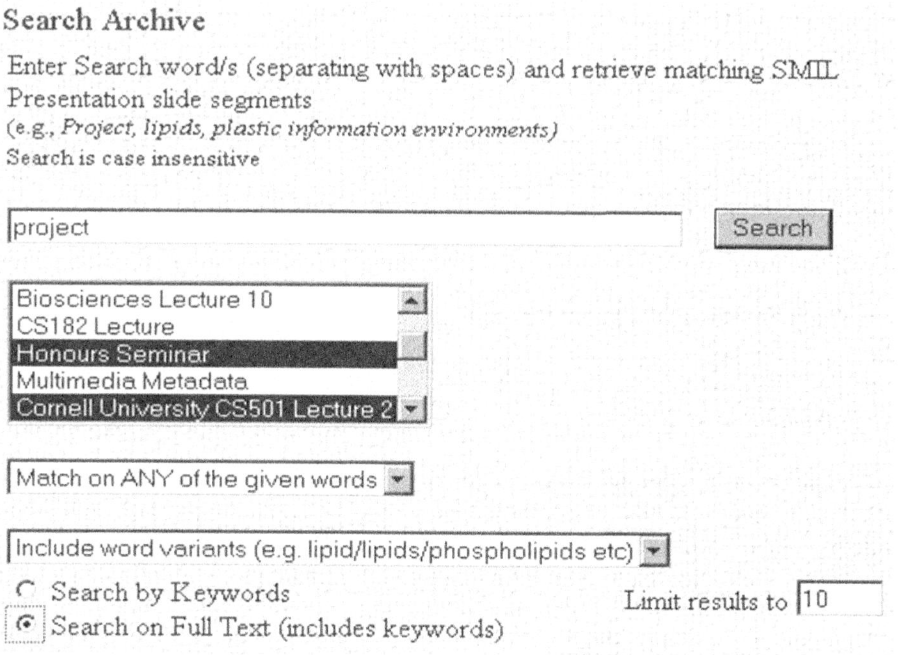

Fig. 7. Presentation Archive Search Interface

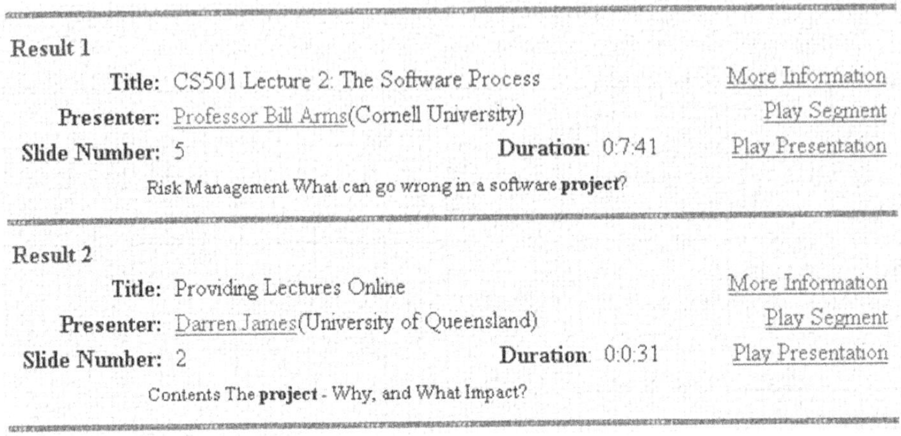

Result 1

Title: CS501 Lecture 2: The Software Process

Presenter: Professor Bill Arms(Cornell University)

Slide Number: 5   Duration: 0:7:41

Risk Management What can go wrong in a software **project**?

More Information

Play Segment

Play Presentation

Result 2

Title: Providing Lectures Online

Presenter: Darren James(University of Queensland)

Slide Number: 2   Duration: 0:0:31

Contents The **project** - Why, and What Impact?

More Information

Play Segment

Play Presentation

Fig. 8. Search Results

Figure 7 shows the search interface to the archive and Figure 8 shows the corresponding results page with the matching query string "project" highlighted. Users can choose to replay just the presentation segment which contains the query string or they can replay the complete presentation.

Server scripts dynamically generate the relevant SMIL segments from the stored metadata descriptions which reference the media content stored on the Real Media servers (the streaming video/audio components) and the web server (the text and slide images). Either the complete SMIL presentation or the selected segment is then streamed to the client and the RealPlayer plugin is invoked. Figure 4 illustrates the browse and replay interface for a retrieved presentation. Users can play the video (using the buttons in the left hand corner) and the corresponding slides will appear automatically or they can jump to any slide number and the corresponding video component will begin playing.

5 Conclusions and Future Work

5.1 Conclusions

In this paper we have presented an automated, cost-effective system for developing a distributed archive of indexed multimedia presentations. By appropriately combining complementary metadata derived from the individual digital objects, we have been able to provide fine-grained, free-text and keyword search and retrieval across multimedia presentations.

Metadata generation is often a prohibitively expensive exercise. During the development of this system, we have demonstrated how the costs of generating high-quality, fine-grained metadata for complex objects can be reduced by:

- generating metadata at the time of content creation. Both the DSTC and Cornell systems capture the temporal, as well as certain descriptive and administrative metadata at the time of lecture delivery and capture;
- applying automatic feature extraction techniques to generate metadata. The Cornell system applies image recognition techniques to the digitized video to determine precisely when slide changes occur. This enables automation of the synchronization and temporal indexing processes;
- exploiting any pre-existing, default or duplicated metadata values where possible e.g., contextual metadata such as institution, lecturer, course etc.;
- inferring metadata where possible. For example, the size of the collection is automatically incremented each time a new lecture is added;
- constraining metadata input via an XML Schema [19]. By validating and constraining metadata input to the structures and data types defined within the specified schema, the quality of the metadata descriptions can (to a certain extent) be controlled;
- constraining metadata input to controlled vocabularies. A number of pull-down lists are built into the PresentationIndexer application to constrain input to values from a set of controlled terms or a thesaurus;
- using open standards (such as SMIL and Dublin Core) which maximize access, re-use and interoperability.

Our evaluations of SMIL 1.0 have shown that, although it provides a simple, platform independent and network independent approach to specifying and delivering composite mixed-media objects, it has certain limitations. These include limited text support, hyperlink support and interactivity capabilities within presentations. However we expect the extended functionality of SMIL 2.0 (which is expected to be published as a W3C Recommendation later this year) to overcome the majority of these limitations.

5.2 Future Work

Plans for future work include investigating the development of presentation editing tools which permit updates, additions and concatenations of existing presentations without loss of synchronisation. Functionality such as cut, paste and delete of presentation segments would enable educators to: reuse existing presentation segments; update presentations with more recent or topical material; and customize presentations for particular audiences, without having to refilm the entire lecture each time.

Future work also includes upgrading the system to SMIL 2.0 when it progresses to a W3C Recommendation and when more players which support the extended functionality of SMIL 2.0, become available. SMIL 2.0 will allow the integration of interactive search facilities and hyperlinks to related resources within the presentations. This will provide students with even greater flexibility, enabling them to navigate through presentations according to their particular needs.

Acknowledgements

The authors wish to acknowledge the use of lecture material belonging to the University of Queensland and Cornell University. We also wish to acknowledge the generosity and cooperation of the presenters whose lecture content is contained within the archive: Bill Arms, Simon Kaplan, Susan Hamilton, Shazia Shadiq and Darren James.

The authors also wish to acknowledge the valuable contributions which the Harmony project collaborators, Carl Lagoze and Dan Brickley have made to this work. The authors also wish to acknowledge that this work was carried out within the Cooperative Research Centre for Research Data Networks established under the Australian Government's Cooperative Research Centre (CRC) Program and acknowledge the support of CITEC and the Distributed Systems Technology CRC under which the work described in this paper is administered. Travel funding for this work was provided by a grant approved under the Technology Diffusion Program of the Commonwealth of Australia's Department of Industry, Science and Resources.

References

1. Synchronized Multimedia Integration Language (SMIL 1.0) Specification, W3C Recommendation, 15 June 1998, http://www.w3.org/TR/REC-smil/
2. Presenter Inc., http://www.presenter.com/
3. Vision 360 EZPresenter, http://www.vision360.net/companyinfo/01.html
4. Real Presenter Plus, http://www.realnetworks.com/products/presenterplus/index.html
5. StreamAuthor, http://ipw.internet.com/development/rich_media/985015125.html
6. Dublin Core Metadata Initiative, http://www.dublincore.org/
7. IMS Metadata Specification 1.1, June 2000, http://www.imsproject.org/metadata/
8. MPEG-7 Home Page, http://www.darmstadt.gmd.de/mobile/MPEG7/index.html/
9. Synchronized Multimedia Integration Language (SMIL 2.0) Specification , W3C Proposed Recommendation, 05 June 2001, http://www.w3.org/TR/smil20/
10. SMIL Players , http://www.w3.org/AudioVideo/#SMIL
11. Sugata Mukhopadhyay and Brian Smith, Passive Capture and Structuring of Lectures. , ACM Conference on Multimedia, 1999
12. Dublin Core Element Set , http://www.dublincore.org/documents/dces/
13. XML Schema Language, http://www.w3.org/XML/Schema
14. XML Spy 3.5 , http://www.xmlspy.com/
15. The SMIL 2.0 metadata element, http://www.w3.org/TR/smil20/metadata.html#edef-metadata
16. SMIL Presentation Archive Search Interface , http://sunspot.dstc.edu.au:8888/smil/search.html
17. RealPlayer 8, http://www.real.com/playerplus/index.html
18. SMIL Presentation Archive Browse Interface , http://sunspot.dstc.edu.au:8888/smil/search.html#browse
19. Appendix A: XML Schema for the Presentation Archive, http://archive.dstc.edu.au/RDU/staff/jane-hunter/ECDL01/ECDL01.html#AppendixA
20. Appendix B: An Example XML Description for a Presentation http://archive.dstc.edu.au/RDU/staff/jane-hunter/ECDL01/ECDL01.html#AppendixB

Digitization, Coded Character Sets, and Optical Character Recognition for Multi-script Information Resources:
The Case of the *Letopis' Zhurnal'nykh Statei*

George Andrew Spencer

Digital Library Program
Indiana University, Bloomington IN 47405, USA
gaspence@indiana.edu

Abstract. Multi-lingual information resources that consist of texts in more scripts than can be represented by a single 8-bit encoding scheme can currently be best represented by use of the Unicode multi-byte character-encoding scheme. However use of Unicode could lead to a decrease in the accuracy of Optical Character Recognition (OCR) software because of the similarity of glyphs between certain scripts. This decrease in OCR accuracy can dramatically increase the amount of time needed to proofread the resulting electronic texts. An Indiana University - Digital Library Program project for digitizing a 20-year portion of the *Letopis' Zhurnal'nykh Statei* is presented as an example of a digital library project dealing with a multi-script information resource for which Unicode has been used.

1 Introduction

In recent years, there have been numerous large-scale digital library projects carried out by various institutions around the world. However digital library projects encompassing the large-scale digitization of information resources in multiple scripts are relatively new. As the Internet continues to grow far beyond its English language ARPAnet roots, multi-lingual information resources and digital library projects using multiple scripts will continue to become more common. Beginning in the fall of 1999, the Digital Library Program [3] at Indiana University began a project to digitize and mark-up in XML (Extensible Mark-up Language) a twenty-year span (1956-1975) of the *Letopis' Zhurnal'nykh Statei*, the Russian/Soviet national journal index. This project [4] has presented specific technical challenges due in part to the fact that the *Letopis' Zhurnal'nykh Statei* contains material not only in the Russian sub-set of the Cyrillic script but also in Greek as well as in the base Latin alphabet and the Latin alphabet composite characters (characters modified by diacritics) used in many Western and Eastern European languages.

2 Choice of Coded Character Set for Multi-script Texts

Most individual electronic text documents produced by digital library projects contain text in only one or two scripts. Over the years, numerous organizations in many

P. Constantopoulos and I.T. Sølvberg (Eds.): ECDL 2001, LNCS 2163, pp. 429-437, 2001.
© Springer-Verlag Berlin Heidelberg 2001

countries have developed a wide variety of code pages for electronic text[5]. These code pages have developed from the early codes such as CCITT (Comité Consultatif International Telegraphique et Telephonique) #2 and BCDIC (Binary Coded Decimal Interchange Code) through the seven-bit codes of the 1960's such as the German DIN 66003-1967 and the United States military's FIELDATA, and on to the early eight-bit code pages such as EBCDIC (Extended Binary Coded Decimal Interchange Code) and ASCII (American Standard Code for Information Interchange)[6]. Through the 1980's and 1990's, eight-bit code pages were the most commonly used. At the beginning of the first decade of the 21st century, this has slowly begun to change with the development of multi-byte encodings, but eight-bit encodings still remain very widely used.

Eight-bit encoding schemes usually suffice to represent the needed characters for texts with one or two scripts because eight-bit character schemes allow for 256 characters to be represented.   Scripts derived directly or indirectly from the Phoenician alphabet (eg. Greek, Latin, Cyrillic, etc.) generally have less than 100 separate characters (counting upper and lower cases separately as they are in code pages). As a result, the 256 possible characters usually permits the representation of both upper and lower case characters for more than one script (plus punctuation marks and computer control characters) within a given code page. Such 8-bit code pages are usually constructed with the basic Latin alphabet in the lower range and various combinations of scripts or composite characters in the upper range. Therefore a single code page, for example КОИ-8 (8-битный код обмена и обработки информации)[2], can represent text both in any language which uses the base Latin alphabet without composite characters, such as English, and also in Russian, with the characters needed for Latin alphabet based languages in the lower numeric range of the code page and the Russian sub-set of Cyrillic characters in the upper range. This eight-bit encoding leads to what is termed "restricted multilingual" language support [1]. However 256 characters is clearly insufficient for representing several scripts present in the same document.

2.1 The *Letopis' Zhurnal'nykh Statei* as an Example of a Multi-script Text

Because of the nature of the materials indexed in the **Letopis' Zhurnal'nykh Statei** this project was faced with the presence of multiple scripts within a single electronic document. Each weekly issue of the **Letopis' Zhurnal'nykh Statei** indexes all fields of knowledge: social sciences, humanities, exact sciences, medicine, technology and industry, etc. While the bulk of the **Letopis' Zhurnal'nykh Statei** is in the Russian sub-set of the Cyrillic script, in some of the exact sciences sections of the index there exists Greek alphabet characters as well as Latin alphabet single characters, words and phrases as well as scientific/mathematical notations and formulae. In the Latin script words and phrases that occur throughout the text of the **Letopis' Zhurnal'nykh Statei** there are also composite characters both from the Western European (Latin-1) code pages (CP-1252, ISO-9959-1) as well as the Eastern European (Latin-2) code pages (CP-1250, ISO-8859-2). In addition to original articles, the **Letopis' Zhurnal'nykh Statei** also indexes translations in Soviet journals of articles published in other countries. Such citations would typically contain a statement citing, in the original vernacular script, the name of the journal in which the original article was published. Many of these articles originate in journals published in the former

COMECON nations, but many also originate in publications from western nations as well, thus the need to represent all the characters used in the languages of both Eastern and Western Europe.

Because of the multiple script nature of the **Letopis' Zhurnal'nykh Statei**, use of one of the more commonly used Cyrillic character sets such as CP-1251, КОИ-8 or ISO8859-5 alone is clearly not sufficient. To fully represent the content of the **Letopis' Zhurnal'nykh Statei**, one needs access to not only the Cyrillic and basic Latin scripts together with the West European composite characters but also the Eastern European composite characters and the Greek script as well. Thus were one to use for example, the Microsoft character sets (Code Pages) one would simultaneously need, at the minimum, characters from not only CP-1251 but also CP-1252, CP-1250 and CP-1253 [7], or if one were to use the corresponding ISO character sets, one would need characters from ISO-8859-5, -1, -2 and -7 [12].

2.2 Moving beyond the 256-Character Limit: WGL-4 and Unicode

If an information resource were to contain only a very few instances of characters from outside the base character set chosen, various workarounds such as imbedded images of the individual characters or words or character entity-references are often used. However such expedients often can render computerized searching of such texts problematic. There is a larger character set that was an attempt to move beyond the 256 character limit, WGL-4 (Windows Glyph List 4), which is essentially a superset of Windows Code Pages CP-1250, 1251, 1252, 1253 and 1254 [7], but with the adoption of Unicode for the Windows NT/2000 family of operating systems, WGL-4 has not been widely implemented [8].

Currently the best remaining option for encoding multi-script texts is the use of a multi-byte character encoding such as Unicode. Unicode was developed in part to be a solution to the "proliferation of multiple, incompatible and inadequate character sets."[1] In the years since the development of Unicode began, there has been a proliferation of character encoding schemes within the Unicode standard, such as UTF (Unicode Transformation Format)-8, UTF-16 big-endian, and UTF-16 little-endian. Nevertheless, the use of a multi-byte encoding does allow character sets to move far beyond the 256-character limit imposed by eight-bit encodings. A sixteen-bit encoding allows for up to 65,536 characters to be encoded, although Unicode version 3.0 has only actually defined 49,194 characters [10].

3 Unicode Compliant Software

The decision to use Unicode for the text files which were to be marked-up in XML for the **Letopis' Zhurnal'nykh Statei** project then caused the project to be faced with several other related decisions, such as which text editor to use for the mark-up and what search engine to use for data access. The XML specification requires all XML parsers be able to read text in the UTF-8 and UTF-16 versions of Unicode[13]. However, the combination of Unicode and XML has only slowly been implemented both by XML editors and by XML search engines. For example, one of the most widely used commercial XML editors, XMetaL did not have a Unicode compliant version until April 2001, well after the ***Letopis' Zhurnal'nykh Statei*** project was under way. In addition, some software packages use UTF-8 as their default Unicode scheme while others use one or the other of the types of UTF-16.

We found in testing various Unicode compliant plain text editors as well as Unicode compliant XML editors that Unicode text created or edited in one editor was not necessarily even readable in another Unicode editor. We tested several Unicode editors including: Yudit, a Linux open source Unicode editor; Unipad, a Windows based Unicode editor; Microsoft Word 2000 and WordPerfect 9. Several of the editors we tested seemed to have slightly different implementations of the Unicode standard, or have odd Unicode character substitutions. For instance we found one editor that would automatically convert all Russian style double angle bracket quotation marks, (guillemets: Unicode U+00AB and U+00BB) to Latin alphabet style quotation marks (Unicode U+0022) every time the file was saved then closed and reopened. Thus use of Unicode encoded text for the ***Letopis' Zhurnal'nykh Statei*** project in some respects created as many problems as it solved.

However for the end-user of a Unicode encoded Internet resource, the software situation is relatively good. The current generation of web browsers, such as Netscape 4.x and 6 and Internet Explorer 4 and 5 support Unicode display with a minimum of configuration. The amount of configuration needed is based mainly on the operating system being used on the computer. For Microsoft Windows NT 4.0, Windows 2000 or Windows 98/ME no configuration is usually necessary. Computers running Windows 95 may or may not have Unicode fonts installed. The same is the case for Linux/Unix machines which may need to have suitable Unicode fonts installed. For the Macintosh, Unicode support was added with OS 8.5. In the Macintosh OS 9, the Language Kit for Unicode may need to be installed [11].

4 Optical Character Recognition in a Multi-script Unicode Environment

One of the Unicode Consortium's stated goals is that "Duplicate encoding of characters is avoided by unifying characters within scripts across languages; characters that are equivalent in form are given a single code"[9]. The critical part of this statement is the "within scripts."

4.1 Unicode: Glyphs Versus Characters

Characters that are equivalent in form (glyph) but are categorized as being in different scripts are treated as wholly different entities with distinctive Unicode hexadecimal values. Thus, Unicode characters that appear to have similar or identical shapes in several scripts are treated as totally separate Unicode characters. For example, the Latin alphabet capital letter "X" has the Unicode hex-code value of U+0058, the Greek alphabet capital letter chi "X" has value U+03A7 and the Cyrillic alphabet capital letter "X" has the value of U+0425. Eight-bit code pages also had this problem, КОИ-8 for example also has both Latin A and Cyrillic A, etc., but the much larger character set of Unicode multiplies the number of similar glyphs contained in the single code page and exacerbates the problem from an OCR standpoint.

While separation of similar or even identical glyphs into separate scripts would have advantages in certain situations and has a certain logic in the abstract (Latin H and Cyrillic H carry very different phonetic values, for example), in practical terms this obviously can have a serious detrimental impact on the accuracy of OCR software, which in turn affects the ability of search engines to locate specific text strings within digital text documents which have been created by an OCR process. In mixed script text such as the **Letopis' Zhurnal'nykh Statei**, if the OCR software is configured to recognize multiple scripts there is great danger that what looks to a human reader as a proper transcription is actually incorrectly recognized. For example, a Latin alphabet capital H or a Greek alphabet capital eta could be substituted for a Cyrillic alphabet capital H. Depending on the font face and size chosen, this would perhaps be indistinguishable to the person reading the text but a computer search engine would obviously fail to find the text because it would actually be searching for character U+041D but the text would contain character U+0048 or U+0397.

The problem is particularly evident in the capital letters where, for instance, there is (again depending on the specific fonts used) no difference in appearance between the Greek alpha glyph, the Cyrillic A and the Latin A. In the lower case forms at least, the Greek glyphs are more often distinctive in form from the Latin and Cyrillic glyphs. The magnitude for this problem is readily apparent when one considers the number of similar glyphs in the Latin, Greek and Cyrillic alphabets given the fact that all three scripts are derived from common roots. Just in the case of capital letters, there are well over fifty possible error combinations when all three alphabets are present in the text. Even in a simpler case where only Cyrillic and Latin alphabets are present in the text there remain numerous possible error combinations. The Appendix presents some examples taken from the basic Greek character set, the English sub-set of the Latin-1 character set and the Russian sub-set of the Cyrillic character set to illustrate the magnitude of this problem. Use of the full Cyrillic, Greek, Basic Latin, Latin-1 supplement, Latin Extended-A, and Latin Extended-B character sets would lead to even more cases of similar glyphs.

4.2 Factors Contributing to Incorrect Recognition

It was found in our experience that most occurrences of the OCR software mistaking a character from one script for another character in a different script occurred when the character was in relative isolation, for example an initial of a person's name or isolated characters such as roman numerals. Because the OCR software that we are using checks complete words against internal dictionaries it is much less likely to place a letter from one script in the midst of a complete word from another script that has been verified against one of the dictionaries. Two factors then caused lower case letters to be less liable to OCR uncertainty: lower case letters are generally found in whole words and these words were usually checked against the dictionary which is built into the OCR software, and there are actually fewer cases of identical (or nearly so) glyphs among lower case letters in the three scripts.

Unfortunately, the structure of the citations that make up the **Letopis' Zhurnal'nykh Statei** follows standard Russian bibliographic practice such that virtually all personal names are presented as surname plus only initials for forename and middle or patronymic names.   This is precisely the situation where OCR confusion is most likely: single capital letters in isolation with no context from which the OCR can ascertain from which script to choose the nearest matching character. The fact that the initial is followed by a period is of no help in distinguishing between scripts since common punctuation is universal across scripts in Unicode. A period (Full Stop) is Unicode character U+002E regardless of whether the surrounding text is Russian, Greek or some language using a Latin based alphabet and thus the presence of a period adds no information as to which script is being punctuated.

An additional well-known source of errors common with all types of OCR is the interpretation of stray marks or blemishes on the paper as punctuation or diacritics. This problem in the *Letopis' Zhurnal'nykh Statei* manifested itself especially with the Greek characters where there exist in the Greek Unicode character set certain letters which have additional composite forms with the added tonos (U+0384) or dialytika (U+0308). It was found in our experience that often a poorly printed or indistinct Latin capital I (U+0049) was interpreted by the OCR software as a capital Greek iota with dialytika (U+03AA) or a capital Greek iota with tonos (U+038A). Thus in addition to the OCR software mistaking characters with identical glyphs, also the problem of composite characters leads to a decrease in accuracy. The capital iota with its associated composite forms was found to be more of a problem because Latin capital I (U+0049) for which it is most often incorrectly recognized is more likely to occur in relative isolation especially as part of Roman numerals. Other Greek letters which have composite forms such as the epsilon with tonos (U+0388) and eta with tonos (U+0389) and the Latin and Cyrillic letters that they are mistaken for, tend to only occur within complete words so the verification against the OCR software's dictionaries tends to weed out most such errors. However this problem was not exclusively limited to recognition of Greek composite characters since composite characters also exist in many variants of the Latin script used for such languages as French, Czech, Polish and many others.

4.3 Increasing Overall Accuracy by Limiting the Number of Languages Recognized

In the specific case of our *Letopis' Zhurnal'nykh Statei* project where the bulk of the text is in Cyrillic, the possible approaches to the problem of similar glyphs that we considered were: disabling Greek recognition entirely and then correcting the text where Greek appears during the manual proofreading stage, disabling both Latin and Greek recognition and correcting both manually or allowing full recognition of all three scripts and correcting all the resulting the errors during the manual proofreading stage.

It was eventually decided for the *Letopis' Zhurnal'nykh Statei* project that the occurrences of actual Greek characters in the document were significantly fewer than the number of erroneous Greek characters that the OCR software was introducing into the text. Thus we found that in our specific case that we could actually increase the overall accuracy of the raw OCR output texts by disabling Greek character recognition entirely. In this respect the *Letopis' Zhurnal'nykh Statei* project was fortunate because the relative occurrence of Greek script was low enough that it was practical to disable Greek script recognition and add the occasional Greek characters back into the text manually.

Further it was also found that the number of incorrectly recognized composite Latin characters were far outnumbering the actual occurrences of such characters. Therefore it was decided to limit recognition of Latin characters to only the base set without any composite characters and as with the case of Greek characters add any composite Latin characters back into the text at the proofreading stage. Had the text consisted of a more equally balanced mix of scripts this perhaps would not have been an acceptable solution.

The ***Letopis' Zhurnal'nykh Statei*** project was also somewhat fortunate in that virtually all of the Cyrillic text was in the Russian language, and thus we were able to configure the OCR software to recognize only those Cyrillic characters used in the Russian language. This had the benefit of excluding several more characters that have glyphs similar to Latin characters such as the J (U+0408) and S (U+0405) used in the Serbian sub-set of Cyrillic.

5 Conclusion

For other potential digitization projects with multiple character sets it will be important at the planning stage to carefully assess the number of scripts that it will be necessary to include in the OCR stage of the project. The fewer scripts that need to be recognized, the lower the number of potentially similar or identical glyphs that the OCR software may incorrectly recognize. We have estimated that the presence in the ***Letopis' Zhurnal'nykh Statei*** of scripts beyond the Russian sub-set of Cyrillic and the resulting decrease in OCR accuracy has conservatively tripled the amount of time needed to proofread the OCR output texts over what would have been the case with purely Russian text.

As digital library projects move beyond documents with text only in a single or at most two languages, Unicode will likely be used more frequently to encode these multilingual electronic documents. In the short term, adherence to the Unicode standard should continue to improve in plain text editors, XML editors and XML search engines. As a result, selecting software packages for use with Unicode texts will require less intensive testing.

However, the problem of similar glyphs across scripts does seem to present specific problems for the current generation of Optical Character Recognition software, which are not as evident when using traditional eight-bit encodings and thus more strictly limited character sets. Thus use of Unicode in the situation for which it is most appropriate (multi-script texts) is also the case where Unicode can lead to potential problems for maintaining OCR data accuracy. This possibility of character substitution between similarly shaped glyphs from different scripts can have potentially serious consequences for accuracy of OCR. The potential inaccuracies in the resulting texts can lead to a decrease in the accuracy and completeness of result sets from search engines. The use of Unicode for some information resources is necessary for certain types of multi-lingual documents. However the added complexity of using Unicode coupled with the types of pitfalls outlined in this paper should be taken into account in the planning stages of any project that may potentially require the use of the Unicode character set.

References

[1]   Adams, Glenn: Introduction to Unicode. Cambridge, Mass.: Institute for Advanced Professional Studies, 1994.

[2] Гончаров, М. В., [и др.]:   Проблемы представления кириллической информации в электронной форме. **Элуктронные библиотеки** (1998) том 1, вып. 2
http://www.iis.ru/el-bib/1998/199802/EGHS/eghs.ru.html

[3] Indiana University Digital Library Program:
http://www.dlib.indiana.edu/

[4] Indiana University Digital Library Program, *Letopis' Zhurnal'nykh Statei* Project.
http://www.dlib.indiana.edu/collections/letopis/letopismain.html

[5]Internet Assigned Numbers Authority (IANA): Character Sets:
http://www.iana.org/assignments/character-sets

[6]   MacKenzie, Charles E.: Coded Character Sets, History and Development. Reading, MA: Addison-Wesley, 1980.

[7]   Microsoft Corp.: Character sets and codepages
http://www.microsoft.com/typography/unicode/cscp.htm

[8]   Phinney, Thomas: TrueType & PostScript Type 1: What's the Difference?
http://www.fontsite.com/Pages/Features/T1vsTTb.html

[9]   Unicode Consortium: The Unicode Standard: A Technical Introduction.
http://www.unicode.org/unicode/standard/principles.html

[10]   Unicode Consortium: The Unicode Standard: Version 3.0. Reading, Mass.: Addison-Wesley, 2000.

[11]   Wood, Alan: Setting up Macintosh OS 9 Web Browsers for Multilingual and Unicode Support.
http://www.hclrss.demon.co.uk/unicode/macbrowsers.html

[12]   World Wide Web Consortium (W3C): i18n/l10n: languages, countries and character sets.
http://www.w3.org/International/O-charset-lang.html

[13]   World Wide Web Consortium (W3C): Extensible Markup Language (XML) version 1.0 (Second Edition) section 4.3.3
http://www.w3.org/TR/REC-xml#charencoding

Appendix

Some Examples of Similar Glyphs for Capital Letters in the Greek, Basic Latin and Russian Cyrillic scripts and their Unicode values

Greek script		Latin script		Cyrillic script	
A	U+0391	A	U+0041	A	U+0410
B	U+0392	B	U+0042	B	U+0412
Γ	U+0393			Γ	U+0413
E	U+0395	E	U+0045	E	U+0415
Z	U+0396	Z	U+005A		
H	U+0397	H	U+0048	H	U+041D
Θ	U+0398			θ *	U+0472
I	U+0399	I	U+0049	I *	U+0406
K	U+039A	K	U+004B	К	U+041A
M	U+039C	M	U+004D	M	U+041C
N	U+039D	N	U+004E		
O	U+039F	O	U+004F	O	U+041E
Π	U+03A0			Π	U+041F
P	U+03A1	P	U+0050	P	U+0420
T	U+03A4	T	U+0054	T	U+0422
Y	U+03A5	Y	U+0059	У	U+0423
Φ	U+03A6			Φ	U+0424
X	U+03A7	X	U+0058	X	U+0425
		C	U+0043	C	U+0421

* Cyrillic character no longer used in modern Russian following the orthographic reform of October 1918.

Document Clustering and Language Models for System-Mediated Information Access

Gheorghe Muresan and David J. Harper

School of Computer and Mathematical Sciences,
The Robert Gordon University,
Aberdeen AB25 1HG, Scotland, UK
{gm, djh}@scms.rgu.ac.uk
http://www.scms.rgu.ac.uk/research/ir/

Abstract. This paper presents the novel concept of system-mediated information access, i.e. system support for the user in clarifying and refining a vague information need and in generating a good formulation for it. The concept is based on two main assumptions: firstly, on document clustering's ability to reveal the topical, semantic structure of a domain of interest, represented by a specialized collection, and secondly, on the capacity of language models to convey content. Experimental results show that these assumptions are correct and that there is potential to significantly improve the retrieval performance by generating a better query through mediation.

Keywords: Mediated Access, Document Clustering, Topic Model

Acknowledgement. The WebCluster Project was sponsored by Ubilab, Union Bank of Switzerland, Zurich.

1 System-Based Mediated Access

1.1 Introduction to the Idea of Mediated Access

Mediation usually means the involvement of human intermediaries who assist the user in clarifying, formulating, refining, and hopefully meeting an information need. For complex information needs, the intermediaries (typically librarians or professional searchers) would first try to understand the context of the user's task, the various aspects of the information need, and the level of detail or abstraction required. Based on their expertise, these mediators would subsequently follow a certain search strategy, formulating a series of queries, varying the precision, scope and vocabulary according to the number of hits and to the user's reaction to the list of hits.

Mediated searches have a far higher success rate than unmediated ones[11], so it is desirable to design retrieval systems that emulate, at least partially, the

P. Constantopoulos and I.T. Sølvberg (Eds.): ECDL 2001, LNCS 2163, pp. 438–449, 2001.

assistance provided by the human mediators. WebCluster, mainly targeting topical searches on the Web, is our attempt to provide such functionality[1].

Our approach to *mediated information access* is based on the existence of
specialised collections of documents or abstracts maintained by various companies and organisations. These collections are kept up to date in terms of validity
of the information and of completeness with regards to the domain covered.
The task they typically support is searching for information in that particular
domain. We propose to apply clustering techniques in order to reveal their structure and to extend the use of these 'source collections' to support mediation[2].
Tools are offered for exploring the structure, the topics and the terminology of
the domain, thus supporting a learning process for the user un-familiar with the
domain. Moreover, the user is invited to explore the use of tools that implement
various retrieval strategies, and can therefore learn what strategies are available,
which are more appropriate in a given situation, and how they can be combined.
Based on the user's exploration of the collection, and on her selection of relevant
documents, the system builds a *language model* of the topic investigated. It can
then act as *mediator* by generating a query that comprehensively, clearly and
precisely reflects the contents of the documents selected by the user. The user has
the option to edit this query, in order to alter its focus, and can use it to extend
her search to 'target collections' that are heterogeneous, unstructured and too
large to readily afford exploration strategies other than query-based searching,
such as the World Wide Web. Mediation through the right 'source collection'
has the potential to generate a very precise query and to dramatically increase
the quality of the retrieval effectiveness and the perceived completeness of the
user's task.

Fig.1 depicts the mediation process. The user usually starts with an ill-defined
information need based on which she chooses, or is recommended by the system,
the most promising source collection from a bank of specialized collections. She
explores the selected source collection using a combination of search strategies:
ranked document retrieval, cluster-based retrieval, and browsing of the structure.
The outcome is a set of results which may help the user solve her task, but also
a *language model* of the topic represented by the set of documents selected by
the user. If the user intends to do a more comprehensive search ("What else can
I find on the Web on this subject ?") or has a monitoring task ("Has anything
new been published in this area ?"), then this *topic model* is used by the system
to generate a query that can be used to search the Web.

There is a close analogy to the search in a library (so the library metaphor
was used in designing the user interface). The user first chooses a library based

---

[1] WebCluster was first demonstrated at SIGIR'99[9] and a new interface, ClusterBook,
based on the library metaphor, was demonstrated at SIGIR2000[10].
[2] Some of these collections may have previously been structured by manual or automatic classification. In this case, no clustering is necessary.

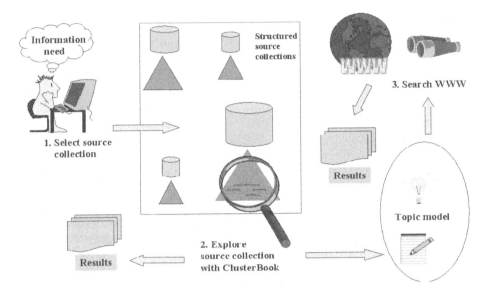

Fig. 1. The mediated access model.

on the domain of interest, then she explores the library. She can ask the librarian's assistance with regards to the terminology and structure of the domain of interest, or search the catalogue, then she can browse the shelf that covers the topic of interest and pick the items that are best for the task at hand.

1.2 Comparison to Other Approaches

It is mainly the concept of *relevance feedback* (RF) that inspired this research: some systems allow users to mark retrieved documents as relevant or non-relevant, so that the system automatically builds a better query and repeats the search or, alternatively, suggests query terms to the user. This approach has been shown to substantially improve the quality of the retrieved set of hits[3]. However, there is typically insufficient support for users formulating the initial query. Moreover, users often ignore the RF functionality[1], or do not recognise the value of the good terms proposed by the system[7].

Campbell's ostensive model[2], applied to searching a collection of photographs, addresses the latter of these problems. It is a query-less system which forces the users to select items and to ask for "more like this". However, there is no support for users to explore a certain structure of the collection. Neither are knowledgeable users supported in going straight to highly relevant documents.

In contrast, the ClusterBook interface, depicted in fig.2 offers a combination of exploration strategies. The **Overview** (leftmost) panel supports the browsing of the hierarchic, topical structure of the source collection. The currently se-

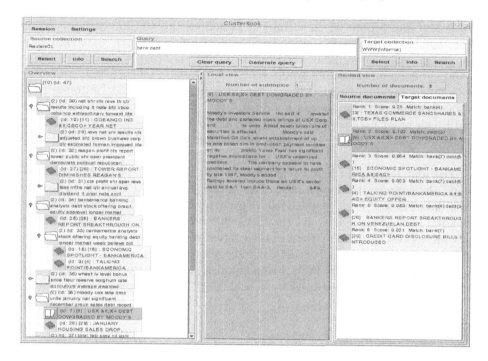

Fig. 2. A snapshot of the ClusterBook interface.

lected document or cluster is shown in detail in the **LocalView** (centre) panel. The **GenerateQuery** button generates a query based on the current selection. The **RankedView** (rightmost) panel displays the hits following a query-based search. If a hit is selected, the corresponding document is displayed in the LocalView and also highlighted in the Overview, indicating a potential 'pocket' of relevant documents. Browsing can suggest search terms and has potential for serendipitously discovering relevant documents, while searching can reveal starting points for browsing, and can find good documents if the searcher can formulate a decent query.

A similar approach of combining a ranked view and a structured view was taken by Leuski[6]. Apart from the interface metaphor, an essential difference is that his system uses clustering to support the exploration of a retrieved set of documents, while WebCluster uses clustering a priori, in order to reveal the structure of a domain to be explored. From this point of view, WebCluster is closer to the Yahoo portal[3], which offers a manually built hierarchic structure of categories, in support of users that have problems formulating a query. Even more similar to WebCluster are systems that use ontologies of specialised domains. For example, a user searching the National Library of Medicine's Medline

---

[3] http://www.yahoo.com

collection[4] can browse Medical Subject Headlines (MeSH) in order to become more familiar with a certain topic and generate a decent query. Although manual classification is arguably better at revealing the 'real' topical structure of a specific domain, clustering is automatic and domain independent. Moreover, WebCluster builds topic models and generates 'mediated queries' automatically. It can bookmark these queries for future use, in support of monitoring tasks, and it can build *user profiles*, following multiple search sessions on a variety of topics, in order to put future queries into context.

Zizi and Beaudouin-Lafon's Shadoc system, based on *interactive dynamic maps*, also supports the exploration of a topical space and allows users to indicate their information need by selecting relevant documents[14]. However, we feel that the library metaphor and the hierarchic organisation of topics, employed by ClusterBook, is more relevant in the context of emulating the librarian's role. Moreover, the approach of structuring the target collection may be infeasible for very large collections. WebCluster applies clustering to homogeneous and relatively small specialised collections, which are used as tools for mediation.

1.3   Applications

There is a wide range of applications envisaged for system mediated information access. The main one is *specialised content portals* to the Web. By applying the mediated access approach to existing collections of documents, abstracts or bibliographic references in domains as diverse as agriculture, finance, health-care, engineering or psychology, the exploration of these specialised domains can be extended to the Web. The user would select documents on a topic of interest and would ask for "more like this". The system would formulate a precise query and would send it to a Web search engine.

The "more like this" approach also suggests applying this paradigm to other media such as image or sound, for which expressing a content-based information need is problematic. For example, a large collection of pictures can be indexed automatically based on content (colour spectrum, texture, etc). A small but representative sub-collection can be annotated, in order to support textual queries, and clustered or categorised. The user can then explore the sub-collection through textual queries combined with browsing. When relevant pictures are found, the system can generate a content description of the relevant items and extend the search to the full collection.

2   Representatives and Language Models

WebCluster supports exploration through browsing and searching, and also the generation of a mediated query. Therefore, an essential issue is the representation

---

[4] http://www.ncbi.nlm.nih.gov/entrez/query.fcgi

of content for documents, clusters and collections. Documents and collections can be viewed as particular cases of clusters (having a single document and, respectively, all the documents) so it is sufficient to discuss the generation of *cluster representatives* (also called *labels* or *centroids*).

For all systems using clustering, as found in the literature, a unique cluster representative is considered. Terms that are deemed typical for a cluster, usually based on their frequency, are selected to be in the centroid. Both un-weighted[5] and weighted[12] centroids have been described. However, getting the right balance between *accuracy* in representation and *power of discrimination* is problematic and can involve adjusting thresholds and re-generating representatives for particular applications.

Our novel approach is to generate multiple representatives, each adapted to a specific purpose: browsing, searching or mediation. The technique used for the label generation is based on the *Kullback-Liebler (KL) divergence* or *relative entropy*, which indicates how different two probability distributions are[8, p.72]. In our context, if P and Q are clusters, viewed as bags of terms, for each term t_i we can calculate its probability distribution in the two bags:

$$p_{i,P} = \frac{number\ of\ occurences\ of\ term\ t_i\ in\ P}{total\ number\ of\ term\ occurences\ in\ P},$$

$$p_{i,Q} = \frac{number\ of\ occurences\ of\ term\ t_i\ in\ Q}{total\ number\ of\ term\ occurences\ in\ Q},$$

and the KL formula

$$KL_i = p_{i,P} \log \frac{p_{i,P}}{p_{i,Q}}$$

indicates the *relative specificity* of t_i in P, compared to Q. The terms that have positive values for this measure are more specific to P than to Q and high levels of relative specificity indicate terms that are much more typical for P than for Q. The set of terms weighted and ranked according to KL form the representative of P in the context of comparing P with Q.

We will now explore how the Kullback-Liebler divergence can be used to generate various cluster representatives.

2.1   Relative Cluster Representative for Browsing

Imagine a user browsing the hierarchic cluster structure. In order to decide which of the subclusters of the current cluster is worth expanding for further exploration, she needs to know what is specific about each subcluster. For that she relies on the cluster labels displayed in the user interface. Therefore, the browsing label of each cluster needs to indicate in what way the cluster differs from its parent. This suggests the use of the Kullback-Liebler divergence measure between the probability distribution in the cluster, and the corresponding probability distribution in the parent, for each term t_i in the cluster:

$$R_i = KL_i(cluster, parent) = p_{i,cluster} \log \frac{p_{i,cluster}}{p_{i,parent}}.$$

This weight indicates the relative specificity of each term in the cluster, compared to the parent cluster. The terms with negative weight are ignored (they are not specific) and the remaining terms are ranked according to their R_i weights in order to generate the browsing label, or *relative representative*.

2.2   Absolute Cluster Representative for Searching

When searching the source collection, based on the user's query, the system needs to find the cluster that best matches the query, and therefore the representative needs to distinguish each cluster from the rest of the collection. The weights of the cluster terms are computed by applying the KL formula between the term probability distribution in the cluster, respectively in the collection:

$$A_i = KL_i(cluster, collection) = p_{i,cluster} \log \frac{p_{i,cluster}}{p_{i,collection}}.$$

Additionally, we introduce the option of taking into account the uniformity of the term distribution in a cluster by altering the above formula with a *uniformity factor*. For example, consider a cluster with 10 documents. A term t_1 may appear once in every document, while another term t_2 may appear 10 times in one document and not at all in the other documents. While both terms have the same frequency, t_1 is more uniformly spread, which may indicate that it is more typical for the cluster. We propose the following uniformity factor:

$$u = \frac{1}{1 + k \cdot \sigma},$$

where σ is the standard deviation of the term frequency over the documents of the cluster and $k \geq 0$ a parameter that can be set to indicate how important uniformity is for specificity (if $k = 0$, then $u = 1$, so there is no influence).

The terms with negative weight are ignored and the remaining terms are ranked according to their A_i weights in order to generate the *absolute representative*.

2.3   Expanded Cluster Representative for Mediation

The *topic model* of a cluster selected by the user and the mediated query generated subsequently need to convey the content of the cluster, and additionally its context. Our approach is to employ a *combined model*, by summing gradually reduced contributions of the absolute representative of the chosen cluster, of its parent, and of all the clusters on the path to the root of the structure. The weight of term t_i in the *expanded representative* is:

$$E_i = (1 - w) \cdot A_{i,0} + (1 - w) \cdot w \cdot A_{i,1} + (1 - w) \cdot w^2 \cdot A_{i,2} + \dots$$
$$+ (1 - w) \cdot w^{r-1} \cdot A_{i,r-1} + w^r \cdot A_{i,r},$$

where $A_{i,0}$, $A_{i,1}$, ..., $A_{i,r}$ are the weights of t_i in the absolute representative of the chosen cluster, its parent, ..., the root cluster, and $w \in (0, 1]$ is the decay rate of the contribution as the context goes from specific to general.

When applying the combined model, all the terms in the vocabulary are considered, not only the terms in the selected cluster. The mediated query will contain the top ranking terms.

3   Evaluation

In order for our mediation approach to work it is necessary that:

1. The clustering algorithm applied to the source collection is good at separating topics and subtopics. For each query, most relevant documents are contained in a small number of clusters.
2. Users are able to identify the 'best' or a 'good' cluster by combining browsing and searching.
3. The mediated query, generated by the system following the interaction with the user, accurately conveys the user's topic of interest.

Test collections can be used for evaluating the first assumption (that the cluster hypothesis holds for specialised collections) and can support user simulations that provide upperbounds of performance for the other two issues. However, real users may conceivably be expected to have problems understanding and applying the idea of mediation. Therefore, an experiment is needed in order to assess if the expected improvement exists for real users. Such an experiment was conducted informally during the development of the software and it was successful[4]. However, a formal experiment is needed in order to quantitatively measure the improvement of retrieval effectiveness and to compare real user performance with the optimal, upperbound performance, obtained by simulating 'ideal' users.

Experiments to verify the first two assumptions listed above have been successfully conducted. The formal user experiment has been designed and is ready to be conducted. Due to the space limitations imposed, we will not enter in details, but will just summarize the purpose and the results of the experiments.

3.1   Cluster Hypothesis Experiments

The *cluster hypothesis* ("closely associated documents tend both to belong to the same clusters and to be relevant to the same requests"[5]) has traditionally been tested in a non-interactive setting, with a batch-retrieval scenario. A test was successful if it indicated a clear separation between relevant and non-relevant documents (for each topic of a test collection) or if it identified a high-quality cluster containing most relevant documents.

These experiments and their results are essentially irrelevant for the interactive setting of WebCluster and its use. Moreover, visual inspections of clustered collections using ClusterBook indicated that clustering offers no guarantee that most relevant documents are grouped in one cluster. Relevant documents seemed to concentrate in 'pockets' of relevance which, for complex topics, seemed to reflect the *aspects* of the topic.

We therefore relaxed the traditional requirement of the cluster hypothesis, proposing that for a specialised collection most relevant documents tend to be grouped in a small number of high-quality clusters. In order to assess the spread of relevant documents, the hierarchical structure obtained by clustering was cut at various levels and the *recall* (R) and *precision* (P) of the clusters in the obtained partitions were computed, as well as their harmonic mean (F) biased towards precision. As the 'good' clusters are the ones envisaged to generate topic models, preference was given to precision more than recall when computing cluster quality: a cluster needs to have high precision (most of its documents should be about the same topic) and some degree of recall (so that more aspects of the topic are covered).

The experiment was repeated for two clustering algorithms (complete link and group average) and five weighting schemes (two biased towards representativeness of terms, two biased towards the terms' power of discrimination, and one balanced). The *cosine coefficient* had been shown to be better than other similarity coefficients at identifying common topics and at contributing to a better concentration of relevant documents in clustering experiments[13], so it was the chosen coefficient for WebCluster and for these experiments.

The results did indeed indicate that most relevant documents were grouped in a small number of clusters, and the skewness of the cluster quality distribution was significantly different compared to that obtained by randomly allocating documents to clusters. An interesting experimental result is that the weighting scheme had no effect on the quality of clustering. The consequence for the administrators of the system and of the collections is that the most convenient (or no) weighting scheme could be used.

A practical consequence of the experiment is that the WebCluster user manual can recommend (for the source collections tested) the typical number of

pockets of relevance that need to be found in order to assure a good completeness of the task as well as the typical size of good clusters that the user should
be looking for.

3.2   Finding Good Clusters

No systematic evaluation of the *browsing labels* was conducted. However, they
were evaluated indirectly, through informal user experiments during the iterative
cycles of the development of WebCluster. The formula initially used for generating (unique) labels selected terms that occurred in a minimum percentage of
the documents in the cluster, and ranked them based on document frequency.
Various threshold values were tried, but no optimal value was found: for high
threshold some clusters corresponding to low similarity levels had empty representatives, while low threshold produced large representatives, with common
terms highly ranked. The new, language model-based labels proved significantly
better: no empty labels are generated, and the top ranked terms do convey the
specificity of clusters in the context of their parent.

Informal observations of searchers using WebCluster have also indicated that
many users prefer to see titles rather than sets of keywords as document representatives, although both could be ambiguous. The users solved the occasional
ambiguity by opening the document and scanning or reading the full text. Consequently, a dual title-keywords representation was used in ClusterBook.

For testing the search labels, the clusters in the hierarchy were ranked based
on the similarity between the search representative and the topic description
(using the cosine metric). Separately, they were ranked based on the quality
value F, derived from relevance judgements. The consistently high correlation
indicates that good queries identify the good clusters.

3.3   Mediation – The User Experiment

The Interactive track of TREC-8, organised by the National Institute of Standards and Technology (NIST), was designed to investigate the exploration of
complex information needs, with a multitude of aspects. This is the very situation in which a user would have problems formulating precise and comprehensive
queries, and therefore would find mediation helpful. Therefore, we adapted the
Interactive TREC-8 experimental design[5] and will compare a) a simple search
system; b) a mediation system that uses a searchable source collection; and c)
ClusterBook, which mediates through a clustered collection that can be searched
and browsed. Mediation is expected to improve the queries submitted to the target collection, and the structure of the source is expected to increase the speed
of finding good documents, the feeling of task completion, the usability of the
system and the user satisfaction.

---

[5] http://www-nlpir.nist.gov/projects/t8i/t8i.html

We simulate an appropriate specialised collection, to be used as source collection for mediation, based on the documents assessed by NIST for the test topics. It contains half of the relevant documents and all of the non-relevant documents of the assessed set, together with their k ($= 6$) nearest neighbours. The obtained collection (of 1241 documents) is quite homogeneous and also small enough to be clustered.

We will conduct the TREC-8-like user experiment after finalising user simulations to establish:

1. upperbound performance levels attainable by the 'ideal user'. These values will be compared to real user performance values.
2. how many documents are needed in order to build a topic model (e.g. choosing just 2 documents may be insufficient, while selecting more than 7, for instance, may not lead to an improvement).
3. robustness to error, or the percentage of relevant documents needed in a cluster selected as relevant (e.g. choosing a cluster with 2 relevant and 3 non-relevant document may be not be representative for a topic, while a cluster with 6 relevant ones and 2 non-relevant ones will).
4. optimal values for the size of the mediated query and the decay rate in its formula.

4   Conclusions

This paper proposes the novel concept of system-mediated access as a tool for supporting users during the information seeking process, and especially in exploring a new domain, for refining an information need and formulating good queries. Such a solution is badly needed today, with searching tools widely available to people not trained in how to search. It is not possible to provide a human mediator for every Web searcher, but an automatic mediator could dramatically improve searching effectiveness and, implicitly, the users' satisfaction. Some of the possible applications of mediated access are suggested in the paper.

Although clustering has been around for over 30 years, its use as a mediation tool in an interactive setting is new. Also new is the idea of using multiple cluster representatives, used to different ends. Although inspired by recent work in language models, the use of the Kullback-Liebler divergence in generating cluster representatives is quite new.

The paper proposes an evaluation methodology for mediation and reports conclusions of some experimental results. The analysis of the results conducted so far confirms the assumptions made regarding mediated access based on clustered specialized collections, and shows its potential in improving the effectiveness of retrieval. User experiments are expected to indicate that the mediated queries generate significantly better retrieval results compared to the original queries.

Plans for future work include an investigation of mediation through various other types of source collections, such as clustered sets of results following an initial search, categorized specialised collections, and user sets of bookmarks. Alternative metaphors and visualization techniques such as maps, town-scapes or hyperbolic trees will also be investigated as means of exploring the structured source collection.

Of course, the results may be dependent on the choice of the target and source collection, and on the clustering method and parameters, so the validity of system-mediated information access can only be proved by more experiments, with different data and parameters.

References

[1] M. Beaulieu, T. Do, A. Payne, and S. Jones. Enquire okapi project. British Library Research and Innovation Report 17, Centre for Interactive Systems Research, City University, London, January 1997.

[2] I. Campbell. Applying ostensive functionalism in the place of descriptive proce-duralism: "the query is dead". In *Workshop on Information Retrieval and Human Computer Interaction*. University of Glasgow, September 1996.

[3] D. Harman. Relevance feedback revisited. In *Proceedings of SIGIR'92*, pages 1–15, Copenhagen, Denmark, 1992. ACM.

[4] D. J. Harper, M. Mechkour, and G. Muresan. Document clustering for mediated information access. In *Proceedings of the 21st Annual BCS-IRSG Colloquium*, Glasgow, April 1999.

[5] N. Jardine and C. J. v. Rijsbergen. The use of hierarchic clustering in information retrieval. *Information Storage and Retrieval*, 7:217–240, 1971.

[6] A. Leuski and J. Allan. Improving interactive retrieval by combining ranked lists and clustering. In *Proceedings of RIAO2000*, pages 665–681, Paris, April 2000.

[7] M. Magennis and C. J. v. Rijsbergen. The potential and actual effectiveness of interactive query expansion. In *Proceedings of SIGIR '97*, pages 324–332, Philadelphia, July 1997. ACM.

[8] C. D. Manning and H. Schutze. *Foundations of Statistical Natural Language Processing*. MIT Press, Cambridge, Massachusetts, 1999.

[9] G. Muresan, D. J. Harper, and M. Mechkour. Webcluster, a tool for mediated information access. In M. Hearst, F. Gey, and R. Tong, editors, *Proceedings of SIGIR'99*, page 337, Berkeley, August 1999. ACM.

[10] G. Muresan, D. J. H. Harper, A. Goker, and P. Lowit. Clusterbook, a tool for dual information access. In N. J. Belkin, P. Ingwersen, and M.-K. Leong, editors, *Proceedings of SIGIR 2000*, page 391, Athens, July 2000. ACM.

[11] R. Nordlie. Unmediated and mediated information searching in the public library. In *Proceedings of ASIS 1996*, 1996.

[12] E. M. Voorhees. *The Effectiveness and Efficiency of Agglomerative Hierarchic Clustering in Document Retrieval*. PhD thesis, Department of Computer Science, Cornell University, Ithaca, NY 14853, October 1985.

[13] P. Willett. Similarity coefficients and weighting functions for automatic document classification: an empirical comparison. *International Classification*, 10(3):138–142, 1983.

[14] M. Zizi and M. Beaudoin-Lafon. Hypermedia exploration with interactive dynamic maps. *International Journal on Human Computer Interaction*, 43, 1995.

Research and Development of Digital Libraries in China: Major Issues and Trends

Guohui Li[1] and Michael Bailou Huang[2]

[1]The Library, Capital Normal University
Beijing, 100037, China
ghlee@263.net
[2]Health Sciences Center Library
State University of New York at Stony Brook
Stony Brook, NY 11794-8034, USA
Michael.B.Huang@sunysb.edu

Abstract. This paper presents an overview on research and development of digital libraries in China, introduces three digital library prototypes being built, and analyses problems and countermeasures of Chinese digital libraries construction.

1 Introduction

Digital libraries have become a hot research topic in library and information sciences fields since the mid 1990's coinciding with the rapid and extensive popularity of computers and the Internet in China.

Still in its infancy stage, the "digital library" is a new phenomenon in this era of networks. "Virtual libraries," "electronic libraries," "digital libraries," and other similar concepts coexist because connotation and extension of digital library concepts are vague. We did a search to find the number of research papers written on digital libraries in *China Journal Net*, the largest full text database of journals in China (http://www.chinajournal.net.cn). It was very hard for us to classify and categorize published articles on this subject. Based on current development of digital libraries, we unified the three concepts and counted them together.

By 2000, we found that there were 327 articles on digital libraries and 2391 related articles in professional journals in China. Judged by depth of research and levels of development of digital libraries, there have been three distinct stages.

Before 1995, there was little research about digital libraries in China with mainly some translations about digital library developments in foreign countries. Most translated articles focused on definitions, characteristics, and relationships among virtual libraries, electronic libraries, and digital libraries. The term "electronic libraries" appeared mostly during that period.

Between 1995-1997, specialized articles on digital library research began to emerge in China and the number of related articles gradually increased. The terms for virtual libraries, electronic libraries, and digital libraries were used equally. Discussions

P. Constantopoulos and I.T. Sølvberg (Eds.): ECDL 2001, LNCS 2163, pp. 450-457, 2001.
© Springer-Verlag Berlin Heidelberg 2001

gradually extended to related concepts and definitions of digital libraries, ideological basis and realistic background of the advent of digital libraries, and effect of digital libraries on traditional libraries. These discussions initiated the beginning of digital library experimentation with library automation being put forward on the agenda. Large-scale library automation facilities and hardware equipment construction projects were implemented. Most medium and large-sized libraries upgraded or purchased new computers, and began to build their local area networks.

Since 1998, but especially during the past two years, digital library research and development has reached an unprecedented level in China. Not only quantity but also research scope and depth have greatly increased. The term "digital libraries" is now used instead of "virtual libraries" or "electronic libraries." This demonstrates that "digital libraries" have become a major concept in the fields of library, information, and computer sciences. Discussions extend to concrete problems in building digital libraries, such as; automated network systems, information resources, intellectual property protection, copyright, metadata, digital library requirements for librarians, digital library prototype designs, and trends of digital library development. Digital library construction plans began with an implementation period, with local area networks connected to the Internet by cables. With financial support by the Chinese government, a number of embryonic digital libraries were built. One of the best representatives is the Chinese Digital Library (http://www.d-library.com.cn/index.php).

2 Central Issues of Digital Library Research in China

Table 1 Searching Results on Various Digital Library Research Topics from *China Journal Net**

	1994 -1997	1998 – 2000*	Total
General	22	305	327
Definitions	6	80	86
Traditional Libraries	12	110	122
Comparative Studies	3	48	51
Automated Networks	7	115	122
Information Resources	10	142	152
Intellectual Property	5	42	47
Librarians	4	47	51
Trends	2	38	40
Metadata	0	24	24

*http://www.chinajournal.net.cn
*Figures for 2000 are not complete.

2.1 Definitions and Characteristics of Digital Libraries

The concept of "digital library" is ever changing. There is no unified definition of what a digital library is, many definitions are still being explored and researched. Various viewpoints summarize essential characteristics of digital libraries from different perspectives, such as: database information systems based on computer and network technologies; organizational method of connected networks; digitized sharing of document resources; collection with no time and space limitations; new storage and management technologies; multi-media, multi-languages, and full-text searching model; and unified user interface and reference services systems.

2.2 Comparative Studies between Digital and Traditional Libraries

The advent of digital libraries has brought revolutionary changes to all library fields. Digitized collection formats, super powerful searching and retrieval, and evolving service functions have had strong impact on traditional libraries [1]. To accommodate continuing developments, traditional libraries should strengthen digital literature resource construction, standards construction, and increase the depth of information services. Judging from China's current status quo, both digital and traditional libraries are mutually dependent and will complement each other for a long time [2].

2.3 Digital Library Technologies

In building digital libraries, Chinese researchers inevitably face problems in system development and management technologies; production technology of information digitization; and searching, dissemination, and safety protection technologies [3]. The following key technologies are discussed most frequently by Chinese researchers: digitization technology of multi-media information; searching technology of graphics, sound, text, and other multi-media; storage, management, and searching of hyper-media information; copyright protection technology of digitized literature; web server and multi-media database connection technology; and digital library prototype design technology [4].

2.4 Digital Library Information Resources

National information policies and cultural modes of thought greatly influence digitization and sharing of information resources in digital libraries. Digitization of information resources will bring about corresponding changes to library collection development. Therefore, we must pay attention to how construction of digital resources influence sharing. In the process of digitizing and sharing, related infrastructure construction should be strengthened. Supported by computer and communication facilities, we need to build a number of databases, especially Chinese information resources with special characteristics. Meanwhile, problems in languages, standards, and securities will need to be resolved.

2.5 Intellectual Property Protection of Digital Libraries

Digital and network environments make sharing of information resources (a main function of digital libraries) a reality. At the same time, it contributes to the ever-deteriorating problem of intellectual property protection [5]. How to fully realize information resource sharing while protecting intellectual property and how to protect intellectual property while sharing information resources has become a heatedly discussed topic among scholars. National policy development, improving laws and regulations, the increasing maturity of computer and network technologies, and the binding power of social ethics are all powerful weapons for intellectual property protection [6].

2.6 Digital Libraries and Librarians

Digital libraries are differentiated from traditional libraries by integrating large numbers of new and high technologies, along with ever-increasing varieties of digital information resources. Librarians who are accustomed to traditional working methods, procedures, and collections should accommodate to this new environment as soon as possible. Not only should they learn computer and networks applications and familiarize themselves with more and more digital information resources, but also learn to develop, organize, select, and evaluate networked information resources in any format. Reference librarians should receive training in real-time reference services and other new formats and contexts. Curriculum for library and information science education and on-the-job-training of practicing librarians should both be strengthened [7].

2.7 Developmental Trends of Digital Libraries

It is commonly understood in Chinese library and information sciences fields that digital libraries are developmental objectives of libraries in this information era. At the same time, they realize that digital library construction is a gigantic and systematic project [8]. Only coordinated financial and technological strengths can fulfill this hugely difficult task. Cooperation from the library, computer, software engineering, communication network engineering fields, as well as the broad society is needed. However, Chinese digital library professionals have differing opinions on achieving multi-level goals and formats in different stages. Nevertheless, effective prediction of future trends will help us discover research problems, increase people's interest, and deepen people's understanding of digital libraries.

2.8 Metadata

With ever-increasing varieties of information resources, metadata as a "classification rule" of digital information resources has become a hot research topic in Chinese library fields and related disciplines. Their research results have been put into practice within the last couple of years. Liangsichen Architecture Database of Tsinghua University, the Ancient Monographs Database of Peking University, and other databases that used metadata were build. Presently, however, there is no unified metadata form in China. An upsurge in research, initiated by Dublin Core, is likely to make it a unified standard in China [9].

3 Some Examples of Chinese Digital Library Construction

3.1 Chinese Digital Library (http://www.d-library.com.cn)

Developed by the National Library of China, Shanghai Library, and six other large public libraries, the Chinese Digital Library is a new, national scale digital library web site, which became fully operational on June 30, 2000. The main purpose of the Chinese Digital Library is to publicize basic digital library concepts and explore developmental path of digital libraries in China. Presently, it provides searching utility for classified multi-media information resources. It will soon provide an information center, book e-business system, and other service platforms. As an important service demonstration window, the Chinese Digital Library web site will continue to adopt new digital library technologies, and provide complete services to clientele throughout the world.

3.2 Liao Ning Provincial Digital Library (http://www.lnlib.com) [10]

Liao Ning Provincial Library chose IBM digital library technology, the first commercial digital library system in the world, as its technological platform. Advanced technology from IBM sped up the digitization and construction process of Liaoning Province Digital Library. With digitization of ancient books as its emphasis, they provide Essence of Ancient Books, Index to Pictorial Documents of Northeastern China, Scenic Spots of Liaoning, Cultural Information Resources, and other multi-media databases with a capacity of 20GB. Users can search library catalogs, news in Liaoning, cultures in Liaoning, historical pictures of Northeastern China, ancient books, famous authors of Liaoning in 1930's, and major news of Liaoning since China's founding in 1949.

3.3 Digital Library in Shanghai Jiao Tong University (http://www.lib.sjtu.edu.cn) [11]

In 2000, Shanghai Jiao Tong University built a thoroughly digital library model with a digitized collection of over 300GB including online catalogs; electronic reference books such as indexes and abstracts, dictionaries, and encyclopedias; as well as electronic journals; conference proceedings; videoimages; multimedia, and computer software. The library has become an important node in CERNET (China Education and Research Network) and CALIS (China Academic Library and Information System). Information provided met the needs of over 90% of patrons who sought energy and transportation materials.

4 Problems and Countermeasures of Chinese Digital Library Research and Construction

4.1 Lack of Digital Library Funding

Libraries are information institutions for the public good and their funding mainly comes from government executive allocations. The Chinese government pays special attention to digital libraries with Vice-Premier Li Lanqing visiting a number of libraries and writing instructions and comments on digital library construction. The Chinese government has planned, organized, and coordinated digital library projects, and offered support in funding and policies. However, digital library construction is a comprehensive and gigantic project extending across different units and industries and it is impossible for short-term research and construction to accomplish. For developing countries like China, just government involvement is not enough. International cooperation and donations from Chinese citizens must be solicited for digital libraries to become a reality.

4.2 Overall Backwardness of Information Technologies

Digital library construction is based on a well-equipped information infrastructure and advanced information technologies. Computer and network popularity levels in Beijing, Shanghai, and other large cities are comparable to international standards. Most elementary and high schools, colleges and universities, and newly build residential areas have cable access to the Internet. However, network development is weak and computer ownership is low in small to medium cities and remote areas. The needs of rapidly increasing numbers of users cannot be satisfied by slow networks connected by telephone lines, serving now by slightly over 100 Internet service providers (ISP's).

Presently, China is making special efforts to popularize computer and Internet utilization, raise users computer competence levels, reduce Internet fees, and develop super high speed cable communication system technologies, multimedia communication terminal and system technologies, and intelligent network technologies. In addition, they have started to build second generation high speed Internet suitable for multimedia transfer, and transform low to medium speed networks that already exist.

4.3 Lack of Information Resources in Chinese on the Internet

There is a tremendous amount of information resources already on the Internet, but most of them are in languages other than Chinese. The objectives of Chinese digital library construction are to provide rich digitized information resources in Chinese and to build digitized collections with special characteristics.

China is a country with a long history along with a huge amount of precious historical literature. According to "A Bibliography of Ancient Race Books in China," ancient rare books since the Song Dynasty are collected by over 780 libraries in China with

60,000 types and 130,000 copies [12]. If these rare books are digitized, they will greatly enrich information resources on the Internet, at the same time, preserving and publicizing China's ancient civilizations and cultures.

4.4 Lack of Social Impact and International Cooperation

Chinese digital library project is a large-scale high technology project that crosses boundaries between various units and industries. It will initiate a flourishing development for related industries, but especially for information and culture industries. Eventually, it will be related to all trades and professions creating huge economic returns and social changes. This is the essential point why Chinese digital library project is so important. Unfortunately, this understanding is now limited to library and information sciences fields, and does not prevail to society in general. Even in library and information sciences fields, discussions are quite limited. So far, there have been no large symposiums or international conferences on digital libraries held in China. This situation does not correspond with the worldwide vigorous digital library movement. International cooperation is a trend in digital library environment, technologies, information resources, standards, intellectual property protections and other aspects. For China, publicizing and strengthening international exchange and cooperation must be a top priority.

Acknowledgements

The authors wish to thank Colleen Kenefick, Associate Librarian of the Health Sciences Center Library, SUNY at Stony Brook, for her useful comments.

References

1. Lin, X.: How Traditional Libraries Face Challenges from Digital Libraries. Journal of Huaibei Coal Industry Teachers College (Philosophy and Social Sciences), May 2000, 21(2).
2. Lu, S. J., Yin, J. H.: On Relations between Electronic Libraries and Traditional Libraries. Journal of Library Science, 1999, 3.
3. Wu, X. N.: Development of Digital Library Technology. Library and Information, 2000, 2.
4. Xing, C. X., Pan, Q., Zhang, H. C., Dai, G. Z.: Studies on Some Key Technologies of Digital Libraries. Journal of Northwestern Polytechnic University, August 1999, 17(3).
5. Qin, K.: Fair Use and Copyright Problem of Digital Libraries. Journal of Library Science, 2000, 4.
6. Huang, M. B., Li, G.: Electronic Resource Sharing and Intellectual Property Protection in the Digital Environment. In C. C. Chen, editor, Global Digital Library Development in the New Millennium: Fertile Ground for Distributed Cross-Disciplinary Collaboration, pages 507-508, May 2001, Tsinghua University Press, Beijing, China.
7. Zeng, L., Zhang, J., Yang, Z. Y.: Digital Libraries: Where to Go? – An Analysis of the Definitions, Architectures, and Projects of Digital Libraries. Journal of the China Society for Scientific and Technical Information, 2000, 1, 64-67.
8. Gao, Y., Gu, Z. M., Huang, J. M.: Digital Libraries – Developmental Trend of the 21st Century Libraries. Journal of Wuhan Textiles and Technologies Institute, September 1999.

9. Sun, Y.: Metadata – Catalog Rule of Digital Library. New Technology of Library and Information Service. 1999, 5.
10. Wan, R. G., Li, D. L.: Construction of Library Networks and Digitization in Liao Ning Province. Journal of Library Science, 2000, 3.
11. Lin, H. M., Ye, A. F., Yang, Z. Y.: Digital Library Model Design of Shanghai Jiaotong University. Journal of Shanghai Jiaotong University (Social Sciences Edition), 2000, 1.
12. Editorial Committee of Chinese Ancient Rare Book Bibliographies: A Bibliography of Ancient Rare Books in China. 1989-2000, Shanghai Ancient Book Press, Shanghai, China.

What's Holding Up the Development of Georeferenced DLs?
(Panel 1)

Michael Freeston[1] and Linda L. Hill[2] (Organizers)

[1] Professor of Information Science
Department of Computer Science
King's College, University of Aberdeen
Aberdeen AB24 3UE Scotland, UK
[2] Alexandria Digital Library Project
Department of Geography
University of California, Santa Barbara
Santa Barbara, CA 93106, USA

Abstract. The implementation of georeferenced digital library technologies in the collection development efforts of various subject domains has been slow in advancing beyond the original geographic and map collections. The panel members will speak from the experience of georeferencing applications in specific subject domains and discuss the issues presented by georeferencing - including aspects of cognition (understanding of the meaning and usefulness of geospatial searching, display, and evaluation), culture (established ways of doing things and identification of geospatial indexing solely with GIS), technologies (e.g., geospatial search functionality and representation of spatial location), and funding (magnitude and availability of funding needed to georeference objects and redesign systems). The session will provide a significant segment of time for discussion among the audience and panelists. The aim is to generate a good exchange of ideas and get closer to understanding the barriers to wide spread integration of georeferencing in DL application domains.

Moderator:
Mike Freeston, University of Aberdeen and University of California, Santa Barbara

P. Constantopoulos and I.T. Sølvberg (Eds.): ECDL 2001, LNCS 2163, pp. 458–458, 2001.
© Springer-Verlag Berlin Heidelberg 2001

Open Archive Initiative, Publishers and Scientific Societies: Future of Publishing – Next Generation Publishing Models
(Panel 2)

Elisabeth Niggemann[1] and Matthias Hemmje[2] (Organizers)

[1] Die Deutsche Bibliothek Frankfurt
[2] GMD-IPSI, Darmstadt

Abstract. This panel will look into the future of publishing as a process between authoring communities such as scientific associations and publishers, i.e. , non profit organizations on the one hand, and commercial enterprizes responsible for performing the production, marketing, sales and distribution of publications on the other hand.

Just recently and especially triggered by the activities of, for example the Open Archive Initiative and other similar movements, the discussion between the different stake holders in the scientific publishing process has become more intensive.

It is generally questioned whether the traditional publishing models are still valid since the advent of electronic publishing tools enable publishing from the desktop, and public distribution mechanisms like the web enable distribution at virtually no cost. These developments have produced a totally different scenario from the past.

In this context the passing of intellectual property rights from authors to publishing companies is questioned in the same way as the validity of traditional business models, pricing policies, and access regulations. On the other hand, issues like quality assurance etc. and the cost of high quality production, distribution, and maintenance of intellectual collections cannot be neglected. The members of the panel are exemplary representatives of the different stakeholders in the scientific publishing process and will report on what has been achieved so far in the discussion and on still open questions. Their presentations will include their view on which agreements have to be achieved in the future for organizing and supporting the scientific publishing process in a fair way, at the same time paving the ground for organizational innovation in other areas of publication.

Moderators:
Elisabeth Niggemann, Die Deutsche Bibliothek Frankfurt
Matthias Hemmje, GMD-IPSI, Darmstadt

Panelists:
Arnou de Kemp, Director Marketing, Sales, and Logistics, Springer Verlag
Carl Lagoze, Open Archive Initiative
n.n., Elsevier Science
n.n., German Physical Society

P. Constantopoulos and I.T. Sølvberg (Eds.): ECDL 2001, LNCS 2163, pp. 459–459, 2001.
© Springer-Verlag Berlin Heidelberg 2001

Digital Library Programs: Current Status and Future Plans
(Panel 3)

Erich J. Neuhold (Organizer)

GMD-IPSI and T.U. Darmstadt

Abstract. For this panel, as for the conference itself, the term Digital Libraries has been broadened to include besides library organisations also museums and archives as well as any other digital collections that are assumed to be of continuing interest for human users. In this way we distinguish them from other kinds of information collections that are of current interest but are of little value for long term availability and preservation.

The members of the panel come from different countries and governmental organisations and will report on what has been achieved so far in the context of various governmental programs. Their presentations will include their views on what has to be done in the future for the Digital Library field, and what governmental programs may come forward to support research, development and use of these collective memories. Special emphasis can be expected on the cultural heritage aspects implied by these collections.

Moderator:
Erich J. Neuhold, GMD-IPSI and T.U. Darmstadt

Panelists:
Chin-chih Chen, Simmons College, USA
Sigrun Eckelmann, Deutsche Forschungsgemeinschaft, Germany
Edward Fox, Virginia Tech, USA
Steven Griffin, National Science Foundation, USA
Bernard Smith, European Commission, Luxemburg

P. Constantopoulos and I.T. Sølvberg (Eds.): ECDL 2001, LNCS 2163, pp. 460–460, 2001.

Author Index

Lecture Notes in Computer Science

For information about Vols. 1–2098
please contact your bookseller or Springer-Verlag

Vol. 2099: P. de Groote, G. Morrill, C. Retoré (Eds.), Logical Aspects of Computational Linguistics. Proceedings, 2001. VIII, 311 pages. 2001. (Subseries LNAI).

Vol. 2100: R. Küsters, Non-Standard Inferences in Description Logocs. X, 250 pages. 2001. (Subseries LNAI).

Vol. 2101: S. Quaglini, P. Barahona, S. Andreassen (Eds.), Artificial Intelligence in Medicine. Proceedings, 2001. XIV, 469 pages. 2001. (Subseries LNAI).

Vol. 2102: G. Berry, H. Comon, A. Finkel (Eds.), Computer-Aided Verification. Proceedings, 2001. XIII, 520 pages. 2001.

Vol. 2103: M. Hannebauer, J. Wendler, E. Pagello (Eds.), Balancing Reactivity and Social Deliberation in Multi-Agent Systems. VIII, 237 pages. 2001. (Subseries LNAI).

Vol. 2104: R. Eigenmann, M.J. Voss (Eds.), OpenMP Shared Memory Parallel Programming. Proceedings, 2001. X, 185 pages. 2001.

Vol. 2105: W. Kim, T.-W. Ling, Y-J. Lee, S.-S. Park (Eds.), The Human Society and the Internet. Proceedings, 2001. XVI, 470 pages. 2001.

Vol. 2106: M. Kerckhove (Ed.); Scale-Space and Morphology in Computer Vision. Proceedings, 2001. XI, 435 pages. 2001.

Vol. 2107: F.T. Chong, C. Kozyrakis, M. Oskin (Eds.), Intelligent Memory Systems. Proceedings, 2000. VIII, 193 pages. 2001.

Vol. 2108: J. Wang (Ed.), Computing and Combinatorics. Proceedings, 2001. XIII, 602 pages. 2001.

Vol. 2109: M. Bauer, P.J. Gymtrasiewicz, J. Vassileva (Eds.), User Modelind 2001. Proceedings, 2001. XIII, 318 pages. 2001. (Subseries LNAI).

Vol. 2110: B. Hertzberger, A. Hoekstra, R. Williams (Eds.), High-Performance Computing and Networking. Proceedings, 2001. XVII, 733 pages. 2001.

Vol. 2111: D. Helmbold, B. Williamson (Eds.), Computational Learning Theory. Proceedings, 2001. IX, 631 pages. 2001. (Subseries LNAI).

Vol. 2113: H.C. Mayr, J. Lazansky, G. Quirchmayr, P. Vogel (Eds.), Database and Expert Systems Applications. Proceedings, 2001. XIX, 991 pages. 2001.

Vol. 2114: Y. Kambayashi, W. Winiwarter, M. Arikawa (Eds.), Data Warehousing and Knowledge Discovery. Proceedings, 2001. XIV, 361pages. 2001.

Vol. 2115: K. Bauknecht, S.K. Madria, G. Pernul (Eds.), Electronic Commerce and Web Technologies. Proceedings, 2001. XI, 347 pages. 2001.

Vol. 2116: V. Akman, P. Bouquet, R. Thomason, R.A. Young (Eds.), Modeling and Using Context. Proceedings, 2001. XII, 472 pages. 2001. (Subseries LNAI).

Vol. 2117: M. Beynon, C.L. Nehaniv, K. Dautenhahn (Eds.), Cognitive Technology: Instruments of Mind. Proceedings, 2001. XV, 522 pages. 2001. (Subseries LNAI).

Vol. 2118: X.S. Wang, G. Yu, H. Lu (Eds.), Advances in Web-Age Information Management. Proceedings, 2001. XV, 418 pages. 2001.

Vol. 2119: V. Varadharajan, Y. Mu (Eds.), Information Security and Privacy. Proceedings, 2001. XI, 522 pages. 2001.

Vol. 2120: H.S. Delugach, G. Stumme (Eds.), Conceptual Structures: Broadening the Base. Proceedings, 2001. X, 377 pages. 2001. (Subseries LNAI).

Vol. 2121: C.S. Jensen, M. Schneider, B. Seeger, V.J. Tsotras (Eds.), Advances in Spatial and Temporal Databases. Proceedings, 2001. XI, 543 pages. 2001.

Vol. 2123: P. Perner (Ed.), Machine Learning and Data Mining in Pattern Recognition. Proceedings, 2001. XI, 363 pages. 2001. (Subseries LNAI).

Vol. 2124: W. Skarbek (Ed.), Computer Analysis of Images and Patterns. Proceedings, 2001. XV, 743 pages. 2001.

Vol. 2125: F. Dehne, J.-R. Sack, R. Tamassia (Eds.), Algorithms and Data Structures. Proceedings, 2001. XII, 484 pages. 2001.

Vol. 2126: P. Cousot (Ed.), Static Analysis. Proceedings, 2001. XI, 439 pages. 2001.

Vol. 2127: V. Malyshkin (Ed.), Parallel Computing Technologies. Proceedings, 2001. XII, 516 pages. 2001.

Vol. 2129: M. Goemans, K. Jansen, J.D.P. Rolim, L. Trevisan (Eds.), Approximation, Randomization, and Combinatorial Optimization. Proceedings, 2001. IX, 297 pages. 2001.

Vol. 2130: G. Dorffner, H. Bischof, K. Hornik (Eds.), Artificial Neural Networks – ICANN 2001. Proceedings, 2001. XXII, 1259 pages. 2001.

Vol. 2132: S.-T. Yuan, M. Yokoo (Eds.), Intelligent Agents. Specification. Modeling, and Application. Proceedings, 2001. X, 237 pages. 2001. (Subseries LNAI).

Vol. 2133: B. Christianson, B. Crispo, J.A. Malcolm, M. Roe (Eds.), Security Protocols. Proceedings, 2001. VIII, 257 pages. 2001.

Vol. 2134: M. Figueiredo, J. Zerubia, A.K. Jain (Eds.), Energy Minimization Methods in Computer Vision and Pattern Recognition. Proceedings, 2001. X, 652 pages. 2001.

Vol. 2136: J. Sgall, A. Pultr, P. Kolman (Eds.), Mathematical Foundations of Computer Science 2001. Proceedings, 2001. XII, 716 pages. 2001.

Vol. 2138: R. Freivalds (Ed.), Fundamentals of Computation Theory. Proceedings, 2001. XIII, 542 pages. 2001.